*Active*Book included

endorsed for edexcel

Paper 1&2:

# Revolutions in Early Modern and Modern Europe

Oliver Bullock | Dan Nuttall | Alan White |
Series editor: Rosemary Rees

ALWAYS LEARNING

PEARSON

Published by Pearson Education Limited, 80 Strand, London, WC2R 0RL.

www.pearsonschoolsandfecolleges.co.uk

Copies of official specifications for all Edexcel qualifications may be found on the website: www.edexcel.com



Designed by Elizabeth Arnoux for Pearson

Typeset and illustrated by Phoenix Photosetting, Chatham, Kent

Produced by Out of House Publishing



Cover design by Malena Wilson-Max for Pearson

Cover photo/illustration © Bridgeman Art Library Ltd: Private Collection/Archives Charmet



First published 2015

18 17 16

10 9 8 7 6 5

**British Library Cataloguing in Publication Data**

A catalogue record for this book is available from the British Library

ISBN 978 1 447 985327



Printed in Great Britain by Ashford Colour Press Ltd



**A note from the publisher**

In order to ensure that this resource offers high-quality support for the associated Pearson qualification, it has been through a review process by the awarding body. This process confirms that; this resource fully covers the teaching and learning content of the specification or part of a specification at which it is aimed. It also confirms that it demonstrates an appropriate balance between the development of subject skills, knowledge and understanding, in addition to preparation for assessment.

Endorsement does not cover any guidance on assessment activities or processes (e.g. practice questions or advice on how to answer assessment questions), included in the resource nor does it prescribe any particular approach to the teaching or delivery of a related course.

While the publishers have made every attempt to ensure that advice on the qualification and its assessment is accurate, the official specification and associated assessment guidance materials are the only authoritative source of information and should always be referred to for definitive guidance.

Pearson examiners have not contributed to any sections in this resource relevant to examination papers for which they have responsibility.

Examiners will not use endorsed resources as a source of material for any assessment set by Pearson.

Endorsement of a resource does not mean that the resource is required to achieve this Pearson qualification, nor does it mean that it is the only suitable material available to support the qualification, and any resource lists produced by the awarding body shall include this and other appropriate resources.

# Contents

# How to use this book

## STRUCTURE

This book covers Route C of the Edexcel A Level and AS Level History qualifications. Route C consists of three papers which are linked by the theme '**Revolutions in early modern and modern Europe**'.

- Paper 1: Britain, 1625–1701: conflict, revolution and settlement
- Paper 2a: France in revolution, 1774–99
- Paper 2b: Russia in revolution, 1894–1924

To take Route C, you must study Paper 1, plus **one** of the two Paper 2 options. You do not need to study the other Paper 2 topic for your exam, but you might like to read it for interest – it deals with similar themes to the topics you are studying.

If you are studying for A Level History, you will also need to study a Paper 3 option and produce coursework in order to complete your qualification. All Paper 3 options are covered by other textbooks in this series.

## AS LEVEL OR A LEVEL?

This book is designed to support students studying both the Edexcel AS Level and A Level qualifications. The content required for both qualifications is identical, so all the material in the papers you are studying is relevant, whichever qualification you are aiming for.

The questions you will be asked in the exam differ for the two different qualifications, so we have included separate exam-style questions and exam preparation sections. If you are studying for an AS Level, you should use the exam-style questions and exam sections highlighted in blue. If you are studying for an A Level, you should use the exam-style questions and exam sections highlighted in green.

**AS Level Exam-Style Question Section A**

Were the actions of Charles I the main reason for the political instability that existed in the years 1625–46? (20 marks)

**Tip**

*Charles' actions before personal rule, during the 1630s and during the search for a settled government should be weighed up against other reasons for instability.*

**A Level Exam-Style Question Section A**

To what extent did the failures of English government in the years 1625–49 arise from a lack of money? (20 marks)

**Tip**

*It is essential to plan your arguments before you start writing. These may include lack of money, religious issues and the personality of the king, among others.*

The 'Preparing for your exams' section at the end of each paper contains sample answers of different standards, with comments on how weaker answers could be improved. Make sure you look at the right section for the exam you are planning to take.

## FEATURES

### Extend your knowledge

These features contain additional information that will help you gain a deeper understanding of the topic. This could be a short biography of an important person, extra background information about an event, an alternative interpretation, or even a research idea that you could follow up. Information in these boxes is not essential to your exam success, but still provides insights of value.

**EXTEND YOUR KNOWLEDGE**

**Nicholas II (1868-1918)**

Nicholas II was the shy and sensitive son of an overbearing and bullying father who scorned him as a 'girlie'. He became tsar in 1894 aged only 26 when his middle-aged father, Alexander III, died suddenly. Little had been done to prepare Nicholas to carry out his responsibilities as a ruler, and he was ill at ease in the world of politics and administration. He was happiest in the company of his wife, Alexandra, and five children, to whom he was devoted.

## Knowledge check activities

These activities are designed to check that you have understood the material that you have just studied. They might also ask you questions about the sources and extracts in the section to check that you have studied and analysed them thoroughly.

ACTIVITY
KNOWLEDGE CHECK

**Laud's reforms**

1 Explain what Arminianism is in your own words.

2 Why did Laud cause resentment? Who resented his reforms?

3 What impression do you get from Source 3 of the way in which the Court of High Commission worked?

4 What similarities existed between Laud and the Puritans, according to Extract 2?

## Summary activities

At the end of each chapter, you will find summary activities. These are tasks designed to help you think about the key topic you have just studied as a whole. They may involve selecting and organising key information or analysing how things changed over time. You might want to keep your answers to these questions safe – they are handy for revision.

ACTIVITY
SUMMARY

**Economic change**

Create a graph of the period 1625-88, outlining developments in trade and the economy. Ensure you cover the following issues. It would be useful to use highlighter pens to establish when each category of change was most significant.

Agriculture; Cloth trade; London; Banking and insurance; Colonies; Trade rivalries

The *x* axis should represent time, starting in 1625 and ending in 1688. The *y* axis should include major changes at the top and minor changes at the bottom. Decide how important each change is and place it on the *y* axis accordingly.

Based on your graph, decide what the three most important changes were between 1625 and 1688, and explain why you have chosen each one.

## Thinking Historically activities

These activities are found throughout the book and are designed to develop your understanding of history, especially around the key concepts of evidence, interpretations, causation and change. Each activity is designed to challenge a conceptual barrier that might be holding you back. This is linked to a map of conceptual barriers developed by experts. You can look up the map and find out which barrier each activity challenges by downloading the conceptual map from this website: www.pearsonschools.co.uk/historyprogressionapproach.

conceptual map reference

THINKING HISTORICALLY Evidence (3b)

**It depends on the question**

When considering the usefulness of a piece of evidence, people often think about authenticity in the case of artefacts, reliability in the case of witness statements or methodology and structure in the case of secondary accounts. A better historical approach to the usefulness of a piece of evidence would be to think about the statements that we can make about the past based on it. Different statements can be made with different degrees of certainty, depending on the evidence.

Work in small groups and answer the following:

1 Look at the photograph of the decorated font (Source 2).

a Write three statements that you can reasonably make about the impact of Laudianism based solely on the photograph.

b Which of the statements can be made with the greatest degree of certainty? Why is this? Which statement can be made with the smallest degree of certainty?

c What else might you need to increase your confidence in your statements?

2 The photograph is an artefact and Source 3 is a witness statement. Which is more useful to the historian studying the impact of Laudianism?

3 Look at Extract 2. How would the historian have gone about constructing this piece? What kinds of evidence would they have needed?

## Getting the most from your online ActiveBook

This book comes with three years' access to ActiveBook* – an online, digital version of your textbook. Follow the instructions printed on the inside front cover to start using your ActiveBook.

Your ActiveBook is the perfect way to personalise your learning as you progress through your AS/A Level History course. You can:

- access your content online, anytime, anywhere
- use the inbuilt highlighting and annotation tools to personalise the content and make it really relevant to you.

Highlight tool – use this to pick out key terms or topics so you are ready and prepared for revision.

Annotations tool – use this to add your own notes, for example links to your wider reading, such as websites or other files. Or, make a note to remind yourself about work that you need to do.

*For new purchases only. If the access code has already been revealed, it may no longer be valid. If you have bought this textbook secondhand, the code may already have been used by the first owner of the book.

# Introduction
# AS/A Level History

## WHY HISTORY MATTERS

History is about people and people are complex, fascinating, frustrating and a whole lot of other things besides. This is why history is probably the most comprehensive and certainly one of the most intriguing subjects there is. History can also be inspiring and alarming, heartening and disturbing, a story of progress and civilisation and of catastrophe and inhumanity.

History's importance goes beyond the subject's intrinsic interest and appeal. Our beliefs and actions, our cultures, institutions and ways of living, our languages and means of making sense of ourselves are all shaped by the past. If we want to fully understand ourselves now, and to understand our possible futures, we have no alternative but to think about history.

History is a discipline as well as a subject matter. Making sense of the past develops qualities of mind that are valuable to anyone who wants to seek the truth and think clearly and intelligently about the most interesting and challenging intellectual problem of all: other people. Learning history is learning a powerful way of knowing.

## WHAT IS HISTORY?

**Figure 1** Fragment of a black granite statue possibly portraying the Roman politician Mark Antony.

History is a way of constructing knowledge about the world through research, interpretation, argument and debate.

Building historical knowledge involves identifying the traces of the past that exist in the present – in people's memories, in old documents, photographs and other remains, and in objects and artefacts ranging from bullets and lipsticks, to field systems and cities. Historians interrogate these traces and *ask questions* that transform traces into *sources of evidence* for knowledge claims about the past.

Historians aim to understand what happened in the past by *explaining why* things happened as they did. Explaining why involves trying to understand past people and their beliefs, intentions and actions. It also involves explaining the causes and evaluating the effects of large-scale changes in the past and exploring relationships between what people aimed to do, the contexts that shaped what was possible and the outcomes and consequences of actions.

Historians also aim to *understand change* in the past. People, states of affairs, ideas, movements and civilisations come into being in time, grow, develop, and ultimately decline and disappear. Historians aim to identify and compare change and continuity in the past, to measure the rate at which things change and to identify the types of change that take place. Change can be slow or sudden. It can also be understood as progressive or regressive – leading to the improvement or worsening of a situation or state of affairs. How things change and whether changes are changes for the better are two key issues that historians frequently debate.

Debate is the essence of history. Historians write arguments to support their knowledge claims and historians argue with each other to test and evaluate interpretations of the past. Historical knowledge itself changes and develops. On the one hand, new sources of knowledge and new methods of research cause *historical interpretations* to change. On the other hand, the questions that historians ask change with time and new questions produce new answers. Although the past is dead and gone, the interpretation of the past has a past, present and future.

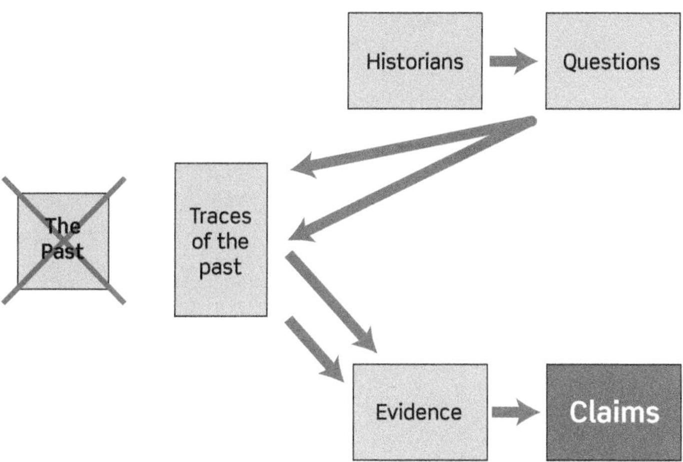


**Figure 2** Constructing knowledge about the past.

## THE CHALLENGES OF LEARNING HISTORY

Like all other Advanced Level subjects, A Level and AS Level history are difficult – that is why they are called 'advanced'. Your advanced level studies will build on knowledge and understanding of history that you developed at GCSE and at Key Stage 3 – ideas like 'historical sources', 'historical evidence' and 'cause', for example. You will need to do a lot of reading and writing to progress in history. Most importantly, you will need to do a lot of thinking, and thinking about your thinking. This book aims to support you in developing both your knowledge and your understanding.

**QUOTES ABOUT HISTORY**

'Historians are dangerous people. They are capable of upsetting everything. They must be directed.'

Nikita Khrushchev

'To be ignorant of what occurred before you were born is to remain forever a child. For what is the worth of human life, unless it is woven into the life of our ancestors by the records of history?'

Marcus Tullius Cicero

History is challenging in many ways. On the one hand, it is challenging to build up the range and depth of knowledge that you need to understand the past at an advanced level. Learning about the past involves mastering new and unfamiliar concepts arising from the past itself (such as the Inquisition, Laudianism, *Volksgemeinschaft*) and building up levels of knowledge that are both detailed and well organised. This book covers the key content of the topics that you are studying for your examination and provides a number of features to help you build and organise what you know – for example, diagrams, timelines and definitions of key terms. You will need to help yourself too, of course, adding to your knowledge through further reading, building on the foundations provided by this book.

Another challenge is to develop understandings of the discipline of history. You will have to learn to think historically about evidence, cause, change and interpretations and also to write historically, in a way that develops clear and supported argument.

Historians think with evidence in ways that differ from how we often think in everyday life. In history, as Figure 2 shows, we cannot go and 'see for ourselves' because the past no longer exists. Neither can we normally rely on 'credible witnesses' to tell us 'the truth' about 'what happened'. People in the past did not write down 'the truth' for our benefit. They often had clear agendas when creating the traces that remain and, as often as not, did not themselves know 'the truth' about complex historical events.

A root of the word 'history' is the Latin word *historia*, one of whose meanings is 'enquiry' or 'finding out'. Learning history means learning to ask questions and interrogate traces, and then to reason about what the new knowledge you have gained means. This book draws on historical scholarship for its narrative and contents. It also draws on research on the nature of historical thinking and on the challenges that learning history can present for students. Throughout the book you will find 'Thinking Historically' activities designed to support the development of your thinking.

You will also find – as you would expect given the nature of history – that the book is full of questions. This book aims to help you build your understandings of the content, contexts and concepts that you will need to advance both your historical knowledge and your historical understanding, and to lay strong foundations for the future development of both.

Dr Arthur Chapman, UCL Institute of Education

# Britain, 1625–1701: conflict, revolution and settlement

## What is a revolution?

Historians use the term 'revolution' in circumstances of sudden and rapid change. It is most often used in connection with political events, but developments of other kinds have been called revolutions too – think, for example, of the 17th-century 'Scientific Revolution' or the Industrial Revolution.

Defining precisely what constitutes a revolution in the political sense is not a straightforward matter. It is, however, widely agreed that a number of elements are involved:

- the overthrow of an established political order and reconstruction of this along new lines
- violence – non-violent or 'bloodless' revolutions are not unknown, but they are rare
- mass participation – in other words, revolutions are at least to some degree popular uprisings.

**EXTEND YOUR KNOWLEDGE**

*Coup d'etat*
In contrast to revolution, a *coup d'etat* (literally, a blow at the state) involves one elite group seizing power from another. Some historians have insisted that important changes, such as the execution of Charles I in 1649 and the 'Glorious Revolution' of 1688-89, actually came about as a result of a *coup* organised by a small number of men and not through 'revolution'.

## The significance of the English Revolution

Between 1625 and 1701, Britain experienced two revolutions.

Source 1 is an image of a momentous date in British history: 30 January 1649. Revolutionary events that had begun in 1640 would result in the trial and execution of the king, Charles I. The causes of this revolution were founded on one important issue: where power should lie. The relationship between Charles and his parliament broke down between 1640 and 1642. Charles believed he had a divine right to rule, given to him by God. Fundamental differences developed over religion, parliament's distaste for Charles' advisers, but most importantly the future direction of government and what the power of monarchy really meant. Whether the ensuing war could have been predicted years earlier or not is a matter of debate among historians. Although the king held the early advantage in this Civil War, the forces of parliament were victorious in 1646 and later held the king in custody. Negotiations between the king and parliament stalled, and he was executed. This revolution led to 11 years of republican rule, resulting in Oliver Cromwell becoming Lord Protector, the first commoner to become head of state in England. The revolution was arguably not successful, as the monarchy was then restored in 1660, under Charles II.

The second revolution occurred in 1688 and 1689. Popularly known as the Glorious Revolution, it took place when the Catholic King James II, son of Charles I, vacated his throne

**1603** – Death of Queen Elizabeth and the accession of James VI of Scotland as James I of England 1603

**1624** – Charles and Buckingham ally with parliament to bring England into the war with Spain, but misuse the money granted 1624

Charles agrees to marry a French Catholic princess

**1629-40** – The personal rule, ended by the Bishops' Wars and recall of parliament in 1640 1629-40

**1649** – Execution of Charles I and abolition of monarchy 1649

**1651** – The First Navigation Act is passed 1651

**1660** – Restoration of Charles II 1660

Pro-French foreign policy and concessions to Catholics at home lead to Popish Plot and Exclusion Crisis

The Royal Society is founded

**1688-89** – The Glorious Revolution and the accession of James' daughter, Mary, and her husband, William of Orange, as joint monarchs 1688-89

**1694** – The Bank of England is founded 1694

**1702** – Death of King William 1702

**SOURCE 1** The execution of Charles I, 30 January 1649. This image was featured on the front cover of a pamphlet supposedly containing the confession of Charles' executioner, Richard Brandon.

1621 **1621** – King and parliament quarrel over MPs' attempts to influence foreign policy as a result of war in Europe

1625 **1625** – Accession of Charles I, leading to a cycle of clashes between Charles and parliament over money, war and religion, and the dissolution of parliament in 1629

1642 **1642** – Outbreak of the English Civil War

1649-60 **1649-60** – Republican rule

1655 **1655** – The English capture the island of Jamaica

1685 **1685** – Accession of James II: his open Catholicism and attempts to create religious equality alienated the religious and political elites

1689 **1689** – England entered the War of the League of Augsburg against Louis XIV; John Locke publishes his *Two Treatises of Government*

1701 **1701** – Act of Settlement laid down the succession to the throne, excluding the Catholic Stuarts

1714 **1714** – Hanoverian Succession: King George I

in the face of opposition from the political classes. Again, the key issue that caused this revolution was that of power. Like Charles I, James felt he had the right to be an absolute monarch, unrestrained by laws. The Dutch Prince William of Orange was invited by parliament to take the throne with his wife, Mary, James' daughter. Some historians believe that the revolution and resulting political settlement was a peaceful and sensible affair, and should not be termed a revolution at all. Others believe that it marked an important change in British history and laid the foundations for parliamentary democracy and the end of divine right monarchy.

As well as the political revolutions, the 17th century was also a revolutionary age for science, economy, trade, religion and ideas. All of this enabled Britain to undergo a rapid rise to become a world power. The scientific revolution led to modern, objective methods of investigation being utilised, the revolution of ideas led to the development of theories that would result in the founding of liberal democracies around the world, and changes in religious attitudes would lead to religious toleration for both Christian and non-Christian groups.

## Causes of revolutions

Historians have distinguished between the preconditions and triggers of revolutions.

Preconditions refer to long-term economic, social and attitudinal developments that undermine and destabilise the established political order to the point that a revolution is a distinct possibility.

- In the 17th century, a rising population put pressure on scarce resources. Starvation and food riots became commonplace. This led to the political elites fearing the breakdown of law and order.
- The Protestant Reformation that occurred in England between 1529 and 1547 led to the development of beliefs that focused on having an individual relationship with God. This led to a rejection of many Catholic practices, which were viewed with suspicion in the 17th century.
- Since James VI of Scotland became James I of England in 1603, the monarch faced the prospect of ruling Ireland, England and Scotland as separate kingdoms. Each of these kingdoms had separate cultural and religious identities and any attempt to suppress these could affect the fragile balance that existed.
- The institution of parliament had risen in prominence, but still had little genuine power. This would change in the 17th century.

The triggers of revolutions are chance, unforeseen events that dramatically illuminate the failings of the established political order and spur critics and opponents of the established order into taking action.

# 1.1 The quest for political stability, 1625–88

**KEY QUESTIONS**

- Why did monarchical government fail in the years 1625–49?
- To what extent did republican rule provide a stable government, 1649–60?
- Why was the Stuart monarchy restored in 1660, only to collapse 28 years later?

## INTRODUCTION

In 1625, against a background of political and religious conflict across Europe, Charles I inherited the thrones of three British kingdoms: England (with Wales), Ireland and Scotland. Although he ruled all three kingdoms, they did not constitute a single unit: each kingdom had its own culture, its own religious arrangements and its own parliament. He was king by inheritance – as the eldest living son of King James I – and by **divine right**, chosen and approved by God himself, as symbolised in the coronation ceremony.

Civil War in England was sparked by rebellions in Scotland and Ireland in 1642, and the king was eventually defeated by an army organised and led by the English parliament. From 1646 to 1648, the victorious parliamentarians attempted to negotiate a settlement with the king, but Charles refused to negotiate honestly and used the time to raise new forces and renew the war with the help of the Scots. In 1649, this divine right monarch was executed in a public beheading outside the Banqueting Hall of his own Palace of Whitehall in London. Moreover, the death of the king was followed by the formal abolition of the monarchy and England's only period of **republican** government.

This action, and the ideology that motivated it, led some historians to view these events as an English Revolution, a forerunner of the similar events that took place in France in 1789 and Russia in 1917. Charles was not the first British monarch to meet a violent death, but he was the first to be publicly tried in the name of the people and executed according to judicial procedures while still king. The implication of this was that kings could be held responsible by their subjects, and not by God alone. Although the monarchy was restored in 1660, and Charles' sons still claimed to rule by divine right, in practice Charles II and then James II knew the possible consequences of conflict with parliament. When James faced the prospect of a new civil war in 1688, he fled into exile in France rather than risk his father's fate. The Glorious Revolution of 1688–89, and the settlements that followed it, owed much to the lessons learned in 1649.

**KEY TERMS**

**Divine right**
This principle is founded on the belief that the monarch was God's representative on earth, and answerable to God alone. It was a sin against God therefore to stand against the monarch.

**Republican**
In a republic, supreme political power is held by elected representatives rather than a hereditary monarch.

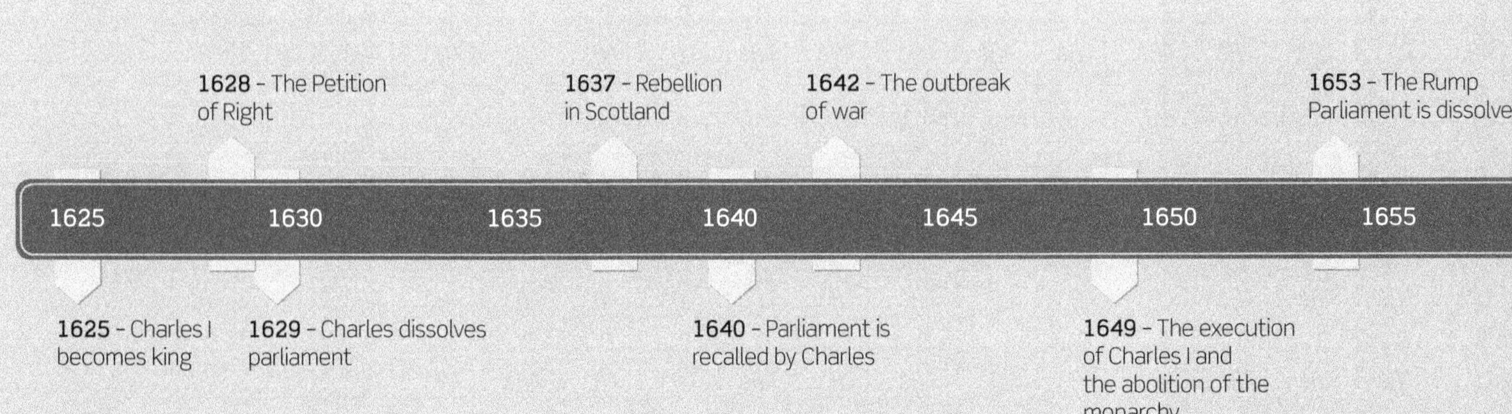

## Monarchy in 1625

The source of law and government in all three British kingdoms was the monarch, deriving power from God. The centre of political life was therefore the Royal Court, made up of the monarch's friends, servants and associates, as well as important office-holders and some foreign ambassadors. Within this there was an inner circle of close friends and advisers, known as the Privy [private] Council, whose members advised the monarch. Each of the three kingdoms had its own council, but the greater wealth and power of England, and the inclusion of Wales, made the English kingdom the dominant seat of government. The king's power was not unlimited, because it was generally recognised that the highest form of law was statute law, made by the **King-in-Parliament**, which took precedence over **prerogative** actions.

Beyond the confines of the court, there were a number of other important institutions, all coming ultimately under royal control. As head of the Church of England, the king appointed the bishops and archbishops who controlled the lower clergy, and exercised authority over the laity (non-clergy). The Church of England was a Protestant Church, as Henry VIII had broken away from the Catholic Church and his daughter, Elizabeth, had imposed a Protestant settlement. The senior archbishop, the Archbishop of Canterbury, was normally a member of the Privy Council. The common law courts were staffed by judges appointed by the king. At a local level the law was administered and enforced by Justices of the Peace (JPs). At the lowest level, they were assisted by parish officials – constables, overseers of the poor and church wardens – whose actions the JPs were expected to supervise. By comparison, the institution of parliament played only a limited role in government – while its functions were important, its meetings were occasional and entirely at the discretion of the monarch. Nevertheless, by 1625, parliaments were a vital and increasingly regular part of the system.

Charles I did not take on a simple or straightforward task when he ascended the throne in March 1625. The main issue that faced Charles was the war with Spain that had been fought by his father, James I. The origins of the war lay in the religious conflicts that had erupted in central Europe and developed into open warfare in 1618. James I had tried to avoid entanglement in the fighting, instead seeking to intervene by diplomatic means. He tried to negotiate a marriage for his son, then known as Prince Charles, with the daughter of the King of Spain, in order to bring a rapid end to the war or, at the very least, restore his daughter Elizabeth and her husband to the **Palatinate**. In order to strengthen his diplomatic credentials, he called a parliament and sought financial backing to prepare for war. The anti-Catholic feeling in England ensured he received support from members of parliament (MPs), who promptly granted taxes as required, but also embarked on a debate about how the war should be conducted.

### KEY TERMS

**King-in-Parliament**
The power of the monarch to make laws with the assistance and approval of parliament.

**Prerogative**
The powers that could only be wielded by the king, such as the power to declare war and sign treaties.

### KEY TERM

**Palatinate**
The territory in Germany ruled by the Count Palatine of the Rhine. The territory was fragmented, with no continuous border, and spread over a large area.

**1660** - Restoration of Charles II

**1662** - First Declaration of Indulgence

**1672** - Second Declaration of Indulgence

**1679-82** - The Exclusion Crisis

**1685** - Death of Charles II and accession of James II

**1688** - Invasion led by William of Orange - James escapes to exile in France

1660 | 1665 | 1670 | 1675 | 1680 | 1685 | 1690

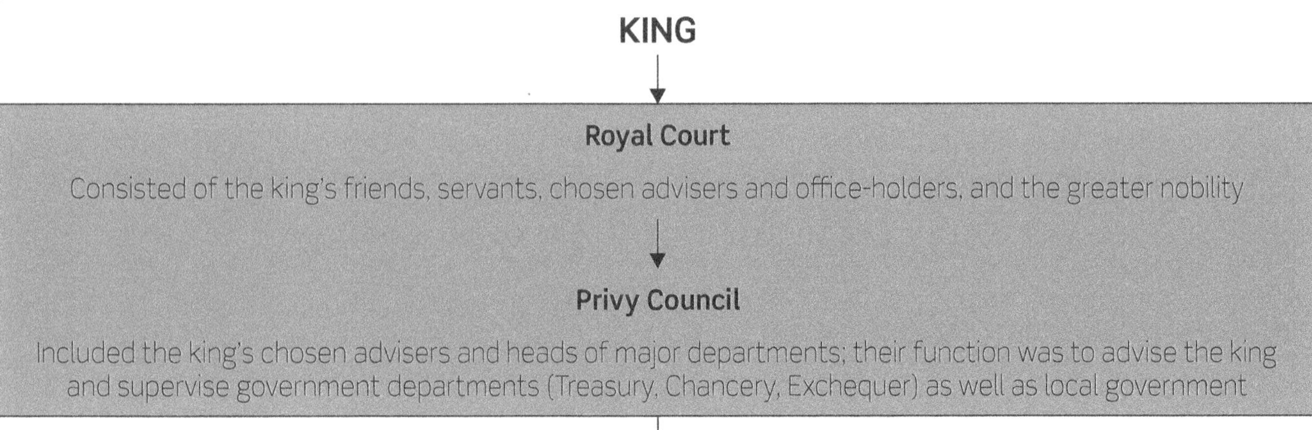


| Parliament | Common Law Courts | Local government in counties and boroughs | Prerogative Courts | The Church |
|---|---|---|---|---|
| House of Lords (including 26 bishops) and House of Commons<br>• 2 MPs from each county and borough<br>• called and dismissed by the king<br>• able to pass statute laws to add to the common law (custom, precedent and royal proclamations) | 1 Exchequer, King's Bench and Common Pleas in London<br>• judges appointed by the king<br><br>2 Judges on circuit held County Assizes<br><br>3 JPs met in petty and Quarter Sessions, sent serious cases to the Assizes | • Lords Lieutenant (in charge of militia)<br>• Sheriffs (in charge of gaols and elections)<br>• JPs, who administered law and supervised parish officials (constables, overseers of the poor and churchwardens) | Run by Privy Councillors, representing the king's direct authority<br><br>• Chancery and Star Chamber in London<br><br>• Court of High Commission dealing with Church affairs<br><br>• Regional Councils of the North and Welsh Marches | Governed by archbishops and bishops chosen by the king<br><br>Lower clergy, supported by churchwardens |

**Electorate**: consisting mainly of gentry and merchant elite. but with some of the 'middling sort' – yeomen and master craftsmen. These also provided local government personnel at appropriate levels.

**The people – tenant farmers, craftsmen, labourers and paupers.** Without any means of expressing their concerns other than to sympathetic local gentry, their tendency had been to resort to riot and disorder, including attacks on the property (and occasionally the persons) of their betters. They were therefore regarded as a danger to society, in need of control if stability was to be assured.

**Figure 1.1**: The structure of government and society in England, 1625.

**ACTIVITIES**
**KNOWLEDGE CHECK**

**Government and society**

1 Who exercised the most power in England, other than the monarch?

2 What is the significance of the fact that most positions outside the royal court were unpaid?

To obtain the necessary subsidies (parliamentary taxes), James had used the influence of his chief adviser, the Duke of Buckingham, to encourage MPs to debate the strategy for war and agreed to conduct a naval war. Meanwhile, Buckingham had negotiated a marriage for Charles with Henrietta Maria, the sister of the French king, in 1625 and an agreement to send troops to support a joint intervention to assist the Protestant cause in Germany. When the troops were dispatched under the command of a mercenary, Count Mansfeld, the poorly equipped English wasted away on the Belgian coast, ravaged by bad weather and disease. By the time this became clear, James was already dead, and it was King Charles I who had to deal with the consequences.

EXTEND YOUR KNOWLEDGE

**George Villiers, Duke of Buckingham (1592-1628)**
George Villiers was born into a minor gentry family in Leicestershire, but was introduced to the king in 1614 in an attempt by court rivals to undermine James' favourite, Robert Carr. Given James' noted fondness for handsome and charming young men, it was not surprising that the Villiers' fortunes rose rapidly.

Although skilled in court politics, Buckingham had little to offer as a statesman, but this did not cause great damage until he extended his influence to the young Prince Charles (who had actively disliked him at first) in 1623. Recognising that the heir to the throne lacked confidence, he set out to gain his friendship and support.

The occasion of their new relationship was the attempt to negotiate a marriage for Charles with the Spanish Infanta (daughter of the Spanish king) and in 1623 they embarked on a diplomatically disastrous adventure by secretly travelling to Madrid so that Charles could woo her in person. The Spanish were shocked and the plan failed, but the visit seems to have enabled Buckingham to gain the affection of the young prince, which never wavered thereafter.

# WHY DID MONARCHICAL GOVERNMENT FAIL IN THE YEARS 1625-49?

## Charles I and parliament, 1625-29

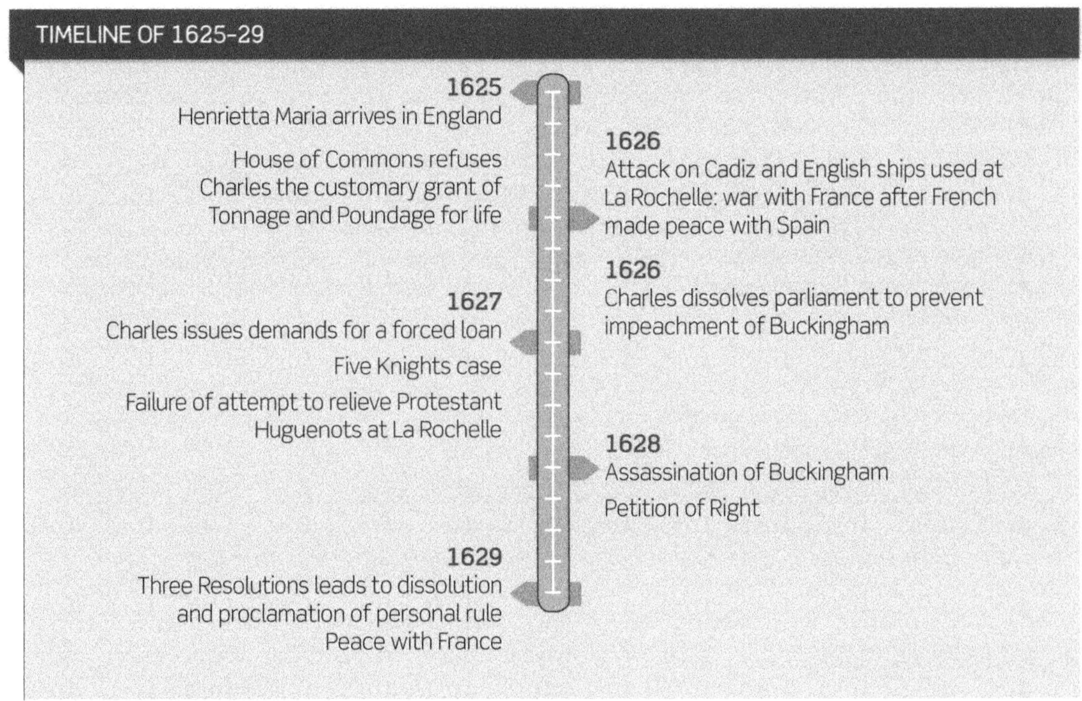


### The 1625 parliament

When Charles succeeded to the throne in March 1625, he found an empty Treasury and dwindling credit. Charles moved to gain a loan from City of London merchants of £60,000, but this was not enough and he had little choice but to face a parliament. The actions of MPs, and the few Lords who worked with them in 1625–29, were mainly focused on the recognised parliamentary functions of taxation, defence of the common law and the occasional attempt to bring 'evil counsellors' to book through the process of **impeachment**. Nevertheless, the meeting of parliament in June 1625 initiated a sequence of quarrels that destroyed any co-operation between king and parliament and led Charles to embark on a period of personal rule in 1629.

Disagreements began when the Commons refused to grant Charles the right to collect an excise tax, Tonnage and Poundage, for life, in response to the disastrous Mansfeld campaign. Instead, the MPs suggested that a grant should be made for a year, so he would be forced to call a parliament regularly.

KEY TERM

**Impeachment**
A process whereby government advisers and officers could be accused of crimes by the House of Commons and tried in the House of Lords. As a method of bringing 'evil counsellors' to justice it was open to manipulation by court factions, but it was an important way of demonstrating public anger to the king and of removing men who were genuinely incompetent or worse.

KEY TERMS

**Arminian**
A follower of the Dutch theologian Jacobus Arminius (1560–1609). Arminius rejected the Calvinist notion of predestination, believing that all Christians have free will and can influence whether they enter heaven or hell. Arminianism in the 1620s and 1630s is associated with 'high church' practices (similar to those of the Catholic Church) such as the use of organs, hymns and bowing to the cross.

***Habeas corpus***
A demand made by a prisoner to their custodian. When issued, the prisoner has the right to go before a court and demand to know the reason for their detention.

**Prerogative Court**
A court where the powers of the sovereign are exercised, often by judges nominated by the king or queen.

The mood darkened when the new Catholic Queen Henrietta Maria arrived in England, establishing her own court of Catholic advisers. Meanwhile, Charles had shown more of his religious sympathies by promoting **Arminian** clergy in the Church and offering a position at court to Arminians such as Richard Montagu. Additionally, the foreign policy failures mounted. The planned war had led to conscription of troops and the forced billeting of troops in people's houses, at a time when a serious outbreak of the plague had already disrupted the economy. In late 1625, a naval expedition was sent to attack the port of Cadiz in Spain. Poorly trained and equipped, and badly led by Buckingham's nominee, Viscount Wimbledon, it failed completely. When the Commons began discussing impeachment proceedings against Buckingham, Charles hastily dissolved parliament.

## The 1626 parliament and prerogative rule

In these circumstances, Charles' decision to call another parliament in early 1626 indicates a serious lack of awareness. When parliament met, the issue of subsidies was set aside to launch an attack on Buckingham. An angry Commons combined with the Lords, and court rivals whom Buckingham had driven from office, to launch an impeachment against him. Forced to dissolve parliament without any grant of taxation in order to stop the process of impeachment, Charles responded by demanding a forced loan from all taxpayers, and this time any who refused payment were to be punished by being imprisoned or conscripted into military service. For many of the political nation, this was a direct challenge to the law and the existence of parliaments, and some began to show their unhappiness. Lord Chief Justice Carew refused to endorse the legality of the loan and was dismissed. In 1627, a group of five knights who had refused to pay the loan and been imprisoned sued for release under ***habeas corpus***. They were refused the opportunity to go to court, because the king claimed a right to an emergency power of arrest.

## Confrontation and dissolution, 1628–29

The result of the 'Five Knights case' was a major confrontation in 1628, when Charles summoned another parliament to provide funds for the now desperate need for national defence. The attack on Cadiz had been followed up by a further deterioration in relations with the other Catholic power, France, in which Buckingham's inept diplomacy led to war and a failed attempt to support a Protestant rebellion in La Rochelle. At war with both France and Spain, Charles had no choice but to seek further subsidies. Aware that outright confrontation could lead to another dissolution, attacks on Buckingham by parliament were abandoned in favour of a more subtle strategy. On the one hand, the Commons voted a total of five subsidies in taxation. At the same time, they prepared a carefully worded document, named the Petition of Right, and offered it to the king, asking him to reverse the decision made in the Five Knights case. They also demanded that, in future, citizens would not be asked to pay forced loans, imprisoned without trial, subjected to martial law or forced to provide free lodgings for soldiers.

After ending the session of parliament because of continuing complaints about Buckingham and the promotion of Arminians in the Church, Charles published a revised version of the Petition that asserted his right to continue collecting Tonnage and Poundage without a parliamentary grant. Using the same justification of emergency powers in the national interest, he also imprisoned any merchants who refused. When one of them, Richard Chambers, was granted bail by the common law courts, Charles had him imprisoned by the **Prerogative Court** of the Star Chamber on direct royal authority. Meanwhile, he also appointed William Laud, a noted Arminian cleric, as Bishop of London.

The Petition of Right had briefly offered the opportunity for reconciliation between Charles and parliament, but the chance of this diminished rapidly as a result of his actions. On top of this, Buckingham was assassinated by a disgruntled army officer named John Felton while reviewing the fleet at Portsmouth. While Charles grieved, the public celebrated with bonfires and, when parliament reassembled in January 1629, the news was further celebrated by MPs. When the reassembled parliament began to look into breaches of the Petition, and the treatment of merchants who had refused to pay Tonnage and Poundage, Charles ordered parliament to adjourn.

On the day of the adjournment, a group of MPs led by Denzil Holles and Sir John Eliot demanded the passing of three formal resolutions against the growth of Arminianism, the levying of Tonnage and Poundage, and the actions of those who paid it. When the Speaker refused to delay the adjournment, they held him in his chair until the resolutions passed, amid shouting and confusion.

ACTIVITIES
KNOWLEDGE CHECK

**Charles, parliaments and Buckingham, 1625–29**

1 Write a summary paragraph to explain why Charles failed to work with parliament between 1625 and 1629.

2 Create a flowchart outlining the process by which relations between king and parliament broke down.

## Personal rule and its failure, 1629–40

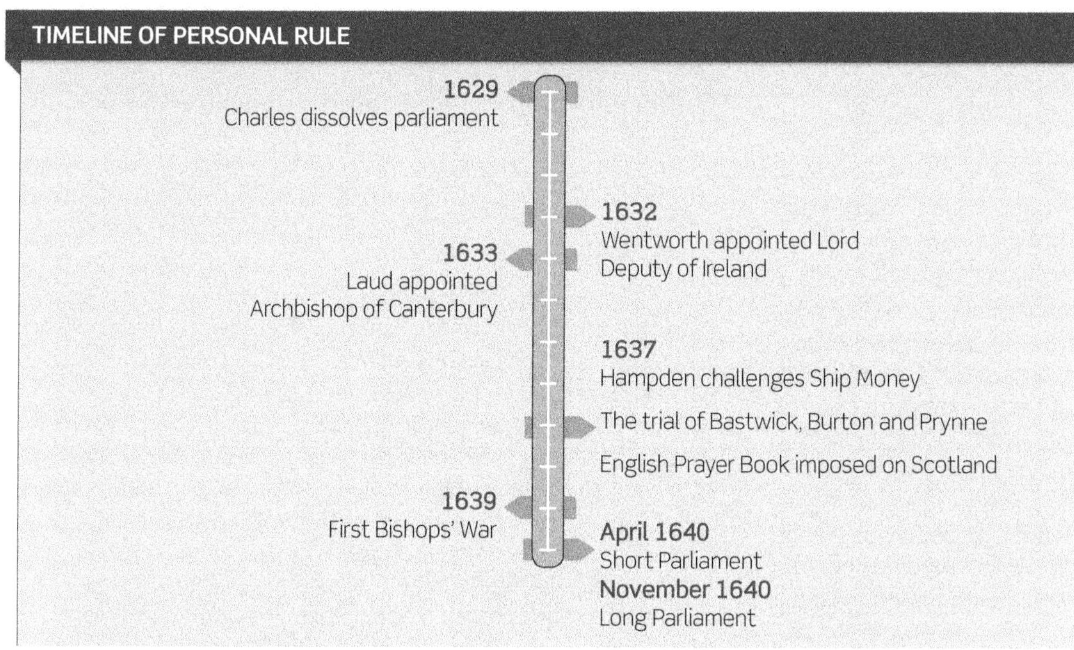


### The significance of the dissolution, 1629–30

With hindsight, it is possible to see that the events of 1629 had significant effects on the quest for stable government in England; it is considered by some historians to mark a turning point in the development of the conflict that led eventually to civil war. Following the views of those who opposed Charles in these years, a number of historians writing in the 19th and early 20th centuries argued that Charles was seeking to create an **absolute monarchy**, similar to those that existed in Spain and, later, in France under Louis XIV. In their view, the dissolution of 1629 and the personal rule that followed constituted a deliberate attempt to destroy parliament as an institution and govern entirely by the authority of a divine right monarch, responsible only to God. Parliamentary opponents were imprisoned, most notably John Eliot, who died in the Tower of London in 1632. Their term for what is now mainly labelled the personal rule was the 'Eleven Years Tyranny'. More recent historians have challenged this argument and concluded that what Charles intended in these years was to create an efficient and stable system of government, based on his own political and religious beliefs. Source 1 offers some clues to his thinking.

KEY TERM

**Absolute monarchy**
A system of government in which the monarch holds unrestricted power over the state and people. Absolute monarchies are often hereditary.

SOURCE 1

From 'The Declaration of Charles I', published 10 March 1629.

Howsoever princes are not bound to give an account of their actions but to God alone... we have thought good to set thus much down by way of declaration, that we may appear to the world in the truth and sincerity of our actions... As we have been careful for the settling of religion and quieting the church, so we were not unmindful of the preservation of the just and ancient liberties of our subjects... [but] the House [of Commons] hath of late years endeavoured to extend their privileges by setting up general committees for religion, for courts of justice, for trade and the like... So as, where in former times the Knights and Burgesses were wont to communicate to the House such business as they brought from their countries [counties], now... they make enquiry upon all sorts of men... to break through all respects and ligaments of government, and to erect a universal over-swaying power to themselves, which belongs only to us, and not to them...

If Charles was attempting to establish an absolute monarchy, contemporaries seem to have been unaware of it. Across the country, the dissolution provoked very little reaction, in part because the behaviour of the MPs who forced the Three Resolutions through the House seemed to justify it. Far from causing a dangerous reaction from the political nation, the first few years of the personal rule seem to have been remarkably calm and orderly. Charles proved to be an effective ruler, devoting many hours to the daily business of government and meeting regularly with a Privy Council led by two efficient administrators, William Laud, who became Archbishop of Canterbury in 1633, and Sir Thomas Wentworth, later Lord Strafford. Wentworth had made a name for himself as President of the Council of the North from 1628, and was appointed Lord Deputy of Ireland in 1632.

### Government and finance, 1630–36

Charles signed the Treaty of Madrid in 1630, ending hostilities with Spain. This would lead to Charles' annual spending on war reducing from £500,000 in the years 1625–29 to less than £70,000 in the 1630s. Charles gave his attention to the Crown's finances, reorganising the management of Crown lands, adding new impositions to the collection of Tonnage and Poundage and reviving a number of feudal payments, such as fines for building on, or otherwise encroaching on, royal forests. The practice of selling monopoly licenses was revived, which would give one individual or company the right to dominate production of certain products. In 1634, Charles issued a monopoly patent for the production of soap, claiming that it would improve both the quality and the supply. It generated considerable resentment and became the subject of public debate in 1641, when opponents claimed that many people had been driven out of business and prices to the public had significantly increased in order to benefit the king's revenues. The greatest controversy of all, however, came with the establishment of an annual levy of Ship Money across the country, eventually worth about £200,000 a year to the Exchequer.

The levying of Ship Money for the upkeep of the navy was not new. Unlike parliamentary taxes, it was a demand for payment of an amount set by the government and collected by the county sheriffs, normally from the counties that lined the coasts. Most monarchs had levied Ship Money once or twice during their reign. The difference with Charles was that he introduced it as an annual tax, and levied it across the entire country, thereby greatly increasing its value. The first year of the levy, in 1634, was carried out in the traditional way, and provoked little comment. But, in 1635, it was repeated and extended to the inland counties. By 1636, it had become an annual tax, with the capability of providing a regular income that was independent of any parliament. If the king had no need of parliamentary grants, then he had no need of parliaments. Even if they were called, they would have little power to influence the government. As early as 1610, MPs had remarked that the main reason for summoning parliaments was to obtain money and that, if that need ceased, it was unlikely that parliaments would survive. Other financial devices included distraint of knighthood, a medieval custom whereby all those with land worth over £40 per annum were expected to be knighted by the monarch. If they had failed to present themselves at Charles' coronation, they were fined. Over 9,000 individuals were charged, and a brief campaign against the tax began in Yorkshire in 1634, but gained little support when the Exchequer judges supported Charles' right to collect the tax.

### The new order in Church and state, 1629–36

It is not surprising that those who opposed the general direction of Charles' government were deeply concerned by the issue of finance and attempted to mount resistance. It is also unsurprising that the same group had strong **Puritan** connections, and were disturbed by the ongoing reforms in the Church as well as state and society.

**KEY TERM**

**Puritan**
A Protestant who believed that the Reformation of the Church under Elizabeth I had not gone far enough, and sought to simplify worship and 'purify' it from the taint of Catholic ceremony and superstition.

In the Church of England, the promotion of Arminians like Laud brought a new insistence on control of the clergy by the bishops and of the laity by the clergy. Charles and Laud demanded strict adherence to rules and the substitution of ritual and formality in place of the Puritan emphasis on individual prayer and preaching. Those ministers who resisted were brought before the Church courts or the prerogative Court of High Commission and, if they failed to conform, were deprived of their livings. It has been pointed out that the number of clergy forced out did not rise greatly during the 1630s, but these numbers exclude the hundred or more clergy who chose to emigrate to the Puritan colonies of New England in America. The practice of Puritan gentry buying up the right to appoint the local minister or the right to collect the tithes that formed his salary was strictly forbidden, and a group known as the Feoffees, who had organised the practice to ensure the appointment of Puritan clergy, were forced to disband.

An emphasis on order, formality and hierarchy coloured Charles' Church policies, and it was no coincidence that Catholic influence at Court was perceived to have increased in line with the changes elsewhere. Unlike the chaotic, and sometimes corrupt, court of King James, Charles had created a well-ordered regime with an emphasis on hierarchy and ceremony designed to instil respect for monarchy and emphasise the religious roots of his power. Churches were decorated with statues and colour, organs were restored, and the altar was moved to the east end of the Church in order for a traditional communion to take place.

Charles' most loyal servants during his personal rule were Archbishop Laud and Thomas Wentworth. Wentworth was based mainly in the North, until sent to Ireland as Lord Deputy in 1632, while Laud's residence as archbishop lay outside the court itself. The queen's influence had also become considerable. Not only did she maintain her own chapel and Catholic clergy, she actively encouraged others, including her children, to participate in Catholic worship. From 1635, Charles welcomed to his court an ambassador from the pope, whose interest in art and royal imagery led to a close relationship between the two men. For those who did not share Charles' vision, the unfolding picture of his government in Church and state was ominously clear, uniform and threatening to all that they valued.

ACTIVITIES
KNOWLEDGE CHECK

**Personal rule**

1 Read Source 1.

a) What accusation does Charles make against MPs in the House of Commons?

b) What does he see as their legitimate role in government?

c) What does the declaration suggest about his view of his own role and function as king?

2 Which groups in society would resent the financial and religious reforms made by Charles? Look at each reform in turn.

**EXTRACT 1**

From C. Carlton, 'Three British Revolutions and the Personality of Kingship' in J. A. Pocock (ed.) *Three British Revolutions: 1641, 1688, 1776* (1980).

An authoritarian personality, Charles was incapable of conceding at a time when compromises were desperately demanded from the English monarchy. He was full of that outward self-certainty (manifest in such doctrines as divine right) that only intense inner doubt can engender... Charles saw his kingly role as a judge to whom issues were taken for decision... not that of a bargainer who settled disputes between rival branches of government, and negotiated settlements with other powerful interest groups. No wonder Charles' parliaments all ended in discord... Charles was psychologically incapable of dealing with a parliament that was anything more than a rubber stamp.

**SOURCE 2**

*Charles I on horseback*, by the Flemish court painter, Anthony Van Dyck, 1633.

ACTIVITIES
KNOWLEDGE CHECK

**The image of Charles I**

1 What image of monarchy does the painting by Van Dyke (Source 2) seek to portray? Bearing in mind that Charles was a small man, how is his figure given presence and stature?

2 To what extent does the painting support the analysis of Charles I's personality provided in Extract 1?

## Reaction and resistance, 1636–40

The first attempts at organised resistance came in 1636 from a group of Puritan gentry and nobility who had been active in parliament before 1629 and maintained contact thereafter through a privately organised shipping company, the Providence Island Company. The leaders of the group were John Pym, the Earl of Warwick, the Duke of Bedford and Lord Saye and Sele. Their contacts stretched to a number of family members in East Anglia and the lawyer Oliver St. John, as well as a Buckinghamshire gentleman named John Hampden. Hampden refused to pay his Ship Money in 1636 and initiated a legal challenge, which Charles decided to use as a test case in 1637. St. John acted as Hampden's counsel. Unsurprisingly, the judges in the Court of the King's Bench found in the king's favour when they made their decision in early 1638, but the margin of their decision was a narrow seven to five. Equally significant, the reaction of the gentry in various parts of the country was, according to the future moderate royalist, Sir Edward Hyde, generally hostile.

Nevertheless, the case represented a defeat for the opposition, and once again the lack of a parliament to speak for them revealed the weakness of their position. Those who did attempt to speak out were quickly silenced by action from the Privy Council and Prerogative Courts. In 1637, one of these courts, the Star Chamber, sentenced three Puritan writers, who had published attacks on the government, to have their ears cut off and be branded on the cheeks before being imprisoned at the king's pleasure. The defendants, Henry Burton, John Bastwick and William Prynne, became notorious. That the sentence had been imposed by Laud emphasised the increasing influence of the Laudian bishops in the government of the state as well as the Church. The presence of clergymen in government was also evident in the appointment of William Juxon, Bishop of London, to the post of Lord Treasurer in 1636.

Although opposition to Ship Money increased, and the yield fell to just 20 percent of expected money in 1639, this was not so much because resistance was stronger or better organised, but because the Privy Council and county sheriffs were increasingly distracted and overburdened by the need to raise an army to fight in Scotland.

### KEY TERMS

**Calvinist**
A follower of the religious teachings of John Calvin (1509-64), who stressed that people can only achieve salvation through God's grace, and not through their own merits. Calvinists in the 17th century believed that if they showed outward signs of godliness, it may be a sign that they had been predestined by God to enter heaven.

**Presbyterian**
A church governed by an assembly of elders or officials rather than a hierarchy of bishops.

### ACTIVITIES
KNOWLEDGE CHECK

**The collapse of personal rule**

1 Why was John Hampden's Ship Money case significant?
2 Why do you think Charles was so determined to fight the Scots, despite the costs this would incur?

## The Scottish troubles and collapse of personal rule

If Charles had ever formed a conscious intention to establish an absolute monarchy, his decision to extend his programme of reform to Scotland ensured his failure. In provoking a war that he could not sustain, he weakened his grip on government and demonstrated an inability to understand the impact of his decisions in the three kingdoms. Despite being born there, Charles had little understanding of his Scottish kingdom and only visited in order to be crowned King of Scotland in 1633. Nor did he trust the Scottish Privy Council to make decisions, preferring to rely on the advice of a few Scottish exiles who lived permanently in London. Unlike the Church of England, the Scottish Kirk (Church) had undergone a thoroughly **Calvinist** reformation led by John Knox in 1560, and emerged as a highly organised **Presbyterian** institution run by an assembly of ministers and lay Elders. A number of events in Scotland caused Charles to recall parliament in 1640.

- In 1636, Charles issued a Book of Canons to the Scottish clergy. This listed instructions as to how they should lay out their churches and introduced a number of practices associated with the Church of England.
- In 1637, Charles introduced the English Prayer Book to Scottish churches. When the book was first read in St. Giles Cathedral, Edinburgh, a riot broke out. Disorder spread across the lowlands and, in 1638, the Scottish clergy and nobility met and drew up a National Covenant to defend the Kirk and restore their religious rights.
- Both Charles and the Covenanters raised armies, but Charles, lacking money, had to rely on the county militias from England. Realising he could not win, Charles signed the Treaty of Berwick in 1639, ending what became known as the First Bishops' War.
- Many of the gentry were unhappy with the idea of funding a war with the Scots, and there was a 'taxpayers' strike' in the years 1639–40. Lacking funds, and unable to borrow money from the London merchants, Charles turned to Wentworth, who advised him to call a parliament. When this so-called Short Parliament assembled in April 1640, amid a flood of petitions against various aspects of personal rule, Charles had the opportunity to save the situation by making concessions. Instead, after Charles demanded money from parliament, the Commons entered into a series of debates, and he was compelled to dissolve parliament after only three weeks.
- Charles collected together an ill-organised and under-equipped force in order to fight a Second Bishops' War. Most of his soldiers actually sympathised with the Scots, and occupied themselves burning altar rails and other symbols associated with Catholicism. Charles was defeated at the Battle of Newburn, near Newcastle, and under the terms of the subsequent Treaty of Ripon in October 1640 he was forced to pay the Scots £850 a day while they occupied Newcastle.

# The failure to compromise, 1640-49

### TIMELINE OF CIVIL WAR AND THE SEARCH FOR A SETTLEMENT

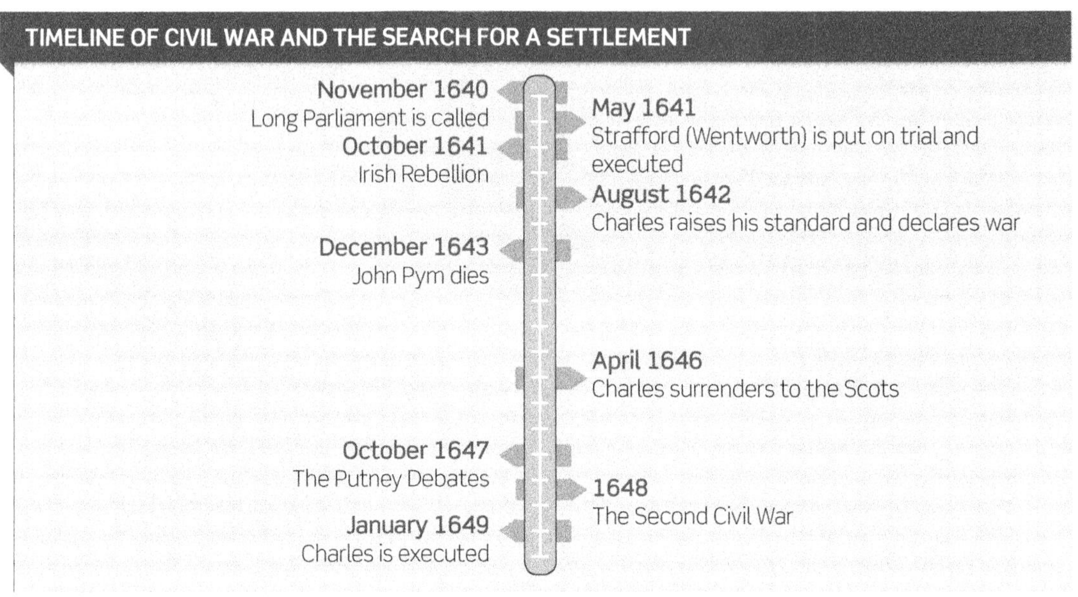

## Parliament attacks the prerogative, 1640–41

When the **Long Parliament** assembled, Pym and his allies were ready to seize the opportunity for which they had waited so long. The early months of the parliament saw the arrest and impeachments of Laud and Strafford, steps to forbid the financial strategies used by Charles to raise money outside parliament, and the passing of two Acts to ensure the future security of parliaments. The group that led the opposition, known as '**Pym's Junto**' by later historians, was certainly a new element in English politics, but the emergence of an organised opposition of this kind was the result, rather than the cause, of the build-up to the political crisis. Relations between both sides broke down over the course of 1640–42.

- The opposition began by removing the king's 'evil counsellors', who had been blamed for the policies enacted during personal rule. Wentworth (now Earl of Strafford) and Laud were both arrested in November 1640 and impeached. In February 1641, parliament introduced the Triennial Act, which laid down an obligation for Charles to call a parliament at least once every three years.
- Strafford was put on trial in April 1641, but to be found guilty of treason he would have to be tried in the House of Lords. Knowing that the Lords would find him not guilty, as he was one of their own, the opposition resorted to passing an **Act of Attainder** against Strafford and he was beheaded in May. To secure the passage of the Act, Pym revealed the existence of a plot by Catholic army officers to release Strafford and dissolve parliament by force. This became known as the First Army Plot and was followed by another at the end of 1641 aimed at bolstering support for Charles. An angry mob surrounded parliament after the Attainder was passed, and Charles, who had promised to protect Strafford, was compelled to sign his death warrant. At the same time, Pym secured another Act, against the Dissolution of this Parliament without its Own Consent.

### KEY TERMS

**Long Parliament**
So-called because, although it was purged and unable to assemble for long periods, it was not dissolved until March 1660.

**Pym's Junto**
The group that organised the opposition strategy to the king in the Long Parliament, led by John Pym, John Hampden and Arthur Haselrig. Pym's training as a lawyer and meticulous work in recording Charles' illegal actions in the 1630s made him an ideal leader for the opposition.

**Act of Attainder**
An Act of parliament that effectively acts as a death warrant. The Act only required a suspicion of guilt, and, as long as it was passed by both Houses and signed by the monarch, no trial was required.

- Some MPs thought that Pym had gone too far in pursuing Strafford and, when a bill was introduced to exclude bishops from the Lords and then establish a new Church along Presbyterian lines, clear divisions among the MPs started to become clear.
- In June 1641, Pym pushed for more constitutional changes, including the abolition of the Prerogative Courts and the abolition of Ship Money. A 'middle group' of moderates emerged in the Commons, led by Sir Edward Hyde and encouraged by allies in the Lords such as Lord Falkland. They favoured a settlement with both king and parliament, and would become known as Constitutional Royalists.
- The opposition drew up Ten Propositions to be considered by the king and requested he accept them before he left for Scotland to make peace. These propositions included significant extensions of parliamentary power, such as the right to approve the king's advisers and measures to protect themselves from royal vengeance.

## The build-up to war, 1641–42

The MPs returned to Westminster in October, and they were greeted by growing rumours of a rising among Irish Catholics and attacks on Protestant settlers in Ireland. These rumours quickly developed into tales of massacre, at least 200,000 deaths, and the landing of an Irish army in north-west England. Nothing could have been better calculated to induce panic among the population, with the possibility of English Catholics rising to join the Irish and tales of brutality and torture increasing daily. The reality, of course, proved much less dramatic, with only a few thousand deaths, but the conjunction of Irish influence, Catholicism and a king who was already mistrusted had done the damage.

Despite the spread of panic over the Irish rebellion, Charles remained in Scotland until November and, in his absence, parliament decided that an army must be raised to tackle the rebellion. Some MPs feared that Charles might use the army against parliament, so Pym devised a plan to unite the Commons behind a demand that parliament should be allowed to approve the king's choice of commander. He sent the king the 'Grand Remonstrance' on 22 November 1641, a document that asserted much of what had been included in the Ten Propositions. When the Grand Remonstrance was put before parliament, it passed the Commons by only 11 votes, thereby revealing the extent of its divisions. When Arthur Haselrig presented the Militia bill to provide an army under the control of parliament to tackle the Irish Rebellion, outraged moderates flocked to Charles' side.

In early January 1642, rumours reached the king that Pym was planning to impeach the queen. On 3 January, Charles ordered the House of Lords to begin impeachment proceedings against the opposition leaders; on 4 January, he arrived at the House of Commons with a warrant for the arrest of five leading members, including Pym and Hampden, backed by an armed escort of 300 soldiers. Such an open attack on the rights of parliament might have been worth the risk if it succeeded, but the five members in question had been warned and had already taken refuge in the City. By 10 January, the king abandoned London for the safety of his family and retired to Hampton Court. From there he would move the court to his northern capital of York. In June, parliament issued Nineteen Propositions as the basis for a negotiated settlement, but the list of demands, including that parliament should oversee the education of the king's children, suggests that their primary purpose was to state the case for parliament and rally support. The kng's reply did the same. Both sides attempted to protect themselves by raising forces, and the king finally raised his standard at Nottingham in August 1642 to declare war.

Historians have attempted to explain the causes of the Civil War and it is a topic that excites much debate. Two interpretations are offered in Extracts 2 and 3.

**EXTRACT 2** From John Morrill, 'What was the English Revolution?' in *History Today*, March 1984.

Those living through the period 1570-1640 would have felt themselves much closer to civil war in the first two decades than in the last two... The Crown had weathered the storm induced by a century of population growth and price inflation. By the 1630s... the economic and social outlook was rosier... Far from being a state sliding into civil war and anarchy, the early Stuart state saw fewer treason trials, no revolts, fewer riots... It can thus be argued that the civil wars grew out of the policies and out of the particular failings of a particular king, Charles I.

**EXTRACT**

From Antony Fletcher, *The Outbreak of the English Civil War* (1981).

Great events do not necessarily have great causes, though it is natural for historians to seek them. Most of [the MPs] who rode up to Westminster in November 1640 had no concept of a parliamentary cause in their minds. Reconciliation and settlement were seen as the purposes of parliaments, and the reforms that most MPs envisaged seemed perfectly compatible with such an end. Only Pym and a few close friends saw the matter in totally different terms: for them the parliamentary cause was the rooting out of a conspiracy that struck at the core of the nation's life... All this, though, is only one side of the picture. Charles I had a jaundiced [sceptical] view of parliaments and a strong sense of distrust of certain individuals who, he believed, were ready to challenge his monarchy for private and selfish ends. [This] would have been less serious if his character had been different. He was a man who magnified distrust even in the most loyal hearts...

What happened in 1641 and 1642 was that two groups of men became the prisoners of competing myths that fed on one another, so that events seemed to confirm two opposing interpretations of the political crisis that were both originally misconceived and erroneous.

**ACTIVITIES**
**KNOWLEDGE CHECK**

**The causes of the Civil War**

1 Why did the Civil War break out, according to Extracts 2 and 3?

2 The historians offer different interpretations of the causes of the Civil War, but are they incompatible?

3 Using the information on the build-up to war, how far do you agree that the Civil War was the intended outcome of an effort to reform the monarchy and secure stable government?

**THINKING HISTORICALLY** Causation (4a&b)

**Fragile history**

Nothing that happens is inevitable. There are causes of change that did not have to develop as they did. Something could have altered or someone could have chosen differently. What actually occurred in the past did happen, but it did not have to be like that.

Work on your own and answer the questions below. When you have answered them, discuss your answers in groups.

Perceived reasons for the outbreak of the English Civil War:

| Development | Event | State of affairs | Event | Trigger event |
|---|---|---|---|---|
| The rise in distrust between Charles and parliament | The attempted introduction of a new Prayer Book in Scotland in 1637 | Tension within the Protestant movement between Arminians and Puritans | The impeachment of the Earl of Strafford | Charles' attempt to arrest five MPs in parliament |

1 Consider the introduction of the English Prayer Book to Scotland and the religious tensions of the time.

a) How did the introduction of the Prayer Book affect the tension between Protestants?

b) Had there been no tension, would the Prayer Book still have been important?

c) What other aspects of the situation existing in 1637 would have been affected had there been no religious tension?

2 Consider the distrust between Charles and parliament, and the incidents involving Strafford and the five MPs.

a) How important is the distrust between Charles and parliament as a causal factor of the two events?

b) What might have happened had Charles refused to sign Strafford's death warrant?

3 What other consequences came about as a result of the information in the table? Try to identify at least one consequence for each.

4 Choose one factor. How might the English Civil War have developed differently if this factor had not been present?

### The victory of parliament, 1642-46

In military terms, the Civil War of 1642–46 consisted of three main phases.

- In 1642–43, the advantage lay with the king, who controlled much of the country and benefitted from the support of the majority of gentry and nobility. In addition, he controlled the existing officer corps and was ably assisted by his nephews, Prince Rupert of the Rhine and Maurice of Nassau, both of whom had gained experience of fighting in the Thirty Years War (1618–48). In October 1642, the royalist forces gained a marginal advantage at the Battle of Edgehill.
- In 1643, Pym established an excise tax in the parliamentary areas to maintain parliament's forces. With some difficulty, Pym maintained parliamentary unity in the face of military defeats and a strong desire among many MPs for peace. Although he had to agree to peace negotiations at Oxford, he had prevented the 'peace party', who wanted a negotiated settlement with Charles, from making the kind of concessions that Charles would have required. By late 1643, Pym was seriously ill (probably with a form of cancer) but, before his death, he succeeded in persuading the Commons to sign a Solemn League and Covenant with the Scottish forces, thereby bringing an effective and experienced force to the aid of parliament's forces in the North. The Scottish army was instrumental in the parliamentary victory at Marston Moor in July 1644.
- Poor performances by the parliamentary leader, the Earl of Essex, created a crisis within parliament and among its military commanders. After failed peace talks at Uxbridge in early 1645, a motion was presented in parliament for a Self-Denying Ordinance, under which all the military leaders, such as Essex and Lord Manchester, would resign their commands to facilitate the creation of a single 'New Model' army. An army of 22,000 men was created, led by the Yorkshire gentleman, Sir Thomas Fairfax, which drew from all of the existing forces. Fairfax was a man with proven talent as a soldier, and little interest in politics, making him acceptable to both the 'peace' and 'war' parties that had emerged in parliament. Another commander who had achieved his status through merit rather than title was Oliver Cromwell, who was appointed cavalry commander.

The creation of the New Model Army marked the third phase of the war and effectively secured parliamentary victory. Its first major success came at the Battle of Naseby in June 1645, and Fairfax moved south and mopped up resistance in much of the south-west. Its success has been attributed to its character as an army of the godly, but in fact it owed much more to training, discipline and leadership.

### The search for settlement, 1646-47

When Charles surrendered to the Scots in April 1646, the overwhelming reaction among parliament's supporters was one of relief and a desire for a speedy settlement. It is clear that, at this time, there was no thought of removing or replacing Charles, and even less consideration of government without a monarchy. One of the initial sources of discontent in parliament, Charles' advisers, had been removed when Laud was finally executed in 1645. While Charles was held by the Scots at Newcastle, he received separate proposals for a settlement from the Scots and from the English parliament, both of which would have restored him to his throne, albeit with some restrictions. Of the two, the Scottish proposals were more generous in political terms.

The Scots entered the war in order to secure the future of the Presbyterian Church. They had been left dissatisfied at the authorities in Westminster, who offered disappointing religious settlements. As parliament were not going to give them their desired reformation, they turned to Charles, although he delayed his response to the Scottish proposals. The Scots gave up in February 1647 and handed him over to the English.

### Divisions in parliament

Parliament offered Charles its own Proposals at Newcastle in July 1646. The group now dominating parliament had been labelled 'political Presbyterians' because of its desire to restrict religious freedom and bring the more radical elements under control. The Newcastle Propositions consisted of the following demands:

- parliament would nominate the key officers of state
- parliament would control the militia for 20 years
- bishops would be abolished and a Presbyterian Church would be created for an experimental three years.

Charles delayed his answer, although he was never likely to accept all of the proposals. While parliament waited for his response, the radical Levellers, who had started as a group advocating religious toleration, developed a political programme. The Levellers had support from within the New Model Army, but the main concern of most soldiers was the arrears of pay that had not been given to them. Despite Cromwell speaking up in their defence, parliament voted to disband the army without pay. Within a few months, the army emerged as a rival political force. They elected their own political spokesmen, known as Agitators.

On 4 June 1647, a junior officer, Cornet Joyce, arrived with an escort at Holdenby House to take possession of the king and escort him to join the army at Newmarket, from where he was later transferred to Hampton Court and held under army supervision. The next day, the leading officers (including Oliver Cromwell) signed an Engagement to stand with the army, and established a General Council consisting of both officers and Agitators. Cromwell was at this point still subordinate to Thomas Fairfax, commander-in-chief of the parliamentary army. Cromwell, however, was more politically astute and ensured he was at the centre of negotiations. Cromwell had chosen to place army unity above other concerns and he was quickly supported by other leading officers, including his son-in-law, Henry Ireton. By mid-June, a document penned by Ireton, the *Representation of the Army*, was published. In it, he demanded the expulsion of 11 Presbyterian MPs and reasonable religious toleration, as well as fresh elections with a wider electorate.

For the army leaders, the priority was a fair settlement with the king and, on 2 August, they presented him with the Heads of the Proposals, drafted by Henry Ireton, as the basis for negotiation. The Proposals included the following.

- The Triennial Act would be repealed and replaced with Biennial parliaments.

- Parliament would nominate key officers of state for 10 years.
- Parliament would control the militia for 10 years.
- There would be continued use of bishops in the Church but a restriction on their coercive powers.

ACTIVITIES
KNOWLEDGE CHECK

**The victory of parliament**

1 In what ways would MPs learn from the experience of governing the areas held by parliament during the Civil War?

2 In what ways did the experience of warfare encourage radical religious and political ideas?

## Politicisation of the army

The Leveller influence in the army became more pronounced and many demanded a more radical blueprint than the Heads of the Proposals. In October 1647, the Leveller-influenced soldiers offered alternative proposals in the *Case of the Army Truly Stated*, which was drawn up into a potential settlement under the title of *The Agreement of the People* and presented to the Army General Council by the Agitators, with the support of some junior officers. In the ensuing debates at Putney, the gulf between the radicals and the leading officers became clearer and wider. The spokesman for the radicals was Colonel Thomas Rainsborough, the highest-ranking Leveller officer. He demanded complete religious freedom and annual parliaments elected by all adult males. Ireton, speaking for the army 'grandees', or senior commanders, countered with the claim that voters must have enough property to prevent them from easy migration. Cromwell focused on maintaining a level of civility between participants and avoiding a complete breakdown of relations between the two groups. The debates were brought to an abrupt end by the news that Charles had escaped from captivity at Hampton Court.

Charles was soon in custody again at Carisbrooke Castle on the Isle of Wight, but his escape meant the Agitators had to return to their regiments. At one army muster at Ware in Hertfordshire, a group of London Levellers appeared with copies of *The Agreement of the People* and urged the troops to mutiny. Cromwell quickly rode into the ranks to restore order and punish their leaders. On 26 December, the king had signed a secret Engagement with the Scots, where he promised to establish a Presbyterian Church in England for three years in return for their military assistance. While an angry parliament voted in early January to hold no more negotiations with Charles, the army readied itself for more action.

ACTIVITIES
KNOWLEDGE CHECK

**Conflicting agendas**

1 What did the political Presbyterians want from the post-war settlement?

2 In what ways did the army take political actions?

## The Second Civil War and the execution of Charles I, 1648–49

The Scots entered England in April 1648, triggering the brief Second Civil War, and were easily defeated by an army commanded by Cromwell in August. Some MPs were still having doubts about ending negotiations, although Charles refused point blank to abolish bishops for more than three years. After a prayer meeting at Windsor, the army presented a Remonstrance to the Commons on 20 November. Written by Ireton, it demanded that Charles be brought to justice. Cromwell agonised about his own stance, but eventually decided that, by deliberately renewing the war in 1648, Charles had betrayed the trust of his people in the eyes of God. Parliament sent four bills to Charles as a final demand, which consisted of a slightly modified version of the Newcastle Propositions. Charles replied that he would consider allowing parliament to have some control of the militia, although he had already confided to friends that he had no intention of standing by his answer.

The Commons promptly voted the king's reply to be a basis for further negotiation. Ireton, already set on punishing the king, acted to forestall this settlement. On 5 December, the Commons was surrounded by soldiers from the regiment of Colonel Thomas Pride. He excluded 186 MPs who supported continued negotiations, and arrested another 45 who had been active in promoting further discussions. This left a 'Rump' House of 240, of whom 71 would become actively involved in the trial and execution of Charles I. A High Court of Justice was created to try Charles. He was found guilty on 27 January 1649 and beheaded on 30 January.

ACTIVITIES
KNOWLEDGE CHECK

**The search for a settlement**

Create a table to explain why a settlement was not reached between 1646 and 1649. The headings for your columns should be 'Political Presbyterians', 'Scots', 'Charles' and 'The army'. Under each heading, explain why that group or individual was responsible for the lack of a settlement.

**AS Level Exam-Style Question Section A**

Were the actions of Charles I the main reason for the political instability that existed in the years 1625–46? (20 marks)

**Tip**

*Charles' actions before personal rule, during the 1630s and during the search for a settled government should be weighed up against other reasons for instability.*

**A Level Exam-Style Question Section A**

To what extent did the failures of English government in the years 1625–49 arise from a lack of money? (20 marks)

**Tip**

*It is essential to plan your arguments before you start writing. These may include lack of money, religious issues and the personality of the king, among others.*

# TO WHAT EXTENT DID REPUBLICAN RULE PROVIDE A STABLE GOVERNMENT, 1649–60?

## Reasons for the failure of republican governments, 1649–53

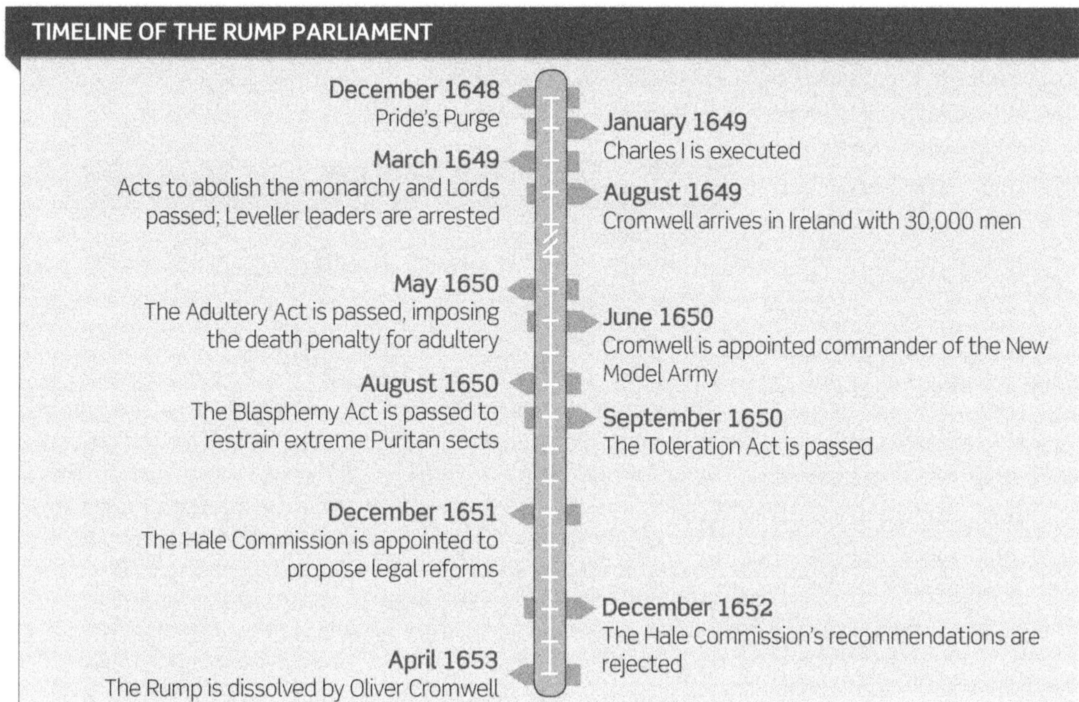


### The rule of the Rump

From the very beginning, those who carried through the execution of Charles I faced problems in establishing a government to replace him. Ireland was already a royalist stronghold and, when news of the execution reached Scotland, Charles II was immediately proclaimed king there in February 1649, although he was still in exile in Holland at the time and would not be crowned until 1651. Within England, the situation was no better. The haste with which the regicides had been forced to act prevented any attempt to plan ahead. Ireton had intended to dissolve parliament and hold new elections, but the mood of the country made that impossible, and power simply had to pass to the MPs who remained at Westminster. On 4 January 1649, the remaining MPs, collectively known as the Rump, reassembled. When the few Lords who had remained as allies refused to return, the assembly declared itself to be the sole legislative authority and elected a **Council of State** to govern in its name. It was not until March 1649 that the monarchy and House of Lords were abolished and then two months later that England was declared to be a **Commonwealth** governed by a single-chamber parliament.

#### KEY TERMS

**Council of State**
A government council that considers high-level policy, similar to the Privy Council.

**Commonwealth**
The official name given to the government of England from the abolition of the monarchy in 1649 to the establishment of the Protectorate in 1653.

#### EXTEND YOUR KNOWLEDGE

**The Rump and radicalism**
Other than the Anabaptists and Levellers within the army, by 1650 a number of more eccentric groups had emerged. These included the Fifth Monarchists and Ranters, who took ideas that were quite widespread to extremes that made them a threat to society.

The Fifth Monarchists believed, as a number of people did, that Christ would eventually return to earth to rule in person, but the events of war also convinced them that this return was imminent and it was the duty of true believers (the Saints) to seize control of government and prepare the way.

The Ranters took the idea of predestination and argued that, if they were predestined to be saved, then they were incapable of sin – apparently sinful actions simply demonstrated the purity of their minds. The most important group to emerge, however, were the Quakers, who believed in complete spiritual equality and the right of all people to follow the spirit of God within them.

Although these groups expected religious toleration, it was not forthcoming. The Toleration Act of 1650 removed the requirement for people to attend church as long as they took part in a religious service each week. However, nothing was done to remove tithes (church taxes) and, in April 1652, the Rump declared that the collection of tithes should continue. The Blasphemy Act of August 1650 was aimed at restricting radical religious sects.

## The failure of the Rump

The fundamental issue facing the new regime was already clear. The 'revolution' of 1649 was the work of a minority, who needed wider support in order to establish an effective government, and across the country local government and order still depended on the active co-operation of the political nation. The first task of the new regime was therefore to restore stability, to calm the fears of the men of property and win their confidence. Unfortunately, the main source of those fears was the very army on which the regime's existence depended.

The problem was demonstrated clearly in the first two years of the Commonwealth's existence. The army fulfilled its role by suppressing threats from the Levellers, in particular a mutiny of Leveller soldiers at Burford in May 1649 that resulted in several of their leaders being shot. The army also continued to counter the threat from the royalists in Ireland and Scotland. The Council of State turned its attention to the reform of government. Reform of the law, a greater measure of social justice – for example, the ending of imprisonment for debt and an end to high taxation – would help to win over opinion across a range of social classes.

While many of the greater gentry and nobility refused to co-operate with the regime, the lesser gentry had taken over much of local government. The distinct lack of support that greeted Charles II's attempted invasion in 1651 suggested that a combination of reform and stability from the new regime could succeed in generating the acceptance that it needed. Charles was easily defeated at the Battle of Worcester, although it served as a reminder that the threat of royalism was not extinct.

Two factors prevented the Rump from providing stability.

- The first was that the proposed reforms involved complex areas such as the law that could not be agreed upon. The Hale Commission was set up in 1651 to investigate reform of the legal system. The Commission met regularly for a year, but its recommendations were never adopted. The rate of reform in general slowed down with time. In 1649, 125 Acts of parliament were passed, reducing to just 51 in 1652.
- The second was the necessity of maintaining a large standing army, the maintenance of which was the major reason for high taxation. Without reliable support from the political nation, the regime could not reduce or dispense with the army, but as long as the army existed, that reliable support would not be forthcoming. In April 1649, the Rump began the sale of Crown lands to raise money, but wars in Ireland, Scotland and against the Dutch led to a shortfall in revenue of £700,000 in 1653.

Cromwell had landed in Ireland in August 1649 to suppress Catholic royalist sympathisers. He expected a swift victory, but only achieved success after he had stormed the strongholds of Drogheda and Wexford, controversially slaughtering thousands of defenders after they had surrendered, and civilians, in the process. He returned to England in 1650 to conquer Scotland, and left Ireton to complete the Irish campaign. Although they had been parliament's allies, the Scots had cut ties with the English after Charles was killed. After Charles II was declared king in Scotland and made peace with the Covenanters, they assembled an army to invade England. With Fairfax reluctant to take on the task of marching to Scotland to attack first, Cromwell was appointed commander-in-chief and, in September 1650, defeated the Scots at Dunbar. Charles led his army south a year later, hoping to gain support, but a dispirited army was defeated by Cromwell at Worcester on 3 September 1651. The First Anglo-Dutch War (1652–54) also took its toll on the treasury. In order to pay for the construction of warships, the **monthly assessment** was raised to £90,000. The assessment alone now raised as much as Charles' entire annual revenue.

**KEY TERM**

**Monthly assessment**
A tax modelled on the Ship Money system, originally collected in areas under the control of parliament during the Civil War.

In the end, a combination of repressive measures and apparent self-seeking by parliament drove Cromwell to dissolve the Rump by force in 1653 and take on himself the role of combining stability with measures of reform. Since the victory over Charles II at Worcester, he had sought to restrain the demands of the Army Council while doing all that he could to persuade the Rump to enact reforms, but in April 1653 he ran out of patience. The final straw appears to have been the decision taken by MPs to hold new elections in order to replace those MPs who had been excluded or had chosen to stay away. Given the mood in the country, it was clear that the elections would increase the representation of conservative views, and Cromwell was aware that any chance of further reforms would disappear. When he discovered that the Rump planned to rush through a bill for elections before addressing any of the reforms desired by the army, he ordered its dissolution. Sources 3–5 provide differing accounts of the dissolution.

**SOURCE 3**

Edmund Ludlow's account of the dissolution, from *The Memoirs of Edmund Ludlow* (1698–99). Ludlow had recently acted as an officer in the army against Irish royalists.

[Cromwell] suddenly standing up, made a speech, wherein he loaded the Parliament with the vilest reproaches, charging them not to have a heart to do anything for the public good, to have espoused the corrupt interest of the Presbytery and the lawyers, who were the supporters of tyranny and oppression, accusing them of an intention to perpetuate themselves in power... the General stept into the midst of the House, where continuing his distracted language, he said 'Come, come, I will put an end to your prating [idle chatter]'; then walking up and down the House like a madman, and kicking the ground with his feet, he cried out 'You are no Parliament, I say you are no Parliament; I will put an end to your sitting; call them in, call them in'. Whereupon... Lieutenant-Colonel Worsley with two files of musketeers entered the House.

**SOURCE 4** A report by Lorenzo Paulucci, Venetian ambassador to the Venetian court, May 1653.

The dissolution is viewed with admiration rather than surprise and gives general satisfaction. The popular voice and the press shows how much the nation disapproved the administration of the parliament, which is principally reproached for having constantly promised law reform but never having done anything, and with having broken faith with those who advanced considerable loans during the civil wars. While instead of seeking to relieve the people, as they promised, they always deceived and taxed them more and more and finally they saddled the country with a troublesome and expensive war with Holland.

**SOURCE 5** Cromwell dissolving the Rump, from a contemporary Dutch engraving. Cromwell says: 'Be gone you rogues. You have sat long enough.' On the wall, the words 'This House to Let' are written.

## ACTIVITIES
### KNOWLEDGE CHECK

**The failure of the Rump**

1 For what reasons were the army and the political nation dissatisfied with the Rump?

2 According to Sources 3 and 4, why did Cromwell dissolve the Rump?

3 Why do you think animals are included in the engraving of Cromwell dissolving the Rump (Source 5)?

## THINKING HISTORICALLY Evidence (3a)

**The value of evidence**

Read Sources 3 and 4, and complete the following.

1 Write down at least three ways in which Ludlow's account is useful for establishing the causes of the dissolution of the Rump, and three ways in which the Venetian ambassador's report is useful.

2 Compare your answers with a partner, then try to come up with at least two limitations of each source for establishing the causes of the dissolution of the Rump.

3 Discuss with a partner whether you think Ludlow or the ambassador is more useful for establishing the causes of the dissolution of the Rump.

4 What if the sources were used to answer the question 'What was the role of Cromwell in the dissolution of the Rump?' Copy and complete the diagrams to show the usefulness and limitations of the two sources for this question and for two questions of your own.

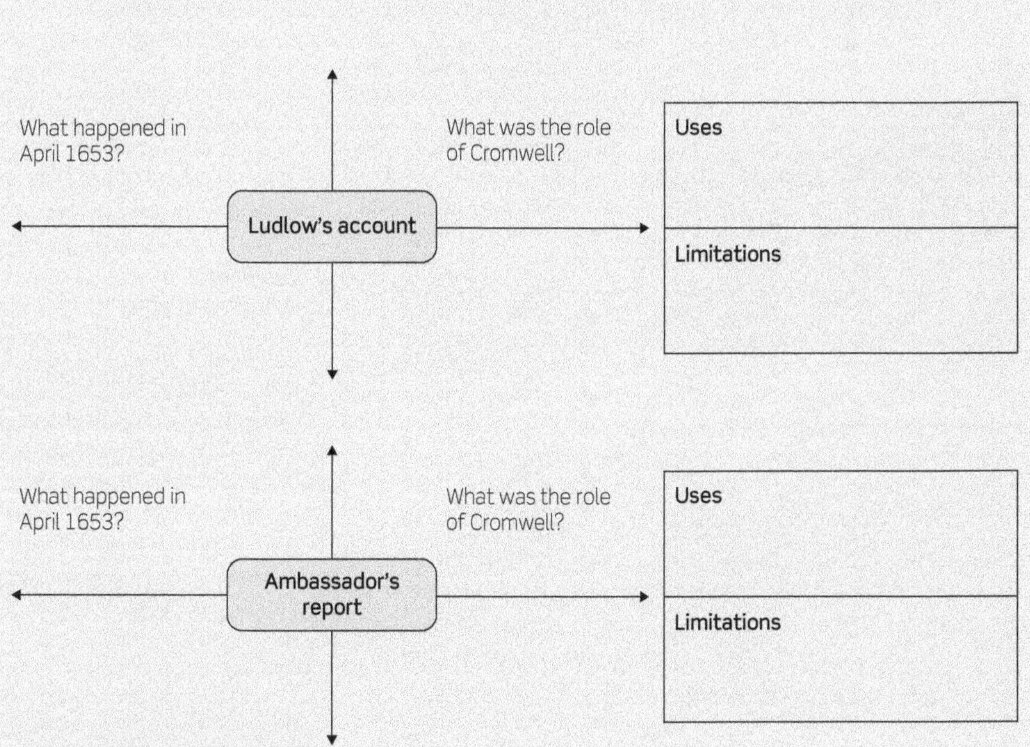

## The role of Oliver Cromwell, 1653-60

### EXTEND YOUR KNOWLEDGE

**Oliver Cromwell's early life**

Cromwell was born into the landed gentry in East Anglia, although as a younger son his father inherited property in the town of Huntingdon rather than the main family estate at Hinchinbroke. Brought up a Protestant and partly educated by a local Puritan, Thomas Beard, Cromwell nevertheless underwent a process of 'conversion' before adopting his characteristic beliefs and embarking on a life dedicated to God's service.

By his own account, Cromwell indulged in a range of youthful sins during his education at Sidney Sussex College in Cambridge. He served as MP for Huntingdon in 1628, suggesting that he had attained some status in the town. There followed a crisis that seems to have arisen from a quarrel within the Huntingdon Corporation about the spending of money that had been given to the town to endow a public lecture by a preacher. Cromwell objected to the way that the money was being used and apparently spoke out, but his opponents were able to use contacts in the Privy Council to uphold their actions, and he was forced into a humiliating public apology.

As a result, he had to sell his father's house at a loss and use the remains of his inheritance to purchase land at St. Ives, where he worked as a yeoman farmer, a degrading experience for one brought up as a gentleman. It would appear that this experience led to some kind of depression, from which he recovered through prayer and the study of similar trials endured by individuals in the Bible, becoming convinced that God had punished him for his worldliness as a means of bringing him to salvation.

Thereafter, Cromwell's life is an illustration of the powerful and active faith that Puritanism engendered. Dedicating his life to God's service meant using his energy and talents to promote godliness in whatever way they permitted. Shortly after his conversion, he inherited a house in Ely and the role of Steward (business manager) for the Cathedral there, which included management of its land and property. Thus restored to a level of prosperity, he nevertheless remained sufficiently outspoken to stand as champion for the Fen dwellers, whose livelihoods were threatened by schemes for drainage and land improvement, insisting that they be compensated.

This would not be the last occasion when he showed sympathy for the poor and humble, and much of his military success arose from a willingness to recognise talent, reward hard work and discipline, and promote men on merit, regardless of their status. In 1640, he was elected to the Long Parliament as MP for Cambridge, where his family links brought him into contact with the opposition leaders, and when war was imminent in 1642 he returned to Cambridge and raised a force of local volunteers to take control of Cambridge Castle.

### Nominated Assembly, 1653

Unsure of the next step after dissolving the Rump, Cromwell was advised by Colonel Lambert to introduce a new constitution. He seems to have listened to the suggestion made by Colonel Thomas Harrison to ask the various churches and radical groups to nominate an assembly of good men to consider and formulate a government. Cromwell formed a committee of four generals, which asked the Independent Churches to nominate members for a new parliament that would become known as the Nominated Assembly. Once the members had been nominated, the Council of Officers added several more names and reduced the total down to 140. This assembly even included members from Wales, Scotland and Ireland, and Cromwell told the members that they were to answer the call of God and enact a godly reformation in his opening speech (Source 6).

**SOURCE 6** Oliver Cromwell's speech to the Barebones Parliament, 14 July 1653.

Truly you are called by God... And you are called to be faithful with the Saints who have been instrumental to your call... Therefore, I beseech you,—but I think I need not,—have a care of the Whole Flock! Love the sheep, love the lambs, love all, tender all, cherish and countenance all, in all things that are good. And if the poorest Christian, the most mistaken Christian, shall desire to live peaceably and quietly under you,—I say, if any shall desire but to lead a life of godliness and honesty, let him be protected.

The commonly used nickname for this parliament, the 'Barebones Parliament', comes from the name of one of its more radical members, 'Praise-God' Nicholas Barbon, a leather seller and preacher from London. However, the majority of its members were of the lesser gentry, who were conservative by nature and had little interest in godly reforms.

A number of moderate and relatively progressive reforms were enacted, as follows.

- The war with the Dutch was continued, as the members of the Assembly were well aware of the need to secure trade routes.
- Legal measures to help debtors were introduced.
- Regulations concerning the treatment of lunatics were introduced.
- Civil marriage was allowed, officiated by JPs.

Although nowhere near as eccentric as its nickname suggested, this nominated assembly did include a radical minority of Fifth Monarchists, whose schemes for godly government frightened the more cautious members. Cromwell was faced with the question of how to deliver reform without alienating the conservative members. The radical 'saints' felt they could not work with the 'sinners' of the conservative gentry and the propertied members were unhappy at the suggestion that the Assembly abolish tithes, which were often key to their financial well-being.

In December 1653, the more moderate members met and voted to dissolve the Assembly. Major-General John Lambert produced the **Instrument of Government** three days later, offering an entirely new constitution, formalised in a Protectorate, with government by a single person in Oliver Cromwell and a parliament designed by Lambert.

### KEY TERM

**Instrument of Government**
The constitutional document that established the Protectorate. It contained 42 articles and vested executive authority in Cromwell and a Council of State of 21 members. It was replaced by the Humble Petition and Advice in May 1657.

ACTIVITY
KNOWLEDGE CHECK

**The Nominated Assembly**

Why did the Barebones Parliament fail to deliver the stability and reform that it promised?

## The First Protectorate Parliament, 1654–55

The Instrument of Government served as the constitutional basis of Cromwell's power, and was modelled on the Heads of the Proposals issued by Ireton in 1647. It was designed by Lambert with the Army Council, and stated that the Lord Protector would be supported by a Council of State and single-chamber parliament with 460 members. Parliaments were to be elected every three years by voters with at least £200 of personal property, and they would sit for a minimum of five months. On top of this, Cromwell would remain head of the New Model Army. On Cromwell's death, a new Protector would be elected by the Council of State. There would be a state Church, but freedom of worship was granted for all except Catholics and the supporters of bishops. This government would rule over England, Scotland, Wales and Ireland.

There was some initial success for this First Protectorate Parliament. 84 ordinances were issued, which included banning bear-baiting and cock-fighting, improving postal services and allowing for the maintenance of roads. Laws were also passed to prohibit blasphemy and drunkenness. Despite some success in the role of Lord Protector, Cromwell faced the same fundamental problems as the Rump, compounded by his own concern for the army and the interests of the men who served in it. He also faced bitter resentment from the republican MPs whom he had excluded from power after the dissolution of the Rump. When they succeeded in destabilising his first parliament by refusing to recognise the Instrument of Government, Cromwell dissolved it in January 1655.

## The rule of the major-generals, 1655–56, and the Second Protectorate Parliament

In the spring of 1655, a royalist rising led by John Penruddock broke out in Wiltshire and, although it was easily defeated, Cromwell decided it showed that greater control of the provinces was needed. He imposed centralised military rule over the entire country by dividing it into 11 districts, each under the command of a major-general. They would be responsible for local government and security, and were encouraged to attempt a 'reformation of manners' across the social spectrum.

The major-generals were to be assisted in their task by a new militia, to be paid for by a ten percent tax on the estates of royalists. The effectiveness of the government of major-generals was mixed. In Lancashire, Major-General Worsley closed down 200 alehouses and, in Lincolnshire, Major-General Whalley suppressed traditional entertainments including stage plays and horse racing. Others seem to have neglected many of their duties and did not apply themselves with the same enthusiasm.

Meanwhile, Cromwell had established **Commissions of Triers and Ejectors** to supervise the running of the Church, with an emphasis on quality of preaching and flexibility of belief. It is a measure of his achievements that, in 1657, he was offered the Crown by a second parliament, elected on a reasonably broad franchise. It is also significant that, by offering the Crown, they sought to direct his power into traditional channels, which would define and limit this power by law. While the major-generals had proved reasonably efficient, their military nature, the restrictions imposed on social activities and the replacement of the local elites by outsiders imposed by central government was unpopular. Hence, the new Second Protectorate Parliament (1656–58) was determined on their replacement, and Cromwell recognised the need to compromise and accepted the idea of a new constitution.

KEY TERM

**Commissions of Triers and Ejectors**
Established in 1654, these commissions served to vet members of the clergy and eject unsuitable individuals. In five years, judgements were passed on 3,500 Church appointments.

ACTIVITIES
KNOWLEDGE CHECK

**King Oliver?**

1 Did the Instrument of Government fulfil the original aspirations of the parliamentary opposition between 1640 and 1642?

2 What concerns would contemporaries have had over its use?

3 Why was the rule of the major-generals so short-lived?

## The Humble Petition and Advice, 1657

When it came, the new constitution proved to be based on the restoration of monarchy. The Humble Petition and Advice was a new constitutional document offered to Cromwell by the Second Protectorate Parliament, and consisted of the following.

- Government by a king (changed to Lord Protector when Cromwell refused the Crown).
- The Lords and Commons to govern with the Protector.
- Provision for a hereditary succession.
- Parliament to control the army, and officers of state to be approved by parliament.
- Regular elections and limited religious toleration.

The use of the term 'king' would automatically confirm that traditional laws and the courts system would be used. According to Edward Hyde, the Humble Petition was welcomed by some royalists as a step towards a Stuart Restoration but, if Cromwell himself was declared king, he would face a severe backlash.

SOURCE

Oliver Cromwell between two pillars, from an illustration produced in 1658. Cromwell is presented as the bringer of prosperity and defender of moral virtues.

There is no doubt that Cromwell sympathised with the idea, and agonised over whether to accept. The Humble Petition and Advice would have done much to restore stability, and made provision for the succession. He was prevented from accepting the offer by the two considerations that had motivated his career from 1648 onwards – his desire for a 'godly reformation' in which all men (and to some extent women) should be free to find God in their own way, as long as it did not harm others, and his belief that God had chosen the army as the means of achieving this. It was the opposition of the army, including many of those closest to him, that led Cromwell to reject the Crown. Whether or not the experiment of the Humble Petition and Advice could have produced a genuinely constitutional monarchy is still a matter of debate. What is clear is that the death of Cromwell in September 1658 marked the end of the opportunity.

Cromwell was succeeded by his son, Richard, who hastily summoned the brief Third Protectorate Parliament in January 1659. Richard was a civilian and, unlike his father, he had no experience of warfare. He was unacceptable to the Council of Officers, who forced him to resign later in 1659 and then recalled the Rump – who proved to have learned nothing from their earlier failures. With the ruling minority disintegrating rapidly, the initiative was taken by General George Monck. Monck was a professional soldier who had fought for the royalists in the Civil War, and later fought with Cromwell at Dunbar and in the Anglo-Dutch War. Stationed in Scotland, Monck decided to act when he realised Richard Cromwell would not be an effective leader. He marched his forces to London to restore a free parliament on the understanding that the ultimate outcome would be the restoration of the Stuarts.

**THINKING HISTORICALLY** Causation (3a&b)

**The might of human agency**

1 'Our lack of control'. Work in pairs.

Describe to your partner a situation where things did not work out as you had intended. Then explain how you would have done things differently to make the situation as you would have wanted. Your partner will then tell the group about that situation and whether they think your alternative actions would have had the desired effect.

2 'The Tyranny of failed actions'. Work individually.

Think about the following event: Cromwell accepting a modified version of the Humble Petition and Advice in 1657.

a) Write down three ways that he could have acted differently in that situation.

b) Now imagine that you are Cromwell. Write a defence of your actions. Try to think about the things you would have known about at the time and make sure you do not use the benefit of hindsight.

3 'Arguments'. Work in groups of between four and six.

In turn, each group member will read out their defence. Other group members suggest ways to reassure the reader that they were not a failure and that in some ways what happened was a good outcome.

4 Think about the following event: the escape of Charles from Hampton Court and its impact on Cromwell's position.

a) In what ways were the consequences of Charles' escape not anticipated by Cromwell?

b) In what ways did the escape turn out better for Cromwell than intended?

5 Think about the following event: Charles' attempted arrest of five leading members of parliament in January 1642.

a) In what ways were the consequences of the five members' incident not anticipated by Charles?

b) In what ways did the five members' incident turn out worse for Charles than the intended consequences?

6 To what extent are historical individuals in control of the history they helped to create? Explain your answer with reference to specific historical examples from this topic and others you have studied.

**ACTIVITIES**
**KNOWLEDGE CHECK**

**Cromwell and the Protectorate**

1 What impression of Cromwell is the artist of Source 7 trying to create?

2 Were there any differences between the role of Lord Protector in the Humble Petition and Advice and the role of king?

3 Was the restoration of the monarchy inevitable?

**AS Level Exam-Style Question Section A**

Was the conservative nature of parliament the main reason for the failure of republican governments to find a political settlement in the years 1649–60? (20 marks)

**Tip**

*Assess all the attempts at a political settlement you have encountered in this period – the Rump, Nominated Assembly, Protectorate Parliaments and rule of the major-generals.*

## WHY WAS THE STUART MONARCHY RESTORED IN 1660 ONLY TO COLLAPSE 28 YEARS LATER?

In January 1660, troops led by General Monck entered London to restore order after an attempt by the army to remove the Rump had led to riots and demands for free elections. In February, he enabled the members of the Long Parliament who had been purged in 1648 to return so that it could dissolve itself. In April, a newly elected assembly (calling itself the Convention Parliament because it had not been summoned by the king) met and was presented with a copy of the Declaration of Breda, issued by Charles II on 4 April 1660, with the advice of Edward Hyde and of Monck himself.

Charles had spent most of his exile at the court of Louis XIV in France but, as the likelihood of a restoration increased in late 1659, Monck had advised that he move into Protestant Holland, and it was in the Dutch city of Breda that the Declaration was devised. The Declaration made a number of promises as follows.

- Co-operation and harmony with the political nation.
- An amnesty for actions taken in the years of war and **Interregnum**, except for those who had signed the death warrant of Charles I.
- The settlement of outstanding issues in partnership with parliament.
- Arrears of pay would be given to the army and religious toleration would continue if the monarchy was restored.

**KEY TERM**

**Interregnum**
The time in which a throne is vacant between two successive reigns, i.e. from Charles I's execution in 1649 to Charles II's restoration in 1660.

On 5 May, parliament voted that government should now consist of the king, Lords and Commons, and on 25 May Charles II landed at Dover to an ecstatic welcome. Because the Declaration of Breda had promised all that parliament required, there were no preconditions for the king's return, but his claim to have returned in the twelfth year of his reign, with its indication that the moment of his accession was the moment of his father's death, should perhaps have raised some questions. However conciliatory his words, and however sincere his desire to co-operate in creating a lasting settlement, King Charles II saw himself as monarch by the will of God, not by parliament.

## The Restoration Settlement, 1660-64

Because the Declaration of Breda pre-empted any attempt by parliament to lay down terms for the monarch's return, the restoration of the Stuarts in 1660 was effectively unconditional. This meant that the details of settlement had to be worked out after the king's return, by parliaments that were open to royal manipulation and subject to the pressure of public opinion. The first part was the work of the Convention Parliament but, in December 1660, it was dissolved and new elections were held. After a failed rebellion in London in 1661, led by the Fifth Monarchist Thomas Venner, had reignited fears of radical groups and soured the political atmosphere, these elections produced a massive royalist majority that gave it the nickname of the **Cavalier Parliament**. Unlike its predecessor, this parliament was seeking not reconciliation but revenge. As a result, the settlement settled little, and certainly not the problems that had been responsible for war and revolution in the first place.

The main features of the settlement are laid out below. The effect of the Cavalier Parliament was to weaken the restrictions on the king's power and undermine the clarity that had been achieved by the Convention Parliament. By retaining the 1641 Triennial Act and ensuring parliamentary control of the militia, as well as confirming the abolition of the Prerogative Courts, the legislation of 1660 had set clear limits on the royal prerogative and protected the powers of parliaments and the common law. The work of the Cavalier Parliament served to undermine this and leave a number of grey areas that would cause uncertainty and tension in the years that followed. For example, the Militia Act of 1661 stated that the king alone was in supreme command of the armed forces, and a revised Triennial Act in 1664 did not provide any mechanisms to enforce the calling of parliament every three years.

The Cavalier Parliament also had the effect of renewing the religious conflicts that had undermined effective political development since 1625. The Convention Parliament had restored the Anglican Church and the bishops, but the details of organisation were to be left to a meeting of the clergy to be held at the Savoy Palace in London. In broad terms, those who attended the Savoy Meeting fell into three categories.

- At one end of the spectrum were the Presbyterian royalists, who sought a reformed Church that would allow moderate Puritans to remain within it.
- At the other end were the High Church party led by Gilbert Sheldon, Bishop of London, who sought the restoration of the Laudian system.
- Between them were a number of clergy who can be labelled **Latitudinarians**.

When the meeting began, in April 1661, the impact of Venner's rising and the election of a vengeful parliament had greatly strengthened the numbers and determination of the High Church party. This was compounded by the tendency of the Presbyterians to become bogged down in detail as the debates progressed.

By the summer of 1661, the opportunity for genuine reconciliation had disappeared and, in religious terms at least, the royalists had their revenge. The Act of Uniformity, passed in 1662, restored the Laudian Church and set conditions so stringent that around 1,800 ministers were unable to conform and were expelled from their livings. Having created these non-conformists (also known as dissenters), the High Church party, with the aid of parliament, set about driving them out of existence.

Already, in November 1661, an Act had been passed to ensure that only those who took Anglican Communion could be chosen to sit on the borough corporations that governed many of the ports and market towns, which had shown themselves to be Puritan strongholds. Now the Act of Uniformity ensured that few

**KEY TERMS**

**Cavalier Parliament (1661-79)**
So-called because it was overwhelmingly royalist. 'Cavalier' was a derogatory term used by the parliamentarians to describe the royalists; it derives from the Spanish word *caballero*, meaning armed soldiers or horsemen. The word 'roundhead' was used in return by the royalists to describe the parliamentarian soldiers, a reference to the shaved heads of the London apprentices who fought for parliament.

**Latitudinarian**
Member of moderate clergy who desired a flexible regime that would accommodate a broad range of religious ideas.

Puritans would qualify. This was followed up when Sheldon, now Archbishop of Canterbury (as had been his mentor, Laud), secured a Conventicle Act ensuring harsh punishment for those who tried to conduct a religious life in separate congregations meeting outside the Church. Ironically, this attempt to destroy Puritanism did much to ensure its survival. The Congregationalists, Baptists and Quakers who made up the bulk of the separatists were relatively few in number and had limited contacts and influence. Left to suffer this persecution alone, their isolation and weakness would have made them vulnerable, but by driving the much larger number of Presbyterians and their contacts among the gentry and merchant classes into the same category, the legislation made dissent a significant religious and political influence in English society. The impact would be seen in the political conflicts of the next three decades.

ACTIVITY
KNOWLEDGE CHECK

**Restoration**

Why was religion a major issue for the Cavalier Parliament?

| Date | Parliament, Church and king | Politics and parties | Government: finance, administration and foreign policy |
|---|---|---|---|
| **1660** | Monarchy and Church of England restored, Bishops appointed<br><br>Desire for reconciliation indicated by offer of Bishopric to Presbyterian, Richard Baxter | Act of Indemnity and Oblivion: only regicides and 9 individuals exempted from pardon | |
| **1661** | Convention Parliament dissolved<br><br>April: Savoy Conference begins<br><br>May: Cavalier Parliament assembles<br><br>Failure of the Savoy Conference<br><br>November: Corporation Act, first measure of so-called Clarendon Code designed to destroy Puritan influence | Elections to parliament produce royalist/anti-Puritan majority<br><br>Support of royalists in parliament strengthens High Church party at the expense of Latitudinarians | Abolition of Feudal Tenures ended monarch's right to feudal taxes such as Forced Loans; failure to restore Prerogative Courts meant other taxes such as Ship Money also disappeared; king compensated with regular income from taxation, mainly customs duties and excise tax, of £1,200,000 p.a.<br><br>Charles doubled size of the Privy Council to 120, in an attempt to accommodate different factions (unwieldy, so relied on unofficial inner group, at this time led by Clarendon) |
| **1662** | Quaker Act: subjected Quakers to severe penalties by authorising magistrates to offer them the Oath of Allegiance; many imprisoned by this device | King Charles issued a Declaration of Indulgence, suspending the Act of Uniformity, but majority in parliament forced its withdrawal | Licensing Act: reintroduced censorship of the press, i.e. any printed matter, not just newspapers<br><br>Hearth Tax voted to increase royal revenues |
| **1664** | Act of Uniformity: about 1,800 Puritan ministers, possibly one-quarter of clergy, ejected<br><br>Conventicle Act passed; expired 1668, renewed 1670<br>Triennial Act of 1641 repealed and replaced by a weaker version – provided no machinery for a parliament to assemble in the event of the king failing to summon one | | Dunkirk sold to Louis XIV, ending English possessions in France |

**Figure 1.2**: Table showing the main features of the Restoration Settlement, 1660–64.

### Charles II and finance

The Convention Parliament had already offered Charles less money than he needed and, although the Cavalier Parliament granted him some funds, he needed to raise regular taxation. The abolition of Feudal Tenures had ended the monarch's right to feudal taxes, such as Forced Loans, and to restore taxes such as Ship Money was unthinkable. Charles was compensated with a regular income from customs duties and excise tax, which stood at around £1.2 million per year. The Hearth Tax was authorised by parliament in November 1661 and levied in 1662, and was assessed based on the number of hearths in each house. The Hearth Tax was a disappointment as only one-third of the expected revenue of £250,000 was collected in the first year, and it struggled to raise significant amounts in the years that followed. Many MPs were pleased with this outcome as they endeavoured to retain financial control over the king.

## Conflicts between king and parliaments, 1665-81

The Restoration Settlement, therefore, did not solve the problems that had led to war and revolution, and left the future of the monarchy to be worked out in practice by Charles and his parliaments. One problem was the series of contradictions created by the piecemeal process of settling the immediate issues. By claiming to be in the twelfth year of his reign when he returned, Charles had laid down a claim to divine right. The reality was that he had been recalled by a parliament, which had provided him with a proper income, but one that was never sufficient to give him independence, even in the areas that undoubtedly lay within his prerogative, such as foreign policy. Similarly, he had shown his desire for a tolerant Church, of which he was the theoretical head, but had been denied this by the actions of parliament.

Given the lack of clarity over key powers, and the difference between theory and practice in government, it is not surprising that conflict re-emerged. What made it more serious, however, was the growing suspicion within the political nation that the king had a secret agenda to pursue, and that the agenda was one which favoured Catholicism.

### Renewed suspicions, 1665-78

The first signs of this had been seen when the king attempted to suspend the Act of Uniformity in 1662 and provide a measure of religious toleration. The immediate benefits would have been felt by the dissenters and Latitudinarians, and there is no reason to doubt that Charles was genuinely opposed to religious persecution – unless it served a wider purpose or was made necessary by the actions of the persecuted. An added effect, however, was that a more tolerant atmosphere would also help the English Catholics, as well as easing religious divisions in Ireland and Scotland, and by 1665 there were indications that Charles' policies were intended to work in that direction.

Given his French Catholic mother and his years in Catholic France, it was not surprising that Charles' foreign policy was decidedly pro-French. In 1665, he embarked on the Second Anglo-Dutch War, justified by commercial rivalry but also designed to aid Louis XIV in his campaign to destroy the Protestant Dutch Republic and extend French territory. Unfortunately for Charles, the war was badly managed. Its leading exponent, James, Duke of York (the king's brother), was Lord High Admiral and hoped that success would help to free the Crown from its financial dependence on parliaments. Despite his victories at Lowestoft and Sole Bay, the Dutch were able to break the chain that blocked the Medway River and destroy the English ships at anchor on the other side.

The political impact of this humiliation by the Dutch was increased by the outbreak of the Great Plague in London in 1665 and the Great Fire that followed a year later. Suspicions abounded that the Plague was the work of Catholic advisers to the king, and rumours sparked that the fire had been started by Papists who were plotting to seize power, helped by Papists at court. Charles was able to deflect some of the criticism by allowing parliament to blame Edward Hyde, now Earl of Clarendon (who had, in fact, opposed the war), and replacing Clarendon in 1667 with a group of advisers known as the **Cabal**, which included two Catholics. In 1668, Charles' brother James announced his conversion to Catholicism and, when Charles signed a treaty with the French at Dover in 1670 that committed England to further war with the Dutch, Charles' Catholic leanings were confirmed. It was as well that the political nation, in and out of parliament, were unaware of a secret clause committing Charles to announce his own conversion to Catholicism at an appropriate time, and that a French subsidy that accompanied the Treaty was designed to free the king from dependence on parliaments.

**KEY TERM**

**Cabal**
The Cabal Ministry refers to a senior group of privy councillors under Charles II, active from approximately 1668 to 1674. Power was shared by this group rather than a single royal favourite, as had been the case under Charles I and James I.

### Suspicions confirmed

In this context, the second attempt by Charles to establish religious toleration, the Declaration of Indulgence issued in 1672, was bound to cause conflict. Charles had attempted a Declaration of Indulgence in 1662, although he had been forced to withdraw it by a strongly Anglican parliament. Although hostility to the Puritan dissenters had declined, and many people had come to dislike the persecution of otherwise respectable and peaceable members of their communities, there were two significant problems with the Declaration.

- The first was that it included Catholics, which many suspected to be its main purpose.
- The second was that it was based on a claim that the monarch's prerogative powers included the right to 'dispense with', i.e. suspend the operation of, the law. It was one thing to accept such powers in the case of individuals, where, for example, a particular law was operating unfairly, but the Declaration did not come into that category – it involved the suspension of the law for a whole section of the nation on a permanent basis and, as such, it was a challenge to the rule of law itself. Even many who sympathised with the dissenters realised the significance of the precedent it would set, and felt obliged to oppose it.

As long as parliament was not in session, the Indulgence could be maintained, but by 1673 financial problems forced Charles to recall parliament. In 1672, Charles found himself unable to pay his debts so he had suspended repayments to his creditors in what became known as the Stop of the Exchequer. Obliged by the Treaty of Dover to begin the Third Anglo-Dutch War, he had little choice but to ask for parliamentary grants. The price demanded in the Commons was the withdrawal of the Indulgence. An attempt to provide toleration for Protestants passed the Commons in March, but was blocked in the Lords by the combined opposition of the king and the bishops. Charles could not, however, prevent the passing of a Test Act, which forced holders of public office to deny key Catholic doctrines and led immediately to the resignation of Lord Treasurer Clifford and Charles' brother James as Lord Admiral.

Unlike his father, Charles was capable of recognising when he had overstepped his powers, and he now accepted political reality by appointing as Treasurer Thomas Osborne, Earl of Danby, whose views and credentials were impeccably Anglican and Protestant. Danby now pursued a foreign policy that favoured the Dutch – sealed by a marriage in 1677 between Mary, the Protestant daughter of the Duke of York, and William of Orange, leader of the United Provinces. In the process, he offended a number of parliamentary groups and individuals, not least Antony Ashley Cooper, by now Earl of Shaftesbury. Shaftesbury had served Charles in the Cabal and throughout the period of the Indulgence, and had a genuine desire for toleration for dissenters. The presence of an orthodox Anglican in Danby threatened this toleration because he only favoured strict conformity. Shaftesbury's disillusionment with Charles led him to gather like-minded allies and form a potential opposition, that would become known as the Whigs, but as long as Danby could rely on the support of the king and dispense royal patronage, along with appropriate gifts and inappropriate bribery, his position would remain secure.

ACTIVITIES
KNOWLEDGE CHECK

**Conflict between Charles and parliament, 1665–78**

1 What was the impact of Charles suspending the Act of Uniformity?

2 Who would oppose the Declaration of Indulgence? Why?

3 Why did Charles appoint Danby as Treasurer?

### The Popish Plot

Nevertheless, the religious fears that Charles (and his brother's conversion) had created lay close to the surface and reappeared with the emergence of the so-called Popish Plot. In August 1678, an Anglican priest named Titus Oates, who had been educated at a **Jesuit** school in France, approached the London magistrate, Sir Edmund Berry Godfrey, with a story of a plot organised by the Jesuits and the French to murder Charles II and replace him on the throne with his Catholic brother. The story lacked credibility and the character of Oates still more so but, shortly afterwards, Godfrey was found dead in a London park and the plot began to seem more believable.

KEY TERM

**Jesuit**
A member of the Roman Catholic religious order the Society of Jesus, founded in 1534.

Investigations revealed correspondence written by Edward Coleman, a former employee of the Duke of York, to Jesuit and French agents, which seemed to confirm Oates's story. With broadsheet publications appearing that detailed the plot and wove in real events, both parliament and public accepted its existence. For the next year, Oates was able to accuse whomever he chose, until his imagination went too far and doubts emerged. By then, however, the rumours had sparked a full-scale political crisis when the opposition in parliament attempted to pass a law to exclude James from the succession.

**SOURCE 8** Example of a contemporary broadsheet showing details of the Popish Plot. This was produced and distributed around London in late 1678.

## Whigs and Tories: the Exclusion Crisis, 1679–81

For Shaftesbury and his associates, the Popish Plot provided a golden opportunity to challenge Danby's power and influence parliament to move in the direction they desired. His methods of parliamentary management had included a level of bribery and corruption, funded by French subsidies, that could now be linked to the activities described by Oates to suggest betrayal of the national interest, if not outright treason. In 1678, they sought to impeach him, using evidence provided by the French ambassador that he had accepted subsidies from France. An attempt by Charles to save him by dissolving the Cavalier Parliament in January 1679 failed, because new elections produced an anti-Danby majority. These MPs were by now known as Whigs – a term used to describe those MPs who favoured reform at the expense of the Crown. In reply, the Whigs labelled their High Church enemies Tories, a reference to Irish Catholic bandits.

The new parliament then forced Charles to appoint a new Privy Council, chosen by parliament. The next step was the introduction of a bill to exclude the Catholic Duke of York from the throne and replace him with Charles' illegitimate but Protestant son, the Duke of Monmouth. Whether or not the Whigs believed the details of the Plot, it was likely that – in the event of Charles' death – his brother would become king and James had made no secret of his faith. It was inevitable that, if he became king, he would adopt pro-Catholic policies and might well be prepared to impose them by force. The association of Catholicism with absolute monarchy that had helped to sour relations with Charles I had reached new heights in the contemporary example of Louis XIV, who had not only secured absolute power in France, but used it to persecute French Protestants. Although this persecution would not reach a peak until 1685, both Anglicans and dissenters were aware of the pattern of events through tales brought by French refugees. There was no reason to believe that James would behave differently and, as the childless Charles II and his wife grew older, every reason to fear that this nightmare would become reality.

For Charles, however, the attempt to exclude his brother from his rightful inheritance was a step too far, and he was determined to resist. There is no evidence of personal sentiment: when details of the Popish Plot reached Charles, he was reputed to have told James that he did not fear assassination if the only alternative was to place James on the throne. What he would not tolerate, however, was a blatant attack on hereditary divine right monarchy, and he set out to defeat it. In this he showed a determination and resolve that contrasted with his apparent apathy in other matters. However willing to avoid confrontation and compromise with parliament on other issues, he showed that – in defence of the principles of divine right – he was not only determined, but also tactically aware. The Exclusion Crisis played out in three stages.

- In 1679, the first Exclusion bill had passed the Commons but was prevented from going to the Lords when Charles dissolved parliament.
- In 1680, a new parliament presented another bill, which was defeated in the Lords by heavy pressure from the king, including personal attendance at the debates. He thus prevented Whig triumph by using his powers of delay and, by 1680, the anti-Popish hysteria that had encouraged uncommitted MPs to support the Whigs was subsiding. 35 Catholics had been tried and executed, or fled into exile, but Oates was running out of credible victims.
- Charles had made a secret agreement with Louis XIV in 1675. This stated that if parliament showed hostility to France, Charles would suspend it. When he suspended parliament in 1675, the first payment of £100,000 reached Charles, and in 1681 he was financially independent. In addition, he decreed that the 1681 parliament should meet in Oxford, away from the Whig stronghold of London and any possible interventions by the London mob. When the Whigs passed yet another Exclusion bill, he dissolved parliament and ordered the arrest of Shaftesbury for treason.

ACTIVITIES
KNOWLEDGE CHECK

**The Popish Plot and Exclusion Crisis**

1 What was the political impact of the Popish Plot?

2 Why did Charles defend his brother, despite the fact that he was a Catholic?

## Personal rule and the collapse of royal power, 1681-88

### The Rye House Plot and decline in Whig power

Although he was acquitted by a sympathetic jury, Shaftesbury found himself facing new charges and was forced into exile in November 1682. In desperation, a group of old Cromwellian soldiers concocted a plot to kill Charles at Rye House in April 1683 and to replace him with Monmouth. The plot failed and they were arrested, but it provided the necessary means to destroy the remaining Whig leaders. Some of them had undoubtedly known of the plot; others such as Lord William Russell were convicted on doubtful evidence because of their political role. Russell had been a long-standing opponent of a Catholic succession and was an acknowledged leader of the 'Country' party and later the Whig faction.

The Rye House Plot was a serious mistake on the part of those leaders who were aware of it, because it discredited the Whigs and sparked a royalist backlash that allowed Charles to avoid calling a parliament for the rest of his reign, in direct contravention of the Triennial Act he had revised in 1664 (although Charles' reissued Act did not include a mechanism to enforce the calling of regular parliaments). In the meantime, he began a process of recalling and revising the borough charters that controlled elections to the corporations and the selection of parliamentary candidates. By vesting the power to vote in a small group of aldermen, who could be hand-picked as supporters or subjected to government pressure, it was possible to ensure the election of more compliant parliaments in future. The process would take time, and was only partly executed when Charles died in 1685, but it was continued by James, who succeeded his brother without opposition.

### James II and personal rule

The parliament called on James' accession proved remarkably co-operative and, when Monmouth raised a rebellion in Dorset in June 1685, he received little support from the political nation. His army was ill-equipped and poorly prepared and, when his supporters had been defeated, they were subjected to bloody punishments. Distraught at the slaughter, Monmouth himself was captured and beheaded on his uncle's orders.

The extent of this victory has led some historians to label the 1680s as a second period of Stuart despotism, a demonstration of the power still held by the monarch if used in the right way, and it is clear that Charles had left his brother in a strong position. A generous financial settlement from the 1685 parliament, elected in many places on the remodelled charters, gave James some independence and the lack of support for Monmouth indicates both respect for the king's hereditary rights and fear of further upheaval. The Exclusion Crisis had revealed a willingness among some MPs to challenge the hereditary principle and insist on a monarch who could be trusted to govern with the consent of the people, or at least of parliaments. In practice, the Whigs had overplayed their hand, but Charles II had shown unusual determination and skill in defeating them. On balance, the crisis reveals that the legacy of civil war and the execution of the monarch was a mixed inheritance. On the one hand, the king could rely on fear of the upheaval that civil war would bring and a desperate desire for stability to rally support. At the same time, both the king and those who opposed him knew that a monarch had been replaced and that parliaments had proved capable of governing.

### James II in decline

Within three years, the strong position in which Charles had left the monarchy had disintegrated and a second Stuart monarch was forcibly removed from the throne. The main reason for this lay in the character and beliefs of James II, but the underlying issues bore strong resemblance to those that had destroyed his father. James was deposed because he represented a threat to the Protestant religion and the rule of law. The determination with which his enemies plotted his downfall arose from that fear of Catholic absolutism that had divided kings from parliaments throughout the century and created problems that had never been fully resolved. The importance of James' personality, and the decisions that he made, lies mainly in the fact that, unlike his father and brother, he did not divide the nation. Instead, he managed to alienate most sections and interests to the point where his authority, and that of the Crown, collapsed completely.

James' primary aim on his accession was to establish religious freedom and legal equality for Catholics, and his reaction when parliament refused to co-operate was that of an autocrat – he would establish their rights by royal prerogative. In 1685, he issued personal dispensations to allow Catholics to become army officers, and used the case of *Godden v Hales* in 1686 to obtain a judicial declaration that he could issue such dispensations as and when he thought necessary. Sir Edward Hales, a Catholic, was prosecuted by his coachman, Arthur Godden, for holding a military command without taking Anglican Communion and the oath of allegiance prescribed by the Test Act. When the case was brought to trial, it was judged that only the king could judge whether Hales was at fault.

In 1687, he used this ruling to issue a new Declaration of Indulgence, granting freedom of worship to both Catholic and Protestant dissenters. It is highly likely that James was sincere in his desire for toleration – his close friendship with the Quaker, William Penn, would suggest that this was the case. It is also possible that he had no secret design to establish Catholic superiority, but in the context of events in France and the persecution of continental Protestants, it was unlikely that this would have been believed. The behaviour of his cousin, Louis XIV, who had revoked the Edict of Nantes in 1685 on which the rights of Protestants in France depended, offered an ominous example, and his own autocratic methods reinforced fears that he threatened parliament and the rule of law.

- Borough charters were further remodelled, and Catholics were appointed as magistrates.
- An Ecclesiastical Commission was set up to act as a Court for Church affairs, with powers similar to those exercised by the Prerogative Court of High Commission, abolished in 1641. These included the ability to make and revise appointments and property settlements, which James used to expel the Fellows of Magdalen College, Oxford, and replace them with Catholics. Where James believed that he was creating equality and redistributing privilege, others saw a blatant attack on the Church, the Protestant religion, and the security of law and property. The result was predictable, even if the form and outcome were not.
- In 1688, James renewed the Declaration of Indulgence and ordered that it be read from the pulpit in every parish, forcing the Church to rubber-stamp the reduction of its own power. When seven bishops refused to obey the order, they were arrested, charged with sedition, tried and acquitted amid public celebration. By now the king had threatened the existence of parliaments, the supremacy of law, the rights of property-holders and the security of the Church.

Two days later, James' young second wife, Mary of Modena, gave birth to a son. Up to this point, those who were threatened by James' actions had been held back from mounting a challenge by the equal, or greater, fear of renewed civil war and by the knowledge that James was an old man with two Protestant daughters to succeed him. Now, however, they faced the prospect of a Catholic heir who would take precedence over his sisters. If James could establish a succession of Catholic monarchs, then there was no prospect of relief and no alternative to taking action.

ACTIVITIES
KNOWLEDGE CHECK

**Charles II, James II, parliament and personal rule**

1. Was the Rye House Plot beneficial to Charles?
2. Why is the case of *Godden v Hales* significant?
3. Other than his Catholicism, are there any other reasons why James was destined to fail?

## Collapse of royal power

In the summer of 1688, a letter was carried to Holland, signed by seven leading political figures, representing virtually all sections of the political nation in England. Its purpose was to invite William of Orange, the husband of James' daughter, Mary, to intervene in England with an armed force. This was not an invitation to take the Crown, but to mount an invasion, and it was accepted for two reasons.

- The first is that the seven names represented almost all of the interests and institutions that formed the political elite in England. The names of Russell, Sidney, Lumley and Devonshire represented Whig traditions, the Earl of Danby (whose impeachment had been rescinded in 1685) and Bishop of London (Henry Compton) were well-known Tories. Shrewsbury was a Catholic who had been persuaded to convert to Anglicanism. Such names were a sign of how many factions James had alienated, and of the potential support for William.

- The second factor was that invasion offered a way of pursuing the purpose that had become William's life work – to ensure the survival of the Dutch Republic in its struggle with Louis XIV, who had waged a campaign to destroy it since 1667. If William could secure control of England, and bring England into the war, then the balance of resources that had always favoured France might be tipped against Louis. It was for this reason that the Dutch authorities supported William's expedition with the necessary ships, supplies and a small, but well-prepared, army.

After a series of delays occasioned by bad weather, William's forces landed at Torbay in Devon in November 1688. Their victory was by no means assured, especially if James showed the determination to resist. He had an effective army at his disposal, and a call to resist foreign invasion was always capable of rallying support. Instead he hesitated and, while he hesitated, his supporters deserted him. Finally, as William approached London in December, James panicked and fled into exile. When he was recaptured and brought back to London, an opportunity was provided for him to escape once more, since it was the ideal outcome for those who wished to remove him.

There would be no High Court, no trial and no public execution to create a martyr for the Stuart cause. By leaving the throne vacant, James allowed his opponents to claim that he had abdicated, and to invite William and Mary, his Protestant heir, to take his place. There is a good deal of evidence to suggest that his tame surrender to revolution was encouraged, if not determined, by the memory of what had happened to his father 40 years earlier. If James had learnt a lesson from the fate of Charles I, the management of the coup by his enemies suggests that they had also learned from the experience of 1640–60, and that they would try to use that experience in providing a stable and lasting settlement for the future.

**ACTIVITY**
**KNOWLEDGE CHECK**

**The collapse of James II**

How far do you agree that the only reason for the collapse of the monarchy after 1685 was differences over religion?

**ACTIVITY**
**SUMMARY**

**The search for political stability, 1625-88**

1. Why are the following dates important when assessing the quest for stable government between 1625 and 1688? 1628, 1641, 1647, 1653, 1657, 1660, 1665, 1672, 1685.
2. Were there significant changes in the powers of the monarchy between 1625 and 1688? What elements remained unchanged?
3. What changes were there in the demands and proposals made by the political nation (or a significant section of it) over the period?
4. What issues continued to cause problems throughout the period?
5. Do any of your answers to the questions above suggest that the attitudes and expectations held by king and parliament had changed over the period?

**A Level Exam-Style Question Section B**

How accurate is it to say that the main cause of political instability in England in the years 1665–88 was the Restoration Settlement? (20 marks)

**Tip**

*You should introduce your answer with a paragraph that analyses the main features of the Restoration Settlement, and use that to begin your explanation of how it caused problems.*

## WIDER READING

Anderson, A. *An Introduction to Stuart Britain*, Hodder (1999) An overview of the Stuart period, including the major political events

Coward, B. *Stuart England 1603-1714*, Routledge (2011) Provides in-depth discussions of the political events of the period

Kishlansky, M. *A Monarchy Transformed, Britain 1603-1714*, Penguin (1997) Provides in-depth discussions of the political events of the period

Scarboro, D. *England 1625-1660: Charles I, the Civil war and Cromwell*, Hodder Murray (2005) Provides similar coverage to Seel

Seel, G.E. *Regicide and Republic: England 1603-1660*, Cambridge University Press (2001) Provides detail on the political situation up to the Restoration

Smith, D.L. *A History of the Modern British Isles 1603-1707*, Blackwell (1998) Provides in-depth discussions of the political events of the period

Worden, B. *The English Civil Wars*, W&N (2010) An accessible overview of the current state of the historical debate surrounding the period 1640-1660

# 1.2 Religion: conflict and dissent, 1625–88

## KEY QUESTIONS

- How effectively did the Church of England evolve in conditions of conflict and revolution?
- Why did religious dissent and non-conformity increase in the years 1625–88?
- Why, and with what effects, did fear of Roman Catholic influence increase under the Stuart monarchs?

### KEY TERMS

**Confessional state**
A state where a single type of religious practice is enforced.

**Book of Common Prayer**
The English Prayer Book, first introduced in 1549, and modified by James I in 1604. The book contained the instructions and details of structured Church services.

## INTRODUCTION: THE CONFESSIONAL STATE

The term '**confessional state**' is used to describe a state in which a single national Church is established and maintained by the government, and a failure to attend its services on a regular basis is treated as a crime. It is, therefore, a state or country with a compulsory state religion. In 1625, England was a confessional state in which the beliefs (or 'confession') of the Church of England, as set out in the **Book of Common Prayer**, were formalised and maintained by the government. In 1688, England was no longer a confessional state because toleration had been granted to most Christian groups.

In 1517, a key figure in the Reformation, Martin Luther, challenged the authority of the Church across Europe. He claimed that the Catholic Church had replaced prayer and preaching with ritual and superstition, which was seen as the work of the devil. He believed that the right path to God was through the Bible, which should be published in the language of ordinary people (rather than just in Church Latin). Protestants such as Luther favoured a state Church in each country, to which all subjects could belong, but where variety of religious practice was protected. This Reformation was taken up in England by Henry VIII, who established the Church of England.

By 1625, the Church of England had existed for nearly a century as the centre of spiritual life and preaching. As an institution with a base in every parish, it was a major source of news, education and social control. The Christian monarch was inclined to insist that all subjects attend their church regularly, for their own spiritual benefit and for the maintenance of royal authority. After Henry's death, there were more changes made to the Church and, after his Catholic daughter Mary reversed the Protestant reforms, her sister Elizabeth I re-established the Church of England after 1558. As Elizabeth sought to pursue a 'middle way' between Catholic traditions and the Protestant emphasis on preaching and Bible study, she retained a number of Catholic ceremonies, such as baptism and Holy Communion, as well as some priestly robes and formal prayers.

**1625** – Accession of Charles I
Arrival in England of Charles' Catholic wife, Henrietta Maria

**1628** – William Laud appointed Bishop of London

**1633** – Laud becomes Archbishop of Canterbury

**1637** – Burton, Bastwick and Prynne sentenced by Court of Star Chamber

**1637–40** – Scottish Rebellion and Bishops' Wars

**1645** – Presbyterian Directory of Worship published, despite objections from Independents – never fully implemented

**1650** – Ranter scare; Rump attempts to restrict the activities of the Puritan sects by passing Blasphemy and Adultery Acts

**1650–52** – Emergence of the Quakers

**1656** – James Nayler case

1625 | 1630 | 1635 | 1640 | 1645 | 1650 | 1655

To some Protestants, who became known as Puritans, the Church left by Elizabeth was too focused on the rituals and superstition that they associated with Catholicism and these practices distracted the congregation from strengthening their faith in Jesus. As well as this, Elizabeth retained the hierarchy of bishops and Church courts. The Puritans conveyed their dissatisfaction with this from the pulpit and, when possible, through the press. When James I succeeded to the throne in 1603, he attempted to steer clear of the Puritans, although he never sought to silence them completely.

The central ideas upon which many Puritans based their belief was that God had **predestined** some individuals to find salvation while others were pre-condemned to hell. The Church (known as the Kirk) in Scotland had already been established on Puritan principles, and it operated a Presbyterian system under a group of elders. To ensure God's purpose was understood, Puritans read the Bible, prayed and debated, and considered the events around them as signs of God's Providence, by which they meant a direct intervention in human affairs to signal divine approval or rejection.

The Puritan reformers hoped their movement would be respected under the new king. James continued along the path set by Elizabeth, insisting on the recognition of rules while allowing a measure of practical freedom to Puritans. Meanwhile, Catholics were subject to fines for **recusancy** and some did attend church. By 1625, when James died, the Church of England covered several strands of religious and political opinion, existing within an accepted framework, if not always in harmony.

KEY TERMS

**Predestined**
The notion that all things have been preordained by God before they happen, and that God has already decided who will and will not go to heaven: in other words, there is no way to 'earn' passage through merit or behaviour.

**Recusancy**
Resistance to the authority and beliefs of the Church of England.

**EXTRACT 1**

From A.G.R. Smith, *The Emergence of a Nation State* (1997).

James showed that he was prepared to distinguish between moderate and radical Puritans, making concessions to the former while showing his determination to suppress the latter... [James] is best remembered today for [his] authorisation of a new translation of the Bible. Only a few Puritan ministers - probably not more than ninety - were so dissatisfied with the results... that they were prepared to refuse conformity to the Prayer Book as it was reissued... These radical Puritans were the ancestors of the independents who were to make such an impact on English religious and political life in the middle years of the seventeenth century, but in James' reign their influence was small.

ACTIVITIES
KNOWLEDGE CHECK

**The Reformation**

1. What were the main features of the Elizabethan Church settlement?
2. To what extent was the England of 1625 a 'confessional state'?

**1660** – **1665** – **1670** – **1675** – **1680** – **1685** – **1690**

**1661** - Fifth Monarchist, Venner's rising in London

**1662** - Act of Uniformity restores High Church control in the Church; c1,800 ministers ejected

**1664** - First Conventicle Act

**1665** - Five Mile Act

**1668** - James, Duke of York announces his conversion to Catholicism

**1672-73** - Charles II issues Declaration of Indulgence in attempt to establish toleration for Catholics and dissenters

**1678** - The Popish Plot

**1679-82** - The Exclusion Crisis

**1685** - Accession of James II; Protestant Monmouth rebellion crushed

**1688** - Second Declaration of Indulgence and trial of Seven Bishops sparks invitation to William of Orange and Glorious Revolution

# HOW EFFECTIVELY DID THE CHURCH OF ENGLAND EVOLVE IN CONDITIONS OF CONFLICT AND REVOLUTION?

## Laud's policies and religious uniformity, 1625–40

### The emergence of the Arminians

The Church of England inherited by Charles I was an apparently effective means of limiting religious conflict and ensuring respect for royal authority. Nevertheless, within that framework there were already signs of change by 1625, the most obvious being the growth of an Arminian theology among a section of the clergy. Their name was derived from the work of a Dutch theologian, Jacob Arminius, who had challenged the Calvinist doctrine of predestination. It would probably be more accurate to label the English Arminians as simply anti-Calvinist, since their attack on Calvinist practice went well beyond the issues of predestination and free will. By the early 1620s, there were signs of an anti-Calvinist reaction on a number of issues, not least on the part of James himself, who found the strident anti-Catholic reaction of many Calvinists in, and out of, parliaments to be an irritating restriction on his pursuit of rational policies at home and abroad. Anti-Catholic feeling was already well established, as England's great rivals, France and Spain, were ruled by Catholic monarchies.

**EXTEND YOUR KNOWLEDGE**

**Jacob Arminius (1560–1609): the interaction of ideas**

The central argument of Arminius's work was the denial of predestination and the argument that God gave man free will to choose or reject the gift of salvation. In this, his argument was close to Catholicism, but the Catholic Church also claimed that the path to salvation lay only in the Catholic Church - hence, the effective choice was to accept or reject Catholic authority. Arminius made no such links, and his ideas were taken up by theologians and clergy from a number of different groups.

The doctrine of predestination had already been softened by many Calvinists to suggest that it referred to God's foreknowledge of which souls would accept and reject the gift of faith, rather than to an active choice to save some and condemn others. In fact, the doctrine of free will was accepted by a number of the more radical Protestant groups, since it was perfectly compatible with the doctrine of salvation by faith alone, and with the idea of the Bible as the source of authority.

Among these were a number of Anabaptist churches in Holland – notable because they were the first to practice adult baptism – which came to influence English refugees who fled from James' drive for conformity between 1603 and 1610, and led to the founding of the English Baptists when some returned to England in 1612.

### The early Arminian challenge

To many Protestants, the Catholic Church was a force for evil, which had corrupted the early Christian Church and destroyed the essential doctrines of salvation by faith alone. Arminius argued, however, that the Church of Rome was mistaken and misguided rather than evil. The English Arminians were thus able to build on claims that the Anglican Church had found the correct balance in stripping out the more superstitious and misleading elements to restore the purity of the early faith, while retaining enough ceremony and hierarchy to ensure order and respect. Hence, they argued that churches should be decorated with the colour, statues and ornate carvings of the early Church, that the clergy should wear robes and symbols of their office to ensure respect and that the laity (non-clergy) should be denied access to certain areas.

This apparent move towards elevating the clergy to a special status challenged the accepted Protestant belief that all men were spiritually equal before God. It also raised fears of a desire to restore the clergy's role and authority as dispensers of God's grace, able to command obedience. Combined with an emphasis on the role and power of bishops in governing both Church and state, the theology and practice put forward by the English Arminians was offensive to Puritans and many others in two ways – it threatened the rights of the individual to a direct relationship with God, and it reeked of Catholicism.

The first public expression of Arminian ideas came in 1624, when Richard Montagu published an attack on Calvinist doctrine entitled *A New Gag for an old Goose*. When complaints were made against him in parliament in 1625, King Charles took him under his personal protection with a place at court. Already, the atmosphere and arrangements at court had changed since the death of James, with a new emphasis on formality and order: the appointment of a succession of Arminian clergy to the role of royal chaplain seemed to confirm the drift of policy. A conference in 1626 at York House, the home of another high-profile Arminian, the Duke of Buckingham, resulted in a debate between the Arminians and their opposition. This resulted in no change of policy on Charles' part. Having dissolved the parliament of 1626, Charles issued a proclamation that forbade the public discussion of sensitive religious doctrine, an action widely interpreted as a restriction on preaching that would affect Calvinists and other Protestants far more than those, like the Arminians, who favoured formal prayers and ritualised responses. The Archbishop of Canterbury, George Abbot, was briefly suspended in 1627 for refusing to grant an Arminian sermon, and William Laud, the Arminian leader, was appointed to the Privy Council a year later when he became Bishop of London, the largest and most important **diocese** in the country.

**KEY TERM**

**Diocese**
A district under the supervision of a bishop.

**SOURCE**

A cartoon taken from a satirical play, showing William Laud dining off the ears of Puritans, circa 1635.

*CAnterbury*, is here all the diſhes, that are provided?
*Doct.* My Lord, there is all : and 'tis enough, wert for a Princes table,
Ther's 24. ſeverall dainty diſhes, and all rare.
*B, Cant.* Are theſe rare : no, no, they pleaſe me not,
Give me a Carbinadoed cheek, or a tippet of a Cocks combe :
None of all this, here is meate for my Pallet.
*Lawyer.* My Lord, here is both Cocke and Pheſant.

## EXTEND YOUR KNOWLEDGE

**William Laud (1573–1645)**
Born the son of a Reading clothier and educated at Oxford, Laud entered the Church as a career and advanced quickly. Ordained in 1601, Laud served as chaplain to the Earl of Devonshire and was promoted to a royal chaplaincy by James I in 1608. Associated with Buckingham, he became Bishop of St. David's in 1621, but access to real influence came in 1625 through his friendship with Charles I. He encouraged the king to promote Arminian clerics only, in order to ensure reform of the Church and to weaken Calvinist influence.

Not really concerned with doctrine, his interest was in the management of the Church and the creation of a regime that ensured order, decency and respect for God and for the Church itself. For Laud, the decoration of churches and the elevation of the clergy served that purpose.

**The religious spectrum**

| Areas of belief | Puritan/Calvinist | Anglican | Arminian | Roman Catholic |
|---|---|---|---|---|
| Faith and salvation | Salvation by faith to those predestined; shown by a willingness to accept discipline and a godly life | Salvation by faith alone | Salvation open to all who seek it through a true Church; God offers it to all, mankind free to accept or reject it | Salvation open to all through the Catholic Church |
| Role of the Church | To guide and teach according to the Bible<br>Use discipline to support the godly and control the sinners | Guidance through authority of the Church based on the Bible | The Church guides through a priesthood given special status and symbolised by robes and ceremonies | The Catholic Church and its sacraments provide the path to God; taking part counts for salvation |
| Preaching and ritual | Preaching is the primary function of the clergy, supported by Bible study, private prayer and reading; rituals are a superstitious distraction | Preaching and providing some rituals is the function of the clergy<br>Rituals can support some aspects of faith, e.g. baptism, Holy Communion | Rituals and ceremonies create reverence and can bring the ignorant to God; beauty is in itself an act of reverence; preaching is useful, but so are set prayers and rituals | Ritual is part of worship and brings people together before God; only the priesthood can conduct rituals that count for salvation |
| Role of bishops | Bishops have no special power; the true leader of the congregation is the minister, chosen by them, and a national Church should be led by a committee of ministers | Bishops have authority to govern the Church in the name of the monarch | Bishops have a special authority passed down from Christ himself through St. Peter and the Church before it went astray; they receive power of enforcement from the monarch | Bishops have a special authority passed down from Christ through the Papacy |
| Attitude to authority | Those in authority should be obeyed unless they threaten God's will and true religion | Obedience is due to higher authority except on matters essential to salvation | Obedience to authority in Church and state should be complete; if you cannot obey in conscience you must surrender to punishment | The authority of the pope is from God; he is therefore infallible and obedience is essential |
| Attitude to Catholic Church | The Catholic Church is evil, seeking to corrupt true faith<br>The pope is the servant of the devil | The Catholic Church is a threat to true faith, but some issues are not essential | The Catholic Church is the early Church misled by error; it is a sister Church like those set up by Luther and Calvin; they should all be treated in the same way | |

**Figure 2.1**: The various beliefs held by different factions within the Church of England, as well as basic Catholic beliefs.

## The Laudian reforms, 1628–40

The fears of a proto-Catholic conspiracy promoted by these events, and expressed by the fears of parliament before it was dissolved in 1629, were undoubtedly an overreaction on the part of Puritan members of parliament (MPs), clergy and their supporters. Given Charles' personality, love of order and interest in the arts, the Arminians were his natural companions in religion and, given their respect for hierarchy and dislike of Puritan attitudes, their support for royal authority was inevitable. Nevertheless, it was a sign that neither Charles nor Laud understood those fears that they now embarked on a programme of reform in the Church that would alienate a large section of the population.

The situation was exacerbated by the existence and behaviour of an actively Catholic queen, the appointment of Catholics to important offices in government and a background of Catholic aggression in Europe. Neither Charles nor Laud were Catholic in belief, but the changes that they were making in the Church in the 1630s raised fears that they might be and that, even if not, they were making the Church of England an institution where Catholics could find a place and work towards further change.

Although Laud's influence was increasing from 1626, it was when he became Archbishop of Canterbury, the most important clergyman in the Church of England, in 1633, that his programme began to take effect. New instructions were to be enforced by the local bishop in every diocese. They focused on the decoration of churches and the conformity of the clergy but, by implication, they also affected the role and status of bishops.

Dissenting ministers were summoned before the Church Courts, but could also be punished by the Star Chamber, as in the case of John Bastwick, who published a satirical *Litany* that criticised Laud and others. Among the laity, it was the changes in the decoration and layout of the churches that seem to have had most impact, in part because they were visible, but also for their significance.

- Organs were installed, to the dismay of Puritans who believed music distracted the congregation from prayer and Bible study.
- Fonts were decorated.
- Statues and colour returned to the churches.
- The most objectionable change for the Puritans was the removal of the communion table from the centre of the congregation to the east side of the Church, where the Roman Catholic altar had always stood. Protected by a rood screen and often richly ornamented, it symbolised the growing differentiation of clergy from laity. It also shifted the emphasis of the communion service, from an act of remembrance of Christ's sacrifice towards the Roman Catholic doctrine of transubstantiation, in which the bread and wine was miraculously changed into the actual blood and body of Christ. On several levels, the change offended the sensibilities of many Protestants, not only those of a Puritan persuasion.

**SOURCE 2**

The decorated font in the Church of St Botolph, Cambridge, dated 1637.

**SOURCE 3**

From J. Rushworth, *Historical Collections* (1659). Rushworth, a lawyer and politician, was a contemporary of Laud.

This year (1634) being the first of Bishop Laud's translation to Canterbury, great offence was taken at his setting up pictures in the windows of his Chappels at Lambeth and Croydon... his bowing towards the Table or Altar, and using Copes [religious clothing] at the Sacrament, which the people clamoured against as popish, superstitious and idolatrous...

Mr Chancey, Minister of Ware in Hartfordshire, for opposing the making of a rail about the communion-table in that parish Church was brought into the High Commission (1635) and suspended from his ministry till he made in open court a recantation after a prescribed form, acknowledging his offence and protesting he was persuaded that kneeling at the sacrament was a lawful and commendable gesture; and that the rail set up in the chancel with a bench thereunto annexed for kneeling at the communion, was a decent and convenient ornament.

EXTRACT 2

From B. Coward, *The Stuart Age: England, 1603–1714* (2011).

What was Laudianism? When he was asked what Laudians held, a contemporary tried to get round this question by saying that they held all the best bishoprics and deaneries in England. One difficulty in going further than that is that Laudianism in the sense of a group of people all holding exactly the same set of beliefs did not exist. Moreover, the gulf between Laudians and other Protestants on some issues can be exaggerated. It is not hard to find 'Puritanical' traits in the life of William Laud. When William Cavendish (later Earl of Newcastle) broke his horse's neck in a fall on Good Friday, Laud noted in his diary, 'should not this day have other employment?' Moreover, was not Laud's concern to reform the Church by recovering ecclesiastical endowments from lay hands in order to finance an educated clergy similar to that of many 'Puritan' reformers since the reign of Elizabeth I?

THINKING HISTORICALLY — Evidence (3b)

**It depends on the question**

When considering the usefulness of a piece of evidence, people often think about authenticity in the case of artefacts, reliability in the case of witness statements or methodology and structure in the case of secondary accounts. A better historical approach to the usefulness of a piece of evidence would be to think about the statements that we can make about the past based on it. Different statements can be made with different degrees of certainty, depending on the evidence.

Work in small groups and answer the following:

1 Look at the photograph of the decorated font (Source 2).
   a) Write three statements that you can reasonably make about the impact of Laudianism based solely on the photograph.
   b) Which of the statements can be made with the greatest degree of certainty? Why is this? Which statement can be made with the smallest degree of certainty?
   c) What else might you need to increase your confidence in your statements?
2 The photograph is an artefact and Source 3 is a witness statement. Which is more useful to the historian studying the impact of Laudianism?
3 Look at Extract 2. How would the historian have gone about constructing this piece? What kinds of evidence would they have needed?

When the opposition found its voice in the parliaments of 1640, the most serious attacks were directed at the Laudian bishops, but these complaints had a political as well as a religious character. To some extent, the bishops paid a price for their role as enforcers, but there were also complaints of their arrogance, pretentious lifestyles and willingness to impose their own views. Some of these complaints, however, were directed at their activities in government rather than in the Church. Many of the bishops came from humble beginnings (like Laud) and were entirely dependent on royal favour for their advancement. If placed in the role of Privy Councillor like Laud, or Lord Treasurer like Bishop William Juxon, they not only deprived the lay nobility and gentry of a role that they had come to regard as their own, but could also be relied upon to obey the king's wishes regardless of their impact on others. It was not only Puritans who drew parallels between the Laudian bishops and earlier churchmen-politicians (such as Cardinal Wolsey), or compared Laud to the French cardinals who were building an absolute monarchy across the English Channel. Few things demonstrate more clearly the intertwining of religion and politics in 17th-century England than the career of Laud and the opposition that it evoked.

ACTIVITIES — KNOWLEDGE CHECK

**Laud's reforms**

1 Explain what Arminianism is in your own words.
2 Why did Laud cause resentment? Who resented his reforms?
3 What impression do you get from Source 3 of the way in which the Court of High Commission worked?
4 What similarities existed between Laud and the Puritans, according to Extract 2?

## Parliament's re-ordering of the Church, 1640–60

### The rejection of Arminianism in the Long Parliament, 1640–43

In 1640, the opposition to Charles within parliament was able to launch an attack on the bishops, and on the wider effects of Arminian influence, with substantial support in the House of Commons. Again, it is difficult to define the measures taken as 'religious' or 'political' since many were both. The abolition of the Prerogative Courts centred on the nature of the law, but it also removed some of the most repressive apparatus used to control the Church and the ability of individuals to discuss it. The strength of the discontent generated by the reforms, and its limits, are both indicated in the struggle over the bishops. In December 1640, the Commons received a **Root and Branch Petition** supported by many in the City of London, which listed religious grievances relating to the treatment of the clergy, restrictions on preaching and the encouragement of Arminian and Catholic ideas. In short, it asked for the abolition of **episcopacy**, which the Covenanters had already done in Scotland in 1638. Given the strength of Puritan support in London and the South East, this was not surprising.

KEY TERMS

**Root and Branch Petition**
A petition that attempted to remove the perceived root of all problems in the Church: the rule of bishops. It was signed by 15,000 Londoners.

**Episcopacy**
Government of a church by bishops.

Of more significance may be the number of complaints supported by Anglicans like Edward Hyde, the future royalist, and some of these at least were specifically religious. He refers to honourable men being brought before the Court of High Commission and subjected to punishment for their beliefs. In some cases, however, it was their moral conduct at issue, which may indicate a concern for their status and privacy. The leaders of the opposition in the Commons (distinctly Puritan in attitude) were able to draw on widespread support to force the king to remove the bishops from the Privy Council and to pass a bill in the Commons to exclude them from the House of Lords, but the attempt to abolish episcopacy failed.

There is, therefore, significant doubt whether the activities of the Long Parliament had a significant impact on daily religious life before the outbreak of civil war, although it is likely that many parishes were able to revert to older habits and reverse unpopular changes. Of far greater significance for religion was the signing of the Covenant with the Scots in 1643 and the attempt to establish a Presbyterian form of organisation. It is perhaps an indication of the limited support for such a change, even among conservative Puritans, that Pym agreed only to set up an assembly of clergy, to meet in Westminster and draw up a model to be established, rather than accept and implement the Scottish version.

## Radicalism and reaction during the Civil War

As a delaying tactic, the Covenant worked well. The Assembly met in early 1644, but it was not until 1645 that parliament officially resolved that the government of the Church should be Presbyterian in form. In 1646, parliament passed resolutions confirming the collapse of episcopacy and the commitment to a form of Presbyterianism. Before Presbyterianism could be imposed effectively, however, the attention of parliament was distracted by the growing quarrel between the Presbyterian leaders in parliament and the City of London on the one hand, and those labelled Independent, who supported the rights of the godly to set up their own independent churches, on the other. The latter were led by a small number of ministers in the Assembly, supported by a minority of MPs and key members of parliament's New Model Army.

There was no reason for the ministers who met in the Westminster Assembly in early 1644 to suppose that they would have difficulty in agreeing a scheme of Presbyterian organisation and achieving their cherished hopes of a godly Church and society. The vast majority of Puritans, both clergy and laity, were essentially conservative supporters of a national Church as a means of promoting their faith and ensuring social control. To the horror of the majority, however, they were presented with an *Apologetical Narration* on 3 January 1644, put together by five of their number, which appealed for the right to establish independent churches outside the national establishment. This was not designed to prevent such an establishment being created, nor was it an appeal for general religious toleration. Nevertheless, it would set a precedent and open the way to other such developments, and was therefore rejected. Despite this, neither the ministers in question, nor their demands, were about to go away.

The complaints voiced by Presbyterian ministers like Richard Baxter about the radicalism of the army were certainly exaggerated, but they were not without foundation. In many ways, the army was an ideal breeding ground for radical ideas, and it was particularly easy to organise groups among men who were brought together to live in close proximity and shared danger. Separated from the other influences and relationships that were used to maintain social control, they would almost inevitably develop a sense of identity and loyalty to their comrades, many of whom were drawn from areas like East Anglia and Lincolnshire, which had strongly Protestant traditions and a history of radical protest. This also applied to some of their officers, without whose support their meetings could not take place.

Among the volunteers who had committed themselves to parliament's (and God's) cause were a number of preachers who had been active in the small and secretive meetings held by groups of religious enthusiasts outside the normal services of the Church. With experience of religious leadership, they would naturally step forward if the services of an ordained minister were not available. What made the New Model Army particularly dangerous to the Presbyterian plans for a new, disciplined national Church in 1645 was its mobility. As the army moved across the country in the aftermath of Naseby, to mop up the remaining royalist forces, a clear pattern emerged, in which its presence stimulated or emboldened existing religious groups and encouraged further conversions. In some cases, an army chaplain actively sought to create a new congregation – as John Canne did in Presbyterian Hull – but, in others, it was a matter of strengthening the resolve of those who had previously remained hidden. Either way, the reaction of the Presbyterian leaders in parliament and the Church was both hostile and ultimately counter-productive.

The attempt to disband the army in 1647 led directly to its politicisation and the collapse of Presbyterian hopes. Despite the demand in every set of peace proposals (except those made by the army) for a Presbyterian Church, it was unlikely that the king would have agreed to any meaningful change. However, the sight of his enemies falling out strengthened his resolve and led to the renewal of civil war in 1648, which, in turn, brought about the purge of parliament and Charles' execution. With those events, the greatest opportunity for the Presbyterians disappeared but, even worse, the execution of the king sparked a new and yet more dangerous wave of radical ideas and groups. These differed from the Independents and **Baptists** – who both had relatively organised churches, despite their Puritan principles – in rejecting any external authority over the conscience of individuals and demanding complete religious toleration for all.

**KEY TERM**

**Baptist**
Starting in the early 17th century, a Baptist Church became identifiable because it carried out the practice of 'believer's baptism', where a person could only be baptised if they were able to understand and profess their beliefs, usually as an adult. Therefore, infant baptism was seen as unnecessary.

## The Rump and the radicals

To compound the problems, it was clear as early as 1650 that the emergence of such radical ideas had provoked a conservative reaction that was both intense and widespread. Complaints about radical groups led the Rump to pass a harsh Blasphemy Act, under which radical religious activity could be subjected to severe penalties. Many of the more eccentric groups were short-lived anyway, prone to internal dissent and dying out with the death or imprisonment of the inspiring leaders who created them. The exception was the Quaker movement, which spread rapidly in the North in 1650–52 under the leadership of George Fox and sent out preachers to convert other areas in 1654.

When the fighting in Ireland and Scotland ceased, many of the soldiers returned to their civilian lives, and the more extreme of those who remained were subjected to discipline or forced to resign in a series of purges carried out by the Council of Officers. However, many of the army leaders and the Independents in the Rump sympathised with the desire of the godly for toleration for their own churches. However, they were far too conventional and far too aware of the dangers that they posed to tolerate claims to complete freedom. While Independent ministers such as John Goodwin and Philip Nye, who had helped to write the *Apologetical Narration*, were determined to maintain the right of their congregations to govern themselves, they also stressed that in everything except Church government they shared the views and habits of the Presbyterian majority. A widespread desire for a restoration of religious and social discipline, demonstrated across the country and especially in the City of London since the end of the war, was only increased by the shock of regicide and the upheavals that followed.

ACTIVITIES
KNOWLEDGE CHECK

**The reversal of Laudianism**

1 How did the Presbyterians want the Church to function?

2 Why is the *Apologetical Narration* significant?

3 Why was the New Model Army a danger to the newly established Presbyterian Church?

## The Protectorate

When Cromwell took power after the dissolution of the Rump and the failure of the Barebones Parliament, he had three aims:

- to reform government
- to help build a godly society
- to encourage a 'reformation of manners', ensuring that people adhered to the word of God and lived morally virtuous lives.

As with many other aspects of his government, his preference was for sensible compromise. The Church had continued to function during the years of the Commonwealth, using a variety of practices based on the preference of individual minsters and their communities. Those who met outside the Church were largely left in peace as long as they were discreet. Now the Church was placed under the control of two committees of ministers, the Triers and Ejectors, whose role was to ensure that the ministers who served in it were competent, well-educated and capable of preaching the word of God. Presbyterian and moderate Anglican ministers found employment, while a number of the Independents served as parish ministers while also meeting their own church members in a separate place. These groups ignored parish boundaries and drew their members from a wide area. The Calvinist sects were thus able to meet and worship outside the Church with relative impunity. Those who posed a greater danger to the regime, or sought to disrupt society, were at risk, but Cromwell himself was averse to persecution, believing that all people were entitled to find their own way to God as long as they did not cause harm to others. By definition, Catholic and Arminian churches did pose a risk to others, since they sought to impose their views, but individuals who utilised traditional forms could often continue in their own way, as long as they were discreet. At the other extreme, the Quakers were subjected to persecution when they tried to spread their views, but in remote areas their meetings were often left in peace. In 1656–57, it was Cromwell who objected to the treatment of the Quaker James Nayler imposed by the political nation in parliament.

The Nayler case is significant for the attitudes that it revealed, and as a forerunner of what was to come. James Nayler had been one of the preachers sent by Fox to convert the South and had gathered a Quaker meeting near Bristol. Although the Quakers had already adopted their **pacifist** ideas and placed great emphasis on personal morality, the early leaders were often intensely excitable in their style of preaching and some were inclined to extravagant gestures, including appearing naked to demonstrate their purity of mind. In one such gesture, Nayler appeared riding a donkey into Bristol on Palm Sunday 1656, accompanied by female Quakers who strewed branches and flowers in his path in a re-enactment of Christ's entry into Jerusalem. Nayler was accused of blasphemy, and some MPs called for him to be executed. At this point, Cromwell intervened and challenged parliament's right to inflict such severe punishment, but was unable to prevent him being publicly flogged, bored through the tongue and imprisoned. While Cromwell saw him as foolish rather than evil, the attitude of MPs reflected a widespread fear, especially among the elites, that such unconventional behaviour threatened the moral and social discipline upon which good order depended.

KEY TERM

**Pacifist**
A person who believes that war and violence are unjustifiable in any circumstances.

ACTIVITIES
KNOWLEDGE CHECK

**The Church under Cromwell**

1 What does the Nayler case suggest about the attitude of the Protectorate government towards radicals?

2 To summarise the failure of the attempt to establish a Presbyterian Church in England in the years 1640-60, construct a diagram to show the steps and stages by which it failed.

SOURCE 4 James Nayler was put in the pillory for two hours before being whipped through the streets. From a near-contemporary anonymous etching.

## The restoration of Anglicanism in 1660–62 and its dominant position in religious life

### The Restoration Church

When the republican regime that followed Cromwell began to disintegrate in 1659 and collapse in 1660, one of the symptoms of the growing royalist reaction was another Quaker scare. Under Charles II, the Convention Parliament of 1660 re-established the Church of England and restored the bishops in the Worcester House Declaration, leaving the details to be worked out by the Savoy House conference in 1661. Both MPs and many of the ministers themselves were hopeful that the differences among them could be resolved to create a broad and flexible national Church, and the prospect also had the support of the king. The Presbyterian Richard Baxter, for example, was offered an appointment as a bishop, as were a number of the moderate Anglicans now known as Latitudinarians because of their support for allowing latitude (width) in defining acceptable beliefs.

Unfortunately, two related events in the winter of 1660–61 soured the atmosphere and prevented these hopes from being realised.

- The first was the ill-conceived and ineffectual rising in London, organised by the Fifth Monarchist Thomas Venner, which gave new life to the old fear of religious radicals. Although the Fifth Monarchists had been active since 1649, they believed that the second coming of Jesus would take place in 1666.
- The second was the election in the aftermath of the rebellion of a conservative parliament of Cavaliers, who were bent on revenge. For the Puritans and moderates at the Savoy, this was a disaster.

Alongside the moderates, the Anglican representatives included a significant number of Arminian thinkers, including the Bishop of London, Gilbert Sheldon. With the backing of the parliament and the bishops in the Lords, Sheldon was determined to establish strict uniformity on the model favoured by Laud, and to drive out of the Church any who would not conform to it. Although the moderates resisted as best they could, their efforts were undermined by a tendency among the Presbyterians to become bogged down in arguments over non-essential details that played into the hands of Sheldon's supporters. In May 1661, the conference ended without agreement, leaving the decisions about the nature of belief, the role of the Prayer Book and the requirements demanded from the clergy in the hands of the High Church Arminians and the anti-Puritan parliament. The result was an Act of Uniformity in 1662 that imposed formality, rituals, priestly robes and episcopal control, resulting in the restriction of non-conformists from Church appointments, and drove 1,800 ministers from their livings. In 1663, Sheldon was promoted to the post of Archbishop of Canterbury, effectively the clerical head of the Church.

The nature of the post-Restoration Church was therefore shaped by the Act of Uniformity and the anti-Puritan attitudes that were responsible for it. These had already been demonstrated in places where an Anglican minister had been ejected in favour of a Puritan one during the 1640s, by the immediate reversal of the process. The bishops appointed in 1660 had begun to ordain new minsters and recreate the machinery of the Church Courts. Those who had survived in their livings were now faced with three requirements that were designed to make their continued service impossible.

- The first was that, if they had not been ordained by a bishop, they were now to accept re-ordination. Not only did this emphasise the status and power of the bishops, it also suggested that their previous ministry was invalid.
- The second requirement was that they renounce the Presbyterian Covenant, to which many had sworn an oath of loyalty.
- The third was the acceptance of every element of the Prayer Book.

According to the historian Mark Goldie, in 1662 the Act was a way of achieving retribution against the Puritans, and it drove from the Church many people who dearly wished to stay within it. For those who made it, this was a declaration and defence of the Anglican faith developed by Laud, a balanced and ordered Church midway between the corruptions of Catholicism and the anarchy of Puritanism. It was also, however, a political act, motivated by dislike of dissent in any form and a conviction that the right form of governance in Church and state was based on a firm alliance between Church and king.

### The dominance of Anglicanism

In this form, the Anglican Church was socially dominant and politically significant after the Restoration. The Corporation Act of 1661 had laid down the requirement of conformity (by the taking of Holy Communion for those holding any position in local government) and this was later extended to cover a range of institutions, such as the universities. Effectively, the social, intellectual and political elites were to be predominantly Anglican.

Although the royal approval that such elites required was intermittent while Charles II reigned, political necessity ensured that he would eventually comply. In 1662, his attempt to suspend the Act of Uniformity and issue a First Declaration of Indulgence offering religious toleration was defeated by a combination of bishops and Cavaliers in parliament, and he was powerless to prevent the persecution that followed. The so-called Clarendon Code (the four Acts designed to restrict non-conformists) was the work of the same Anglican alliance, and the Second Declaration of Indulgence, issued by Charles in 1672, was followed by a Test Act that increased the requirement for conformity and led to the resignation of the future James II from his post as Lord High Admiral.

When Charles appointed Thomas Osborne, Earl of Danby, as Lord Treasurer in 1673, he allowed Danby to renew persecutions of Protestant dissenters and exercise royal social and political patronage to build up majorities in both Houses of Parliament. This strengthening of royal and Anglican authority soon became known as 'Tory' policies. After the problems posed by the Popish Plot and Exclusion Crisis in 1678–82, Charles returned to this strategy with a vengeance, embarking on what was probably the harshest period of persecution in the entire reign for Protestant dissenters, combined with the remodelling of borough charters to ensure Tory and Anglican control. By 1685, the Anglican establishment was truly the 'Church of England', but the one thing that it had not achieved was the level of uniformity desired by its leaders and required in a confessional state. In 1688, Anglican supremacy was demonstrated in the trial of the Seven Bishops who opposed James II's Second Declaration of Indulgence, which offered toleration to both non-conformists and Catholics. They were firm supporters of Anglicanism, and crucially were found not guilty.

**ACTIVITY**
**KNOWLEDGE CHECK**

**The restoration of Anglicanism**

Had England returned to being a confessional state after 1662? Provide arguments for and against.

**AS Level Exam-Style Question Section B**

How accurate is it to say that Archbishop Laud and Laudian beliefs and practices were the greatest threat to the Church of England between 1625 and 1688? (20 marks)

**Tip**

*Choose three or four other possible factors and evaluate them against the threat posed by Laud.*

# WHY DID RELIGIOUS DISSENT AND NON-CONFORMITY INCREASE IN THE YEARS 1625–88?

## Puritanism under Charles I

### The emergence of the sects

The origins of religious radicalism can be traced back to well before the reign of Elizabeth, when the first small groups of separatists seem to have appeared. In terms of ideas and beliefs, links can be found with anti-clerical ideas and preachers who emphasised the authority of the Bible above that of the Church, first seen in the Peasants Revolt of 1381. The development of such ideas and the paths they took went well beyond religion; these will be addressed more fully in Chapter 3. In the reign of Elizabeth, there were isolated examples of European sects such as the Family of Love (a forerunner of the Quakers) and arguments against the confessional state were aired by the Brownists and Barrowists, but such examples were so isolated as to have little impact.

**EXTEND YOUR KNOWLEDGE**

**Brownists and Barrowists**

Two of the dissenting groups that existed in the later Tudor period. The Brownists took their name from Robert Browne (c1550–1633). At Cambridge University he had been taken with Puritan ideas, and although he took up a number of positions within the Church of England, he soon decided that godliness could only be achieved outside the established Church.

Browne was arrested for setting up a separate, Congregationalist church in Norwich. He then attempted to set up a Puritan community in Holland, which failed after two years.

The Barrowists, named after Henry Barrow (1550–93), also believed that each congregation should be independent. Barrow believed that separation from the national Church was necessary in order to avoid the influence of Catholicism. He was executed for his views.

Some increase in the number of ministers who left the Church to form separatist churches was seen during Archbishop Bancroft's drive for uniformity in 1604–10, and two examples had some significance. Two ministers who were educated and ordained at Cambridge, John Robinson and John Smyth, gathered groups of adherents in Lincolnshire and were driven into exile along with the remnants of a congregation led by a lay preacher in Sandwich and another Cambridge graduate, Henry Jacob. While living in Holland, the group – led by Robinson – seem to have prospered, but tiring of life in a foreign country, they acquired a ship named the Mayflower and set out for the newly settled colony of Virginia in America. Blown off course by a storm, they eventually established the first New England colony in 1620. Here, their Congregational Church became the model for later settlers and provided a refuge for fellow Puritans, especially during the period of Laudian reforms.

### Charles and the Puritans

Meanwhile, John Smyth adopted Baptist ideas – rebaptising his congregation as a symbol of their free choice in joining him – and later established the General Baptist movement, which rejected both infant baptism, where the sprinkling of water onto a child's head was supposed to initiate them into the Church, and predestination. In the 1620s, there were at least five such churches in England, with a total membership of 150. Under Charles, then, there was already a small but well-established tradition of Puritanism. Archbishop Laud placed restrictions on preaching and imposed the use of a **Catechism** to teach the laity set prayers and Church doctrines, which were to be learned by heart. Historians have disagreed on their impact.

- **Whig historians** detected widespread opposition to Laud's focus on Catechism, suggesting that it contributed to the conflicts between king and parliament.
- The Whig claims were later challenged by **revisionist** historians who believed that ordinary members of the Church generally welcomed the reform.

Undoubtedly, the pattern varied in different areas according to the strength of Protestant and Puritan support. Clerical ejections increased, as did the number of dissenters who met outside the Church, but it is impossible to provide exact numbers for either. There were certainly more ministers affected than the 90 who had objected to James' religious policy in 1604 – at least 100 emigrated to Puritan New England (in North America) to avoid ejection – but there were nowhere near the 1,800 ejections that took place after the Act of Uniformity in 1662.

Charles and Laud's fear of the Puritans is evident in the extensive use of Prerogative Courts to punish dissent. As well as John Bastwick, who had written anti-Arminian texts, Henry Burton and William Prynne were presented to the Star Chamber and punished in 1637. Burton was a minister whose sermons deviated from the set texts and often resulted in his attacking the bishops. Prynne was a lawyer and author who had written his *Histriomastix* in the early 1630s, denouncing stage plays and actresses as ungodly. All were released by the Long Parliament and their sentences declared illegal.

It is no coincidence that the leading members of the opposition in the Long Parliament were Puritans. John Pym had been keeping a dossier on Charles' mismanagement of government between 1629 and 1640, and John Hampden, who earned notoriety in the Ship Money case, was part of the same Puritan circle. The historian J.P. Kenyon has asserted that those who resisted Ship Money before the taxpayers' strike of 1639, such as Hampden, the Earl of Warwick and Lord Saye and Sele, would have opposed Charles regardless of his financial policies, simply because they were Puritan and therefore natural opponents of Charles and Laud.

**KEY TERMS**

**Catechism**
A book that contains questions and answers that can be read and learnt in order to take part in Church ceremonies and sacraments.

**Whig historian**
A historian who presents a progressive model of the past. He or she sees modern liberal democracy as the ideal form of government, is suspicious of absolute rule and follows the tradition set by the original 17th-century Whig MPs.

**Revisionist**
A historian who practises historical revisionism - the process of reinterpreting the orthodox view of events based on changing social or political influences. Revisionism of the 17th century has been taking place since the 1960s.

## Presbyterians and religious radicalism

By 1616, Henry Jacob had returned to England and established a Congregational Church in London. By 1640, this had multiplied into eight such churches, in part because of opposition to the Laudian reforms. The excitement caused by the Long Parliament encouraged further development that included the practice of allowing laymen to preach but, on the eve of the Civil War in 1642, there were only about 1,000 active separatists in a city of around 350,000 – a supposed hotbed of radicalism.

The course of the war saw further growth, arising from various factors. The breakdown of normal restraints allowed existing separatist groups and their preachers to become more active, attracting new members and strengthening the old. A number of the more radical ministers were able to take on parish responsibilities, or preach as lecturers in towns and boroughs that were sympathetic to parliament. They also established separate groups who attended meetings and debated the Bible (and the events of this providential war), gradually building up a separate identity although not necessarily any formalised separation.

Of particular importance was the relative freedom of the press, where new ideas were propagated and public debate stimulated more radical thinking. The work of the Independent preachers and the role of the New Model Army has been explored above. By 1647, when the quarrel between parliament and army intensified, the arguments for religious freedom and radical social change were already well publicised and available to those who were interested through both the press and the pulpit. The radical political ideas associated with the sects are discussed further in Chapter 3.

Source 5 was written by a Presbyterian minister who disapproved of the religious sects and set out to warn of the danger that they posed.

SOURCE 5 From Thomas Hall, Presbyterian minister, *A Looking Glass for Anabaptists* (1645).

Their first tenet is that infant baptism is a childish, needless thing, and that none must be baptised till he come to a perfect age and can make a confession of his faith: that infant baptism came from the pope and the devil.

2 That all gifted persons may preach without ordination.

3 That God reveals his will, not only by the written word, but also by dreams and visions; which they believe more than the word.

4 That the Saints, in this life, are pure, without spot, and need not use that petition, 'Forgive us our sins'...

6 They are rigid separatists. They separate themselves from all reformed Churches...

9 They hold free will by nature in all spiritual things.

10 That a man may have more wives than one.

11 That clothes discover sin; therefore they, being as perfect and pure as Adam in his innocency, they ought to go naked.

12 That Christ died intentionally for all.

13 That a Christian cannot with a safe conscience take an oath, nor by oath promise fidelity to a Magistrate. [i.e. a monarch or ruler]...

26 After rebaptisation, we cannot sin.

27 We may dissemble our religion for our own protection, if we keep it safe in our hearts. God delights not in our blood.

28 That Scripture is no more than allegories.

29 That Heaven and Hell are nowhere but within a man.

ACTIVITY
KNOWLEDGE CHECK

**Non-conformity during personal rule and Civil War**

Using what you have read about the sects to guide you, decide the following.

**1** Why do you think non-conformity survived the persecutions of Charles and Laud?

**2** Read Source 5. Which of the statements about the Baptists and their beliefs do you believe to be accurate? Which are designed to shock? Does Thomas Hall approve of any of the beliefs he lists?

KEY TERM

**Confession of Faith**
A formal statement of belief, often taken by all members of a congregation.

By September 1658, when Cromwell died, his efforts to balance freedom in religion and stability in society had achieved mixed results. Most of the more dangerous sects had disappeared, but the Quakers posed a threat (and had become a refuge for a number of earlier radicals such as Lilburne the Leveller and Winstanley the Digger, both of whom were converted in the 1650s). The freedom given to the Independents (now increasingly known as Congregationalists) and the different orders of Baptists had allowed them to become organised and established, setting up national organisations and specific **Confessions of Faith** to apply to all of their members. The importance of this would be shown after 1660, in helping both movements to survive renewed persecution. The Presbyterians had also gained from the opportunity to work in the Church and set up voluntary organisations such as regional associations of ministers. At the same time, fear and suspicion of religious radicalism had not abated, as the Nayler case demonstrated, and its links with the army intensified the unpopularity of both.

In part because of these fears, the focus of the reaction was against the sects, and for a number of reasons their significance was seriously exaggerated by contemporaries and historians. The shocking nature of their beliefs, especially as portrayed by the likes of Thomas Hall, created a reaction out of all proportion to their numbers.

The core of separatism before 1660 lay in three groups – the Congregationalists, the Baptists and the Quakers – and while it is impossible to be precise about numbers, their sum total was still dwarfed by the Presbyterians, whose aim remained a reformed, national Church. Hall, Baxter and other Presbyterian writers were, if anything, even more disturbed by the activities of the sects than the nation at large, and made no secret of their desire to see the return of authority in both Church and state. In 1660, it was two Presbyterian ministers, John Shaw of Hull and Edward Bowles of York, who liaised between Sir Thomas Fairfax and General Monck to arrange the seizure of York and clear the way for Monck's march to London. The 1,200 deserters who left John Lambert's regiment of the army and backed Fairfax are testament to both the respect in which the Presbyterian Fairfax was still held and to their own desire for stability.

As part of their intervention, Shaw and Bowles travelled to Breda to meet King Charles II, and Shaw was appointed as a royal chaplain. When the king landed in England in 1660, another Presbyterian minister in Yorkshire, Oliver Heywood of Coley, wrote of his excitement in his diary, comparing the dark and gloomy winter of the Interregnum with the heart-reviving spring of the Restoration. Heywood was to live throughout the reigns of Charles II and James II, and his diary is an important source of information about the development of Puritanism in those years. Unfortunately, it was to record more clearly than anything else the painful and protracted process in which the Puritanism of its author was transformed into non-conformity.

**EXTEND YOUR KNOWLEDGE**

**Oliver Heywood and non-conformity**

Oliver Heywood fell victim to many of the laws and regulations surrounding non-conformity after 1660. He was born in Lancashire in 1630 and enrolled at Trinity College, Cambridge, in 1648. His parents had raised him in a Puritan household, and in 1650 he became a non-conformist minister. The religious freedom associated with the Interregnum enabled him to flourish for a time.

He was forced to move in 1665 under the terms of the Five Mile Act, when he was unable to obey the Act of Uniformity. He eventually set up a moderate Presbyterian church in West Yorkshire, but his licence to preach was revoked in 1675.

In 1685, he was banned from preaching again when it was discovered he was holding non-conformist meetings in his house, but under the Toleration Act of 1689 he was able to establish another church. He died in Halifax in 1702.

**ACTIVITY**
**KNOWLEDGE CHECK**

**Non-conformity and Presbyterianism**

How would you describe the relationship between the Presbyterians and non-conformists between 1649 and 1660?

## The persecution of dissenters under Charles II and James II

### The development of non-conformity, 1660–69

The persecution of the 1660s was not an entirely new experience for the English Puritans. The efforts of Bancroft and Laud to enforce uniformity in the Church would have provided similar experiences for those who left the Church (by choice or otherwise) and they would have received similar support from supporters. Three things, however, made the Clarendon Code (so named because it was promoted under the ministry of Edward Hyde, Earl of Clarendon, 1660–67) a different experience.

- One was its scale and the numbers affected.
- Another was the bitterness and desire for revenge with which it was enforced in many (but not all) places.
- The third was the fact that it was directed primarily at those who wanted to remain within the Church and had no desire to establish separate congregations.

Four Acts made up the Clarendon Code.

- The Corporation Act (1661) was intended to make it impossible for non-conformists to hold municipal offices.
- This was followed by the Act of Uniformity (1662), which excluded them from Church offices.
- As soon as it became apparent that meetings of some kind would continue, this was followed by the Conventicle Act of 1664, intended to widen the targets to include the laity who attended meetings and to isolate the ministers.
- This was followed by the Five Mile Act (1665), which sought to drive non-conformists away from their friends and allies that remained.

Although the Acts were spread over four years, they were undoubtedly part of a coherent strategy on the part of the High Church party to create uniformity of worship across the kingdom and silence dissent of any kind. By 1669, it was clear that the strategy had failed.

For many, the impact of Restoration was felt long before the Act of Uniformity was passed in 1662. Shaw was employed in Hull as a preacher at Holy Trinity Church and as master of a nearby almshouse. Nevertheless, in the wake of the Corporation Act in 1661, the Corporation received a letter ordering the dismissal of three aldermen and of Shaw from Holy Trinity. Shaw appealed to the king, who he served as chaplain, and was given permission to retain his post at the almshouse and continued with his preaching. Reports indicated that much of the congregation had followed him, leaving the church half empty. The result was a campaign of persecution by the garrison, probably on Sheldon's orders, including one occasion when they closed the town gates early and forced 300 people to sleep in the almshouse for protection. By June 1662, Shaw had been banned from entering Hull and, aware of the imminence of ejection (being removed from his post) under the Act of Uniformity, he returned to his native Rotherham. There he assisted the vicar, Luke Clayton, until both were ejected. Thereafter, they preached to those who would attend their private meetings.

Shaw's experience, which was replicated many times across the country, illustrates the combination of formal and informal methods used to exact revenge on the ministers, but such experiences were not confined to the clergy. Oliver Heywood recorded the trials and tribulations of a neighbour, Captain John Hodgson, who had served under Monck but was known as the friend of Independent preachers, Thomas Jolly and Henry Root. Not only did his past make him vulnerable, but his religion was a provocation to local royalists, who warned him that they would take revenge. In October 1660, he was arrested on false charges and was forced to take the oath of allegiance to the Crown and Church of England before being imprisoned for several weeks to await trial. He was eventually acquitted, but underwent similar experiences four more times within the next 18 months.

The worst suffering of all was endured by the Quakers, who were already experiencing problems in the wake of the Quaker Scare in 1659. The Scare led to several of their number being executed by the fearful authorities. The Quakers were particularly vulnerable because they refused to meet in secret, and because their peculiar methods of worship – meeting in silence until one of those present was moved to speak by God – roused suspicions that they met for other, secret purposes. By early 1662, the Quaker Act was in force, allowing them to be arrested and tendered the Oath of Allegiance, in the full knowledge that their beliefs did not allow them to swear an oath of any kind. Most offered to make a declaration rather than an oath of allegiance, an offer normally rejected. By this means, many were imprisoned without charge and for indefinite periods, including some Baptist preachers like John Bunyan.

With all this in place well before the Act of Uniformity, its impact might be expected to be reduced, and certainly many of those who were ejected were aware of what was coming. Nevertheless, its impact was considerable, especially on the Presbyterians (and a few Congregationalists) who served within the Church and believed that a national establishment was necessary for both religious and social reasons. Of the 1,800 ministers who left the Church, around 1,000 were ejected in the summer of 1662. It is impossible to generalise about their reactions, but many refused to give up their ministry as long as there were followers who sought their support, and meetings continued in private houses despite the danger of arrest.

Joseph Wilson, Vicar of Hessle and Hull, was ejected in 1660 at the behest of his predecessor, William Styles, but was appointed to preach in St. Mary's, Beverley, until the Act of Uniformity forced him out once more. When his successor arrived, a riot ensued, in which the congregation barred the doors of the church and refused to allow the new minister access. Wilson continued to preach in nearby Anlaby until the Five Mile Act of 1665, which stated that he was not to live within five miles of where he was ejected, drove him further afield.

Other minsters benefitted from association with wealthy merchants or landowners, and were offered chaplaincies and payment for preaching. Ralph Ward, ejected in York, was provided with an income and accommodation by Sir John and Lady Hewley, and conducted meetings from there for the rest of his life. The Stricklands of Boynton, near Bridlington, supported several ministers in the area with regular gifts and sometimes legal help. The main beneficiaries of this generosity from within the ruling elite were the Presbyterians, but some Independent congregations also received help. A group founded by John Canne received £20 a year to help with the salary of a minister from Lady Dorothy Norcliffe.

**EXTRACT**

From F. Bremer and T. Webster, *Puritans and Puritanism in Europe and America* (2005).

Although some of the earlier acts were security measures designed to ensure that urban corporations and hence parliamentary elections were under the control of loyal men, later legislation demonstrates the conviction among churchmen and members of Parliament that the Nonconformist clergy were the root of the problem. The Five Mile Act, for example, was designed to cut the links between ejected clergy and their former flocks... There was little popular enthusiasm for this legislation, and many disliked the use of paid informers. Neither central government nor local authorities enforced the acts consistently or effectively, although some groups, such as the Quakers, suffered more than others for their Nonconformity.

**ACTIVITY**
**KNOWLEDGE CHECK**

**Non-conformity and the Restoration**

1 How did the authorities take revenge on non-conformists after the Restoration?

2 What was the Clarendon Code? Why was it significant?

## Improvements for dissenters in the 1660s

It is as difficult to generalise accurately about the strength of dissent in 1669 so as to assess the extent of suffering in the years before that, but there is significant evidence to support the contention that, by 1669, the worst was over for the dissenters in many areas. By 1666, the mood of revenge was beginning to soften and, in 1667, the first Conventicle Act expired. There were also signs that a new network was developing, even among the Presbyterians. Much of this relied on personal contacts – Oliver Heywood, for example, was preaching in several places in West Yorkshire and over the border into Lancashire as a result of links with other ministers and invitations from sympathetic acquaintances, both within and outside the Church. In addition, his friendships with Thomas Jolly and Henry Root had encouraged him to meet with fellow dissenters of both Presbyterian and Congregationalist views to establish an informal association of ministers.

Perhaps most significantly in terms of changing attitudes, growing concern with the declining numbers of dissenting clergy available to support the meetings that existed led dissenters to consider how to provide replacements. The need would certainly increase as age took its toll on the ejected ministers, and both denominations were opposed to reliance on lay preaching. In 1669, with the support of Heywood and others, the ejected Presbyterian, Richard Frankland, founded an Academy to provide an education for potential clergy. In 1678, the first ordinations of new pastors took place and, by 1689, over 100 new recruits had been added to the ranks of the dissenting clergy. Perhaps most importantly, the development reflected a changing attitude, in which the ejected Presbyterians were beginning to accept an existence outside the Church and plan for the future.

### Continued difficulties

This did not mean that by 1669 survival was assured. Difficulties and hostility remained, as did the internal conflicts between the different denominations. The impact of persecution on the Quakers had been immense, and their organisation was shattered. The organisation of the Quaker movement was unusually orderly.

- Each meeting was self-sufficient in terms of daily worship and local support, and did not require orders to be given from a central office.
- Poor relief was given to members separately in each congregation.
- The movement as a whole was linked by travelling preachers, district monthly meetings and an Annual Meeting held at Skipton.

Between 1661 and 1664, the men who led this organisation were effectively removed, to prison or worse. Their leader, George Fox, was imprisoned in Scarborough Castle in 1664. Here he was kept in chains in one of the guard towers in a single chamber whose arrow-slit windows, devoid of glass, let in very little light and a great deal of cold and damp from the nearby North Sea.

When Fox was finally released in 1666, he was faced with a movement on the verge of collapse. Discussions had already begun about how to restore some organisation and unity, which Fox encouraged as he began to travel the length and breadth of the country. Despite some resistance from those who feared that free expression might be undermined, a meeting was held in York in 1668, in which proposals for a new structure were put together. Based on a system of district monthly meetings and an Annual Meeting in London run by a central committee. This system succeeded in transforming a powerful but diffuse gathering of enthusiasts into a highly organised, disciplined Church. In 1669, however, this development was in its early stages.

The situation that existed in 1669 was reflected in the reaction of Gilbert Sheldon, by now Archbishop of Canterbury, in campaigning for a renewal of the Conventicle Act. Dissent had not only survived, it had begun to organise more effectively, and Sheldon sought to draw attention to the need for firm action by conducting a survey to show its extent. There is evidence that orders were given to minimise numbers, and many meetings were not included, although some of this may well have resulted from sheer inefficiency. Certainly, Sheldon intended to raise the alarm and renew persecution, but he did not believe, or wish to suggest, that the destruction of the dissenting groups had become impossible. The result was the Second Conventicle Act of 1670 and a renewed onslaught but, in so far as accurate records exist, they indicate a limited impact. To some extent, this reflected the improved organisation within the dissenting groups, but it also reflected a change in the attitude of many outside the ranks of dissenters, who were simply offended by the deliberate harassment of people whom they knew to be otherwise peaceable, respectable neighbours.

### Charles II and sympathy with the dissenters

The change had already been foreshadowed in 1669 by an attempt led by two judges, Sir Orlando Bridgeman and Sir Matthew Hale, and supported by John Wilkins, Bishop of Chester, to introduce a scheme for revising the Act of Uniformity in parliament to allow the **Comprehension** of most dissenters within the Church. The attempt rapidly failed, but it was a significant indication of opposition to persecution within the ruling elite and the Church itself. In 1672, that opposition took on a new face when the Conventicle Act and other persecuting laws were suspended by the king himself, in a Declaration of Indulgence that would allow dissenters the freedom not to attend church and to meet in licensed gatherings of their own.

> **KEY TERM**
>
> **Comprehension**
> The inclusion of a group, specifically non-conformists, within the Established Church. This was proposed several times between the 17th and 19th centuries but never fully adopted.

Charles had already demonstrated some sympathy with non-conformists by attempting to suspend the Act of Uniformity in 1662, but the strength of anti-Puritan sentiment in parliament and the Church had made effective action impossible. Despite this, there were many who found the persecution that followed to be unacceptable. Within the Church, there were many who held Latitudinarian views, which signified a belief that some variation of religious views was both rational and sensible. Among those holding to such views was Bishop John Wilkins, whose scientific and academic background enabled him to find common ground with scholars of all kinds and to maintain a good relationship with Oliver Cromwell, into whose family he had married. Wilkins and others argued from the outset that persecution was both irrational and counter-productive.

There were many others in the Church whose views were only slightly different from those of the non-conformists, and who were well aware of that fact. John Tillotson, who became Archbishop of Canterbury in 1691, had thought long and deeply before conforming himself in 1664. Similarly, among the wealthy classes and the aldermen and JPs who were responsible for enforcing the laws against dissenters were many who shared their views and conformed without enthusiasm. In the mood of the early 1660s, these men (and women) had offered help to individual ministers, but had found it difficult to speak out against persecution as a whole.

Changing attitudes, disgust against the excesses of the law, and the dignity with which many of the non-conformists bore their sufferings, brought a change in the political climate, of which Charles could take advantage. After the fall of Clarendon in 1667 – unfairly blamed for the failings of the Dutch war as well as the code that bore his name, neither of which he supported,

Charles appointed a group of close advisers who included two Catholics, one near-atheist, and two who had close associations with moderate Puritanism. With their support, and possibly as a first step to alleviating the position of Catholics, he now felt able to challenge the High Church Anglicans and their parliamentary allies for control of policy.

ACTIVITIES
KNOWLEDGE CHECK

**Non-conformity in the 1660s**

1 What measures were taken to reduce dissent between 1660 and 1669?

2 Why was dissent still strong by 1669?

EXTEND YOUR KNOWLEDGE

**Richard Baxter (1615-91)**

Baxter was born in 1615 in Shropshire, and, although he did not go on to Oxford or Cambridge University, he studied divinity with the help of a number of local clergymen. From an early age, he rejected the episcopal structure of the Church of England and became a moderate non-conformist.

After preaching in Kidderminster, Baxter became a chaplain in the New Model Army during the Civil War. After the Restoration, he showed his Presbyterianism by rejecting the offer of a bishopric and, throughout the reign of Charles II, he was persecuted by the authorities. At the age of 69, Baxter was sent to prison for 18 months for insulting the Church of England.

By the time Baxter died in 1691, he had written 141 books on theology and had become a major influence on the dissenting groups.

## Non-conformity, 1669-88

Within a year, it was clear that Charles had misjudged the mood of parliament, and with war against the Dutch and a financial crisis on his hands, he withdrew the Indulgence. Nevertheless, that year had enabled the dissenters to consolidate the gains made by 1669, and lay the foundations of future development. In some cases, those foundations were physical – the building of purpose-built meeting houses, the formation of ministers' associations, and the development of education and training academies – but of equal importance for the Presbyterian majority was the psychological impact of taking out a licence and defining their ministry outside the national Church.

Some refused – Baxter took out a licence to preach but refused to be designated a Presbyterian – but, for most, that step was not only taken, but never reversed. Although the Indulgence was withdrawn in 1673, the licences were not recalled until 1675, by which time the patterns of worship, links with sympathisers and practice of occasional conformity by some were well established. In addition, when persecution was renewed, there was a distinct lack of enthusiasm among many of those charged with the task, and the application of the law was patchy and intermittent.

As always, the extent of local and individual variation and the limited range of records available make accurate generalisations impossible, but in Hull the Presbyterian and Congregationalist groups worshipped largely undisturbed, and even the Quaker meetings outside the borough were subject only to intermittent problems at the hands of individual justices or clergy. In 1676, when Danby mounted a census of dissenting groups in a bid to persuade Charles that persecution should be renewed, it was only partially completed and failed in its main purpose. The king argued that both dissenters and Catholics were too numerous to be suppressed. From 1678 to 1683, the impact of the Popish Plot and the Exclusion Crisis cemented the alliance between the dissenters and their Whig allies even more firmly, in a development that ultimately backfired for the former.

In 1682–83, the failure of Exclusion, the Rye House Plot and the collapse of Whig support freed Charles to pursue his own agenda, part of which was to renew the attack on dissent and on the sources of Whig power associated with them, especially the corporate boroughs and urban centres where both thrived. The persecution of 1683–86 was the harshest ever experienced in many places, and in many areas meetings had to be abandoned for a certain length of time. Reports from all areas indicated that royal determination was achieving what Sheldon and his associates could not – a nationwide onslaught. In Devon, the County Committee reported that dissenting groups had ceased to meet, in West Yorkshire they were meeting at night, in Bristol the efforts of the mayor and corporation to alleviate the impact led to a temporary suspension, and even the Quakers were reduced to meeting in the most remote places in the hope of avoiding detection. When Charles embarked on the recall and amendment of borough charters, with the intention of gaining control of both local administration and the MPs it produced, there was a prospect that things might become even worse.

For all this, however, when the persecution ceased in 1686–87, its failure was apparent in the speed with which the dissenters re-emerged, reconstituted their organisations and took up their spiritual life. Despite the scale of this last persecution, it had failed in its purpose. Not only were the dissenting chapels stronger and better organised, and therefore more able to withstand the onslaught, but public opinion had already shifted away from the desire for uniformity. When the Earl of Plymouth ordered his local courts to enforce the laws against dissenters with full rigour, one alderman threatened to resign, explaining that after many years of observation he found the dissenters to be pious, peaceable men and loyal subjects to the king. Such resistance could not prevent the persecution, but it could and did blunt the impact. More than any other factor, the gradual shift in public perception about the Church, religion and the nature of dissent worked in favour of its survival. This shift, however, did not only result from the behaviour of the dissenters and their allies, but also from a growing fear of an older enemy – the influence of Catholicism.

ACTIVITY
KNOWLEDGE CHECK

**The survival of non-conformity, 1669-87**

Why had the persecution of dissenters ceased by 1687?

## Conclusion: Why did the dissenters survive the years of persecution?

It is difficult to prove conclusively that, by 1686, the survival of dissent was assured. Had Charles II lived longer, or had James II continued with a policy of Anglicanism and persecution, it is possible that resistance would have been worn down. However, an analysis of the reasons for their survival from 1660–86 provides some indication of their prospects. Three factors were crucial in aiding survival:

- the commitment and dedication of those who left the Church, either voluntarily or by ejection, to their beliefs and their need to retain them
- the level of support given by sympathisers, at first as individuals, but increasingly through social and political organisations; these included some in positions of influence and power, who for reasons of their own were opposed to the attempt to destroy the dissenters
- finally, a number of mistakes made by their enemies, of which the greatest was probably the decision to define uniformity on a narrow basis, thereby increasing the number and range of those who became dissenters. Had the desire of most Presbyterians for more diversity within the Church been met, then dissent would have consisted of relatively tiny numbers of the more radical sects, whose unpopularity and isolation would have made survival far more difficult.

It was no coincidence that, in the 1660s, it was the Quakers who came nearest to extinction, despite their organisation and commitment. Although relations between Presbyterian and Congregationalist groups improved under the shared pressure of persecution, significant differences remained and could surface at any time. Without the Presbyterians and their contacts, the remaining groups would have lacked the level of support that was so crucial to survival in the early years, especially that which was forthcoming from within the political and social elites. It is possible to argue, therefore, that while survival can be attributed to a combination of factors, the crucial element was the misjudgement of their enemies in 1662, in defining and creating non-conformity on a scale and with a range of support that gave the non-conformists a fighting chance. Thereafter, and certainly by 1686, their own efforts and development combined with further errors on the part of the persecutors were probably enough to ensure their survival. In the event, any remaining doubt was quickly removed by the decisions made by the new king, James II.

ACTIVITIES
KNOWLEDGE CHECK

**Non-conformity, 1625-88**

**1** Re-read the concluding section above and write a list of the causal factors that are mentioned that explain why dissent survived.

**2** Write a paragraph about each factor, adding supporting examples and explaining its impact.

**3** Write a conclusion that shows how the different factors worked together - for example, the importance of early sympathisers in giving the dissenters time to build their organisation.

**A Level Exam-Style Question Section A**

To what extent was the Act of Uniformity of 1662 responsible for the survival of the dissent that had existed since 1649? (20 marks)

**Tip**

*The Act of Uniformity had a very broad definition of what dissent was. Discuss how dissenting groups could take advantage of this.*

THINKING HISTORICALLY **Causation (3c&d)**

**Causation and intention**

**1** Work on your own or with a partner to identify as many reasons for the survival of religious dissent as you can. Write each cause on a separate card or piece of paper.

**2** Divide your cards into those that represent:

**a)** the actions or intentions of people

**b)** the beliefs held by people at the time

**c)** the contextual factors or events (i.e. political, social or economic events)

**d)** states of affairs (long- or short-term situations that have developed in particular ways).

**3** Focus on the intentions and actions of three key people (Oliver Cromwell, George Fox and Charles II) involved in the survival of dissent. For each person, draw on your knowledge to create a table identifying:

**a)** their intentions

**b)** the actions they took to achieve these

**c)** the consequences of their actions (both intended and unintended)

**d)** the extent to which their intentions were achieved.

**4** Discuss the following question with a partner. How important are people's intentions in explaining the survival of dissent between 1625-88?

# WHY, AND WITH WHAT EFFECTS, DID FEAR OF ROMAN CATHOLIC INFLUENCE INCREASE UNDER THE STUART MONARCHS?

## Catholic influence within Charles I's court

### The origins and development of anti-Catholicism

In 1621, the House of Commons petitioned James I to take England into the Thirty Years War that had started in 1618 and led to the expulsion of his Protestant son-in-law from his lands in the Palatinate. This war was fought in order to resist the expansion of Catholic power that appeared to be under way. Those in the Commons who pushed for war believed that, if Catholics were given any power and influence in England, they would press for toleration and, if that should be obtained, they would demand equality. If they gained equality, they would then aspire to superiority and the destruction of Protestantism. These were not the sentiments of Puritan extremists but, as the voice of the Commons, the expression of a powerful mainstream view: that, by its very claim to be the only true Church, and in the light of long experience, the Catholic Church intended the destruction of other religions and the absolute control of religious life wherever it gained influence. It was this that had led Luther and Calvin to regard it as evil – the servant of Antichrist – and it was backed up by English experience in both myth and reality.

This did not necessarily mean hostility to every individual Catholic, as it was the Church as an institution led from Rome that was feared. However, the application of terms such as popery and papist indicated that every Catholic was suspect if they maintained loyalty to the Catholic Church as an institution. In 1570, the pope excommunicated Elizabeth I, which imposed on Catholics a duty to withdraw and work for her deposition, if not her death. While many Catholics continued their attendance at a parish church and found ways of combining private worship with loyalty to the queen, a minority did not.

The arrival of priests trained in the English **seminary** at Douai in France, the links established between some of the nobility and Mary, Queen of Scots, the plotting against Elizabeth's life and occasional outright rebellion created a powerful mythology with enough basis in fact to ensure that, by 1587, anti-Catholic feeling was widespread. To this was added the massacre of Protestants in France and the Low Countries, the Spanish attempt to invade England in 1588 and, in the course of the war that followed, the fomenting of rebellion in Ireland. The Gunpowder Plot of 1605 and the Hapsburg assault on Protestants in central Europe, which culminated in the outbreak of war in 1618, reinforced this mythology with recent experience. By 1625, most English people shared an intense fear of Catholicism.

**KEY TERM**

**Seminary**
A training college for priests.

### Charles I and Catholicism

In this context, the policies adopted by Charles I in 'reforming' the Church of England on Arminian lines were both tactless and naïve, but outside the Church his actions added fuel to the fire. There is no doubt that Charles was, and remained, a faithful Anglican throughout his life, but his actions sometimes indicated otherwise. Source 6 is taken from a letter written to the pope in the course of Prince Charles' visit to Spain in 1623, seeking approval for his proposed marriage to the Infanta. When this failed it was followed up by a marriage to Henrietta Maria of France, the terms of which allowed her to bring and maintain a retinue of Catholic clergy to serve her at court.

In 1624–25, there were complaints in London about the boldness of Catholics in the court, and it was clear that high profile Catholic gentry were residing in the City. The survival of Catholic belief had been greatest among those who could afford to employ a priest in residence, and some noble families had held on to their faith and used their wealth and influence to support others of their religion who lacked such facilities. In Lancashire and parts of the North particularly, but in pockets throughout the country, recusancy laws and restrictions on Catholic meetings were only enforced intermittently. In London itself, the existence of foreign communities of merchants and diplomats added to a Catholic presence. These conditions were not new, but with Charles' marriage, his accession to the throne and the arrival of Henrietta Maria, the activities resulting from them became significantly more open and intrusive. Although the words of Charles' letter would have been private, his actions would have made his sentiments clear and their impact very public.

**SOURCE 6** From a letter written by Prince Charles to the pope from Madrid, 20 April 1623.

> What cruel slaughters, what deplorable calamities have arisen from the dissensions of Christian princes. The judgement your Holiness hath formed of my desire of contracting affinity and marriage with the house of a catholic prince is a test both of your charity and wisdom, for never should I feel so earnest as I do to be joined to anyone living in that close and indissoluble bond, whose religion I hated. Wherefore be your Holiness persuaded that I am, and ever shall be, of such moderation as to keep aloof from every undertaking which may testify any hatred towards the Roman Catholic religion. Nay, I will seize any opportunities... so that we all confess one undivided Trinity, and one Christ crucified, we may be banded together unanimously unto one faith.

Unfortunately for Charles, his sentiments were shared by relatively few of his subjects, but most damaging of all, his actions suggest that he was unaware of the impact that such sentiments would have in England. Hence, he not only fulfilled the terms of his marriage to Henrietta Maria, but made no attempt to restrict her influence. A strong personality, she not only worshipped as a Catholic, but encouraged others to join her and allowed her priests to officiate outside her private chapel. After the death of Buckingham in 1628, the marriage became close, and Charles enjoyed a domestic companionship and family life that many kings lacked. The effect, however, was to reinforce his natural tendency to be reserved, and his unwillingness to explain his actions and the reasons behind them was a major political weakness. The promotion of Arminians in the Church and at court, the increasing role taken by bishops in the secular administration and the exclusion of the Puritan nobility from office and influence inevitably appeared to be part of a pattern directed towards some purpose, and Charles did nothing to dispel this impression. In addition, his authoritarian behaviour towards parliament, the crisis over the forced loan and the Petition of Right suggested a desire for the kind of autocratic powers that were increasingly exercised by his wife's brother in France.

To this was added a style of court that elevated monarchy to a semi-religious mystique, using an imagery and approach perfected in Catholic Rome. The Catholic painter, Peter Paul Rubens, was summoned to provide the decorated ceilings and murals in the new Banqueting House at Whitehall, and provided a commentary on the glory of monarchy by placing it at the shoulder of God himself. In 1633, when he finally had himself crowned in Scotland, Charles left the Scottish nobility and parliament bemused by the pomp and ceremony employed. By the mid-1630s, high profile members of the Privy Council, Francis Windebank and Francis Cottington, had Catholic wives. The royal children and a growing number of courtiers worshipped in the queen's Catholic chapel, and the king's closest companion, apart from his Catholic queen, was the papal ambassador, George Con, with whom he shared a love of art.

**SOURCE**

Henrietta Maria with Jeffrey Hudson, her court dwarf. This painting by Van Dyck (1633) was designed to show her love of fun and entertainments. Most members of Henrietta's household, including Hudson, were expected to practise Catholicism.

Outside the court, Puritans were harassed and Catholics left largely undisturbed. A group of Catholic courtiers were making large profits from a lucrative soap monopoly, while the regional nobility and gentry were ordered to spend time in their localities. Those who protested were silenced and subjected to brutal punishment by the bishops and Privy Councillors who staffed the Prerogative Courts of High Commission and Star Chamber and acted explicitly in the king's name. Authoritarian government, the lack of parliaments and overriding of common law seemed to many, loyal Anglicans as well as Puritans, to be leading only in one direction – towards the kind of absolutism associated only with Catholicism.

The question of Charles' motives and the importance of his personality has already been addressed in Chapter 1 and few modern historians would suggest that he was consciously or deliberately attempting to establish an absolute monarchy, let alone a Catholic Church in England. The unity of opposition that his errors created in parliament and the political nation quickly dissipated when there was a need to agree on what should replace the structures of the personal rule and, by 1642, Charles had rallied sufficient support to believe that he could suppress what to him was the Great Rebellion.

Within the ranks of royalists, the English Catholics formed a significant and loyal minority, to whom both of Charles' sons acknowledged a debt of gratitude, and in both Ireland and western Scotland there were sizeable Catholic armies who played a significant part in the war. Whatever their military value, however, it came at a cost. The widespread fears generated in England by the Irish rebellion in 1641 were reinforced in 1645 by the news that the king's correspondence, captured with his baggage train after the Battle of Naseby, revealed plans to use Irish troops in England and an offer of help from the pope. The fears and prejudices that existed in 1621 could only be intensified by the events of the personal rule, and the struggles that followed, while its political legacy was to bring into sharp focus the perceived links between absolute monarchy, the Catholic Church and tyranny.

**ACTIVITIES**
**KNOWLEDGE CHECK**

**Charles I and Catholicism**

1 Read Source 6. What do you perceive to be Prince Charles' motives in writing this letter? What does it reveal about his beliefs and his personality? In what different ways could his words be interpreted?

2 Look at Source 7. What impression do you get of Henrietta Maria? What might Puritans think of her?

3 How much of an impact did the inclusion of Catholics at court have on the reign of Charles?

## The exclusion of Catholics from religious toleration

### The Civil War and its aftermath

When religious toleration was offered by the Rump Parliament, it automatically excluded Catholics. The Toleration Act of 1650 removed the requirement to attend an Anglican church, but Catholics were still not given freedom. The 1640s had been the key decade in the development of tolerationist ideas and these were grounded in radical Puritanism. For the first time, in the context of war, the issue of toleration could be freely and openly debated. In 1644, the Puritan theologian Roger Williams opened the debate when his call for toleration included embracing heretics, blasphemers, Catholics and pagans. Williams had emigrated to North America in the 1630s as a result of the persecutions of Archbishop Laud, and most Puritans disagreed with his views.

The first explicit law against Catholics after 1640 was passed by the Long Parliament in August 1643, requiring all Catholics aged over 21 to swear an Oath of Abjuration denying their basic beliefs. If this was refused, they had two-thirds of their land and goods confiscated. Catholics were also required to pay the assessment tax at twice the normal rate. The Oath was reissued in 1656 with even stricter terms, and the Act of Parliament that accompanied it called for the closing down of Catholic chapels in foreign embassies, with a fine of £100 for anyone caught worshipping at them. Many Catholics had their estates confiscated after the Civil War, and some were left with no option but to conform, as Extract 4 makes clear.

EXTRACT

From A. Loomie, 'Oliver Cromwell's Policy towards the English Catholics: The Appraisal by Diplomats, 1654–1658', in *The Catholic Historical Review* (2004).

Catholic peers felt compelled to take the oath of abjuration as the only alternative for the family's survival. The near penniless 2nd Earl Rivers took the oath in 1649, and the 4th Baron Petre, overcome by his losses during the civil war, had to salvage his diminished estate by taking the oath in May, 1652. It was an ironical result of this type of persecution that each time a Catholic conformed, the Commonwealth or the Protectorate lost money.

### The Protectorate

Cromwell was not prepared to grant Catholics toleration, and even Henry Vane, who wrote a pamphlet calling for religious freedom for Catholics in 1652, stated that he would not extend it to **idolaters**. Most calls for sustained Catholic persecution cited the use of statues and reverence of saints as a primary reason for their continued actions.

KEY TERM

**Idolater**
A person who worshipped false idols (idolatry), such as the statues of saints revered by Catholics.

Cromwell issued an order in January 1654 stating that the laws against Catholics enacted under Elizabeth I and James I were to continue. Disturbed at this, a group of Catholics led by three peers met Cromwell privately to plead for restraint. Although Cromwell gave them the impression he would resist further calls to limit Catholics, the meeting was followed in April 1655 by a proclamation demanding that the laws against Catholic influence in the priesthood be adhered to. In September 1655, a report sent to Cromwell stated that 992 people refused to take the Oath of Abjuration in Lancashire, far more than in any other county. Contemporaries reported that mass was still being carried out and the authorities turned a blind eye to many Catholic practices. The contradictory nature of Cromwell's anti-Catholicism is also shown in his friendship with Sir Kenelm Digby, a leading Catholic in the household of the exiled Henrietta Maria. Digby visited London in 1654 and was able to secure the release of his family's confiscated property.

Although persecution of Catholics was clearly widespread, in the years between the end of the First Civil War and the fall of Clarendon in 1667, the problem of Catholic influence was not the major focus of the political battles and religious tensions that dominated affairs. The existence of monarchy itself and the threat posed by unrestricted religious enthusiasm was a far more immediate threat to the moderate majority and their perceptions of stability. Neither Catholics nor hostility towards them disappeared, but if they remained discreet they were able to worship privately. The Irish Catholics endured a further invasion in 1649, but the fighting was between parliamentary and royalist armies and, despite the supposed massacres of civilians at Drogheda and Wexford, the evidence of local records shows remarkably few civilian deaths. The population probably suffered more from the ensuing land settlement, in which Scottish and English soldiers were paid with Irish land.

With the Restoration of Charles II, the Catholics in England gained a measure of safety, in some cases reward for faithful service, and a measure of religious freedom because there were other, more immediate targets. In Scotland, a similar situation developed as the restored parliament, dominated by the nobility, was primarily concerned to restrict the power of the Kirk and suppress rebellious dissenters. Ireland was governed by a governor and the Church of Ireland restored, leading to persecution of both Catholics and dissenters with variable consistency.

## Anti-Catholic sentiment, 1660–88

### Charles II and continental Catholicism

Nevertheless, after the Restoration, there were signs of a renewed concern among some in both court and country factions with the threat of Catholic influence. In 1666, the Great Fire of London sparked rumours of Catholic agents at work and, while war with the Dutch was generally popular, the disasters that followed (such as the destruction of the fleet) created a range of reactions. While the House of Commons blamed and impeached Charles' chief adviser, Clarendon, others saw events as a judgement of God on the activities of a dissolute court and the influence of Papists within it.

In 1667, the great absolutist Louis XIV invaded the Spanish Netherlands and launched an attack on the Dutch, feeding a growing awareness in England that Catholic France was now a greater threat to English and Protestant independence than the Hapsburgs in the Holy Roman Empire and

Spain. In 1668, while English diplomats were negotiating a Triple Alliance with Sweden and the United Provinces, Charles was in talks with Louis through his sister Henrietta, who was married to the French king's brother. In the same year, the Duke of York converted to Catholicism, a fact that became public knowledge by 1669. Having replaced Clarendon with a group of courtiers who included two known Catholics, Clifford and Arlington, Charles entertained his sister in an extended visit in 1670, signed the Treaty of Dover with France, and took a new French mistress – Louise de la Valliere.

Charles' commitment to a French alliance caused grave concern, while his receipt of subsidies from Louis raised questions about a desire to escape financial dependence on parliaments. It was as well for Charles and for most of his subjects that they were unaware of a secret clause in the Treaty, in which Charles promised to announce his conversion to Catholicism as soon as it was safe and appropriate.

### Charles II and Catholicism at home

Although the details of these decisions were not all widely known, the direction of events was enough to raise suspicions and rumours. Hence the announcement of a new Declaration of Indulgence in 1672, which explicitly permitted Catholics to worship in private, did not come as a shock. It did, however, produce hostile reactions in parliament and across the Anglican establishment. This was primarily for two reasons.

- One reason was a dislike of the king's claim to be able to dispense with the law, rather than any religious implications that the Declaration had.
- The other was that the Catholic sympathies of both the king and his brother and heir were increasingly apparent.

It is difficult to assess Charles' motives. There is no reason to doubt that he genuinely opposed persecution in matters of religion, and his association with Latitudinarians like Lord Ashley, Chancellor of the Exchequer from 1661, indicates that his attitude towards dissent was sympathetic. Ashley was one of the group who replaced Clarendon and, in 1672, he was promoted to the office of Lord Chancellor and created Earl of Shaftesbury. However, when Charles was forced to withdraw the Indulgence in 1673, Shaftesbury's obvious reservations regarding the French alliance led to his dismissal and the beginning of a career in opposition to royal policy. The main reason for this was Charles' decision to ally with the Anglican establishment. This decision and his acceptance of the Test Act, excluding all but Anglicans from public office, indicates that, whatever his motives, they were not strong enough to persuade Charles to risk a repetition of his father's fate.

Nevertheless, from this point on, fear of Catholicism and absolutism increased significantly. While Danby concluded a Dutch alliance and a marriage between William of Orange and Mary, the elder daughter of the Duke of York, the Duke himself was permitted to marry the Catholic, Mary of Modena, in 1673. As the queen's childlessness became less and less likely to change, the likelihood that James would succeed his brother increased. Although he had two Protestant daughters to follow him, a Catholic king with a Catholic wife might well produce a Catholic son, who would supersede his half-sisters. Meanwhile, Danby built up control of parliament using royal patronage and French subsidies. The old equation of Popery with arbitrary government was encouraged by publications like the pamphlet issued by Shaftesbury in 1675, entitled *A letter from a Person of Quality to his Friends in the Country*. This argued that Anglican bishops were promoting persecution of Protestants and arbitrary government under the guise of protecting the Church.

The political attitudes and beliefs that were to become Whig and Tory were beginning to take shape and, in that shape, the Whigs appealed to the Protestant majority, occasionally tainted by association with dissent, while the Tories stood for Church and king, increasingly tainted by association with Catholic absolutism.

It was therefore no coincidence that the Exclusion Crisis, which threatened Charles II with a repeat of his father's problems in 1640–42, was preceded by the hysteria generated by the Popish Plot. Whether or not the Whig leaders believed the claims made by Oates, it was the perfect opportunity to undermine Danby, remove the threat of a Catholic king and strengthen the rights and independence of parliamentary government. In the event, Charles was able to outmanoeuvre them for a number of reasons.

- A more astute politician than his father, he played his cards with patience and skill, aided by French subsidies so that he could afford to dissolve parliament at will.
- Meanwhile, English control of Ireland and Scotland, established after 1649 and strengthened by the Restoration, enabled him to focus entirely on events in England.
- Most important of all, however, the memories of upheaval and the Protestant extremism of the 1640s and 1650s allowed him to paint the Whigs as potential rebels and regicides, drawing on loyalty to the Crown and the belief that only the Crown could guarantee stability.

In 1683, this was reinforced by the Rye House Plot to assassinate Charles, and for the remainder of Charles' life he was able to focus public fears on dissent and away from Catholicism. The period from 1682 to 1686 has been labelled by some historians as a Second Stuart Absolutism, in which loyalty to Church and king enabled the Triennial Act to be ignored, the corporations to be brought under Tory control and financial independence to be secured by French subsidies. Whether this could have been extended permanently is debatable, but the possibility rested on two things – the skills and determination of Charles II and the quietening of anti-Catholic fears by focusing on the non-conformist threat. In 1685, both were lost with the accession of James II.

**ACTIVITIES**
**KNOWLEDGE CHECK**

**Toleration to Restoration**

1 In what ways were Catholics excluded from toleration in the aftermath of the Civil War?

2 Why was Cromwell's anti-Catholicism contradictory?

3 How was Charles II able to overcome rumours about his Catholic sympathies?

### James II and anti-Catholic sentiment, 1685–88

However difficult it is to assess the aims of Charles II in the policies that he pursued, the same cannot be said of his brother. From the moment of his accession, one aim was crystal clear – to ensure equality as citizens for his fellow Catholics, by using his power as monarch. That this would entail overriding existing laws or ignoring the rights of parliaments did not seem to constitute a problem to him and the actions he took from 1685 to 1688 provided a series of straightforward steps in that direction.

Whether he desired to extend royal power for its own sake is less clear and subject to some debate, as is the extent to which he was genuine in opposing persecution of other faiths. A close friendship with the Quaker William Penn suggests that he was sincere, but whether a Catholic monarchy would have maintained toleration over a period of time is questionable. Certainly, the action of his brother-in-law, Louis XIV, in withdrawing toleration from the Protestant Huguenots in 1685, sending a stream of refugees to England, raised serious doubts at the time and contributed significantly to James' eventual failure. The historian Barry Coward summarises the situation in Extract 5.

**EXTRACT 5** From B. Coward, *Stuart England, 1603–1714* (1997).

Whether or not James II intended to establish royal absolutism in England is not known. What is certain - and of more importance in explaining the course of events in his reign - is that most of his subjects came to *believe* that he did.

In 1686, James issued instructions to the bishops forbidding the preaching of anti-Catholic sermons, and set up the Court of Ecclesiastical Commission, reminiscent of the Prerogative Court of High Commission (abolished in 1641), to oversee enforcement. When Bishop Compton of London refused to suspend a cleric for preaching such a sermon, he was, himself, suspended by the Court. In a similar exercise of prerogative powers, James set up a licensing office to sell permits to dissenters, exempting them from the laws of the Clarendon Code. Meanwhile, a legal decision in the case of *Godden v Hales* confirmed the king's right to exempt individuals from the Test and Corporation Acts, and James used this to force Magdalen College, Oxford, to accept a Catholic President, despite the opposition of the fellows.

Having dismissed his Anglican advisers, the Earls of Clarendon and Rochester (sons of Edward Hyde), James now authorised the Earl of Sunderland and Judge Jeffreys (infamous for the trials conducted against the Monmouth rebels known as the Bloody Assizes) to question JPs and parliamentary candidates in a campaign to pack the next parliament with members who would vote in favour of repealing the Acts. He had already issued a Declaration of Indulgence in 1687, allowing both dissenters and Catholics to worship freely; in 1688, this was followed up in a another Declaration, more explicit on the rights of Catholics and allowing dissenters to meet without a specific licence, which he ordered to be read from the pulpit of every parish church. When seven of the Bishops, including Sancroft, Archbishop of Canterbury, petitioned against this order, they were tried and acquitted to public celebration. Shortly after this, the birth of a son to James and Mary of Modena led seven leading political figures – three Whigs, three Anglican lords and the Bishop of London – to write an appeal to William of Orange to invade England and forestall any further action by the king.

**ACTIVITIES**
**KNOWLEDGE CHECK**

**A Catholic king**

1 Analyse the actions described in the final section, and list those which:

a) established freedom of worship for Catholics and others

b) created political and social equality for Catholics and others

c) placed Catholics in positions of power and influence

d) involved the extension or strengthening of royal power.

2 In conclusion, explain why James' actions could be interpreted as a desire to create absolute monarchy in England.

**ACTIVITY**
**SUMMARY**

**Religious conflict and dissent, 1625-88**

1 Create three parallel timelines of the period 1625-88. One should cover the growth of non-conformity and dissent, one should show the development of the Church of England, and one should demonstrate the threat of Catholicism.

2 On each timeline, pick out the five most important turning points and provide an explanation of why you have chosen them.

**A Level Exam-Style Question Section B**

How accurate is it to say that non-conformity was a greater threat to the monarchy than the fear of Catholicism, 1660–1688? (20 marks)

**Tip**

*Be prepared to argue that, at different points in the chronology of this answer, the balance of evidence will change in favour of both non-conformity and Catholicism.*

## WIDER READING

Acheson, R.J. *Radical Puritans in England*, Longman (1990) For the development of non-conformity, including the radical sects

Anderson, A. *An Introduction to Stuart Britain, 1603-1714*, Hodder Education (1999) A textbook giving the impact of religious reform

Coward, B. *Stuart England*, Longman (1997) A textbook giving the impact of religious reform

Smith, D.L. *A History of the Modern British Isles: the Double Crown 1603-1707*, Blackwell (1998) Contains detail on the development of the Anglican Church and the Catholic question

Spurr, J. *The Post-Reformation: 1603-1714*, Pearson (2006) A book covering the developments in religion

# 1.3 Social and intellectual challenge, 1625-88

**KEY QUESTIONS**

- Why did the population of Britain increase in the years 1625–88, and what impact did this have?
- In what ways did the revolutionary events of the century affect the structure of society?
- What changes came about in the fields of science, philosophy and political ideas?

## INTRODUCTION

Between 1625 and 1688, changes not only came about in religious belief and the structure of the Church and government, but also in society as a whole. Historians have long debated the significance of the revolutionary events of the century, particularly the Civil War, in causing the great social developments of the age. Away from Civil War and revolution, changes to the economy, employment, migration and disease all contributed to changes in society.

- The **gentry** class, which had grown rapidly since 1500, began to increase in wealth and status, thus threatening the power of the traditional ruling nobility.
- A new merchant class emerged, as well as a professional class of doctors, lawyers and other professionals.
- The gradual population growth that had taken place since the country was decimated by the plague in the 14th century continued to build.
- With a rising population came increasing urbanisation, as more people moved to towns in order to find work.
- The role of women in driving social change was significant, with a number of women having noteworthy roles within the radical religious groups that flourished in the middle of the century.
- These developments led to new pressures on society. The few larger towns that existed were experiencing a gradual expansion, contributing to food shortages and widespread poverty as population growth led to new pressures on scarce resources. However, the lives of the poor had arguably been improved by the Elizabethan Poor Laws, which provided basic relief for those most in need, and indeed there were fewer food riots in the 17th century than in the 16th century.

**KEY TERM**

**Gentry**
The class immediately below the nobility. They were free from the need to work the land and had the wealth and leisure time to become involved in politics. Many of the leading MPs and political figures of the period, including Oliver Cromwell and John Pym, were from gentry backgrounds.

1600 | 1605 | 1625 | 1630 | 1635 | 1640 | 1645 | 1650

**1601** - The Poor Relief Act is passed

**1626** - Francis Bacon dies

**1629** - Charles I begins his personal rule

**c1638** - The population of Britain reaches five million

**1649** - The Leveller leaders are imprisoned in the Tower of London

Gerrard Winstanley establishes the first Digger commune

**1651** - Thomas Hobbes publishes *Leviathan*

The 17th century was also a time of growth in the areas of science and philosophy, and at least some of the changes developed as a result of the religious radicalism discussed in Chapter 2. The idea that the monarch should have an undisputed divine right to rule had been questioned during the Civil War and informed the great philosophical debates of the day. The works of Thomas Hobbes and John Locke heavily influenced modern ideas of the **nation state** and democracy, and new discoveries in the fields of science and mathematics enabled Britain to become both a world leader in trade and an intellectual powerhouse.

KEY TERM

**Nation state**
A country that is united by a combination of political ideas, cultural or ethnic ties. Modern nation states have fixed boundaries, centralised public administration and a united economic system.

## WHY DID THE POPULATION OF BRITAIN INCREASE IN THE YEARS 1625-88, AND WHAT IMPACT DID THIS HAVE?

Between 1520 and 1680, the population of England doubled, from around 2.5 million to more than 5 million. This expansion was far from equal across regions and changed pace at various points; however, on average, the rate of population growth across the Stuart era was around 0.5 percent per year. This was significantly higher than the growth experienced in the 14th and 15th centuries. The population was scattered unevenly, with around three-quarters of the entire population living in the South East. Large swathes of the North were effectively uninhabited, and in all areas towns were still a rarity. London bucked this trend as it continued to dominate in terms of population, making it the largest city in Western Europe. After the First Civil War (1642–46), population growth slowed in the context of conflict and uncertainty.

## Reasons for the increase in population

### Migration

Migration had some impact on population growth, particularly around times of revolution and war. For example, a large number of foreign immigrants arrived in 1651, two years after the Commonwealth was established and when religious toleration appeared to be an established policy. Migration was most noticeable in towns and, by 1600, migrants made up 35 percent of the population of Norwich. These were economic migrants – skilled weavers from the Low Countries. Migration within Britain was also taking place, and the traditional view that people lived their entire lives close to their place of birth has been questioned by historians in recent years. As people moved in order to find work, they would invariably find themselves living in towns. More job security would lead to more children being born. As historian Barry Coward discusses in Extract 1, migration had both positive and negative effects on the British population.

EXTRACT 1

From B. Coward, *The Stuart Age, 1603–1714* (2003).

[A] study of 206 witnesses before two church courts in Sussex between 1580 and 1640 concludes that over 75 per cent of them no longer lived in their birthplaces; most had moved only once and over short distances of up to twenty miles... Long-distance migration was more common among people at the upper and lower ends of the social spectrum. Wealthy landowners, merchants and professional people and their families, habitually travelled to London to take advantage of the many attractions of the capital; while landless labourers, vagrants and unemployed young people travelled long distances in search of work. Between 1580 and 1640 poor migrants from all parts of Britain poured into three Kentish towns. Some travelled even further afield, emigrating to Ireland or boarding ships at ports like Bristol, taking the hazardous gamble of sailing to the newly established colonies in north America to become indentured servants.

**1662** - The Settlement Act modifies the Poor Relief Act

**1689** - John Locke publishes *Two Treatises of Government*

1655 1660 1665 1670 1675 1680 1685 1690

**1660** - The Royal Society is founded

**1686** - Newton presents his theory of gravity to the Royal Society

The Kentish towns that were so attractive to migrants, such as Cranbrook, Tenterden and Maidstone, were well established centres of the cloth trade, and had already seen migration from skilled Dutch weavers. English migrants were following their lead, and hoped to benefit from the prosperity of these towns. In 1585, 120 Dutch workers lived in Maidstone and, as they took on apprentices, English migrants were able to take on much of the work. The widespread poverty that existed in both town and country contributed to large numbers of the poor leaving for a better life elsewhere. Although it is difficult to ascertain precise numbers, it is clear that many moved to the towns. Despite this, only 5 percent of the population outside London lived in towns with over 5,000 inhabitants in 1700. There is no reason to believe that Coward's reference in Extract 1 to 75 percent of the Sussex population moving between rural parishes was not comparable with other counties.

### Mortality and fertility

Mortality [death] rates were lower than in the preceding three centuries, primarily because of a decline in incidences of plague. The infamous bubonic plague, or Black Death, that reached England in 1348 had a dramatic impact on the population, which was just 1.5 million in the 1450s, compared with 5 million before the plague struck. By the 1520s, the population was around 2.5 million and it continued to increase rapidly. In the mid-16th century, short-lived epidemics of other viral diseases hampered growth, but these had reduced greatly by 1625. This was not necessarily due to advances in medical techniques; rather, it was because the population had become adept at isolating individuals and containing the spread of diseases. It was common in the late Tudor and early Stuart period for the theatres of London to be shut for months at a time when an epidemic hit.

It also seems that the population was able to recover rapidly from bouts of disease. For example, when the plague of 1665 hit the parish of Eyam in Derbyshire, parish records show that the children who died were replaced within ten years by the surviving adult population. When elder members of a family died, the younger members would gain more of an opportunity to marry and, if they married younger, the marriage was more likely to result in a large number of children. Historians have discovered that this pattern existed throughout the early modern period. When death rates were high, fertility was often high. When death rates were lower, not as many children were born.

Despite the emphasis placed by some historians on dramatic population growth, it is clear that the population expanded and contracted throughout the period and did not always follow a clear pattern. Fertility rates were high during the 16th century, falling slowly until reaching a low around 1650, with rates only beginning to rise again by 1680. This high was driven almost exclusively by the massive growth of London. The unusual decline after 1650 appears to be due in part to the late average age of first marriages. In the middle of the century, the average age for men and women to marry was 28 and 26 respectively, compared to 26 and 24 in 1600. The resulting number of children per marriage would therefore be lower.

**ACTIVITIES**
**KNOWLEDGE CHECK**

**Population growth**

1 What was the impact of migration on society?

2 Which words would you use to describe the nature of population growth? Explain why you have chosen them.

**SOURCE**

A contemporary illustration showing weekly burials in the City of London, 1665.



## The impact of population growth on the development of towns

### London

At some time around 1650, London overtook Paris (France) and Naples (Italy) to become the largest city in Western Europe. Contemporaries estimated the population to be around 500,000 and the modern estimate has settled at 400,000, making London more than ten times bigger than the next largest English towns of Norwich and Bristol. Around 7 percent of the English population lived in London, increasing to over 9 percent in 1700. This compares with 2.25 percent in 1520. Many historians believe that the growth of the Stuart economy and the success of the fledgling empire were due to the drastic growth of London. The growth of London also impacted on the rural economy, as huge amounts of agricultural goods, including nearly 400 percent more grain between 1600 and 1680, were needed to feed the City. London was ideally placed to power the Stuart economy, as it was at the heart of the road and shipping network, and could support the increasing demand for goods. The growth of London and its impact on the economy is discussed further in Chapter 4.

SOURCE 

Image of London as viewed from Bankside, 1647, by Wenceslaus Hollar, who was resident in the City at the time. London was the political, economic and religious centre of England and was vital to the rapid population growth experienced in the 17th century.

## Other towns

In 1600, there were eight towns with a population over 5,000, and this had increased to over 30 in 1700. Towns that did expand in the period, such as Bristol, were generally ports or industrial centres and did so because of the increase in trading activity. In the first quarter of the 17th century, Norwich was the most populous town outside London, with 30,000 inhabitants, up from 10,000 in 1500. Norwich was the centre of the East Anglian cloth industry, and welcomed a number of foreign migrants, particularly from the Low Countries. The next largest town was Bristol, with 20,000 inhabitants, followed by York and Newcastle with around 12,000 each. The 17th century would see early trade with the Americas and the Indian subcontinent, and port towns like Bristol and Liverpool also became industrial centres, processing the goods imported from abroad. The North East of England was the centre of the coal extraction industry and Newcastle continued to develop as a result. The importance of Newcastle was shown when the Scots invaded England in 1640. They occupied the city, as well as the rest of the north-east, resulting in massive coal shortages in London. Population growth on smaller market towns had a mixed impact, primarily because these towns had little to offer potential migrants, especially when compared with London.

| Town | Population in 1500 | Population in 1625 |
|---|---|---|
| Norwich | 10,000 | 30,000 |
| Bristol | 9,500 | 20,000 |
| York | 10,000 | 12,000 |
| Newcastle | 10,000 | 12,000 |

**Figure 3.1**: Table showing the populations of major towns in 1500 and 1625.

Outside these major population centres, there were between 600 and 750 provincial towns, and at least 500 of these had populations less than 2,000. In the South East and Midlands, there was more of a need for market towns, where crops could be traded. The North, dominated as it was by cattle and sheep farms, contained fewer large towns. Ten of these smaller towns were on the coast and were involved in fishing. The growth of manufacturing (which was almost exclusively restricted to textiles) led to a growth in the size of Ipswich, where the population increased from 4,000 in 1600 to 7,500 in 1680. Chester was a centre for the leather industry, and this is reflected in a growth in population from 4,600 in 1563 to 7,100 in 1664.

**Figure 3.2**: England in 1603 and 1714: maps of England showing county boundaries and towns with a population over 5,000.

**KEY TERMS**

**Vagrant**
Traditionally a person who, due to poverty, would wander from town to town in order to beg or to seek out employment. By the 17th century, they were defined as being able to work but choosing not to. They were subject to harsh punishments under the law, such as whipping and branding.

**Poverty line**
The minimum level of income needed to secure the basic necessities of life.

## Impact of population growth

The main impact of population growth on the towns was undoubtedly an increase in poverty, and in the number of people officially classified as **vagrants**. The increase in population caused a shortage of work in both town and countryside, although government policy blamed vagrants for not being able to find work. Towns were the most obvious places to look for work, although the cloth industry, perhaps the biggest employer outside agriculture, began to move to the countryside after 1600 in order to avoid the regulations and taxes placed upon it by the administrators of towns. Two-thirds of the urban population lived near the **poverty line**, and although this fraction did not increase nationally, the number of poor rose as the population increased. In Norwich, for example, many of the inhabitants engaged in trades related to the dominant cloth industry, such as tailors, lived below the poverty line, suggesting that there was not enough work to go round. This was because there were a large number of people who had served apprenticeships and were fully qualified.

A unique glimpse into town life and development can be found in the surviving writings of Celia Fiennes, who travelled throughout England between 1685 and 1698. She was the daughter of the Civil War parliamentarian Nathaniel Fiennes, and was able to travel freely because although she was from a gentry family, she never married. In Source 3 she records what she saw when she visited Colchester, where she apparently finds abundant wealth.

SOURCE

From *The Journeys of Celia Fiennes, 1685–1698* (1947). Fiennes was the daughter of the Civil War parliamentarian Nathaniel Fiennes, and was able to travel freely because although she was from a gentry family, she never married and was not required to run an estate. She wrote a travel memoir in 1702, but it was not published in her lifetime.

Colchester... the whole town is employ'd in spinning weaveing washing drying and dressing their baize [cloth], in which they seeme very industrious; there I saw the Card they use to comb and dress the baize, which they call them teazels which are a kind of rush tops or something like them which they put in frames or laths of wood; the town looks like a thriveing place by the substantiall houses, well pitched streetes which are broad enough for two Coaches to go a breast... out of these great streetes runs many little streetes but not very narrow, mostly old buildings except a few houses builded by some Quakers that are brick.

According to Fiennes, the entire town was employed in the cloth industry, resulting in apparent prosperity for the inhabitants. In reality, the population and way of life in towns like Colchester changed very little in the Stuart period, with the majority of economic migrants choosing to move to London.

EXTEND YOUR KNOWLEDGE

Alternative interpretations

Although many historians agree that population growth increased the importance of provincial towns, some, such as Barry Coward, are careful not to overstate their importance. Coward, in *The Stuart Age* (1980), argued that the development of provincial towns before 1650 was slow, and that in the context of the national economy, their significance was minimal. He believed that English agriculture had not yet become efficient enough to feed a large urban population, and the manufacturing sector of the economy was not diversified enough to enable a large number of towns to develop as industrial centres.

## The impact of population growth on rural life

Any discussion of the British economy in the 17th century usually begins by emphasising that it was dominated by agriculture. Even in counties where fewer people were employed in agriculture, it was still at the heart of all local economies. One of these counties was Gloucestershire, where a census for 1608 shows that half of the population was engaged in other professions, mainly related to the cloth industry. Agriculture, however, was still vastly important in a country experiencing steady population growth. Around 9,000,000 acres of English land were devoted to the growing of crops, the majority consisting of wheat (which was necessary for baking bread) and barley (which was needed for brewing beer).

It was relatively easy for farmers to make a profit in the first half of the 17th century, as the population was increasing at a reasonable rate. After 1650, however, inflation meant that many small landowners were unable to invest in their farms, and had no choice but to sell their land. This left the wealthy aristocracy and higher gentry as the only landowners able to invest in improving their yield from agriculture. New methods of agriculture were needed, which are discussed further in Chapter 4. As the population increased, more farms were amalgamated and enclosed in order to make larger farms that could focus on the production of a single crop or rear animals. The owners of small farms who were pushed out as a result of this drive for efficiency would often become eligible for poor relief (discussed on pages 72–73), and some even joined the ranks of the vagrants.

Regardless of trends in the countryside, the number of people living in towns was growing, reaching around 15 percent of the population by 1701, up from 12 percent a century earlier. This meant that the countryside had to continue to support this growth at a rate not seen before, and employment in agriculture became more reliable than in the cloth industry. As London and other towns expanded, new markets needed supplying, which in turn made it necessary to improve the transport infrastructure of the countryside. Large landowners and some town councils invested in improving the condition of rivers (in order to make them navigable) and roads (including the first toll roads after 1662). They also invested in wagons, transforming the lives of those employed in the rural economy.

## Growth of poverty

As we have already established, competition for work as a result of population growth led to an increase in poverty. The early Stuart period was marked by population growth, falling wages and rising prices, leaving many people vulnerable, with little to fall back on. Contemporary writers, many of whom belonged to the gentry and aristocracy, were convinced that the numbers of poor were huge, with some estimating that half of the population fell into this category. Taxation records from the 1670s show that this figure may be exaggerated, but the real figure was certainly more than one-third of the population. This is similar to the numbers of poor under the Tudors; however, the increased enclosure of common land, leading to a lack of space for the poor to graze animals, and a shortage of food meant that the living conditions of the poor were getting worse.

The poor can be divided into two groups: the *settled* poor and the *vagrant* poor.

- The settled poor were those who were established in one parish and did not move around to beg or find work. They made up around one-quarter of the population.
- The vagrant poor were traditionally those who travelled in order to sustain themselves, and were treated as criminals under the law. Accurate figures for the population of vagrant poor are hard to come by, although contemporaries believed their numbers were great and that they were a genuine threat to stable society. In reality, their numbers were much lower than the settled poor: it is known that 26,000, or roughly 0.5 percent of the entire population, were arrested for vagrancy in the 1630s, although many more undoubtedly escaped and were not recorded.

There can be no doubt that the poor got poorer in the 17th century and, without government help, they may well have threatened the social and political order. Added to the mix was

**price inflation**, which was running at around four percent per year for consumable goods in the first half of the century. This may not seem particularly high by modern standards, but this level had been sustained since around 1500, and it outstripped wage rises by two-to-one. If such a high proportion of the population struggled to support themselves through work, then how did they survive? There is no doubt that the grinding poverty experienced by so many was only helped by limited state and voluntary relief, which is discussed later in the chapter (see pages 72–73).

**KEY TERM**

**Price inflation**
The rate at which the general level of prices for everyday goods rises, leading to a fall in purchasing power.

To escape the poverty trap, around two-fifths of the workforce in villages took up jobs as servants, living and working in the households of others. In towns, the proportion was higher, certainly more than half. This system was common for two reasons: first, the able-bodied poor were required to have 'masters' by law and could not live entirely independently; and second, apprenticeships for most trades took seven years to complete and were out of reach for the very poorest. This option was also popular because workers were given free housing, clothing and food from their masters, thus safeguarding them from rising prices. This option was not without its hazards, as the diarist Samuel Pepys recorded in relation to his own servant (see Source 4).

**SOURCE**

From Samuel Pepys's Diary, published 1825. Pepys was a naval administrator for both Charles II and James II, but became most famous for the diary he kept of the period 1660 to 1669.

Dec. 1st, 1660. This morning, observing some things to be laid up not as they should be by the girl, I took a broom and basted her til she cried extremely, which made me vexed, but before I went out I left her appeased.

Feb. 19th, 1665. At supper, hearing by accident of my mayds letting in a rogueing Scotch woman to helpe them to washe and scoure in our house, I fell mightily out, and made my wife, to the disturbance of the house and neighbours, to beat our girle, and then we shut her down into the cellar, and there she lay all night.

Another option for the poor was migration, whether within a county, to one of the expanding industrial towns or even abroad. It is estimated that, within any given decade of the 17th century, around a third of the population of each village would leave to find work. Of course, many of these would leave to work in the households of the better-off in nearby villages, but some would move further afield, perhaps to towns or even to discover the supposed wealth of opportunities promised in London. Migration away from Britain entirely was the last resort, with perhaps 200,000 people following the Puritan founders to the American colonies.

The sheer numbers of poor meant that the state struggled to keep check on expanding poverty, as Extract 2 suggests.

**EXTRACT**

From A.L. Beier, *The Problem of the Poor in Tudor and Early Stuart England* (1983).

In London and elsewhere, the suburbs were on the point of being overwhelmed with the hordes of displaced indigents. In both town and country officials began to drive them out by using settlement by-laws. Under the early Stuarts, Whitehall (government) even attempted to check immigration by restricting building in London, and to rid woodland areas of squatters by reviving the forest laws... In the forest regions, officials were rebuffed by riots involving thousands. Vagrants in fact came overwhelmingly from suburbs and woodland areas, a result partly of official clear-outs, but mainly because of the high degree of distress in such places.

**THINKING HISTORICALLY** Change and continuity (4a)

**Significance**

Look at the accounts contained in Source 3 and Extract 2 of the state of urban life in the 17th century.

1 How does Celia Fiennes present Colchester in Source 3?

2 Why does Colchester appear to be important, according to Fiennes?

3 Compare this to the historian A.L. Beier in Extract 2. What does he think of the state of towns in the 17th century?

4 Why do you think these views might differ so greatly?

**ACTIVITY**
**WRITING**

**The impact of population growth**

Write a paragraph explaining why population growth took place and its impact on urban and rural life. Ensure you include the following words: mortality, fertility, vagrants, migration, employment, encouraged, dependent, triggered.

## The Poor Laws and actions against beggars and vagrants

### Before the Restoration

A number of Poor Laws were passed under the Tudors, culminating in Elizabeth's Poor Relief Act of 1601, which is often referred to as the Old Poor Law. Although not passed by a Stuart monarch, the Act is important as the basis for the treatment of the poor until 1662. The basic principle behind the original Poor Laws was that provision should be made for the relief of those unable to work through disability, with punishments handed out to those who were able to work but did not. The earlier laws were inevitably interpreted to suit local circumstances, with some able-bodied people receiving relief and disabled people punished, so the Act of 1601 was passed to end any ambiguity surrounding the treatment of the poor. In reality, the 1601 Act simply recorded for the first time principles that already existed.

The Act of 1601 is often considered to be the crowning glory of Tudor poor relief legislation, primarily because it was not followed by anything significantly new until the 19th century. The Act included the following.

- Overseers of the poor became the chief local officials in charge of the collection of poor relief taxes.
- Overseers were appointed in all parishes and were responsible for deciding who would receive relief.
- Provisions were made to compel people who had previously refused to pay a poor tax.
- The poor could be sent to a poorhouse at the expense of local parishioners.
- Begging was allowed in a person's home parish, but only to provide food.

This Act provided the basis of poor relief throughout the reign of Charles I, and was supported by his policy of 'Thorough', aimed at making local government more efficient and at enhancing poor relief. In 1631, Charles issued a Book of Orders to all Justices of the Peace (JPs) in the counties, which included provisions for the relief of the poor and treatment of vagrants. Although promising much, the Book contained no new principles and was motivated more by Charles' fear of rioting than any sympathetic feelings he may have had. Direction from central government came to an end in 1642, with the advent of civil war, and JPs continued to keep the system going under the original Elizabethan principles without any major issues. According to surviving records, three-quarters of the money that was allotted by overseers by 1660 came from rural parishes, and in 1650 state relief stood at at least £188,000 nationally, compared with £30,000 in 1614.

It seems clear that, in times of both peace and war, poor relief was being well enforced before the Restoration. Local inhabitants charged with paying the poor tax may have had similar motives to Charles, in that they were most interested in keeping order and preventing vagrancy. According to historian Keith Wrightson, as poverty grew, those paying the Poor Rates began to regard local labourers and transient vagrants as more of a threat than ever before. They were no longer seen as individuals and were instead treated as an inconvenience.

Although the poor laws were administered reasonably successfully, there still existed a gap in in the provision for the poor that was only filled through the actions of the Church and the wealth of generous individuals. Charitable gifts and endowments from members of the gentry, who saw it as their duty to look after the poor, were relatively commonplace before the Restoration. For example, Sir Hugh Cholmondley, a wealthy Yorkshire landowner, recorded in the 1630s that he made gifts of food to the poor twice a week from the gates of his manor house.

### After the Restoration

After the restoration of the monarchy in 1660, the Poor Rates were grudgingly paid and the wealthier parishes began to complain that vagrants from poorer districts were squatting on their common land and eventually claiming poor relief from the community. This coincided with an economic depression that began after the death of Oliver Cromwell in 1658. Under pressure, the Cavalier Parliament passed a Poor Relief Act (often known as the Settlement Act) in 1662, which gave more powers to local administrators and attempted to restrict the movement of individuals claiming poor relief. The negative effects of this reform are clear: the labour force was now not as mobile as it had been, and the poor had less economic and personal freedom.

Under the Act, 'settlement certificates' could be issued to prove that a person lived in a parish, thus entitling them to poor relief in their original parish if they moved and got into difficulty. If a resident of a parish decided to move to a new parish, they were entitled to poor relief there if they remained resident for 40 days. If, during the 40 days, a complaint was made to the local overseers or churchwarden, they could be sent back to their original parish. The Act is significant for two reasons: the settlement certificates meant that, for the first time, a poor person could actually prove where they lived; and a definition of what constituted 'poor' had been given for the first time, as only people renting property worth less than £10 were considered worthy of help. The Act was manipulated by local officials, who would send their poor to other parishes, sometimes with instructions that they should avoid detection until they became eligible for relief. After the Glorious Revolution of 1688, the Act was modified in order to close this loophole, as any new entrants to a parish had to be declared public.

All of this had a significant impact on beggars and vagrants. The idea that each person had a place of settlement was essential to the Settlement Act, and this was principally concerned with limiting migration. It was now easier for parish officials to expel newcomers, and wandering from a parish was technically a criminal offence. The Act also authorised the arrest of vagrants, and their committal to workhouses or prisons. The most severe punishment under the act was transportation to the English colonies for seven years. The owners of large estates benefitted more than any other group from the Act, as they were able to demolish empty houses on their land, thus preventing the return of those who had left. Labourers from other parishes could be hired in their place, reducing the amount paid by the landowners in poor relief if these workers were laid off, as they were officially 'settled' in other parishes, who bore the responsibility of their welfare.

**ACTIVITIES**
**KNOWLEDGE CHECK**

**The growth of poverty**

1. Did towns benefit or suffer as a result of population growth?
2. Were the existing Elizabethan Poor Laws adequate? Explain your answer.
3. Did the Settlement Act of 1662 improve the prospects of the poor?

**AS Level Exam-Style Question Section B**

To what extent did the lives of the poor improve in the years 1650–85? (20 marks)

**Tip**

*The poor can include both settled poor and vagrants. Make sure you compare the earlier Elizabethan legislation with that passed after the Restoration.*

# IN WHAT WAYS DID THE REVOLUTIONARY EVENTS OF THE CENTURY AFFECT THE STRUCTURE OF SOCIETY?

## The power of the nobility

As we can see from Chapter 1, society in the 17th century can be described as strictly hierarchical. It was, however, technically possible to move up or down the social scale in certain circumstances. The group that commanded the highest status was the nobility, who made up the class immediately below the monarch. Many of the nobility held land, property and titles that had been in their families for generations, and the heads of noble families were often members of the House of Lords. The boundary between the nobility and the gentry is difficult to define, as it was possible for a 'gentleman' to be wealthier and wield more influence than a noble. It is easiest, then, to define the nobility as **peers**, who historically controlled a majority of wealth and power. It is also important to note that only 2 percent of the population belonged to the nobility and gentry. It was in the later years of Elizabeth's reign that the nobility began to decline in significance, and this appears to have continued throughout the 17th century. Inflation undoubtedly had a role in this, as did the high levels of spending expected from an aristocratic family, as the historian R.H. Tawney identifies in Extract 3.

EXTRACT 3

From R.H. Tawney, 'The Rise of the Gentry, 1558–1640', *Economic History Review* (1941).

Such a (noble) family, inheriting great estates, often inherited trouble. Its standards of expenditure were those of one age, its income that of another... The overheads of a noble landowner - a great establishment, and often more than one; troops of servants and retainers; stables fit for a regiment of cavalry; endless hospitality to neighbours and national notabilities; visits to court, at once ruinous and unavoidable - had always been enormous. Now, on top of these traditional liabilities, came the demands of a new world of luxury and fashion... The wealth of some of the nobility, and especially of the older families, was not infrequently more spectacular than substantial. It was locked up in frozen assets... Side by side with more lucrative possessions, their properties included majestic, but unremunerative franchises - hundreds, boroughs, fairs and markets; a multitude of Knights' fees, all honour and no profit.

Although historians such as Tawney have argued that the fortunes of the nobility were suffering, there is no doubt they continued to wield considerable power; many lived very comfortable lives with vast reserves of wealth. The Marquis of Newcastle and the Earl of Worcester were in a position to donate £900,000 and £700,000 respectively to the royalist cause in 1642. These were colossal amounts by 17th-century standards, especially when compared with the wealth of an average labourer, whose earnings could reach around £10 per year.

## The rise of the gentry

As we can see in Chapter 1, many of the key individuals who shaped the political events of the century were members of the gentry: John Pym, Oliver Cromwell, George Monck and many others. During the Civil War, the gentry were divided in their loyalties and revisionist historians generally agree that class had little to do with the taking of sides among this group. There can be no doubt that this class were of growing importance in the Stuart period, with their numbers increasing by approximately 300 percent between the early Tudor period and the middle of the 17th century, which is slightly higher than the rate of population growth as a whole. More importantly, they were beginning to dominate politics and could be elevated to the peerage for service to the Crown – as was the case with Thomas Wentworth, who became Earl of Strafford. The very term 'gentleman' conveyed an air of superiority and helped them to stand apart from the rest of the non-aristocratic group. The total number of gentry was around 15,000, made up of 3,000 higher and 12,000 lesser gentry. Across the counties, their numbers were small in the context of the entire population (Yorkshire, for example, had 256 higher and 323 lesser gentry, out of a population of more than 300,000). Yet they controlled an immense amount of land and wealth. Across the country, half of all wealth and property belonged to the gentry, with 15 percent controlled by the nobility and most of the rest in the hands of the Church or monarch.

**KEY TERM**

**Peer**
A titled individual (such as a duke, earl, marquess, viscount or baron) who was entitled to a seat in the House of Lords. The majority inherited their status, although the monarch was able to grant titles.

Although this group is often viewed by historians as a single unit, there was a good degree of variation in the wealth of the gentry. Some held property in a single parish, some owned a number of estates and manors, and the richest and most influential could effectively control the politics of an entire county. The lesser members of the gentry could own an estate as small as 50 acres, while it was not unusual for the greater gentry to control estates of 5,000 acres or more. At county level, the gentry could become JPs, constables or judges, whereas the higher gentry could aspire to become members of parliament.

There is no doubt that the gentry became more powerful and influential between 1625 and 1688, although the extent of this power, and how far it was due to a decline in the fortunes of the nobility, is debatable. The so called 'gentry controversy', which produced countless works of research and argument among historians in the mid-20th century, became one of the most heated debates seen in the academic world. The historian Hugh Trevor-Roper discusses the rise of the gentry in Extract 4.

**EXTRACT**

From H. Trevor-Roper, 'The Gentry 1540–1640', *Economic History Review* (1953).

But there nevertheless is a phenomenon, which still may be called 'the rise of the gentry', and this phenomenon, even if it needs to be differently stated, still needs to be explained. The rising class... undoubtedly did prosper and acquired, through their political machine the Houses of Parliament, a political power at the expense of the Crown. The question is, who were these families, and to what did they owe their prosperity?... Almost without exception they were office-holders. Cecils and Howards, Herberts and Villiers and their numerous kindred... Office rather than land was the basis of many undoubtedly 'rising' families.

Trevor-Roper argued that members of the gentry were not necessarily increasing their land and holdings, but instead had more influence due to their participation in politics, at both a local and national level. This participation increased for a number of reasons.

- It became normal for the second or third sons of gentry to enter a career in law, which was seen as an ideal prerequisite for becoming a member of parliament (MP) or joining the Privy Council.
- As parliament became more important in the build-up to the Civil War, the role of the gentry was enhanced. Most MPs were members of the gentry and, after personal rule, Charles had no choice but to turn to them to help fight the Scots.
- Many of the officers who fought for parliament in the Civil War and later became high profile figures in the Republic were from the gentry. With the abolition of the House of Lords in 1649, new opportunities were created.

This contrasts with Tawney's view, found in Extract 3, that the gentry benefitted due to the decline in the fortunes of the nobility. In the middle of the century, the power of the gentry peaked, and during the Interregnum they were essential for the running of government. The Lord Protector himself, Oliver Cromwell, came from a relatively minor gentry background, and was able to achieve his position through his skill in political manoeuvring and godly zeal. Despite their apparent rise in importance, the majority of lower gentry lived out their lives within a few miles of their manor house, without taking part in national or even regional affairs.

**EXTEND YOUR KNOWLEDGE**

**The gentry controversy**

One of the most significant historical debates of the mid-20th century, the so called 'gentry controversy' was started by R.H. Tawney in 1941. He argued that the crisis that caused the Civil War and the toppling of monarchy was due to the shifting fortunes of the nobility and gentry. Inflation caused the fortunes of the nobility to decline and the rising gentry, many of whom had experience in the fields of business and finance, filled the vacuum. Lawrence Stone also supported Tawney's theory, and added that the nobility's poor management of finances caused their decline.

In the 1950s, the theory was challenged by Hugh Trevor-Roper, who claimed that the gentry themselves were actually in decline, leading them to become disgruntled and eventually form the anti-court faction against Charles. Marxist historian Christopher Hill challenged Trevor-Roper, claiming that his analysis lacked reliable statistical evidence and relied too much on assumptions.

## Urbanisation and the growth of the professional and merchant classes

### Merchants

As London and some of the major towns grew, the merchant class, like the gentry, began to grow in power and influence. It was estimated at the time that 64,000 merchants were trading in 1688, a number that had grown by at least 30,000 since 1580. Their status in society was quite different from that of the gentry discussed above. It is true that they were looked down on by the landed elites; however, merchants often maintained connections with the gentry. This rise in numbers and status would not have been possible without increased urbanisation. Many of the towns that grew were involved in trade, and ports such as Bristol and Liverpool became centres of international trade. Some were the younger sons of landowning families and some married into them. It was also possible for merchants to accumulate as much wealth as members of the gentry and hold positions of power in towns equal to those occupied by the gentry in the countryside. In London, in particular, a small but extremely wealthy class of merchants developed in the context of increasing urbanisation. London also witnessed a consumer boom after 1650, as a result of improved trading conditions. This led to an increased demand for shops and traders began to flourish.

Merchants were never able to command the same amount of respect and prestige as the landed elites, and most were unable to pursue a scholarly education as they had little leisure time. Despite this, the gentry were not excluded from trade, as the younger sons in landowning families would often embark on business careers, with the help of their inheritance. Some merchants became hugely wealthy, which meant they could buy the land that they may have been deprived of previously and they could enter public office as aldermen, or even become a mayor in their town. Despite the large numbers of urban businessmen, there was always room for more. This was because many successful merchants would aim to retire and set up home on a country estate as early as possible, allowing others to fill the void. Merchants were often keen to leave towns due to the threat of disease and the instability associated with the world of commerce.

Although the merchant class grew in all major towns, there is no doubt that the growth of London contributed most to their growing importance. The merchant community in London expanded because the City was the centre of trade within Britain, as well as overseas, leading to the formation of a well-established and respected group by the outbreak of the Civil War. Further growth in the 1650s can be attributed to safer overseas trading conditions. The Navigation Act of 1651 restricted the use of foreign, particularly Dutch, ships in trade out of England, and the Navigation Act of 1660 listed a number of commodities that could only be shipped in English vessels. The owners of the larger international trading companies were as rich as the nobility, and some purchased earldoms to ensure their family's future as part of the aristocracy. A number of merchants, as well as those in the professional classes, however, refused to aspire to this traditional elite status. Historian Mark Kishlanksy has claimed that newly successful merchants did not value family lineage and land, but instead valued money. In the 16th century the gentry could buy the aristocracy, but in the 17th century, the professional classes, most notably merchants, could buy their way into the gentry. Many received knighthoods for commercial success and public service rather than their family background.

KEY TERMS

**Professional**
A person employed in a job that requires specific qualifications, often associated with a high level of learning.

**Inns of Court**
The four legal societies given the right to confer the title of barrister on law students.

### Professionals

Like the merchant class, the number of **professionals** rose considerably in the Stuart period as a direct result of the rising living standards experienced by the gentry and merchants. As quality of life grew, there was an increased demand for legal services, healthcare, new buildings and education, which led to a growth in the numbers of lawyers, doctors, architects, academics and bankers. Records containing precise numbers of these professionals do not survive, but the records of Gray's Inn, which became the largest of the four **Inns of Court**, show that its membership increased from 120 barristers in 1574 to more than 200 in 1619. The only notable profession before this period was the clergy, members of which would usually have received a university education, but now doctors and lawyers in particular were beginning to achieve a similar status. Like merchants, many of the professional class were from, or related to, gentry families. At another of the Inns of Court (the Inner Temple) where lawyers would undertake training, 90 percent of the 1,700 students admitted between 1600 and 1640 were sons of the nobility and gentry, with the rest being the sons of professionals or merchants. This reflects the lack of educational opportunities for the lower orders, as entry to the grammar schools was not possible for most yeoman farmers and certainly not for girls.

## The impact of religious and legal changes on the status of women

### The status of women

Women in the 17th century had very few rights and, under law, they were under the complete control of their husbands and fathers. Unmarried women were viewed with suspicion. It is no coincidence that the vast majority of women accused of witchcraft in the 17th century were unmarried women, and the accusations were normally founded in rivalries and disputes between neighbours. Progress for women was slow or even non-existent until the time of the Civil War. The role of a woman was generally to run a household and bring up children; a woman would very rarely be expected to give advice to her husband. Household record-keeping required some women to be able to read and write, which meant they were also able to teach their children if required, but education for women would normally go no further. The role of women would vary depending on their background: the wife of a member of the gentry would direct servants and staff, whereas the wife of an agricultural labourer would be required to carry out physical work herself.

The prevailing view of women as irrational, devious and a threat to the good functioning of society was based on the moral teachings of the Bible, with some ministers even questioning whether women possessed souls. A number of well-established punishments existed for women found guilty of gossiping or becoming a nuisance, including the brank, a metal device that fitted over the head, humiliating the victim and making it impossible to talk. Women who deviated from the behaviour expected of them could still be accused of being a witch, a crime punishable by hanging in England and being burnt at the stake in Scotland.

Although very little progress was made to enhance the status of women in the early years of the 17th century, after 1642 opportunities came about as a result of the Civil War. Like the First and Second World Wars in the 20th century, women took on the roles of men who had gone away to fight, although this was more common in gentry families where large estates needed to be managed. Brilliana Harley directed forces to defend her family's estate in Herefordshire while her husband was away fighting, Lucy Hutchinson managed the estate of her parliamentarian Colonel husband John, and Mary Banks, a royalist, commanded a detachment of troops in the defence of Corfe Castle. When the fighting ended, so did any apparent hope of an improvement in the conditions of women, although during the Commonwealth (see below) some radical women were at the forefront of political events.

### The impact of Puritanism on women

The spread of Puritanism in the late 16th and early 17th centuries affected the status of the poor, middling and gentry in several ways. A number of richer Puritans advocated more widespread education, and grassroots schooling became influenced by Puritan morals and values. These values advocated a religious structure where the family was at the heart of worship, rather than the Church, making it necessary for women to be able to read in order to instruct their children in religious education. Other than this, education for women, even in Puritan circles, was limited and there was still a widespread belief that women who were too highly educated were dangerous. Even the Quakers, who advocated women's education, founded just four schools willing to teach girls out of a total of fifteen established before 1671.

Despite the apparent lack of progress in family life and education, Puritan women found themselves at the forefront of political and social campaigns, particularly around the time of the Civil War. A number of examples of protests by women exist, including the crowd of up to 6,000 women who petitioned parliament for peace in August 1643. When John Lilburne, the Leveller leader, was imprisoned in 1649, during the early months of the Commonwealth, his wife Elizabeth, along with other high profile Leveller women such as Katherine Chidley (see 'Extend Your Knowledge'), organised a petition for his release. The petition, which was signed by 10,000 women, was presented to parliament and, in it, they argued that women were created in the image of God and should therefore have as much freedom as men. The reaction from parliament was typically sexist, informing the women that they should return home and continue with housework, and Lilburne was not released.

#### EXTEND YOUR KNOWLEDGE

**Katherine Chidley (c1596–c1660)**

Katherine Chidley was the wife of Daniel, a Shrewsbury tailor. In 1626, she committed her first controversial act when she refused to be 'churched' after the birth of her first child. This practice dictated that women were not to touch any sacred items in church after childbirth, as they were seen as unclean and in need of purification.

When she moved with her family to London in 1640, she began writing religious tracts and aligned herself with the radical Levellers. She argued for women to have the right to preach and even referred to herself as a minister. She also wrote the first English publication that advocated religious toleration under a woman's name.

The middle of the century appeared to offer the best chances for women to advance their social position, and some radical Puritan groups, such as the Diggers, advocated both male and female **suffrage**. The Levellers, however, never pushed for women to have the vote. Despite their lack of political power, women did preach in Puritan circles, although this was not necessarily unique to the age, as women in the Protestant countries of mainland Europe had been involved in preaching since the late 16th century. The status of women varied across the Puritan sects, with the Quakers offering women the most freedom.

#### KEY TERM

**Suffrage**

The right to vote in elections. Most modern Western democracies are based on the principle of universal adult suffrage, where all men and women can vote.

### The impact of legal changes

The Quakers believed that, as God's light was in every person, male and female, women had the right to speak up in church, preach and give their opinion. Over one percent of the population were Quakers in 1680, and they were able to flourish after the legal changes brought about by the Toleration Act of 1650, although they would later be restricted by the Quaker Act of 1662 and then given further toleration. As they were tolerated after 1650, they were able to hold separate meetings for women and also allowed women to speak in mixed meetings. Their founder, George Fox, argued in 1676 for the continuation of separate women's activities. After the Restoration in 1660, Charles II

**AS Level Exam-Style Question Section A**

Was the rise of the gentry the main reason for the structure of society changing between 1625 and 1688? (20 marks)

**Tip**

*Remember to explain the causes of the rise of the gentry, to show how that relates to other factors such as the decline in the nobility.*

lifted the legal restriction on women performing in stage plays, though this may have had more to do with Charles II's love of theatre than any interest in enhancing the status of women.

The legal changes that came about during the Republic affecting women were founded out of Puritan beliefs. The Marriage Act passed by the 'Barebones' Parliament in 1653 had the potential to be a truly revolutionary reform, as it allowed civil marriages to take place, overseen by JPs. It was largely ignored and evaded, primarily because it did not give men as many rights over their wives as Church marriages did. Both men and women could be sentenced to death under the Adultery Act of 1650, although a man's sexual misdemeanours were considered a lesser crime than a woman's, and it was most often used against women. For example, in Middlesex, 24 women and 12 men were tried for adultery in the 1650s, and in Devon, male suspects made up only ten percent of the 255 charged between 1650 and 1660.

ACTIVITIES
KNOWLEDGE CHECK

**Changing society**

1 Create a table with the following headings: nobility, gentry, merchants, professionals and women. Under the headings, explain the key changes that affected each group.

2 Explain whether you believe each group was better or worse off in 1688 compared to 1625, and explain why.

# WHAT CHANGES CAME ABOUT IN THE FIELDS OF SCIENCE, PHILOSOPHY AND POLITICAL IDEAS?

## Radical political ideas

KEY TERM

**Millenarianism**
The belief that the second coming of Christ is near. Millenarians believe that this will lead to the establishment of the Kingdom of God on earth, lasting for a thousand years.

The Civil War, and the execution of Charles in 1649, led to the collapse of censorship and opportunities arose for radical political ideas to emerge. Many of these ideas were promoted by the Puritan sects, who flourished for a limited time. The sense of living through momentous events had already intensified **millenarianism** within the ranks of the Puritans, but the collapse of earthly monarchy in England was enough to convince some that the coming of Christ and the rule of the saints was imminent. Fifth Monarchists believed that the fifth great empire (after the Greek, Roman, Persian and Assyrian) would come to earth imminently with the return of Jesus. The followers of two preachers, Lodovic Muggleton and John Reeve, became convinced that they had been chosen to begin preparing for Jesus' return and, as 'Muggletonians', claimed to be the forerunners of Christ himself.

### Levellers

The most important of the radical groups was the Levellers, who were active from 1645 and had their origins in the religious radicalism of the army and parliament. Their leaders, John Lilburne, William Walwyn and William Overton, issued pamphlets calling for a widening of the voting franchise, new elections and equality under the law. Their most influential work was *An Agreement of the People*, which was released in several versions between 1647 and 1649. The Levellers became particularly influential in the aftermath of the Civil War, when Leveller elements of the army began to call for change. The highest-ranking Leveller in the army was Colonel Thomas Rainsborough, who spoke on behalf of the radical soldiers against the army grandees, Cromwell and Ireton, at the Putney Debates in late 1647. His argument, as reproduced in Source 5, was that there was nothing written in the Bible to justify the fact that the poor were excluded from politics. Overall, the Leveller demands consisted of the following.

- The House of Commons should be the central body in the political system.
- The House of Lords should be abolished.
- The new system should be based on universal male suffrage.
- There should be a new constitution.
- People should be equal before the law and have religious freedom.

The Levellers were certainly political radicals, but were they socially revolutionary? They argued for reform to the legal system and wanted local courts to be staffed by locally elected judges and officials, as well as calling for an end to imprisonment for debt. They did not advocate bringing women into the voting franchise, and some Levellers even suggested servants and those receiving poor relief should not be able to vote. Their treatment of women, as we have seen, was mixed. Some Leveller women were influential and were able to organise protests, however these protests were easily dismissed by parliament, as the MPs claimed they could not take a petition presented by women seriously.

**SOURCE 5** Thomas Rainsborough's speech at the Putney Debates, 1647.

I thinke that the poorest hee that is in England hath a life to live as the greatest hee; and therefore truly, Sir, I thinke itt's cleare, that every man that is to live under a Government ought first by his owne consent to putt himself under that Government; and I doe thinke that the poorest man in England is nott att all bound in a stricte sence to that Government that he hath not had a voice to putt himself under... I doe thinke that the maine cause why Almighty God gave men reason, itt was, that they should make use of that reason, and that they should improve itt for that end and purpose that God gave itt them. And truly, I thinke that halfe a loafe is better then none if a man bee an hungry, yett I thinke there is nothing that God hath given a man that any else can take from him . Therfore I say, that either itt must bee the law of God or the law of man that must prohibite the meanest man in the Kingdome to have this benefittc as well as the greatest. I doe nott finde any thinge in the law of God, that a Lord shall choose 20 Burgesses, and a Gentleman butt two, or a poore man shall choose none.

### How successful were the Levellers?

There can be no doubt that the Levellers were the most successful revolutionary group of the age and, although their existence was short-lived (the leaders were imprisoned in 1649 and the Rump Parliament crushed the movement), the ideas that they promoted influenced later democratic movements. In terms of the history of the English Revolution, however, they are also responsible for encouraging conservatism in others. Even in the New Model Army, their influence was not widespread after 1647, and they actually served to encourage the conservatism that began to emerge from the grandees and Rump between 1649 and 1653. Cromwell and the other leaders of the Rump were not socially radical, and it would not be beneficial to them to support a group that would threaten their privileged status as members of the gentry.

Another limit to their success was due to disagreements between individual leaders. Different pamphleteers would include rival proposals in their publications, and they lacked a cohesive, consistent message. National support for the movement was also relatively minor, as much of what they offered was of no interest to the majority of the rural poor.

### Ranters

A small group of preachers, calling themselves Ranters, appeared in London in 1650, arguing that those predestined to be saved by God were incapable of sin and could therefore ignore man-made codes of social morality. They believed, therefore, that immoral sexual behaviour, drinking, swearing and crime were legitimate activities. That they indulged in the drunken orgies of which they were accused is doubtful, but the claims were certainly believed and, by 1651, their leaders were in prison.

Although the Ranters were effectively banned by the Blasphemy Act of 1650, there is doubt about whether they were a significant force. Sources discussing the Ranters were all written by their natural enemies, those conservatives who would benefit from a population too fearful to stray from the Protestant path. Regardless of their level of support, what matters more is that the fear of the Ranters was more important than any genuine threat they posed. The Rump was able to use this fear to pass Acts that actually reduced religious toleration.

### Diggers

Equally scandalous in the eyes of the political nation, a number of groups calling themselves the True Levellers claimed that the ownership of land was based on man-made laws invalidated by the king's death, and set up rural communes for the poor on common land. The first such group, nicknamed the Diggers, began to dig vegetables on common land in Weybridge, Surrey, in April 1649. The group gradually grew in size and became a small community, much to the dismay of the locals. The leaders of the group were interviewed by the leader of the New Model Army, Thomas Fairfax. They refused to remove their hats in his presence – a profound insult in 17th-century England. They eventually left, after nearly four months, when they lost a court case brought by local landowners. A few more Digger communities emerged in Northamptonshire and Buckinghamshire in the course of 1650, to meet the same fate.

The Diggers had developed surprisingly modern ideas about society, which they believed should consist of common ownership of the means of production, compulsory education for both boys and girls, and the abolition of the monarchy and House of Lords. The source of their ideas, Gerrard Winstanley (see 'Extend Your Knowledge'), continued to write in favour of these ideals until he found a spiritual home in the Quakers.

**EXTEND YOUR KNOWLEDGE**

**Gerrard Winstanley (1609-76)**
Winstanley was a cloth merchant, originally from Wigan, who moved to London in 1630. When his business failed, he moved to Surrey and became a cattle farmer, where he began to write religious pamphlets. He claimed he had received a message from God telling him that Britain should return to a 'golden age' before the Norman conquest, when Winstanley believed common ownership of land was the norm. Little is known about his later life, although he became a Quaker before his death in 1676.

The ideas of the Diggers were more revolutionary than those of the Levellers, and it is for this reason that they received less attention and support. Their message was relevant to rural communities, as they advocated setting up agricultural communities, but their communes repeatedly faced angry opposition from local farmers and landowners. In many ways, they were too revolutionary for the 17th century.

### Seekers and Quakers

Meanwhile, groups of loosely organised dissenting groups called Seekers emerged in the 1620s, defined by their belief that churches and the traditional clergy were unnecessary because God was to be sought and found within each individual. The Levellers and Diggers were primarily a threat to the social hierarchy and could be dealt with on that basis, but, among the purely religious ideas that flourished, the Seeker claim that God existed within each individual would prove both dangerous and enduring. Whatever the threat posed to political and social control by the independent sects, those like the Congregationalists, who believed every individual church should be autonomous, and the Particular Baptists, who had demanded toleration in earlier years, were essentially Calvinist, recognising the authority of the Bible and seeking privileges for the godly rather than freedom for all. The General Baptists had gone a step further in challenging predestination, and this had encouraged claims for natural rights and political equality, as advanced by the Levellers. The new Seeker sects, however, were beginning to deny any religious or moral authority outside the individual conscience or the voice of God within.

Between 1650 and 1652, this claim was taken up in the North of England by George Fox, founder of the largest and most enduring of all the new groups, the Quakers. The appeal of his ideas was in his belief that religion comes from the voice of God within. This, combined with the impact of his personality and his tireless missionary work, and the fact that Quaker groups needed no external support or organisation in order to function, made them ideal for the more remote rural districts. In these districts, the formal provision provided by the Church was often inadequate and, in 1654, Fox launched a 'mission to the South' to be carried out by 60 'First Publishers of Truth'. Quaker preachers appeared throughout the country to gather adherents, with considerable success. The wandering preachers could be arrested and imprisoned (or worse) under laws made to deter vagrants, but, despite harsh persecution, the movement flourished and it has been estimated that, by the early 1660s, there were some 35,000 Quakers in England. Long before that, however, the activities of the more eccentric groups had ensured a conservative reaction that would threaten to destroy them all.

SOURCE 6

'The world turn'd upside down', from a pamphlet produced shortly after the Civil War, shows the chaos and confusion that was thought to have taken hold.

# THE World turn'd upſide down:

OR,

A briefe deſcription of the ridiculous Faſhions of theſe diſtracted Times.

By T.J. a well-willer to King, Parliament and Kingdom.

*London*: Printed for *John Smith*. 1647.

**ACTIVITIES**

**KNOWLEDGE CHECK**

What does Source 6 suggest about the state of the country in 1647?

Change and continuity (4b&c)

The bird's-eye view

| The Development | Medium-term Consequences | Long-term Consequences |
|---|---|---|
| The rise of the Levellers | Their demands had to be taken into account when the army were negotiating after the Civil War. Their ideas were a threat and were crushed under the Rump. | Groups like the Levellers set a precedent for the questioning of divine right monarchy and traditional political institutions. Some of their ideas were adopted after the Glorious Revolution. Many of their ideas influenced the development of political and legal rights in the 19th and 20th centuries. |

Imagine you are looking at the whole of History using a zoomed-out interactive map like Google Maps. You have a general view of the sweep of developments and their consequences, but you cannot see much detail. If you zoom in to the time of the Levellers, you can see the events in detail but will know nothing of their consequences in the medium or long term. If you zoom in to look at the medium or long term consequences, you will know about them in detail but will know very little about the events that caused them. For example, the fact that a Dutch prince in William of Orange would become king could not be predicted if you could only zoom in on the rule of Charles I.

Look at the table above and answer the following.

1 What were the immediate consequences of the rise of the Levellers?

2 In what ways are the medium-term consequences different to the long-term consequences?

Work in groups of three.

3 Each student takes the role of the teacher for one of the above (the development, medium-term or long-term consequences) and gives a short presentation to the other two. They may comment and ask questions. After each presentation, the other two group members write a 100-word paragraph showing how the presentation links to their own.

Answer the following individually.

4 What happens to the detail when you zoom out to look at the whole sweep of history?

5 What are the advantages and disadvantages of zooming in to look at a specific time in detail?

6 How could you use the 'map' (Q3) in order to get a good understanding of history as a whole?

## The end of divine right monarchy and a confessional state

In 1625, England was a confessional state; in 1688, it was not. The nature of the confessional state in 1625 is outlined in Chapter 2. Although complete uniformity of practice was not enforced, or enforceable, the concept of a single national religion, upheld by government power, was so widely accepted as to be unchallengeable. The number who opposed the concept were so few as to be effectively non-existent, and even those who could not conform accepted the right of the state to punish them and paid their fines, accepted ejection or left the country. The vast majority of those who avoided conforming did so, not because they disagreed with the idea of uniform practice, but because they disliked the particular version that was being imposed.

In 1640, those questioning the confessional state were sufficiently numerous and organised to bring about the collapse of authority in religion, and in the conditions of civil war and upheaval, others began to explore and debate alternatives to the Church of England of Charles I. Many of the radical groups mentioned above pushed for an end to divine right monarchy, and some believed in an end to all traditional state institutions. Although they never received widespread support, a debate had started that would lead to a change in the role of the monarchy. In the course of these debates, the concept of uniformity itself began to be seriously challenged and, although the confessional state was restored in 1660, the intervening years of increased freedom and toleration had strengthened the opposition to the point where it could not be eradicated. As a result, a growing number of thinkers questioned the necessity, or even the desirability, of compulsion and argued that political loyalty did not, and need not, depend upon agreement over religion. In these discussions lay the seeds of a secular state, in which government concerned itself with non-religious matters and religion became part of the private domain. By 1688, another king, James II, had attempted to establish a political model based on a confessional state, and many of those who opposed him did so for political, or secular, reasons.

It can therefore be argued that, by 1688, the confessional state was no more and that any attempt to re-impose it would fail. Attempts at removing the confessional state had failed after the Civil War, but after the Glorious Revolution there could be no doubt that the monarchy had changed forever. The monarch was now subject to law; an idea that was espoused by philosophers such as John Locke (discussed on pages 85–86). Tories and Whigs in parliament continued to argue, however, about the monarch's place in both Church and government. The opinions of clergymen shifted by 1688, and Richard Claridge, the rector of Peopleton in Worcestershire, announced to his congregation that God should not have a role in civil government and that government should only be formed by the people. Although he was an Arminian priest, Daniel Whitby wrote at the time that no single individual could claim to rule by divine right because God never intended it.

**ACTIVITIES**
**KNOWLEDGE CHECK**

**Radical political ideas**

1 Create a table with two columns. In one column, create a list of reasons why the radical groups were successful, in the other create a list to show why they were not successful.

2 On balance, do you think the existence of these groups helped influence the future direction of government and the Church?

**Causation and consequence (5a)**

**Connections**

Inter-relations: causes never simply come one after another. They are often present simultaneously and have an effect on one another. Sometimes new causes develop and interact with existing ones.

**Causes of social change in the 17th century**

| Population growth | Radical ideas | Urbanisation | The decline of the aristocracy | Price inflation | Increased international trade |
|---|---|---|---|---|---|

Work in groups to produce a diagram of causes and the links between them.

1 On an A3 piece of paper, write all the causes of social change. Write these in boxes, the size of which will reflect how long they were a relevant factor. For example, if you argue that 'population growth' had been an important factor since the Black Death, then this will be quite a big box, whereas the 'radical ideas' would be a lot smaller. Spread these boxes over the page.

2 Then make links between all the causes. Draw lines between the boxes and annotate them to explain how the causes are connected and in which ways each affected and altered the other. For example, between 'population growth' and 'urbanisation' you could write something like: 'without population growth, urbanisation would not have happened and poverty would not have spread in the same way'.

Answer the following questions.

3 How do the causes differ in their nature? (Think in terms of events, developments, beliefs, states of affairs, etc.)

4 How do the causes differ in the roles they played in causing social change? (Think about whether each cause created the right conditions, was a trigger in causing immediate change or acted in some other way.)

5 Write a 200-word paragraph explaining how important it is to recognise the relationships between causes. Give examples from your diagram. Try to include connective phrases such as: 'this created conditions conducive to...' or 'this made the development of that situation more/less likely'.

## Philosophy: the significance of Hobbes and Locke

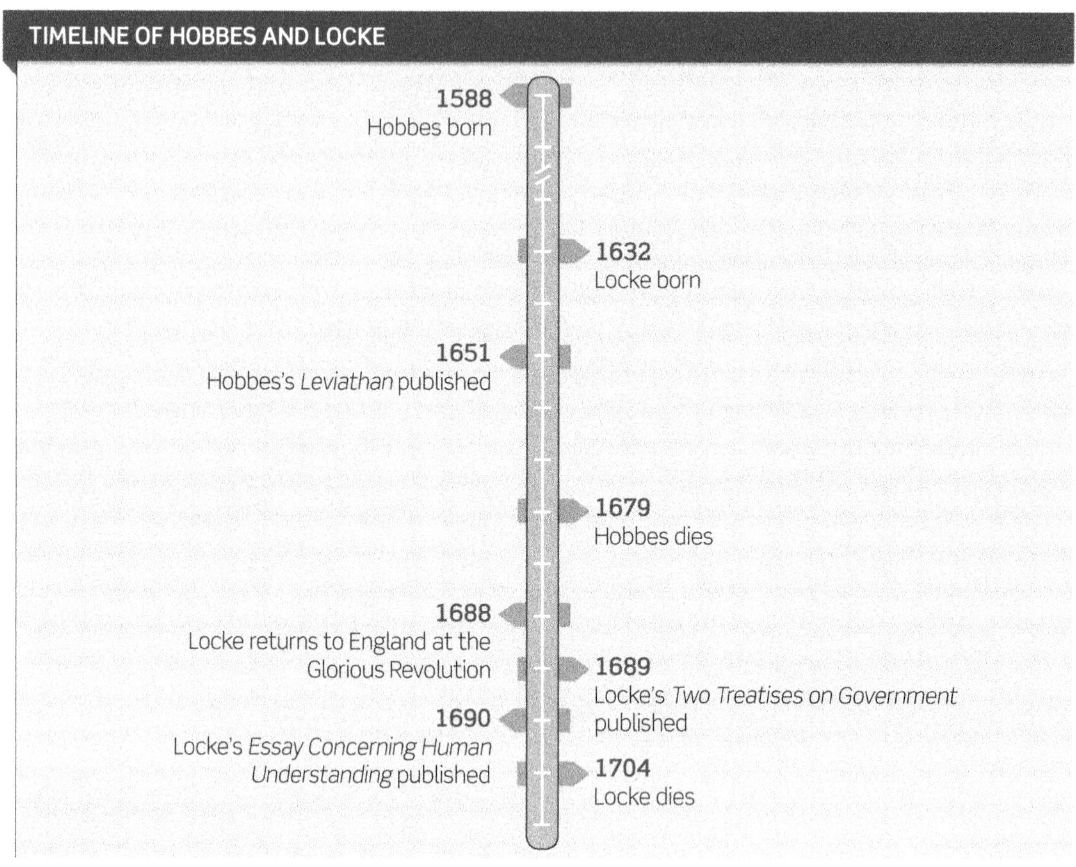


The political writings of the Levellers in the late 1640s were certainly significant for a time, and had a limited impact on the thoughts of leading politicians. As we have seen, however, the Levellers served to encourage more conservatism among the political nation, and they had little effect on the later history of **political philosophy**.

> **KEY TERMS**
>
> **Political philosophy**
> The ideas about the way in which government and power are organised.
>
> **Liberalism**
> A belief in the notions of individual rights, freedom, tolerance and social reform. By their nature liberals tend to oppose absolute monarchy.

### Thomas Hobbes

A small number of political philosophers did make an impact during the Interregnum, the most widely recognised of which was Thomas Hobbes. Hobbes, the son of a vicar, was born in 1588 and attended Oxford University. He worked as a tutor to the sons of the landed elite and travelled extensively around Europe, where he developed an interest in philosophy. When the Civil War broke out in 1642, he was in Paris, after fleeing there fearing that he would be targeted for his royalist sympathies. While in Paris he worked for a time as tutor to the young Charles II, and it was here that he began to formulate his most important ideas, published in 1651 in his book *Leviathan*.

*Leviathan* is a great contradiction; while it has been an inspiration to those aspiring for absolute monarchy, it also underpins a number of principles that are now associated with **liberalism**. The underlying principle behind *Leviathan* is that people are guided by a lust for power or by the fear of what will happen to them as a consequence of their struggle for power. Because people are naturally afraid of each other, they are compelled to agree to a social contract, whereby they confer all power to one man or one political body, the Leviathan, and give up some liberties in order to be protected. People will always concede to the Leviathan because they know that, if they do not, anarchy will ensue; so the Leviathan is able to make the law and decide who should be imprisoned. Hobbes believed that, before the age of governments, human existence was defined by perpetual war and that, if there was not a strong government, society would revert to this state. His overarching belief, therefore, was that people should have individual liberties, but that they should only have these if a strong ruler is placed in charge. This was Hobbes's justification for advocating the Stuart monarchy.

SOURCE 7 From T. Hobbes, *Leviathan* (1651).

The office of the sovereign, be it a monarch or an assembly, consisteth in the end for which he was trusted with the sovereign power, namely the procuration of the safety of the people, to which he is obliged by the law of nature, and to render an account thereof to God... it is the office of the sovereign to maintain those rights entire, and consequently against his duty, first, to transfer to another or to lay from himself any of them. For he that deserteth the means deserteth the ends; and he deserteth the means that, being the sovereign, acknowledgeth himself subject to the civil laws, and renounceth the power of supreme judicature; or of making war or peace by his own authority; or of judging of the necessities of the Commonwealth; or of levying money and soldiers when and as much as in his own conscience he shall judge necessary; or of making officers and ministers both of war and peace; or of appointing teachers, and examining what doctrines are conformable or contrary to the defence, peace, and good of the people. Secondly, it is against his duty to let the people be ignorant or misinformed of the grounds and reasons of those his essential rights, because thereby men are easy to be seduced and drawn to resist him when the Commonwealth shall require their use and exercise.

SOURCE 8 Frontispiece to the first edition of Hobbes's *Leviathan*, representing the power of monarchy to unite the nation, 1651.

THE LEVIATHAN OF HOBBES.—BY ABRAHAM BOSSE.

This curious figure forms the upper half of the frontispiece of the first edition of Thomas Hobbes's book, "Leviathan," published in 1651. It represents the spiritual and temporal power united in the person of the King, and ruling over the whole earth.

## John Locke

If Hobbes was the most prominent defender of absolutism in 17th-century England, then John Locke was the most vocal proponent of what would today be termed liberalism. He helped to create a new era of liberal philosophy, which set the scene for the next century. His ideas influenced not only the Whigs in Westminster, but also the great thinkers of the 18th century, such as Rousseau and Voltaire, and helped to inspire the French and American Revolutions. He is generally viewed as opposing absolute monarchy in favour of individual rights and liberties, in contrast to Hobbes's justification for a strong state.

Locke was born in 1632 and his Puritan father fought for parliament during the Civil War. Locke studied medicine at Oxford, although he also spent much time learning about ancient philosophy, which he quickly grew tired of. He entered the service of the Earl of Shaftesbury, a prominent founder of the Whig movement and England's Lord Chancellor, and, as a result of his patronage, was able to write and publish a number of important works of political philosophy. When Shaftesbury's political career appeared to be floundering in 1675, Locke fled to Holland and only returned permanently in 1688, accompanying the new queen Mary.

Although Locke had been writing for a number of years, it was only after the Glorious Revolution that the majority of his works were published. His ideas became influential extremely quickly and, by the time of his death in 1704, his theories were well known to practically the entire political nation. Locke is seen as the father of **empiricism**, as he sought to make his conclusions only through experience or through observing the experiences of others. His ethical and philosophical ideas were published in *Two Treatises on Government* (1689) and his *Essay Concerning Human Understanding* (1690). The *Treatises* have been seen as his most important pieces of work and were generally accepted to be a justification for the Glorious Revolution, although they were almost certainly written years earlier.

**KEY TERM**

**Empiricism**
A belief that knowledge can only come about as a result of experience. Empiricists tend to seek out evidence and carry out experiments in order to formulate theories. Empirical ideas were essential to the development of the scientific revolution.

Locke's significance for the world of politics is in the contribution he made towards the contemporary debate between the Whigs and Tories. He rejected the Tory view that absolutism was necessary for a fully functioning society, and believed that men were born free and that no one had divine right, as all are equal in the eyes of God. He strongly believed that the confessional state should not be resurrected, an idea that was also championed by his patron, Shaftesbury, who campaigned against the succession of James II. Like Hobbes, he believed that people entered into a social contract but, unlike Hobbes, he believed that this contract meant that no government could interfere with basic human rights. He believed the role of government should be to protect the basic rights of life, liberty and property, and that if government overstepped the mark then citizens could destroy it, as they did in the Glorious Revolution. To prevent the government from abusing its power, the legislative, executive and judicial branches should be kept separate, an idea that underpins Western democracies today.

**ACTIVITIES**
**KNOWLEDGE CHECK**

**Hobbes and Locke**

1. According to Source 7, what does Hobbes believe the role of the sovereign should be?
2. 'Hobbes and Locke are both products of their age.' How far do you agree with this statement?

## The scientific revolution

The 'scientific revolution' refers to the emergence of modern scientific beliefs and methods after approximately 1550, although new discoveries and debate peaked in the 17th century. New developments in biology, chemistry, physics and mathematics helped to fundamentally alter established views on nature. The revolution began when Nicolaus Copernicus (1473–1543) questioned the ancient astronomical belief that the earth was at the centre of the universe. Other important contributors to the scientific revolution included Johannes Kepler (1571–1630), whose laws of planetary motion would inspire Newton's theory of gravity, and Galileo (1564–1642), whose many achievements include the discovery of four of the moons of Jupiter and an early appreciation for the role of tides in relation to the rotation of the earth.

### Francis Bacon and the experimental method

Two figures tower over the world of scientific thought in Stuart Britain: Francis Bacon and Isaac Newton. While Newton came to prominence towards the end of the period, and was known for his breakthroughs in mathematics and astronomy, Bacon did not make a single scientific discovery. He is remembered instead for his contribution towards the scientific method, as he discusses in Source 9.

**SOURCE 9** From F. Bacon, *Novum Organum* (1620).

Those who have handled sciences have been either men of experiment or men of dogmas. The men of experiment are like the ant; they only collect and use: the reasoners resemble spiders, who make cobwebs out of their own substance. But the bee takes a middle course, it gathers its material from the flowers of the garden and of the field, but transforms and digests it by a power of its own. Not unlike the true business of philosophy; for it neither relies solely or chiefly on the powers of the mind, nor does it take the matter which it gathers from natural history and mechanical experiments and lay it up in the memory whole, as it finds it; but lays it up in the understanding altered and digested. Therefore from a closer and purer league between these two faculties, the experimental and the rational (such as has never yet been made) much may be hoped.

Bacon wanted to pursue the 'experimental and the rational', concepts that appear normal to the scientists of today, but were not part of the vocabulary of pre-17th-century thinkers. At the time, scientific thinking was heavily influenced by the beliefs of the Church and this restricted scientific advancements for centuries. There are a number of key elements to Bacon's method.

- He believed that scientific discovery is best aided by accumulating as much data about the subject as possible.
- His method involved rejecting any preconceived theories or conclusions about the subject matter.
- He thought that the methodical and meticulous observation of facts was the best way to understand natural phenomena.

Bacon was accomplished in a number of fields, including philosophy, law, politics (he was both Attorney General and

Lord Chancellor), but it was the scientific method he is most remembered for. After his death in 1626, other scientists attempted to emulate his 'Baconian Method' and the empirical nature of his work was developed by philosophers such as Locke. His ideas about science were not widely implemented before 1640 but, with the change in social attitudes that came about as a result of the Civil War, his work was revisited and emulated by others. Perhaps the best evidence of Bacon's influence is in the founding of the Royal Society (see below) nearly 40 years after his death. Regular mentions of his guiding genius were cited at early meetings.

While Bacon applied his empirical thinking to the study of nature, others adopted his ideas when they attempted to understand religion. Lord Falkland (1610–43) opened his house and estate at Great Tew in Oxfordshire to learned thinkers, where they used the rational method to question the problems that faced the Church of England. Falkland's group reached the conclusion that the Church would benefit from religious toleration, as a rational interpretation of the Bible shows that it contains many contradictions that will inevitably be interpreted in different ways by different people. Because of this, no single denomination has the right to dictate the way people worship. The rational method also spread to be used in the study of society, philosophy and eventually history.

### Isaac Newton

Isaac Newton (1643–1727) is widely recognised as one of the most influential scientists in history. His theories about calculus, classical mechanics, gravity and the laws of motion have remained relatively unaltered since his lifetime. His first letters to the Royal Society, written around 1672, concerned his research into the spectrum of light and he was soon invited to present his new invention, the reflective telescope. His work built on the advances in astronomy, mathematics and physics that had been made before him, including Kelper's laws of planetary motion. Galileo had previously suggested that the movement of heavenly bodies could be related to physics on earth, but was effectively banned from promoting this by the Catholic Church in Italy. By 1687, Newton was able to present this idea, along with his most famous discovery of universal gravitation, in his most respected work, *Philosophia Naturalis Principia Mathematica*.

Despite these achievements, Newton was well aware of the fact that he would not have been so successful if it was not for the earlier thinkers who began the scientific revolution. His work represents the final stage of a long process of theory and discovery that had evolved for over a hundred years. *Principia* represents an important break from the mindset of the Middle Ages and, although his works were not accessible to many at first, later interpreters such as Voltaire provided simpler versions of his work for the masses. In 1703, Newton was elected as the twelfth president of the Royal Society, a post he held until his death.

SOURCE

The title page of Bacon's *Instauratio Magna* (1620). It depicts a ship sailing past Gibraltar, out of the Mediterranean and onwards to the great expanse of the Atlantic Ocean. This represents the new investigative and exploratory method he hoped to encourage.

## The significance of the Royal Society

The need for a national scientific association was understood as early as 1645, when a group of natural philosophers formed what became known as the 'invisible college', a loosely organised collective who shared an interest in experimental investigation. It was not until the Restoration in 1660 that the political climate was suited to the formation of a more formal organisation, and Charles II's interest in science inevitably contributed to the swift royal charter given to the Society. The Society was formally proposed in November 1660, at a lecture by the architect Christopher Wren, and was established in July 1662. It met once a week and its membership included men from all areas of intellectual study. John Locke; Samuel Pepys, diarist and civil servant; John Dryden, poet; and the Earl of Sandwich joined an array of botanists, astronomers, mathematicians, chemists and biologists. The aims of the Society are outlined in Source 11.

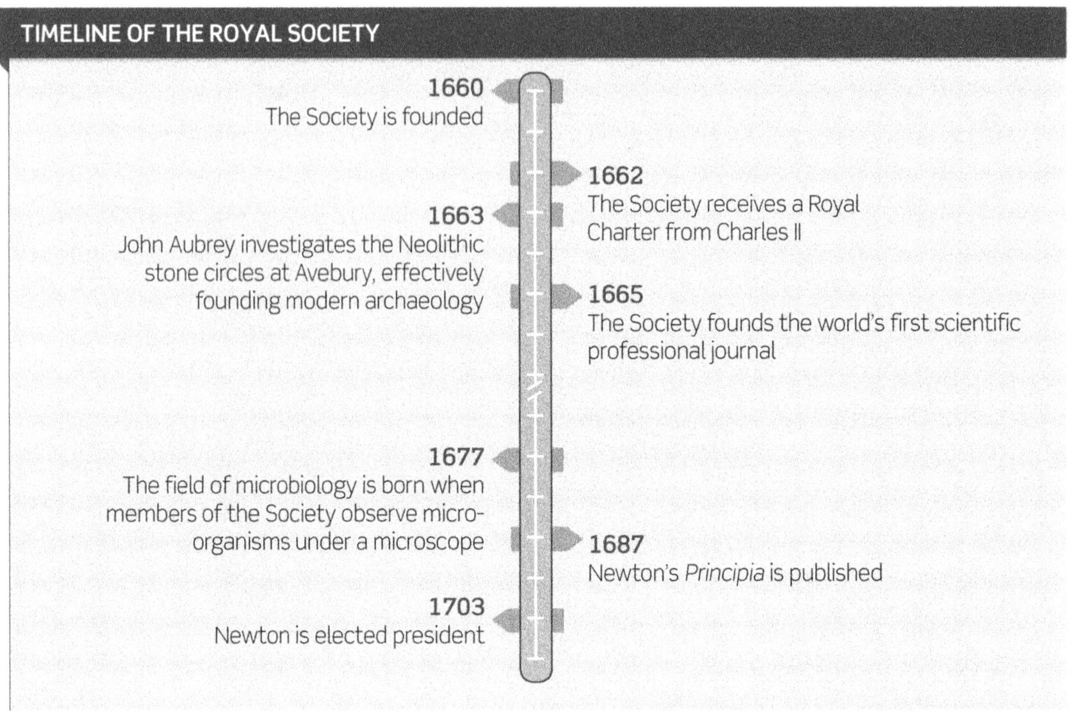


**SOURCE 11** From E. Chamberlayne, *Angliae Notitia, or The Present State of England* (1687).

> The design of the Royal Society is, in brief, to make faithful records of all the Works of Nature, or of Art, which can come within their reach, so that the present Age and Posterity may be able to put a mark on the Errors which have been strengthened by long Prescription; to restore the Truths that have been neglected, to push on those which are already known to more various uses; to make the way more passable to what remains unrevealed.

The Society was divided into a number of committees, each responsible for a different area of study. The first few years were marked by a genuine variety of research in areas other than science, including an investigation into the best way to improve the English language. Most early experiments followed Bacon's method in all areas of intellectual endeavour, and it was only after 1684 that the Society dedicated itself solely to scientific pursuits. Isaac Newton, who was working at Cambridge University at the time, was consulted about his theory of gravity and so began a long relationship with the Society, of which he was president for 24 years. In fact, the pull of Oxford and Cambridge was not as great as that of the Royal Society in the post-Restoration period, and the universities appeared to be falling behind as they were not always able to attract the best scholars. Religious nonconformists were excluded from both universities, and many would attend for the status that a degree gave them rather than for any serious desire to learn. Those who were genuinely engaged in pushing the boundaries of science did so through the Society.

The Society has been seen by some historians to be less than significant, as it was simply a channel for scientists to air their discoveries, and did not necessarily give them any assistance. However, its Baconian aim to gather all knowledge about nature made it extremely well respected. The Society also agreed that the knowledge it would gather would only be used for the public good, rather than to fulfil the interests of a small clique of intellectuals. As well as English scientists, the Society encouraged foreign scholars to share their discoveries and, from 1665, these discoveries were presented in the first scientific journal, *Philosophical Transactions*. This sharing of information was perhaps its greatest strength. For example, in 1661, Marcello Malpighi wrote to the Society after he observed capillary action in the lungs of frogs. This turned out to be the missing link in William Harvey's theory of blood circulation. The Society also created a model that would be followed by groups on the continent. In 1666, the French Royal Academy of Sciences was established and the Prussian Academy of Sciences was founded in Berlin in 1700.

The Royal Society could not survive without funding, and this came in the form of endowments from wealthy supporters, as well as gifts from wealthy men from all over Europe who saw themselves as amateur scientists. The aim to carry out work that was beneficial to the public good was achieved through regular public demonstrations and a number of members carried out public anatomy lessons, with dissections taking place on the bodies of criminals. Crucially, by 1688, science was part of the public consciousness, was no longer viewed with suspicion and had been greatly supported by Charles II. The Society gave a boost to the increasing belief in Europe that humans could progress without divine assistance and contributed to the overall aims of the Enlightenment, or Age of Reason, that had begun in the 1650s.

## Conclusion: society transformed?

In many respects, the structure of society in 1688 was not dissimilar to that of 1625 and attitudes towards the poor, religion and women would not have been that different for most people. The poor were still poor, although they had received limited help from expanded poor relief. The increase in population put huge pressures on society and London in particular felt the benefits of this change, as well as the inevitable downsides. Changes to the overall structure of society did not affect the majority of landless peasants, who were still subject to the will of local landowners, whether the landowners had become members of the higher gentry or not. The place of women had not shifted drastically after the extraordinary events that took place in the middle of the century, although their near-equal status had been accepted in groups that would continue to flourish, such as the Quakers. Religious conformity was established in law after the Restoration, which restricted those groups that also favoured a fairer society as well as equality under God. It is clear, though, that the seeds of change had been sown in the 17th century and the ideas of Locke in particular would serve to influence the development of liberal government in the 18th and 19th centuries. Scientific methods of studying the natural world spilled over into the study of society and politics, and the desire to question accepted systems and traditions is certainly one major achievement of the century.

ACTIVITIES
KNOWLEDGE CHECK

**The scientific revolution**

1 Why is the Baconian method a radical change from what came before?

2 How did the Royal Society help to advance the scientific revolution?

**A Level Exam-Style Question Section B**

How far do you agree that population growth was the most important factor in causing social change between 1625 and 1688? (20 marks)

**Tip**

*Ensure you compare the factor of population growth to at least three other possible reasons for social change.*

ACTIVITY
SUMMARY

**Society in the 17th century**

1 Create a graph showing the major changes in society and intellectual thought between 1625 and 1688. The *x*-axis should denote time, and the *y*-axis should represent periods of drastic change. From this you should be able to establish when the most significant changes took place.

2 Choose three changes that you feel are the most noteworthy, and explain why they are important.

WIDER READING

Coward, B. *The Stuart Age*, Routledge (2011) Provides an assessment of how society changed in the period

Dunn, J. *Locke: A Very Short Introduction*, Oxford (2003) Sums up the ideas of Hobbes and Locke

Hill, C. *The World Turned Upside Down: Radical Ideas During the English Revolution*, Penguin (1991) A classic of Marxist historiography detailing the impact of the radical groups, particularly the Levellers

Tuck, R. *Hobbes: A Very Short Introduction*, Oxford (2002) Sums up the ideas of Hobbes and Locke

Wrightson, K. *English Society 1580-1660*, Hutchinson (1982) A look at Stuart society in general, including the poor, towns and the class system

# 1.4 Economy, trade and empire, 1625–88

**KEY QUESTIONS**

- How far did changes in agricultural techniques and investment impact on the economy?
- What impact did changing trade patterns, banking and insurance have on economic development?
- How significant was imperial expansion between 1625 and 1688 to the economy?

## INTRODUCTION

In 1688, Britain's economy was in a remarkably strong state considering the difficulties the country had faced earlier in the century. Over 40 years of war, revolution and religious conflict had taken their toll on the nation, yet the British state, as well as those engaged in trade, were more affluent than they had ever been. 1688 was the year when, for example, Edward Lloyd began inviting merchants and ship owners to his coffee house in London, where he would share crucial shipping news and those involved in trade would discuss insurance deals. This informal arrangement evolved to become what is today the oldest insurance market in the world, Lloyd's of London.

But Britain's prosperity was not simply based on banking and finance. The rural economy played its part, as the population growth outlined in Chapter 3 created a need to change agricultural techniques in order to avoid famine. New methods and new crops from abroad, as well as increased investment in agriculture, meant that the all-too-regular fear of a bad harvest was less of a problem. New techniques were also evident in the cloth industry, with new methods and fabrics, as well as skilled workers, arriving from the Low Countries. The economy also improved as a result of improved trading conditions, especially after 1650 with the end of Civil War hostilities. Britain fought the First Anglo-Dutch War from 1652, which ended with the once dominant Dutch being forced to accept Britain's control of the sea, although in 1674 war began again and the Dutch defeated the navy of Charles II. A major advancement surrounding these wars was the passing of the Navigation Acts, designed to boost British trade at the expense of the Dutch.

## HOW FAR DID CHANGES IN AGRICULTURAL TECHNIQUES AND INVESTMENT IMPACT ON THE ECONOMY?

### Changes to agricultural techniques

A number of new crops were introduced into Britain in the 17th century, including artichokes, asparagus and clover. This led to a revolution in eating habits and improvements in soil fertility. Diets became more varied, but among the poor a heavily bread-based diet continued. Population growth,

**1600** – The East India Company founded

**1636** – The first money-scrivening (banking) firm founded

**1649** – Walter Blith's *A New Survey of Husbandry* advocates the use of new agricultural techniques

**1651** – The first Navigation Act is passed by parliament to counter the economic threat posed by Dutch shipping

**1655** – The island of Jamaica is captured

1600 | 1630 | 1635 | 1640 | 1645 | 1650 | 1655

together with the need to guarantee good harvests, required a more effective agricultural output. The development of the **market garden**, many of which served to feed Britain's largest city, London, required new and more efficient techniques. By the 1640s, agricultural production in Britain had exceeded that of all other European countries except Holland and, in 1700, the average number of days worked per agricultural family was 405, compared with 266 in 1450. This figure reflects both the rise in population growth that led to a need to boost production and the drive for efficiency that resulted from it. How, then, did this revolution in all areas of agriculture come about?

**KEY TERMS**

**Market garden**
A specialist producer of fruits and vegetables for sale. Today the term refers to small-scale enterprises, but 17th-century market gardens could be extremely large and serve many thousands of people.

**Common land**
Land owned by one person but over which other people have certain rights - such as the right to graze animals or collect firewood.

## Enclosure

One major change to the structure of rural life was the enclosure of land. Enclosure involved consolidating scattered holdings into blocks of land, usually by fencing them off. The enclosed land would then be reserved for the sole use of a single landowner or tenant. This ensured that crop production was not unnecessarily duplicated as fewer rivals would exist in each region, and it could be combined with the upkeep of separate pastures for animals. Enclosure was nothing new, as it had been common in the medieval period to enclose **common land** in order to stimulate wool production, but it intensified in the 17th century. By 1650, peasants had come to accept that the only way they could break out of the cycle of subsistence farming was to accept enclosure. Most enclosure agreements were informal affairs, with a loose agreement made between landowners, tenants and families, and after 1660 enclosure was proceeding briskly. There were, naturally, protests by small landowners and those peasants who would suffer if common land was no longer accessible, but the fact that enclosure led to improved agricultural efficiency was difficult to deny. The social conditions created by enclosure were, however, less than harmonious and successful. An example of its impact can be seen at Sherrington in Buckinghamshire, where modest freeholders, who had gradually been gaining land since the 16th century, were driven out because of indebtedness after 1660 as a result of enclosure. They were unable to compete with the larger enclosed farms that had been created nearby. Added to this, a number of counties where enclosure was not widespread, such as Oxfordshire, were also very successful centres of agricultural innovation.

## Farming techniques

The development of more modern farming techniques began under the Tudors and spread widely under the Stuarts. Increased levels of literacy after 1600 meant that more **yeomen** and **husbandmen** were able to make use of books, such as those written by Walter Blith, containing information about new agricultural techniques. There was a new awareness that, in order to run an efficient farm, as much land as possible should be utilised, reducing the number of fields left fallow, or left to regain nutrients for a year, and that crops should be selected based on their suitability for different soil types. Enclosure was instrumental in allowing these new techniques to be used and improvements in crop rotation took place. Traditionally, one field in three would be left for pasture (fallow) in any given year, in order for nutrients to be restored to the soil. This led to a lower than desired yield and, as only three fields were being rotated at any one time, there was often not enough time given for the soil to return to its most productive level. After enclosure, more fields were generally available for rotation, leading to better yields. New nitrogen-rich crops such as clover were also used to provide nutrients. In 1420, just over 7 million acres were given to arable farming, with 3 million left fallow. This had increased to nine million acres in 1700, with just 1.8 million left fallow.

**KEY TERMS**

**Yeomen**
Farmers who owned their own land, often consisting of a large farm, although they could hold as much property as a member of the gentry.

**Husbandmen**
Tenant farmers or small landowners.

**1660** - The second Navigation Act is passed under Charles II, reaffirming the new regime's commitment to mercantilism

**1663** - The Turnpike Act allows for the construction of toll roads

**1674** - Charles II is forced to make peace with the Dutch after losing the Third Anglo Dutch War

**1681** - In France, forced conversions to Catholicism begin, compelling many Protestants to migrate to England

**1688** - Lloyd's Coffee House becomes the focal point of the London insurance industry

1660 | 1665 | 1670 | 1675 | 1680 | 1685 | 1690

EXTEND YOUR KNOWLEDGE

**Walter Blith (1605-54)**
Walter Blith was the son of a Warwickshire yeoman and played an active part in the Civil War on the side of parliament. He is best known for his writings on agricultural practice, which were published during the Interregnum (1649-60). He was concerned with improving agricultural output and was naturally wary of enclosure, although he accepted that it was necessary in order to intensify production.

Blith advocated the use of water meadows, improved drainage and the use of manure as fertiliser, and believed that subsistence farming was no longer viable. He believed that the long hours worked by small farmers for little reward would be better spent as tenants on specialised farms.

More efficient crop rotation meant that new crops could be introduced and more experimentation could take place. Potatoes were planted in some areas, although their use was not widespread, as a new type of frost-resistant turnip that had been imported from the Low Countries was more economical. Indeed, much of the work needed to improve irrigation and cultivate new crops was carried out by Dutch immigrants, many of whom settled in the South East. One of these immigrants, Cornelius Vermuyden, was commissioned to drain the Fens of East Anglia after he had been knighted by Charles I for similar work he had done in Lincolnshire. Crops that aided industry also benefitted from crop rotation, such as flax for the manufacture of linen, hemp for rope-making and hops for brewing beer. The German-born writer, Samuel Hartlib, was responsible for promoting other Dutch innovations in Britain, such as the use of nitrogen-rich crops, like clover and cabbage, which would help to fertilise the soil for the following year.

### Water meadows

Another improvement in agricultural practice was made through the use of water meadows. Water meadows, which had been in existence for at least 100 years before 1625, worked by diverting water from a nearby river or stream to a field. This diversion would be regulated by a network of gates and dams. The aim of a water meadow was not to flood the ground, but to provide soil that was always damp, thus reducing the chances of frost in early spring and encouraging grass to grow earlier. Sheep or cattle would feed on this grass in the spring and, by early summer, they would be moved on to ordinary pasture, leaving the grass to grow and hay to be harvested. This ensured the animals were well fed throughout the next winter. Figures on the number of water meadows are hard to come by, although contemporaries noted that their use expanded dramatically in the 17th century.

Water meadows enabled farmers to maintain more working and non-working animals. The number of working animals increased, and it is estimated that around 630,000 horses were used on farms in 1700, compared with 300,000 a hundred years before. Horses were quicker and often lived longer than oxen, which were gradually replaced, although there were still around 130,000 working oxen in 1700. The number of non-working animals also increased and enclosure meant that individual breeds of sheep or cattle could be kept together in single enclosures. The breeds of sheep that produced the most wool could now be selected and intensively bred for the cloth industry.

## The development of specialised farming and the growth of employment

### Specialised farming

With new techniques came a new appreciation for the fact that different regions could specialise in types of farming more suited to local conditions. Before the 17th century, there were no national markets for agricultural products and farmers generally produced what was needed for their local community. It had, however, long been known that the warmer, drier South East was more suited to **arable**, rather than **pastoral farming**. The geography of the North and West was more suited to the rearing of livestock, as much of the terrain was more rugged and hilly, with higher levels of rainfall.

As transport infrastructure improved, opportunities to develop national markets presented themselves and farmers could concentrate on farming products that suited local conditions, as seen in Figure 4.1.

KEY TERM

**Arable and pastoral farming**
Arable farmers cultivate crops, usually with the aid of the plough, whereas pastoral farmers aim to produce livestock.

| Region | Local conditions | Specialised produce |
|---|---|---|
| South East | Deep soil, dry, warm | Wheat, oats, hops, hemp |
| East Anglia | Dry, flat, chalk soil | Wheat, barley, rye, flax |
| Yorkshire | Mixture of fertile, deep soil and hills | Mixed sheep farming and some arable |
| Midlands | Damp, heavy soil, some fertile plains | Cattle, sheep, some crops |
| Cheshire | Damp soil | Cattle (cheese) |
| Scotland | Hills, higher rainfall | Cattle, sheep |
| Wiltshire and Somerset | Damp, heavy soil, warm | Dairy products (milk, cheese) |

**Figure 4.1**: Table showing the types of produce associated with each region.

Specialised farming helped to improve economic conditions for many farmers, and the group that benefitted more than any other were the yeomanry. They owned a large amount of land and as such they were generally sheltered from the possibility of poor harvests. They were therefore able to experiment with new techniques and crops, although they could not always afford large-scale changes. Husbandmen grew in number, but had mixed fortunes. As they farmed land that usually covered less than 40 acres, they were actually at an advantage if they were shrewd enough to farm produce that was in demand and suited to local conditions, as they could dedicate their entire farm to one product. However, they were less able to exploit opportunities, as – regardless of where they focused their energies – they would often produce too little to make a substantial profit. Contemporary commentators noted that husbandmen were slow to take up specialisation and new techniques, as they had to be absolutely sure they would benefit from changing the way they organised their farms.

## Growth of employment

Small tenants suffered as a result of enclosure and smallholding became an unsustainable employment for many. At their expense, the number of wage-dependent agricultural labourers grew, although inflation reduced the real value of their wages for much of the 17th century. Employment on the farms of larger landowners was relatively secure, but many also had to work in the small-scale cloth industry in order to feed their families, with 240,000 people involved in skilled crafts by the end of the period. After the Settlement Act was passed in 1662, it was easier for landowners to hire labourers from other parishes and let them go when the harvest ended, as these workers were officially 'settled' in other areas and the employers did not have to worry about contributing to the Poor Rates. With the growth of towns, particularly ports, more stable employment grew, but job security was poor for those who had not served a seven year apprenticeship. Historian Christopher Hill believed that the growth of stable employment had a mixed impact on agricultural labourers, as shown in Extract 1.

**EXTRACT**

From C. Hill, *The Penguin Economic History of Britain: Reformation to Industrial Revolution 1530–1780*, (1991).

Enclosure of common land not only increased corn production: it also deprived the poor of a source of fuel and pasture, and so by increasing their dependence on wages forced them to work harder and more regularly than they otherwise would have done... Enclosure for pasture would *increase* employment in the clothing industry, at the same time as it reduced the number of those who lived off the commons without working, and so released labour for industry. Enclosure had always been profitable, but in the sixteenth century most moralists had disapproved of it. It now became a pleasurable religious and patriotic duty in the eyes of all but disreputable radicals.

It was estimated in 1688 that there were 364,000 families of labourers, which means over 1 million people must have been employed in this way. Figures showing the situation earlier in the century do not exist, but the proportion of labourers to small farmers increased throughout the century. Changes to a pattern of life in the countryside that had existed for hundreds of years naturally resulted in opposition, as shown in Source 1. By the time Source 2 was produced in 1727, the process of enclosure followed by the inevitable employment of the local poor on large farms was well established.

SOURCE

From a complaint contained in a petition to parliament by the commoners of Wootton Bassett, 1650s.

That soon after the manor came into the possession of Sir Francis Englefield, he did enclose the park, leaving out to the free tenants of the borough that part of it which was called Wootton-Lawnd, and contained only 100 acres... and he thereby knowing that the town had nothing to show for the right of the common, but by prescription, did begin suits in law with the said free tenants for their common, and did vex them with so many suits in law for the space of seven or eight years at the least, and never suffered anyone to come to trial in all that space; but did divers times attempt to gain possession thereof by putting in of divers sorts of cattle... And as for our common we do verily believe that no corporation in England is so much wronged as we are, for we are put out of all common that ever we had, and hath not so much as one foot of the common left unto us, nor shall have any; we are thereby grown so in poverty, unless it please God to move the hearts of this Honourable House to commiserate our cause, and to enact something for us that we may enjoy our right again.

SOURCE

Advice to the stewards of estates, from Edward Laurence's *The Duty of A Steward To His Lord*, (1727).

A Steward should not forget to make the best enquiry into the disposition of any of the freeholders within or near any of his Lord's manors to sell their lands, that he may use his best endeavours to purchase them at as reasonable a price, as may be for his Lord's advantage and convenience - especially in such manors, where improvements are to be made by inclosing commons and common-field; which (as every one who is acquainted with the late improvements in agriculture, must know) is not a little advantageous to the nation in general, as well as highly profitable to the undertaker. If the freeholders cannot all be persuaded to sell, yet at least an agreement for inclosing should be pushed forward by the steward... the poor will be employed for many years, in planting and preserving the hedges, and afterwards will be set to work both in the tillage and pasture, wherein they may get an honest livelihood.

THINKING HISTORICALLY **Evidence (4a&b)**

**Balance of evidence**

Sources 1 and 2 could be used by a historian to build up a picture of the state of enclosure in the 17th century.

Answer the following.

**1** Explain why Sources 1 and 2 offer two views on the impact of enclosure. How might this affect their value as pieces of evidence in appraising attitudes towards enclosure? Explain your answer.

Discuss the following in groups.

**2** Suppose the historian had ten more accounts that agreed broadly with Source 1 and only four that agreed with Source 2. What would that tell them about enclosure?

**3** How far should the balance of the evidence play a role in constructing written history? What else must the historian consider about the evidence being used before drawing conclusions?

## Capital investment in agriculture

In order for farmers to take risks and experiment with new techniques, investment was needed to ensure that productivity increased. Most of the yeomen and husbandmen were unable to afford much investment, so it was left to the higher gentry and the aristocracy to invest in large-scale modernisation. They were able to buy land from neighbouring farms, enclose it and invest in new crops. The large farms that resulted from this process flourished after 1650, as population growth slowed down and deflation meant that large landowners could improve their estates relatively cheaply, as labour and materials became more affordable. Farmers were also free of the need to supply only their local market, where they would receive lower prices for their goods. Instead, they could concentrate on supplying markets where demand for their goods was high. The impact of this investment in larger farms can be seen, for example, in the south Midlands, where, in 1700,

53.6 percent of agricultural land was part of large estates of over 100 acres, compared with 32.2 percent a hundred years earlier.

Some farms became huge as a result of this investment and, in East Anglia, some were over 500 acres in size. Numerically, small family farms still outnumbered these large 'capital farms', although small farms were only predominant in the pastoral North and the moorland of the South West. The counties that specialised in wheat or mixed wheat and livestock production – lowland plains in the Midlands, as well as East Anglia and the South East – became dominated by landowners able to invest heavily. With the expansion of size, owners required more assistance in managing production, so leased out sections to tenants, and it was often more profitable to work as a large tenant farmer than remain a small landowner.

As large landowners delegated work to their tenants, capital investment once again improved production. This was because the rents that were charged by the owners of large farms were high, and tenants were expected to maintain buildings at their own expense, as well as ensure hedges and fields were kept in good condition. In order to meet demands for rent, tenants had no choice but to specialise and produce what was most suited to local conditions, which meant investment was required. Landlords would invest in their tenants by offering them loans to help them modernise, in the expectation that they would profit from increased production. This investment could also consist of road improvements and the widening of water courses in order to sell goods at regional markets.

### EXTEND YOUR KNOWLEDGE

**The transition from feudalism to capitalism**
A number of historians, particularly those who would be described as Marxist (such as Christopher Hill and Lawrence Stone), believe that the 17th century represents a transitional period in British economic history, as part of a wider, Europe-wide 'crisis of the 17th century'.

Marxists see society as inherently unequal, and believe that those who possessed land and property in the medieval period were able to act as feudal overlords, with peasants or serfs being dependent on them for their livelihood. In a capitalist system, economic power is based upon the acquisition of wealth (capital) and the ability to exploit wage labourers.

Marxist historians believe that the continuing enclosure of land, transition to large estate farming and capital investment in wealth-creating projects point to the development of an early capitalist system in the 17th century. The group that stood to benefit from this system were those middle and upper gentry immediately below the aristocracy.

### ACTIVITIES
KNOWLEDGE CHECK

**Agricultural techniques**

1 How did enclosure benefit agriculture? Who lost out as a result?

2 Which new agricultural practice do you think is the most innovative and why?

## The development of national markets

The gradual growth of population in towns resulted in an increased demand for food, and the traditional markets that had been established by charter and regulated by the government were no longer fit for purpose. Nowhere was the demand for food more evident than in London, where shipments of grain brought to the City via the Thames increased from 500,000 quarters (6,350,000 kg) in 1605 to 1,150,000 (14,605,000 kg) in 1661. The demands of London and other towns necessitated better organisation of the markets. This required improved roads and infrastructure, as well as specialist merchants who would source stock to be taken to market. Market gardens began to develop in the immediate vicinity of London, in places such as Fulham and Whitechapel, in order to provide fresh food for the London market. The London market thrived partly because of the abundance of agricultural land to the west, as far as Oxfordshire, that was easily linked to the City via the Thames.

In order for markets to develop, transport infrastructure needed to improve. The road system did not develop considerably until the second half of the century, primarily as a result of increased demand for goods rather than in order to create new markets. Before this, roads were the responsibility of local parishes and many were in a poor state of repair. The exceptions to this were the routes that followed the old Roman roads, which were passable by cart throughout the year. The first Turnpike Act was passed in 1663, which allowed for the creation of brand new toll roads opened by merchants and businessmen. The toll paid by travellers on these roads helped to pay for their upkeep, and they were invaluable in linking major market towns. The development of the stage coach was also important for communication, and the first coaches from London to Bristol and Bath appeared in 1657. The first road atlas ever published was produced by John Ogilby in 1675. The 300-page book, which weighed over 7 kilogrammes, covered all of England and Wales, and mapped more than 7,500 miles of road. It was well regarded for its accuracy and became essential reading for merchants by the end of the century.

Water transport was crucial if markets were to develop and, although travel along the east and west coasts of Britain was relatively straightforward, at the start of the 17th century many rivers were not navigable for their entire length. Coal was transported from Newcastle to London via the east coast and Charles I ensured that the Royal Navy was able to protect ships following this route. The dredging and widening of rivers began in Tudor times and, by the end of the 17th century, the Severn, Ouse and Thames were used to transport manufactured goods as well as agricultural produce.

Although national markets did exist, it cannot be said that they dominated the economy until the late 18th and early 19th centuries. A large proportion of farmers still supplied small local markets, and a national market did not develop as clearly in Scotland and Ireland, as transport was inadequate and the Westminster government was reluctant to invest heavily in improving agriculture there. Ireland was viewed as a colonial possession with few towns large enough to create a market system and it was difficult to provide effective communications in the Scottish Highlands. The more fertile soil of lowland Scotland was being exploited more effectively and new agricultural techniques here enabled farmers to trade in markets at Edinburgh, Newcastle and Carlisle. The dominance of the London market was not entirely beneficial to the economy as a whole, as the huge demand for food in the capital drained the resources of other communities in the South East, reducing the standard of living in those areas. The prices of basic agricultural commodities in 1650 were six times higher than they were in 1500. This pressure is also evident in the supply of barley for brewing, as London brewers regularly outbid those from other towns for the purchase of barley from the Home Counties, effectively destroying the brewing industry in surrounding small towns.

SOURCE 3

The roads from London to Aberystwyth, via Oxford, from John Ogilby's *Britannia* (1675). Ogilby travelled extensively after the Civil War and was appointed official Cartographer to the Crown in 1674.

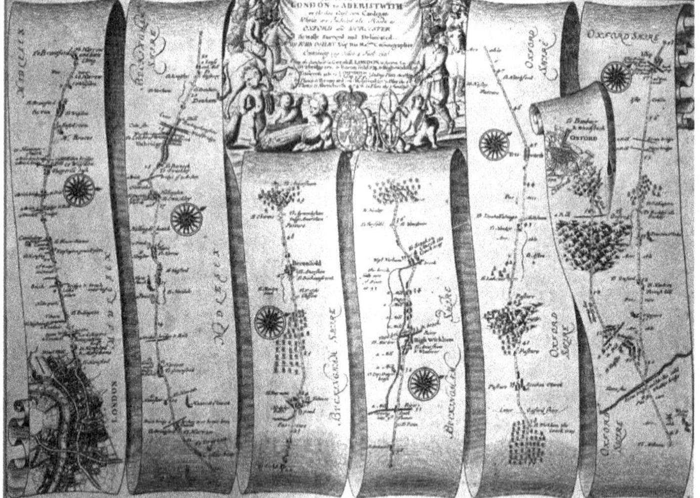

The development of national markets would not have been possible without improved trading conditions and infrastructure. Improvements in agricultural techniques meant that more food was produced, which in turn meant that London and other large towns were able to expand. Improved transport to and from London, although relatively late in the century, as well as the growth of banking and overseas trade discussed later in the chapter, enabled the standard of living of most people to improve.

ACTIVITIES
KNOWLEDGE CHECK

**Agriculture and markets**

1 Create a table with two columns. One column should include groups in 17th-century society that benefitted from the following changes, and one should include groups that would suffer: changes in agricultural techniques, the growth of specialised farming, capital investment in agriculture, the development of national markets.

2 Once you have created both lists, write a paragraph to explain whether or not you think the rural economy was transformed between 1625 and 1688.

**AS Level Exam-Style Question Section B**

How significant were improved agricultural techniques for the success of the British economy, 1650–88? (20 marks)

**Tip**

*Note that this question only refers to the later part of the period. Evidence from the whole of 1625–88 can be included but ensure it is tailored to the question.*

# WHAT IMPACT DID CHANGING TRADE PATTERNS, BANKING AND INSURANCE HAVE ON ECONOMIC DEVELOPMENT?

## The changing cloth trade

The wool trade was central to economic prosperity in the Middle Ages, and the production of cloth had always been small-scale and often home-based. Cloth ranged from the low-quality product worked by small farmers for their own use to high quality textiles for the national and international markets. The textile industry expanded substantially, although this followed a trend that had begun in the 14th century and was now sustained by population growth in the Tudor and Stuart periods. With increased population, more labour became available and the **putting-out system** flourished in the first half of the 17th century. The boom in international markets benefitted the cloth industry and the value of exports rose from £600,000 in the 1560s to London alone exporting £1.5 million of textiles in the 1660s. The historian D.C. Coleman has estimated that the monetary value of textile exports multiplied 15-fold between 1485 and 1714, which means that the cloth industry exceeded the growth in population and the value of textiles rose much faster than overall prices for commodities. Cloth accounted for 92 percent of exports out of London in 1640 and, even when rival products entered the market in large numbers, it still accounted for 74 percent of exports in 1660 and 72 percent in 1700.

KEY TERM

**Putting-out system**
Also known as the *domestic system*, this refers to the subcontracting of labour to those able to carry out work from home. This meant that anyone in a family could work and women could combine the production of cloth with the rearing of children. Merchants would usually provide the raw materials necessary and would collect the finished product to be sold at market.

### The growth of the domestic system

The cloth industry lent itself well to the use of a domestic labour force, as the process of working cloth was divided into a number of steps that could be carried out by different members of a family. The resulting products of the domestic system varied according to region. The weavers of Lancashire produced a coarse cloth unsuitable for clothing, whereas those in the West Country manufactured hard-wearing 'broadcloths' that would be sent to the continent, usually the Low Countries. East Anglia, the south Midlands and Yorkshire were also centres of the industry. Merchants who supplied the raw materials would first provide wool to be made into yarn and then, through the putting-out system, would hire weavers to make it into cloth. These merchants could make enough money to marry into landowning gentry families and, by the start of the 17th century, this system was already well-established, as displayed by the official government survey of the cloth industry from 1615 (see Source 4).

SOURCE

*State Papers Domestic, James I, Vol 53* (1615). The State Papers contain the accumulated correspondence of government. This extract is taken from a report sent by a government agent to the Privy Council.

[T]hey [the clothiers] buy but little or no wool, but do weekly buy their yarn in the markets, and presently make it into cloth and sell it for ready money, and so buy yarn again; which is weekly brought into the markets by a great number of poor people that will not spin to the clothier for small wages; but have stock enough to set themselves on work, and do weekly buy their wool in the market by very small parcels according to their use, and weekly return it in yarn, and make good profit thereof, having their benefit both of their labour and of the merchandise, and live exceedingly well.

The domestic system continued throughout the 17th century because it was easy to hire and let go of labour as the market dictated, and the skills involved were familiar to peasant families. As the industry was primarily based in the homes of workers, it was also free of the taxes and regulation experienced by guild-based industries in towns. The general trend in the cloth industry, therefore, is a continuation of what already existed, although new textiles and skills were developed as a result of contact with the continent.

### 'New draperies' and Protestant immigration

The British workforce did not posses the skills required to finish and dye cloth for sale on the general market, so it was shipped to Holland in order to be sold on. This system was interrupted early in the century as fashions changed and 'new draperies' became popular in Europe. The heavy woollen cloth that had been the staple of the British textile industry was replaced with lighter mixtures of wool, linen, cotton and silk. The domestic cloth trade remained relatively buoyant, but output would not increase significantly until the second half of the century.

Many of the traditional centres of the cloth industry fell into decline and changed their economic focus, but Norwich and Colchester flourished and became the focus of production for those employed in making the new draperies. Just over 1,500 Protestant Dutch immigrants had settled in Colchester in 1565–68 and the level of immigration decreased markedly after the foundation of the Dutch Republic in 1581, ending Catholic Hapsburg rule. This meant that Protestants were no longer persecuted there. Even so, by 1585, there were 13,000 immigrants working in the cloth industry in England. The existing population resented the new arrivals at first and some even attempted to expel the immigrants from the town, as the Dutch were allowed privileged access to the hall where all new draperies were taken for inspection before sale. If they approved of the product, whether it was made by an immigrant or a native of the town, they were able to put their seal on it as if it were their own. Regardless of this, the innovative techniques and skill of the immigrants had a positive impact on the native workers, as they were able to be trained in new continental methods. In Colchester, those employed in the textile industry rose from 26.4 percent in 1619 to 40 percent in 1699.

The key achievement of the Dutch in East Anglia was the introduction of new **worsted draperies**, in particular bays and says, types of cloth that were woven from wool rather than carded, a simple process where wool is brushed between two paddles in order to prepare it for the next stage of the process. The new worsteds therefore required a higher level of skill. This cloth was relatively versatile and cheap, and most crucially appealed to a wider market than traditional English wares. As the Dutch immigrants were involved in quality control, the reputation of Colchester and Norwich cloth meant that merchants on the continent were happy to buy products without reviewing samples first.

KEY TERM

**Worsted draperies**
Named after the village of Worstead in Norfolk, a group of cloth types created through combing and weaving rather than the simpler method of carding.

Away from the urban centres of East Anglia, other forms of textile manufacture were established and work was still undertaken by the rural workforce. Again, the impetus for change came from Dutch immigrants, whose most important innovation was the introduction of the frame knitting machine. This drastically reduced the amount of time required to produce cloth because it imitated the movements of hand knitters at a much faster pace.

In 1681, French Protestant **Huguenots** began to emigrate after Louis XIV started a process of forced conversion to Catholicism and, in 1685, Protestantism was declared illegal in France. Although most men and women in France were also employed in agriculture, the Huguenots had large numbers of skilled craftsmen among their ranks and many lived in towns. Silversmiths, watchmakers, gardeners and artisans came to settle in England, as well as a large number of weavers. Many settled in Kent and London, establishing a major weaving industry in the East End.

KEY TERM

**Huguenot**
A member of a group of French Protestants who followed the teachings of John Calvin.

## The growth of London and its impact on economic development

In the mid-17th century, London became the largest city of Western Europe, with a population of around 400,000. By 1700, the population increased to 575,000. Many historians believe that the growth of the Stuart economy and the success of the fledgling empire were due to the drastic growth of London. London was ideally placed to power the Stuart economy, as it was at the heart of the road and shipping network and could support the increasing demand for goods, as well as being home to the new investment banking industry.

Although the climate for economic growth in London existed in the 16th century, the City saw a boom under the Stuarts. Revisionist historians, writing since the 1970s, have generally concluded that London's economy grew as a result of a number of minor developments that happened to occur at the same time, rather than any one major advance in a particular area. London had much to offer.

- The banking and insurance industries were based in London, which provided employment as well as the capital needed to maintain merchants and businesses.
- It was the centre of the legal system – the Inns of Court, where legal training would take place, were all in the City and most high-profile lawyers were based there.
- Transport had been improving since Tudor times. Some roads in the area had seen investment and the Thames was navigable for much of its length. This was contrary to the situation in other towns, where less investment was made in transport.
- Demographic growth in London surpassed other towns, as the wealth of opportunities made it a more attractive place to live and work.
- Skilled and educated workers were more likely to move to London as it offered more than simply subsistence work.
- The number of markets meant that London was the focal point for economic activity in the South East. By the middle of the century, the national prices of livestock, grain and cloth were dictated by the London market.

London was the economic, political and religious capital of England, resulting in migration of not only poor workers from the countryside and other towns, but also the gentry and their families. If the son of a wealthy landowner wanted to gain favour at the royal court, they would naturally gravitate to London. If they did not succeed in politics, they were able to forge a career in the higher echelons of the military, especially the Admiralty, which was also based in London. Training in law was also a well-respected career path among the gentry, and membership of one of the Inns of Court was essential for any aspiring barrister. A number of chartered companies, whose interests were in trade and exploration, were based in London. These included the East India Company (established in 1600), as well as the Levant Company (founded in 1581) and the Muscovy Company (founded in 1555).

By 1688, not only was London at the centre of British trade but also it was the hub of a European market that relied on the port of the City. As world trade grew, London grew and the risk associated with trade became greater. In order to respond to this risk, merchants became acutely aware of the need to insure their ships and goods, leading to a boom in the insurance industry, as discussed below. The presence of merchants, insurers, bankers, barristers and government civil servants in London led to a growth of employment in service industries, as Source 5 illustrates.

**SOURCE 5** A satirical broadside designed to denounce the Puritan preachers of London for being low born. It shows the wide variety of occupations available in the City, 1647.

**ACTIVITIES**
**KNOWLEDGE CHECK**

**London and the cloth trade**

1 Using the information on the changing cloth trade and the growth of London, create a mind map to explain the different factors that explain why economic change happened in the 17th century.

2 Choose the three factors that you believe are most important and explain why you have chosen them.

### Banking

Banking was essential for the development of both the British economy and international trade, although money-lending services associated with banking existed before the Stuart period. Under the Tudors, rich merchants, such as Sir Thomas Gresham, obtained loans from Antwerp, at the time the base of most major European financers. Antwerp declined in importance towards the end of the 16th century and Gresham was able to secure finance from wealthy London inhabitants instead. Gresham would work as

## The growth of banking and insurance

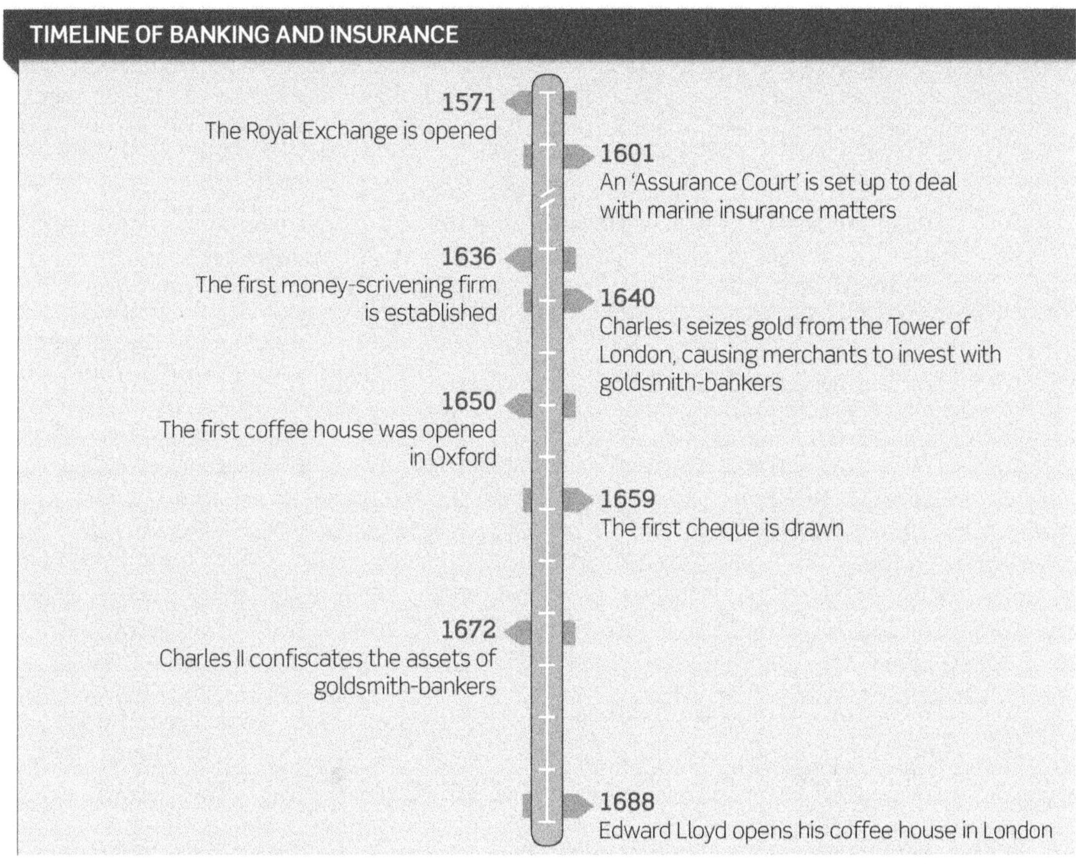


a broker, finding suitable finance for clients to invest with. The Royal Exchange, the first commercial building in Britain, was opened by Gresham in 1571 and provided space for brokers to do deals.

Before the development of banking, goods were traded for cash or bartered for. Bills of exchange were developed in the Middle Ages, which were essentially a form of credit. When used in a transaction, the bill of exchange would make it clear that the purchaser would pay for the goods they had received at a future specified date and, as the supplier of the goods was always taking a risk, interest was added to the loan. This meant that the supplier would eventually receive more than the true value of the goods. The growth of lending was made possible due to the lowering of interest rates. The legal limit for interest rates between 1571 and 1624 was ten percent, followed by eight percent between 1624 and 1651, finally reducing to six percent between 1651 and 1714. This reduction made credit more attractive, and banks and brokers were needed to provide it. As the demand for credit increased, brokers established networks of contacts that could provide money, particularly in London. In 1640, the market rate for a 'good' loan was eight percent, the legal limit, and in 1688 it was between four and six percent, below the legal limit.

### Money scriveners

The first **money-scrivening** firm was established by Robert Abbott, who had moved to London to be apprenticed to a financer, in 1636 and flourished in the 1650s. Royalist landowners faced disaster in the decade after the Civil War, as a result of the Commonwealth's move to confiscate their land and remove their capital, so they turned to London for loans in order to protect their assets and estates. This encouraged men with wealth to offer their own capital as loans and Abbott was able to act as a very successful broker in these transactions. He charged a fee for his services, and between 1652 and 1655 a staggering £1,137,646 passed through his accounts.

Abbott's firm was taken over on his death by his nephew, Robert Clayton. By 1672, Clayton's wealth was enormous and his accounts show he received £3,515 per year in interest from loans alone. Clayton and his business partner, John Morris, were also responsible for writing the first English cheque in 1659, which acted as a promise to pay the receiver a specified amount.

**KEY TERM**

**Money scrivener**
Someone who lends money, or arranges the lending of money on behalf of others, usually to those wanting to raise money on guarantee or security. They may also invest money at interest for clients.

### Goldsmith-bankers

The second half of the 17th century saw a boom in the success of goldsmith-bankers. Traditionally, a goldsmith's job was to forge items out of gold and silver for sale, which meant that they had secure, private vaults for the storage of precious metals. Merchants who accumulated large amounts of gold usually deposited this at the Royal Mint but, when this was seized by Charles I in 1640, storing valuables with goldsmiths was seen as a safer option. Goldsmiths were able to lend the money they held in storage with interest. London had an estimated 32 goldsmith-bankers in 1670, rising to 44 in 1677. Records show that, because they were seen as trustworthy, goldsmiths were also able to borrow at between four and six percent, which meant that they could offer short-term loans at a rate above six percent. The system used by both goldsmiths and money scriveners was paper-based, and goldsmiths would often accept bills and notes from other banks and then attempt to raise the funds to pay off the debt. Bankers were keen to take business from each other and acceptance of bills from others was an opportunity to do this. The historian Stephen Quinn has argued that the goldsmiths knew each other well because of the guild system of apprenticeship, which meant that they had a familiarity and reputation that improved the stability of banking in London.

Banking was not always allowed to flourish. The Commonwealth attempted to regulate finance through the Hale Commission, formed in 1652, which discussed a number of legal reforms. For example, it suggested the establishment of a register of property transactions, but this, like the vast majority of recommendations, was not acted upon. In the early 1670s, Charles II was heavily indebted to a group of goldsmith-bankers, who were borrowing money at six percent and lending to the Crown at ten percent. This led to Charles reforming banking in 1672, so that loans to the Crown were levied from the general public, resulting in him paying a lower rate of interest. The goldsmiths received notification that the funds deposited by them in the royal treasury had been confiscated, and they were not refunded. Any confidence the public had in the Crown to keep investments safe was completely lost, resulting in another boom for private financers. Confidence was not regained until 1688, when William III restored the status of goldsmith-bankers by repaying the original loans.

**EXTEND YOUR KNOWLEDGE**

**Robert Clayton (1629-1707)**

Born in 1629, Robert Clayton's career encompassed banking, politics and the military. He was apprenticed to his uncle, Robert Abbott, and it was during this time that he met his lifelong business partner, John Morris. The two would go on to found Clayton and Morris Co., one of the most successful banking companies in London.

Clayton's career was successful and his interests outside banking were many. He became an MP, Sheriff of London, a knight, Lord Mayor of London, Colonel of the Orange Regiment of the militia and director of the Bank of England in 1702.

### Marine insurance

**KEY TERM**

**Marine insurance**
Financial coverage provided against risks to shipping, including loss or theft of a ship or damage to cargo.

The growth of insurance was instrumental in fostering the economic conditions required for successful trade and an expanding empire. **Marine insurance** was well established by the 17th century, although a developed industry did not appear until after 1688. Dutch merchants had understood the value of marine insurance in the late 16th century, often visiting London to meet with financers, although formal insurance policies were unusual. Italian merchants had brought the practice to Britain in the 15th century and the insurers Filippo Borromei and Co. had a branch in London. Records show that, as far back as 1483, they were insuring shipments of broadcloth from Essex to Bruges.

A marine insurance law was introduced in 1601 in order to regulate the market and create a separate 'Assurance Court' to deal with insurance matters. In the first half of the century, many British merchants were reluctant to part with large amounts of money in order to take out insurance due to the high rates charged for premiums and it was common for as little as half of the value of goods on a ship to be covered. The London merchant, William Freeman, expressed his view on this in a letter written in 1680 (see Source 6).

SOURCE 6 From a letter by merchant William Freeman to a friend, written in 1680.

It's my general custom to insure when adventures are anything considerable, whether at peace or war. When the danger is least, premium is low, and so I look upon it as a safe way.

Freeman was interested in taking out the minimum amount of insurance possible and some companies even felt they were wealthy enough to avoid insurance entirely, as the East India Company did, preferring instead to accept the risk. The Dutch were apparently more conscious of the risk associated with international trade and, by 1657, it had become normal for ships from Holland to be insured through English brokers.

London merchants began to replicate the Dutch in seeing the calculation of risk as a wise practice and the use of insurance services increased. In the course of the 17th century, marine insurance prices to all destinations dropped by up to 75 percent as the industry became more established and more policies were taken out, and London became the leading insurance market in the world. The usual risks insured for included piracy, fire and natural disaster and, in time, underwriters were able to find a balance and charge a price that was both attractive to those buying policies and profitable for themselves. In 1688, Edward Lloyd opened his coffee house in London, which would eventually develop to become the world's first insurance market, Lloyd's of London. Lloyd welcomed merchants and ship owners and would share information about everything from weather conditions to the latest prices of tradable commodities. Insurance brokers began to descend on his coffee house, which ultimately moved to larger premises in 1691.

Before Lloyd, insurance business was carried out primarily by bankers and moneylenders, who 'underwrote' their names for a particular sum against a risk. Coffee houses such as Lloyd's proved to be convenient meeting places, saving the underwriter time in visiting their clients around the city. The first coffee house was opened in Oxford in 1650, followed by the first in London in 1652, set up by a Turkish merchant and many more sprang up in quick succession. The other resource available to insurers was the *City Mercury*, the principle newspaper of London: it published shipping announcements and surviving copies include some of the earliest records of those engaged in the marine insurance business. From 1680, advertisements for insurance services began to appear in the *Mercury*.

### Fire insurance

As well as marine insurance, fire insurance enjoyed a boom in the 17th century. State-funded fire insurance began in Germany in 1623, with a central 'fire fund' established in Prussia, but the first fire insurance companies were established in London. Records exist from 1615 referring to a Mr Havers, described as an assurer of fire insurance, with an estate worth up to £40,000. In 1627, an office within the Royal Exchange had been created to deal with insurance of ships and fires, and records exist of a scheme created by Charles I in 1638 to insure London citizens and business owners against fire, although this probably passed into oblivion once parliament was recalled and the Civil War began. Fires were common in the tightly packed streets of London and the Great Fire of London in 1666 increased the need for formal insurance policies, especially for businesses. An Act was passed in 1667 for the rebuilding of the City after the fire and reference is made to the settling of insurance claims at the Royal Exchange. Two specialist companies were set up towards the end of the period: the Fire Office in 1681 and the Friendly Society in 1683. It was not until 1720, however, that a company specialising in policies for private housing was established. Despite the expansion of fire and marine insurance, categories of insurance that would later become essential for many people, such as policies to cover life and accident insurance, were still unheard of in the 17th century.

It is clear that the insurance industry was still in its infancy, especially when compared with the booming market that developed in the 18th century. Insurance was still, however, an essential ingredient in the growth of a prosperous economy and the development of more formal banking made this possible.

ACTIVITIES
KNOWLEDGE CHECK

**Banking and insurance**

1 Why did banking and insurance develop in the 17th century?

2 Why do you think the true 'boom' in banking and insurance did not take place until the 18th century?

3 Do you believe the success of banking and insurance was due to the actions of a small number of individuals rather than the state?

Change (5a)

The strands of complex change

### The cloth trade, banking and insurance

| Strand | Explanation of how the strand links to the opening of Lloyd's Coffee House, 1688 |
|---|---|
| Increased dominance over the Dutch | • The Navigation Act was passed (1651) in an attempt to reduce Dutch dominance<br>• The Anglo-Dutch Wars were fought as a consequence and there was an increased need to provide insurance services in the light of new dangers at sea |
| The development of marine insurance | • Marine insurance law was passed in 1657<br>• Dutch merchants were using English insurance brokers by 1657<br>• Advertisements for insurance services appeared in newspapers from 1680 |
| The 'new draperies' and a successful cloth trade | • Cloth accounted for 92 percent of London's exports, 1640<br>• Large numbers of weavers arrived from France (1685), increasing European demand for woven cloth |
| The development of banking | • First evidence of banking in London from 1636<br>• Charles I seized gold from the Tower of London in 1640, leading to the rise of goldsmith-bankers<br>• 44 goldsmith-bankers were working in London in 1677, providing loans to fund foreign ventures |

Create two graphs. On each, the *y* axis should show the likelihood of an organised insurance market developing. At the top write 'An insurance market was likely to develop'; at the bottom write 'An insurance market was unlikely to develop'.

On the first graph, plot the individual strands against the *y* axis. Use a different colour for each. You don't need to label it with the events. On the second graph, plot a single line that is a combination of all four strands (for example, at a given point two of the four strands are plotted high up on the *y* axis, while two are plotted lower; the combined strand would have to be plotted somewhere in the middle to represent a summary of those four individual strands).

Answer the following.

1 How have the strands combined to make change less or more likely?

2 Why did an insurance market develop in 1688 and not before?

**A Level Exam-Style Question Section A**

To what extent was the development of banking and insurance more important than the changing cloth trade to the success of the British economy in the years 1650–88? (20 marks)

**Tip**

*Ensure you focus on the impact of these industries after 1650, and only include information from the period 1625–50 to provide context.*

# HOW SIGNIFICANT WAS IMPERIAL EXPANSION BETWEEN 1625-88 TO THE ECONOMY?

## The significance of North America and Jamaica

### North America

There is no doubt that imperial expansion had an important impact on the development of the Stuart economy, although much of the trade was one-way, as imports of raw materials from the New World vastly outnumbered any exports. Columbus had discovered America in 1492, and much of the early interest in the continent was from the Spanish and Dutch. The defeat of the Spanish Armada and the growth of Puritanism in England created an atmosphere suited to expansion westwards, although it was the desire to find precious metals, particularly gold, that drove exploration further. The Jamestown colony in Virginia, named after James I, had been established in 1607 and this marked the beginning of a lucrative tobacco trade with England. Tobacco was not as valuable as gold, but became the first **cash-crop** to be exploited by the English gentry and was such an important part of life in the colony that, in 1669, the crimes of adultery and fornication were punished in Virginia by a fine of up to 1,000 lbs of tobacco. It is difficult to estimate precisely how much tobacco was imported from Virginia, although the maximum limits on imports can give an impression of how significant the trade was (Source 7). Tobacco became particularly important because it helped the British to compete with other European powers in North America, principally the Dutch. The Stuart economy was boosted as customs duties could be levied on tobacco when it was transported back to England, and would be crucial in funding William III's military campaigns.

**KEY TERM**

**Cash-crop**
Any crop that is considered profitable and easily marketable.

**SOURCE**

**7** Table showing maximum proposed imports of tobacco to England, 1620–1638.

| Year | Maximum proposed imports of Virginia tobacco (lbs) |
|---|---|
| 1620 | 55,000 |
| 1625 | 200,000 |
| 1627 | 250,000 |
| 1635 | 600,000 |
| 1638 | 1,600,000 |

The slave trade had not yet become the dominant method of providing workers for the tobacco trade, although vagrants and **indentured servants** were regularly shipped over from Britain. This went some way towards solving the problems of unemployment and vagrancy in Britain, but the amount paid in poor relief was still high. The majority of settlers in Virginia and, later, Maryland (founded in 1632) were Anglican and Catholic refugees, although by 1680 there were enough Scots in the Virginia port of Norfolk to form a Scottish Presbyterian congregation. Further colonies in North and South Carolina were established after the restoration and, by 1700, 22 million lbs of tobacco were being exported from the North American colonies.

**KEY TERM**

**Indentured servant**
A worker contracted from one person to another without pay for a fixed period of time in exchange for free passage to their new country. When the fixed period had ended, they were freed. Most labourers in 17th-century Virginia and Maryland arrived as indentured servants.

Puritan colonies were established in the Americas, such as the one established by the Providence Island Company in 1629 in present-day Nicaragua. Prominent Puritans, such as John Pym, John Hampden and the Earl of Warwick, had financial interests in the company. North of Maryland and Virginia along the east coast, a number of other colonies developed with a markedly different focus. The *Mayflower*, carrying Puritan settlers, arrived at modern-day Massachusetts in 1620 and the Massachusetts Bay Colony, established in 1629, received around 20,000 Puritans in the 1630s, at the height of Archbishop Laud's persecutions. The Puritan New England colonies emerged as farming and fishing communities and were able to strengthen the British economy by creating markets for the trade of fur. Although these colonies were established partly as a result of economic problems in Britain, the primary motive for the establishment of both Puritan and Catholic colonies was contempt for the religious policies of Charles I. Despite this, according to the historian Barry Coward, a desire to cure the problem of overpopulation in England and open up new markets were the two factors that lay behind all colonisation schemes in North America.

The northern colonies, which continued to grow, included Rhode Island and Maine as well as Massachusetts. They were never as lucrative as Virginia and Maryland, although the population of the northern colonies was slightly smaller than the south in 1688. As well as farming and fishing, shipbuilding became an essential industry that fuelled further economic growth. Newfoundland, which was established as England's first colony in 1583, provided useful economic resources – especially fish – which were transported to England to be traded on the continent. Overall, the story of colonisation in North America between 1625 and 1688 is one of contrasts. On the one hand, High Church, Catholic and Anglican settlers were running large plantations for the export of tobacco and, on the other hand, largely Puritan colonies attempted to implement a deeply religious society where all were equal under the eyes of God. Both, however, had a generally positive impact on the Stuart economy.

## The Caribbean

As with South America, initial colonial success in the Caribbean was the result of Spanish conquest. The Spanish had a powerful navy and occupied the important islands of Cuba and Jamaica. Experimental expeditions were carried out by the English at the turn of the 17th century, culminating in Bermuda being occupied in 1612 and a small number of settlers moving to St Kitts in 1624. The founder of the English colony of St Kitts, Sir Thomas Warner, began growing tobacco on the island and some limited trade with Europe took place.

Spanish sea power declined after the 1620s, as a result of regular incursions by pirates and economic depression in Spain itself. This gave British colonists the opportunity to occupy Montserrat, Barbados and Antigua. Sugar became Antigua's primary crop after 1674, when Christopher Codrington established the island's first sugar plantation. Other Caribbean islands followed suit and the large plantations needed to support the sugar trade led to the expansion of the Atlantic slave trade.

**Figure 4.2**: Map of Caribbean islands, and inset, the North East coast of America in 1660 showing major European claims.

During the Interregnum (1649–60), British interest in the Caribbean increased, as Cromwell's Protectorate committed itself to expanding foreign trade and influence, in what became known as the 'Grand Western Design' to disrupt the Spanish monopoly on trade in the region. Massive investment in the navy resulted in 109 vessels being built and 111 captured by the British between 1646 and 1659. Although this investment was initially designed to counter the threat of the Dutch and Spanish, it also gave the government the opportunity to intervene in the Caribbean. In order to rid the Caribbean of the Spanish, the navy attempted to capture Hispaniola in 1655. When this failed, Jamaica was seized instead.

Jamaica was discovered by Christopher Columbus in 1494 and it was settled by the Spanish in 1509. Here they benefitted from the opportunity of controlling a safe natural harbour. After the invasion by the English, the Spanish, knowing that defeat was imminent, released their slaves and encouraged them to attack the invaders. The Spanish were not defeated until 1660. Once Jamaica was secure, the English government granted patents to wealthy merchants and members of the gentry for most of the land that was fit for cultivation. The large estates that were created would eventually be farmed through the use of large-scale slavery. Although, in 1670, the island had a slave population of just 7,000, this would grow to 55,000 in 1713. The English expected Jamaica to be another colony on which to grow tobacco, but it soon became clear that sugar was well suited to the climate and environment, and the price of tobacco had already been reduced by the success of the North American colonies. The abundance of tobacco being exported from the North meant it was not financially viable for Jamaican landowners to produce it, and the increasing taste for sugar in Britain and Europe made it a more lucrative prospect.

By 1662, there were 4,000 British settlers in Jamaica, many of whom were English, but also included were a number of impoverished Scottish and Welsh families. While sugar dominated output, cocoa and coffee also became popular and production of these followed fresh demand from the London economy. Overall, Jamaica was important between 1655 and 1688 for two reasons, as follows.

- The English capture of Jamaica, as well as the Cayman Islands, led to the Treaty of Madrid with Spain in 1670. Spain recognised English possessions in the Caribbean and English ships were permitted to sail freely between the Caribbean islands.
- The sugar trade became extremely successful, especially after slaves began to replace British indentured servants. This success was particularly dramatic after 1688, as Jamaica was not part of the previously established transatlantic trade routes.

ACTIVITIES
KNOWLEDGE CHECK

**North America and the Caribbean**

1 What was the attraction of North America and the Caribbean for British merchants and the government?

2 What was the impact of the North American colonies on the British economy?

3 Why were the British so keen on maintaining their possessions in the Caribbean?

## The Navigation Acts and the development of mercantilism

The sudden growth of international trade may seem surprising considering the slow pace of development in the 16th century, although a number of factors working together can help to explain why this happened.

- The Royal Navy, which had been growing in influence since the early 16th century, was able to enforce English supremacy at sea.
- A combination of war, the spread of Protestantism and loss of territory led to the gradual decline of the Catholic Spanish Empire.
- The Navigation Acts, outlined below, helped to reduce the trading strength of other naval powers.
- A policy of **mercantilism** developed, whereby the state took a lead role in organising economic policy.
- This policy had been encouraged by all Tudor and Stuart monarchs to an extent, but mercantile activity reached its peak during the Interregnum (1649–60). The transformation of trade in the 17th century has been described by the historian Ralph Davis as a commercial revolution based on mercantile shipping and the Navigation Acts did much to promote this. The first Navigation Act (see Source 8) was passed by the Rump Parliament in 1651.

KEY TERM

**Mercantilism**
The practice of accumulating wealth through trade with other countries. This is normally done by building overseas empires and colonies, restricting all but necessary imports from other rival nations, creating a self-sufficient economy and exporting any surplus manufactured goods for profit.

SOURCE 8 The Navigation Act, 9 October 1651.

No goods or commodities whatsoever of the growth, production or manufacture of Asia, Africa or America, or of any part thereof; or of any islands belonging to them, or which are described or laid down in the usual maps or cards of those places, as well of the English plantations as others, shall be imported or brought into this Commonwealth of England, or into Ireland, or any other lands, islands, plantations, or territories to this Commonwealth belonging, or in their possession, in any other ship or ships, vessel or vessels whatsoever, but only in such as do truly and without fraud belong only to the people of this Commonwealth, or the plantations thereof.

According to the Act, goods imported to England and its territories had to be carried on English ships. This was designed to remove the Dutch monopoly on freight trade across northern Europe and North America. It also required that all crews of English ships had to be at least half English by nationality. The historian Christopher Hill has argued that the Act was important because it represented the victory of a *national* trading interest over the separate interests of the various private trading companies, though the Levant Company found that it helped to boost their activity particularly. This was because their trade routes to the Middle East had been saturated by merchants from Holland, Spain and France, resulting in a decline in their share of trade. The Act helped the English new draperies to dominate the textile trade instead of the Dutch, as well as reducing imports of cheese and agricultural staples. This exercise in mercantilism contributed towards customs revenues increasing by three and a half times between 1643 and 1659.

All Acts passed by the Commonwealth were repealed at the Restoration, although a modified version of the Navigation Act appeared in 1660. The chief promoter of the new Act, Sir George Downing, had been Cromwell's ambassador to the Dutch Republic, which demonstrates the continued influence of a Republican anti-Dutch faction after 1660. The new Act confirmed the earlier legislation, but also banned exports, as well as imports, from being carried in foreign ships. It also included a long list of goods, including tobacco and sugar, which could only be shipped to England and her colonies. The Navigation Act and associated Staple Act of 1663, which stated that all goods shipped from the continent to the colonies had to pass through England, became the cornerstone of commercial expansion and success in the second half of the century. Both imports and exports were now protected, and the raw materials that came from the colonies could be re-exported to the continent. As the colonial population grew, the empire became wealthier through increased exports of raw materials. The Navigation Act was updated again by the Plantation Duty Act of 1673, which ensured that captains of English ships delivered specified goods to England only or faced a financial penalty.

**SOURCE 9** Mercantilism and the dominance of the Royal Navy was made possible through the construction of warships such as *Sovereign of the Seas*, active 1637–96, shown here in a contemporary engraving.

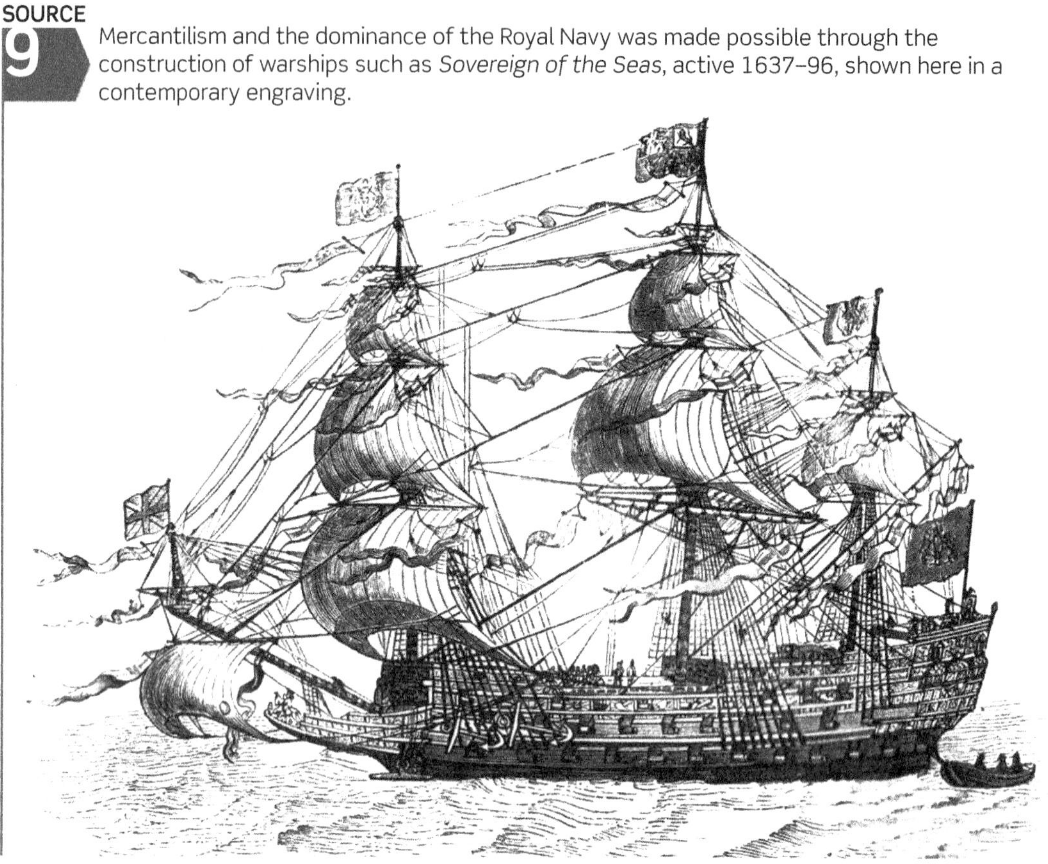

## The effects of Anglo-Dutch commercial rivalry

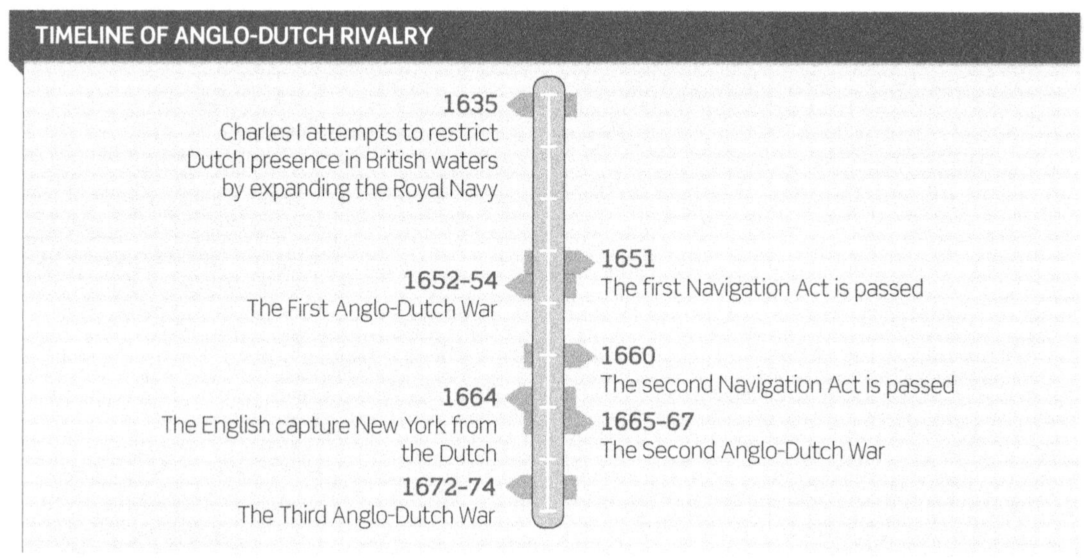


### Early rivalry

The Navigation Acts were devised primarily to deal with the threat of the Dutch, who had a monopoly on much European shipping trade. Rivalry over international trade and manufacturing, as well as New World colonies, caused three Anglo-Dutch Wars in the period (1652–54, 1665–67 and 1672–74). England and Holland were united by William of Orange in 1688, although William administered the two states as separate countries. This ended the political rivalry, but it did not stop Anglo-Dutch commercial rivalry, which would continue for another century. Anglo-Dutch rivalry evolved through a number of major stages in the 17th century. The first, from 1609–49, is marked by Dutch dominance and the beginnings of a commercial rivalry. By the middle of the century, England was stronger militarily but had become less efficient economically, and in the next stage, 1649–74, the commercial rivalry developed into direct conflict and war. The third stage, 1674–88, involved a gradual decline in rivalry as the two states allied against France. Why, then, did this rivalry last for so long? The historian Jack S. Levy argues that it was due to fundamental differences between the economic policies followed by England and Holland (Extract 2).

**EXTRACT**

From J.S. Levy, 'The rise and decline of Anglo-Dutch commercial rivalry, 1609–1689' in William R. Thompson (ed.), *Great Power Rivalries* (1999).

The conflicting economic interests of England and the Netherlands were reinforced by a conflict of ideology between English mercantilism and Dutch economic liberalism, though these ideologies closely paralleled the economic interest of each side. English writers... asserted that power and wealth were mutually reinforcing, that economic activity should promote the mutual interests of the merchants and the state... The Dutch, by contrast, articulated doctrines of economic liberalism and the principle of the freedom of the seas. Dutch political leaders and merchants alike perceived war as a costly and inefficient activity and strongly preferred peace to war, because it allowed them to pursue expansive trade policies abroad while lowering taxes and the national debt at home. The role of the state was to promote a liberal trading order and a peaceful international system; economic activity and diplomacy were separate.

Rivalry over trade with the East typifies the competition that existed between the two nations. The English East India Company was founded in 1600 (discussed below) and, two years later, the Dutch United East India Company was formed. Both companies traded predominantly in spices, and received the same price and paid the same acquisition cost for their goods; however, the profits of the Dutch Company were higher. This was for two reasons: first, the Dutch Company had closer ties with their own government, who were able to provide capital and assistance; second, they had more shareholders who expected dividends to be paid annually, thus leading to greater efficiency as the shareholders expected maximum returns for their investments. The Dutch soon began to overtake the English in terms of success in the East, returning 65 ships to England's 35 between 1615 and 1625. Considering this rivalry, it is surprising that a commercial war did not break out until 1652, although tensions often led to occasional hostilities, including the Dutch seizure of four English ships between 1617 and 1619. This early rivalry held the British economy back and the economic growth of London was slower in the first half of the century.

Anglo-Dutch rivalry involved much more than just trade with the East. There was competition over American colonies, culminating in the English capture of New Amsterdam (renamed New York) in 1664. The finishing process of raw English cloth also created tensions, as the Dutch traditionally captured much of the profit when unfinished cloth was exported to Holland to be finished and re-exported to the rest of Europe. There was also rivalry over access to English fishing grounds, as one-fifth of the Dutch population were employed in fishing and relied on fisheries off the British coast. The issue of fishing provoked a particular challenge, as Charles I decided to make an exclusive claim to the seas around Britain in 1635, demanding all vessels make a salute to English ships in the English Channel and North Sea. As well as this, the English began to deliberately search out and seize Dutch ships in their waters, which posed a significant threat to the Dutch role as the carriers of international trade.

## The Anglo-Dutch Wars

By 1649, the balance between the two nations changed, as the Dutch had ended their war with Spain in 1647, closing a longstanding Spanish embargo against them. The Dutch economy prospered, while the English economy hit a new low as a result of general depression, coupled with the impact of the Second Civil War, royalist uprisings in Ireland and Scotland, and the execution of Charles I. The new Commonwealth committed itself to enforcing English sovereignty on the seas once again. The Navigation Act of 1651 was designed to protect English trading interests, and the refusal of a Dutch ship to salute the English resulted in a short naval battle and the resulting First Anglo-Dutch

War in July 1652. The Navigation Act was the most important development in the rivalry between the two nations, as it helped to strengthen the British economy by excluding the Dutch from trade. Oliver Cromwell became Lord Protector in 1653 and, hoping for an alliance with the Dutch, ended the war on fairly lenient terms in the Treaty of Westminster in 1654.

### EXTEND YOUR KNOWLEDGE

**Treaty of Westminster, 1654**
Negotiations over the terms of a peace treaty between the English and Dutch began long before the war ended and, when terms were agreed, the Dutch were required to adhere to the terms of the Navigation Act, including saluting English ships in the Channel. Both sides also agreed to allow Swiss representatives to arbitrate any future disputes between England and Holland.

The Treaty stipulated that William III, Prince of Orange, was prevented from becoming Head of State in the Netherlands. This clause was inserted to allay fears in England that William would assist the Stuarts in restoring the monarchy, as he was the son of Mary, daughter of Charles I and Henrietta Maria.

The Treaty failed to resolve the underlying causes of the war, which led to several crises later in the 1650s and 1660s. For example, the Anglo-Spanish War (1656–59) severely affected Dutch trade with Spain, bringing England and Holland close to war once again. War was also narrowly avoided in 1658, when both sides sent fleets to intervene in a war between Sweden and Denmark. The Dutch provided a force to assist the Danish and the English sent a fleet to fight for the Swedish king, Charles X, although they were forced to withdraw due to a combination of Dutch naval superiority and political crisis at home under Richard Cromwell.

After the Restoration, parliament passed another Navigation Act in 1660 that excluded all foreigners from British trade. A number of goods could only be shipped to England under the provisions of the Act, such as tobacco, sugar, rice and cotton. This strengthened the Stuart economy at the expense of the Dutch, and the tax revenue from these products was given to the English treasury rather than the colonies from which they originated, but the Dutch were able to continue trading with their own colonies and other European countries. Charles also insulted the Dutch by demanding that foreign ships did not fish within ten miles of the British coast and tensions escalated further when Mary Stuart, wife of the late William II, died, leaving Charles II as the guardian of the young William of Orange. The pro-Stuart House of Orange was strengthened and Dutch merchants feared that, if the House of Orange returned to rule Holland, trade policy would be centralised and their freedoms restricted.

Colonial rivalry was also a factor in increased tensions, as Charles issued a Royal Charter in 1663, giving the Royal African Company a monopoly over West African trade. This brought the company into direct conflict with the Dutch, who had previously laid claim to the region. Pressure reached tipping point when an English captain seized a number of Dutch colonies in Africa in 1664 and, although Charles had the captain imprisoned, a skirmish followed in which the Dutch destroyed a number of English ships off the African coast. Charles ordered a blockade of Dutch ships using the English Channel in November 1664 and war was declared by Holland in January 1665. The Dutch were better prepared for this Second Anglo-Dutch War than they were in 1652 and they were able to pay for Denmark to join the war on their side. The English, demoralised by the effects of the Great Plague and the Great Fire of London, performed poorly and their humiliation was complete when the Dutch were able to sail up the Thames and capture the warship *Royal Charles*. The Dutch were then in a position to secure a relaxation of the Navigation Act as a condition of victory at the expense of the British economy. This war had a profound effect on the City of London, and for a time it was difficult for merchants to find insurers willing to cover their voyages.

In 1670, the English negotiated the Treaty of Dover with France, which called for an offensive partnership against the Dutch. The French king, Louis XIV, was angered when he found out that the Dutch had formed an anti-French alliance with Sweden (and, to begin with, England). When the next war broke out in 1672, Charles' motivations were again clear: he resented Dutch republicanism, demanded that the seas around Britain be free of Dutch ships and wanted international trade to be more favourable to the English. The war that Charles entered into was part of the wider Franco-Dutch War, which continued until 1678, although parliament feared that Charles would resort to absolutism if he remained in a close alliance with the French and encouraged him to withdraw from the war. A second Treaty of Westminster was signed in 1674, which reverted relations between the two states to that of 1667.

Throughout these years of rivalry, competition with the Dutch served to both help and hinder the British economy. When victories and peace treaties were gained, the British usually gained an advantage in international trade, but when the often long and drawn out battles of the Anglo-Dutch Wars were taking place, the economy in London would often come to a standstill, with merchants, insurers and bankers all feeling the knock-on effects. The historian Nigel Heard has argued that the British were able to survive the cycle of conflict and suspicion because of the strength of the colonies (Extract 3).

**EXTRACT 3** From N. Heard, *Stuart Economy and Society* (1995).

England was assured of a constant supply of cheap raw materials from her colonies. This promoted industrial growth and provided a growing volume of goods for the re-export trade. At the same time the colonies provided a protected market for English manufacturers. This steadily increased as the colonial population grew and became more wealthy through the export of raw materials. However, before this benign situation could be achieved England had to be able to enforce her monopoly against foreign competition.

## The end of Anglo-Dutch rivalry

Opinion in parliament and among the public by the 1670s was firmly against war and merchants had suffered greatly as a result of the disruption to trade brought about by the First and Second Anglo-Dutch Wars. In the end, however, the decline in rivalry between the two states had little to do with commercial interests and more to do with the political and religious situation faced at home. First, William III became **Stadholder** of the Dutch Republic in 1672 and married Mary, daughter of the future James II, in 1677. Charles promptly agreed to an alliance with William against France, and sent the army and navy to fight with the Dutch. Louis revoked the Edict of Nantes in 1685, which had provided protection for Protestants in France. A number of French Protestants migrated to England and Holland, leading to a mutual anti-French feeling in both states. The rivalry was entirely over when William was invited to take the English throne from the Catholic James II in the Glorious Revolution of 1688.

ACTIVITIES
KNOWLEDGE CHECK

**Colonies and rivalries**

1 Create a flowchart of the period 1600-89, highlighting when Anglo-Dutch rivalry was particularly pronounced and why.

2 Read Extracts 2 and 3. Outline the contrasting reasons given for Anglo-Dutch rivalry between 1625 and 1689.

KEY TERM

**Stadholder**
A steward. Although the Dutch Republic did not have a monarchy, those who held this office in the Republic had developed to have equivalent powers to that of a monarch. William III of Orange would go on to become William III of England and Ireland.

## The role of the East India Company

English rivalry with Spain culminated in the defeat of the Armada in 1588 and the gradual decline of Spanish sea power. Elizabeth I, and later James I, felt confident enough to develop trade with the East. The Portuguese and Dutch still had a monopoly on trade with the East at the beginning of the 17th century, although English ships made a number of voyages between 1590 and 1600 with limited success. In 1600, 242 London merchants agreed to found the East India Company and their fleet travelled to India for the first time in 1601, under the command of Captain James Lancaster, with funds totalling £68,000, including money for ships, as well as gold and silver to trade with. Lancaster established a trading post at Bantam, on the island of Java.

The local rulers in the East Indies and India were reluctant to trade their commodities for British goods, which they did not have a use for, and asked to trade in silver, a request to which the company agreed. The English policy of mercantilism favoured accumulating gold and silver, therefore the strategy of the East India Company contravened official government policy, although due to its success the trading model was given the freedom to flourish. A number of further trading posts were established in the East Indies between 1601 and the 1620s, although Portugal still had a monopoly over trade with India and the first trading post there was not established until 1613.

**Figure 4.3**: Map of India in 1700, showing the chief colonial settlements.

KEY TERM

**Saltpetre**
A chemical compound used as fertiliser and in gunpowder, also known as potassium nitrate.

English activity in the East Indies ended abruptly when, in 1623, a number of company officials were executed by the Dutch for attempting to expel the Dutch from their base on the island of Ambon in present-day Indonesia. This led to a change of direction for the company and it now focused its energies on India. The first shipment of **saltpetre** arrived from India in 1626, which was then re-exported to the continent. Pepper was sold in bulk by the company from 1627 and the trading post of Madras was established in 1633. Madras grew quickly to become a centre for the trade of calico textiles, which were made from woven cotton. A lasting peace was made with the Portuguese, who controlled the Indian region of Goa, in 1635, improving trading conditions on the west coast of India.

The company's success continued into the 1640s and it established a trading post at Basra to support Persian trade interests. However, the fortunes of the company would soon fall foul of Oliver Cromwell's suspicion surrounding its royalist sympathies. The company's charter was finally withdrawn by Cromwell in 1657 and, on his restoration, Charles II granted a new charter with the same privileges and returned capital assets totalling £740,000 back to the company. Relations with the Portuguese improved further when Charles II married Catherine of Braganza in 1662 and her dowry included the island of Bombay, which Charles allowed the company to use. There was a great demand for Indian textiles in the 1660s, and the company made loans to the Crown of £10,000 in 1660 and £50,000 in 1667. As Charles was indebted to the company, any financial irregularities regarding their practices were not investigated. The 1660s were also a successful decade for trade with India as the first shipments of tea arrived in 1664, although this success was briefly threatened when the Great Fire of London destroyed warehouses containing large quantities of pepper and other goods in 1666.

The importance of the East India Company was highlighted in 1672, when it was given permission to mint coins in India, and in 1675 the mint began the production of the Indian rupee. All English subjects in India were subject to the authority of the company, and a private army was created to protect English citizens and trading interests, as well as new armoured ships from the 1670s, designed to a specialised set of specifications. By 1688, the company was a popular choice for investment by wealthy courtiers and profits equalled, and often exceeded, the Caribbean and North American tobacco and sugar trades. In the 1680s, it was normal for annual profits to exceed £600,000, compared with no more than £100,000 between 1600 and 1640. The company was, therefore, key to both the advancement of trade in a lucrative part of the world, and crucial in ensuring the English were able to compete with the other major European powers.

ACTIVITIES
KNOWLEDGE CHECK

**The East India Company**

1 How did the East India Company's methods contradict the policy of mercantilism?

2 Why was the East India Company so successful?

## The significance of British control of the triangular trade

KEY TERM

**Triangular trade**
A system of trading in which a country pays for its imports from one country with exports from another.

A basic system of transatlantic slave trade had existed since 1510, when the first 50 slaves were transported by the Spanish to Hispaniola. The Spanish and, in particular, Portuguese dominated the trade in its infancy. The Portuguese had been trading with West African tribes in the 16th century and established outposts that would serve as collection points for the transportation of slaves across the Atlantic. A **triangular trade** soon developed, where slaves would be taken to Caribbean and North American colonies and sold for local produce such as tobacco, sugar, cotton or mahogany, which would then be taken to Europe. Merchants were attracted to the triangular trade because the profits made from the process could be significant; slaves were purchased from African chieftains in exchange for cheap European goods and the cargo they ultimately acquired in exchange for the slaves could be sold in Europe for a much higher rate than their original shipment to Africa. The first involvement of the British in what could be termed a triangular trade did not occur until later in the 16th century. In 1562, sea captain John Hawkins set sail from Plymouth in order to capture slaves on the Guinea Coast and then transport them to the Caribbean in exchange for commodities that could be used in Britain.

Although British merchants had a role in the transportation of slaves, in 1640 there were no slaves in the English colonies of North America. By 1660, slavery was written into law in most American colonies and, by 1700, there were nearly 120,000 slaves, primarily in Caribbean colonies such as Jamaica and Barbados. The barbarity associated with slave labour was not acknowledged by the English government, who still saw slaves as nothing more than property. This extraordinary expansion took place for a number of reasons, as outlined below.

- Early in the 17th century, the Dutch controlled most of the major West African trading posts. As a result of English successes in the First Anglo-Dutch War, the Royal Adventurers of England Trading in Africa was set up in 1663. This company was able to acquire a number of Dutch trading posts.
- After the Restoration in 1660, colonies such as Montserrat and Antigua were already experiencing severe labour shortages and the system whereby British migrants would settle in these colonies as indentured servants was no longer adequate. The triangular trade was therefore mutually beneficial for both English slave traders and plantation owners.
- The establishment of the Royal African Company in 1672 enabled the British to dominate the slave trade into the 18th century. This company was a restructured version of the one founded in 1663, although it now had the right to levy its own army, and set up military bases and trading posts. The company maintained control over slave trading across the entire West African coast with the use of this army, as well as ships that were more advanced than their rivals.

The significance of increased British control over the triangular trade is shown in the fact that the profits made from huge numbers of slaves transported after 1660 were able to add massively to the wealth of the City of London. The gold taken from Africa in this trade contributed to the **Royal Mint**, strengthening the economy and the Crown's hand further. Ports that had been involved in North American trade, such as Liverpool and Bristol, became the primary centres of the slave trade. The slave trade continued to grow after the Glorious Revolution in 1688, although the monopoly that had been given to the Royal African Company was broken when William III allowed all English merchants to trade in African goods and slaves. The Royal African Company was given the right to supply slaves to the Spanish possessions in South America in 1713, resulting in Britain controlling approximately half of the entire transatlantic slave trade.

The Royal African Company's strength in the City of London is also important. 15 Lord Mayors of London, 25 sheriffs and 38 aldermen were shareholders in the company between 1660 and 1690. The 'Guinea' coin, named after the part of Africa where Britain's gold and slave supply was located, was first minted in 1663.

ACTIVITIES
KNOWLEDGE CHECK

**Triangular trade**

How were the British able to dominate the triangular trade?

KEY TERM

**Royal Mint**

An institution whose primary role was to produce coins on behalf of the Crown. It first became a single unified institution in 886. From 1279, it was based in the Tower of London and, until Charles I removed large quantities of gold in order to finance war with Scotland, it was also used to store the profits of many London merchants.

Change (5b)

**Impetus and disruption**

### Changes to trade and empire, 1625–88

| | | |
|---|---|---|
| The East India Company is founded, 1600 | The Navigation Act is passed, 1651 | Imports of Virginia tobacco reach 1,600,000 lbs, 1638 |
| Edward Lloyd opens a coffee house that would later develop to become the world's first insurance market, 1688 | A marine insurance law is passed, 1601 | The Treaty of Westminster ends the First Anglo-Dutch War, 1654 |
| The first money-scrivening firm is founded, 1636 | The island of Jamaica is captured from Spain, 1655 | The Royal African Company founded, 1672 |

Patterns of development consist of changes that, at given times, converge and have a bearing on one another and, at other times, diverge and have little in common. In the above example, the changes come together to form a pattern of development that results in British dominance of international trade.

Work in groups.

Write each change on a small piece of paper and arrange them on a large A3 piece of paper as you think best. Then link them with lines and write along the line what it is that links those changes. Try to make sure that you think about how those links may have changed over time.

Answer the following questions individually or in pairs.

1 Why is 1651 an important year when considering the changing relationship between Britain and Holland?
2 Which changes were significant when assessing Holland's more belligerent attitude?
3 What changes were important in encouraging economic change in Britain?
4 Where can you see failure or a lack of growth in economic policy?

# CONCLUSION

## Was the economy transformed between 1625 and 1688?

Although Britain was yet to see the transformative change brought about by the commercial and industrial revolutions of the 18th and 19th centuries, it is clear that changes made between 1625 and 1688 provided the seedbed for further growth. Changes in agricultural techniques undoubtedly contributed to a growth in agricultural output, particularly in 'cash-crops' that could be used in the textile industry, such as hemp and flax. The crops grown in the colonies contributed to an improvement in economic conditions, as tobacco and sugar production became vastly profitable. London's newfound role as the centre of European trade and commerce ensured that there would be long-term prosperity in Britain. Finance was widely available for the first time and the chance to acquire credit meant that merchants were able to invest in new ventures and trading companies.

A clear theme that runs throughout the period is rivalry with the Dutch. The textile industry, once dominated by skilled workers from the Low Countries, had undergone a resurgence as a result of the 'new draperies' pioneered in the towns of East Anglia. The policy of mercantilism also enabled Britain to compete with Holland on the world stage, and one of the most important effects of this policy was undoubtedly the passing of the Navigation Acts. These Acts enforced English supremacy at sea and enabled North American colonies to prosper. The beginnings of a British monopoly of the triangular trade can also be seen in the period at the expense of other powers, such as Portugal and Spain. However, it has been argued that mercantile regulations were unnecessary in North America and the Caribbean, as in many cases England was the only trading partner of the newly settled colonies. Resentment towards mercantilism gradually developed in the colonies, as the government, based in London, that was giving direction and regulations was seen as distant and out of touch. In New England, colonists would routinely ignore the Navigation Acts by trading with other European powers.

Although economic development was generally strong, there is a clear correlation between the slowdown in population growth in the second half of the 17th century and a slowing in economic progress. This, coupled with a conservative approach to aspects of the rural economy such as the continuation of the 'putting-out' system for the production of cloth, as well as a lack of agricultural progress in some regions, meant that economic development was not felt by everyone. This lack of progress is most evident in Ireland, which saw little industrial investment and did not reap the benefits of improved agricultural techniques until later. The issue of land ownership in Ireland hampered progress, as English Protestant settlers were almost always favoured over the native Catholic population when land disputes broke out. Rivalry in Ireland came to a head during the rebellion of 1641 and the restoration monarchy failed to address these grievances further.

Finally, although some changes were made to transport and industry, they were limited. The development of road transport was piecemeal, with turnpikes only appearing towards the end of the century, and water transport was often unreliable and easily disrupted by seasonal changes and the weather. Heavy industry, which would be the backbone of the industrial revolution, was virtually non-existent. Coal and tin mining were well-established industries, although the processes by which they were extracted were still slow and inefficient.

**ACTIVITY**
**SUMMARY**

**Economic change**

Create a graph of the period 1625-88, outlining developments in trade and the economy. Ensure you cover the following issues. It would be useful to use highlighter pens to establish when each category of change was most significant.

Agriculture; Cloth trade; London; Banking and insurance; Colonies; Trade rivalries

The *x* axis should represent time, starting in 1625 and ending in 1688. The *y* axis should include major changes at the top and minor changes at the bottom. Decide how important each change is and place it on the *y* axis accordingly.

Based on your graph, decide what the three most important changes were between 1625 and 1688, and explain why you have chosen each one.

### A Level Exam-Style Question Section A

To what extent did the British economy radically change in the years 1625–88? (20 marks)

**Tip**

*Make sure you include the various strands of the economy, including trade rivalries, the cloth trade, the growth of the industries associated with London and agricultural change.*

### WIDER READING

Coward, B. *Stuart England 1603-1714*, Routledge (2011) Includes an accessible introduction to economic developments

Heard, N. *Stuart Economy and Society*, Hodder and Stoughton (1995) Provides an overview of the Stuart economy, including agriculture and overseas trade

Hill, C. *Reformation to Industrial Revolution*, Penguin (1991) Contains a detailed discussion of mercantilism and the impact of the Navigation Acts

Seel, G.E. *Regicide and Republic: England 1603-1660*, Cambridge University Press (2001) Contains an accessible overview of economic developments

# 1.5 How revolutionary, in the years to 1701, was the Glorious Revolution of 1688–89?

**KEY QUESTIONS**

- How significant were revolutionary ideals in the establishment of a constitutional monarchy?
- What was the impact of the Toleration Act of 1689 and the end of Anglican supremacy?
- How significant was the Triennial Act of 1694 in promoting parliamentary power?
- How important were William III's wars in the development of a financial revolution?

## INTRODUCTION

The Revolution of 1688–89 has retreated somewhat from public consciousness and is not generally viewed as a significant event, on a par with the signing of the Magna Carta in 1215, the Civil Wars of the mid-17th century or the Act of Union of 1707. This is primarily because the consensus among historians from the 18th century to the present day is that it was a bloodless revolution that restored an ancient English constitution, rather than a revolution that fundamentally changed the make-up of social, political and religious life. Some historians have countered this consensus by suggesting that the Revolution represents a radical shift in the history of Britain. Ideas of absolute monarchy and a confessional state were questioned and parliament became pre-eminent in the political system. When Charles I was faced with limits on his prerogative powers in the form of parliament's Nineteen Propositions in 1642 (see Chapter 1), his reply was that parliament's only duty was to levy taxes and ensure that monarchs did not become tyrants. Within 100 years, parliament was to become an integral part of the political system, controlling most taxation and public spending, deciding who would succeed the king and meeting more regularly than ever before. As well as this, factions developed in the form of the Whigs and the Tories, who would dominate politics for the following 200 years. Eventually, they would evolve to become the Liberal and Conservative parties.

Religious reform was a key element of the settlement established by William and Mary. Catholics were to be excluded from public life through the Toleration Act, which allowed nonconformists to worship without persecution. A revolution also came about in public finances, culminating in the foundation of the Bank of England in 1694. William's Nine Years' War with France (1688–97) put a heavy strain on government funds, necessitating a restructuring of government finances and more scrutiny of public spending. The financial revolution was also a political one, as parliament was increasingly involved in controlling and scrutinising public finances and royal expenditure.

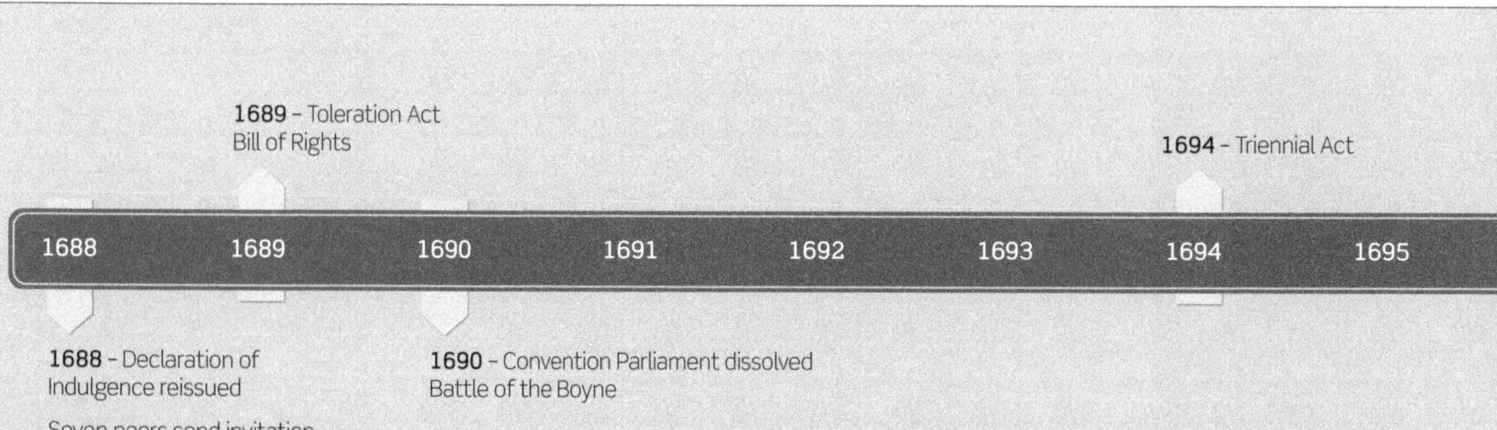

### The course of events, 1688–1701

In April 1687, James II issued a Declaration of Indulgence, suspending penal laws against Catholics as well as allowing some religious toleration for dissenters. His dissolution of parliament in the summer and his attempt to repeal the pro-Anglican Test Acts led to increased opposition from the political establishment. After seven bishops refused to read another Declaration of Indulgence in May 1688, their acquittal after they were arrested was met with public rejoicing. Seven leading figures from the political nation, terrified at the prospect of a Catholic heir after James' wife finally fell pregnant, sent an invitation to William of Orange to bring a force against James.

William arrived, and in December 1688, James fled the country. A 'convention parliament' was established in January 1689, and it declared that William would rule jointly with his wife, Mary, the Protestant daughter of James. They were presented with a Declaration of Rights, which affirmed a number of constitutional principles, such as the prohibition of unparliamentary taxation and the need for regular parliaments. Pressure from William ensured that a Toleration Act was passed in May 1689, granting many Protestant groups, but not Catholics, religious freedom.

Meanwhile, James attempted to amass a force in Ireland in order to take back the throne, which led to William leading an army and securing victory against him at the Battle of the Boyne in 1690. William spent much of the years 1690–97 on campaign, against the supporters of James and the armies of Louis XIV of France. In 1694, Mary died, and parliament secured the passing of a Triennial Act, which ensured parliament would be called regularly, and in the same year, the Bank of England was created, primarily to finance William's war with France, which ended in 1697. The importance of parliament in these years is highlighted by the creation of the civil list in 1698, which gave William a fixed financial allowance that could only be approved by parliament. Parliament was also able to scrutinise public spending in a way they had not been able to before.

Fears of a potential Catholic succession once again became pronounced in the late 1690s and, in 1701, the Act of Settlement was passed, which would lead to a German prince, George of Hanover (later George I of England) becoming king in 1714. James II died in 1701, and the Security of the Succession Act was passed, requiring nearly all public office-holders to take the oath of abjuration, denouncing James' son, also called James, as heir to the throne. Before the succession of George, when William died in 1702, he was immediately succeeded by Queen Anne, Mary's Protestant sister.

## Evaluating interpretations of history

The job of the historian is to provide judgements about what happened in the past based on research and an assessment of the available evidence. It is inevitable that this process will result in their opinion or beliefs influencing the outcome of their research. This chapter contains a number of interpretations that will help you prepare for Section C of your exam. Although the interpretations historians present are based to some extent on opinion, this does not mean they should be discarded by the student. Evaluating and comparing a number of interpretations of an event can be just as useful as evaluating different primary sources in order to ascertain the truth. Some historians will clearly state their agenda throughout their work, and others will attempt to remain as neutral as possible. Either way, it is important to note that every interpretation created is informed, whether consciously or unconsciously, by factors including the political, religious, moral or cultural viewpoint of its author.

Sound interpretations need to be backed up with evidence, and it is important for the historian to show how they have arrived at their interpretation. When reading the extracts in this chapter, consider the following questions.

- Is the author actually giving an interpretation or are they simply stating facts?
- Is the interpretation based on generalisations or is it backed up by evidence?
- Does the historian make clear the methods they have used to arrive at their interpretation?
- Do any other interpretations agree with the one given?

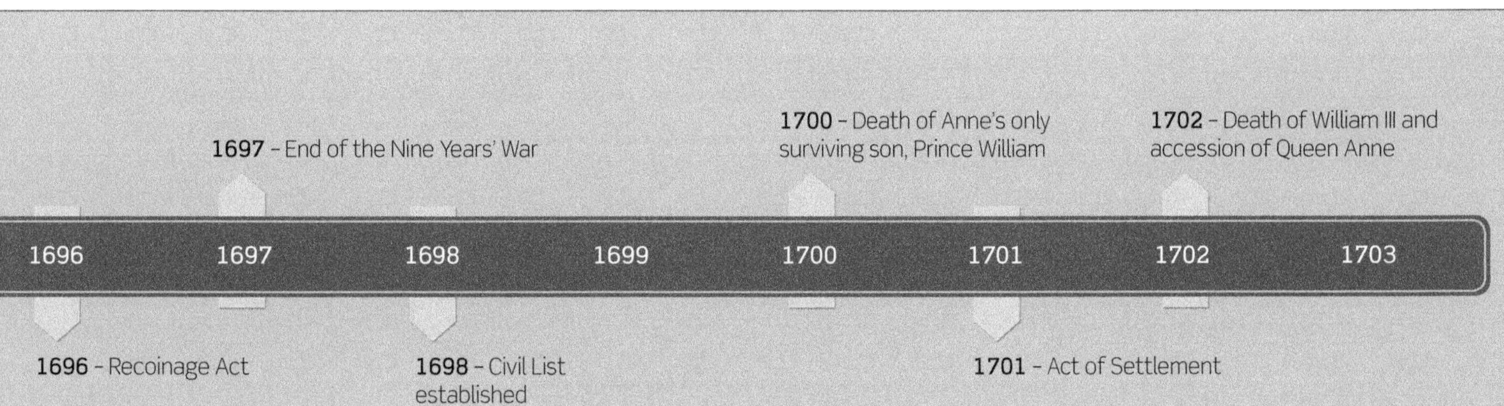

Interpretations (5a)

**What I believe is how I see**

Below are three descriptions of the perspectives of very famous historians.

| Herodotus | Leopold von Ranke | Christopher Hill |
|---|---|---|
| • Research consisted of conversations<br>• Identified that accounts had to be judged on their merits<br>• Some believe that certain passages in his writing are inventions to complete the narrative | • Believed in an evidence-based approach and relied heavily on primary sources<br>• Desired to find out the 'facts' and discover the connections between them<br>• Stressed the role of the individual in shaping history | • As a Marxist, he believed that history would go through stages leading to a state where everybody was equal<br>• Believed that historical changes were ultimately determined by changes to the economy<br>• Was often driven by political considerations and looked for evidence to support his point of view; looked to draw links between the 17th century and political problems that existed in the 20th century |

Work in groups of between three and six. Each member, or a pair, will take the perspective of one of the historians in the table above and argue from that perspective. Work through Questions 1–4 as a group and answer Question 5 individually.

1 Herodotus did not use written evidence to construct his history. Does this mean that his history is less useful than the others?

2 Ranke based his writing almost exclusively on primary sources from the time he was investigating, rather than secondary sources. How might this affect his ability to see larger patterns in history as opposed to the other two?

3 Hill put his philosophy of history, and perhaps politics, first and research second. Would this make his history weaker than the others?

4 'Colourful' individuals populate the writing of Herodotus and Ranke, while Hill concentrates on the difference between classes. Write three historical questions that each historian might ask.

5 The three historians mentioned above all had different methods and motivations and yet their writing has been valued ever since it was created. Explain how the prior knowledge that we bring to the history that we write does not invalidate it.

# HOW SIGNIFICANT WERE REVOLUTIONARY IDEALS IN THE ESTABLISHMENT OF A CONSTITUTIONAL MONARCHY?

## The revolutionary ideals behind the overthrow of James II

In 1688, it was evident that James II had lost the confidence of much of the political nation. It seemed that the fears that had caused the Civil War earlier in the century had come to fruition: a Catholic was on the throne and he was aspiring to be an absolute monarch. After he had successfully defeated Charles II's illegitimate son, the Duke of Monmouth, in 1685, James consolidated his power by apparently modelling his rule on the despotism seen in France under Louis XIV. Many Protestants had been holding on to the hope that James would be succeeded by his Protestant daughter, Mary, wife of William of Orange. This changed, however, when the queen gave birth to a son and potential Catholic heir in June 1688. It is easy to depict the Glorious Revolution as a popular uprising of the Protestant majority against a tyrannical and unpopular king, leaving the path clear for William to gratefully receive the throne. However, the reality was very different from this and the beliefs that drove the actors in these events were wide-ranging.

Historical interpretations of the overthrow of James II tend to explain the events with reference to a number of key themes.

- Most traditional interpretations accepted that the Glorious Revolution was the result of a foreign invasion and was not instigated by the native population of England.

Another common view is that the Revolution was a bloodless one. The 19th-century Whig historian Thomas Macaulay contrasted it with the French Revolution and concluded that it was the least violent revolution known to history. More recent interpretations, as put forward by historians such as Edward Vallance, have claimed that the Revolution should be reassessed as one typified by violence, especially in Ireland and Scotland.

- Macaulay also believed that the overthrow of the king came about due to a moderate political consensus between Whigs and Tories. More recently, John Morrill has built on this and described the events of 1688–89 as the 'Sensible Revolution'.
- Marxist historians have presented 1688 as a continuation of the 'bourgeoisie revolution' of 1649, where the propertied classes overthrew a monarchy that restricted their economic livelihoods. According to the Marxists, the propertied classes were again the only group to benefit from the events of 1688–89.

A key motive for those who prompted the overthrow of the king was religious conviction. Many Whig members of parliament (MPs) shared the view of John Locke, that enforcing religious uniformity would lead to social disorder and that imposing a single 'true religion' is impossible as humans are not capable of judging which religious standpoints are the most legitimate. The Anglican Tories who opposed James had to find a way to oppose his initiatives without contradicting their established principles of non-resistance and **passive obedience.** In Extract 1, Tim Harris outlines the reasons why some Anglican Tories felt compelled to oppose James II.

KEY TERM

**Passive obedience**
Unquestioning obedience to the authority of a monarch, even when the monarch abuses his or her powers.

**EXTRACT 1**

From T. Harris, *Revolution: The Great Crisis of the British Monarchy, 1685–1720* (2006).

To appreciate the logic behind Tory-Anglican non-compliance, we have to be clear about two key doctrines: the doctrine of passive obedience, and the maxim that the king could do no wrong. Although one was supposed to 'yield obedience' to the king 'in all Things' that were 'agreeable to God's Commands', the Church had always held that if the king commanded something that was contrary to God's law, one had to obey God rather than man. One should not commit an immoral act even if commanded to do so by the king. Nor should one violate one's oaths - since perjury was a sin as well as a crime - or go against one's conscience. Nevertheless, one could not resist the king, and one had to accept whatever punishment was meted out for non-compliance. Thus the fellows of Magdalen College had no option but to stand up to James II, but they also accepted the consequences, namely ejection from their fellowships. This was a classic example of the application of the principle of passive obedience, although in modern-day parlance it might more accurately be styled passive disobedience.

ACTIVITY
WRITING

**Passive obedience or passive disobedience?**

Read Extract 1 and complete the following.

1. Identify words and phrases used to express degrees of doubt or certainty about the subject matter.
2. Identify words and phrases used to describe the relationships between cause and consequence.
3. Identify words and phrases that show the historian's attitude towards the importance of passive obedience.
4. Write a short paragraph explaining the historian's views, using quotes from the extract to back up your points.

Steve Pincus summarises the Whig attitude towards the idea of passive obedience, particularly among Whig supporting bishops, in Extract 2.

**EXTRACT 2** From S. Pincus, *1688: The First Modern Revolution* (2009).

The Whig political commitments of the Williamite [those loyal to William III] bishops suggest a shift in the views of a culturally significant portion of the clergy... The events of James II's reign convinced many passive obedience men to reconsider their political ideas. 'Those English divines who preached and wrote most for passive obedience and non-resistance, mostly perceive that they laboured under a mistake', recorded the Scottish Episcopalian minister Robert Kirk in 1690 after months of discussions with English divines... The Whig party was now much broader than the party of Dissenters and their friends. The revolution made it clear that the political principles of many in the Church of England had been dramatically transformed. 'I can but blush and admire that the bishops of the English Church should be so changed since the days of pious Laud. Then it was submit and obey, now it is resist and rebel,' lamented one High Churchman in the wake of the revolution.

### ACTIVITIES
### KNOWLEDGE CHECK

**Revolutionary ideals**

1. Why is it not adequate to depict the Glorious Revolution as a popular uprising against an unpopular king?
2. What are the different reasons given for the ideological opposition to James II in Extracts 1 and 2?
3. How far do the authors differ in their view of the extent of opposition to passive obedience?

James reissued the Declaration of Indulgence in 1688, giving toleration to all religious groups, both Protestant and Catholic. As well as the obvious friction created by James' attempt to allow Catholics and, potentially, those of non-Christian faiths freedom of religion, opponents of the Declaration objected to the fact that James was attempting to overrule parliament by going against their wishes. Pamphleteering against the Declaration began promptly and the Marquis of Halifax argued that, although he understood why the dissenters were attracted to the idea of toleration offered by James, they should resist his overtures towards them and wait for parliament to pass its own law: one offering true religious freedom that did not favour Catholics and did not set a precedent for absolute rule. Gilbert Burnet offered a similar view in his *Ill Effects of Animosities among Protestants in England Detected.* Burnet was a clergyman who had been invited by William to live in The Hague in the Netherlands, and took up his offer in 1686, thus making his work an early piece of Williamite propaganda.

Burnet explained that, since the Restoration, both Charles II and James II had attempted to create divisions among Protestants in order to pursue their agenda of promoting Catholicism and arbitrary government. He believed that both dissenting nonconformists and conformists should work together to defend the Established Church. He also claimed in 1687 that James had transgressed the constitution and laws of England, thus virtually deposing himself from government. The idea that James had abdicated himself from government would be taken up again by William's supporters in the winter of 1688–89.

**SOURCE**  'The Protestant Grind-Stone', from an unknown anti-Catholic author in London, produced in 1690. William III and Queen Mary press the Pope's nose to the grindstone being turned by Anglican bishops Sancroft and Compton. Three of William's supporters, Marshal Schomberg, Lord Halifax and Bishop Burnet, look on.

In the end, political change resulted from James resigning his throne voluntarily. This was necessary for the Revolution to take place because, although it was likely that the Commons would have managed to secure a majority against James' continued reign, the Lords would probably have rejected any proposal. The clergy, too, would not have approved of a change of personnel. There were, of course, precedents for the overthrow of the monarch dating back to the Middle Ages, and the execution of Charles I, still within living memory for many, was a more recent example. Many within the political and religious establishment were generally in favour of divine right and hereditary monarchy in order to prevent the return of the unstable governments experienced during the Interregnum, so there is a strong chance that James would have kept his crown if he had not resigned it voluntarily.

The Whig argument at the time for the deposal of James II was that he had broken a solemn contract with his people. Some moderates in the Commons would argue that government existed as a result of an agreement between the king and the people, and John Locke's *Two Treatises of Government* (1689) tends to suggest that the Revolution was an opportunity for those who represented the people in parliament to alter the constitution. Locke's work, although published after the Revolution itself, is often seen as a justification, or even a manifesto, for the kind of government the Whigs wanted to create after James abdicated. As discussed in Chapter 3, Locke rejected the view that the Crown should have unquestioned authority and suggested that the monarch did not necessary have a divine right to rule. He believed in freedom, although he only advocated freedom from government interference in order to protect life and property and was not interested in **universal suffrage**.

### KEY TERM

**Universal suffrage**
The right of all adults, both male and female, to vote in elections.

Locke and the Whigs believed that, if a ruler attempted to behave as an absolute monarch, citizens had the right to remove them. In the opening days of the Convention Parliament in January 1689, some Whig MPs voiced similar concerns to Locke. Sir Robert Howard argued that the government was grounded on a pact between king and people and, if the king broke that pact, members of parliament were within their rights to appoint another ruler.

Despite the fact that James II had openly defied both parliament and the religious establishment, prompting actions that would become revolutionary, historians are generally agreed that William's invasion was equally as important in leading to a change in government, whether William intended to take the throne or not. His invasion was invited by those who rejected James' government, but they did not necessarily have a plan in place when they sent their invitation.

ACTIVITIES
KNOWLEDGE CHECK

**The fall of James II**

1 Why was the Declaration of Indulgence unpopular?

2 What was the contemporary Whig view of the overthrow of James II?

## The significance of the Bill of Rights, 1689

After William arrived in London and James slipped away to France in December 1688, the terms for a political settlement were not immediately clear. Had James abdicated his throne? Was William intent on working with parliament or against them? Could a parliament be summoned without a king to summon it? On 26 December, William arranged for a meeting of sympathetic peers and MPs in order to plan for the future of the monarchy and the country. A Convention Parliament was hastily elected, with its first meeting due for 22 January 1689. Radical Whigs wanted to declare William king immediately, but many others favoured a role for his wife, Mary, by hereditary right. Thus, the Crown was offered to them both, and a Declaration of Rights was presented to both William and Mary at the same time as the offer of the Crown and read out at their coronation ceremony. Although William would claim that he did not accept the throne with conditions, it was clear that both William and Mary had been placed on the throne based on terms put forward by the elected representatives of the people. At the end of 1689, the Declaration was modified and many of its terms placed on the statute book as the Bill of Rights.

**SOURCE 2** The Bill of Rights, 1689.

1 That the pretended power of suspending laws, or the execution of laws by regal authority, without consent of parliament, is illegal.

2 That the pretended power of dispensing with laws, or the execution of laws by regal authority, as it hath been assumed and exercised of late, is illegal.

3 That the levying money for or to the use of the Crown, by pretence of prerogative, without grant of parliament, for longer time or in other manner than the same is or shall be granted, is illegal.

4 That it is the right of the subjects to petition the king, and all commitments and prosecutions for such petitioning are illegal.

5 That the raising or keeping a standing army within the kingdom in time of peace, unless it be with consent of parliament, is against the law.

6 That elections of members of parliament ought to be free.

7 That the freedom of speech, and debates or proceedings in parliament, ought not to be impeached or questioned in any court or place out of parliament.

8 That excessive bail ought not be required, nor excessive fines imposed; nor cruel and unusual punishment inflicted.

9 And that for redress of all grievances, and for the amending, strengthening, and preserving of the laws, parliaments ought to be held frequently.

ACTIVITIES
KNOWLEDGE CHECK

**The Bill of Rights**

1 Read Source 2. Which clauses in the Bill of Rights are aimed at protecting the rights of a) parliament and b) ordinary citizens?

2 According to Source 2, what is suggested about the nature of James' rule?

The Bill of Rights is often cited as a significant constitutional document, as important as the Magna Carta of 1215 and the Petition of Right of 1628. Most of the clauses included in the bill referred to specific abuses of the royal prerogative under Charles II and James II, and the important clause calling for elections to be both regular and free reflected resentment among MPs at attempts by the Crown to intimidate them and tamper with elections. The bill is also important because it made certain the legal position of the army, which had been in some doubt. The clause stating that a force could not be raised or kept in times of peace without the consent of parliament was inserted in direct reaction to the forces created by Charles II, which could have been used to enforce absolutism. As well as this, a number of Mutiny Acts were passed from 1689, ensuring that the king could not court martial at will without the consent of parliament, and as each Act was only valid for a year, the king had no choice but to turn to parliament regularly for approval.

**EXTEND YOUR KNOWLEDGE**

**The legal status of the Bill of Rights**
There are subtle differences between the Declaration of Rights that was presented to William and Mary at the beginning of the Revolution and the final Bill of Rights that became law. The Declaration was a restatement of traditional rights, but continued conflicts between Whigs and Tories meant it had to be watered down. In particular, there was debate about whether to include a clause suspending the maintenance of a standing army in peacetime, and the Whigs were able to have this included in the final document.

Many of the original declarations around issues such as free elections and regular parliaments were included in the final Bill but, importantly, they were not part of any conditions that William was subject to in taking the crown.

A number of other Acts complemented the Bill of Rights, and the Crown and Parliament Recognition Act (1689) confirmed all the Acts of the Convention Parliament. This Act also acknowledged William and Mary as sovereigns. The parliament had been summoned in a legitimate manner and the Acts passed were therefore seen as constitutional and legal. The Bill of Rights stood in England and Wales, but in Scotland corresponding legislation was passed under the Claim of Right Act (1689).

Parliament asserted its control of the military through the Bill of Rights, but many of the other clauses simply restated what was already known to be part of the constitution and cleared up grey areas of the royal prerogative. The Marxist historian Christopher Hill has argued that the Bill of Rights was vague and that references in particular to holding frequent parliaments could still allow for absolutism to creep in. The Bill made no provision for ensuring that elections were regular or free and made no definition of what 'free' actually meant. This vagueness would be partially, although not completely, removed by the Triennial Act of 1694. According to the historian John Morrill, the Bill of Rights was not as significant as some historians suggest, as it was a statute law that could be revoked by any future parliament. He believed that the Bill was not a yardstick by which other laws could be judged and did not form part of a contract between the king and the people. It did not create a new procedure by which arbitrary monarchs could be removed and, if this was to happen, it would need to be done in the same way it was done before 1688: as a result of rebellion or through parliamentary pressure. The monarch was still free to decide on issues surrounding war, peace and foreign policy, and William was still able to choose his own advisers.

**EXTEND YOUR KNOWLEDGE**

**Mutiny Acts**
When William invaded England, a number of troops remaining loyal to James refused to fight on his behalf. As mutiny was not recognised as a crime under common law, parliament passed the Mutiny Act in 1689, allowing the Crown to hold courts martial in order to punish the mutineers.

As the existence of a standing army during peacetime was prohibited under the terms of the Bill of Rights, the first Mutiny Act was only enforceable for one year. Parliament renewed the Mutiny Act every year until 1879, thus making it possible to revoke the right of the Crown to punish mutineers if a new Act was not passed.

The Mutiny Act benefitted both Crown and parliament: William was able to freely punish those who had mutinied and parliament was able to place limits on the royal prerogative if it wished.

## The significance of the Act of Settlement, 1701

Restrictions on the rights of the Crown were not simply limited to the revolutionary years of 1688 and 1689. The Act of Settlement appeared in 1701 and stated that, in order to bypass potential Catholic heirs to the throne, the succession would be vested in the House of Hanover, a German royal dynasty, after the reign of Queen Anne (the Protestant daughter of James II), who became queen after William's death. The House of Hanover was linked to the Stuarts through Sophia, the granddaughter of James I, and as William and Mary (and Anne) had no surviving children, she was the next suitable heir. Sophia married Ernst Augustus, Elector of Hanover, and died before she could inherit the throne, thus passing the succession down to her son, George I, who became King of England, Scotland and Ireland on Anne's death in 1714. Under the terms of the Act, Catholics, and those married to Catholics, were barred from the succession and all future monarchs were required to be members of the Church of England.

The Act was not simply limited to providing for a smooth succession and it enabled a number of legislative proposals first put forward in 1689 to finally reach the statute book. Judges could no longer be dismissed without the consent of parliament, a reaction to James' removal of disloyal members of the judiciary. Another demand that had been discussed in 1689 was for royal pardons to be declared irrelevant in cases of impeachment, but this was only included in the Act as Tories hoped to impeach William's Whig advisors. The Act can be seen as a reaction against the policies of William and not simply an attempt to resurrect some of the reforming zeal of 1689. The clause concerning the religion of the monarch reflected concerns over William's Calvinism as much as a fear of Catholicism and another proviso preventing the monarch from leaving Britain without the permission of parliament is rooted in a fear of William doing just that. It is no coincidence that the clause concerning the flight of the monarch was repealed in 1716, when it was no longer seen as necessary as William was no longer king.

The fear of absolutism and a desire to rein in the king is clear throughout the Act. No future foreign monarch was allowed to enter England into a war in order to defend the monarch's home country without the consent of parliament, which serves as a clear response to the potential threat of William. William had entered England into the expensive Nine Years' War (the implications of which are discussed later in the chapter – see pages 129–130). All matters regarding the governing of Britain had to be discussed with the full Privy Council and not decided by the monarch alone. No foreign-born man was allowed to join the Privy Council, sit in either House of Parliament, have a military command, or be granted lands or titles.

## How far did the Bill of Rights and Act of Settlement confirm the end of divine right monarchy?

There can be no doubt that the concept of divine right monarchy was severely damaged by the Revolution settlement and many historians see it as a watershed moment in the reduction of the Crown's prerogative powers. After the Bill of Rights was passed, it was no longer possible for monarchs to claim their power came from God, as their authority was approved by the people through their representatives in parliament. The concept of divine right was one of the issues over which the original Civil War had been fought in 1642, and the victors had briefly established a republican system between 1649 and 1660. The concept again came to the forefront of politics after the Restoration in 1660.

### The establishment of a constitutional monarchy - differing interpretations

Historians have developed different views over the centuries on the impact of the Bill of Rights and Act of Settlement. The Whig domination of parliament that began during the reign of William continued with Robert Walpole, who became prime minister in 1721, and Whig writers maintained that the Bill of Rights preserved England's 'ancient constitution' from the absolutism of James II; therefore, it represented the restoration of previous political stability, rather than creating an entirely new settlement. The Whig view gradually developed to present the political settlement as a starting point of a new constitution, a revolution where both Tories and Whigs compromised and a constitutional monarchy was established. This view became so well established that it was included in school textbooks, most famously Edward Baldwin's *The History of England for the Use of Schools* (1806). This interpretation presented parliament as the supreme authority in the political system after the settlement and the post-revolution era was seen as the beginning of a new period of English history. Even the Marxist historians Christopher Hill and A.L. Morton borrowed much from Whig theorists and went on to present the settlement as one that created a constitutional monarchy in the interests of the existing ruling elites.

Some revisionist historians such as John Morrill (Extract 3) have attacked the importance given by Whigs and Marxists to the Revolution and have instead presented the events as changing virtually nothing except the line of succession. They believe that a constitutional monarchy was not fully established, although the concept of divine right was effectively destroyed. Parliament was still officially an advisory body only and the office of prime minister did not emerge until Robert Walpole informally took the title alongside the already established office of First Lord of the Treasury in 1721. The monarch was still pre-eminent within the political system, parliament still represented only the richest two percent of the population and the electorate was still small. It was not until 1760 that the 'crown estate' was created and most of the monarch's property was placed under the control of parliament.

**EXTRACT 3**

From J. Morrill, 'The Sensible Revolution, 1688' in *The Nature of the English Revolution* (1993).

The Sensible Revolution of 1688-9 was a conservative Revolution. It did not create damaging new rifts in the English nation, although it did sharpen and to some extent extend divisions in Scotland and Ireland that were of lasting consequence. The constitutional settlement and the ecclesiastical settlements were both fudges. It was possible in 1689 for all kinds of people to continue to believe all sorts of contradictory things... [such as that] James had been lawfully resisted by his subjects because he had violated their civil rights and threatened the true religion; or that there had been no resistance in 1688, only passive disobedience, and that William's expedition had been intended merely to remonstrate with his uncle about the violations of Englishmen's rights, and to secure his wife's rights to the succession in the face of a possible dynastic fraud... If the actors in 1689 were confused, largely unprincipled, living from day-to-day and scrambling for solutions, then there can be no turning-point, no great divide. The 'revisionist' question precludes the Whig answer. In establishing a new pattern of constitutional relationships (many of them unanticipated); in creating a new context within which men and women had to make sense of spiritual and moral imperatives; in crystallizing out the two great parties which, in constant evolution, would dominate English politics for the next 200 years; in forcing a redefinition of England's relationship to Europe and the world... the events of 1688-9 quickened and nurtured a distinctive phase in British historical development.

What was created through the political settlement can best be described as a monarchy of parliament's choosing. Parliament effectively decided who the next monarch would be and parliament could suspend the Mutiny Act at any time in order to restrict the king's control of the army. It could also be argued that the framework for a constitutional monarchy had initially been established with the Magna Carta in 1215, as the monarch was compelled to consult a 'great council' over at least some issues. It is perhaps best to describe the Bill of Rights and Act of Settlement as the further foundations of a constitutional monarchy, rather than the end product. Royal interference with the law was now restricted, elections were to be regular and free from the interference of the monarch, and taxation by royal prerogative was theoretically no longer possible.

**ACTIVITIES**
**KNOWLEDGE CHECK**

**The political settlement**

1. How could it be argued that the political settlement was revolutionary?
2. What evidence can you find to show that the political settlement favoured William rather than parliament?
3. Which historical interpretation of the political settlement are you most convinced by and why?

# WHAT WAS THE IMPACT OF THE TOLERATION ACT OF 1689 AND THE END OF ANGLICAN SUPREMACY?

## The importance of the Toleration Act

As well as a political settlement, a religious settlement was also established after the Glorious Revolution. Anglican Churchmen were concerned with ensuring that worship within the Church remained uniform and was not modified. In early 1689, William urged the removal of the sacramental test for public office holders, which would mean repealing the Test Act that expected all office holders to take Anglican Communion. As a compromise, William suggested that a Toleration Act be passed with a promise for Tory and Anglican demands for uniformity to be referred to **Convocation** later in the year. William was well aware of the need to maintain good relations with both dissenters and Anglicans, so attempted to pursue a middle path.

The Act was passed by the reluctant Tories and it was influenced most obviously by John Locke's **A Letter Concerning Toleration**, printed in 1689 but prepared in the years before. William, who favoured toleration and was originally suspicious of the Anglican Church, was met with confrontation from the Tories, who were fearful that he wanted to impose Dutch Calvinism. Under the terms of the Act, dissenters were exempted from punishments if they took the oath of allegiance to the Crown and accepted the 1678 Test Act, meaning they could not enter public employment without swearing loyalty to the Anglican Church. Dissenters were therefore not expected to attend an Anglican church, but their meetings were closely monitored and the doors of their meeting places could not be locked. The Act even made special dispensations for certain dissenting groups: as the Quakers refused to take oaths, they were allowed to declare, rather than swear, that they denied the pope's authority. The Act certainly made it easier for dissenters to worship freely and, by 1714, there were around 400,000 dissenters in England.

The Toleration Act served to humiliate the Anglican clergy and Tories in the Commons. The Whig majority in parliament, who had been keen for the Act to be passed, then insisted that the clergy take an oath of allegiance to William and Mary. As they had already sworn allegiance to James and believed in the concept of passive obedience to his royal authority, many were troubled by this demand, and over 400 parish priests refused and were deprived of their livings. This gave the Whigs a perfect excuse to attack the Tories and High Church clergy, accusing them of being more loyal to James than to William. The clergy that were removed from office were replaced by more moderate men, sympathetic to the Whig cause.

### Who was excluded from the Act's provisions and why?

The Act excluded Catholics, **non-Trinitarians** and Jews. As the Test Act was not repealed, non-Anglicans could still not sit in parliament or hold public office. Those who did not swear allegiance to the Anglican Church could not attend university, work in the legal profession or practise medicine. Even those dissenting groups that were tolerated under the terms of the Act were not fully equal to Anglicans, as they still had to pay tithes to a Church to which they did not attend and did not belong. In reality, Catholics had little to fear from William, as he had effectively guaranteed their safety by entering into an alliance with a number of Catholic powers against the French in the League of Augsburg in 1686. (This alliance would later fight together in the Nine Years' War.) A number of Whigs commented that Catholics were really the group that gained most from the Revolution and, when Frenchman Henri Misson commented on the state of England in the 1690s, he noted that, despite legal limitations, Catholics appeared to enjoy universal toleration.

**KEY TERMS**

**Convocation**
An assembly of the Church. Members of the clergy, including bishops and representatives of the ordinary clergy, meet to discuss issues surrounding the future policy of the Church, the collection of Church taxes and the content of sermons.

**A Letter Concerning Toleration**
A letter to an unnamed individual, originally published without Locke's knowledge. Locke argued that having a wide variety of religious groups in society actually prevents civil unrest, as minority religious groups would not feel the need to protest against their oppression. He also argued that the state and Church should be separate institutions, as they cater for different aspects of people's lives. The state promotes political liberty and welfare, the Church only exists to promote spiritual salvation.

**Non-Trinitarian**
Someone who does not believe in the doctrine of the Trinity – the notion that divinity exists within God, Jesus and the Holy Spirit equally.

## The end of Anglican supremacy

### Was the Anglican Church and confessional state undermined?

The Toleration Act and events of the period 1688–1701 served to undermine the established Anglican Church in a number of ways, and the historian Christopher Hill has argued (Extract 4) that the role of religion in local government and the legal system was also reduced.

- It was now accepted that the Church of England could not enforce complete uniformity and that some allowances had to be made for dissenters. The dissenters flourished and made up nearly eight percent of the population by 1714.
- Catholics enjoyed a reasonable degree of freedom despite being excluded from the provisions of the Toleration Act. Contemporaries reported that many Catholics were able to participate in mass without any trouble.
- William used his royal authority to influence judges and curb Church interference in the lives of Catholics and dissenting sects not covered by the Act.
- The power of Church courts, which had been crucial in upholding the authority of the confessional state earlier in the century, was severely restricted by the Toleration Act.

**EXTRACT 4**

From C. Hill, *The Century of Revolution* (1961).

The Toleration Act of 1689 finally killed off the old conception of a single state Church of which all Englishmen were members. The parish became more exclusively a local-government area, whose officers regarded themselves as responsible to secular rather than to ecclesiastical authority. The attempt to punish 'sin' by judicial process was virtually abandoned. The laity had won its centuries-long struggle against the Church courts. In this respect too the Middle Ages were over... The Toleration Act served a political purpose: It was necessary for national unity and the safety of the regime that dissenters should be allowed freedom of worship. But they remained excluded from political life.

However, a number of historians (see Extract 5) argue that the Anglican Church still had an important role.

- Crucially, the statutes enforcing uniformity (Test Act and Act of Uniformity) that had been passed under earlier Stuart monarchs were not repealed, which meant that public officials were duty-bound to swear allegiance to the Church.
- To gain public employment or join parliament, there was no choice but to swear allegiance to the Crown and take Anglican Communion.
- There was no great theological debate between MPs and peers before the Toleration Act was passed. It can be seen as a reactionary attempt to maintain order and preserve the Anglican Church.
- As Extract 5 makes clear, further Toleration Acts were passed in Scotland and Ireland, and these did not give dissenters the opportunity to participate in national or local government.

There was a fear in the royal court that the alternative to Anglican supremacy was a dangerous slide into religious radicalism and social revolution.

**EXTRACT 5**

From J. Champion, 'Toleration and Citizenship in Enlightenment England' in O.P. Grell and R. Porter, *Toleration in Enlightenment Europe* (1999).

To some extent, England remained a confessional state: the Toleration Act (1689) and succeeding acts in Scotland (1712) and Ireland (1719), while establishing rights to public worship to Protestant dissenters, did not break the connection between religious identity and civil rights. Penal laws removed did not enfranchise even Protestant dissenters to participate in local and national office: the Test and Corporation Acts (1673, 1661) meant that to be a fully competent subject all individuals had to swear oaths of allegiance and supremacy to the Crown and certificate that they had taken Anglican sacraments. These statutory requirements excluded not only the obvious minorities - Catholics, Quakers, Jews, Muslims, atheists - but also many of the more mainstream Protestant dissenters. This compromise between full toleration of a diversity of religious beliefs and the restriction of full civil liberties to the Anglican confession was the result of the theological origins of the Toleration Act itself. The statutory legislation of 1689 was the result of complex and careful negotiation between Anglican and dissenting interests rather than the conclusion of conceptual considerations about the rights of conscience. Such statutory provisions were calculated to avoid much more dangerous alternatives being advanced: the overwhelming imperative was to preserve the authority and legitimacy of the 'true' Anglican religion.

**THINKING HISTORICALLY** Interpretations (4a)

**The weight of evidence**

Work in pairs.

Read Extracts 4 and 5, then complete the activity and answer the questions.

1. Use highlighter pens to colour-code copies of the extracts. Use one colour for 'evidence', another colour for 'conclusions' and a third for language that shows the historian is 'reasoning' (e.g. 'therefore', 'so'). Alternatively, draw up a table with three columns, headed 'Evidence', 'Conclusions' and 'Reasoning language' and copy the relevant parts of the extracts into the columns.
2. How do the extracts differ in terms of the way that the evidence is used?
3. Which of these extracts do you find more convincing? Which has the best-supported arguments?
4. What other information might you want in order to make a judgement about the strength of these claims?
5. Write a paragraph of 200 words explaining the importance of using evidence to support historical claims.

**ACTIVITIES KNOWLEDGE CHECK**

**The end of Anglican supremacy**

1. In your opinion, was the confessional state undermined? Explain your answer.
2. Read Extract 5. Why does the author believe that the confessional state did not end after the Toleration Act was passed?

**AS Level Exam-Style Question Section C**

***Study Extracts 4 and 5 before you answer this question.***

Historians have different views about how revolutionary, in the years to 1701, the Glorious Revolution was. Analyse and evaluate the extracts and use your knowledge of the issues to explain your answer to the following question.

How far do you agree with the view that England was no longer a confessional state in the years 1688–1701 as a result of the Glorious Revolution? (20 marks)

**Tip**

*Both extracts focus heavily on religious matters and the concept of toleration, but links should be made with the wider political issues.*

# HOW SIGNIFICANT WAS THE TRIENNIAL ACT OF 1694 IN PROMOTING PARLIAMENTARY POWER?

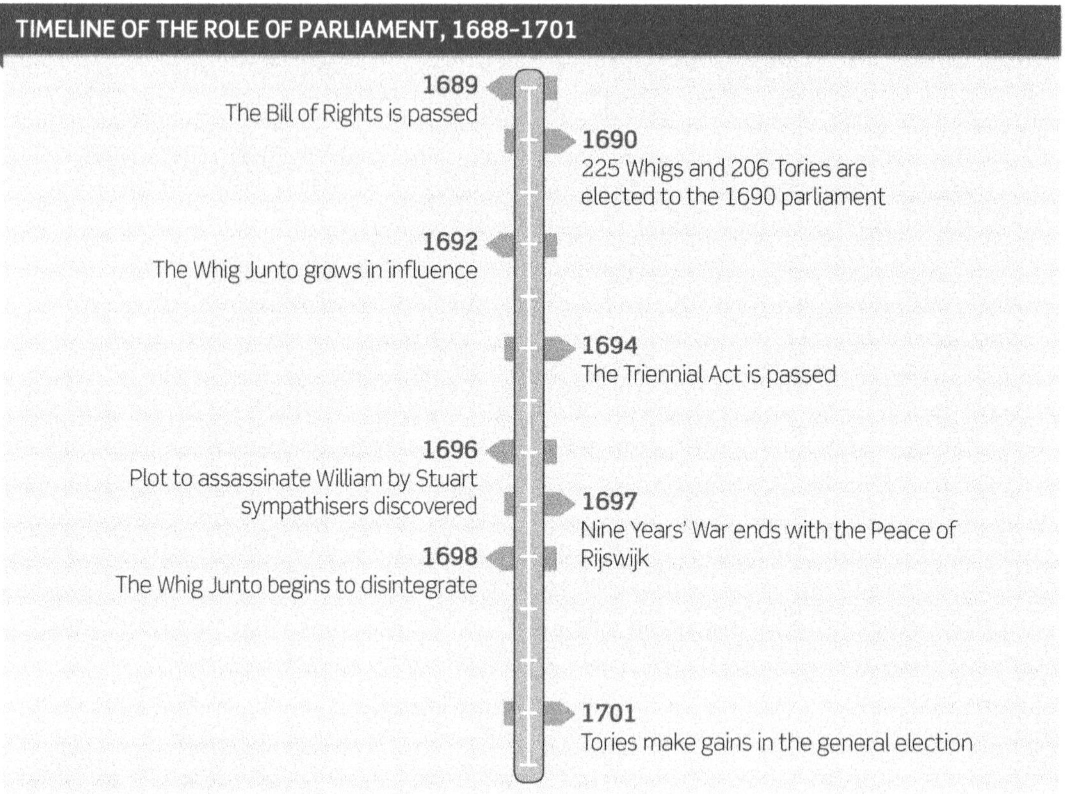


## The role of Parliament, 1688-93

### William's advisers

William used his prerogative powers immediately after becoming king in order to form a Privy Council of his own choosing. His choice of Lord Halifax as Lord Privy Seal was not surprising, as he had become a close advisor to William after being dismissed by James. Halifax had led the House of Lords in their discussions about the political settlement during the Convention Parliament and, perhaps most crucially, he was not loyal to either the Tory or Whig parties. William struggled to understand the system of political parties and was keen to appoint someone who would be able to transcend their differences. The Earl of Danby, who had helped arrange the marriage of William and Mary in 1677, was appointed Lord President of the Council. A carefully selected balance of Whigs and Tories were appointed to other posts, although they struggled to command the respect of the Commons.

**EXTEND YOUR KNOWLEDGE**

**George Savile, First Marquess of Halifax (1633-95)**

Savile came from a Yorkshire gentry family and was first elected as an MP in the Convention Parliament of 1660. In 1667, he was elevated to the peerage and became a privy councillor under Charles II in 1672. He was active in the passage of the Test Act, earning him the scorn of the Catholic James II, who was at the time the Duke of York.

In the early 1680s, Savile concentrated on improving relations between Charles and William of Orange, but when James succeeded Charles in 1685 he fell out of favour. He helped to pave the way for William by supporting the Seven Bishops who had opposed the Declaration of Indulgence but, oddly, he did not sign the invitation sent to William.

Savile succeeded in persuading the Lords to accept William and Mary as joint sovereigns, and enjoyed unrivalled influence on the Privy Council. However, his failure to support either the Whig or Tory factions in parliament left him isolated and his career fell into decline. Amid suspicions that he was beginning to sympathise with the Stuart cause, he was removed from the Privy Council in June 1692.

### William's relationship with the political parties

The parliament of 1690 consisted of 225 Whigs and 206 Tories. William's natural allies should have been the Whigs, who favoured progressive reform and had originally called for a Protestant succession. William originally believed they were too radical and had suspicions that a number of them were, in fact, republicans. He hoped to woo the Tories, who he knew to favour tradition and strict loyalty to the monarchy and the Anglican Church. The first session of the 1690 parliament saw a strengthening in the position of the Privy Council over parliament and an opposition attempt to establish a parliamentary commission to investigate government accounts was rejected. Meanwhile, James was amassing a force in Ireland in an attempt to return to power, and William left to fight him in the summer of 1690, culminating in his victory at the Battle of the Boyne in July. The councillors who he left in charge in his absence reflected his clear preference for loyal Court Tories.

The war in Ireland, which became known as the Williamite War (1689–91) had started when James held a parliament in Ireland in 1689, where the majority of the Catholic gentry of Ireland offered their support to his cause. Over 80,000 soldiers fought on both sides and, although William achieved a relatively swift victory, some historians have used the war as evidence that the Glorious Revolution was not the peaceful and sensible transition suggested by the Whigs. Over 8,000 people died when William's forces defended the Siege of Derry in 1689, and half of James' soldiers were killed or captured at the Battle of Aughrim in July 1691. The cost of the war in Ireland was a concern for parliament and the Whigs, headed by Robert Harley, were able to establish a commission of accounts in an attempt to control expenditure. In 1691–92, divisions in William's council over strategy led to a series of defeats to the French in the Nine Years' War (1688–97) between Louis XIV and an alliance of other European states. The Williamite War in Ireland, as well as a **Jacobite** rising in Scotland (1689–92), which resulted in a massacre of James' supporters by Williamites at Glencoe in 1692, have been interpreted by historians as extensions of the wider Nine Years' War.

A group of Whig rebels known as the '**Whig Junto**' became influential between 1692 and 1693. They favoured a strong executive and supported William's war. There was an attempt to push through a triennial bill in order to ensure regular parliaments. This was passed by both Houses and William was forced to use his royal veto to deny the bill becoming law. The king was only holding onto his position of predominance within the political system with difficulty.

#### KEY TERMS

**Jacobite**
A supporter of James II and his descendants in their claim to the British throne.

**Whig Junto**
A group of Whig leaders who influenced the direction of policy. The group consisted of Edward Russell, John Somers, Thomas Wharton and Charles Montagu. They held considerable influence in government between 1694 and 1699, but as the members of the group gradually inherited or were given peerages, their influence in the Commons began to wane. Despite their success in the Commons, their success in the Lords was limited. They favoured war with France in order to promote the Protestant cause in Europe.

## The significance of the Triennial Act, 1694

By the beginning of 1694, the Whig Junto was beginning to dominate government: Montagu became Chancellor of the Exchequer, Somers Lord Keeper and Russell First Lord of the Admiralty. The triennial bill was debated again and received the royal assent in January 1694. Under the terms of the Triennial Act, a parliament could not last longer than three years, which meant general elections would be held more regularly. More seats were contested in these regular elections, as Edward Vallance discusses in Extract 6. Rivalry between Whigs and Tories was stronger than ever, but regular elections meant that it was difficult for the Crown to establish a party in the House of Commons, leading to William becoming more reliant on securing support from MPs. The Act was repealed in 1716 and replaced with the Septennial Act, which allowed for elections every seven years.

The period from circa 1690 to 1715 has been referred to by historians as the Rage of Party, characterised by the instability caused by frequent elections. With more regular elections came a renewed interest in politics from those outside the immediate political nation and the electorate were better informed than they had ever been as a result of the lapsing of the Licensing Act of 1695, which had previously led to heavy censorship of the press. This new press freedom allowed for political pamphleteering and journalism to influence the votes of the 200,000 men that could vote. The impact that the Act had on both parliament and government is discussed in Extracts 6 and 7.

**EXTRACT**

From E. Vallance, *The Glorious Revolution: 1688 – Britain's Fight for Liberty* (2006).

Military success made Parliament more ready to lend money... William's assent to the Triennial Act of 1694... ensured regular Parliaments and ushered in a period of feverish electioneering and deeply partisan politics. Between 1689 and 1715 there were twelve general elections: in 1689, 1690, 1695, 1698, 1701 (two), 1702, 1705, 1708, 1710, 1713 and 1715. Each of these saw on average 100 out of 269 seats contested... Over that period only nineteen constituencies managed to avoid having contests at all, meaning that in almost every constituency in England the local electorate was at some point asked to decide between rival candidates... politics was increasingly being governed by loyalty to one or other party. There is strong evidence that after 1695 voting in the Commons was conducted largely along party lines, with only 14 percent of MPs regularly engaging in cross-party voting.

EXTRACT 7

From H. Horwitz, *Parliament, Policy and Politics in the Reign of William III* (1977).

It was the conflict over issues and the competition for places among those loyal to William that principally shaped domestic politics between 1689 and 1702. Pre-Revolution issues were not all resolved in 1689. The Revolution itself was a subject of controversy, and the King's policies engendered new disputes. And despite the enlargement of the government apparatus during the war, there was never a shortage of suitors for offices of profit in the crown's gift... William is said to have exclaimed on occasion 'that he wished every man, that was in any office, immortal', so that he would not be badgered about the disposition of their posts. The competition for place was affected, in turn, by the enhanced importance of parliament. Seats in the Commons were more and more stepping-stones to office, so that Harley's prediction before the general election of 1695 that the new triennial legislation would help to 'render gentlemen less willing to spend money to come into the House' proved to be mistaken. As Lord Cheyne observed... 'In truth, a seat in parliament is not worth the pains we undergo to attain, but a place at Court with a seat there is most people's aim.'

ACTIVITY
KNOWLEDGE CHECK

**The Triennial Act**

Outline the impact that the Triennial Act had according to Extracts 6 and 7. Where do their interpretations differ?

Interpretations (3a)

**Differing accounts**

Carefully read the two historical interpretations of the impact of the Triennial Act in Extracts 6 and 7 before completing the activities that follow.

1 For each of the historians, create a summary table of their views. The table should include the following headings down the left-hand side:

- Why was the Triennial Act important?
- What impact did it have on parliament?
- What impact did it have on William's government?

Across the top of the table, you should include these headings:

- Interpretation of the issue
- Evidence they provide
- Evidence that supports or challenges this view (from own knowledge)

2 In pairs discuss which historian's interpretation seems to best fit with the available evidence. Which seems the most convincing?

3 Make a note of any issues that made it difficult to compare the two interpretations directly.

**Challenge:** Seek out another historical interpretation of the state of parliament and government after the Triennial Act and compare this to the views you have explored already.

## The role of parliament, 1694–1701

The Triennial Act gave the Commons a new-found confidence and, in 1695, a number of inquiries were set up to investigate corruption in government. The Speaker, Sir John Trevor, was accused of accepting a bribe of 1,000 guineas in order to assist with the passage of a bill and William was convinced that parliament would have to be dissolved in order to prevent the inquiries from continuing. When this happened, another election was held in October 1695. This election favoured the Whigs, who cemented their dominance over parliament and the Privy Council. When, in February 1696, a plot by Stuart sympathisers to assassinate the king was discovered, the Whigs became more united than ever and, with the potential of a French invasion never far away, William seemed more dependent than ever on the Whig faction in parliament and the Whig Junto in the Privy Council. Both Houses adopted a Whig proposal acknowledging William as the lawful king and reasserted their belief in him through a loyal 'Association', although 89 Tories did not sign it. A reminder that opposition to the Whig faction was still lingering was given in 1697, when the opposition to the Junto in the council were able to secure a vote that limited William to sustaining an army of just 10,000 men through government grants.

**SOURCE 3** The Lords Justices placed in charge of William's government while he was on campaign in 1695. His choice of administrators included three Whigs: John Somers, Baron Somers; Charles Talbot, First Earl of Shrewsbury; and William Cavendish, First Duke of Devonshire; one Tory: Sidney Godolphin, First Earl of Godolphin; a poet: Charles Sackville, Sixth Earl of Dorset; and the Archbishop of Canterbury, Thomas Tenison. From an engraving by Robert White, a professional artist and portrait painter, 1695.

The tug-of-war between the king's ministry and the Commons continued throughout 1697 and 1698, although the Junto usually garnered enough support to govern as they pleased. The election of 1698 was marked by a distrust of the Whig Junto, and the rivalry between **Court and Country** interests was as strong as ever. The Country opposition were able to secure a bill that restricted the size of the army in England to 7,000 and refused to allow the retention of William's Dutch guard. As well as this, a commission was set up to investigate the Crown's choice of recipients for confiscated lands in Ireland. In 1698, it seemed clear that William had little room for manoeuvre and parliament was dictating policy.

### KEY TERMS

**Court and Country**
The two broad factions within parliament in the period c1680–1740. The Court party were loyal to the Crown, and the Country party consisted of disaffected Whigs and some Tories who believed that the Court party were corrupting politics.

**Bill of resumption**
The bill of resumption stated that any grants of land in Ireland given to members of the Privy Council were illegal. 13 trustees were to be appointed in order to hear claims to estates in Ireland and sell them to the most appropriate individuals. The money arising from the sale of lands was to go towards the arrears of pay due to the army.

Initial amendments made by the Lords were rejected by the Commons, who seemed exasperated with the government, and when the Lords suddenly gave up their opposition to the bill, William gave it the royal assent.

The heavy blows sustained by the government in 1698 contributed to the Junto dismantling. Montagu was demoted within the Privy Council and Russell was forced to resign his rank within the Admiralty. Only Somers survived. In 1699, the commission investigating confiscated lands in Ireland issued its report and found that William had made excessive grants to loyal courtiers. The Commons put forward a **bill of resumption**, which infuriated William, who saw it as an infringement of his royal prerogative and a personal insult. After an attempt by the Lords to stall the bill, William reluctantly gave it the royal assent, allowing the parliamentary session to be brought to an end. The Commons also petitioned for the resignation of Somers, which William again saw as a personal affront to his authority, and, although the opposition lost the vote on Somers's future, he resigned. In the election of 1701, the Tories made gains and instigated impeachment proceedings against Somers, Montagu and Russell, although they were eventually acquitted by their fellow parliamentarians.

### ACTIVITY
KNOWLEDGE CHECK

**The role of parliament**

Was parliament in a strong position after the Triennial Act was passed? Explain your answer.

**AS Level Exam-Style Question Section C**

***Study Extracts 6 and 7 before you answer this question.***

Historians have different views about how revolutionary, in the years to 1701, the Glorious Revolution was. Analyse and evaluate the extracts and use your knowledge of the issues to explain your answer to the following question.

How far do you agree with the view that the power of parliament increased in the years 1688–1701 as a result of the Glorious Revolution? (20 marks)

**Tip**

*Consider both the benefits and drawbacks of the Triennial Act for William and parliament, as well as the other Acts that were passed.*

## How far did parliament become a partner in government?

If the Revolution did not represent the dawn of parliamentary democracy, it certainly represented a move towards parliamentary government. William needed parliamentary taxes to fight the French and this resulted in parliament gaining increased control over government finance, as discussed later in the chapter. Through the Triennial Act, it became an institution that the monarch could not ignore. Political necessity had forced William to appoint men he loathed (he refused to speak to Wharton) and he was forced to reduce the size of the army as a result of a parliamentary decision. The argument in favour of parliament becoming a partner in government is a strong one.

- Parliament was able to encroach on areas that were once firmly part of the royal prerogative, such as the king's appointment of ministers and control of the army.
- The Triennial Act did enhance the power of parliament, but this authority would not have been possible without the Bill of Rights. Under its terms, parliament had to give approval for a standing army to be kept in peace time and taxation without parliamentary consent was illegal.
- Earlier monarchs, such as Charles I, had refused demands for parliament to be given more power on the grounds that its only purpose was to raise money for the Crown. This was no longer the case and the monarchy was faced with no option but to work with parliament.
- The Bill of Rights gave guarantees that the abuses of power experienced under James II would not be repeated.
- The monarch was not allowed to interfere with elections and the proceedings of parliament could not be questioned by judges.
- The financial settlement reached ensured that William and Mary would be financially dependent on parliament, as discussed further in the chapter.

Although parliament had become an integral part of the political system, there was still a desire among many of the political class to join the royal court, which strengthened William's hand. Much of the royal prerogative was left intact, such as the sovereign's power to declare war, to dissolve parliament and veto legislation if he desired. Through the Civil List Act of 1697, parliament decided to give a grant of £700,000 per year to William for life, in order to cover the expenses of the royal household, as well as salaries for diplomats and judges. This is perhaps the best example of king and parliament working in unison; he still had vast power and commanded deep respect, but was more aware than any previous monarch of the need to gain the approval of the elected representatives.

**ACTIVITIES**
**KNOWLEDGE CHECK**

**King and parliament**

**1** Create a timeline to show the key events in the relationship between king and parliament between 1689 and 1701. Mark on the timeline:

- events that show parliament was becoming a partner in government
- events that show that William was using his prerogative in order to resist or reduce parliamentary power.

**2** Read Extracts 6 and 7. Which interpretation are you most convinced by and why?

# HOW IMPORTANT WERE WILLIAM III'S WARS IN THE DEVELOPMENT OF A FINANCIAL REVOLUTION?

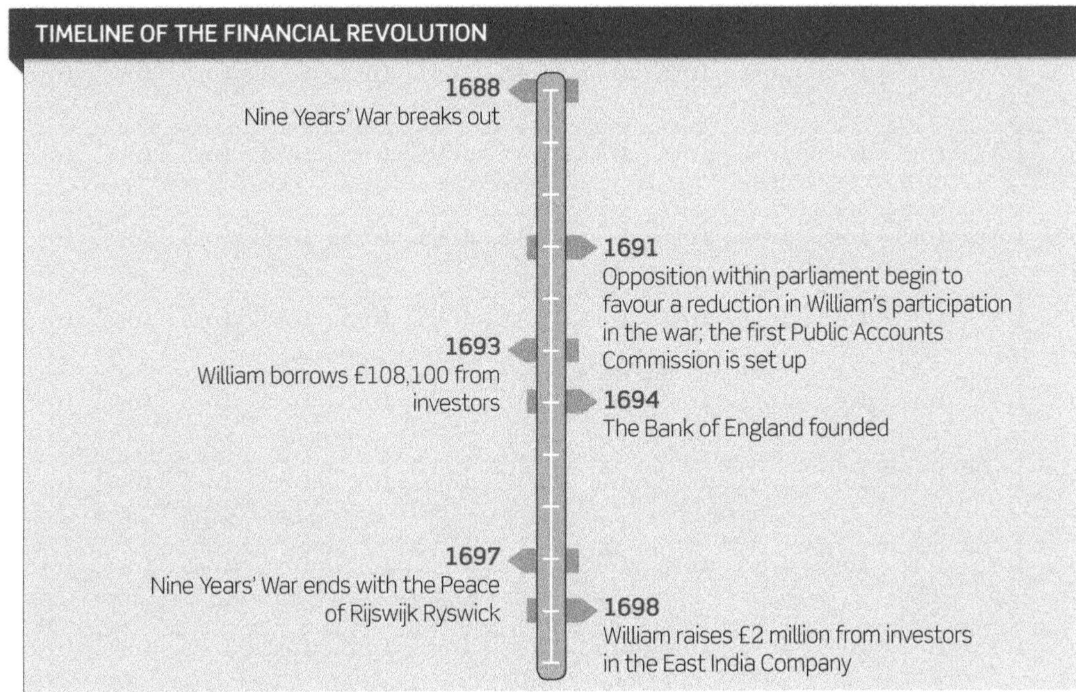


## The Nine Years' War and the restructuring of government finances

### The course of the war

The Nine Years' War (1688–97) was fought between the League of Augsburg, led by Holland, England, Spain and the Holy Roman Empire, and France under Louis XIV. William, as head of state in both Holland and Britain, spent a total of six years on campaign, making many key strategic decisions himself. He was concerned with ensuring that France was not able to dominate, and that balance was restored to, European politics. This marked a complete transformation in British foreign policy, and William was certainly taking a risk by committing millions of pounds and thousands of troops to the war effort. The war caused strain between William and parliament, as the huge sums he was demanding to fund the war had never been approved by a parliament before.

Louis appeared to have a number of advantages, including authority through divine right in his own country and a larger number of troops. After 1691, the opposition within parliament favoured a reduction in William's participation and only voted him funding for 10,000 troops. Merchants in particular were unhappy with the continuing hostilities and trading routes in the North Sea, Mediterranean and African coast became too dangerous after 1693. William succeeded in recruiting 68,000 men at a cost of £2.8 million through borrowing, via the newly established Bank of England in 1695, and attempted to keep parliament informed of his progress at regular intervals. Despite this, criticism of the campaign was heaped on William for the impact it was having on trade, his use of foreign commanders and his poor performances. In the face of opposition from parliament, William took many key decisions himself, such as the placement of troops and negotiations with other states. Although he entered peace talks with the French after 1696, Louis did not offer a satisfactory settlement to William and French negotiators refused to acknowledge William as the legitimate King of England.

Despite the stalling of peace talks, both sides were bankrupt by 1697, and William was facing increasing opposition from the Tories and non-Junto Whigs in parliament. They argued that the army should be reduced in size again and that the taxes that had been used to pay for the war should be reduced. Peace talks resumed and with both sides weary of war and the French suffering an economic crisis, a settlement was reached under the terms of the Treaty of Ryswick in September

1697. Peace was officially declared between France and the three powers: England, Spain and the Dutch United Provinces. The French agreed to abandon their claims for land in Germany and Holland, and Louis was forced to accept that William was the legitimate King of England, and promised to give no assistance to James II. The French had also made gains from the English in North America, and so the borders were returned to those that existed before 1688.

SOURCE 

4 The battle of La Hogue between a combined Anglo-Dutch fleet and France, May–June 1692, from a contemporary engraving by the Dutch artist Romeyn de Hooghe. Battles such as this cost the Crown huge sums of money and forced a change in the structure of government finances.

### Restructuring of government finances

The average annual expenditure in the Nine Years' War was just over £5.4 million, however the average tax revenue was just £3.6 million. William was able to achieve this level of revenue primarily through excise taxes on items such as tea, tobacco and alcohol. The most significant revenue stream was the land tax, which provided for around a third of all required funds. The landed elites were most liable to pay this tax and the efficiency with which it was collected suggests that the war had the tacit approval of many of them.

An administrative revolution was taking place, similar to that seen under Henry VIII when royal income from the dissolved monasteries buoyed the treasury. The unprecedented levels of taxation meant that royal income doubled after 1688. The land tax was introduced in 1692 and yielded £1 million in its first year. In order to meet the shortfall in funding for the war, a new system of public credit was established. This involved the Crown taking out long-term loans from merchants and City traders and repaying them with interest, effectively selling the government's debt. This would, in turn, lead to the creation of the National Debt. The National Debt stood at £16.7 million by 1698 and repayments took up around 30 percent of the Crown's annual revenue. This was a relatively secure debt, since it had been underwritten by parliament and the loans employed by William were long-term.

| Date of loan | Amount borrowed | Interest (%) | Details of loan |
|---|---|---|---|
| January 1693 | £108,100 | 10 | Investors received an annual dividend on their investment |
| January 1693 | £773,394 | 14 | Investors received return payments for life |
| February 1694 | £118,506 | 14 | Investors received return payments for life |
| March 1694 | £1,000,000 | 14 | 100,000 £10 tickets sold as a lottery |
| April 1694 | £1,200,000 | 8 | Investors were incorporated into the Bank of England |
| April 1697 | £1,400,000 | 6.3 | A 'malt lottery' where the benefits were to be paid to investors from excise taxes on malt |
| July 1698 | £2,000,000 | 8 | Investors incorporated into the East India Company |

**Figure 5.1**: Table showing the loans levied by William to fund the Nine Years' War.

By the end of the war, Dutch merchants could not endure further disruption to trade and the English gentry could no longer tolerate the burden of the land tax. William had raised more in tax than any previous monarch, but it was not enough. As we have seen, by the end of the war, government debt stood at nearly £17 million. The financial settlement of 1690 had been designed by parliament to be insufficient for William to live off. A further settlement was established in 1698 when the Civil List Act was passed. The king was now given a 'civil list' of income estimated at £700,000 per year, with any surplus only granted with the consent of parliament. This money was allocated to meet the expenses of William's government, including the salaries of civil servants and judges, and the expenditure of the royal household. Importantly, all military and naval expenditure, in times of peace and war, was the responsibility of parliament. King and parliament had to meet regularly in order to renew the civil list, so it can be concluded that it was the financial settlement of the 1690s, rather than the Triennial Act or Bill of Rights, that necessitated regular meetings of parliament.

## Public scrutiny of government income and expenditure

During William's reign, concerns among backbenchers about the huge sums of money spent on war led to a number of parliamentary commissions being set up to investigate government expenditure. The commissions were the forerunner to modern-day select committees within parliament, made up of MPs. The commissions had the power to interrogate ministers and call for papers from government to be read and consulted in order to establish whether money had been spent appropriately. The commissioners would then publish reports, which would often expose corruption or waste at William's court. William was actually the first to suggest he opened up his accounts to inspection and such scrutiny had rarely been permitted before. For a while in 1689, the MPs were unsure about how they would go about their investigations as there was no precedent for this kind of procedure. The commissions were successful in bringing a number of ministers to account.

In 1690, William had agreed to the Public Accounts Act and the first commission was set up in 1691, with nine commissioners voted to their positions by the MPs. The commission was renewed each year until 1697, although William blocked more being established. The commission would be revived again during Queen Anne's reign. When the first commission met, Whig members, such as Robert Harley, and Tories such as Sir Benjamin Newland worked well together in their common concern to expose deficiencies within government expenditure. The nine-strong commission were paid £500 per year each and were ultimately responsible to parliament rather than the monarch. When two members, Sir Robert Rich and Robert Austen, were given roles in the Admiralty by William, they were removed from the next commission. After this, it comprised seven members for the rest of William's reign.

The scrutiny was carried out with unprecedented attention to detail. Meetings took place daily and interviews were regularly carried out, although government officials would often obstruct the process. As a result of this obstruction, many of the intended reports were never completed and it became difficult to make definitive suggestions for financial improvement. Despite this, the reports would make clear where ministers had evaded questions and refused to present accounts, thus implicating them in mismanagement. William was generally happy to adopt suggestions made by the commission and it was successful in compelling him to reassess the size of the army and navy.

Members of the commission were able to criticise government expenditure in the chamber of the Commons and members such as Robert Harley became members of the Country opposition. In the second half of the 1690s, the commission lost some of its initial impact and was increasingly used to attack unfavourable ministers rather than to act as a check on finances. High profile members of the House, such as the speaker Sir John Trevor, were expelled for financial malpractice.

ACTIVITIES
KNOWLEDGE CHECK

**Restructuring of finances**

1 How did the Nine Years' War change the relationship between William and parliament?

2 Was the restructuring of government finances revolutionary or necessary?

3 Was the Public Accounts Act a success or failure?

KEY TERM

**Tontine loan**
A method for raising capital. Investors can pay into the fund in order to provide a loan, which is paid back with interest. Each investor receives annual dividends on the money they originally paid in. As each investor dies, their invested share is reassigned to the surviving members, thus increasing their yield.

## The establishment of the Bank of England, 1694

The Bank of England was the brainchild of the Whig Chancellor, Charles Montagu, and was supported by many Whigs but opposed by leading Tories. From 1692 onwards, parliament had been increasingly interested in schemes for long-term borrowing, and a **tontine loan** to the Crown had been levied in 1693 and was seen as a reasonable success. The interest received by the investors was to be taken from a number of excise duties for 99 years, although investors were wary of its complexities and it yielded only £108,000 for them, significantly less than expected. The Tonnage Act of 1694 provided a similar loan of £1.2 million at an interest rate of eight percent, although this time the investors were to be incorporated as the Bank of England.

The investors in the Bank were given the authority to deal in bills of exchange. The bills were given by the Bank as £100 bills, which were effectively bank notes, and in return the investors would receive a guarantee that they would be paid through excise duties. Bank notes were soon produced on a larger scale and denominations as small as five pounds were produced. From William's point of view, the Bank was an essential way in which he could attract large numbers of investors who would deposit small amounts to be lent to the government, although the system was only possible as it had the backing of an Act of Parliament. Both the Bank of England and the tontine loan were examples of the long-term borrowing that has kept government afloat ever since. Other loans were levied in the form of 'lotteries', such as the scheme begun in March 1694 that enabled William to raise £1 million. 100,000 tickets with a value of £10 were sold and winners were drawn at random to win larger amounts. In 1698, William raised £2 million at a rate of eight percent by promising investors a stake in the 'new' East India Company. The short-term borrowing associated with earlier Stuart monarchs was always dependent on tax receipts, which were variable, and led to a lack of a confidence from creditors. Despite this, long-term loans accounted for less than half of the money borrowed during the Nine Years' War and William had to rely on high interest, short-term loans for the balance.

The Bank took over affairs related to military funding and opened a branch in Holland from which to attract investors. Confidence in the Bank of England increased significantly after William's death, when more emphasis was placed on long-term investment and government borrowing was increased to over £2.5 million per year in the decade after 1701.

As well as the establishment of the Bank of England, a Recoinage Act was given the royal assent in 1696. Silver coins that had been produced during the reign of Charles II had been regularly clipped on their edges or forged. This meant that their real value in England declined. However, the value of the silver was higher on the continent, leading to increasing numbers of coins being melted down and shipped abroad. Parliament requested that old coins be surrendered and weighed in order to ascertain their true value, and new coins were struck at a number of mints around the country. The effect of the recoinage was promising at first, with the value of the new coins being maintained for a time, and much confidence was restored to the economy. However, within two years silver was again worth more as bullion than it was in coin.

EXTEND YOUR KNOWLEDGE

**Coin clipping**

Coin clipping refers to the process of clipping the edges of a coin in order to reduce the precious metal content of the coin. This can be done to deliberately lower the value of the coin, or to use the precious metal for other purposes, such as making counterfeit coins.

Clipping had been a problem since the ancient Romans and Greeks attempted to manipulate the value of precious metals in their coins. When Isaac Newton was appointed Master of the Royal Mint in 1699, he insisted that all coins be marked on the rim with stripes that would be destroyed if they were clipped.

## The significance of parliamentary control of finance

As John Miller makes clear in Extract 8, a distinction was made between military and civil expenditure. Parliament made significant steps towards relieving the king of any responsibility of the funding of the army and navy. The significance of parliament controlling various aspects of national finance is summed up by the following.

- Crucially, parliamentary control of finance meant that the king had no choice but to meet with parliament regularly, thus increasing its authority.
- Parliament controlled military expenditure and, if desired, it could withhold supply and effectively hold the Crown to ransom.
- Parliament was able to audit government expenditure. This was unprecedented, and the fact that the commission into public accounts was paid by and accountable to parliament rather than the monarch gave it a degree of independence.
- From 1698, the Crown's day-to-day spending was controlled through a grant, the civil list. The monarch would never again be able to use their prerogative to avoid working with parliament.

**EXTRACT 8** From J. Miller, *The Glorious Revolution* (1997).

Having distinguished between the civil and military elements in the Crown's ordinary expenditure, the Commons increasingly took over responsibility for military and naval expenditure, voting money to pay the interest on debts incurred on the various branches of the ordinary revenue. Under the pressures of war, the old distinction between ordinary and extraordinary revenue became so blurred as to be meaningless: some argued that the revenue 'is in the crown as a trust' and that 'what is given to the king... is not as he is king, but for support of the nation'. It was superseded by a more realistic distinction between civil and military expenditure. Such a distinction seemed particularly necessary in 1697-8, when many were unwilling to trust William with the army left over from the war, but it would probably have developed anyway. With the king given a revenue adequate only for his civil expenditure, the tradition that he should 'live of his own', which had received some mortal blows in 1689-90, was buried forever. From the reign of Anne, the monarch was voted the civil list for life, while the army and navy estimates were put before Parliament each year.

The failure to grant William an adequate revenue in 1689-90 was deliberate... Dislike or distrust of William made the Commons determined not to surrender the financial weapon placed in their hands by the Revolution... Whatever the motives, the destruction of all hope of an independent royal revenue transformed the Crown's relationship with parliament. Now the Commons, if they chose, could force their wishes on the king by withholding supply.

The Marxist historian Christopher Hill has interpreted parliamentary control of finance through the Bank of England as a move that benefitted only the propertied classes. Government borrowing was now under the direct control of the MPs, who were the representatives of the tax-paying classes. Hill has argued that this led to a situation where monied interest played an important role in politics, and no future political faction or party could hope for sustained success without the support of the financers of the City of London. Douglass North and Barry Weingast (Extract 9) have interpreted parliamentary control over finance as beneficial to the economy. Those who had previously been reluctant to invest in the government and wider economy had a new-found confidence as parliament was effectively underwriting the Bank of England. Tony Claydon has argued that William saw parliament as the only solution to spiralling debts and increased costs, and would do anything to secure funds for the war with France (Extract 10).

**EXTRACT 9**

From D. North and B. Weingast, 'Constitutions and Commitment: The Evolution of Institutional Governing Public Choice in Seventeenth-Century England' in *The Journal of Economic History* (1989).

After the first few years of the Stuarts' reign, the Crown was not able to systematically raise funds. By the second decade of the seventeenth century, under mounting fiscal pressure, the Crown resorted to a series of 'forced loans,' indicating that it could not raise funds at rates it was willing to pay. Following the Glorious Revolution, however, not only did the government become financially solvent, but it gained access to an unprecedented level of funds. In just nine years (from 1688 to 1697), government borrowing increased by more than an order of magnitude. This sharp change in the willingness of lenders to supply funds must reflect a substantial increase in the perceived commitment by the government to honour its agreements. The evidence shows that these expectations were borne out, and that this pattern extends well into the next century.

**EXTRACT 10**

From T. Claydon, *William III* (2002).

William treasured the legislature as a fierce financial watchdog. Earlier Stuart kings had faced calls for Commons control over how the court spent money. Fears of corruption and extravagance in the royal household had sparked demands that parliament scrutinise and supervise public expenditure to ensure that all sums were used for the public good. Being Stuart kings, William's predecessors had resisted these calls. They had taken the traditional line that money voted for the king became his private revenue, and insisted that parliamentary comments on the king's finances were unwarranted intrusions into the mysteries of the state. By contrast, William saw a use for Commons mistrust. He knew that parliamentarians suspected that money was wasted and embezzled at court. At the same time, he was determined that money his legislators voted for the struggle with France should actually be used for that purpose...William, therefore, saw a central role for parliament in ensuring financial probity [integrity]. He also seems to have had wider views on the usefulness of his assembly. He appears to have had a vision of it as a source of information and counsel which could provide an alternative to his own circle. He apparently believed that a parliament which represented the nation and knew its condition should have a central role in formulating policy.

## THINKING HISTORICALLY Interpretations (4b)

### Method is everything

| **Bad History** | **Good History** |
|---|---|
| Based on gut feeling | Based on an interpretation of evidence |
| Argument does not progress logically | Argument progresses logically |
| No supporting evidence | Evidence deployed to support argument |

Work in pairs.

Historical writing can reveal much about the methods by which it was constructed. Read Extracts 8 and 10 and answer the questions below.

1 Look carefully at the spectrum of methodology.
   **a)** Where would you place each source on the spectrum of historical practice?
   **b)** What evidence would you use to support your choice?
2 Look at Extract 10. How would you change it to make it the same quality of historical writing as Extract 8?
3 Use a dictionary. Explain the following words in their relation to historical writing: substantiation, deduction, inference, cross reference.
4 How important is it that historians understand and evaluate the methods used by other historians?

ACTIVITIES
KNOWLEDGE CHECK

**Parliamentary control of finance**

Read the interpretations in Extracts 8 and 10.

1 Why was the failure to grant William adequate revenue 'deliberate' (Extract 8)?

2 According to Extract 10, why was William content to allow parliament more control over government finances?

3 What is the balance between fact and opinion in each interpretation?

4 Which interpretation do you find the most convincing? Which one provides the most evidence to back up their argument?

**A Level Exam-Style Question Section C**

***Study Extracts 8 and 10 before you answer this question.***

In the light of differing interpretations, how convincing do you find the view that, as a result of the Glorious Revolution, parliament had a 'central role in formulating policy' (Extract 10, line 13)?

To explain your answer, analyse and evaluate both extracts, using your own knowledge of the issues. (20 marks)

**Tip**

*These sources focus primarily on the financial settlement, but connections can also be made between this and the wider political settlement.*

## CONCLUSION: HOW REVOLUTIONARY WAS THE GLORIOUS REVOLUTION?

Among historians, there are two broad schools of thought on the importance of the Glorious Revolution. A well-established view is that the Revolution was little more than a change of dynasty and that the events were unrevolutionary. The Act of Settlement ensured a smooth Protestant succession in line with what had existed for most of the 17th century and the Bill of Rights ensured that England reverted to an 'ancient constitution'. The Toleration Act excluded some groups, such as non-Trinitarians and Catholics, and dissenting groups had to practice their religion in registered places of worship. It was, therefore, a peaceful, Protestant and conservative succession. This view was prevalent among Whig historians and many historians of the 20th century.

**SOURCE 5** An 18th-century allegorical representation of the accession of William and Mary, which reaffirms the dominant Whig view at the time. Magna Carta and Liberty, depicted to the left, are in favour, however the pope is not. This image was drawn by the Dutch engraver Jakob van Schley and featured in French Protestant historian Thoyras de Rapin's *History of England* (1727).

The second school of thought was put forward by a number of Enlightenment thinkers and, more recently, by revisionist historians such as Tim Harris and Steve Pincus. This school focuses on the genuinely revolutionary nature of the settlement by paying attention to a number of key developments.

- The events after 1688 have been reinterpreted to depict them as being characterised by violence (such as that associated with the Williamite War in Ireland) and radicalism rather than peace. It has been argued that the Revolution took place over a number of years, rather than a number of months, and it had long-term causes that can be found in the Protestant Reformation and the authoritarian actions of Charles I, as well as important consequences of which the makers of the Revolution were well aware. It has also been argued by Steve Pincus that the revolutionaries numbered in the thousands, including the thousands of soldiers who fought for William, and were not simply a tiny political elite.
- Events outside England have been reassessed by revisionist historians, who have concluded that the Revolution was not bloodless and that thousands of people lost their lives between 1689 and 1701 in Ireland, Scotland and in William's Nine Years' War. Of course these wars were well known about previously, but they were not seen to form part of the Revolution.
- The constitutional settlement confirmed that divine right monarchy was no more. The Bill of Rights is still an important constitutional document and set into law concepts of freedom of speech, free elections and parliamentary taxation. The judiciary were now independent of the Crown and no longer served 'at the king's pleasure'. After the assassination plot against William in 1696, the '**Association**' was taken not only by MPs, but also by hundreds of thousands of ordinary people. By signing, they were agreeing that the events of 1688–89 had signalled the end of hereditary divine right and accepted William's authority.
- The religious settlement that came about as a result of the Toleration Act of 1689 had widespread support from leading bishops and political figures, and its basic terms were not fully repealed until the 20th century.
- The financial settlement ensured that the Crown's ability to control finance was seriously constrained, and funding for the navy and army was closely controlled by parliament. The creation of the Bank of England in 1694 represented a victory for those who supported the unlimited possibilities of economic growth based on a system of credit.

**KEY TERM**

**The Association**
An oath of loyalty to the Crown, created by the passing of 'An Act for the Better Security of His Majesties' Royal Person and Government' in 1696.

**EXTRACT 11**

From T. Harris, *Revolution: The Great Crisis of the British Monarchy, 1685–1720* (2006).

One scholar has even claimed that the true English revolution occurred neither in mid-century nor in 1688-9 but in the 1690s. [Historians] disagree, however, over whether such changes were the result of the Glorious Revolution itself or of the subsequent war against France... in which England became involved... The English monarchy became limited, bureaucratic and parliamentary. It ceased to be a personal monarchy in quite the same way it had been under Charles II or James II. Yet in many respects it became a monarchy with more real power, as a result of the creation of the fiscal military state and the concomitant [associated] ability to harness the economic wealth of the country in the service of the sovereign - now the king-(or queen)-in-parliament. It is in this sense that the Glorious Revolution, despite the legal conservatism of the Declaration of Rights, truly brought about a revolutionary transformation of the English state.

### A Level Exam-Style Question Section C

***Study Extracts 3 and 11 before you answer this question.***

In the light of differing interpretations, how convincing do you find the view that, as a result of the Glorious Revolution, 'the English monarchy became limited' (Extract 11, line 4)?

To explain your answer, analyse and evaluate both extracts, using your own knowledge of the issues. (20 marks)

**Tip**

*Consider the issues of the parliamentary settlement, William's wars, the financial settlement and the religious settlement brought up in the sources, and relate your own knowledge to those issues.*

| Historian | View of the Glorious Revolution |
|---|---|
| Thomas Macaulay | The Whig view promoted most notably in Thomas Macaulay's *History of England from the Accession of James II* (1848) presented the Revolution as moderate and unrevolutionary. The events were bloodless, the succession was only slightly altered to exclude Catholics and the English had no desire to fundamentally change the constitution. |
| John Morrill | John Morrill (1991) tested the theory of another Whig historian, G.M. Trevelyan, who had seen the Revolution as a progressive event that led to a more modern and balanced constitution. Morrill concluded that, although Trevelyan's scholarship was questionable, his theory that the events constituted a 'sensible' and moderate revolution rather than a 'glorious' one is plausible. |
| Christopher Hill | Marxist historians, most notably Christopher Hill (1980), have tended to downplay the Revolution in favour of the events of the 1640s. They argue that the real revolutionary events took place between 1640 and 1649, when the traditional relationship between landlords and tenants broke down and the ruling elites were undermined by a bourgeois gentry. According to the Marxists, the events of 1688–89 were simply a manifestation of the new power relations in England and only solidified the existing settlement that had been created with the execution of Charles I. |
| Catharine Macaulay | Some 18th-century historians broke away from the prevailing Whig view, including Catharine Macaulay, who completed a history of England from 1603 to 1688 in 1783. She acknowledged, like the Whigs, that the Revolution reduced the power of the Crown and ended divine right monarchy, but claimed that the chance to further erode the royal prerogative was missed. The Whigs who dominated government under William were as ruthless as the 'evil counsellors' who advised Charles I during his personal rule and upheld royal authority. |
| Steve Pincus | Steve Pincus, in *1688: The First Modern Revolution* (2009), rejects what he saw as the orthodox view of the Revolution. Rather than assuming that the Revolution was a peaceful event that took place between 1688 and 1690, he suggests that its effects were felt well into the 1690s and that it was popular, violent and divisive. Rather than finding its origins in the reign of James II, he finds longer-term religious, political and socio-economic causes. Pincus claimed that he was resurrecting ideas that had been promoted by Enlightenment thinkers such as David Hume and Voltaire, as well as Catharine Macaulay, who saw the Revolution as fundamentally transformative. |
| Edward Vallance | The idea that the Revolution is marked by violence and disorder rather than a peaceful transition towards a sensible constitution is put forward by Edward Vallance (2006). Vallance looks beyond the relatively peaceful revolution that took place in England and argues that events in Scotland, such as the Glencoe Massacre of Jacobites in 1692, and Ireland mark the Revolution as one as violent as those that took place later in France or Russia. |
| Douglass North and Barry Weingast | Douglass North and Barry Weingast (1989) have highlighted the revolutionary nature of the financial settlement. According to North and Weingast, financial and governmental institutions changed beyond recognition and those who had previously been reluctant to invest in the economy had a newfound confidence. As the monarch was now constrained by parliament, merchants were assured it was now less likely that their affairs would be interfered with. Confidence was boosted once again as parliament was now able to audit the government's expenditure. |

**Figure 5.2**: The Glorious Revolution and the historians.

ACTIVITY
SUMMARY

### Glorious Revolution dinner party

Throughout the chapter you have encountered a number of interpretations about the Glorious Revolution. On separate sticky notes or pieces of paper, write down as many named historians as you can find in the chapter, together with a basic description of their belief. In the middle of a large piece of paper, draw a dining table and arrange the historians around the table. Your aim is to ensure that historians who would broadly agree with each other are sat together and are sat as far away as possible from historians they would disagree with. Provide a key to show why you have made your selections.

Categories you may wish to focus on could include:

- historians who have commented on the financial settlement
- historians who have commented on the religious settlement
- historians who believe the Revolution was peaceful and bloodless
- historians who believe that the Whig view of the Revolution should be reassessed.

1 If conflict was to arise between two or more historians, between whom would this take place? Draw a line to show this.

2 Where would you seat yourself and why?

### WIDER READING

Coward, B. *The Stuart Age*, Routledge, fourth edition (2011) A clear narrative with concise summaries of the debates

Cruickshanks, E. *The Glorious Revolution*, Macmillan (2000) An academic but accessible overview of the key debates

Harris, T. *Revolution: The Great Crisis of the British Monarchy, 1685-1720*, Penguin (2007) An important work of revisionism

Miller, J. *The Glorious Revolution*, Longman (1997) A clear overview of the revolution and its consequences

Pincus, S. *1688: The First Modern Revolution*, Yale (2009) An important work of revisionism

Trevelyan, G.M. *The English Revolution, 1688-1689*, Oxford University Press (1965) A traditional Whig interpretation of the Revolution

Vallance, E. *The Glorious Revolution*, Abacus (2006) The most accessible revisionist interpretation

# Preparing for your AS Level Paper 1 exam

## Advance planning

- Draw up a timetable for your revision and try to keep to it. Spread your timetable over a number of weeks, and aim to cover four or five topics each week.
- Spend longer on topics which you have found difficult, and revise them several times.
- Above all, do not try to limit your revision by attempting to 'question spot'. Try to be confident about all aspects of your Paper 1 work, because this will ensure that you have a choice of questions in Sections A and B.

## Paper 1 overview:

| AS Paper 1 | Time: 2 hour 15 minutes | |
|---|---|---|
| Section A | Answer 1 question from a choice of 2 | 20 marks |
| Section B | Answer 1 question from a choice of 2 | 20 marks |
| Section C | Answer 1 compulsory interpretations question | 20 marks |
| | Total marks = | 60 marks |

You should familiarise yourself with the layout of the paper by looking at the examples published by Edexcel. The questions for each section are followed by eight pages of lined paper where you should write your answer.

## Section A questions

Section A questions ask you to analyse and evaluate either cause or consequence. You should consider either the reasons for, or the results of, an event or development. You will be asked for coverage of a period of around ten years, possibly a little longer. For example, a question for Option 1C might be 'Was military involvement in politics the main reason for the failure of republican government in the years 1649–60?' Your answer should consider the reasons given in the question, then look at other relevant points and reach a conclusion.

## Section B questions

Section B questions cover a longer timespan than in Section A, at least one-third of the period you have studied. The questions take the form of 'How far…', 'How significant…', 'To what extent…' or 'How accurate is it to say…'. The questions can deal with historical concepts such as cause, consequence, change, continuity, similarity, difference and significance. Again, you should consider the issue raised in the question, consider other relevant issues, and then conclude with an overall judgement.

## Section C questions

There is no choice in Section C, which is concerned with the historical interpretations you have studied linked to the question 'How revolutionary, in the years to 1701, was the Glorious Revolution of 1688–89?' You will be given two extracts totalling around 300 words (printed separately) and the question will take the form 'How far do you agree with the view that …?' There is no need to use source analysis skills such as drawing inferences for the Section C answers. You will need to use the extracts and your own knowledge to consider the view given in the question.

## Use of time

This is an issue which you should discuss with your teachers and fellow students, but here are some suggestions for you.

Do not write solidly for 45 minutes on each question. For Section A and B answers you should spend a few minutes working out what the question is asking you to do, and drawing up a plan of your answer. This is especially important for Section B answers, which cover an extended period of time.

For Section C it is essential that you have a clear understanding of the content of each extract and the points which each extract is making. Read each extract carefully and underline important points. You could approach your answer by analysing the extracts separately and then as a package, and then using your own knowledge before reaching an overall judgement. You might decide to spend up to ten minutes reading the extracts and drawing up your plan, and 35 minutes writing your answer.

# Preparing for your AS Level exams

## Paper 1: AS Level sample answer with comments

### Section A

These questions assess your understanding of the period in breadth. They will ask you about the content you learned about in the four key themes, and may ask about more than one theme. For these questions remember to:

- give an analytical, not a descriptive, response
- support your points with evidence
- cover the whole time period specified in the question
- come to a substantiated judgement.

*Was Charles I's choice of advisers the main reason for the problems faced by the monarchy in the years 1625–49?*

#### Average student answer

Charles regretted his decision to sign Strafford's death warrant until he was executed himself in 1649. His advisers were therefore extremely important to him, and he would not have been able to maintain his personal rule for long if it was not for their help. His choice of advisers was questionable, however, as Strafford, Laud and Buckingham were very unpopular and caused resentment from parliament.

> This is a weak opening paragraph because it does not analyse and define the question. It does not outline the different possible reasons or what problems the monarchy actually faced.
>
> The point made is not very clear. It does have some links to the question, but is not very detailed or convincing.

One reason why Charles had problems was as a result of bad advice from those who he appointed to his privy council. George Villiers, Duke of Buckingham, was previously James I's favourite and became a key adviser to Charles during his early reign. In 1623, he travelled with Charles to Spain in order to secure the 'Spanish Match' which would result in Charles marrying the Spanish Infanta. They returned without the Infanta and Charles had to settle for marrying Henrietta Maria, a Catholic French Princess. As a result of this, the public and parliament were suspicious of Charles and saw him as a secret Catholic. This idea that he was a secret Catholic was also put forward by the promotion and policies of Archbishop Laud. Laud favoured High Church policies such as stained glass windows, organs in churches and a national prayer book for everyone. Laud's policies caused resentment in Scotland, and his introduction of the English prayer book in Scotland caused the First Bishops' War in 1639. Laud was eventually arrested by the Long Parliament and was executed in 1645. Charles' other key adviser was Thomas Wentworth, who became Earl of Strafford. He was made Lord Deputy of Ireland and ruled in a heavy-handed way there in the 1630s. He caused resentment from the Irish parliament because he demanded extra taxes, and alienated the native Catholics by favouring Protestant landowners. The Irish Rebellion in 1641 took place as a direct result of Strafford's policies.

> It is important to keep to the timescale given in the question. Much of the information about Buckingham and the Spanish match is out of the period and would gain little credit. It is also not related to the question itself. The points about Strafford and Laud are relevant and deserve credit, although they are not always concise enough to allow sufficient time to be dedicated to other relevant points.

Another cause of Charles' problems was his own personality and actions. Charles was never meant to be king, as his older brother Henry was the heir to the throne until he died before reaching adulthood. Charles grew up as a lonely individual, and developed a stubborn personality. He also believed strongly in divine right, an idea he inherited from his father. Whenever Charles met with parliament problems were caused. When he asked for money, parliament would often refuse, and this eventually led to him dissolving parliament for eleven years in 1629. During the personal rule his own actions were equally as bad, as he collected illegal taxes such as Ship Money. His policies such as the Book of Orders to JPs reflected his controlling and obsessive personality. When he was negotiating with parliament before the Civil War, his stubbornness again showed itself. When negotiations went badly, he tried to arrest five leading MPs including John Pym, but they found out beforehand and escaped. Charles rejected every offer that was put to him during this time, and when the Civil War was over he rejected further offers, ultimately leading to his execution.

This paragraph is more focused on the timescale in the question. Every point is accurate, but development of material is modest, and lacking in both range and depth. Dates are lacking and it is not made clear how the paragraph helps to answer the question.

Problems were caused for the monarchy as a result of opposition to Charles. There was opposition from parliament between 1625 and 1629, as they were reluctant to give Charles the power to collect taxes such as tonnage and poundage when his failed expeditions to Europe wasted money. The Petition of Right was put forward to restrict the power of the monarchy, and when Charles eventually rejected it his problems became much worse. There was opposition to Charles' policies during his personal rule, such as taxes and religious policy, although it can be argued that this was his fault. Opposition was at its peak between 1640 and 1642, when Charles was forced to give up some of his power in order to fund his war against the Scots. Illegal taxes were banned by parliament, and they issued the Grand Remonstrance. This document stated that Charles could no longer choose his own advisers, and when he rejected it Civil War became much more likely. When Charles had lost the Civil War, he faced further opposition from parliament, who attempted to reach a settlement that the king could not agree with.

The points on opposition are accurate, but once again the material supporting the points made is lacking in depth of development and explanation. This could be improved with some specific examples of how opposition was organised, and the role of individuals such as Eliot, Pym and Cromwell.

The Irish Rebellion caused major problems for Charles. In 1641, the native Catholic Irish rose up against Protestants, and many were killed or forced to leave their land. This created problems back in England as all sides knew that something had to be done about the Irish threat. The big question that was raised in England was who would control the army – the king or parliament?

This paragraph is describing the Irish Rebellion without linking the points to the problems of the monarchy. More development – for example on how it linked to Charles' relationship with parliament – would have made the paragraph more convincing.

In conclusion, I believe that the main reason for the problems faced by the monarchy lie in Charles' own decisions and his character. His advisers played an important part in creating problems, especially Strafford and Laud, and the opposition were always a thorn in his side. However, many of the problems he faced, including the Civil War and his own execution, would not have happened if he did not make mistakes himself.

The conclusion is not very securely developed, and largely just restates points made earlier in the answer. The issue of Charles' problems and what they consisted of is never fully addressed.

## Verdict

This is an average response because:

- the issue in the question (problems faced) is not explored fully or related to the points put forward, and it is too descriptive
- there are no inaccuracies, but many points are made without development and explanation
- it doesn't come to a strong, reasoned judgement
- it shows some organisation, but lacks coherence throughout.

Use the feedback on this answer to rewrite it, making as many improvements as you can.

# Paper 1: AS Level sample answer with comments

## Section A

*Was Charles I's choice of advisers the main reason for the problems faced by the monarchy in the years 1625–49?*

### Strong student answer

The monarchy faced a number of problems between 1625 and 1649. Charles' inability to finance his regime at times led to increased tensions with parliament, and indeed 11 years without parliament came about because of arguments over this issue. As well as this, religion was at the heart of political life in the 17th century and, as head of the Church of England, decisions made by Charles and his advisers had a dramatic impact on the religious lives of citizens. Charles' advisers, in particular Buckingham, Laud, Strafford and even his wife Henrietta Maria, must take some of the blame for the increasing tensions and ultimately Civil War. There are also other factors that must be addressed in order for an adequate conclusion to be drawn. Charles' own actions caused many issues, such as the implementation of the English Prayer Book in Scotland, and opposition from religious and political figures added to his problems.

This is a good opening statement. The events that need to be covered are made clear, and some key themes that will be referred to throughout the answer are made clear.

Also, a firm conclusion is not reached at the start, but the fact that other factors need to be addressed before such a conclusion can be reached is made clear.

Charles' advisers link to a number of problems for the monarchy. A theme that runs through the entire period 1625–49 is the poor relationship between king and parliament. It can be argued that figures such as Buckingham encouraged this poor relationship. Buckingham led the expeditions to La Rochelle that caused fury from parliament and a reluctance to allow the king to collect further subsidies. It can also be argued that the Petition of Right was put forward in 1628 as a reaction to the questionable advice the king was getting from Buckingham. During his personal rule, Charles surrounded himself with high church Arminians such as Laud and Wentworth, as well as so called 'crypto-Catholics' such as Cottington and Windebank. This fuelled the suspicion among the political nation that there was a Popish Plot at court, a situation that was made worse by Charles' marriage to Henrietta Maria in 1625. Henrietta became a close adviser during Charles' personal rule, and assisted Charles in his preparations for the Civil War in 1642 and 1643. Wentworth was selected as Lord Deputy in Ireland in 1632, and ruled in a heavy-handed way, as he had done as President of the Council of the North. Wentworth was chosen because Charles was well aware of his uncompromising reputation, and he ended up alienating all the key interest groups in Ireland. It is clear, then, that a great deal of political resentment was caused as a result of Charles' choice of advisors.

The issue of Charles' advisers is the key concern of the question, so it is right to dedicate a large paragraph to it. The paragraph has secure knowledge, but an explanation of why the advisers link to specific problems could be stronger.

Another major problem Charles experienced was religious opposition. It can be argued that much of this opposition came about as a result of him choosing William Laud as Archbishop of Canterbury. Laud, like Charles, was authoritarian and believed strongly in divine right. He encouraged Charles' drive towards religious uniformity, and personally oversaw the 'beauty of holiness' project. This consisted of returning organs to churches, putting in stained glass windows, placing statues in churches and most crucially ensuring that hymns were sung and the Book of Common Prayer enforced. It is true that many happily accepted the reforms, and indeed encouraged them: in 1642, a large crowd gathered around Norwich Cathedral in order to prevent the organ being destroyed by parliament. His reforms did however create new resentment and opposition not seen before. Church taxes were levied to pay for the new additions to churches, and outspoken Puritans caused problems for Charles and Laud. In 1637, Bastwick, Burton and Prynne, Puritans who had spoken out against the regime, were punished in the Star Chamber, with Laud acting as chief judge. William Prynne, for example, had written a book attacking stage plays and the theatre as ungodly, and was imprisoned for life and mutilated. They became heroes of the opposition cause, and were promptly released when the Long Parliament met. The problem of religion continued, aided by Charles' choice of advisers throughout the Civil War, when parliament depicted Charles' followers as ungodly Papists.

There is a clear explanation that demonstrates why advisers were to blame for religious opposition. Perhaps too much space is dedicated to Laud, although he is the chief architect of religious reform and should be discussed in relation to this question.

Charles' advisers cannot take all the blame for the problems faced by the monarchy, although they often encouraged him in his mistakes. In the fields of finance and religion, as well as government administration, Charles was the author of his own downfall. He continued to rule without parliament for 11 years between 1629 and 1640, and in this time relied on dubious prerogative taxation. Though not technically illegal, innovations such as Ship Money, which raised an average of £200,000 per year, created resentment and ultimately problems for Charles. In 1639, after Charles' decision to enter into war with the Scots, the majority of taxpayers simply went on strike and refused to pay Ship Money. This led to him recalling parliament and began the chain of events that would end in Civil War. Despite Charles' role in enforcing prerogative taxation, the responsibility can again be given to his advisers. It was William Noy, Attorney General under Charles, who revived many of the medieval taxes such as Ship Money and Forest Fines that Charles relied on.

> There is good understanding shown here of Charles' role in causing resentment to his financial policies. This is linked to the factor given in the question, as the role of advisers is also addressed.

After the Civil War Charles continued to anger the opposition as a result of his stubborn nature and unwillingness to compromise. The opposition themselves can be blamed for some of the problems faced by the monarchy. John Pym's Nineteen Propositions, issued to Charles in June 1642, were far too radical for him to ever accept, and included clauses that would mean the education of the king's children would be controlled by parliament. The Newcastle Propositions, associated with the Presbyterian Party and Denzil Holles in 1646, were also unrealistic, and were the basis for the negotiations between Crown and parliament that would lead to Charles' execution in 1649. However, Charles delayed his response to the Propositions for a year, and never intended to accept them. He instead entered into secret negotiations with the Scots, and a Scottish army entered England on Charles' behalf in order to start the Second Civil War. This would seal Charles' fate as he could no longer be seen as trustworthy.

> There is a good understanding of the issues that informed negotiations between 1640–42 and 1646–49. This might have been strengthened with some more specific references, such as the role of Ireton in the negotiations and a reference to the Civil War itself.

In conclusion, there can be no doubt that Charles' choice of advisers contributed to a number of problems. His choice of Wentworth in Ireland alienated key interest groups and helped to cause the Irish Rebellion, his choice of Buckingham began calls from parliament to restrict the king's ministers, his choice of Laud caused friction and enhanced the idea that a Popish Plot was taking place at court. The role of the opposition is also important, as parliament could have negotiated with Charles on more realistic terms if they wished, but time after time they failed to offer settlements that would be acceptable. The factor that caused many of the problems is undoubtedly Charles' own personality and actions. If it was not for Charles, more moderate advisers may have been chosen, and if a monarch who had more sympathy with the opposition was on the throne, the Civil War may have been avoided.

> This is a strong evaluative conclusion. The role of advisers is discussed and other factors are commented on briefly. Charles' personality and actions are given as the most important factor explaining the problems, and the point is made convincingly.

## Verdict

This is a strong response because:

- the answer considers a number of problems and addresses advisers, opposition and the role of Charles before reaching a persuasive conclusion
- sufficient knowledge is demonstrated and there are no inaccuracies at all
- there are some less strong passages, but it must be remembered that the answer covers a long period
- the quality of written communication, logical coherence and conceptual understanding are all excellent.

# Paper 1: AS Level sample answer with comments

## Section B

These questions assess your understanding of the course in breadth and will cover a period of 30 years or more. They will ask you about the content you learned about in the four key themes, and may ask about more than one theme. The questions will also require you to explore a range of concepts, such as change over time, similarity and difference, as well as significance. For these questions remember to:

- identify the focus of the question
- consider the concepts you will need to explore
- support your points with evidence from across the time period specified in the question
- develop the evidence you deploy to build up your overall judgement
- come to a substantiated judgement that directly addresses the question set.

*How significant were improvements in agricultural techniques for the success of the British economy, 1650–88?*

### Average student answer

The British economy changed drastically between 1650 and 1688 and changes in agricultural techniques were important in making this change. Better techniques were needed to feed a growing population, and to make Britain a world power. A large number of people had moved to towns and many people were so poor that they had become vagrants.

This is a weak opening statement. The issue of agricultural techniques is addressed, but other potential factors are not considered and the demands of the question are not fully set out.

Enclosure was an important aspect of agriculture in the 17th century. By 1650, farmers were starting to enclose small farms to make larger ones, so they could concentrate on growing just one crop. These farms became very profitable, and it was often more sensible for farmers to become tenants on large farms, rather than purchase their own. Some new crops were introduced, such as cabbage and clover, which would fertilise the soil and increase productivity. Water meadows were used to create more animal feed. Farmers focused on growing specialised crops that had particular uses, such as hemp and flax for the cloth trade. Barley was also concentrated on for the brewing of beer, and many areas in South East England were dedicated to this and other crops. All of these improvements helped the economy to do well between 1650 and 1688.

This paragraph is accurate and has appropriate content, but is too brief to gain a high mark. The point about enclosure is relevant but too brief to gain much credit. Water meadows are discussed, but a full explanation of their use and how they functioned is not given. As this paragraph discusses the main factor given in the question, it needs to be more detailed.

Improved transportation helped the success of the economy. Rivers were cleared, which meant goods could be transported further inland. Many of the major towns were on rivers so this was essential. The Thames was cleared which enabled London and Oxford to be better connected, and the Ouse at York was made more navigable. The first Turnpike roads were set up after 1663, which meant that goods could be transported on good quality roads for the first time. The turnpike roads eventually created a network that spread out from London towards the North and West. Travellers on these roads were assisted by the production of the first road atlas in 1675.

A fairly brief paragraph that discusses the relevant issue of improved infrastructure. Clearer links could be made between transportation and improved agricultural techniques, as well as the growth of national markets. The statement about the first road atlas is relevant, but not explained and made relevant to the question. The drawbacks and shortcomings of transportation and infrastructure are not mentioned.

The main economic rival to Britain in the 17th century was Holland. The Dutch were particularly good at producing textiles, and most of the cloth produced in England had to be shipped to Holland in order for it to be dyed and finished because the English did not have the skills required. The domestic system of cloth production continued after 1650, and cloth became so important that in 1660 74% of all exports out of London were textiles. The domestic system consisted of families working cloth at home, with each family member having a different role. Families could often take on this work while also working in agriculture, the dominant area of employment across the entire country. This system continued to be favoured after 1650 because it was easy to hire and fire workers, so market conditions could decide who was employed and how much cloth was needed. The cloth industry had continued this way for over a century, so very little changed. Therefore, the cloth trade is not as important as changes in agricultural techniques.

A fairly convincing paragraph, with good use of factual information. The domestic system is well explained and related to why the economy was successful. The key issue of the 'new draperies' is missing, however, and should be included in any discussion of the cloth trade.

The Royal Exchange was opened in 1571. This was the first commercial building in Britain and helped bankers to do their jobs. Loans started to be given out to ex-Royalists after the Civil War because their estates had been confiscated. London was the centre of this trade and many bankers and insurance companies opened offices there. Goldsmiths, who had large vaults for storing their precious materials, also started giving out loans after 1650. They even lent money to Charles II. Insurance was also an important business in London, and insurers offered policies on merchants' ships so they could go to the American colonies. The American colonies produced goods that could not be made in Britain, so they became extremely valuable after 1650. There were colonies in North America and the Caribbean, and Spain and Holland also occupied islands and territory in the area. Britain was able to compete with the Dutch thanks to the wealth of its colonies.

This paragraph relies strongly on narrative material and lacks sufficient explanation. Simple statements are made and are not expanded on with accurate facts and dates. There is no link made to how finance and trade helped the overall success of the economy.

In conclusion, there were many reasons why the economy was more successful after 1650, and I believe that the improvement in agricultural techniques was the most important reason. Agricultural techniques improved a lot between 1650 and 1688, and they were definitely crucial in making sure that farming was more productive and the right kind of crops could be grown. If these techniques did not improve, the growing population would have struggled to flourish.

The conclusion focuses solely on the issue of agricultural techniques, rather than investigating other relevant factors. However, there is some understanding shown here of change over time: population growth and agricultural techniques are linked.

It could be improved by including a balanced assessment of all the factors discussed in the response.

## Verdict

This is an average response because:

- the answer considers a number of relevant factors, but not in sufficient detail to merit a higher mark, and few links are made between different factors
- most knowledge included is accurate and relevant, although it is not always used to tackle the demands of the question, and the factual material used lacks range and depth
- there are too many descriptive passages that simply provide information without evaluation and judgements are not substantiated
- there is a lack of precision throughout the response and the conclusion is weak because it only discusses the factor given in the question.

Use the feedback on this answer to rewrite it, making as many improvements as you can.

# Paper 1: AS Level sample answer with comments

## Section B

These questions assess your understanding of the course in breadth and will cover a period of 30 years or more. They will ask you about the content you learned about in the four key themes, and may ask about more than one theme. The questions will also require you to explore a range of concepts, such as change over time, similarity and difference, as well as significance. For these questions remember to:

- identify the focus of the question
- consider the concepts you will need to explore
- support your points with evidence from across the time period specified in the question
- develop the evidence you deploy to build up your overall judgement
- come to a substantiated judgement that directly addresses the question set.

*How significant were improvements in agricultural techniques for the success of the British economy, 1650–88?*

### Strong student answer

A number of changes to the British economy came about after 1650, and by 1688 Britain was at the centre of European and world trade. A number of innovations and improvements working together led to this situation, not least the improvements seen in agricultural techniques. They led to a growing population being sustained and the growth of national markets meant further efficiencies could be achieved. As well as agricultural techniques, improved transport infrastructure, the growth of banking and insurance and improvements in key industries such as textiles meant that the economy was in a position to expand further in the 18th century.

This is a strong opening paragraph, emphasising the importance of agricultural techniques and covering all the factors that are going to be discussed in the answer.

The population of Britain had doubled between 1520 and 1620, which led to a crisis in food production. In order to sustain this population and for Britain to be a successful economy, agricultural techniques needed to improve. Enclosure was absolutely essential to the success of the economy. Large farms developed as a result of the enclosure of scattered holdings, and farmers could ensure there was no duplication in crop production or animal rearing. Enclosure also meant that fewer fields were left fallow each year, and more could be fully utilised. Added to this, nitrogen-rich crops such as cabbage were farmed, which would fertilise the soil for the following year. Although enclosure increased after 1650, it was already well established in many areas, and small farmers suffered when they could not compete with larger farms. As well as this, some counties where enclosure was not used widely, such as Oxfordshire, thrived and managed high levels of production as a result of general improvements in techniques.

This paragraph provides a balanced assessment of the importance of enclosure, focusing not only on the successes of enclosure but also providing some evidence of the limited nature of improvements.

A number of new agricultural techniques were imported from the continent, particularly from Holland. Dutch immigrants brought with them new crops, such as a frost-resistant turnip, and improved methods of irrigation. Enclosure and specialised farms also meant that crops that aided industry could be produced on a large scale and less was wasted. Hemp and flax were used in the textile industry, and hops were used to brew beer. The use of water meadows also expanded after 1650. Water would be diverted from rivers onto fields, ensuring that there was less frost in early spring. This meant that there was more food for sheep and cattle. New techniques helped the economy, but some groups did not benefit. Small tenant farmers suffered because smallholding became an unsustainable employment as a result of enclosure. The numbers of wage-dependent agricultural labourers grew, but their wages were reduced as a result of inflation. Despite the improvements in agriculture, there was a lack of progress in some areas. In Ireland, for example, there was virtually no investment in new techniques.

Statistical evidence could be used here to elaborate on the strength of agricultural output. There is, however, enough evidence to show that improvements to agricultural techniques were a success and a counter-argument is given to show the drawbacks.

There can be no doubt that the textile industry improved greatly after 1650. The production of wool had been a staple industry since medieval times, and the arrival of Dutch immigrants led to innovations in techniques and a wider variety of textiles being produced. Dutch immigrants settled in towns such as Norwich and Colchester, where up to 40% of people were employed in the textile industry by the end of the century. Dutch weavers used their skills to introduce new types of cloth that appealed to a wider market than traditional English cloth. The Dutch also introduced the frame knitting machine, which reduced the amount of time and effort required to produce cloth. The domestic 'putting out' system continued throughout most of the country, and this made it easy for employers to hire and release labour as market conditions dictated.

> This is a relevant paragraph that addresses a key reason for the success of the economy. It could be improved with some more relevant statistics.

The economy would not have been so successful if it was not for the development of London. A number of industries were based in London, and innovations in these helped to make Britain an important world economic power. London was by far the largest city in Britain, with a population of around 400,000 in 1650. It was at the heart of the road and shipping network and, after the Turnpike Act was passed in 1663, the first well-maintained turnpike roads led to London. London became an attractive place to live and work, which led to the population increasing to nearly 600,000 in 1700. Of course, this population growth would not have been possible without the improvements in agricultural techniques. London was the hub of a European market that relied on its ports and shipping industry and it was the centre of the fledgling British Empire. The growth of insurance, particularly against threats to shipping, was essential to the success of the economy. Some companies were so large that they felt no need to insure their ships, such as the East India Company. The East India Company and other Companies given royal charters were important to the success of the economy as they were able to help Britain compete with Spain and Portugal, and the significance of the Company is shown by the fact that it loaned the Crown £50,000 in 1667.

> The role of London and industries based there are examined successfully. A link is made between the improved agricultural techniques and the growth of London, although this could be developed further.

As well as the insurance and shipping industries, London was the centre of banking and investment. Merchants would not have had the opportunity to expand if capital was not available to them. The first money-scrivening firm was established in 1636, and after the Civil War millions of pounds were lent. Goldsmith-bankers also flourished after 1650, and at least 44 were active in London in 1677. Charles II came into conflict with the goldsmith-bankers after he became indebted to them, and their significance reduced until William III became king in 1688.

> A relevant paragraph, but relatively short.

In conclusion, there were a number of reasons why the economy was successful between 1650 and 1688, and I believe that the role of London was of crucial importance. It is true that London could not have flourished without improvements in agriculture, but industries such as banking, insurance and shipping ensured that Britain became a world economic power. The textile industry was important, but its success was largely based on a system that had been established long before 1650.

> A strong answer to this question must consider the relative importance of different reasons for success. Here the growth of London and its industries is put forward as the most important factor, but the roles of agriculture and industry are also considered.

## Verdict

This is a strong response because:

- it puts forward a number of relevant factors and explains them well, making links between them
- it has a wide range of evidence that is used to support the points made and meets the demands of the question
- it reaches a strong and persuasive judgement by weighing up the evidence
- it is well organised and communication of material is clear and precise, and the argument is logical.

# Paper 1: AS Level sample answer with comments

## Section C

These questions require you to read and analyse two sources carefully in order to develop a response which examines and makes an informed judgement about different interpretations. The best answers:

- need to show an understanding of the extracts and identify the key points of interpretation
- deploy own knowledge to develop points emerging from extracts and provide necessary context
- develop a judgement after developing and weighing up different interpretations.

***Study Extracts 6 and 7 (pages 125 and 126) before you answer this question.***

Historians have different views about how revolutionary, in the years to 1701, the Glorious Revolution was. Analyse and evaluate the extracts and use your knowledge of the issues to explain your answer to the following question.

*How far do you agree with the view that the power of parliament increased as a result of the Glorious Revolution?*

### Average student answer

Parliament became very important as a result of the Glorious Revolution. After James II had fled London, the path was clear for William of Orange to become king, and his and Mary's rule was approved of by parliament. There became an ideal balance between king and parliament, and it set the scene for the parliamentary democracy that we enjoy today. Horwitz states in Extract 7 that 'the enhanced importance of parliament' led to more competition for places in William's government.

This is a weak opening paragraph that does not target the specific question and only mentions one of the extracts, at the end of the paragraph. It also provides a very simplistic review and suggests a very rosy view of the situation after William became king. There is nothing included that supports the alternative view that the power of parliament did not increase.

Two of the most important Acts that were passed by parliament after 1689 were the Bill of Rights and Act of Settlement. They helped to make up the overall political settlement that William agreed to when he accepted the throne. The Bill of Rights stated that laws could not be passed without consent of parliament, the Crown could not raise taxes without parliament, and only parliament could approve the use of a standing army in peace time. This was partly a response to the absolutism seen under James II and to an extent, Charles II, and William had to agree to this before he could become king. The Act of Settlement stated that future monarchs could not be Catholics, but also gave parliament the power to select judges. This was also a response to the absolutism and Catholicism of James II, and as William was Protestant he had no problem signing the Act into law.

Although the Bill of Rights and Act of Settlement are relevant to the issue of parliamentary power, this is a descriptive account and does not relate the information to the demands of the question. Opportunities to refer to the extracts are missed, and no evidence is put forward to suggest that these Acts did not increase the power of parliament.

Extract 6 shows that parliament and William worked well together, and hints at the alliance William made with the Whig party. The Whig party had developed as a reaction against absolutism, and were generally suspicious of autocratic power and High Church policies. In response to this, the Tories defended the traditional status of the monarchy. Extract 6 also shows that William had to agree to the Triennial Act in order to stay in power. This Act stated that a parliament could not last longer than three years, which resulted in more regular elections. This meant that parliament became more important. In the aftermath of the Triennial Act, the rivalry between the Tory and Whig parties became more pronounced, and William included members of both factions in his ministry throughout the 1690s.

Identifies an important point made in Extract 6 about the significance of the Triennial Act. This paragraph fails to assess any of the other issues raised in the extract, such as the increase in party divisions as a result.

Parliament did become more important, but the king also benefitted from the Glorious Revolution. Extract 7 emphasises this when Horwitz says 'a place at Court with a seat there is most people's aim'. The Triennial Act was actually seen as enhancing the king's power, and Horwitz mentions the fact that the government became larger as a result of the Nine Years' War. The Nine Years' War acted as a huge financial strain on Britain and the government because it was so costly. William had to find new ways to raise funds, and he raised loans and ultimately founded the Bank of England in 1694 in order to find investors. William still had important powers, as he was still head of the Church, and members of parliament still had to swear allegiance to the Crown. Parliament was not a democracy in any way, as it still represented only the richest 2 percent of the population. The gentry were the only people who could realistically enter politics, and voters could still be bribed or influenced. In many constituencies, very small numbers of people, sometimes in single figures, could decide election results.

This paragraph does attempt to provide balance by discussing what the monarchy gained from the Revolution. The extract from Horwitz could be put into context and fully explained.

Overall the evidence seems to agree that there was a real change to the power of parliament after the Glorious Revolution and that the king was now subject to their agreement on most issues. There was rapid progress towards a more balanced constitution, and parliament had to approve many aspects of government policy. The absolute monarchy exercised by James II and, to an extent, Charles II was definitely no more. The Triennial Act in particular meant that the monarch had no choice but to rely on parliament and call them regularly and the Bill of Rights gave a level of protection to parliament and became an important part of the constitution.

The conclusion argues a point of view, but it lacks the specific illustration and explanation to be substantial.

## Verdict

This is an average response because:

- it attempts some analysis of the extracts by describing points given in them, but does not use them sufficiently to further the debate in the question
- there is some deployment of contextual knowledge, but a significant amount provides background to the topic rather than being focused on the specific question
- there is an attempt to weigh up the argument and provide a judgement, but the answer is too one-sided and focuses too much on the argument that parliament did gain more power
- Communication is adequate, but the answer does not follow a logical structure.

Use the feedback on this answer to rewrite it, making as many improvements as you can.

# Paper 1: AS Level sample answer with comments

## Section C

These questions require you to read and analyse two sources carefully in order to develop a response which examines and makes an informed judgement about different interpretations. The best answers:

- need to show an understanding of the extracts and identify the key points of interpretation
- deploy own knowledge to develop points emerging from extracts and provide necessary context
- develop a judgement after developing and weighing up different interpretations.

***Study Extracts 6 and 7 (pages 125 and 126) before you answer this question.***

Historians have different views about how revolutionary, in the years to 1701, the Glorious Revolution was. Analyse and evaluate the extracts and use your knowledge of the issues to explain your answer to the following question.

*How far do you agree with the view that the power of parliament increased as a result of the Glorious Revolution?*

### Strong student answer

The two extracts have quite different perspectives and develop points related to their arguments. Vallance in Extract 6 argues that the Triennial Act led to a period of 'feverish electioneering', while Horwitz in Extract 7 states that, as parliament became more important, the power of the king's government, and demand for places in it, became more pronounced. Both authors provide evidence to advance their arguments: Vallance gives election statistics, whereas Horwitz refers to the accounts of contemporaries involved in parliament and government. Vallance also refers to the Nine Years' War as an important turning point, suggesting that William became closer to the Whig Party in order to 'prosecute his war against Louis more effectively'.

An effective opening paragraph that is driven by the extracts and identifies their key arguments. It cites some of the evidence put forward and begins to set up the debate.

Horwitz argues that the Revolution resulted in 'the enhanced importance of parliament', and it is important to be aware of the reasons why historians have come to this conclusion. Although the prevailing Whig view was that the Revolution was peaceful and sensible, resulting in minimal change, some Enlightenment thinkers, as well as more recent revisionist historians, have suggested that the Revolution was a transformative event that enhanced the power of parliament. There is certainly evidence to show that the Bill of Rights of 1689 enhanced the power of parliament. The monarchy was severely restricted in its control over the army and taxation, as well as making it clear that elections should be regular and free. The Bill of Rights has been criticised, however, for not making it clear how arbitrary monarchs could be removed and for not actually setting out how often elections could take place. Vallance, too, says that the Triennial Act ushered in a period of 'feverish electioneering', suggesting that as elections became more regular, political passions became stronger. Although both authors give weight to the role of the Triennial Act, parliamentary authority would not have been possible without the Bill of Rights.

This paragraph argues the case that parliament gained from the Glorious Revolution. Some effective specific evidence is deployed and a good knowledge of the historical debate is shown.

In order to put Vallance's argument about parliament becoming more important into context, it is important to stress that William needed parliament in order to legitimise his rule. He was invited to England by parliament as a result of James II's absolutist policies. William's wife, Mary Stuart, was the closest living appropriate successor and, most importantly, they were both Protestant. William effectively had no choice but to concede power to parliament. Earlier monarchs, such as Charles I, had argued that parliament's only role was to approve taxes, but in 1689 this was simply not an option. In 1697, parliament illustrated their power when they passed the Civil List Act. This granted £700,000 per year to William for life, in order to cover his expenses. Although he was still vastly powerful, he still needed to gain the approval of parliament.

This paragraph demonstrates a good understanding of the context of Vallance's argument, and uses factual knowledge to back up the argument.

While it is true that parliament became an important part of the political system, Horwitz suggests that, with increasing parliamentary power, William actually benefitted. Horwitz states that 'there was never a shortage of suitors for offices in the Crown's gift'. Here, Horwitz is putting forward the argument that parliamentarians were keen to take up appointments in the Privy Council and royal court. Horwitz also states that 'seats in the Commons were more and more stepping-stones to office', and that gentlemen were more interested in gaining a seat at court than in parliament. There is much evidence to support the view that the Crown benefitted from the Revolution. For example, many of the demands contained within the Declaration of Rights were not implemented through the Bill of Rights, and William still behaved as a fiercely independent monarch.

Shows an attempt to provide balance and context. Horwitz's argument is backed up with some contextual knowledge of the Declaration of Rights, although this could be expanded further.

Vallance states that William formed a close alliance with the Whig party, in part to mount a successful war against France. The 'Whig Junto' that formed around William became very influential, and this caused suspicion and jealousy from Tory MPs. Parliament became more fragmented as a result of this rivalry, and Vallance continues 'voting in the Commons was conducted largely along party lines'. This actually enhanced the power of the king, as he could be presented as a figure of continuity and strength when pitted against the disjoined parliament. After all, William still had the power to appoint his own advisers, and he controlled foreign policy as he still had the power to declare war, meet foreign delegations and sign treaties. He spent several years away from England fighting in the Nine Years' War, and there was nothing that parliament could do to prevent him doing this. They attempted to restrict his financial independence by limiting the amount of troops they would fund for him, but he resorted to levying a variety of short-term and long-term loans to cover the huge expense of the war.

This is attempting to show that, as parliament became more divided, the power of the monarch was enhanced. Some more statistical or factual information to back up the argument would help here.

Overall, the balance of the argument seems to favour Vallance's argument that the Revolution, in particular the Triennial Act, enhanced the power of parliament and ensured regular elections. This is especially evident when the situation after 1689 is compared with what came earlier in the century. Under Charles I, for example, parliament had little role in the governing of the country, and it was generally accepted that parliament simply existed in order to assist the king in raising taxes. Horwitz is correct in asserting that William still commanded great respect and parliamentarians were keen to join his Council, but the Bill of Rights and later Act of Settlement ensured that parliament was now a permanent and important part of the constitution.

The concluding paragraph comes to a clear judgement based on the balance of the evidence.

### Verdict

This is a strong response because:

- it identifies and illustrates the arguments of the two extracts, and demonstrates an excellent understanding of them, analysing the issues raised through comparison of them
- it deploys a sound range of specific evidence in most cases to develop points emerging from the extracts in order to provide a sense of the context
- it develops an argument that considers both interpretations and tries to provide balance, and a clear judgement is made that is supported by a combination of source analysis and contextual knowledge.
- Communication and organisation are excellent throughout.

# Preparing for your A Level Paper 1 exam

## Advance planning

- Draw up a timetable for your revision and try to keep to it. Spread your timetable over a number of weeks, and aim to cover four or five topics each week.
- Spend longer on topics which you have found difficult, and revise them several times.
- Above all, do not try to limit your revision by attempting to 'question spot'. Try to be confident about all aspects of your Paper 1 work, because this will ensure that you have a choice of questions in Sections A and B.

## Paper 1 overview:

| AL Paper 1 | Time: 2 hour 15 minutes | |
|---|---|---|
| Section A | Answer 1 question from a choice of 2 | 20 marks |
| Section B | Answer 1 question from a choice of 2 | 20 marks |
| Section C | Answer 1 compulsory interpretations question | 20 marks |
| | **Total marks =** | **60 marks** |

You should familiarise yourself with the layout of the paper by looking at the examples published by Edexcel. The questions for each section are followed by eight pages of lined paper where you should write your answer.

## Section A and Section B questions

The essay questions in Sections A and B are similar in form. They ask you to reach a judgement on an aspect of the course you have studied, and will deal with one or more historical concepts of change, continuity, similarity, difference, cause, consequence and significance. The question stems which will be used will include 'To what extent…', 'How far …', 'How significant was …' and so on. You should consider the issue raised by the question, develop your answer by looking at other relevant points, and reach a judgement in your conclusion.

The main difference between Section A and Section B questions will be the timespan of the questions. Section A questions will cover a period of ten years or more, while Section B questions will be concerned with at least one-third of the period you have studied.

A Section A question for Paper 1C might read 'To what extent was fear of Catholicism responsible for the discontent faced by the monarchy in the years 1667–88?' Your answer should consider the fear of Catholicism under both Charles II and James II, look at other issues such as conflicts between king and parliament, fears of absolutism, and discontent over the Anglo-Dutch Wars, before reaching an overall judgement on the question.

A Section B question on the same paper will cover a longer period of time, but have a similar shape. For example, 'How far do you agree that society was transformed in the years 1625–88?' Here you should consider various transformational changes, such as the changing class system and changing attitudes and ideas, but also point out elements of society that had changed little, such as the role of women and the conditions of the poor. You should conclude by reaching a judgement on the question.

## Section C questions

There is no choice in Section C, which is concerned with the historical interpretations you have studied linked to the question 'How revolutionary, in the years to 1701, was the Glorious Revolution of 1688–89?' You will be given two extracts totalling around 400 words (printed separately) and the question will take the form 'How convincing do you find the view that …?' There is no need to use source analysis skills such as drawing inferences for the Section C answers. You should approach your answer by analysing the extracts separately and then as a package, and then use your own knowledge to support, and to counter, the view given in the question, before reaching an overall judgement.

## Use of time

This is an issue which you should discuss with your teachers and fellow students, but here are some suggestions for you.

Do not write solidly for 45 minutes on each question. For Section A and B answers you should spend a few minutes working out what the question is asking you to do, and drawing up a plan of your answer. This is especially important for Section B answers, which cover an extended period of time.

For Section C it is essential that you have a clear understanding of the content of each extract and the points which each extract is making. Read each extract carefully and underline important points. You might decide to spend up to ten minutes reading the extracts and drawing up your plan, and 35 minutes writing your answer.

# Preparing for your A Level exams

## Paper 1: A Level sample answer with comments

### Section A

These questions assess your understanding of the period in breadth. They will ask you about the content you learned about in the four key themes, and may ask about more than one theme. For these questions remember to:

- give an analytical, not a descriptive, response
- support your points with evidence
- cover the whole time period specified in the question
- come to a substantiated judgement.

---

*To what extent were religious differences responsible for the failure to reach a political settlement between 1629 and 1653?*

#### Average student answer

At no point between 1629 and 1653 was a political settlement reached. Charles I acted like a tyrant during his personal rule and alienated a lot of people. He went to war with parliament and after the war the two sides could not agree on how to take the country forward, so Charles was eventually executed. After Charles was executed, a settlement could not be reached and Oliver Cromwell became Lord Protector, making him the first commoner to become head of state. The whole period was a time of upheaval, and the political nation went from one crisis to another.

This is a weak start to the answer. It is a general narrative of the events of 1629–53 and does not address the factor of religious differences given in the question.

Religious differences were important in the search for a settlement. The reason why a settlement was not reached before the Civil War was down to Laud's reforms. Laud favoured High Church policies and alienated puritans. He favoured the decoration of fonts, the presence of organs in churches and the movement of altars from the middle of the church to the east end, railed off from the congregation, something done in the Catholic Church and despised by puritans. Charles promoted Laud's reforms so is equally to blame. The Civil War began as a result of the unpopularity of Charles and Laud's reforms. After the Civil War a settlement could not be reached, partly because of religious differences. The New Model Army became extremely radical and made demands that Charles would never accept. This was partly due to the influence of a radical group called the Levellers. The Levellers wanted society to be equal and were closely related to the puritan movement. After Charles was executed, Cromwell wanted a godly parliament to rule the country, but the Rump Parliament and later the Nominated Assembly were full of people that were not godly enough for Cromwell. Cromwell clamped down on radical groups such as the Ranters and Diggers, closing down their communes and imprisoning their leaders. Overall, religious differences were very important in ensuring that a settlement could not be reached between 1629 and 1653.

The basic content of this paragraph is relevant and accurate, but it is missing sufficient evidence. For example, the discussion on the role of religion during personal rule is weak and makes a broad generalisation about the Civil War being caused by Charles' religious reforms without providing factual evidence.

Another key reason for the failure to reach a settlement was the role of Charles I. During his personal rule he alienated many people when he raised taxes without the consent of parliament. He acted like a tyrant and when parliament was recalled in 1640 many MPs wanted to reduce his powers. In all of the negotiations that followed, Charles refused to negotiate and reach a settlement. He denied all demands offered by the leaders of parliament and Civil War eventually started. Even after the Civil War he did not want a settlement and refused all offers put in front of him. Charles was stubborn by nature, and genuinely believed that everything he did was right and ordained by God. This led of course to his execution in 1649. He had been executed in 1649 so this factor is not important in the years 1649–53.

The key problem with this brief paragraph is a lack of evidence. As well as this, it states that the role of the king is not important between 1649 and 1653 because he had been executed. There was still significant support for the monarchy and the future Charles II, and this could be elaborated on here.

Another reason for the lack of a political settlement was the role of the military in political affairs. The New Model Army was created in 1645 and helped parliament to win the Civil War. They had immense success because they were well trained, well equipped and had a genuine cause to fight for. Some within the Army started asking for political reforms. They felt they had nothing to lose, so they demanded new elections and a widening of the voting franchise. The leaders of the Army would never agree to this, and at the Putney Debates the two sides showed how different their views were. Cromwell and Ireton spoke for the grandees, and said they felt uncomfortable giving political rights to ordinary people, because it would threaten their status as members of the gentry. Pride's Purge was an attempt by the Army to ban Royalist sympathisers and moderates from parliament. After this, the path was clear for Charles to be put on trial. The Rump Parliament of 1649–53 was effectively controlled by the Army, so any chance of a settlement was not possible as the radical groups such as the Levellers were banned entirely. Therefore, the army is a crucial factor in explaining why a settlement could not be reached.

This paragraph relies strongly on narrative, and does not get to the bottom of the reasons why the army was divided and why this caused the lack of a settlement.

In conclusion, there are a number of reasons why a political settlement could not be reached between 1629 and 1653. I believe that differences over religious matters was the most important reason, because if it was not for religion, many of the conflicts seen in these years would not have happened. Charles and Laud followed High Church policies that made them unpopular, resulting in conflicts that would change the monarchy forever, and the government that was created after the Civil War was never willing to give in to demands for religious toleration.

The conclusion focuses solely on the factor of religion rather than investigating other relevant factors. It should contain a judgement that is informed by all of the evidence.

## Verdict

This is an average response because:

- too many paragraphs lack sufficient evidence to back up the arguments being made and it is too descriptive
- most knowledge displayed is accurate, but many points are made without development and explanation, resulting in the answer lacking range and depth
- it doesn't come to a strong reasoned judgement backed up by a strong argument
- although the answer shows a reasonable level of organisation, the quality of written communication is not always clear.

Use the feedback on this answer to rewrite it, making as many improvements as you can.

# Paper 1: A Level sample answer with comments

## Section A

*To what extent were religious differences responsible for the failure to reach a political settlement between 1629 and 1653?*

### Strong student answer

The years 1629 to 1653 were crucial in shaping the constitutional future of Britain, as they include the 'eleven years tyranny' of Charles I, the First Civil War, resulting in the capture of the king and ultimately his execution when a settlement could not be reached. 1649–53 is also important because it marks the country's first attempt at Republican rule under the Commonwealth and Nominated Assembly. This however also failed to provide a lasting settlement and the country would soon be ruled by Oliver Cromwell as Lord Protector, bringing government back to an arbitrary and autocratic system. Religion lay at the heart of national life during the 17th century, and was responsible for many decisions not only in people's everyday lives but also in politics. This is why differences over religious matters are a crucial area of study when assessing these years. As well as religion, the 17th century was the age of personal monarchy, so the role and decisions made by Charles I are essential in understanding the search for a settlement. After the Civil War, the Army became an important part of political life, and this added a further complication to negotiations.

This is a strong introduction that sets out the demands of the question well. Some context to the question is provided and it explains why each of the chosen factors are important.

Religious differences lay at the heart of the search for a settlement between 1629 and 1653. From the outset it was clear that Charles had inherited his father's belief in divine right, and this was evident in many of his dealings with parliament. When he decided to rule without parliament between 1629 and 1640, religious differences that already existed were exacerbated. Whig historians have called these years the 'eleven years tyranny', partly because of Archbishop Laud's persecution of Puritans. The infamous case of Bastwick, Burton and Prynne, who were imprisoned for life and mutilated, highlights the religious tensions evident in the 1630s. When the time came for a political settlement to be reached in order for Charles to fund a war with the Scots, the puritan-dominated House of Commons made it difficult for Charles to get what he wanted. The leader of the opposition, John Pym, pushed for restrictions on religious courts and bishops. Indeed, when the gentry took sides at the outbreak of war in 1642, the issue of whether a hierarchical church with bishops should still exist lay behind the decisions of many. In Scotland and Ireland, too, religious differences meant that settlements could not be reached. The Presbyterian Scots were outraged when Charles attempted to impose the Anglican prayer book on them in 1637, resulting in the formation of the National Covenant in 1638, and the Irish Rebellion of 1641 was partly due to the native Catholic population feeling they had been betrayed by their Protestant overlords.

A detailed section that provides a convincing argument. The issue of religious differences is focused on throughout, with strong supporting evidence.

Religious radicalism became a real force during the First Civil War, when the Leveller movement influenced many rank and file soldiers in the New Model Army. The Levellers demanded religious toleration, as well as equality before the law. The Levellers had an important impact on the search for a settlement between 1646 and 1648, and ultimately the execution of Charles I in 1649. Cromwell envisaged a godly government running the country after the death of Charles, but again religious differences meant this was not possible. Although Cromwell was an Independent, and compulsory attendance at church was repealed through the Toleration Act of 1650, he crushed the Levellers, as well as other radical groups such as the Ranters and Diggers. Cromwell ultimately favoured a settlement that favoured the gentry and did not threaten the existing social hierarchy. The Nominated Assembly, or 'Barebones Parliament', was supposed to be a 'Parliament of Saints', but this collapsed within a few months due to the conservative nature of many of the members.

The actions of Charles cannot be ignored when assessing the failure to reach a political settlement in these years. In the age of personal monarchy, the king's personality and decisions inevitably had an enormous impact on politics. Charles alienated many of the political nation during his personal rule and their frustration would be clear when parliament met again in 1640. Prerogative taxes such as forest fines, distraint of knighthood and ship money, which raised up to £200,000 a year, caused resentment. In 1637, the Buckinghamshire gentleman John Hampden refused to pay ship money and was taken to court. He narrowly lost his case, but by 1639 there was effectively a strike of the taxpayers. Charles had also caused resentment as a result of his Scottish policy and when he recalled parliament he was attempting to finance an expensive war north of the border. Charles was the key figure in the lack of a settlement between 1640 and 1642, as well as during the Civil War itself. When offers of a settlement were put to Charles, such as the Grand Remonstrance and Nineteen Propositions, he maintained that the role of parliament was not to govern jointly but to simply approve taxation. Charles also contributed to the lack of a settlement because he was undoubtedly to blame for starting the Second Civil War in 1648, by entering into secret negotiations with the Scots. However, the opposition can also be blamed for the lack of a settlement. The demands made to Charles were often unrealistic. For example, the Grand Remonstrance in 1641 asked to control the king's councillors and the Four Bills put to Charles in 1647 demanded that parliament control the army for 20 years, something they knew he was unlikely to agree to.

The role of Charles is evaluated well by offering a counter-argument suggesting the opposition within parliament were equally to blame. This counter-argument could be expanded further.

From the creation of the New Model Army onwards, the role of the military in political affairs is crucial in explaining the lack of a settlement. The Army became heavily politicised in 1647. Their original demands amounted to asking for arrears of £3,000,000 to be paid and they soon elected Agitators to advance their political cause. They came to blows with the Presbyterians in parliament who favoured a moderate settlement with the king. At the Putney Debates in October 1647, the rank and file soldiers were represented by Thomas Rainsborough, the highest-ranking Leveller in the Army. He debated with Henry Ireton, who spoke for conservatism and maintaining the existing hierarchy. After the Second Civil War, radical Army officers led by Thomas Pride purged parliament of Royalist sympathisers. After the execution, Leveller mutinies were suppressed by Cromwell and Fairfax, and the Army would be crucial in upholding the experimental Commonwealth and Nominated Assembly. It can be argued that the Commonwealth and Nominated Assembly lacked legitimacy because they were effectively the results of military coups. Royalist feeling was still strong between 1649 and 1653, and if the Army was not so powerful, the monarchy may have been restored earlier than 1660.

Although not as detailed as the previous paragraphs, relevant factual material is deployed to provide a strong argument.

The one party that attempted to prevent a settlement at every stage was undeniably Charles. His commitment to divine right and a genuine belief that he was the only true authority in the country stemmed from his religious beliefs, so both factors worked together to prevent a settlement being reached. The clash of high church Anglicanism and Puritanism that had been building up since the Reformation came to a head in the 1630s and 1640s, so it is clear that Charles would not have been so integral to the events that took place if it was not for religious differences.

The conclusion comes to a substantiated judgement and states that Charles is most responsible for the lack of a settlement. The conclusion also shows an appreciation for other factors and how they are linked.

## Verdict

This is a strong response because:

- it sets out the demands of the question in the introduction and explores a number of key issues, with sustained analysis throughout
- strong supporting evidence is used throughout to respond to the demands of the question
- reasoned judgements are made about the importance of each factor before coming to a strong conclusion
- it is well organised, and the argument is coherent and logical.

# Paper 1: A Level sample answer with comments

## Section B

These questions assess your understanding of the period in breadth. They will ask you about the content you learned about in the four key themes, and may ask about more than one theme. For these questions remember to:

- give an analytical, not a descriptive, response
- support your points with evidence
- cover the whole time period specified in the question
- come to a substantiated judgement.

*How significant was population growth in causing social change between 1625 and 1688?*

### Average student answer

Population growth was an important factor in causing social change between 1625 and 1688. Britain's population grew rapidly after the devastation caused by the plague in 1348, and this caused huge pressures to be put on society. The population roughly doubled in the 100 years before 1625, and towns were starting to grow. As well as this, London grew dramatically, and was far larger than any other population centres. Resources became stretched and towns could not cope with the increasing numbers of people. Food was needed and raw materials were required to meet the demand for housing, heating and day-to-day living. There are also a number of other factors that explain why society changed.

> This is a weak introduction because, although it explains why population growth is important, it does not set up the debate sufficiently. It refers to the fact that there are other factors responsible for social change, but does not elaborate on what they are.

The population roughly doubled in the hundred years before 1625, causing pressures not seen before. One major impact of population growth was on the state of towns. The number of large towns grew significantly between 1625 and 1688. Towns were centres for regional markets, and agricultural produce and other goods would be traded at them. This meant that more people were employed in jobs that were done in towns. As well as changes to employment, population growth led to an increase in poverty, which caused massive social change. As there were not enough jobs to go round, unemployment increased and the number of vagrants became a real problem, and many of the settled poor had to take jobs as servants in the homes of others. Vagrants were people who travelled from place to place, often begging in order to survive. They were classed as criminals under the law. In London, the authorities had to take steps to stop the large number of vagrants from the countryside descending on the city. Population growth was an important factor in social change, especially as the number of towns grew in numbers and size, meaning people's working lives changed drastically.

> A reasonable discussion of population growth. This paragraph could be improved if it included more statistical and factual information rather than making general points. For example, the size of the population is not mentioned, and there are no details about employment in towns.

Social change also came about because of the growth of the professional and merchant classes. Because towns and the city of London grew, more opportunities were available for merchants who could get involved in trading overseas. New markets existed in the colonies of North America and the Caribbean, and the East India Company was pioneering trade with the East. Products were being traded that could fetch high prices in London markets, such as tobacco from Virginia. This led to social change because merchants could become as rich as the gentry class. The gentry class were also of increasing importance in the 17th century and their numbers grew dramatically. The gentry were rich enough to be free of the need to work the land and they could spend time educating themselves. They might own several estates, and have many tenant farmers working for them. The gentry were the class that made up the MPs in parliament, and they were important in causing the Civil War and commanding the armies that fought in the war. As there were more gentry there were more people needed to work for them, providing services

> This is a reasonable discussion of the changing class system, but neglects the important issue of the declining aristocracy making way for the gentry and merchant classes. Accurate points are made about the gentry, but this is not related to the overall argument or backed up with evidence.

and working as servants. At the bottom of society, very little changed, and the lives of the poor were not hugely different to before. The Poor Relief Act of 1601 gave some protection to the poor, and the richer members of a parish were expected to pay towards their upkeep.

The growth of radical ideas also led to some social change. The role of women in Stuart society was as housewives and mothers, and women would often work in the textile industry or in farming. Higher class women had more rights than the poor, and the wives of the gentry were able to look after their houses and estates. This also happened during the Civil War, when some gentry women defended their estates while their husbands were fighting. Puritanism had a huge impact on the lives of its followers, and Puritans tended to see women as more equal to men than the Anglican Church did. Some of the radical sects that emerged in the middle of the century such as the Diggers believed that women should be completely equal to men, and demanded more rights. The Quakers also advocated women's rights, and they became the largest Puritan sect by the end of the period. As well as changing the role of women, radical Puritanism had an impact on political beliefs. Groups such as the Levellers wanted society to be more equal, and they had a large following in the New Model Army. Their ideas were important in the establishment of the Republic in 1649. As well as radical religious ideas, new scientific thinking had an impact on social change. Thinkers such as Francis Bacon and John Locke changed the way science was approached, with a more empirical and rational approach being used.

> This gives too much weight to the idea that women's lives changed and needs to offer the other side of the argument as well. The failure of the radical groups is also not assessed. The reference to science is not utilised effectively and is not made relevant to the answer.

In conclusion, population growth had a big impact on social change as people's way of life in both the countryside and in towns changed forever. Employment, the lives of the poor, living conditions and health were all affected and managing population growth become a huge problem for the government. London grew more than any other town, and the change to the economy and employment there came about as a result of population pressures.

> Only one factor is discussed in the conclusion. Other factors could be evaluated here to make a valid judgement.

## Verdict

This is an average response because:

- there is some analysis, and the answer considers a number of relevant factors, but not in sufficient detail to merit a higher mark
- although most of the information is accurate, there is some irrelevant detail
- some attempt is made to make judgements, but the conclusion is not substantiated
- the general trend of the argument is clear, but at times lacks logic and coherence.

Use the feedback on this answer to rewrite it, making as many improvements as you can.

# Paper 1: A Level sample answer with comments

## Section B

*How significant was population growth in causing social change between 1625 and 1688?*

### Strong student answer

Society changed in a number of ways between 1625 and 1688. The growth of poverty, a changing class system, new ideas and changing gender roles all had an impact on social change at some point in the period. It is clear that population growth was an important determining factor in driving at least some of this change. The population of Britain had grown steadily since the 14th century, and this put new pressures on society that had not been seen before. Other factors can be seen as responsible for social change in these years, including the decline of the aristocracy. In their place, a thriving gentry and merchant class were able to flourish and take advantage of the new economic conditions that were present in the 17th century. As well as this, the growth of radical ideas in philosophy, science and religion helped to change society to an extent.

This is a strong introduction that sets out what is going to be addressed in the essay, and emphasises the importance of population growth as a factor. It introduced a number of factors that will be discussed.

The population of England doubled in the 100 years before 1625, from around 2.5 million to over 5 million. The populations of Scotland and Ireland also went up, but not at the same rate. This impacted on social change in a number of ways, but nowhere more clearly than in towns. In 1600, there were eight towns with a population over 5,000, and this had increased to over 30 in 1700. This naturally changed society as towns provided different employment opportunities, resulting in those employed in agriculture declining from 67% of the population in 1600 to 56% in 1700. One industry that did particularly well was the cloth industry and, as the 'new draperies' from the Low Countries started to be produced in England, people's working lives changed. Despite these changes, the historian Barry Coward has argued that towns did not grow any more than is to be expected, and people's lives changed very little in these years.

Relevant statistics are used to create a convincing argument, although more analysis of these could take place.

Population growth undoubtedly had an impact on levels of poverty, in both towns and the countryside. By the middle of the century, two-thirds of the urban population lived near the poverty line, and between 1600 and 1650 inflation was around 4%. This outstripped wage rises, resulting in a decline in living conditions for some. Population growth led to overcrowding and competition for jobs in towns, and in the countryside, two-fifths of the rural poor had to work as domestic servants. It has been estimated that one-third of the population of rural villages in any given decade had to leave to find work, such was the competition for jobs. It is therefore clear that population growth impacted on social change, and the government were acutely aware of this. The existing Poor Relief legislation that had been passed in 1601 was modified in 1662, as vagrants were becoming a serious problem. This second Act restricted the movement of vagrants, and gave a definition of what constituted 'poor' for the first time, thus showing that the government was acutely aware of the changes that had taken place in the conditions of the poor.

The impact of population growth is addressed again in this paragraph to show the impact it had on poverty and factual information is used well to relate this argument to the demands of the question.

The fortunes of the aristocracy were in decline between 1625 and 1688, and this resulted in some changes to the structure of society. Since Elizabeth's time, the aristocracy had been in decline, partly due to inflation, and partly due to the fact that much of the wealth of the aristocracy was tied up in assets they could not make a profit from, such as their property. As the aristocracy declined, the gentry class were able to flourish. The number of gentry increased by 300% between 1550 and 1650, and some of them even became richer than the aristocracy. Historian Hugh Trevor-Roper has claimed that 'office rather than land' was the basis of their success, and they were able to hold important positions within government and the admiralty. As the economy improved, particularly in the second half of the century, there was an increase in the number of merchants. Many were based in London, and the most successful were given

A strong paragraph on the decline of the aristocracy, and rise of the gentry and merchant classes. Sound evidence is used and a link is made to the previous factor of population growth.

knighthoods for their service, which were previously only awarded through family connections. The Navigation Act of 1651 strengthened the power of the merchants, as British ships were guaranteed to be used in the transportation of British goods. More gentry and merchants meant there was more of a demand for those that were employed in providing services for them. In London in particular, more lawyers, doctors and architects were needed. The decline in the aristocracy and increase in the merchant class had little impact on the lower orders, and at the bottom of society it can be argued that very little changed. 90% of those accepted to the Inns of Court were still the sons of the gentry and nobility, and the sheer number of the poor (26,000 were arrested for vagrancy in the 1630s) shows that radical social change did not happen. This factor can be linked to population growth, because the gentry appear to be the class that benefitted most obviously from the increase in poverty driven by population pressures.

The growth of radical political and religious ideas also encouraged social change. The role of women changed in some social circles, as Puritanism became more popular. Traditional religious teaching stated that women should have a traditional role in the home. Wealthy women had more independence, and the daughters of the gentry would often be literate. There are a number of examples of women running the estates of soldiers fighting in the Civil War, and 6,000 women petitioned parliament for peace in 1643. After the First Civil War, there seemed to be the prospect of some change when radical ideas became more popular. The Levellers advocated giving some rights to women (though not the vote), and 10,000 Leveller women petitioned for John Lilburne's release in 1649. The Diggers went as far as to advocate female suffrage in the middle of the century, although their support was not widespread and they were limited by the Commonwealth. Despite this, the role of women changed little. The Adultery Act passed under the Commonwealth imposed the death penalty on women for adultery, although women were treated better in the North American Colonies. The group that had the most success in promoting the rights of women was the Quakers, who allowed girls to be educated in four of the 15 schools they opened before 1671.

Radical social change was promised by groups like the Levellers, who wanted a fairer and more just society. The Levellers wanted new elections under universal male suffrage, and wanted to abolish the House of Lords. Between 1649 and 1653, the radical groups were crushed and again the only group that had any long-term success was the Quakers, who had 35,000 members in the 1660s. Social attitudes were ultimately changed by the rise in the rational scientific method, first promoted by Francis Bacon. Bacon, and later John Locke, studied science and philosophy through empiricism and observation. This would eventually have an impact on social attitudes, but this was not until after the Glorious Revolution.

Radical political ideas are linked well to social change, and both the successes and failures of this are addressed. The discussion of the scientific revolution is brief and could be expanded further.

In conclusion, population growth had a knock-on effect on a number of changes between 1625 and 1688. The growth of poverty and success of the gentry clearly widened the gap between rich and poor, but it is debatable whether this was caused solely by population growth. The impact of radical ideas was limited because throughout much of the period these ideas were outlawed. The most important reason for social change appears to come from the changing class system, in particular the decline in the aristocracy. If this had not happened, the old social fabric would not have changed, and the Civil War and ensuing radical events would not have happened.

A strong conclusion that weighs up the factors that have been discussed in the essay and comes to a solid conclusion.

## Verdict

This is a strong response because:

- the answer considers a number of relevant factors and evaluates them well and there is a sustained analysis of the key features of the period
- accurate and appropriate evidence is used throughout
- links are made between factors and the conclusion comes to a reasoned judgement
- the answer is well organised and follows a clear, logical structure.

# Paper 1: A Level sample answer with comments

## Section C

These questions require you to read two extracts carefully to identify the key points raised and establish the argument being put forward. For these questions remember to:

- read and analyse the extracts thoroughly, remembering that you need to use them in tandem
- take careful note of the information provided about the extracts
- deploy own knowledge to develop the points and arguments that emerge from the extracts and to provide appropriate context
- develop an argument rooted in the points raised in the extracts and come to a substantiated conclusion.

---

***Study Extracts 3 and 11 (pages 121 and 136) before you answer this question.***

*In the light of differing interpretations, how convincing do you find the view that, as a result of the Glorious Revolution, 'the English monarchy became limited' (Extract 11, line 4)?*

*To explain your answer, analyse and evaluate the material in both extracts, using your own knowledge of the issues.*

### Average student answer

The English monarchy clearly became limited as a result of the Glorious Revolution. The previous Catholic monarch, James II, who had ruled since 1685, fled London in 1688 and William of Orange was able to take his place with the consent of parliament. James was an unpopular monarch, primarily because he was Catholic. He attempted to put Catholics in places of power, and most importantly he resorted to personal rule, and neglected parliament. When he imprisoned seven bishops for their opposition to the second Declaration of Indulgence, his popularity hit rock bottom. A number of leading figures in the political nation sent a letter to William asking him to come to England, and he consented. The monarchy has been limited ever since, but the process that resulted in the constitutional monarchy that exists today started with William and Mary. Harris states in Extract 11 that 'it ceased to be a personal monarchy' in the way it had been under previous monarchs.

This is a weak opening paragraph that does not target the specific question and only mentions one of the sources. It provides only a simplistic view of the events of 1688, and does not show an awareness of the importance of the period 1689–1701. There is nothing included that supports the alternative view that the monarchy was not limited.

There is much evidence to show that the power of the monarch became limited between 1689 and 1701. The most important Act that was passed was the Bill of Rights in 1689. This limited the monarch because it called for free elections, an end to unparliamentary taxation and parliamentary approval for a standing army in peace time. The Bill of Rights was enhanced by the Triennial Act of 1694. This stated that parliament could not sit for longer than three years, resulting in more regular elections. This led to parliament becoming increasingly important in the political system. As well as these Acts, the Act of Settlement limited the monarchy because it ensured that no future monarch could be a Catholic. The Act of Settlement was a response to the Catholicism and absolutism of James, and although parliament knew that William was a Protestant, the Stuarts were still a threat.

This paragraph includes relevant detail, but opportunities to relate this to the extracts are missed. There is no attempt to evaluate the importance of these Acts, which could be done by referring to the rise of the Whig Junto and a strong executive.

Extract 3 calls the events a 'Sensible Revolution' and a 'conservative Revolution', suggesting that the Revolution did not drastically change the way government worked. Morrill also states that the Revolution 'quickened and nurtured a distinctive phase' in British history, and admits that parties were formed that would control the way government and politics worked for the next 200 years. So Morrill's view is that the Revolution was both conservative and radical, and that it caused changes that may have happened regardless of the events that took place. Changes had already started after the Civil War, as the idea of personal monarchy had been questioned. Charles II resorted to consulting parliament, although by the end of his reign he had also reverted to personal rule. Morrill's belief that the revolutionary changes might have happened without the

The extract is used to make quite basic descriptive points. The references here could be backed up with contextual knowledge, particularly around the formation of parties.

events of 1689 is quite flawed, as no member of the Stuart family was prepared to give as much power to parliament as William did.

The monarchy did become more limited, but the king also kept a number of powers after the Glorious Revolution. Extract 11 emphasises this when Harris says 'in many respects it became a monarchy with more real power'. The monarch had more power within parliament as they had to work together in order to fund the Nine Years' War. This war with France was very costly, and normal methods of raising funds were not adequate. William spent much of his time away fighting this war, and parliament attempted to restrict his ability to finance the war by offering him limited subsidies and only enough funding for a small army. In response to this, William attempted to raise money through the use of loans, and set up the Bank of England in 1694. Investors in the Bank of England were paid back with interest, and much of the money used to pay them back came from excise taxes and other methods of royal revenue. As well as this, William still commanded great respect within parliament, and MPs still had to swear an oath of allegiance to him and he had the power to declare war and dissolve parliament.

This paragraph does attempt to provide balance by elaborating on the argument that the Crown was not fully limited. The extract from Harris should be fully explained.

On balance, the evidence seems to agree that the power of the monarchy was limited as a result of the events of 1689 to 1701. The Bill of Rights imposed constraints on the Crown and ensured that parliament was a permanent and important part of the constitution, and the Triennial Act meant that parliament became a part of the political system that the monarch could not ignore. This was because parliament had to meet regularly, and parliament had to approve many of the king's actions.

This paragraph is too brief to fully justify the conclusion the response is making, and makes no reference to the extracts.

## Verdict

This is an average response because:

- it shows a basic understanding of the extracts and shows some analysis, and explains some key points of interpretation found in the extracts
- there is some deployment of own knowledge, but a significant amount provides background to the topic rather than being focused on the specific question and links to the extracts
- a judgement is made in the conclusion, but this is not supported by enough evidence
- the argument is mostly coherent, but there are some issues with quality of communication.

Use the feedback on this answer to rewrite it, making as many improvements as you can.

# Paper 1: A Level sample answer with comments

## Section C

These questions require you to read two extracts carefully to identify the key points raised and establish the argument being put forward. For these questions remember to:

- read and analyse the extracts thoroughly, remembering that you need to use them in tandem
- take careful note of the information provided about the extracts
- deploy own knowledge to develop the points and arguments that emerge from the extracts and to provide appropriate context
- develop an argument rooted in the points raised in the sources and come to a substantiated conclusion.

***Study Extracts 3 and 11 (pages 121 and 136) before you answer this question.***

*In the light of differing interpretations, how convincing do you find the view that, as a result of the Glorious Revolution, 'the English monarchy became limited' (Extract 11, line 4)?*

*To explain your answer, analyse and evaluate the material in both extracts, using your own knowledge of the issues.*

### Strong student answer

The two extracts contain differing perspectives on the issue of the balance between monarchical and parliamentary power. Harris in Extract 11 argues that the monarchy became 'limited, bureaucratic and parliamentary' but also a 'monarchy with more real power', while Morrill in Extract 3 states that the Revolution was sensible and cautious, but that it quickened a transitional phase that had already started. Both authors provide evidence to advance their arguments: Morrill focuses on the contradictory nature of the events and the rise in parliamentary parties, whereas Harris refers to the impact of the Nine Years' War. Harris also refers to the growth of a 'fiscal military state', where the king had no choice but to work with parliament.

A strong opening paragraph that is directed by the extracts and identifies the main arguments contained within them.

Harris argues that the Revolution resulted in a monarchy that became 'limited, bureaucratic and parliamentary', and it is important to be aware of the reasons why historians have come to this conclusion. Whig historians such as Thomas Macaulay concluded that the Revolution was non-violent and in many ways non-revolutionary, as the English had no desire to fundamentally change the constitution. The succession was only slightly altered to exclude Catholics and the basic powers of the monarchy were unchanged. More recently, a number of historians have followed the lead of some Enlightenment thinkers who suggested that the Revolution was a transformative period and that it did limit the monarchy. There is evidence to show that the Bill of Rights and Triennial Act reduced the power of the monarchy. The monarch now had no choice but to submit to regular parliaments and had less control over the army and taxation. There is, however, a vagueness to the Bill of Rights, as it fails to include measures to deal with tyrannical monarchs and does not detail how elections should work or how often they should take place. Morrill, too, says that the Revolution established 'a new pattern of constitutional relationships', suggesting that the role of the monarchy had changed permanently as a result of the events of 1689–1701.

This paragraph argues that the monarchy was limited, with reference to both sources and some effective evidence deployed. An excellent knowledge of the historical debate is shown in order to put the sources into context.

In order to place Harris' argument that the monarchy became limited into context, it is important to note that William's entire rule was based on the concept of a limited monarchy, and when he took the throne he was well aware of this. William's wife, Mary Stuart, was the closest living Protestant heir to the throne, and they were placed on the throne as a reaction to the absolutism experienced under James II. Earlier monarchs, especially Charles I, had failed to reach political settlements with parliament because they believed, justifiably, that parliament was not a partner in government but simply a law-making and tax-raising body that worked on behalf

This paragraph demonstrates a good understanding of the context of the argument contained in Extract II.

of the monarch. This could not be further from the truth in the 1690s and in 1697 parliament approved a grant of £700,000 to cover William's expenses. This emphasises the limited nature of the monarchy.

Despite the fact that both sources show that the monarchy became limited, there is evidence to suggest that the monarchy remained relatively unchanged. Although Morrill accepts that the Revolution caused conflict in Ireland and Scotland, he states that 'it did not create damaging new rifts in the English nation', suggesting that little changed. Harris also follows this thread, when he suggests that the monarchy gained more real power. Here, Harris is stating that as parliament and king were working together in the 'fiscal military state', in the context of the Nine Years' War, William, as commander-in-chief and head of the Church, was able to direct where money could be spent to an extent. Despite this, the Country opposition were able to pass a bill restricting the army to 7,000 men and refused to allow the retention of William's Dutch Guard. When Morrill states that the political and religious settlements were 'fudges', he may be referring to the fact that many of the demands contained in the original Declaration of Rights were not implemented in the Bill of Rights, thus giving the monarchy significant power.

Makes some relevant points about the power that the monarchy still had. Own knowledge is used to put the arguments into context.

Harris emphasises the importance of the Nine Years' War in promoting revolutionary change, and weighs this up against the events of 1688–89. The War was important because it was in these years that the 'Whig Junto' rose in prominence to become key advisers to the king. In 1696, in the face of an assassination attempt against William, the Junto encouraged both Houses to adopt a proposal acknowledging William as the true and lawful king. By the end of the decade, the Junto collapsed in the face of opposition, and William was implored to agree to a bill of resumption depriving some of his advisers of their land in Ireland. This shows that, although the Junto was able to uphold royal authority for a time and govern as they pleased, the monarchy could still be constrained in a way that was not possible before.

This paragraph maintains a focus on the key issues in the question. Some more factual information, perhaps on Whig and Tory voting statistics, would help to advance the argument.

In conclusion, the balance of the argument appears to favour Harris' argument that the Revolution limited the monarchy and enhanced the power of parliament because the monarchy became reliant on parliament for most (but not all) aspects of its existence, especially finance. Morrill is correct in stating that the Revolution was 'conservative' and was relatively organic and peaceful in nature, but it did fundamentally change the relationship between king and parliament. A number of Acts were passed between 1689 and 1701 that ensured that the monarch would have no choice but to work with parliament if they wanted to fund both their wars and their own reigns.

The concluding paragraph comes to a clear judgement based on the balance of the evidence.

### Verdict

This is a strong response because:

- it identifies and illustrates the arguments of the two extracts, and interprets them with confidence in order to analyse the key issues raised
- it deploys a sound range of specific evidence in most cases to develop points emerging from the extracts in order to provide a sense of context
- it presents a sustained evaluative argument throughout, reaching fully substantiated judgements by showing an understanding of the historical debate
- the answer is coherent and the quality of communication is excellent.

# France in revolution, 1774-99

**SOURCE 1** A painting by the contemporary artist Pierre Antoine de Machy showing the Place de la Révolution in Paris during the 1790s. This was the square where many people were guillotined during the French Revolution. This image has been interpreted by some as showing the execution of King Louis XVI.

The guillotine is one of the most iconic symbols of the French Revolution: a symbol of death and control through fear. The guillotine claimed many thousands of lives, the greatest proportion of which were during the radical phase of the revolution (1793–94), a period known as the Terror. Yet the guillotine also represents the paradox of the French Revolution. To us, in the 21st century, it is an inhumane machine, but when it was introduced as a common method of execution during the revolution, it was based upon ideas of humanity and equality. Unlike methods of execution prior to the revolution, which included strangling and the breaking of suspects' backs, the guillotine was relatively painless and therefore more humane. Furthermore, in pre-revolutionary France, the nature of the execution depended on a person's standing in society. A noble could expect to be despatched quickly through decapitation by axe or sword. A commoner would face a slow and more painful death. In revolutionary France, all those condemned were executed via the guillotine. As such, it was a symbol of equality.

The paradox that the guillotine presents can be applied to the French Revolution more generally. To some, the revolution was, and is still perceived as, a noble fight against tyranny: a fight for liberty, equality and brotherhood (the maxim of the revolution was *liberté, égalité, fraternité*). To others, it is a lesson from the past about the dangers of what can happen when a society attempts to transform itself too quickly, with an inevitable decline into chaos and dictatorship. The debate over both the ethics and the causes of the revolution continues to this very day and will, no doubt, continue into the future. When, in 1953, the Chinese prime minister, a leading communist (many communists looked to learn lessons from the French Revolution), was asked for his view on the French Revolution, he simply replied: 'It is still too early to tell.'

**1770**

1770 – Prince Louis marries Austrian princess Marie Antoinette

**1778**

1778 – France enters the American Revolutionary War (1775-83) on the side of the USA

**1788**

1788 – Aristocracy revolts against King Louis

**1790**

1790 – Political clubs, such as the Jacobins and Cordeliers, and a radical press develop

Aristocrats begin to flee France; they are known as *émigrés*

August – The Civil Constitution of the Clergy attacks the Church's power

**1792**

1792

April – The Revolutionary Wars between France and other European powers begin

July – Austrian and Prussian powers threaten to destroy Paris

August – Louis' palace is stormed by a mob and he is arrested

September – France is declared a republic

**1794**

1794

June-July – The Great Terror, Robespierre increases the Terror to stop opposition to his rule

July – The Coup of Thermidor ends the Terror

Robespierre and his followers are executed

**1795-96**

1795-96 – Rebellion breaks out again in western France

**1798**

1798

May – The Directors overturn election results to purge Jacobins from the Councils in the Coup of Floréal

1774 1774 - Louis XVI ascends to the French throne

1787-88 1787-88 - Financial crisis in France combines with bad harvests

1789 1789 - The French Revolution

June - The National Assembly declares itself the ruler of France

July - The Storming of the Bastille symbolises the collapse of Louis' power

August - The Declaration of the Rights of Man and of the Citizen declares equality and liberty

1791 1791

June - King Louis and the royal family try to flee France

1793 1793

January - Louis is publicly beheaded by guillotine

March - Civil war breaks out in France in opposition to the government

April - The Committee of Public Safety is established to punish 'enemies' of France

September - The Terror, partly led by Robespierre, begins; executions of suspected enemies increase

October-November - The Committee executes its political enemies; rebellious towns are brutally supressed

1795 1795 - Jacobins are persecuted in the White Terror

August - A new constitution comes into effect, establishing the government of the Directory

September - *Émigrés* launch an unsuccessful invasion of France

1797 1797

September - Royalists are purged from the Councils in the Coup of Fructidor

New conscription laws lead to increased unrest

October - The Treaty of Campo-Formio formalises Napoleon's defeat of the Austrians

1799 1799

October - Napoleon returns to Paris with great popularity

November - The Coup of Brumaire leads to the collapse of the Directory

Napoleon seizes power

Despite the division of opinion, what is widely accepted is the massive significance of the French Revolution. So much so that 1789 is often considered the date when the Early Modern period (which followed the Medieval period) ended, and the Modern period began. Using any date to define a period of history is problematic, but the fact that historians use the French Revolution as a threshold in time suggests a lot about its importance. The revolution played a major role in spreading democratic ideals, ideas of equality and the rights of the common man. It is also seen as fundamentally important in challenging ideas about monarchy, the power of the Church and the privilege of aristocracy. Its effects were felt far and wide, from the European colonies in the Caribbean, to the fledgling USA, to almost all of Europe. It inspired revolutionary movements in many other countries and influenced the development of many ideologies, including **nationalism** and **communism**. Its laws, reinterpreted by Napoleon after the revolution, provide the legal framework for many European countries to this day.

A study of the French Revolution takes us through an experiment in political ideas and government, an experiment that was acted out on a national scale. In many ways, it was a series of revolutions rather than a single one. Absolute monarchy gave way, in 1789, to constitutional monarchy. This, in turn, gave way to a radical republic in 1792, characterised by violence and terror. The Terror ended in 1794 with an attempt to restore a more moderate balance of government to France and, when that failed, in 1799, a new period of European history was born: the Napoleonic era. Each of these stages, from the reign of Louis XVI to the fall of the Directory in 1799, is explored in this unit.

### KEY TERMS

**Nationalism**
An extreme form of patriotism, or pride in one's own country. The French Revolution encouraged loyalty to one's country, as opposed to loyalty to a specific king or ruler.

**Communism**
A system where all property is owned by the community and, in theory, people within that community contribute what they can, and receive according to their need. Leading communist thinkers, such as Karl Marx and Vladimir Lenin, used the French Revolution as an example of how oppressed people can overthrow their rulers in order to achieve a more equal society.

# 2a.1 The origins and onset of revolution, 1774-89

## KEY QUESTIONS

- Was King Louis XVI doomed from the start?
- How far were the causes of the revolution a question of economic decline, rather than political discontent?
- To what extent were King Louis XVI and his court responsible for the onset of revolution?
- What was significant about the events of 1789?

The storming of the Bastille has become the most enduring image of the French Revolution. Arguably less significant than the events that were unfolding in the political assemblies of Versailles, the attack nevertheless came to symbolise the revolution of 1789; it was a symbol of the collapse of royal power, an end to tyranny and the rise of the liberated populace. Predictably, the reality of the situation is far more complex and the events of summer 1789 did not suddenly sweep away the despotism of the ***ancien régime*** to create an enlightened society, where the oppressed population were freed from their chains. Whether or not the *ancien régime* was despotic and whether the population were oppressed are even matters of debate. That said, it is undeniable that the political situation in France was very different at the end of July 1789 than it had been at the start of 1788. After years of ruling as an **absolute monarch**, without the obligation to consult any assembly, King Louis XVI now found himself in a situation where decisions on the future of the French nation were being formulated by a National Assembly, created against his wishes and set on rewriting the political and social structures of the state. Not only this, Louis now faced open resistance on the streets of Paris as armed militia staged demonstrations and stormed government buildings like the Bastille.

### KEY TERMS

***Ancien régime***
Used to describe the structure of French society and government prior to the revolution of 1789.

**Absolute monarch**
A monarch who has absolute power over their subjects: their power is not restricted by law or constitution.

**Enlightenment**
A period during the 17th and 18th centuries when philosophers and other academics increasingly began to challenge the views and values of the societies within which they lived.

The causes of this huge shift in power within France have been the subject of much debate, a debate stretching back over two centuries (see 'Extend Your Knowledge', page 178). The debate largely hinges around two central issues: who caused the revolution and what drove these people to action. In terms of 'who', we can consider both social class and the scale of opposition. Some historians have viewed the revolution as a bourgeois (middle-class) one, some have highlighted the role of the nobility (especially in relation to the financial crisis of 1787–88), whereas others have placed more emphasis on the peasants and the urban poor. Some claim the revolution reflected widespread resentment regardless of class, others have pointed to the dissatisfaction of a limited minority, mainly the bourgeoisie. In relation to what drove these groups, a number of different factors have been identified and assessed. Some emphasise the role of the **Enlightenment** in causing the people of France to question the corruptions and inequalities of their society. Others have focused more on the economic causes, arguing that rising food prices caused resentment to spill over into revolution.

**1730s-1770s** - Enlightened *philosophes* publish texts attacking the *ancien régime*

**1756-63** - Seven Years' War leaves France in huge debt

**1770** - Prince Louis, heir to the French throne, marries Marie Antoinette

**1774** - May: Louis XVI ascends to the throne
August: Anne-Robert-Jacques Turgot is appointed controller-general
Winter to spring 1775: Bad harvests combined with free trade reforms lead to Flour Wars

**1778** - France enters the American Revolutionary War (1775-83) on the side of the USA

**1781** - Jacques Necker produces his *Compte rendu au Roi*

**1787** - April: Charles-Alexandre de Calonne is dismissed after the Notables oppose his proposed reforms

**1787** - July: Paris *Parlement* rejects Louis' edicts
August: Paris *Parlement* is exiled

1730s-1770s | 1754-63 | 1770 | 1775 | 1780 | 1785

SOURCE 1 The storming of the Bastille, a royal fortress used as a prison, on 14 July 1789. Armed Parisian demonstrators stormed the fortress, killing Governor De Launay. Although only seven prisoners were freed from the Bastille, the storming and subsequent demolition of the building came to symbolise the downfall of absolute monarchy.

The failings of King Louis XVI, his court and his ministers have also been stressed by certain writers, whereas some have defended him, arguing that he was doomed from the very start of his reign. This chapter seeks to address all of these issues and arguments in an attempt to explain the causes of the 1789 revolution.

1788 | 1789 | 1790

**1788** – Bad harvests cause famine and bread price increases

**1788** – June: Day of Tiles, pro-*parlement* revolt in Grenoble

**1788** – August: France is declared bankrupt
August: Louis agrees to convene the Estates-General

**1789** – May: The Estates-General meets at Versailles

**1789** – 17 June: Third Estate declares itself the National Assembly
20 June: Tennis Court Oath is sworn
27 June: Louis orders the union of the three estates, legitimising the National Assembly

**1789** – July: Louis calls further troops into Paris and Versailles
11 July: Necker is dismissed, causing riots in Paris
14 July: Storming of the Bastille
15 July: National Guard is formed to defend property, with Lafayette as commander

# WAS KING LOUIS XVI DOOMED FROM THE START?

When Louis XVI inherited the throne of France in 1774, he inherited a country governed by a deeply unequal social and political system. As enlightened views spread in the 18th century, an increasing number of people began to question and challenge the nature of their society. This section addresses how politics and society were divided under the *ancien régime* and what criticisms were made of that system at the time.

## Absolutism, court faction and the *parlements*

### Absolute monarchy

Prior to the revolution in 1789, France was ruled by the Bourbon royal family, an ancient aristocratic dynasty who had ruled France since the 16th century. The Bourbon kings ruled France as an absolute monarchy. It was believed and widely accepted that the king's power was God-given; he had a **divine right** to rule with total power.

It is rumoured that Louis' predecessor, King Louis XIV (1638–1715), once said of his position: 'L'État, c'est moi', meaning 'I am the state'. Whether he actually said this or not is perhaps less significant than what it suggests about how France was governed during the *ancien régime*. The French monarchy did, in many ways, have absolute power. There was no elected representative body, like a parliament, to check the power of the king. The king chose a small group of ministers to advise him, the most important of whom was called the **controller-general**. These ministers were appointed or dismissed as the king wished and so courtiers would compete to impress him in order to win appointment. There was no formal meeting of these ministers, they were simply consulted as and when the king desired. The king was also the only person who could initiate new legislation and, while he could consult a council of advisors, he was under no obligation to accept their views. Furthermore, the king had the right of arbitrary arrest and imprisonment, where someone is arrested and detained without a trial, by issuing a *lettre de cachet* (a *cachet* is a royal seal), like an arrest warrant. *Lettres de cachet* became the target of much criticism during the Enlightenment (see page 188) as they were seen as a symbol of **despotism**.

As well as significant political power, the royal families of the *ancien régime* lived in absolute splendour. The royal court was situated at Versailles, some 20 kilometres from Paris, and it was here that the centre of political power resided. One of the largest and grandest palaces in all of Europe, the Palace of Versailles was significantly developed and extended under King Louis XIV. The front of the palace is an incredible 402 metres long, filled with the finest art, furniture and decoration. Versailles would host lavish parties where court factions would compete to win the king's favour. Palace life at Versailles was determined by a strict code of **etiquette**, dictating everything from when people could eat, to what they wore, to what type of chair they were allowed to sit on. Failure to adhere to the expected behaviours could lose a noble their position at court.

**KEY TERMS**

**Divine right**
The belief that monarchs' power is God-given and, as such, they have the right to rule as they see fit. To rebel against a divinely appointed monarch would be a sin against God.

**Controller-general**
The most senior position in the French ministry. The controller-general was in charge of the finances of the state. They would be appointed or dismissed by the king as he wished.

**Despotism**
When absolute power is used in a cruel, abusive or oppressive manner.

**Etiquette**
Traditions and customs of good manners. Customary codes and rules of behaviour that determine how one should act.

### Limits to the monarch's power

Perhaps the biggest limits to the king's power were the *parlements*. These were local law courts or councils, and, by the 1780s, there were 13 situated in regional administrative centres, like Grenoble, Bordeaux and Toulouse. The most important *parlement* was that in Paris. The *parlements* of the *ancien régime* should not be confused with, or considered similar to, the British parliament. The French *parlements* did not create laws and were not elected. The members of the *parlements* would be important local nobles and higher clergymen, such as bishops. It was their responsibility to ensure that the populace performed their civic duties and to prosecute those who did not. They also, like any law court, would try those accused of being outside the king's law.

The *parlements* also had an important political role. They could refuse to register and implement laws created by the king if they felt them to be against the traditions and values of the *ancien régime*. If this happened, the king could issue a *lit de justice*, essentially an edict over-ruling the *parlements* and demanding that the law was registered. Yet, without the support of the *parlements*, it would be very difficult for the monarch to ensure that a law was implemented. Furthermore, if the king did dare to over-rule the *parlements*, he would risk being accused of despotism. This left the king in a somewhat uncertain position, with the power to create laws independently, yet lacking total power to see these laws enacted. In 1788, King Louis XVI would discover for himself the perils of trying to force the *parlements* to obey his command (see page 184).

## The three estates, the rights of nobles and church privilege

Under the *ancien régime*, French society was divided into three classes, known as estates. The First Estate consisted of the Catholic clergy, the Second Estate was the nobility and the Third Estate was everybody else. It should be noted that the estate to which a person belonged was not necessarily an indication of wealth. It could certainly be said that the vast majority of the Second Estate were wealthier than the vast majority of the Third Estate but, as Figure 1 shows, the situation was actually more complex. The estates system was more concerned with determined rights, privileges and responsibilities.

### The First Estate

Members of the First Estate, the clergy, numbered around 130,000 out of a total population of somewhere in the region of 28 million. The majority of this estate were monks, nuns and lower clergy, such as local parish priests, who were often very poor. The remainder of the First Estate were higher clergy: abbots, bishops and archbishops, who would usually be very wealthy and whose positions tended to be passed on within families, much like aristocratic titles.

**SOURCE 2** The palace of Versailles, as painted by French artist Pierre Patel in 1668. This image was painted prior to the significant developments and extension made by King Louis XIV. Even so, the vast wealth of the Bourbon monarchy is clearly evident.

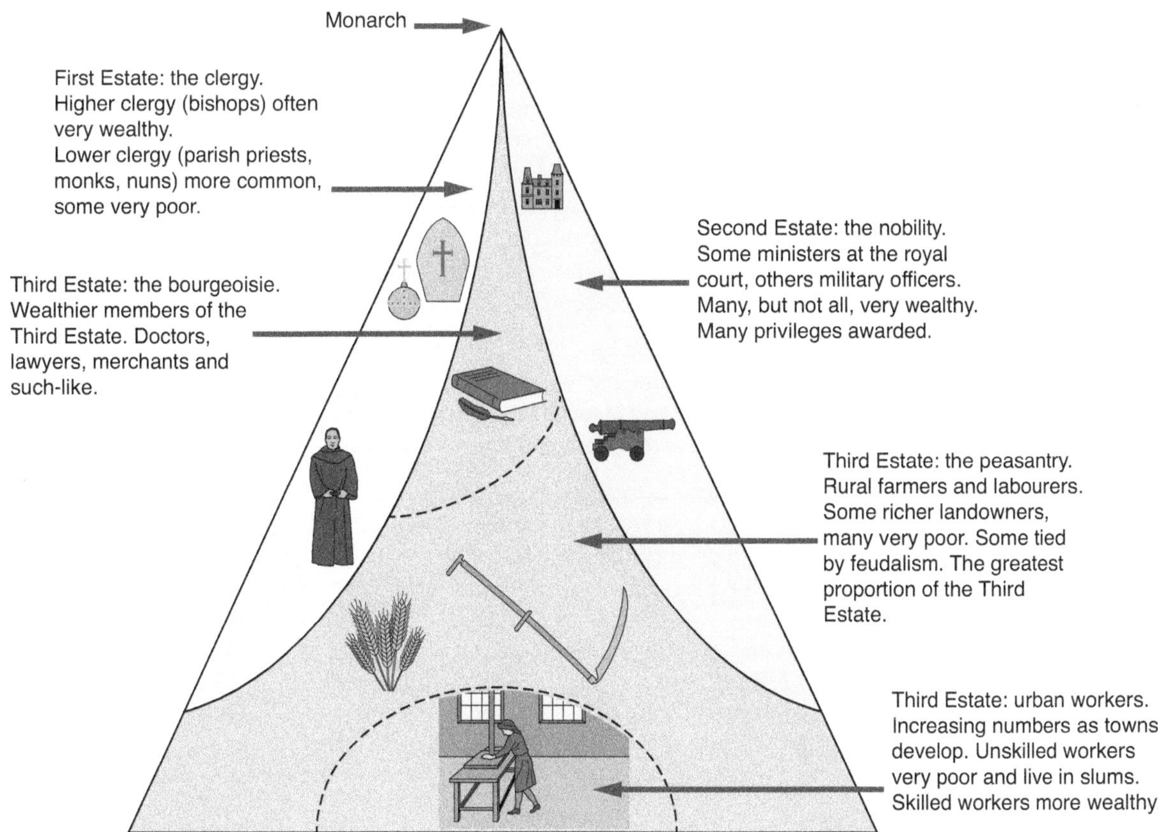


**Figure 1**: A representation of the structure of French society under the *ancien régime*. The higher they were placed within the triangle, the greater a person's wealth.

For most French people in the 18th century, the Catholic Church played a key role in their lives. The Church was responsible for administering poor relief and providing the limited educational facilities and hospitals that existed at the time. Supposedly to fund these services, and to pay for their local priest and church buildings, members of the Third Estate were obliged to pay a tax to the Church known as a tithe. The tithe amounted to one-tenth of a person's earnings or produce. Some resented paying the tithe, as it was felt that the wealth often only went to make the abbots and bishops even more prosperous, rather than benefiting the local community. This resentment was added to by the fact that some bishops rarely visited the dioceses (an administrative district under the supervision of a bishop) they were supposed to represent (a practice known as absenteeism). A further privilege was that the First Estate were exempt from paying direct taxation, such as the *taille* (see page 178). The wealth and privilege of the Catholic Church was an aspect of French society particularly attacked during the Enlightenment.

### The Second Estate

It was the Second Estate who enjoyed the most privilege – as well as the majority of wealth. Estimates vary hugely as to the size of the nobility in France in the 1780s, from around 120,000 to 350,000. Nobles usually acquired their titles through inheritance, the norm with hereditary aristocracy. The most attractive privilege bestowed on the Second Estate was that they were exempt from paying nearly all direct taxation as well as some indirect taxes, such as the much-despised *gabelle* (see page 178). Historically, this was based on the expectation that nobles would fight and lead armies for the king, and this was their duty instead of paying tax. However, by the late 18th century, this expectation no longer existed due to the rise of professional armies. In fact, the Second Estate were even exempt from compulsory military service (although officers within the army would exclusively be aristocrats). Other perks included exclusive hunting and fishing rights, and noblemen were often granted **monopolies** on a local scale over particular goods (such as wine) or small businesses (such as bakeries), to the frustration of some members of the bourgeoisie.

### The Third Estate

The vast majority of the population belonged to the Third Estate and most of them were peasants. Some peasants would own land, employ labourers and sell produce for profit. Far more common, though, were poor labourers who earned little for their labour and often lived at subsistence levels. Other peasants lived on and farmed the land of the nobility, under a system of **feudalism**. In return for the land and their subsistence, they would have to pay feudal, or seigniorial, dues to the landowner. These dues often cost the peasants as much as half their produce and ensured that they could never accumulate enough wealth to purchase their own land. In addition, all members of the Third Estate were expected to pay a host of taxes, as outlined on page 178. As well as dues and taxation, peasants were also required to carry out duties on aristocratic estates, known as *corvée*. By the late 18th century, *corvée* most commonly involved repairing and maintaining roads. With *corvée*, feudal dues and excessive taxation, the burden on the Third Estate was a heavy one.

The Third Estate's urban population could be divided between unskilled poor workers, who lived in overcrowded and dirty city slums, and the higher-paid skilled workers, often craftspeople organised into **guilds**. The majority of urban workers would be employed in small workshops, producing a wide variety of goods and products, from textiles to bread.

At the wealthier end of the Third Estate were the bourgeoisie or middle class. These were educated people such as lawyers and doctors, as well as merchants, bankers and industrialists. With the growth of trade and industry in the 18th century, this class of people began to grow significantly, by an estimated three times across the course of the century. Influenced by enlightened ideas (see page 173), some bourgeois people were dissatisfied by the fact that they were contributing a significant amount to the French economy, with their wealth often rivalling that of the nobility, and yet they had no political say, rights or freedoms.

#### KEY TERMS

**Monopoly**
A monopoly is when a business or an individual has exclusive control over buying or selling a particular produce or service.

**Feudalism**
A social system common in medieval Europe whereby wealthy aristocrats controlled the land. Peasants lived on and farmed this land to provide their own subsistence. In return, they had to pay dues (like taxes) and provide labour for their lord.

**Guild**
An association or group of craftspeople from the same trade (for example, a weavers' guild) who join together to protect their industry and their own interests. Some guilds had significant local power.

SOURCE

*Les Peuple sous l'ancien Régime* (The People under the Ancient Regime): an illustration produced in 1815 reflecting perceptions of French society prior to the revolution. The emaciated man in chains represents the Third Estate, who is being ridden by King Louis XVI, a priest, representing the First Estate, and a nobleman, representing the Second Estate. Louis, holding the whip, is saying 'Faith and honour due to the lord'.

## The Enlightenment and the spread of new ideas

The Enlightenment, sometimes known as the Age of Reason, is the name given to the intellectual movement that occurred in Europe in the 17th and 18th centuries. Writers, philosophers and political thinkers began to question the conventions of the societies within which they lived. Enlightened thinkers, or *philosophes* as they were known in France, promoted the use of reason, logic and evidence as opposed to the reliance on tradition, superstition and religion. The *philosophes* wrote about and considered a wide range of subjects, from politics and history, to religion and theology, to science and nature.

Although enlightened ideas were born across Europe, France could arguably be said to be the home of the Enlightenment. It was in France where many of the most significant *philosophes* wrote their works. At the salons (intellectual gatherings), and in the coffee houses of Paris and the growing mercantile towns, the educated bourgeoisie and nobility would discuss and debate the latest political works and ideas. People began to question the fairness and values of their society, and this meant challenging the structure and inequality of the *ancien régime*. Summarised below are some of the principal works and ideas of three *philosophes* whose views challenged the French establishment in the 18th century.

### KEY TERMS

**Constitutional monarchy**
Where there is a king or queen who acts as head of the state, but laws are created and passed by a separate assembly.

**Republican**
Someone who supports the idea that a state should not have a monarchy.

### Charles-Louis de Secondat, Baron de la Bréde et de Montesquieu (1689–1755)

**Principal political work:** *The Spirit of the Laws* was first published anonymously in 1748.

**Key ideas:** Montesquieu challenged the estates system of the *ancien régime*. He argued that the estates and feudalism should be abolished. He favoured the British model of government, believing that France, like Britain, should be ruled as a **constitutional monarchy**, whereby a monarch's power is restrained by an assembly. However, he also argued that democracy could lead to mob rule and that ruling elites benefited from an understanding of how to govern that common people did not possess.

### François-Marie Arouet, known by his pen name Voltaire (1694–1778)

**Principal political work:** Although largely a historical writer and a playwright, Voltaire did write some political essays such as *Philosophical Letters*, published in 1733.

**Key ideas:** Like Montesquieu, Voltaire looked favourably on the English system of government. He also praised English law, seeing it as more tolerant and more liberal than that in France. This was seen as an attack on the French monarchy and his essays were banned and publicly burnt. He was a major advocate of freedom of expression as well as a critic of the power of the Catholic Church. He was a **republican**, proclaiming that in a republic equality can be more closely achieved.

### Jean-Jacques Rousseau (1712–78)

**Principal political works:** Rousseau's most famous political works are *Discourse on Inequality* (1755) and his most influential work, *The Social Contract* (1762).

**Key ideas:** In *The Social Contract*, Rousseau argued that everyone within a society has a right collectively to choose the laws under which they live, and that everyone should have equal rights. He accepted that citizens should have a responsibility towards the rulers of their society, but that duties should be equal for all. Rousseau strongly argued that everyone has a right to freedom. He was also a republican, believing that monarchies only served the interests of the ruling class.

SOURCE 4

In his most famous political work, *The Social Contract* (1762), Rousseau made the following criticisms of monarchy.

The best kings wish to have the power of being wicked if they please, without ceasing to be masters. A political preacher will tell them in vain that, the strength of the people being their own, it is their greatest interest that the people should be flourishing, numerous and formidable; they know very well that it is not true. Their [kings'] personal interest is, in the first place, that the people should be weak and miserable, and should never be able to resist them... If it is difficult for a great state to be well governed, it is even more so for it to be well governed by a single man; and everyone knows what happens when a king appoints deputies... One essential and inevitable defect, which will always render a monarchical government inferior to a republican one, is that... those who succeed in monarchies are most frequently only petty mischief-makers, petty knaves, petty intriguers whose petty talents, which enable them to attain high posts in courts, only serve to show the public their ineptitude as soon as they have attained them.

ACTIVITY
KNOWLEDGE CHECK

**The estates system and the Enlightenment**

Read the information about the principal ideas of the three *philosophes* on page 173. Create a table like the one below to explain how these ideas could challenge the nature of the *ancien régime*. One example has been completed for you. Note how, in the example, multiple specific details about the workings of the *ancien régime* have been used to support the point made.

| ***Philosophe*** **and their principal idea(s)** | **How the idea(s) challenged the *ancien régime*** |
|---|---|
| Montesquieu believed in constitutional monarchy, with the power of a monarch kept in check by a legislative assembly. | |
| Voltaire advocated freedom of expression. | |
| Voltaire was a critic of the power and privilege of the Catholic Church. | |
| Rousseau argued that rights and responsibilities should be shared equally within a society. | |
| Rousseau believed that everyone has the right to freedom. | EXAMPLE: This challenged the *ancien régime* because many people were not completely free. The system of feudalism meant that many peasants could not acquire enough wealth ever to escape the lives they led. Also, the monarchy had the right to take away people's freedom without trial by issuing *lettres de cachet*. |

## Censorship and repression of enlightened ideas

Under the *ancien régime*, the publication of literature was strictly, although not efficiently, controlled. Printers had to be granted royal licences to own printing presses and all new publications were supposed to be granted approval by an official called the royal censor. In reality, there were many printing presses operating illegally, and there was a thriving black market in books and pamphlets brought into the country from Geneva, where press controls were much more liberal.

Both the Catholic Church and the French government produced lists of banned books, including the works of all three *philosophes* covered above. Furthermore, the authors of such texts could be prosecuted by the state. Rousseau's novel *Émile*, a text containing anti-Catholic and pro-education messages, was quickly banned. Warrants were issued for his arrest, so he fled to Britain, where he lived in exile. As well as spending time in the Bastille prison in his younger days, Voltaire was banned by King Louis XV from living in his home city of Paris, due to his controversial works and views.

## The spread of radical ideas

Trying to measure the common attitudes of a society is never an easy task for the historian. The extent to which the average French man or woman was exposed to these new and often radical ideas would very much depend on who that person was. Pamphlets and books containing enlightened ideas would be printed and circulated in urban areas, especially Paris and Lyon, where there were many bookshops and where a larger proportion of the population would be literate. A feudal peasant living in an isolated rural area would be far less likely to be exposed to these ideas than a literate member of the bourgeoisie, who would have both the wealth to afford books and the time to meet and discuss enlightened philosophy at social gatherings.

It would be easy to assume that the ideas of the Enlightenment would chiefly appeal to members of the Third Estate, but this was not always the case.

SOURCE

**In this account, Louis-Philippe, Comte de Ségur (a count, a member of the Second Estate) explains why the ideas of the Enlightenment appealed to some of the younger nobility.**

We were smiling mockers [people who make cruel jokes] of the ancient ways, the feudal pride of our fathers and their grave etiquettes, and everything was old and boring and ridiculous to us. The gravity of the old-fashioned doctrines was too burdensome for us... Without deeply enquiring into the thought of more serious writers, we admired it [the Enlightenment] because it was instinct with courage and opposition to arbitrary power... Voltaire seduced our minds; Rousseau touched out hearts; we took secret pleasure in the fact that these men attacked the old edifice [system of beliefs] that seemed to us to be Gothic [out-dated] and ridiculous. So, whatever might be our rank or privilege... which were being undermined at that very moment, we took pleasure in this little war; for we did not feel its dangers, we saw it only as a piece of drama... The idea of Liberty, in whatever way it was expressed, pleased us by its courage, its spirit of equality and its general convenience. Men find it a pleasure to stoop below themselves, as long as they feel able to rise up when they please; and since we did not look that far ahead, we were able to sample at one and the same time the advantages of aristocracy and the luxury of plebeian [commoner] philosophy.

A key advocate of enlightened philosophy was Louis-Philippe Joseph, Duc d'Orléans (Duke of Orleans), who, despite being a Bourbon and a member of the royal family, played a significant part in spreading radical ideas in Paris immediately prior to, and during, the revolution. He would hold intellectual gatherings at his Palais Royal, the Duke's royal residence in Paris. As a royal palace, his residence was exempt from censorship laws, so it was used as a base to print and distribute radical **pamphlets**. Louis-Philippe would later gain the nickname Philippe Égalité, meaning 'Equality'.

**KEY TERM**

**Pamphlets**
Pamphlets are like leaflets. They were very common in 18th-century Europe at a time before newspapers became widely available and when books were very expensive. Pamphlets tended to be short, written pieces, but sometimes contained satirical (politically humorous) cartoons. Some would be political attacks, others aimed to tell the news.

**ACTIVITY**
**KNOWLEDGE CHECK**

**The *philosophes***

1 Study Source 4. Identify and explain three criticisms that Rousseau makes of monarchy.

2 Study Source 5.

a) Why does the author mock 'the ancient ways, the feudal pride of our fathers and their grave etiquettes'?

b) Why do you think the author describes the Enlightenment as courageous?

c) The author writes 'we took pleasure in this little war... we saw it only as a piece of drama'. What does he mean by this statement? What is the 'war' he is referring to?

d) Read the final three lines of the source. What is the author referring to when he says 'we did not look that far ahead'?

EXTEND YOUR KNOWLEDGE

**Jean-Jacques Rousseau (1712–78)**

Jean-Jacques Rousseau was a Swiss-born writer and political theorist. He moved to Paris at the age of 30, where he began working with the important *philosophe* Denis Diderot in writing and producing the *Encyclopédie*: an epic work that attempted to bring together the collective knowledge and learning of all the great *philosophes* of the era. Over the next two decades, Rousseau refined his own political theory in a number of works.

The culmination of his thinking was *The Social Contract* (1762), which begins with the sentence: 'Man is born free, yet everywhere he is in chains.' In *The Social Contract,* Rousseau developed his idea of the 'General Will' of the people: how everybody within a society must work towards and follow the rules of the collective, aiming for what is best for society rather than for the individual. He argued that, by being a part of such a society, the General Will would also represent and benefit the individual.

Before the revolution, *The Social Contract* was not widely circulated. However, once the revolution was underway, sales of Rousseau's work increased and his philosophy was widely discussed and quoted in assemblies, newspapers and pamphlets. It is reputed that Maximilien Robespierre (see page 202) was so influenced by Rousseau that he always carried a copy of *The Social Contract* on his person. The concept of General Will allowed Robespierre to attempt to justify his actions during the Terror, by arguing that the good of society came before that of the individual. By 1794, Rousseau's philosophy was so revered that the remains of his body were transferred from their resting place in Ermenonville, a village near Paris, to the Panthéon, a mausoleum in Paris reserved for only the most highly respected people.

The American Revolution (see page 179) also had an impact on the spread of the Enlightenment. French soldiers fought on the side of the soldiers of the USA in their fight against British rule. The USA saw its war as a war against monarchy, tyranny and despotism. When the war ended in 1783, French soldiers returned to France having been influenced by the cries for republicanism, freedom and equality. It is notable that one of the leading French revolutionary figures of 1789 was the Marquis de Lafayette, a French general during the American Revolution.

## Conclusion

From the very beginning of his reign, Louis XVI faced challenges. The nature of French society was unequal, unfair and inefficient. With the spread of the Enlightenment came increasing criticism of the established order. However, the *ancien régime* had existed for centuries and enlightened thinking had been spreading for decades before Louis XVI ascended to the throne in 1774, so it must be further questioned why things came to a head in the 1780s.

ACTIVITY
KNOWLEDGE CHECK

**The estates system and the Enlightenment**

Combine your knowledge of the nature of the *ancien régime* with your knowledge of the Enlightenment to produce a pamphlet in the style of an 18th-century *philosophe*, attacking the social and political structures of pre-revolutionary France. Refer specifically to particular aspects of the system that could be deemed unfair or unequal. It may be necessary to conduct further research on the *philosophes* in order to incorporate more of their ideas and theories into your work.

Cause and consequence (6a)

**Divine right**

Different times and different places have different sets of ideas. Beliefs about how the world works, how human societies should be governed or the best way to achieve economic prosperity can all be radically different from our own. It is important for the historian to take into account these different attitudes and be aware of the dangers of judging them against modern ideas.

In pre-revolutionary France, people had a different attitude towards the role of the monarchy than we do today. It was believed that the king's power was God-given. It was God who had ordained who should be rich, who should be poor and who should be king. As the king had a divine right to rule, he could lead the country as he saw fit; only God had the right to judge him. Although some people in France began to question this idea during the Enlightenment, the divine right of kings was a widely held belief both by the rulers and by those whom they ruled.

1 What attitudes do you think gave rise to the idea that the king had a divine right to rule?

2 If people had known how events would progress, for example that King Louis would lose his power and supporters of the king would be persecuted, do you think that they would have changed their attitudes? Would King Louis have done so? Would the people of France have done so?

3 In the 18th century, French attitudes to the role of the monarchy were different from current attitudes in the UK.

a) Are there any other ways in which 18th-century French attitudes differed dramatically from those that are current in the UK?

b) Why do you think that they are different?

4 How important is it for historians to deal with events in the context of the beliefs and values of people in the past, as well as seeing them as part of a greater pattern?

# HOW FAR WERE THE CAUSES OF THE REVOLUTION A QUESTION OF ECONOMIC DECLINE, RATHER THAN POLITICAL DISCONTENT?

The debate over the causes of the French revolution began in the 19th century. Some historians, such as Alexis de Tocqueville (1805–59), emphasised the impact of the Enlightenment and political discontent in causing the revolution. Others, though, like Jules Michelet (1798–1874), have placed more emphasis on the declining economic conditions of the 1780s. In his view, it was not so much the gradual spread of ideas of **liberty** and equality that caused the revolution, but that it was more of a spontaneous response to dire poverty, hardship and a state on the verge of economic collapse. This section outlines the economic challenges facing France in the 1780s.

KEY TERM

**Liberty**
Liberty means freedom. The concept of liberty was widely promoted by the Enlightenment and became a rally cry for its followers.

## Rural poverty and urban food prices

Rural poverty in France was not a problem new to the 1780s. In an age before state benefits such as pensions and disability allowances, many people could not even afford to feed themselves and had to rely on relief, or charity, provided by the Church. Labourers and feudal peasants (farmers tied to the land they worked) would often find themselves living hand to mouth. During the 1730s to 1770s though, despite occasional bad harvests, agricultural output had grown steadily, allowing the population to increase while avoiding crises. This era of relative agricultural prosperity did not continue into the 1780s, however, as harvest failures became increasingly common. Bad harvests were reported in 1778–79, 1781–82, 1785–86 and 1787. With the population growing, poverty and starvation increased. The harvest of 1788 was a particular disaster, with a long drought followed by a terrible hail storm, which destroyed much of the crop.

As well as impacting on the rural peasantry, some of whom saw their profits drop, and many of whom found that they were unable even to feed their families, the failure of harvests also affected the urban population. For the working classes in towns, bread constituted the main proportion of their diet. When harvests failed, wheat prices increased and so, in turn, did bread prices.

The price of bread in Paris increased by over 50 percent between August 1788 and March 1789. The bad harvests also had an indirect negative consequence for urban workers. As poverty increased, demand for manufactured goods fell and, as a result, urban unemployment increased.

SOURCE

Arthur Young was a British travel writer who, by chance, was visiting France on the eve of the revolution. He recorded his observations of French society in a book called *Travels in France During the Years 1787, 1788 and 1789* (published in 1792).

Sept. 5th 1788. To Montauban [a town in southern France]. The poor people seem poor indeed; the children terribly ragged, if possible worse clad than if no clothes at all; as to shoes and stockings they are luxuries. A beautiful girl of six or seven playing with a stick and sinking under a bundle of rags has made my heart ache to see her. They did not beg, and when I gave them something seemed more surprised than obliged. One-third of what I have seen of this province seems uncultivated, and nearly all of it in misery. What have kings and ministers and parliaments and states to answer for their prejudices, seeing millions of hands that would be industrious, idle and starving, through the execrable maxims of despotism, or the equally detestable prejudices of feudal nobility.

The increasingly challenging socio-economic climate might go some way to explaining why some workers of Paris were easily provoked to take to the streets in rebellion in the summer of 1789, and why, in certain areas, the peasantry rose up in the Great Fear of the same year (see page 194).

### EXTEND YOUR KNOWLEDGE

**Were the poor really becoming poorer?**

According to the historian Alexis de Tocqueville writing in 1856, the poor were not living in abject poverty or at least where they were this was not the cause of the revolution. He pointed out that the practice of feudalism significantly declined during the 18th century, with many peasants winning their freedom. He also highlighted the fact that levels of literacy were increasing among the populace and that one-third of the land in France was owned, not by aristocrats, but by the peasants themselves.

Tocqueville concluded that the revolution was not a spontaneous reaction to the dire poverty of the 1780s. Instead, he argued that, as the peasantry became more literate and free from the ties of feudalism, they were more able to understand the inequality of their society and felt more empowered to act. In Tocqueville's view, it was the improvement in the lives of the peasantry, not the decline, which was key in causing revolution.

The historian George Rudé challenged this view in the 1950s, emphasising that increasing peasant prosperity was by no means universal and that, while across the century agricultural output did increase, this fails to take account of the economic depression that began in the 1780s.

### KEY TERM

**Exemption**

For a person to be exempt from something means they do not have to do it. So, for someone to have an exemption from a tax means they do not have to pay it.

## Taxation and crown debt

The system of taxation in France under the *ancien régime* was extremely complex. Taxes can be divided into two main types: direct and indirect. Direct taxes are applied to an individual person, usually in relation to their wealth or property. Indirect taxes are applied in other ways, most commonly by being added to items or goods purchased. Those members of the First and Second Estate who were wealthy enough could often find ways to buy **exemption** from taxation. The table below outlines some of the main taxes that were applied in pre-revolutionary France.

| Name | Type | Detail | Who paid? |
|---|---|---|---|
| *Taille* | Direct | A tax on land, with landowners paying an amount proportional to the amount they owned. | Only the Third Estate. |
| *Capitation* | Direct | Depending on wealth, property and status, each person would be put into one of 22 categories and pay a fixed sum according to their category. The higher/wealthier the category, the more they paid. | The Second and Third Estates. The First were exempt as long as they paid an annual fee called the *don gratuit* ('free gift'). |
| *Vingtiéme* | Direct | An income tax, equivalent to one-twentieth of a person's income. | In theory, everyone. But the First and Second Estates could buy exemption with a *don gratuit*. |
| *Gabelle* | Indirect | A tax on salt. It was particularly despised as salt was a much-needed basic necessity (to preserve food in a time before refrigeration). | Only the Third Estate. |
| *Tabac* | Indirect | A tax on tobacco. | Anyone purchasing tobacco. |

### Tax farmers

All indirect taxes, which made up 55 percent of state income, were collected by *La Ferme Générale* ('The General Farm') – a large organisation that was the second biggest employer in France after the army, whose officials were commonly known as tax farmers. The tax farmers had the right to confiscate property and use physical force if people failed to meet the payments owed. Tax farmers had a strong reputation for corruption and, with little central regulation from the Crown, could easily abuse their position.

What served to make the system even more unprofitable for the state was the simple fact that the wealthiest estates were expected to pay the least tax. Only 1.6 percent of state revenue was generated from taxation on land directly (perhaps the best indication of wealth in the 18th century). This means that taxation was harder on those who were not landowners, often the poorer classes.

### Crown debt

With corruption rife and the wealthiest paying the least, the system was highly inefficient. Due to this, successive Bourbon kings had to take large loans, especially in times of war. King Louis XV accumulated huge debts during the **Seven Years' War** (1756–63). In the war, France was defeated by the British in North America, costing the French valuable overseas colonies in eastern North America and further damaging the French economy. The result of this was that, when Louis XV's grandson, Louis XVI, came to the throne in 1774, he inherited vast debts. By 1780, the greatest proportion of state wealth was tied up paying interest on loans. 43 percent of state expenditure was committed to debt, compared with just 23 percent being spent on state administration and 25 percent on the war department. With state spending significantly higher than state income (in 1786, state revenue was 472 million livres compared with an expenditure of 633 million livres), the problem of debt was destined only to get worse.

## The impact of the American Revolution

In 1776, the Thirteen Colonies of America, shortly to become the USA, took up arms in rebellion against their British rulers in an effort to win independence. The ensuing war is known as the **American Revolutionary War** or the American War of Independence and lasted until 1783, when the victorious Americans won their independence, striking a major blow to the British Empire. The victory of the USA over Britain can, in part, be attributed to the support provided by the French to their cause. Keen to see Britain's global power reduced and to seek revenge for France's defeat in the Seven Years' War, King Louis XVI signed a military alliance with the USA in 1778. Over the next five years, France provided armies and resources in support of the USA's cause, to a total cost of an estimated 1.3 billion livres. While the USA and France may have been successful in denting British global power, the war came at a cost that the French state could not afford and, by 1788, the proportion of state expenditure on debt had staggeringly grown to over 50 percent.

## Corruption at court

As state debt soared and poverty among the populace grew, the spending of King Louis XVI's court came under increasing scrutiny and criticism, from both bourgeois merchants, who suffered from the economic decline, and from the nobility, who feared for the stability of the nation. Costing six percent of the state's expenditure, it is little wonder that people began to question the expense of the royal court.

The French court, though, could also be a source of income for the state, as offices and positions in the royal court and administration could be bought from the Crown. Buying these positions and titles was a system known as venality. These venal titles were sometimes bought by nobles wishing for positions even closer to the king, or by very wealthy members of the Third Estate wanting to 'buy themselves' into the Second Estate and gain all the privileges that that status awarded. With so many privileges, it is hardly surprising that, during the 18th century, an estimated 30,000–50,000 people bought such titles.

Although the sale of venal titles did provide short-term income for the state, in the long term the system had a detrimental effect, as it meant that wealthy previously tax-paying members of the Third Estate became wealthy tax-exempt members of the Second Estate.

#### KEY TERMS

**Seven Years' War (1756–63)**
A major war that brought all the great European powers into conflict. France, Austria and Russia were aligned on one side against Prussia and Great Britain on the other. In mainland Europe, the conflict largely consisted of warfare between Austria against Russia and Prussia over the central European states of Bohemia, Saxony and Silesia. Meanwhile, British and French forces competed for domination of territories in North America and India. The war was a great success for Britain, but cost the French valuable colonies in North America.

**American Revolutionary War (1775–83)**
Sometimes known as the War of Independence, this was a rebellion by Great Britain's 13 colonies in North America against British rule. The colonies wished to exert more power over their own affairs and resented paying taxes and custom duties to a government which, many felt, had no interest in their affairs and which did not represent them. Ideas of the Enlightenment played an important role in shaping the views of many of the revolutionary leaders: men such as Thomas Jefferson and Benjamin Franklin. The war was presented as war against the tyranny of monarchy and for the virtues of liberty, equality and republicanism.

In the early stages of the war, American forces consisted of small militia brigades but, as the war proceeded, it took on an increasingly international dimension. Wishing to see a reduction in Britain's power and increase their own influence in the region, both Spain and France intervened. Ultimately, not least due to considerable French support, the revolutionaries forced the British into surrender. The USA was thus born.

Venality was also damaging in that it blocked the advancement and promotion of people based upon merit. As a consequence, the royal administration was determined almost solely by wealth, rather than talent or integrity, meaning that corruption and incompetency were commonplace.

## Conclusion

By the late 1780s, the economic situation in France was dire. At a local level, peasants and the urban working classes were struggling to feed themselves, as an excessive burden of taxes was compounded by harvest failure and subsequent bread price rises. At a national level, the inefficiency and corruption of the state system, combined with overspending on wars and at court, meant that France was verging on bankruptcy. As dissatisfaction at the economic situation rose, so did the likelihood of revolution.

ACTIVITY
KNOWLEDGE CHECK

**Poverty, taxation and crown debt**

1 Write down three reasons why poverty increased in France during the 1780s. Explain how these reasons are connected.

2 How was the system of taxation in pre-revolutionary France inefficient? Consider the taxes themselves and how they were collected.

3 Explain the impact of war on France's finances.

4 In what way was venality both beneficial and damaging to the French state?

# TO WHAT EXTENT WERE KING LOUIS XVI AND HIS COURT RESPONSIBLE FOR THE ONSET OF REVOLUTION?

## Louis' character

Louis XVI inherited the throne at the young age of 20. He had not been destined to be king, as he had an older brother who was the *dauphin* (the heir). However, his elder brother died in 1761, leaving Louis as heir. Seen by his parents as inferior to his elder brother, Louis did not receive the specific training and schooling usually afforded to the *dauphin* in order to prepare him for kingship. Instead, Louis was encouraged to pursue other interests and hobbies, most famously locksmithing. It is often said that, perhaps as a result of his upbringing, Louis was a weak character: indecisive, easily led and lacking in court and political experience.

**SOURCE**

Guy-Marie Sallier, a member of the Paris *parlement*, described Louis' character in a memoir written in 1813.

Louis XVI was exempt from the vices which sprung from strong emotions, but he also lacked the energy to which they gave birth. Nature, having given him amiability and the virtues pleasing in the private individual, denied him of the qualities needed by one destined to command. His education had done little to remedy the defects of his nature. Timidity and mistrust of himself were at the centre of his character; and it was soon recognised that, if he were not guided by his own inclinations, others could succeed by skill and perseverance in influencing his decisions.

## Attitudes to Marie Antoinette

Louis married young. He was just 15 when, in 1770, he married the 14-year-old Austrian princess, Marie Antoinette. The marriage formed a union between two of the most powerful families in Europe: the Bourbons and the Hapsburgs. Yet the marriage was not without controversy, as Marie's Austrian roots would prove to be a source of suspicion and distrust throughout the period. Distrust of the princess was furthered at court by her lack of familiarity with, and dislike for, the very complex system of etiquette at Versailles. It was also rumoured that Louis was far too easily led by his wife and that, due to his passive character, she manipulated him for her own, and Austria's, interests.

The popularity of the royal couple was dented further when they initially failed to produce an heir. One of the foremost responsibilities of a royal couple was to produce an heir to continue the family line and ensure stability. This was not entirely surprising, as they were so young, and were almost total strangers when they got married. They did not consummate their marriage until years after their wedding day. In public, Louis behaved coldly towards his wife. All this gave ammunition to critics of the royal couple and obscene pamphlets were produced mocking the couple's infertility. A daughter, born in 1778, helped to quash such slander, as did the arrival of the *dauphin*, a son born in 1781 and also called Louis.

**SOURCE 8** An anonymous painting of the French royal family in 1782. In the centre of the image, Marie Antoinette holds the baby *dauphin*. Louis XVI sits next to them, while family members and close courtiers gather around. The birth of baby Louis was met with excitement in France. Sadly for the royal couple, the *dauphin* died in 1789.

The arrival of an heir was not enough to restore Marie Antoinette's reputation entirely. As France's economy declined in the 1780s, the spending of the royal court, and specifically that of Marie Antoinette, came under increasing criticism. She acquired the nickname 'Madame Déficit' ('déficit' meaning 'debt'), as some blamed the financial crisis on her lavish spending. In 1785, one scandal, known as the Affair of the Diamond Necklace, was particularly damaging to Marie Antoinette's reputation. She was accused of trying to purchase a diamond necklace worth an incredible 1,600,000 livres, a scandalous thing to do when state finances were so low. The reality of the situation, though, was that Marie had never tried to purchase the necklace. There was actually a criminal plot in which a countess, the Comtesse de La Motte, had tried to acquire the necklace by forging Marie Antoinette's signature. De La Motte and her accomplices were eventually brought to justice and the truth was revealed. Yet, despite Marie's innocence, the scandal did little to improve perceptions of the queen.

The interpretation of Marie Antoinette as a frivolous and excessive queen is a matter of debate. It could be said that her spending was no more excessive than that of previous French queens.

Indeed, that as queen, she had a divine right to live in a manner vastly above that of most common people. Either way, in the late 1780s, she became the target of propaganda and open criticism. Louis did not escape opposition either, as he was accused of failing to rein in his wife's expenditure.

Marie Antoinette was accused of being distant from and disinterested in her subjects. As the financial crisis reached a head in 1787–89, she spent her days on her model farm, complete with dairy, farmhouse and mill (built at great expense within the grounds of Versailles), acting like, but certainly not living like, a French peasant girl. Life at Versailles, for both Louis and Marie, seemed like a world that was increasingly distant from the poverty of the peasants and Parisian poor.

## The financial reforms of Turgot

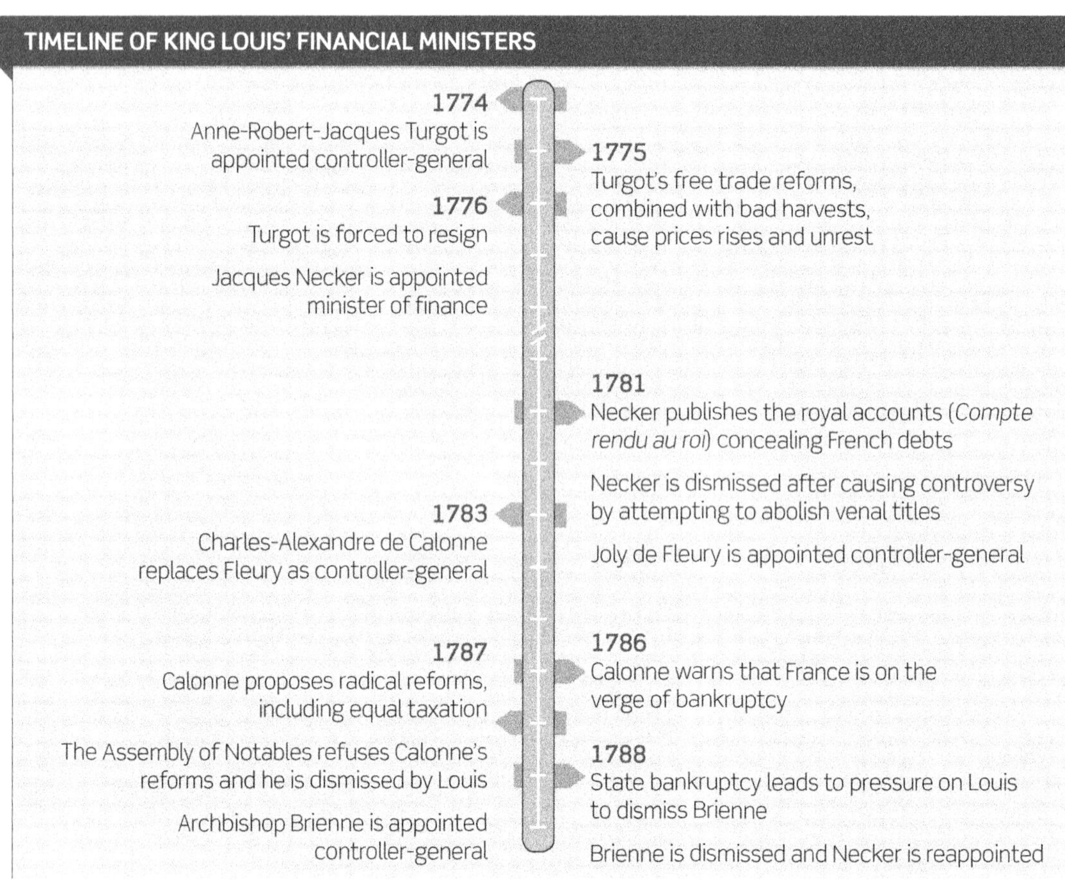


**KEY TERM**

**Physiocrat**
A group of economists during the 18th century. They were influenced by ideas of the Enlightenment. They advocated the idea of free trade, stating that governments should not intervene in trade and business. This was a radical idea in 18th-century France, as prices were often fixed and there was a complex system of customs and trade duties (taxes). Many physiocrats also believed in equality of taxation.

Despite criticism of the luxury and cost of the royal court, Louis and his ministers did act to try to improve the economic situation within France. Anne-Robert-Jacques Turgot was a **physiocrat**, appointed by Louis as controller-general in 1774. In an effort to avoid state bankruptcy (a serious concern as it could leave the Crown unable to pay not only for its court but also for its armies) without further borrowing, Turgot set about trying to increase the efficiency and administration of the state's finances, introducing a number of effective measures to streamline state bureaucracy.

A more controversial, and less successful, measure was the introduction of free trade in grain. Prior to 1774, control of grain trade and grain prices was subject to complex localised rules and regulations. In many areas, certain individuals, usually nobility, held monopolies over the trade, set custom duties or fixed prices in their own interests. Turgot believed in free trade, with duties, barriers and controls on prices removed. Removing such controls and duties would obviously be to the cost of those people who profited from such privileges, thus causing opposition. In theory, however, free trade would be to the benefit of the majority as, providing grain was plentiful, prices would remain low. In reality, Turgot was unlucky as bad weather in winter to spring 1774–75 resulted in bad harvests, which, in turn, caused the price of grain to increase. This sparked violent unrest in some areas, known as the Flour Wars. These were a series of uprisings that occurred within the Parisian basin, the rural areas surrounding Paris. Over 17 days, 180 towns, villages and hamlets witnessed unrest. Often, the targets of the rioting were bakeries and warehouses, as merchants, the bourgeoisie and the nobility were accused of hoarding bread and flour at the expense of the lower classes.

Despite popular unrest and aristocratic opposition to Turgot's reforms, Louis initially showed great firmness in his support for his controller-general. The riots were suppressed and Turgot's ministry continued, but, in 1776, Turgot became even bolder in his proposed reforms. He presented an edict banning the *corvée* and proclaimed his aim to abolish privilege and introduce a property tax payable by all three estates. This was a step too far for the First and Second Estates and the *parlements* refused to sanction Turgot's reforms. His attempted reforms caused such resistance that, in May 1776, Louis ordered Turgot to offer his resignation and, with no other option, he obliged.

## The reforms of Necker

Although court protocol prevented him from taking the title controller-general, because he was a Protestant, the next minister in charge of finance was the Swiss economist Jacques Necker. One of Necker's most influential actions was publicly to publish a record of the state's finances. The report, published in 1781 and called the *Compte rendu au roi* ('Report to the King'), claimed a surplus of ten million livres, concealing the actual deficit of 46 million. By publicly releasing the accounts, Necker won popular support, as he was seen to be trying to increase the transparency and accountability of the royal court. As was his intention, it also made financiers willing to loan further finances to the French state. The state needed money to fund continuing involvement in the American Revolutionary War and Necker was determined to do so without increasing taxation. However, this was to cause problems later, as Necker was simply increasing the state debt. Also, as the *Compte rendu* hid the huge deficit from the public; when the truth was later revealed about the desperate economic situation, the shock and concern was even greater than it would have been had Necker publicised it earlier.

Necker controversially attempted to streamline the state's financial administration by ensuring that venal ministers (see page 179) were replaced by trained and salaried officials. This meant that there was a reduction in the sale of offices and, while being a positive step towards greater efficiency, this also meant that there were fewer opportunities for ambitious, wealthy Frenchmen hoping to buy status. This caused strong opposition and those close to the king pressed for Necker's dismissal. Louis failed to support his financial director and, in 1781, forced Necker to resign.

### EXTEND YOUR KNOWLEDGE

**Jacques Necker (1732-1804)**
As well as producing the *Compte rendu au roi*, Jacques Necker also introduced a number of other reforms. He reduced the number of tax farmers in the state, recognising their corruption and inefficiency. He also took steps to create provincial assemblies in which the Third Estate was represented (unlike in the *parlements*) alongside the First and Second Estates. While two such assemblies were established in Berry and Haute-Guyenne, the plan was not extended any further due to opposition at Versailles.

During his second ministry, from August 1788, Necker's time was largely devoted to making the arrangements for the **Estates-General** and he has been blamed for making the decision that the Estates should vote 'by order' and not 'by head' (see page 187).

Necker's dismissal by Louis XVI on 11 July 1789 was one of the causes of the storming of the Bastille (see page 188), as he was very popular with the Third Estate due to his enlightened views. Following the outbreak of violence in Paris, Louis quickly reinstalled Necker in an effort to regain support. Necker's third and final ministry was to prove less significant and he soon found himself outside events as other figures, such as the nobleman the Comte (count) de Mirabeau, rose to the fore. He retired from politics in 1790.

### KEY TERM

**Estates-General**
An assembly consisting of representatives, or deputies, of the three estates. Kings of the *ancien régime* could convene the assembly when they saw fit, for the purpose of discussing state affairs. Prior to 1789, the last time an Estates-General had been convened was in 1614.

## Charles-Alexandre de Calonne, the Assembly of Notables and the revolt of the aristocracy

Necker's successor, Joly de Fleury, did little to tackle the state's huge deficit, simply continuing to borrow. In 1783, Charles-Alexandre de Calonne was made controller-general. As financiers again became less willing to lend to the French Crown, Calonne was forced to look for other means of salvaging the economy. His eventual reform plan was both radical and controversial. As Turgot had, he advocated free trade and a reduction in government spending.

Most controversially, though, Calonne proposed increasing state income through the sale of Church land, and proposed introducing a universal land tax payable by all estates. It was felt that such a break from the traditions of the *ancien régime* needed the approval of a body representing the people. A meeting of the Estates-General would have been the obvious choice, but Calonne and Louis instead decided to convene an **Assembly of Notables**. When they met in February 1787, some members of the Assembly were sceptical about Calonne's grim assessment of the economic situation, possibly as a consequence of the *Compte rendu*, which had given the impression of healthy state finances just six years earlier. They were also sceptical about the need for such radical reform.

**KEY TERM**

**Assembly of Notables**
A gathering of key figures from the first two estates and the *parlements* that met in February 1787. It consisted of 144 nobles, archbishops and members of the royal family, hand-chosen by Calonne in the hope that they would approve his reforms.

**SOURCE 9**

In 1787, Calonne defended the necessity for significant reform by highlighting what he believed to be the weaknesses of the *ancien régime*.

> I shall easily show that it is impossible to tax further, ruinous to be always borrowing and not enough to confine ourselves to measures of the economy, and that, with matters as they are, ordinary ways are unable to lead us to our goal, and the only effective remedy, the only means of managing to put the finances truly in order, must consist in revising the entire State by recasting [restructuring] all that is unsound in its constitution... A kingdom whose provinces are foreign to one another; where multiple internal frontiers separate and divide the subjects of the same sovereign; where certain regions are totally freed of taxation, the full weight of which is therefore borne by other regions; where the richest class is the least taxed; where privilege prevents all stability; where neither a constant rule or a common will is possible - such a state is inevitably a very imperfect kingdom, full of corrupt practices and impossible to govern well.

Despite some division, the Assembly of Notables refused to approve Calonne's reforms. Once again, realising the strength of opposition, Louis failed to support his controller-general and Calonne was dismissed.

## Opposition in the Paris *parlement*

Archbishop Brienne, Calonne's successor as controller-general, fared little better. Although he succeeded in getting the Paris *parlement* to sanction an edict allowing internal free trade (there had been many complex internal customs duties and barriers under the *ancien régime*), he faced great opposition when he also attempted to introduce a universal land tax. In July 1787, the Paris *parlement* refused to sanction the introduction of a new tax, arguing that such a radical change to the principles of the *ancien régime* would require the consent of an Estates-General. This time Louis took decisive action in support of his minister and, on 15 August, exiled the *parlement* to the town of Troyes, over 160 kilometres from Paris.

**SOURCE**

From a pamphlet of 1788 criticising the actions of the Paris *parlement*.

> What motives have led the *parlement* of Paris to demand the meeting of the Estates-General under the form of 1614? Is it in the virtue of tradition? There are older forms. Is it to conform to present circumstances? The facts are to the contrary... In addition, what right has the *Parlement* of Paris to prescribe any form of the Estates-General? It is not empowered to do so by the nation... It is either error or bad faith to say that it is from a desire not to change the constitution, not to make innovations, not to upset the established order.

Louis' plan backfired. By exiling the *parlement*, he was seen by the nobility to be acting as a tyrant and, when he went further and tried to impose a rule reducing the legislative power of the *parlements*, a series of aristocratic revolts broke out across France, known as the 'revolt of the aristocracy'. The most famous of these was the revolt of Grenoble in June 1788. In defiance of Louis' orders that the local *parlement* should disassemble, the aristocrats of the Grenoble *parlement* refused to be dismissed. When royal soldiers were sent into the town forcibly to dissolve the *parlement* and arrest its members, violence broke out on the streets. Roof tiles were flung down on Louis' troops from surrounding buildings, earning the revolt the name the 'Day of Tiles'. To some, this aristocrat-led revolt, and similar disturbances elsewhere, are seen as the beginning of the French Revolution.

Although the revolts were suppressed, Louis realised that his reputation had been seriously damaged and that his position could be threatened. In August 1788, in an effort to garner support, Louis recalled the members of the Paris *parlement* to the city. It was in the same month that France was declared effectively bankrupt as, on 16 August, the treasury declared that all payments would be suspended, meaning that lenders were no longer willing to provide the state with further loans. This had serious implications as it meant that the state would be unable to pay its soldiers and to finance the royal court. Brienne was pressured to resign and did so. Recognising Necker's popularity with the people, Louis reappointed him as finance director. In a further attempt to appease the nobles and to secure finances, he agreed to convene a meeting of the Estates-General to discuss the economy of the state. When the Estates-General did meet, in May 1789, events would quickly accelerate outside his control.

## Conclusion

It is easy to criticise Louis for his handling of the financial crisis in 1787–88. When his ministers and their reforms met opposition, he repeatedly failed to back them, choosing instead to submit to the pressure of critics. Some might say that this indecision and weakness were character flaws that Louis had carried with him since childhood. However, the reality is more complex. The financial crisis shows us the great challenge and contradiction of the power of the monarchy under the *ancien régime*. Louis did rule as an absolute monarch with the right to introduce new laws. Yet he was also supposed to be the protector and upholder of the traditions of the system. So, when he needed to reform that system for the good of the country, he found himself accused of tyranny and despotism. It could be argued that Louis' position was an almost impossible one.

**SOURCE**

This source was written by Antoine Barnave. He was a lawyer prior to the revolution and became an important politician during the events of 1789, becoming a leading member of the National Assembly. He wrote this reflection on the causes of the revolution whilst he was awaiting execution during the Terror of 1793.

The democratic ideal, virtually stifled under all European governments while the feudal system remained powerful, has gathered strength and continues to grow... Conditions in France were ripe for a democratic revolution when the unfortunate Louis XVI ascended to the throne; the government's actions favoured its explosion. The two privileged orders [estates] who still retained control of the government were ruined through their taste for luxury and had degraded themselves by their way of life. The Third Estate, in contrast, had produced enlightened thinkers and acquired enormous wealth. The people were restrained only by their habit of servitude and the limited hope they had of breaking their chains. The government had succeeded in containing this hope; but it had never-the-less flourished in the heart of the nation.

**AS Level Exam-Style Question Section A**

***Study Source 11 before you answer this question.***

How much weight would you give the evidence of Source 11 for an enquiry into the reasons for the collapse of absolute monarchy in 1789?

Explain your answer using the source, the information given about it and your own knowledge of the historical context. (12 marks)

**Tip**

*Consider whether what Barnave says is fact or opinion. Also, take into account the background of the author: how might his position affect his view of the causes of the revolution?*

**ACTIVITY**
**KNOWLEDGE CHECK**

**The royal family and the financial crisis**

1. Identify and explain as many reasons as you can for Marie Antoinette's unpopularity.
2. Write a script for a debate between Calonne and one of his aristocratic opponents in the Assembly of Notables. Consider why a member of the Second Estate would object to Calonne's proposals and use Source 9 for an indication of how Calonne defended his reforms.
3. Study Source 10. How and why does this source condemn the actions of the Paris *parlement*?
4. Draw a table as a summary of Louis' three key financial ministers. In the table, use one column to record the details of the reforms (actual and proposed) of Turgot, Necker and Calonne and in a second column record the causes of their dismissal.

# WHAT WAS SIGNIFICANT ABOUT THE EVENTS OF 1789?

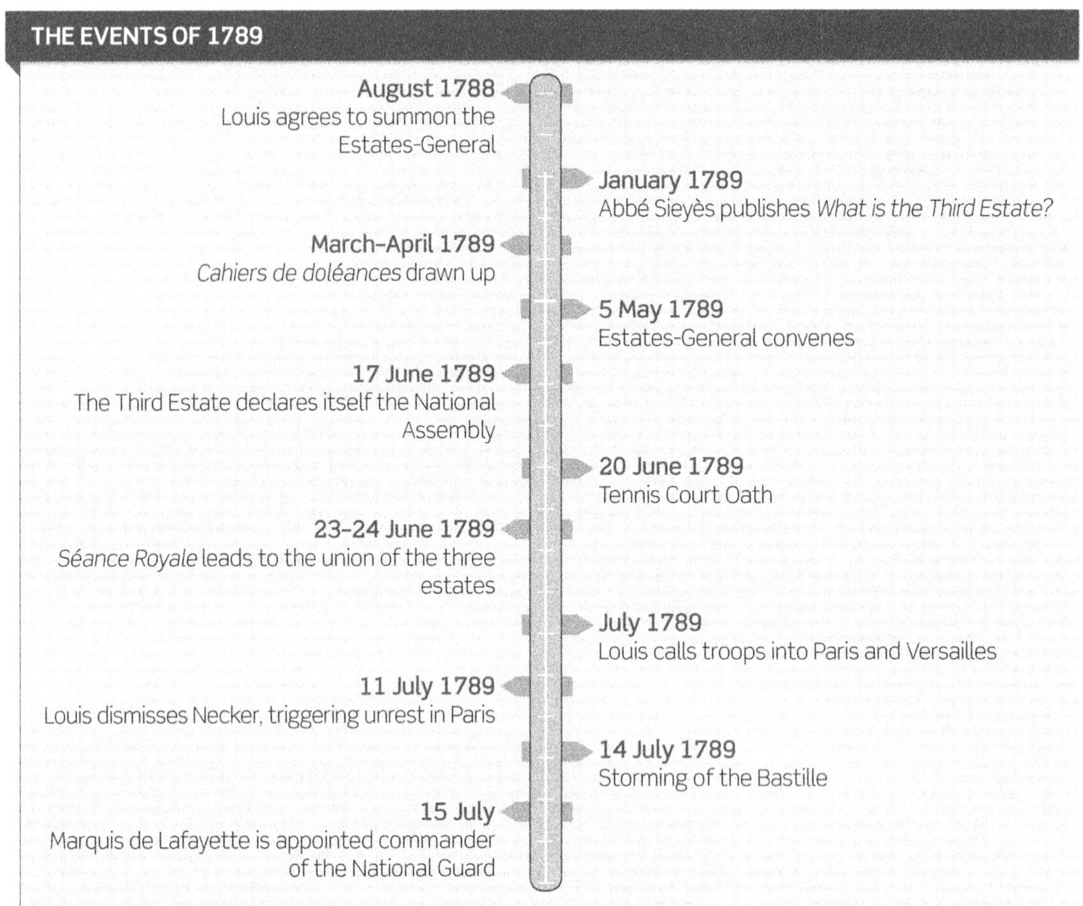


## The summoning of the Estates-General

### *Cahiers de doléances*

With the royal announcement of the Estates-General (August 1788), the people of France were invited to send lists of grievances that they wished to be discussed. These lists were known as *cahiers de doléances*. Each town or region could submit their complaints and proposals, either by individual estate or through one combined list. These *cahiers* give the historian an interesting insight into the attitudes and concerns of the time. Louis hoped that the Estates-General would chiefly be a meeting to discuss the state's finances and allow him to raise new taxes. However, as the *cahiers* show, expectations of the role of the Estates-General were far higher and concerned with much more than just taxation. Many *cahiers* were demanding a new constitution.

**SOURCE 12** From the *cahier* of Gisors, reflecting the views of the wealthier members of the Third Estate of that small town.

The Third Estate of this town invites the deputies to the Estates General to do all they can to encourage the assembly to adopt the following resolutions, but not until they have all joined with all the deputies of the Kingdom in demonstrating to the best of kings the gratitude, respect, love and submission of his subjects of the town of Gisors... That in the matter of taxes and loans the Sovereign's [King's] authority cannot be exercised except by the general agreement of the assembled nation, and with the assistance of its deliberations and its advice in matters of legislation... They shall ask for the abolition of every kind of indirect tax, under whatever description it was set up, and that none be created within the interior of the Kingdom. No citizen may be made prisoner nor deprived of his liberty for any reason whatever without having first taken before his natural judge... for which purpose all arbitrary imprisonment and especially *lettre de cachet* shall be forbidden. Deputies will ask for; abolition of all forms of seigniorial [feudal] justice; abolition of the venality of office; the nation's right to choose its judges in all future tribunals; reform of the civil and criminal codes.

SOURCE 13 From the *cahier* of the rural village of Ménouville, reflecting the grievances of the peasantry.

We beg His Majesty to have pity on our farmland because of the hail we have had. Also, we have a great deal of wasteland which is covered in juniper, and this causes much trouble on account of the rabbits which are very numerous; it is this that makes us unable to pay the dues we owe to His Majesty. We have no help from anyone to bring us relief... We only have a few good fields very remote from the village, the rest is wretched land very full of game and this causes very small harvests... We state that the sale of salt is too dear for poor people. We state that there should not be any tax men... We state that there should be no militia [military] duty, because this ruins many families; it would be better if His Majesty laid a small tax on each young man. We inform His Majesty that our goods are too heavily burdened with seigniorial [feudal] and other charges.

**A Level Exam-Style Question Section A**

***Study Sources 6 and 13 before you answer this question.***

How far could the historian make use of Sources 6 and 13 together to investigate the causes of discontent in France in the 1780s?

Explain your answer, using both sources, the information given about them and your knowledge of the historical context.
(20 marks)

**Tip**

*Take into account the weight of the evidence by considering the extent to which these sources represent the views of the wider French population.*

### *What is the Third Estate?*

As well as the *cahiers*, Necker invited writers to give their suggestions and thoughts on how the Estates-General should be organised and directed. The most famous response to Necker's request was a pamphlet written in January 1789 by Abbé Sieyès, a senior clergyman, entitled *What is the Third Estate?*

SOURCE 14 *What is the Third Estate?* by Abbé Sieyès was a pamphlet that was widely circulated in the months leading up to and during the Estates-General.

We have three questions to ask ourselves: What is the Third Estate? Everything. What has it been in the political order until now? Nothing. What is it asking for? To become something. Who would dare say that the Third Estate does not have in itself all that is needed to form a complete nation? It is a man who is strong and robust but still has one arm in chains. Take away the privileged order, and the nation would not be less, but more. And so what is the Third Estate? It is everything but everything shackled and oppressed. Without the privileged order, what would it be? Everything, an everything flourishing and free.

### The meeting of the Estates-General

Accompanied by great anticipation, the Estates-General finally gathered at the Palace of Versailles on 5 May 1789. Each region and town was represented by elected members, divided by estate. The First Estate, the clergy, was represented by 303 deputies, the largest number of whom were parish priests. The Second Estate was represented by 282 nobles and the Third Estate had 578 deputies, most of whom were bourgeoisie (predominantly lawyers), but also including some members of the higher estates who instead represented the Third Estate. Two notable examples of this were Abbé Sieyès and the Comte de Mirabeau, a nobleman who would play a key role in the events of the revolution (see page 204). Initially it was expected that all estates would have equal representation, but it was later decided that the Third Estate would be given twice the number of deputies than the other two estates. In theory, this would give them equal say to the First and Second Estates combined. However, this was not the reality, as it was decided that voting would be by estate, not by head (i.e. one vote per delegate). Each estate would, in private, discuss any reforms proposed, vote among themselves, and then simply present one 'yes' or 'no' vote. This meant that the First and Second Estates, who had similar interests, would always be able to outvote the Third Estate. It was this voting system that would cause the first debate of the Estates-General, as many deputies pushed for voting by head. It should not be assumed that it was only Third Estate delegates who opposed voting by estate. As the *cahiers* reveal, there were many deputies of the First and Second Estates who stood in support of the rights of the Third Estate rather than standing in defence of the privileges afforded to them.

## The declaration of the National Assembly

As the debate dragged on, Louis failed to take the opportunity to exert his influence over proceedings, possibly because he was distracted by the death of his son and heir. He made no judgement or ruling on how voting arrangements should proceed, allowing the frustration of the deputies to build. The patience of the Third Estate deputies ran out when, on 17 June, inspired by the speeches of Mirabeau and Sieyès, the deputies declared that they were the 'National Assembly': the body representing the greatest proportion of the French people and therefore the body that would singly decide the future of the French constitution. Just two days later, the First Estate voted to join the Third Estate in the National Assembly. Louis was now facing a major threat as the pace of events began to accelerate.

## The Tennis Court Oath

In an attempt to bring events back under his control, Louis acted. He decided that he would call the three estates together in a *Séance Royale* ('Royal Session') and there present a package of proposed reforms. Chance then caused a significant twist in events. On 20 June, the deputies of the Third Estate arrived at the palace to find that the hall where they had met was locked shut and that the door was guarded by royal soldiers. It is said that the hall had been closed so that preparations could be made for the *Séance Royale* scheduled for three days later. To the deputies of the Third Estate, this looked like the king was trying to prevent them from assembling. Determined to assemble by any means, the deputies found another place within the palace to meet, which happened to be a handball court, but is more commonly referred to as a tennis court. It was here that, in a statement of defiance against the king, and under the leadership of Mirabeau, the deputies swore a collective oath. This was the Tennis Court Oath.

**SOURCE 15** The oath taken by deputies of the Third Estate on 20 June 1789 in the tennis court.

> The National Assembly, holding that, when it has been called to settle the constitution of the Kingdom, effect the regeneration of public order, and maintain the true principles of the monarchy, nothing can prevent it from continuing its deliberations and completing the important task for which it has met, in whatever place it is forced to establish itself, and, finally wherever its members meet, there is the National Assembly, has decided that all the members of this Assembly shall at once take an oath never to separate, but to meet wherever circumstances dictate, until the constitution of the Kingdom and public regeneration are established and settled; and that, after the taking of said oath, all members, and each individually, shall confirm this irrevocable resolution with their signatures.

The statement had now publicly been made that France was going to have a new constitution, with or without the approval of the king. Despite the challenge to his authority, Louis pressed ahead with the *Séance Royale,* which met on 23 June. He was willing to accept some significant restrictions to his power, including the abolition of the hated *lettre de cachet,* agreeing to freedom of the press and accepting that any new taxation would have to be approved by a representative body. Yet he was firm in his conviction that the privileges of the First and Second Estates would remain and that the National Assembly, as declared on the 17 June, was void and that instead the three estates should continue to meet separately. However, when Louis attempted to dismiss the estates to their separate meetings, the Third Estate deputies, in accordance with the Tennis Court Oath, refused to leave the hall. The next day, scores of deputies from the First and Second Estate arrived to join with the Third Estate's National Assembly in their defiance of the king. Realising that he had little choice, Louis ordered the remaining deputies of the First and Second Estate to join the Third. The National Assembly was now legitimate.

## Revolt in Paris and the storming of the Bastille

Politically outmanoeuvred, Louis now began seriously to contemplate using military force to reassert his authority. Demonstrations had already broken out on the streets of Paris in support of the National Assembly and, fearing open revolt, Louis ordered troops to be moved into Paris and Versailles. This caused great alarm and anger among the populace of the capital, at a time when tensions were already running high due to rocketing bread prices and poverty. This anger was heightened when, on 11 July, Louis dismissed Necker due to his sympathies with the Third Estate. Incited further by radical speakers at the Palais Royal, such as the Duc d'Orléans and Camille Desmoulins (see page 203), a pamphleteer and journalist, demonstrations began to turn violent as some Parisians armed themselves and attacked customs posts.

**SOURCE 16** Lord Dorset, Britain's special ambassador to France at the time of the revolution, recorded the causes of the outbreak of violence on the streets of Paris in July 1789, as he saw them.

> The atmosphere of unease spread by the pamphleteers and orators [speakers] was intensified by the fact the court had summoned up 20,000 troops from the provinces. The climax came when the court party felt itself strong enough to dismiss Necker, whom the people - for no good reason - idolized. They may still have believed that the persuasive financier might be able to do something about the price of bread; in 1789, a four-pound loaf cost 14.5 sous [pennies], and the effective daily wage of, say, a builder's labourer was only 18 sous. All these irritants combined to persuade the ordinary people of Paris that they were to be crushed under the scarlet heels of the aristocrats, just when they thought they were on the threshold of freedom. It was too much.

The Parisian demonstrators then turned their attention to the Bastille. The Bastille was a huge fortress used for decades as a prison by the rulers of the *ancien régime.* Many a victim of a *lettre de cachet,* including Voltaire, had ended up behind the walls of the Bastille. By 1789, though, the Bastille was used only infrequently as a prison, but nevertheless stood as a symbol of the despotism of absolute monarchy. Of even more significance to the rioters were the vast quantities of gunpowder stored within the fortress (as they had seized 28,000 muskets from an arsenal the day before). On 14 July 1789, the Parisian demonstrators demanded entry to the Bastille. The governor of the building, de Launay, refused. After he ordered his troops to fire on the crowd, violence erupted and the Bastille was stormed. De Launay was stabbed and killed. He was then decapitated and his head was held aloft on a pike (a long spear).

## The significance of the storming of the Bastille

**SOURCE 17** From a journal written immediately after the storming of the Bastille by Edward Rigby, a doctor from England who, by chance, was visiting Paris in July 1789.

> We ran to the end of the Rue St Honoré. We here soon perceived an immense crowd proceeding towards the Palais Royal with acceleration of an extraordinary kind, but which sufficiently indicated a joyful event, and, as we approached, we saw a flag, some large keys, and a paper elevated on a pole above the crowd, in which was inscribed '*Les Bastille est prise et les portes sont ouvertes*.' ['The Bastille has fallen and the gates are open.'] The intelligence [information] of this event thus communicated, produced an impression upon the crowd really indescribable. A sudden burst of almost frantic joy instantaneously took place; every possible mode [way] in which the rapturous [enthusiastic] feelings of joy could be expressed, were everywhere exhibited. Shouts and shrieks, leaping and embracing, laughter and tears, every sound and every gesture, including even what approached nervous and hysterical affection, manifested, among the promiscuous [thoughtless] crowd, such an instantaneous and unanimous emotion of extreme gladness as I supposed was never before experienced by human beings.

While only seven prisoners were 'liberated' from the fortress that day, the storming of the Bastille was a significant event. It showed that King Louis had lost control of the streets of Paris, as well as the political assemblies. Not only this, but Louis' failure to subdue the unrest led to further changes. The Parisian bourgeoisie were concerned that the unplanned and uncoordinated uprisings could spill over into civil anarchy. They attempted to regain control of the situation by establishing a new assembly to govern the city (like a city council). This elected body was to be known as the Commune and would have a significant impact on later events of the revolution.

One of the first acts of the Commune was to establish an armed guard to keep order, largely to defend the interests of property owners against mob violence. This citizens' militia was known as the National Guard, and its first commander was an enlightened nobleman and hero of the American Revolutionary War, Lafayette. The position of the National Guard was a complex one. It was revolutionary in that it was subservient to the Commune and the National Assembly and not to the king. However, it was also there to prevent the revolution from running over into wanton destruction and blood-letting.

As well as its direct consequences, the storming of the Bastille would become the most enduring symbol of the revolution. While to most historians the revolution had begun in the months prior to the storming of the Bastille, in popular culture this event is seen as the start of the revolution and it is for this reason that, in France today, they still commemorate the 1789 revolution on 14 July every year, Bastille Day.

**AS Level Exam-Style Question Section A**

***Study Source 17 before you answer this question.***

Why is Source 17 valuable to the historian for an enquiry into the significance of the storming of the Bastille?

Explain your answer using the source, the information given about it and your own knowledge of the historical context. (8 marks)

**Tip**

*As well as using your knowledge to explain what the source says and implies, also remember to consider the utility of the source. Does the source give us the whole picture of why the storming of the Bastille was significant?*

## Conclusion

In August 1788, when King Louis agreed to summon the Estates-General, little could he have known how rapidly events would escalate. By the end of July 1789, Louis had lost nearly all control over the political happenings at Versailles. There was now a National Assembly, created against his wishes, that represented all three estates combined and that was on course to rewrite the constitution of France. He had lost control of the streets of Paris, as armed demonstrators rioted, attacked government buildings and threatened civil peace. Furthermore, feeling undefended by the king, the bourgeoisie had taken matters into their own hands, establishing the Commune and the National Guard.

However, it should be emphasised that, in 1789, the cries on the streets of Paris and in the National Assembly were, for the vast majority, not cries of republicanism. The tricolour flag, today the national flag of France, was first seen on the streets of Paris in summer 1789. Red and blue were the traditional colours of Paris and to this was added a white stripe, white being the colour of the Bourbon monarchy. The inclusion of white on the flag indicates that the 1789 revolution was not a republican one. Similarly, the *cahiers* reflected that the mood of the nation in early 1789 favoured constitutional monarchy, not its overthrow.

**AS Level Exam-Style Question Section B**

How far was the philosophy of the Enlightenment responsible for the collapse of absolute monarchy in 1789? (20 marks)

**Tip**

*Plan your answer before you begin to write. Consider what other factors, aside from the Enlightenment, contributed to the collapse of absolute monarchy. Also, try to have an overall judgement in mind before you begin writing your answer. This will help you to form a clear and sustained argument.*

ACTIVITY
KNOWLEDGE CHECK

**Estates-General to the storming of the Bastille**

1 Study Source 14. What do you think Abbé Sieyès meant when he described the Third Estate as being 'everything'?

2 Study Source 16. How many different causes of the unrest in Paris in July 1789 can you identify within this source? Draw a table like the one below and record the causes mentioned in the first column. In the second column, explain and expand upon these causes using your knowledge of the period. One example has been done for you. See how many further rows you can add.

| Causes of unrest identified in Source 16 | Expansion and explanation using contextual knowledge |
|---|---|
| 'The atmosphere of unease spread by the pamphleteers and orators [speakers]' | Pamphlets that attacked the *ancien régime* and encouraged resistance were being produced and distributed in Paris from the Palais Royal. The palace became one of the key bases for the demonstrators in July 1789. After Necker's dismissal, speakers such as the Duc d'Orléans and Desmoulins incited the crowds further. |

ACTIVITY
SUMMARY

**Bringing it all together: what caused the revolution of 1789?**

1 Create a mind map summarising the causes of the 1789 revolution. Use the following four key stems: 'The Enlightenment', 'Nature of the *ancien régime*', 'Financial problems' and 'King Louis and his court'. To each of these stems, add details and examples that could be used to support how that factor contributed to revolution. For example, to the 'Financial problems' stem, you might add 'Louis inherited debt due to the Seven Years' War.'

2 Once you have added as many details and examples to the four stems as you can, try to make connections between these examples and other stems, to show how the causes are connected. For example, you may have added 'France ruled as an absolute monarchy' to the 'Nature of the *ancien régime*' stem. You could then draw a line connecting that point to 'The Enlightenment' stem also as enlightened *philosophes* challenged the idea of absolute monarchy.

EXTEND YOUR KNOWLEDGE

**The historiography of the causes of the French Revolution**

One of the first noteworthy people to comment on the causes of the French Revolution was Edmund Burke, a late 18th-century British politician and writer. Burke condemned the French Revolution. He argued that the revolution had been caused by a minority of selfish, disruptive groups. These groups, he said, consisted of the middle-class bourgeoisie, guided by the ideas of the Enlightenment into believing that they deserved more, who saw revolution as an opportunity to replace the traditional aristocracy with their own kind. Burke claimed that the desire for change was not widespread, and that the poor, incapable of political thought in his view, were simply swept along by this minority of self-interested bourgeois-types.

Liberal historians of the 19th century, such as François Mignet, agreed with Burke in that they interpreted the causes of the revolution as being a consequence of the Enlightenment. However, contrary to Burke, they saw the causes in positive terms, arguing that there was a widespread political movement, led by the 'respectable' classes (i.e. the bourgeoisie) that aimed to improve outmoded, inefficient and undemocratic institutions.

Jules Michelet, a French historian writing in the 1840s and 1850s, took a very different view of the causes to Burke. In his interpretation, the revolution was a popular movement; a spontaneous uprising against despotism triggered by the grinding poverty of the 1780s. Alexis de Tocqueville, another French historian of the mid-19th century, challenged Michelet's view. He argued that the condition of the peasants had actually improved in the 18th century and that, as the peasants became wealthier and better educated, they became more aware of their social importance and more able to express their dissatisfaction. He concluded that, once the suggestion of reform was voiced and attempted, this inspired people, already influenced by enlightened thought, to push for greater and greater change. The floodgates had been opened to allow people of all classes to make the vision of the Enlightenment a reality.

In the 20th century, the Marxist interpretation of the French Revolution came to prominence, seeing the revolution, as Marxist interpretations do, as a class struggle: an attempt by the growing bourgeois class to overthrow the old aristocracy. George Rudé, writing in the 1950s, challenged Tocqueville's view (see page 178). Rudé argued that the 'common revolutionary psychology' of the era was fuelled by widespread dissatisfaction due to hardships and oppression. The trigger for this discontent to develop into revolution was the opposition of the *parlements* and aristocratic revolt of 1787-88. However, according to Rudé, the revolution became one from below as both the bourgeoisie and the lower orders joined the cry against the despotism of the ruling classes.

More recent revisionist historians, most famously Francis Furet, have opposed the Marxist interpretation of class struggle. Instead, they have tended to re-emphasise the impact of the Enlightenment, and how the revolution was a cultural movement driven largely by a minority of people within Paris, most of whom were nobles or wealthy bourgeoisie. In this view, it was a revolution 'from above'.

## THINKING HISTORICALLY Interpretations 5c

### Good questions/Bad questions

Below are approaches attributed to three individuals who wrote about the causes of the French Revolution.

| Arthur Young | Edmund Burke | Augustin Barruel |
|---|---|---|
| Young was a British travel writer and agriculturist. He campaigned for the rights of peasants and agricultural workers. He travelled to France in 1787-89 and recorded his reflections. | Burke was a British politician who wrote a famous work criticising the French Revolution entitled *Reflections on the Revolution in France* (1790). He largely focused on the political changes within France and the balance of power between the people and the monarchy. | Barruel was a French Jesuit priest. He wrote an account of the French Revolution published in 1797. In his work, he argued that the revolution has been a secret conspiracy of the bourgeoisie, aiming to overthrow the Catholic institutions of the *ancien régime*. |

Work in groups.

1 Devise three criteria of what makes a good historical question.

2 Consider what you know about the causes of the French Revolution.

a) Each write a historical question based on that subject matter.

b) Put these in rank order, with the best question first, based on your criteria.

3 Using a piece of A3 paper, write the names of the three writers so they form a large triangle.

a) Write your questions from 2(a) on the piece of paper so that their positions reflect how likely it is that the writers would be interested by each question. The more interested they would be, the closer you should write the question to their name. For example, a question about the impact of the bad harvests would be likely to interest Young and perhaps Burke a little (as it has an indirect link to the balance of power), so would be somewhere between those two, but nowhere near Barruel.

b) Add some further questions. Try to think of questions that only one of the three would be interested in.

4 Take it in turns to try and answer the questions you have created in the style of one of the historians. See if the other members of the group can guess which historian it was.

5 Answer the following questions individually using the examples created by the above activity:

a) Does one method of constructing history lead to better reasoning than the others? Explain your answer.

b) Explain why all historians who deploy rigorous methodology are, to an extent, useful sources for the study of the past.

### WIDER READING

Brown, G.S. *Cultures in Conflict: The French Revolution*, Greenwood Press (2003) An academic text; the 'Historical Overview' in the first chapter is particularly useful and the book also includes a timeline, glossary and study questions

Doyle, W. *The French Revolution: A Very Short Introduction*, Oxford University Press (2001) A concise, readable overview with helpful chronology; highly recommended for Chapters 2-4 too

Doyle, W. *The Old Regime*, Oxford University Press (2001) An academic text; chapter 8 explores the politics of Louis XVI reign with particular attention to the financial crisis

Hardman, J. 'Louis XVI and the French Revolution', *History Review*, September 1996, pages 37-41: www.historytoday.com/john-hardman/louis-xvi-and-french-revolution An interesting and accessible essay arguing in defence of Louis XVI; subscription to the website required

Hobsbawm, E. *The Age of Revolution 1789-1848*, Weidenfeld & Nicholson (1962) A challenging academic text; chapter 1 gives a fascinating insight into the world in the 1780s, helping to contextualise the French Revolution and chapter 3 addresses the revolution itself

Waller, S. *France in Revolution 1776-1830*, Heinemann (2002) An A Level textbook written for a previous specification; chapters 1-3 address the causes of the revolution and section 2 includes a useful chapter debating different interpretations of those causesInterpretations (3a)

# 2a.2 Revolution and the failure of constitutional monarchy, 1789–93

## KEY QUESTIONS

- Did the reforms of the Constituent Assembly go too far or not far enough?
- How divided were political views in the period 1789–93?
- How far was the flight to Varennes the key cause of radicalisation in 1791 and 1792?
- To what extent had the radicals triumphed by January 1793?

The execution of Louis XVI on 21 January 1793 sent shockwaves across Europe. James Gillray's cartoon of the execution (Source 1, opposite) reflects an attitude towards the event not uncommon in Britain: that this was a monstrous act by radical extremists. In the image, King Louis is beheaded by guillotine, while a mad-looking revolutionary looks on, incongruously playing the violin and with two bloody daggers tucked into his belt. The dead bodies hanging from lamp posts, the burning palace in the background and the fearful people peeping from their windows only add to the disturbing scene.

While Gillray's cartoon is clearly not an objective portrayal of France in January 1793, it does raise several questions: who is the revolutionary sitting watching the execution? Why are there dead bodies hanging from the lamp posts and why do they appear to be bishops, monks and nuns? Why is the palace ablaze? However, the biggest question is: why was King Louis XVI overthrown and executed?

In the summer of 1789, very few people were calling for a republic, never mind the execution of Louis. The vast majority of the Constituent Assembly favoured constitutional monarchy and the majority of constitutional **monarchists** sought to achieve their aims through peaceful constitutional reform. Yet, in August 1792, a violent uprising would overthrow the king, leading to the declaration of a republic and, ultimately, Louis' execution.

### KEY TERMS

**Monarchist**
An individual who strongly supports the existence and rights of the monarchy.

**Counter-revolutionary**
A person or group who opposed the revolution and attempted to reverse its course.

The debate surrounding why constitutional monarchy failed hinges around a number of key arguments. The blame could be placed upon the actions of a radical minority: journalists, agitators and extremist politicians who attacked the weaknesses of constitutional reform in an effort to advance the republican cause. Others might blame the Constituent Assembly for failing to deliver to the people of France the constitution they sought, and for failing to deliver the poor from their abject poverty. Louis himself is also not absolved of blame. He repeatedly acted in a manner that convinced some people that he was an enemy, not a friend of the revolution, not least when he tried to flee France in June 1791. The trigger of Louis' fall, though, was caused by the coming of war. When the war between Austria and France began in April 1792, the revolution had to fight for its survival. Suspicion and fear of **counter-revolutionary** activity heightened during the war, and when Paris

**1789** – July-August: The Great Fear

**1789** – 5 August: The August Decrees
26 August: The Declaration of the Rights of Man and Citizen

**1789** – 5 October: The October Days

**1789** – November: National Assembly approves sale of Church land

**1789** – December: A law passed distinguishing between active and passive citizenship

**By end of 1789** – Tithes, feudal dues and many taxes and duties abolished

1790

**1790** – April: The Cordeliers Club established by Georges Danton
Maximilien Robespierre elected president of the Jacobins Club

**1790** – July: The Civil Constitution of the Clergy sanctioned

**1790** – November: Refractory clergy refuse to take oath of allegiance

1791

**1791** – January: A new, universal taxation system is introduced
Poor harvests cause strikes and further unrest

**1791** – April: Comte de Mirabeau's death

was threatened with annihilation by a foreign army this fear spilled over into terror and a violent uprising that would forcefully remove the king from power.

ACTIVITY
KNOWLEDGE CHECK

**Explaining Gillray's cartoon**

As you progress through this chapter, refer back to Gillray's cartoon to apply what you have learnt to what you can see in the image. Try to explain the following:

1 What type of person is sitting watching from a lamp post? Why is he wearing no trousers?

2 Why does this person have two bloody daggers in his belt?

3 What is the red cap on a stick next to this figure?

4 Why is there a palace burning in the background? What event could this be alluding to?

5 Why are there dead monks hanging from the lamp posts? Could this be a reference to a specific event?

6 The cartoon is entitled *The Zenith of French Glory; – The Pinnacle of Liberty*. Why do you think Gillray chose this title?

7 Why is a hanged judge shown?

SOURCE 1

The British cartoonist James Gillray presented a grim image of the execution of King Louis on 21 January 1793. From an etching entitled *The Zenith of French Glory; – The Pinnacle of Liberty. Religion, Justice, Loyalty & all the Bugbears of Unenlightened Minds, Farewell!*, published in Britain in February 1793.

## DID THE REFORMS OF THE CONSTITUENT ASSEMBLY GO TOO FAR OR NOT FAR ENOUGH?

In the months following the storming of the Bastille, the National Assembly began the process of dismantling the structures of the *ancien régime*. As we will see in this chapter, the August Decrees, formally abolishing feudalism, and the Declaration of the Rights of Man and Citizen were the first steps in this process. These reforms were set against a backdrop of rural uprisings, known as the Great Fear, and of continuing demonstrations in Paris, culminating in the march on Versailles in October 1789. Over the following two years, the National Assembly, or the Constituent Assembly as it is also known during this period, created a new constitution for France. The resulting constitution of September 1791 can be seen as a radical departure from pre-revolutionary absolutism.

**1791** - 21 June: King Louis and the royal family try to flee France

**1791** - 17 July: Champs de Mars massacre

**1791** - 27 August: Declaration of Pillnitz

**1791** - 3 September: The new constitution of France comes into effect

1792

**1792** - 20 April: France declares war on Austria

**1792** - 20 June: King Louis vetoes *fédérés* and a law against refractory priests

**1792** - 25 July: The Prussian Brunswick Manifesto

**1792** - 9 August: Radicals led by Danton take over the Paris Commune
10 August: The Tuileries Palace is stormed; Louis is arrested

**1792** - September: The September Massacres
20 September: The National Convention meets for the first time
20 September: French victory at the Battle of Valmy
21 September: France declared a republic

**1792** - 10 December: Louis' trial begins

1793

**1793** - 21 January: Louis is publicly beheaded by guillotine

For some, though, it did not go far enough and the extent to which the reforms introduced by the Constituent Assembly directly benefited the general population of France is debatable. For others, it was too much too soon, and heralded a counter-revolutionary movement that would later become a serious threat to the government.

## The Great Fear and the abolition of feudalism

Rural unrest did not begin in the summer of 1789. There had been many rural disturbances in the 1770s and 1780s, such as the Flour Wars (see page 182), often a result of failed harvests and rising grain prices. However, the unfolding events in Paris seemed to give rural discontent a new stimulus. In July and August 1789, uprisings were reported in every province of France, excluding Alsace, Brittany and Lorraine. Although a lot of historical mist surrounds this turmoil, especially regarding who the offenders were and the extent to which the unrest was co-ordinated and connected, there was a clear pattern in the targets of these rural revolts. Peasants were taking up arms against the manors of their lords, targeting, as they saw it, the sources of their oppression. This phenomenon of summer 1789 has become known as 'the Great Fear', sometimes known by its French name, *la Grande Peur*. The 'fear' was of an aristocratic conspiracy. Rumours abounded that, in an attempt to overturn the revolution and defend their power, the nobility were gathering militia forces to suppress the peasantry. It was the fear created by such rumours, seemingly untrue, that triggered the violence.

**SOURCE 2**

The Great Fear of July 1789 as represented in an anonymous engraving from Paris in 1789. Peasants attack and burn an aristocratic château and a chapel, targeting the beneficiaries of their dues, labour and taxation. The Great Fear led to the first wave of aristocratic *émigrés* fleeing France. Perhaps the departing coach in this scene reflects the flight of an aristocratic family.

As news of the Great Fear spread, the Constituent Assembly became increasingly concerned with the nationwide turmoil. The National Guard was deployed to defend the threatened properties of the nobility. In a further effort to stop the unrest, the Constituent Assembly began considering the abolition of feudalism, to appease the peasantry. The Assembly's hand was forced when, on 4 August, the Duc d'Aiguillon, one of the greatest landowners in France and a man with liberal beliefs, encouraged noblemen to declare an end to feudalism on their lands. What followed has been described as 'an orgy of self-sacrifice' as nobles at the Assembly renounced their own privileges. The Constituent Assembly formalised and legalised these changes in a series of decrees between 4 and 11 August, known as the August Decrees. The Decrees abolished many privileges of the nobility, including venality (the buying of titles and official positions). Instead, such positions – Church, military and civil – became open to all. Other privileges attacked included those related to feudalism, with an end to the payment of tithes and equality of taxation across the three estates.

The August Decrees did not bring about a sudden transformation in French society. The process of abolishing something in principle is very different from abolishing something in practice, and few would see an immediate and direct change. The Decrees were more of a statement of intent and that statement was a strong one: to cast aside the noble privileges of the *ancien régime* and to promise a more equal society.

## The Declaration of the Rights of Man

'The Declaration of Rights was the death-warrant of the system of privilege, and so of the *ancien régime*. In this respect it inaugurated a new age.' This was how the renowned historian Alfred Cobban described arguably the most significant document to come out of the French Revolution. The Declaration of the Rights of Man and of the Citizen, to give it its full name, was issued on 26 August 1789 by the Constituent Assembly. It was not a constitution in itself, but a list of principles and core values that were to underpin the new constitution. Although the Declaration was issued collectively by the Constituent Assembly, it is perhaps the Marquis de Lafayette who could be given the greatest credit for it. Lafayette had worked directly alongside the American statesman Thomas Jefferson in drafting the Declaration. Jefferson had been the key author of the American Declaration of Independence (1776) and there are clear parallels between the two documents. Although the Declaration took influences from a wide range of sources: the ideas of Abbé Sieyès' *What is the Third Estate?* are also evident.

SOURCE 3 Selected articles from The Declaration of the Rights of Man and of the Citizen.

1 Men are born and remain free and equal in rights. Social distinctions may be founded only upon the general good.

2 The aim of all political association is the preservation of the natural and imprescriptible rights of man. These rights are liberty, property, security, and resistance to oppression.

3 The principle of all sovereignty resides essentially in the nation. No body nor individual may exercise any authority which does not proceed directly from the nation.

4 Liberty consists in the freedom to do everything which injures no one else...

5 Law can only prohibit such actions as are hurtful to society. Nothing may be prevented which is not forbidden by law, and no one may be forced to do anything not provided for by law.

6 Law is the expression of the general will. Every citizen has a right to participate personally, or through his representative, in its foundation. It must be the same for all, whether it protects or punishes. All citizens, being equal in the eyes of the law, are equally eligible to all dignities and to all public positions and occupations, according to their abilities, and without distinction except that of their virtues and talents.

7 No person shall be accused, arrested, or imprisoned except in the cases and according to the forms prescribed by law...

10 No one shall be disquieted on account of his opinions, including his religious views, provided their manifestation does not disturb the public order established by law.

11 The free communication of ideas and opinions is one of the most precious of the rights of man. Every citizen may, accordingly, speak, write, and print with freedom, but shall be responsible for such abuses of this freedom as shall be defined by law.

13 A common contribution [of taxes] is essential for the maintenance of the public forces and for the cost of administration. This should be equitably distributed among all the citizens in proportion to their means.

## EXTEND YOUR KNOWLEDGE

### Marquis de Lafayette (1757-1834)

The Marquis de Lafayette was a French aristocrat from an ancient noble family. He led French forces in support of the Americans in their Revolutionary War against Britain. He was hailed as a hero when he returned to France in 1782. He was a significant leader of the liberal nobles in the years leading up to the revolution, arguing for religious tolerance, the abolition of slavery and the transfer of power from the aristocracy to the bourgeoisie. He was elected to the Estates-General and, after it became the Constituent Assembly, was instrumental in the formulation of the Declaration of the Rights of Man and of the Citizen.

Despite criticism from the radical press for being too close to the king, Lafayette was a major force in the Constituent Assembly and also led the National Guard. His reputation was damaged when Louis tried to flee France in June 1791, as Lafayette had been charged with the responsibility of ensuring that the royal family did not leave Paris. Although the flight failed, popular newspapers, like Jean-Paul Marat's *L'Ami du peuple* ('Friend of the People'), accused Lafayette of orchestrating the escape. Even greater damage was done to his reputation when he led the National Guard against a crowd of protesters at the Champs de Mars field, resulting in a massacre with some 60 people killed. In October 1791, due to his lack of popularity amongst the populace of Paris, Lafayette resigned his post as head of the National Guard.

When the Tuileries Palace was stormed in August 1792 and King Louis was arrested, Lafayette realised that constitutional monarchy was collapsing and that, as a leading supporter of constitutional monarchy, his life was in great danger. He fled to Austria, where he was imprisoned. Later released, and with the revolution over, he returned to France during the reign of Napoleon Bonaparte (in 1799). He played a role in the later governments of the Bourbon Restoration (1814-30), eventually retiring in 1830. He was one of the great survivors of this turbulent period of history.

## The October Days and the march on Versailles

In August 1789, expectations were running high. It appeared that France was on course to build a new constitution that, while still including a monarch as head of state, upheld values of equality and freedom. However, things were not to run smoothly. On 5 August, King Louis refused to sanction the August Decrees. This was at a time when tensions were already high in Paris.

Bread prices had not dropped, radicals continued to agitate crowds and Lafayette's National Guard was struggling to keep law and order. Fearing further unrest, Louis called his highly disciplined Flanders regiment to Versailles to protect the royal family. Things came to a head in October when, despite the discontent caused by his refusal of the August Decrees, Louis also voiced his objections to the Declaration of the Rights of Man.

**KEY TERM**

**Revolutionary cockade**
The revolutionary cockade was a symbol worn by the French revolutionaries. It was like a rosette, with three concentric circles. It was a tricolour design with red and blue representing the traditional colours of Paris and white being the colour representing the Bourbon monarchy (the Bourbon family's flag was a *fleur-de-lis* against a white background). (See Source 1 for an example of a cockade, in the revolutionary's hat.)

Distrust of the monarchy was compounded when Marat's *L'Ami du peuple* and Camille Desmoulins' *Les Révolutions de France*, radical newspapers that had already fuelled unrest through stories of royal treason and gluttony, published a rumour that Louis' officers had trampled a **revolutionary cockade** during a state banquet. This triggered a huge demonstration, led largely by women, outside the Hôtel de Ville in Paris. The crowd, some 6,000 or 7,000 strong, many of whom were armed with sticks and knives, began to march on Versailles. These women were following a tradition of the *ancien régime* where, in an annual ceremony, common women of the markets of Paris would march to the palace and present the royal family with bouquets of flowers. The mood of the October 1789 march, however, would be very different from this reverent ceremony of the past.

When the crowd arrived at Versailles, some of them broke into the palace, killing a number of royal guards as they did so. Marie Antoinette fled to Louis' side in his private apartment. This was perhaps just in time to save her life, as her chamber was ransacked by armed protesters shortly afterwards. The lives of the royal family were spared by the arrival of Lafayette and the National Guard who, in an attempt to appease the mob, convinced Louis to agree to move the royal court to Paris immediately. The royal family was escorted by the National Guard, followed by a large procession of demonstrators, to the heart of the city.

The October Days, as this event is known, forced the royal family to give up its residence in Versailles and move to the Tuileries Palace, in the heart of Paris. The deputies of the Constituent Assembly similarly had to relocate from Versailles and convene within the city instead. As was the intention of those who forced their move to Paris, this meant that both Louis and the Constituent Assembly were far closer to, and therefore far more easily influenced by, the power of the people in the city. Some deputies of the Assembly feared for their personal safety, believing that they would be attacked by the Parisian mob. As a result, some 56 monarchist deputies refused to attend the Assembly, in effect giving up their positions. The loss of so many deputies was a blow to Louis' support within the Constituent Assembly.

Yet the October Days also had a symbolic significance. The event gave a sense of victory of the revolution over the *ancien régime*. Not for the last time in the revolution, the common people of Paris had successfully taken political events into their own hands.

**ACTIVITY**
**KNOWLEDGE CHECK**

**Events to October 1789**

1. 'Four revolutions had already taken place in France by the end of August 1789.' What 'four revolutions' do you think historian George Lefebvre meant when he wrote this of the period 1787 to August 1789? Do you agree with his view?
2. How far would you blame King Louis for causing the October Days? Who, or what else, could also be said to have caused the march on Versailles?

Cause and consequence (5b)

**Causation relativity**

Historical events usually have many causes. Some are crucial, while some are less important. For some historical questions, it is important to understand exactly what role certain factors played in causing historical change.

**Significant factors in the timing and nature of the August Decrees**

| | | |
|---|---|---|
| Bad harvests contributed to a severe economic downturn in the late 1780s. | The storming of the Bastille had involved large numbers of working-class people. | The structure of government meant that the rising middle classes had no say in the way the country was governed. |
| The Tennis Court Oath placed the Estates-General at odds with the monarchy | The Enlightenment movement had raised questions about the nature of government. | Louis XVI was indecisive in his dealing with opposition. |

Answer the following questions on your own:

**The timing of the August Decrees**

1 How important were the poor harvests in explaining the timing of the decrees?

2 In what ways did the storming of the Bastille change the state of affairs caused by the Tennis Court Oath? How far did this precipitate the August Decrees?

3 How could Louis XVI have delayed the kind of reform contained in the decrees?

**The nature of the August Decrees**

4 How far had the Enlightenment movement changed the attitudes of the people who were involved in writing the August Decrees?

5 What role did the above factors play in the way that the August Decrees reshaped the agricultural economy?

6 Would the nature of the August Decrees have been the same if the Bastille had not been stormed?

7 What roles did each of the above causal factors play in determining the nature and timing of the August Decrees?

## The reforms of the Constituent Assembly

From August 1789, and culminating with Louis' acceptance of the new Constitution on 14 September 1791, the Constituent Assembly set about rewriting how France was to be governed.

### The power of the monarchy

Though the days of absolute monarchy were over, it was generally agreed within the Constituent Assembly that monarchy should remain. The hereditary principle of monarchy was upheld, and Louis retained the right to appoint his own ministers, ambassadors and military commanders. He was also granted 25 million livres to allow the royal family to continue to live in a manner befitting its status. Louis was, however, stripped of significant legislative power. The king could no longer initiate new laws or taxes, all of which would now be written and sanctioned by the elected Constituent Assembly. Completely powerless in regards to taxation, Louis did maintain some legislative power, in that he was given power of a suspensive veto, allowing him to delay or suspend laws created by the Constituent Assembly for up to four years. This power of veto would cause serious problems during the events of 1792 (see page 210).

KEY TERMS

**Universal suffrage**
Where everyone has the right to vote. In the context of the period, when politicians talked about universal suffrage, they were usually only referring to the right to vote for adult males. There were a number of groups and individuals in Paris during the revolution who also argued for female suffrage, but their cause was not commonly supported.

**Franchise**
The right to vote. To be given the right to vote is to be enfranchised. When the right to vote is withdrawn, this is described as being disenfranchised.

***Émigrés***
Beginning in summer 1789, some French nobility and clergy, fearing for their safety, began to flee France. As the revolution became increasingly radical, the rate of emigration greatly increased. These emigrants were known as *émigrés*. Many sought refuge in the Austrian Netherlands, but others fled to Britain, Austria, Italy and Switzerland. As concern about counter-revolution increased during 1791 and 1792, there were fears within France that the *émigrés* might attempt an invasion of France to re-establish the power of the king.

***Biens nationaux***
The land of the Church and *émigrés* that was sold off by the state.

## Political rights

Despite the impact of popular action in forcing the Constituent Assembly's move to Paris, the deputies were mostly keen to see that those involved in popular protest did not play a direct role in government and the idea of **universal suffrage** was dismissed. Instead, in a law of December 1789, it was decided that the vote would only be awarded to those male citizens aged over 25 who paid the equivalent of three days' unskilled labour in local taxes. Those with the right to vote were called 'active' citizens; those who could not were called 'passive' citizens. Yet even most active citizens did not have the right to elect the deputies of the Constituent Assembly. Instead, they would vote in local assemblies. These primary assemblies would determine the 'electors' for the Constituent Assembly. In order to stand to be an elector, a candidate would have to pay the equivalent of ten days' labour in taxes. These electors would then vote in the secondary assemblies, where the deputies for the Constituent Assembly would be elected once every two years. To stand as a deputy candidate for the Constituent Assembly, an individual had to pay one silver mark in taxes.

These complex criteria can make it difficult to assess the extent of the **franchise**. One historian has calculated that around 70 percent of male citizens had some right to vote; however, only 50 percent could afford to be electors and fewer than 10 percent were wealthy enough to become deputies to the Constituent Assembly. This may appear a far cry from the revolutionary principle of equality and a long way from universal suffrage. Yet the system should be considered within its historical context. While voting was limited, a far wider proportion of the population was enfranchised than in any other European state; more than in Britain, whose political system many *philosophes* had held in high regard. Furthermore, when we remember that under the *ancien régime* no-one had any right to elect national representatives, the reforms could be seen as a major step forward. Even at the time, though, not everyone saw it this way, and some political factions strongly opposed the concept of active and passive citizenship (see page 203).

## Economic reforms

In the summer of 1789, the Constituent Assembly swept away many of the unpopular taxes and economic burdens of pre-revolutionary France: the *taille*, the *gabelle*, tithes, feudal dues and internal customs duties (see page 178) were all abolished by the end of 1789. State monopolies and the practice of tax farming were also eliminated. These reforms were of particular benefit to peasant landowners, who had been obliged to pay land tax, and to the bourgeoisie, who had suffered the effects of customs barriers and monopolies. Yet the reforms came at a major cost to the state. There was a time lag between the destruction of the old system of taxation and the establishment of the new one. This left the state with a concerning shortfall, one that the Constituent Assembly tried to fill through the sale of Church land.

On 2 November, the Constituent Assembly nationalised all land belonging to the Catholic Church. It then proceeded to approve the sale of this land and land belonging to ***émigrés***. With the auctioning of 400 million livres' worth of land, this was a major boost to the state's finances. It was also to the benefit of those who could afford to buy the land. Around half of it was purchased by the bourgeoisie, who would in turn lease small plots to the peasantry. In these cases, the labouring peasants would simply be exchanging one lord for another. However, a significant proportion of the land would be bought by the peasants themselves and, with tithes and dues abolished, they could now accumulate greater wealth.

In order to purchase the ***biens nationaux***, prospective buyers would first have to buy bonds from the government, called assignats. These assignats began to be used as paper currency. The problem here was that the government overprinted assignats, leading to depreciation in their value and inflation.

In January 1791, a new system of taxation came into effect. The system was intended to be proportional to wealth, therefore all taxes were direct. Three new taxes were created: a tax on the transfer of goods (not payable by passive citizens, thereby protecting the poorest classes), a tax on commercial/business profits and, most importantly, a universal land tax from which no-one was exempt (as Calonne had proposed in 1787).

## Religious change

The nationalisation and sale of Church land was not without controversy. Some pamphlets celebrated the attack on the Church, arguing that monks and nuns, stripped of their land, would be forced to become useful citizens. Others saw the confiscation of lands as redressing the balance after centuries of Church greed and exploitation. Just as powerful, though, were the voices that argued that an attack on the Church was an attack on God, and bishops condemned the actions of the Constituent Assembly from their pulpits. They denounced those who bought the lands as being in league with the devil. A more practical argument concerned the education and welfare provision that the Church supplied. The Church provided the only education and healthcare that the less wealthy could afford and, as the wealth of the Church waned (due to land confiscations and the abolition of the tithe), these institutions closed as a consequence.

Even more controversial than the sale of Church lands, and perhaps the most divisive reform of the Constituent Assembly, was the Civil Constitution of the Clergy, sanctioned on 12 July 1790. The Civil Constitution essentially put the Church under state control. Priests and bishops were to be paid by the state and were to be elected by the citizens of France. This was seen as a major challenge to the authority of the pope. In the view of most Catholics, the pope was God's representative on earth and therefore only he, and those acting with his blessing, had the right to appoint priests and bishops.

On 27 November 1790, with so many of the clergy opposing and defying the Civil Constitution, the Constituent Assembly insisted that all priests swear an oath of allegiance to the Assembly and the Constitution. Only seven out of 83 bishops took the oath and over half the parish priests refused. Those who refused became known as 'refractory priests'. Over the following years, refractory priests would find themselves being persecuted; many fled, many were arrested. Despite the Legislative Assembly banishing all refractory priests on 27 April 1792, a significant number remained in France, stirring up opposition to the government.

Yet it was not only the clergy who opposed the Civil Constitution. To many people, the Church was the centre of their lives, spiritually and in terms of their communities, and there was considerable resistance to the changes from the peasantry, especially in the western areas of France.

Aside from the Catholic Church, the Constituent Assembly did, true to the values of the Declaration of the Rights of Man, grant full civil rights to Protestants in 1789 and to Jews in 1791.

**SOURCE**

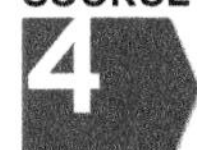

**From an article in the revolutionary newspaper *Les Révolutions de Paris*, published in January 1791. Inspired by the events of July 1789, Louis-Marie Prudhomme established the newspaper to promote the values of the revolution.**

What then is a priest? He is a citizen who, feeling himself endowed with gentleness and humility, [dedicates himself to] those virtues that tend towards the good of society... Under the *ancien régime* and in times when we lacked energy, a good priest would ease our chains and give us hope that sooner or later God, who called us to liberty, would give us the opportunity and provide us with the means for breaking our chains... My friends, my brothers! Three more months, and the country will be saved. Have patience; take courage; the beginnings of liberty are not easy; put on a good face; let harmony reign in our midst. Let us remain united, and we shall stay free. Do not let the refusal of a few bishops and several priests [to take the oath] alarm you; that is their affair. God is on our side, for liberty is his beloved daughter. Liberty is the handmaid of religion. God repulses the incense of slaves. Servitude gives rise only to superstition. Let us then remain free to please God and to makes ourselves respected among men.

**SOURCE**

**The view of the author of Source 4 was not shared by everyone. In the diocese of Vienne, near Lyon, churchgoers had to swear the following oath in order to be confirmed. This was an important ritual in the Catholic Church. The oath was introduced as a reaction to the Civil Constitution of the Clergy.**

In order not to separate myself from the faith of my fathers, but to live in their religion until death, I will remain inviolably [unbreakably] attached and submit to Our Holy Father the Pope, Vicar of Jesus Christ, successor of Saint Peter... I will not recognise any priest who does not hold from [him]... his position and his powers; this is why I will continue to ignore in religious matters all those [priests] who, by their oath to the Civil Constitution of the Clergy... never will I go to their mass; never will receive from them the sacrament; never, in a word, will I communicate with them in spiritual matters.

### AS Level Exam-Style Question Section A

***Study Source 4 before you answer this question.***

Why is Source 4 valuable to the historian for an enquiry into the reaction to the Civil Constitution of the Clergy in 1790?

Explain your answer using the source, the information given about it and your own knowledge of the historical context. (8 marks)

**Tip**

*As well as applying your contextual knowledge to explain and expand on the points raised in the source, also remember to consider its purpose; why do you think the newspaper felt the need to publish such an article?*

### Other reforms

As well as freedom of religion, the Constituent Assembly also upheld freedom of expression, by removing restrictions on the press and ending press censorship; a move true to the revolutionary cause but one that would leave the Assembly vulnerable to attacks from the radical press. Other reforms included the abolition of the *parlements* (August 1790) and the much-despised *lettres de cachet*. These judicial institutions were replaced by the introduction of Justices of the Peace (JPs). Under the Constituent Assembly, France's administrative regions were restructured, with the country being divided into 83 *departments*. The active citizens of each *department* would elect a JP. The JP would then oversee law and order for that region. All citizens would be tried in the same type of trial, against the same laws and with a jury present.

## Conclusion

In the revolutionary fervour of the summer of 1789, the Constituent Assembly was quick to cast aside the values on which the *ancien régime* was based, decrying privilege and oppression, amid much excitement and expectation. The extent to which these dreams were realised depends upon your perspective. By the end of 1791, equality existed in taxation, in rights before the law, in freedom of religion and in freedom of expression. The laws of the country were now created by representatives of the people and the power of the monarchy had been severely curtailed. However, there was still vast inequality of wealth, with the poorest being unable to afford the auctioned-off land, and the political arena remained reserved for those with enough wealth to occupy a seat in the Constituent Assembly. Furthermore, the Civil Constitution of the Clergy was, for some, a step too far in attacking what many people had held dear prior to the revolution.

SOURCE

On 16 January 1790, Adrien Duquesnoy, a deputy for the Constituent Assembly, recorded the following in his diary. Duquesnoy was elected to the Estates-General representing the Third Estate. He was also present during the storming of the Bastille. He was closely aligned with the Comte de Mirabeau (see page 204) in the Constituent Assembly and was a strong advocate of constitutional monarchy.

Putting aside priests, nobility, magistrates and financiers, it is clear that all the rest of the kingdom reaps infinite benefits from the revolution. And indeed, amongst those citizens whom I have just listed there are a great number who judge it advantageous to them, because in truth it is. Thus the clergy of second degree [lower clergy, i.e. parish priests] and almost all provincial noblemen, who were recently oppressed by bishops and court nobles, should consider themselves fortunate to be relieved of this aristocracy... In any case, one thing is certain - it would be difficult for things to be any worse than they were under the former regime. I often hear people around me asking a very strange question: they enquire, 'What has the assembly been doing for the last six months?' I only know of one reply to this question: 'Look, and observe: clergy and nobility abolished, provincial privileges gone, ecclesiastical [Church] property nationalised. Could you have achieved so much in ten years?'

SOURCE

From an article in *Le Fouet National* ('The National Whip'), a revolutionary newspaper, published in September 1789. The author criticises the consequences of the Constituent Assembly's actions.

Never mind, upon the views of the proposal for these articles you are discussing today, the people of all provinces regarded them as fully decreed [made into law]; and they took every advantage which they alone can withdraw. They no longer pay taxes, they have armed themselves for smuggling; they have fixed the price of salt... they have devastated the woods, countryside, estates, destroyed all the game [animals] and even ruined crops at the very time they have become most valuable to us. They refused to acknowledge rights whose abolition was still being discussed [by the Constituent Assembly]; they have ceased to fear the ministers of justice, whose abolition in the villages you have advised. They are acting, then, exactly as people who no longer fear the law, and it is the strongest who enjoy liberty, while your [the Constituent Assembly's] mission is to give it to the weak as well as to those who are powerful.

**A Level Exam-Style Question Section A**

***Study Sources 6 and 7 before you answer this question.***

How far could the historian make use of Sources 6 and 7 together to investigate the impact that the reforms of the Constituent Assembly (1789–92) had on the people of France?

Explain your answer, using both sources, the information given about them and your knowledge of the historical context. (20 marks)

**Tip**

*As well as identifying and expanding on points from the individual sources, also consider them in combination. What points do both sources agree upon?*

ACTIVITY
KNOWLEDGE CHECK

**Did the reforms of the Constituent Assembly go too far or not far enough?**

1 Draw a table with four columns entitled: 'Aspect of French society', 'What existed before 1789?', 'What changed between 1789 and 1792?' and 'Too far or not far enough?'

a) In the first column, list each of the following: 'Role of the monarchy', 'Central government', 'Economy', 'Religion' and 'Division of society'.

b) In the second column, recap the key features of French society under the *ancien régime* against each of the different aspects of French society highlighted in the first column.

c) In the third column, summarise the reforms introduced by the Constituent Assembly between August 1789 and September 1791 relative to each of these aspects.

d) In the final column, for each aspect, assess whether the reforms had met people's expectations or not, and/or whether the reforms had gone too far. Think carefully about different perspectives. Why might some reforms be considered too radical and/or too conservative?

2 'The Constitution was a veritable monster: there was too much republic for a monarchy and too much monarchy for a republic.' What do you think the historian Étienne Dumont meant when he wrote this? Do you agree with his judgement?

# HOW DIVIDED WERE POLITICAL VIEWS IN THE PERIOD 1789–93?

## Key political groups and individuals

In the months following the summer revolution of 1789, a number of **factions** began to emerge in French politics. Different factions would meet in clubs around Paris, where they would discuss the political goings-on of the Constituent Assembly and France in general. These clubs were the first opportunity that large numbers of people had to express their views freely and to be involved in the political life of their country. They would prove to have great influence on the Constituent Assembly and on the people of Paris.

KEY TERM

**Faction**
A faction is a group of people who share similar beliefs and so work together to see their beliefs realised. Factions should not be considered the same as political parties. With factions, the lines are far more blurred and allegiances can change or overlap. For example, Georges-Jacques Danton, the most famous of the Cordeliers (see page 203), would also frequently give speeches at the Jacobin Club. Similarly, Jacques-Pierre Brissot, the leader of the Girondins (see page 203), would speak at both the Jacobin and the Cordeliers Clubs.

### The Jacobin Club

The Jacobins would become the most famous political faction of the French Revolution, closely associated with the violence and extremism of the radical period (1793–94). Yet the Jacobins did not begin life as a radical faction. They met at the Jacobin Club, so-named as the club convened in a former convent belonging to the Jacobin religious order. The club was established in late 1789, after the Constituent Assembly was forced to move to Paris. It aimed to preserve the gains of the revolution, as well as ensuring the stability of the city, in order to protect the property and interests of the bourgeoisie. The club charged high entrance fees and tended to be supported by wealthy liberal constitutional monarchists. The Jacobin Club proved to be very popular, with 1,200 members in Paris and 152 affiliated clubs across France by July 1790.

In July 1791, there was a significant split in the Jacobin Club. Following the flight to Varennes, when King Louis fled Paris to escape the revolution, some of the more radical Jacobins, led by Maximilien Robespierre, supported a petition demanding the removal of the king. Other Jacobins opposed such an extreme measure and so broke away from the club to create their own, more moderate faction, called the Feuillants. With their more moderate elements removed, the Jacobins became a republican faction with Robespierre very much the leader.

SOURCE 8 A 19th-century French engraving of a meeting of the Jacobin Club, in the Jacobin monastery, in early 1792. The style of dress of those present is indicative of the wealthier bourgeoisie. The layout of the hall reflects the fact that, unlike in the coffee houses of Paris, discussions were of a formal nature. Note also that there are a number of women present. While women were excluded from voting and from sitting in the Constituent Assembly, they were allowed to join some political clubs, including the Jacobins.

Club des Jacobins.

## Maximilien Robespierre

The man who was to become the most famous Jacobin was Maximilien Robespierre. Like many a deputy to the Constituent Assembly, Robespierre had previously been a lawyer. Prior to being elected to the Estates-General in 1789, he was a man of standing in Arras, a provincial town in the far north of France. As a lawyer, he had a reputation for supporting the underdog and being driven by a genuine sense of liberal justice. He even opposed the death penalty.

Although elected to the Estates-General, the role of Robespierre in the events of 1789 was limited. Upon arriving at the Estates-General, and as it evolved into the Constituent Assembly, Robespierre found it difficult to obtain a hearing or the attention of those gathered. Yet he quickly developed his craft as a master orator and there is little disputing Robespierre's increasing influence in the events of 1790 onwards. He was to speak more than 500 times during the life of the Constituent Assembly and he gained such a reputation for his unwavering beliefs that he earned the nickname 'The Incorruptible'. He believed that, as a deputy of the Constituent Assembly, he should dedicate himself to his work for the people, not for personal gain. His simple lifestyle upheld these beliefs, as he rented just one room in a house of a working Parisian family where he lived a basic life, denouncing the influence of luxuries, drinking and women. While these might appear noble qualities, Robespierre's idealism would play a key part in causing the Terror (see Chapter 3).

Although he was not a committed republican in 1789–90, Robespierre's views tended to be more radical than many deputies of the Constituent Assembly who, let us not forget, were exclusively wealthy. His speeches appealed to the members of the Jacobin Club who, while not poor, consisted of the middle classes as well as the rich. His popularity was so great at the Jacobin Club that, in March 1790, he was elected president of the club.

### The Cordeliers Club

Also meeting in a former religious building, in the notoriously radical Parisian district of Cordeliers, the Cordeliers Club was established in 1790. The club was formed in the belief that the reforms of the Constituent Assembly fell far short of the principles enshrined in the Declaration of the Rights of Man. The Cordeliers opposed the distinction between active and passive citizens, calling instead for direct democracy, in which universal male suffrage would determine the deputies of the Assembly. They also supported the right of popular action, including **insurrection**, if the government acted contrary to the ideals of the revolution. The Cordeliers saw it as their duty to watch over the government and to stand up for the oppressed.

At only two **sols** per month, the membership fee of the club was well within the reach of most Parisians, barring only the very poor, and was considerably cheaper than the Jacobin Club. Despite this, the club still tended to attract wealthier and better-educated members of the public. Regular speakers at the Cordeliers Club included some of the most notable names of the French Revolution, including Desmoulins, Marat (see page 223), Danton and Brissot.

### Georges-Jacques Danton

Perhaps the most famous of the Cordeliers is Georges-Jacques Danton. Like Robespierre, he was a lawyer by background, but Danton's route into politics was not via the Constituent Assembly. He was practising law in Paris when the revolution broke out. Inspired by the events of July 1789, Danton enrolled in the National Guard for the Cordeliers district, rising to become commander. He also managed to acquire a minor position within the **Paris Commune**. He was therefore much more of a local figure than Robespierre. He is considered to have been very much a man of the people, explaining his close association with the *sans-culottes* (see page 204). It was Danton who established the Cordeliers Club in spring 1790, in response to the feeling that the Assembly was not representing the interests of the lower classes. In stark contrast to Robespierre, with his imposing moral standards and citations of Rousseau, Danton was renowned for his excessive spending and his love of fine clothes, expensive luxuries, drinking and women.

### Jacques-Pierre Brissot and the Girondins

Jacques-Pierre Brissot was from a humble background, the son of a pastry cook from Chartres. He had experienced grinding poverty in his younger years and lived hand to mouth as a writer. Brissot worked as a pamphleteer, authoring liberal texts, many of which argued for the abolition of slavery. When the Estates-General was called, he moved to Paris and launched his newspaper, *Le Patriote Français* ('The French Patriot'), which became one of the most successful within Paris.

Brissot was a committed republican and, through his newspaper, speeches at the Cordeliers and Jacobin Clubs, and, later, in the Legislative Assembly, to which he was elected in September 1791, (see page 203), he argued for the complete abolition of monarchy. Whereas Robespierre tended to work alone, Brissot surrounded himself with like-minded individuals who, like him, were skilled orators. This loosely organised faction became known as the Girondins, as three of Brissot's close associates came from the Gironde region of France. The Girondins later played an important role in countering the views of the more moderate deputies of the Legislative Assembly.

As well as being an important advocate of republicanism, Brissot was also a leading member of the diplomatic committee of the Legislative Assembly. He drove the push for war against Austria in late 1791 and early 1792 (see page 208), seeing such a conflict as a revolutionary crusade necessary for the good of, not just the French people, but humanity at large.

#### KEY TERMS

**Insurrection**
An uprising of the common people.

**Sol: French currency in 1789**
French currency in 1789 was divided into livres, sols and deniers. One livre was worth 20 sols. One sol was worth 12 deniers. This is similar to the pre-decimal system of coinage in Britain, with pounds, shillings and pence. Calculating the relative value of historical currency is highly complex, but to give some idea of value, the following statistics may be useful. In 1789, a Parisian labourer might earn around 30 sols per day, whereas a skilled craftsman would earn as much as 100 sols daily.

**Paris Commune**
The Paris Commune was the administrative body responsible for governing the city. Created in the administrative reforms of 1789, the Commune was essentially a city council, operating out of the Hôtel de Ville (town hall). The Commune initially consisted of members of the bourgeoisie looking to protect the interests of the middle classes, especially their rights of property and protection against *sans-culottes* violence. This bourgeois Commune was forcibly evicted in August 1792 and replaced by a far more radical revolutionary Commune.

#### EXTEND YOUR KNOWLEDGE

**Camille Desmoulins (1760-94)**
Camille Desmoulins was a lawyer prior to the revolution. In summer 1789, he was an active voice on the streets of Paris, encouraging the *sans-culottes* to take up arms. He is often credited with being the agitator most responsible for causing the storming of the Bastille. He wrote and distributed pamphlets attacking the *ancien régime* and in support of the Constituent Assembly. As early as September 1789, he began to promote republicanism. His campaign for King Louis' abdication ran throughout 1789-91 until, in the crackdown on radicals following the Champs de Mars massacre in July 1791 (see page 207), he was forced to go into hiding.

Desmoulins emerged in August 1792 to play a role in the rising that would overthrow the monarchy. In September 1792, he was elected, alongside his close ally Danton, to the National Convention. Danton and Desmoulins advocated a policy of Terror (see Chapter 3) in 1793, calling for enemies of the revolution to be executed. By early 1794, though, Desmoulins had reversed his support for Terror. This brought him into conflict with his childhood friend, Robespierre, who at the time was continuing to push for even greater Terror. Due to his opposition to Robespierre and the government, Desmoulins was himself accused of being a counter-revolutionary traitor and he was executed on 5 April 1794.

## Popular protests and the *sans-culottes*

In the months and years following the revolution of the summer of 1789, economic conditions in Paris continued to decline. Inflation soared, due in part to the overprinting of assignats (see page 198), and a bad harvest in 1791 caused bread prices to rise even higher. The result was a wave of strikes and riots in 1791. Lafayette's National Guard was deployed to maintain order within the city.

The rioters and demonstrators of Paris became known as the *sans-culottes*, so named as they wore a simpler style of trousers to the *culottes* worn by the wealthier bourgeoisie and nobility ('*sans*' meaning 'without'). Although debate exists as to the actual social make-up and political attitudes of the *sans-culottes*, they were essentially the workers of the city: craftsmen, tradespeople, shop owners and their employees. In the local government reforms of 1790, Paris was divided into 48 sections and it was from within these sections that *sans-culottes* tended to be organised.

The unrest on the streets of Paris was both a cause and a consequence of the increasing radicalism of the political clubs and men like Danton, Desmoulins and Marat. Demonstrators, strikers and rioters were fuelled by agitators and the radical press and, at the same time, added strength and legitimacy to those who argued that the revolution had not gone far enough in ensuring equality for the common man.

### Revolutionary culture

In the period from 1789, right through until 1795, there developed within Paris a distinct revolutionary culture. The political clubs and radical press were obviously an important part of this culture, but it also went further into people's day-to-day lives. A revolutionary fashion code emerged. Bright colours and long, curly hair were associated with the aristocracy and so declined in popularity. Instead, the unofficial uniform of the *sans-culottes* became a common sight. This consisted of a red bonnet, or 'liberty-cap' as it was sometimes referred to, striped long trousers and short, straight hair. Supporters of the revolution would refer to one another as 'citizen', a more egalitarian title than the traditional '*monsieur*' and '*madame*'.

## Mirabeau and royalist support

Despite unrest within Paris, there were still strong leaders in support of moderate constitutional monarchy. Two 'heroes' of 1789 had a powerful influence: Mirabeau and Lafayette. Within the Constituent Assembly, Mirabeau, who had played a major role in its birth, held great sway.

The Comte de Mirabeau, Honoré Gabriel Riqueti, was one of the leading politicians of the Constituent Assembly in the early years of the revolution. Despite being born with aristocratic blood, Mirabeau's background was not one of etiquette and noble convention, and he had opposed the traditions of the *ancien régime*. Before the revolution, he was twice imprisoned through *lettres de cachet*. While in confinement, he wrote a number of texts. The subject of his writing was broad, including some erotic literature, but it largely focused on political issues, as did *Of Lettres de Cachet and State Prisons*, which attacked the power of arbitrary arrest. After imprisonment, he spent a number of years working as a pamphleteer, distributing 'enlightened' pamphlets and travelling. He visited England where, as Voltaire and Montesquieu had, he saw a political and social system far favourable to that in France. It was partly for this reason that, from when he was elected to the Estates-General in 1789 until his death in April 1791, he fought to uphold the balance of constitutional monarchy.

Mirabeau was an avid opponent of despotism, but he certainly was not a republican. He believed that the monarchy should remain, sharing power with an elected assembly. While a deputy of the Constituent Assembly, he worked closely with the royal family in trying to reach a compromise between the desires of the more radical deputies and the monarchy itself. His close connection with the royal family gave his political opponents, and the radical press, ammunition with which to attack him as a monarchist. It was rumoured at the time, and many historians now accept, that Mirabeau was actually being paid by the royal family to support its position within France.

Aside from his support for the monarchy, Mirabeau also denounced the violence in Paris, fearing civil chaos. Additionally, he opposed the August Decrees and the Declaration of the Rights of Man and of the Citizen, seeing them as too radical in intent.

Outside the Constituent Assembly, Lafayette, the architect of the Declaration of the Rights of Man, tried to prevent radicalism and unrest via the National Guard. There were also others within the Constituent Assembly who tried to bridge the divide between the bourgeoisie, the nobility and the monarchy. Three leading figures, Adrien Duport, Antoine Barnave and Alexandre, Comte de Lameth, known as the 'triumvirate', were influential in trying to find compromise with the king, and to lead the Assembly in continuing to pursue the cause of moderate constitutional monarchy.

As well as the supporters of constitutional monarchy, there were those who supported the complete restoration of Louis' position. In 1790, the Monarchy Club was established in Paris. This counter-revolutionary club sought links with *émigrés* and produced its own propaganda to counter that of the more **left-wing** Cordeliers. It also tried to create a network of affiliated clubs across France. Its members sometimes came into conflict, on occasion violently, with members of Jacobin Club. By spring 1791, these monarchist clubs had ceased to exist due to lack of popularity and Jacobin dominance, but their existence had helped to increase fear of a counter-revolutionary movement.

**KEY TERM**

**Left wing**
As a simplistic definition, 'left wing' is a term used in politics to refer to individuals or groups who press for reform and tend to be more radical. 'Right wing' tends to be used to describe more conservative individuals or groups. The use of the terms stems from the French Revolution when, in the National Convention (created in September 1792), the more radical faction (the Jacobins) sat on the left of the Assembly hall and the more conservative factions sat on the right.

## Conclusion

By early 1791, French politics was becoming more divided. The impact of political clubs, especially the Cordeliers and their dissatisfaction with the reforms of the Constituent Assembly, played an important role in this. Increasing unrest in Paris, caused in part by challenging economic conditions and encouraged by the radical press, furthered political instability. Additionally, the reputation of Mirabeau, a leading constitutional monarchist, began to suffer in late 1790 as it emerged that he was being paid by the royal court to act in support of its cause. The negative press he received from these revelations made other deputies less willing to work too closely with the king. Mirabeau's death in April 1791 of natural causes was another blow to those favouring constitutional monarchy.

Yet the extent of republicanism should not be overstated. The Jacobin Club, the most popular political club, was largely not republican in early 1791. Also, as the Constituent Assembly worked towards the new constitution, the mood of the deputies remained very much in support of constitutional monarchy.

### ACTIVITY
KNOWLEDGE CHECK

**How divided were political views in the period 1789-91?**

1 Draw a horizontal line representing a continuum of political beliefs in early 1791. The right of the line should represent conservatism and royalism, the left radicalism and republicanism.

Place each of the following people/groups onto the continuum by drawing an arrow to reflect where you believe their views lie and adding notes to explain your decision: Mirabeau, Lafayette, Robespierre and the Jacobins, Danton and the Cordeliers, Brissot, the *sans-culottes* and the Monarchy Club.

For example, you might place Mirabeau in the middle of the continuum line, writing that 'Mirabeau did support moving away from absolute monarchy, but he was not too radical as he worked closely with the king and opposed the violence of the Parisian mob.'

2 Group task: a revolutionary dinner party! In a group of four, allocate each person one of the following individuals: Brissot, Robespierre, Danton or Mirabeau. Conduct further research on your individual's beliefs and views. Then stage a mock dinner party, set in early 1791, where the four individuals sitting together discuss the changes and proposed reforms within France. You should discuss your characters' thoughts about the role of the monarchy, the actions of the *sans-culottes*, actual and proposed constitutional reforms (voting rights, Church reforms, economic changes) and the extent to which the ideals of the Declaration of the Rights of Man (see Source 3) have been realised.

### Using evidence (6a)

**Arguments and facts**

Work in groups. Read the following three extracts.

**Extract 1. From *France in Revolution*, an A Level textbook by Sally Waller, published in 2002.**

> The Cordeliers Club, founded in 1790, was more radical [than the Jacobins]. It did not restrict admission and, although led by members of the bourgeoisie, such as Danton and Desmoulins, it had a widespread working-class following.

**Extract 2. From *France in Revolution*, an A Level textbook by Dylan Rees, published in 2012.**

> The Cordeliers Club, founded in April 1790, was more radical than the Jacobin Club and had no membership fee.

**Extract 3. From *French Revolutionaries and English Republicans: The Cordeliers Club, 1790-1794*, an academic text by R. Hammersley, published by the Royal Historical Society in 2005.**

> The membership fee [of the Cordeliers Club] was set at two sols per month, placing it well within the means of small townsmen. None the less, the club tended to be dominated by the financially better off.

1 Why are facts important in history?

2 Compare Extracts 1 and 2 with Extract 3.

a) How do these sources disagree?

b) Which do you think is correct? Explain your answer.

3 What do you think is the significance of the cost of membership of the Cordeliers Club? Do you think that these authors, whose accounts differ in terms of the facts, would have viewed the significance of the Cordeliers Club much different from you? Explain your answer.

4 All these sources give detailed arguments about the significance of the Cordeliers Club, but they only briefly mention the cost of membership. Which do you think is more important?

5 If we accept that Extract 3 is correct about the cost of membership, do we discount Extracts 1 and 2 as not being useful? Explain your answer.

# HOW FAR WAS THE FLIGHT TO VARENNES THE KEY CAUSE OF RADICALISATION IN 1791 AND 1792?

TIMELINE OF EVENTS LEADING TO THE FALL OF KING LOUIS

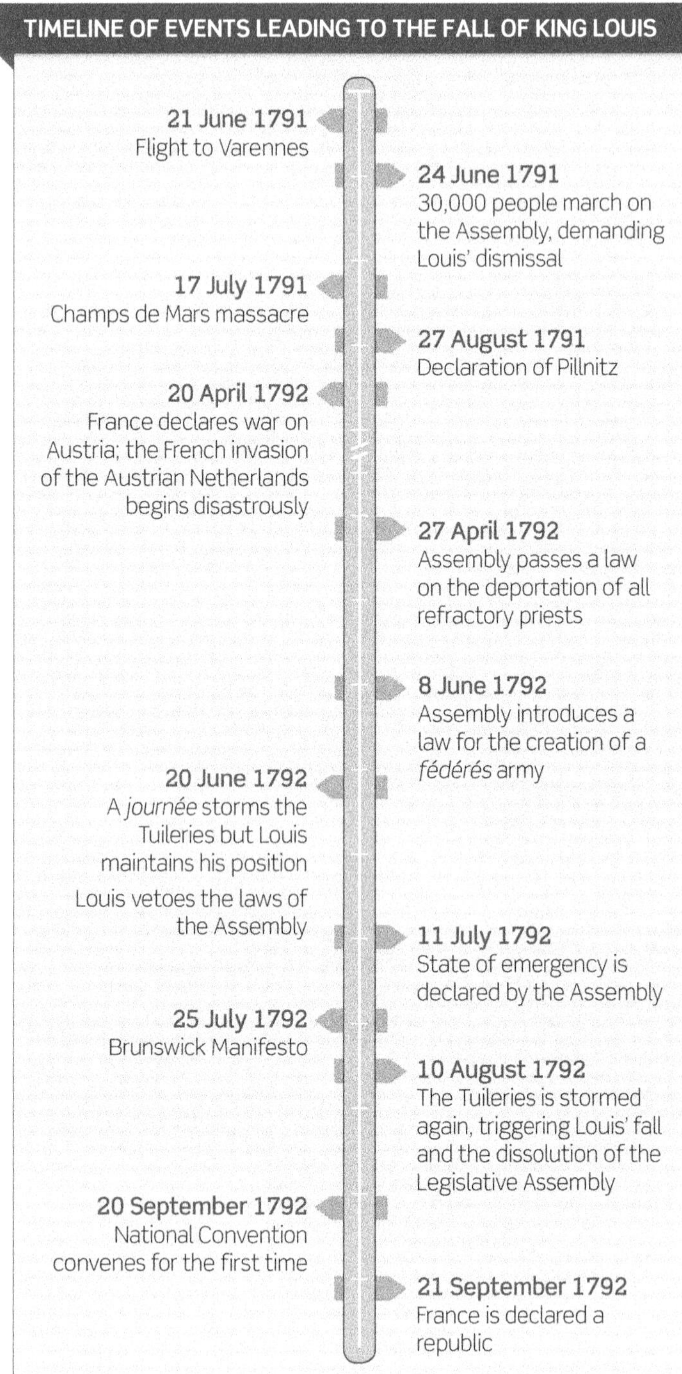


Although, in spring 1791, there was still significant support for constitutional monarchy, by the end of September 1792, the king had been overthrown, the Constitution of 1791 had been abandoned and France had been declared a republic. This major shift in politics can be attributed to a number of events and factors. One of the most commonly cited causes is Louis' failed attempt to flee France in June 1791. This flight to Varennes, the town where Louis was apprehended, significantly damaged the reputation of the royal family. Constitutional monarchy, though, still survived and it was not until the war with Austria that events accelerated and the king was forcibly overthrown.

## The flight to Varennes

On the morning of 21 June 1791, it was discovered that the bedchambers at the Tuileries Palace of Louis, Marie Antoinette and their children were empty. Soon the ***tocsin*** was ringing, as news spread that the royal family had fled the capital, and a crowd of people from across the city surged towards the palace in anger. Lafayette, who had been charged with the responsibility of ensuring that Louis did not flee, immediately set about trying to recapture the royal family.

Louis' plan was to get to the Belgian border, to a French frontier town called Montmédy. Belgium was ruled as part of the **Austrian Netherlands**, so Louis knew he would find protection in the name of his wife's family and from a number of influential *émigrés* who now resided there. However, the royals did not get that far. Their coach had travelled only about 160 kilometres before the king was recognised by a postmaster in the town of Varennes, who reported him to the National Guard. The royal family was arrested and escorted back to Paris among a large procession of both military and civilian personnel.

### KEY TERMS

***Tocsin***
An alarm bell, usually a church bell. The *tocsin* was sometimes 'sounded' or rung as a signal to the *san-culottes* to take to the streets in protest or uprising.

**Austrian Netherlands**
Modern-day Belgium. This was an area to the north of France, ruled by Austria. As the region bordered French territory, it was the area to which many *émigrés* fled and the area that France would first invade after declaring war on Austria in 1792.

It must be questioned why, when Louis had lost so much power in the summer of 1789, he chose to wait until June 1791 to attempt to flee. A key reason was the Civil Constitution of the Clergy. As a devout Catholic, Louis was appalled by the Civil Constitution and his anger was furthered when he was prevented from attending Easter mass, as the priest delivering the communion was refractory. Louis may also have felt that, after the death of Mirabeau, his support was waning in the Constituent Assembly. To add to this, rumours, seemingly untrue, were circulated around court that Austria was planning an invasion of France in order to restore Louis to absolute power. At this time, the king wished to avoid such a conflict. It is for these reasons that he took the decision to escape his country.

The return of the king to Paris was an event that concerned the Constituent Assembly. It was feared that uncontrollable riots would break out in anger at the king's actions and/or that riots could break out in support of the king. Posters were displayed around Paris reading: 'Whoever applauds the king shall be flogged. Whoever insults him shall be hanged.' This ensured that the return of the royal coach to the Tuileries was met by an immense, but silent, crowd.

## The emergence of republicanism

The effect of the flight to Varennes has been described as 'electrifying'. The political clubs of Paris, in particular the Cordeliers, intensified their protests, calling for Louis' **abdication**. Even the Jacobins, who had been more moderate in their views to this point, began to radicalise, causing the club to split. In the Constituent Assembly, views were divided. Many continued to argue for constitutional monarchy, fearing that the revolution could descend into chaos. Others supported the call of the Cordeliers and the radical press in their demand for abdication. A compromise was reached. It was decided that, in return for his pledge to support the new constitution, Louis' powers would be temporarily suspended until that constitution came into force.

KEY TERM

**Abdication**
When a monarch gives up their position.

To legitimise its decision, the Assembly put around the story that Louis had been kidnapped by the enemies of the revolution. This untrue story was significantly undermined by the fact that prior to the flight Louis had written a declaration, left at the Tuileries, declaring that he felt that the political situation in France as it stood was an unworkable one. As the declaration had been published in many newspapers in his absence, it was impossible to maintain the pretence that he had been abducted. The damage done to the king's reputation was huge. The flight had shown that the king himself did not truly believe in constitutional monarchy. On 24 June, 30,000 people marched on the Constituent Assembly, calling for the king's dismissal. Yet the king still had his supporters. Led by Barnave, many in the Constituent Assembly continued to oppose republicanism. A total of 290 deputies abstained from voting on the proposal to suspend the king's power, in protest at an action that they feared would only further fuel the republican cause.

## Counter-revolutionary activity

The flight to Varennes also greatly increased fear of counter-revolutionary activity. Rumours of an 'Austrian Committee' developed. This was the belief that there was a group of 'traitors' led by the royal family, in particular Marie Antoinette, who sought to restore the king's power through Austrian intervention. These traitors included refractory priests, *émigrés* and anyone who was deemed to be too close to the royal family. Barnave was one target of such accusations, as was Lafayette. There is little doubt that Marie Antoinette was in contact with her family in Austria, though the extent to which there was a counter-revolutionary conspiracy occurring within Paris is difficult to ascertain.

Due to suspicion of the royal family, on 17 July 1791 a large crowd gathered at Champs de Mars, a large open area in Paris, in support of a petition created by the Cordeliers demanding the king's abdication. Accounts of the ensuing events vary greatly, with some reporting a crowd of 6,000 people, others claiming as many as 50,000. What began as a protest descended into violence. The trigger for this violence is unclear. It has been said that there were royalist spies, hiding under the altar situated at the front of the demonstration and upon which the petition was placed, attempting to gather the identities of the leaders of the protest. It has also been said that the people hiding under the altar were just a group of men trying to look up women's skirts. Either way, the crowd set about these individuals, sparking a riot. Other accounts put the blame firmly on the 10,000-strong National Guard who, led by Lafayette, brutally tried to disperse a peaceful crowd. Whatever the cause, the violence claimed the lives of some 60 demonstrators and led to a further 200 arrests.

The violence at Champs de Mars resulted in a strong clampdown by the Constituent Assembly. Under pressure from the Assembly, the Paris Commune declared martial law, allowing the civil liberties of Parisians to be suspended. Freedom of the press was curtailed. Printing presses were shut down and radical journalists, like Marat and Desmoulins, went into hiding. Fearing arrest, Danton also fled.

With the suppression of the Cordeliers, republicans and the radical press, it would be easy to state that the moderates had won. Yet it was not as simple as this. The events of June and July 1791 represent an increasing gap between the attitudes of those in the Constituent Assembly and the attitudes of the popular societies and clubs of Paris, and particularly the *sans-culottes*.

**AS Level Exam-Style Question Section A**

***Study Source 9 before you answer this question.***

How much weight would you give the evidence of Source 9 for an enquiry into French attitudes towards monarchy following the flight to Varennes in June 1791?

Explain your answer using the source, the information given about it and your own knowledge of the historical context. (12 marks)

**Tip**

*As well as exploring what we can learn from the source, also consider its limitations. What does it not reveal about the conflict of opinion following the flight to Varennes?*

**KEY TERMS**

**Anticlericalism**
Opposition to the Church and the involvement of the clergy in state affairs.

**Holy Roman Emperor**
The Holy Roman Empire was a union of central European states, incorporating much of modern-day Germany, Austria and the Czech Republic. In contrast to the usual definition of an empire, the Holy Roman Empire was not centrally controlled. It was a complex network of semi-independent states, ruled by separate monarchs who descended from different lines of the Hapsburg dynasty. The Empire, though, did possess a hereditary Emperor who held significant influence over these monarchs. In 1791, the Holy Roman Emperor was the Austrian Leopold II. Leopold was Marie Antoinette's brother.

**SOURCE 9**

In July 1792, following the flight to Varennes, the Cordeliers Club produced the following petition calling for the Assembly to declare France a republic.

We were slaves in 1789, we believed ourselves free in 1790, we are free at the end of June 1791. Legislators! You had allocated the powers of the nation you represent. You had invested Louis XVI with excessive authority. You had consecrated tyranny in establishing him as an irremovable, inviolable and hereditary king. You had sanctioned the enslavement of the French in declaring that France was a monarchy. Good citizens lamented and opinions clashed vehemently. But the law existed and we obeyed it, waiting for the progress of enlightenment and philosophy to bring us our salvation... But times have changed. This so-called convention between a people and its king no longer exists. Louis has abdicated the throne. From now on Louis is nothing to us, unless he becomes our enemy...

The Society of Friends of the Rights of Man [the formal name of the Cordeliers Club] considers that a nation must do everything, either by itself or through removable officers chosen by it. It [the Society] considers that no single individual in the state should reasonably possess enough wealth and prerogatives to be able to corrupt the agents of the political administration. It believes that there should be no employment in the state that is not accessible to all the members of that state... above all hereditary monarchy, is incompatible with liberty. Such is its opinion, for which it stands accountable to all Frenchmen... Legislators, you have a great lesson before your eyes. Consider well that, after what has happened, it is impossible for you to inspire in the people any degree of confidence in an official called 'king'. We therefore call upon you, in the name of the fatherland, to declare immediately that France is no longer a monarchy, but rather that it is a republic.

## Divisions in the Legislative Assembly

In September 1791, the new constitution came into force and with it the Constituent Assembly was dissolved, to be replaced by the Legislative Assembly, a body that ruled France for just one year. The Legislative Assembly consisted entirely of new deputies. This was due to a self-denying ordinance, proposed by Robespierre in an attempt to undermine his opponents, which stated that no deputy who had served in the National Assembly could also serve in the Legislative Assembly.

The outcome of the elections was not entirely the result Robespierre had hoped for. Of the 745 deputies elected, 264 were members of the Feuillant Club (who opposed the Jacobins) and only 136 were Jacobins and Girondins. The remaining deputies were unaligned. The balance of the Assembly, then, was against republicanism. On paper it seemed that, in September 1791, despite the flight to Varennes, constitutional monarchy could survive. However, the figures alone do not take account of the impact of significant individuals. Brissot was one such republican elected to the Legislative Assembly and, along with his Girondin associates, he fought to win over the unaligned deputies to his cause. The Girondins' message was a radical one, based upon the ideas of the Enlightenment, denouncing *émigrés* as traitors and supporting **anticlericalism**. With Lafayette and Barnave excluded from the Assembly due to the self-denying ordinance, the Feuillants, in contrast to the Girondins, lacked the powerful oratory and leadership necessary to dominate the Assembly. As a result, the mood of the unaligned deputies began to move to the left. The dominating influence of the Girondins is exemplified by their success in driving forward the argument for war against Austria.

## The impact of war with Austria and Prussia

### The Declaration of Pillnitz

In spite of pressure from *émigrés*, an Austrian invasion of France seemed unlikely in 1791. The **Holy Roman Emperor,** Leopold II, had refused to take action in defence of the family of his sister, Marie Antoinette. He had pressing enough problems within his own dominions and, as a fairly liberal ruler, perhaps welcomed some degree of constitutional reform. It is also not implausible to say that he welcomed the collapse of French power, as it meant one less potential rival within Europe.

Despite the unlikelihood of an Austrian invasion, following the flight to Varennes Leopold did feel obliged to show some loyalty and support towards King Louis. Co-signed with **Prussia**, Leopold sent a statement to France known as the Declaration of Pillnitz (August 1791). In the Declaration, Austria and Prussia stated that they were willing to restore a monarchical order in France by force. However, this was upon the proviso that other European states would also intervene. As other states were unlikely do to so unless threatened themselves, this made any threat rather remote and, if not remote, certainly not immediate. The Declaration was more of a 'face-saver' than anything else. The insincerity of the Declaration did not go unnoticed by the French royal family, with Marie Antoinette commenting: 'The Emperor has betrayed us.'

KEY TERM

**Prussia**
In the 18th and 19th centuries, Prussia was a powerful European state occupying parts of what are now Germany and western Poland.

## The war debate

Caused partly by the Declaration of Pillnitz, but more by growing concern about counter-revolution due to *émigrés* and suspicions of the Austrian Committee, a debate began in Paris concerning the potential benefits and dangers of a French invasion of Austrian territory, specifically the Austrian Netherlands. Leading the pro-war side of the debate was Brissot. He argued the war case in revolutionary terms, believing that a war would flush out those not truly loyal to the cause. The Girondins also believed that the peoples of neighbouring states were just waiting to be liberated from the despotism and tyranny of monarchy. If France invaded, they claimed, the people would rise up in support of the French invaders, overthrowing those who oppressed them. Brissot also warned that, if France did not strike first, then the Great Powers of Europe, all led by monarchies, would unite to crush the revolution.

**SOURCE 10**

Maximin Isnard was a leading Girondin who sprang to prominence due to his call for war. Here, in a speech made to the Legislative Assembly on 20 November 1791, he argues the war case in revolutionary terms.

Even if the *émigrés* are not thinking of attacking us, the very fact they have assembled in a threatening manner is enough to make it essential that we disperse them by force and put a stop to it all. The French people will become the most outstanding in the world. As slaves they were bold and daring: could they be timid and weak now that they are free? Always ready to fight for freedom, always ready to die for it, and to disappear entirely from the face of the earth rather than be cast back in to chains, that is the nature of the French people... Let us say to Europe that if its ministers engage kings in a war against the people, we will engage the people in a war against kings. Finally, let us say to Europe that ten million French people, fired by freedom, armed with the sword, the pen, reason and eloquence could single-handedly change the face of the world, and make all tyrants tremble on their thrones of clay.

Not all pro-war motives were so idealistic; some were more pragmatic. The royal family, for instance, thought it had little to lose from a war with Austria. Louis believed that France would be defeated in war and then the Austrians would restore his power in France. There were other vested interests in the pro-war movement. Lafayette's reputation had been greatly damaged by his involvement in the Champs de Mars massacre. A war with Austria might provide him with an opportunity to regain his status and position.

There were also those who voiced strong objections to the war. Robespierre was one of the most vocal critics of the war proposal. He argued that, due to serious economic problems and the sheer number of French officers who had fled, France was not in a position to launch an attack and, if it were to do so, it would be rapidly crushed. Robespierre was also suspicious of the royal family's and Lafayette's motives for supporting the war argument, recognising that they sought to do so for their own gains.

In this case, Robespierre's views represented those of the minority and, on 20 April 1792, France declared war on Austria, thus beginning the French Revolutionary Wars (1792–1802). One month later, Prussia joined the fray by declaring war on France. The reputations of Robespierre and the Girondins were now closely linked to the war; who would be proved right in their predictions of the outcome?

### The war starts badly

The war started disastrously for France. This was largely due to a lack of military officers. Following the flight to Varennes, officers had been required to swear an oath of loyalty to France and to the Constituent Assembly. The oath omitted the king's name and many officers objected to this. Partly as a consequence, by the end of 1791, 3,000 officers had left their regiments and fled France. Many officers who remained were not trusted by their men, who suspected them of being royalist counter-revolutionaries, and mutinies were common. The French army numbered less than 140,000, many of whom were volunteers who, while full of revolutionary enthusiasm, were equipped with little in terms of weaponry or training.

When the French soldiers invaded the Austrian Netherlands, on 20 April 1792, it is hardly surprising that panic and confusion swept the French army. Regiments deserted en masse, others mutinied and, in one case, the soldiers even murdered their commanding officer, an Irishman named Theobald Dillon. Within a month, the commanders of the French army were arguing that peace must immediately be made.

### Royal vetoes

The calamitous start to the war, and the threat of invasion by Austria and Prussia, heightened fear of counter-revolutionary activity within France. In May 1792, the Legislative Assembly introduced a number of laws to defend France against such traitors. On 27 April 1792, a law decreed that all refractory priests should be deported. Another sought to disband the king's royal guard, as the soldiers were deemed too loyal to Louis, rather than to the Assembly. On 8 June, a third law called for the establishment of a camp of 20,000 National Guards, known as *fédérés*, recruited from the provinces in order to defend Paris.

On 19 June 1792, Louis refused to sanction these laws and he used his right of suspensive veto to delay their passing. This was an inflammatory act that made it appear as if the king was actively trying to undermine the Legislative Assembly's efforts to defend the country against counter-revolution. Louis had also caused outrage by dismissing a number of Girondin ministers on 12th June. Jean-Marie Roland, a leading Girondin, had written a letter to the king implying that he was an accomplice of the 'conspirators' against the revolution. Louis sacked Roland and his peers. These dismissals only sought to heighten suspicions that Louis was against the revolutionaries.

### The *journée* of 20 June 1792

The king's unwise actions caused a ***journée*** on 20 June. A group of 8,000 *sans-culottes*, incited by the Cordeliers Club, stormed the Tuileries demanding that Louis reverse his vetoes and dismissals. The crowd forced Louis to don the liberty cap, a red hat that had become a symbol of a true revolutionary. Despite such an intimidating situation, Louis did not give in and refused to withdraw his vetoes or to recall the ministers.

**KEY TERM**

***Journée***
Literally translated as 'day', *journée* is a term used to describe days or periods of the French Revolution when the *sans-culottes* rose up in insurrection, such as on 14 July 1789 when the Bastille was stormed. Often these *journée* were planned or co-ordinated by the political clubs and/or by the radical press.

Louis' refusal became an irrelevance though, as bowing to popular unrest the Legislative Assembly went ahead with the creation of the *fédérés* camp anyway. On 11 July, the Assembly went further by declaring a state of national emergency, calling on all men to support the war and stating that, due to the threat France was now facing, they no longer required the sanction of the king to enact their laws. Louis had lost his right of veto.

The arrival of the *fédérés* in Paris only sought to radicalise the city even further. These were, after all, militant people who had volunteered to fight for the defence of the revolution. As well as their militancy, perhaps the most famous thing that the *fédérés* brought to Paris was 'La Marseillaise', a song that is today the French national anthem. In 1792, it was the song sung by the *fédérés* who arrived from Marseilles and it became the anthem of the Parisian *sans-culottes*.

### The Brunswick Manifesto

On 25 July 1792, Charles, the Duke of Brunswick, commander of the advancing Prussian army, issued a proclamation to the French people. The Brunswick Manifesto, as it has become known, promised freedom to those who did not oppose his armies, but strongly threatened those who opposed him or harmed King Louis.

**SOURCE**

The Brunswick Manifesto (25 July 1792)

I, the commander in chief of the two armies [Prussia and Austria], declare: 1. That, drawn into this war by irresistible circumstances, the two allied courts entertain no other aims than the welfare of France, and have no intention of enriching themselves by conquests. 2. That they do not propose to meddle in the internal government of France, and that they merely wish to deliver the king, the queen, and the royal family from their captivity... 3. That our allied armies will protect [French] towns and villages, and the persons and goods of those who shall submit to the king and who shall cooperate in the immediate reestablishment of order and the police power throughout France... 7. That the inhabitants of the towns and villages who may dare to defend themselves against [our troops], either in the open country or through windows, doors, and openings in their houses, shall be punished immediately according to the most stringent laws of war, and their houses shall be burned or destroyed... 8. The city of Paris and all its inhabitants shall be required to submit at once and without delay to the king... If the chateau of the Tuileries is entered by force or attacked, if the least violence be offered to their Majesties, and if their safety and their liberty are not immediately assured, [we] will inflict an ever memorable vengeance by delivering over the city of Paris to military execution and complete destruction.

With the Prussian army already on the border of France, and tensions running high in Paris, the Brunswick Manifesto led to further unrest within the city.

## The attack on the Tuileries: *journée* of 10 August 1792

Counter to Brunswick's intention, the Manifesto actually increased calls for the abolition of the monarchy. Jérôme Pétion, the mayor of Paris, called on the Legislative Assembly to depose Louis and declare a republic. The Assembly refused to do so, reflecting the schism in opinion between the deputies of the Assembly and the *sans-culottes* and political clubs of Paris.

As a consequence of the Assembly's refusal, on 9 August the *sans-culottes*, led by leading Cordeliers such as Danton and Jacques Hébert, took over the Hôtel de Ville (town hall) and established their own revolutionary Commune, forcibly expelling the bourgeois one established in 1789.

The next day, the *tocsin* was sounded, heralding another *journée*, and a crowd marched upon the Tuileries. A total of 30,000 citizens, consisting of National Guard, *fédérés* and *sans-culottes*, stormed the palace. The Tuileries was guarded by almost 1,000 Swiss Guard, soldiers loyal to the king. Realising the sheer weight of numbers against them, the guards tried to flee. What followed could be described as a bloodbath, as the Swiss Guard were chased down by the mob and butchered, their bodies gruesomely mutilated. It is believed that over 600 of the Guard were killed.

Upon seeing the crowd approach, Louis had fled via a secret passage to the chamber of the Legislative Assembly, where he was placed under arrest.

## Conclusion

There was a sizable shift in French politics following the flight to Varennes. The republican movement gained strength, as evidenced by the petitions calling for the king's removal. The radicalisation of the Jacobin Club further supports this point. Yet, at the end of 1791, the deputies of the Legislative Assembly still remained largely in favour of constitutional monarchy and some of the radical elements of Paris had been forced underground or into exile. It was following the disastrous start to the war with Austria that opposition to the monarch really heightened. Fear of counter-revolutionary activity increased suspicions of the royal family, not least due to Marie Antoinette's Austrian roots. Louis exacerbated these suspicions by vetoing laws designed to protect France during a time of war, angering many. This distrust and anger boiled over when the Brunswick Manifesto threatened to destroy Paris. Fuelled by economic hardship, Cordeliers agitators and the influx of *fédérés*, it was a popular rising that was the final trigger for Louis' fall. When the Tuileries Palace was stormed, the views of the Legislative Assembly seemed hardly relevant: the rising rejected its authority as well as that of the king.

SOURCE

12

An oil painting of 1793 by the French artist Jean Duplessis-Bertaux, portraying the assault on the Tuileries on 10 August 1792. Louis XVI's Swiss Guard, wearing their red jackets, try to defend the palace and the royal family from a crowd of 30,000 *fédérés*, seen here in the blue jackets, and *sans-culottes*.

ACTIVITY
KNOWLEDGE CHECK

**Key vocabulary**

Complete the following summary using the key terms below.

Political views became increasingly divided during the period 1789 and 1792, between those who favoured the abolition of the monarchy, known as _______, on one side, and the _______, who wanted to see the restoration of Louis' power. Some, such as Marat, held particularly _______ views. Marat, and others such as Desmoulins, played an important role in mobilising and encouraging the actions of the _______ on the streets of Paris. People who encourage protest and demonstrations like this are sometimes described as _______. Different political clubs emerged. Led by Danton, the _______ felt that the _______ Assembly (later known as the _______ Assembly) had not gone far enough in its reforms. They opposed the fact that only some people, known as _______ citizens, were to be given the vote, whereas others, _______ citizens, were not. The Jacobins were initially less radical than the Cordeliers, but after the flight to Varennes the club split, with the _______ Club breaking away. After this, the Jacobins became increasingly _______. Others, led by Lafayette, Barnave and Mirabeau, were more _______. They challenged the _______ of the *ancien régime*, but also opposed popular violence, and strived to uphold _______ _______. The new _______ came into force in September 1791, new elections were held and the _______ Assembly was born. As fear of _______ activity increased during the war, the Assembly introduced new laws to protect against internal enemies. Louis used his _______ to delay these reforms, sparking a _______, where the *sans-culottes* rose up in protest. Following the Brunswick _______, tension within Paris peaked, causing the Tuileries Palace to be stormed and the end of constitutional monarchy.

*constitutional monarchy, passive, Feuillants, republicans, Legislative,* sans-culottes, *Cordeliers, moderate, counter-revolutionary, Constituent, active, radical, left-wing, constitution, agitators, veto, absolutism,* journée, *monarchists, National, Manifesto*

ACTIVITY
KNOWLEDGE CHECK

**How far was the flight to Varennes the key cause of radicalisation in 1791 and 1792?**

1 Look back at Activity 1 on page 205. Redraw the same continuum but this time to reflect how views shifted *after* the flight to Varennes and the Champs de Mars massacre. You should include the same people and groups as before, apart from the following: you should no longer include Mirabeau (as he had died by then) nor the Monarchy Club (as it had closed). You should also add in the Feuillants Club, which was established after the flight to Varennes, and the Girondins. Once complete, compare this continuum with your previous one. What significant changes can you see? How far had attitudes turned against Louis after the flight to Varennes?

2 Explain why, if the flight to Varennes had damaged Louis' reputation so badly, he still remained head of state at the beginning of 1792.

**A Level Exam-Style Question Section B**

How far was the collapse of constitutional monarchy in August 1792 the result of the actions of a radical minority? (20 marks)

**Tip**

*In the introduction to your answer, try to define what you think the question is asking: what does the question mean when it refers to a 'radical minority'? Who do you consider to have been the 'radical minority'? Refer to specific individuals and groups.*

# TO WHAT THE EXTENT HAD THE RADICALS TRIUMPHED BY JANUARY 1793?

## The creation of the National Convention

During the attack on the Tuileries, Louis had sought refuge in the Legislative Assembly, but the deputies could not protect his position. The rioters invaded the Assembly and demanded the king's imprisonment, recognition of the new revolutionary Commune and the election of a new assembly, a body elected through universal male suffrage. Fearing for their own safety, many of the deputies who had supported constitutional monarchy (still the largest proportion of the Assembly) fled or went into hiding. With the more moderate elements of the Assembly removed, the remaining deputies made a number of more radical changes. In response to the demands of the protesters, the royal family was imprisoned in the Temple Prison, a medieval castle where the family was given just two floors to inhabit, a far cry from the luxury of the Tuileries. The Assembly appointed Danton as minister of justice and also introduced several radical laws, including the arrest and deportation of any remaining refractory priests and the sale of all *émigrés* land. The job of deposing the king was left to the National Convention.

In accordance with the demands of the August rising, the Legislative Assembly was dissolved in September 1792. At the end of August 1792, new elections had been held to appoint a new representative body. All males over the age of 21 had the right to vote and anyone could stand to be a deputy. The resulting elections, though, were much less democratic than this may at first appear. In such a volatile political atmosphere, participation in elections took real courage. Intimidation and fear of reprisals saw to it that fewer than six percent of those entitled to vote actually did so. Royalists and constitutional monarchists, through self-preservation, steered clear of the ballot. As a result, when the National Convention first met on 21 September 1792, it was a far more left-wing body than the Legislative Assembly had been. The 24 deputies for Paris included many of the most militant Jacobins and Cordeliers, who all tend to be known as Jacobins after this time, including Robespierre, Marat, Danton, Desmoulins and an extreme radical named Collot d'Herbois, an actor who was very popular with the *sans-culottes*.

As in the assemblies before it, many of the deputies to the Convention were lawyers; some 47 percent worked in the profession. However, compared with the previous assemblies, the Convention was a body of relatively young men, with the average age of the deputies being much lower. Also, a far wider range of social classes was represented, including at least one peasant and, at the other extreme, the former prince Philippe Égalité (see page 175). The inclusion of radical journalists like Desmoulins in the Convention also added a new dynamic.

Two principle factions were to emerge at the Convention. The Jacobins were led by Robespierre. They sat on the highest benches, to the left of the hall, and gained the nickname '*La Montagne*' ('The Mountain' or '*Montagnards*' ('Mountain people')). Of the 749 deputies, around 300 were Jacobins, considerably the largest faction. The other faction, the Girondins, were led by Brissot and numbered around 150. The remaining deputies of the Convention were known as '*La Plaine*' ('The Plain'). They did not vote in a coherent pattern, supporting neither one faction nor the other. Although not aligned to either faction, the deputies of The Plain should not be seen as a faceless mass. Their numbers included some very adept and experienced politicians, such as Abbé Sieyès.

There was little to distinguish between the two factions in terms of social composition, occupational backgrounds or experience. Both factions were republican, publicly being anything else at this point could have been very dangerous, and both claimed to uphold true revolutionary values. The significant difference between the two, though, was in their attitude towards the *sans-culottes*. The Girondins saw themselves as the protectors of legal justice, opposing the brutality and illegitimate actions of the 'mob'. The Jacobins, however, saw the actions of the *sans-culottes* as a legitimate part of the revolutionary process. To them, the people *were* the revolution.

One of the first actions of the Convention was to formalise Louis' deposal. On 21 September, monarchy was abolished, a republic was declared and King Louis XVI simply became citizen Louis Capet.

## The September Massacres

In the political sphere, one assembly was dissolving and another one was emerging; on the streets of Paris, a very different type of revolutionary action was occurring. In September 1792, Verdun, an important strategic French town, fell to the Prussians. Like the Brunswick Manifesto before it, news of Verdun's fall sparked panic in Paris and agitators once again warned Parisians of the dangers of the enemy within, as well as the foreign enemy without. It has been said that what followed 'has no equal in atrocities committed during the French Revolution by any party'. Paranoid about counter-revolution, and encouraged by radicals, the *sans-culottes* hunted out anyone who may have betrayed the revolution and butchered them. While some brutal murders took place on the streets of the city, the targets of most of the killings were in the city's prisons. After all, it was here that some refractory priests, counter-revolutionary politicians and fallen aristocrats were held. Accounts describe scenes of mass killings, bloodlust, torture and mutilation. In all, at least 1,400 people were killed in cold blood. While this number did include some priests and nobles, the vast majority were probably common criminals, thieves, prostitutes and similar individuals, with no counter-revolutionary desires.

**SOURCE**

**The writer Nicolas-Edme Restif de la Bretonne describes what he saw on the second day of the September Massacres. Restif was a French novelist who lived in Paris during the revolution and recorded his memoirs in 1793.**

I arose, distressed by the horror. The night had not refreshed me at all, rather it had caused my blood to boil... I go out and listen. I follow groups of people running to see the 'disasters'—their word for it. Passing in front of the Conciergerie, I see a killer who I'm told is a sailor from Marseilles. His wrist is swollen from use. I pass by. Dead bodies are piled high in front of the Châtelet. I start to flee, but I follow the people instead. I come to the rue St.-Antoine, at the end of the rue des Ballets, just as a poor wretch came through the gate. He had seen how they killed his predecessor, but instead of stopping in amazement, he took to his heels to escape. A man who was not one of the killers, just one of those unthinking machines who are so common, stopped him with a pike [a spear] in the stomach. The poor soul was caught by his pursuers and slaughtered. The man with the pike coldly said to us, 'Well, I didn't know they wanted to kill him...'

There had been a pause in the murders. Something was going on inside... I told myself that it was over at last. Finally, I saw a woman appear, as white as a sheet, being helped by a turnkey [a person who holds the keys to a prison]. They said to her harshly: 'Shout "*Vive la nation!*"' 'No! No!' she said. They made her climb up on a pile of corpses. One of the killers grabbed the turnkey and pushed him away. 'Oh!' exclaimed the ill-fated woman, 'do not harm him!' They repeated that she must shout 'Vive la nation!' With disdain, she refused. Then one of the killers grabbed her, tore away her dress, and ripped open her stomach. She fell, and was finished off by the others. Never could I have imagined such horror. I wanted to run, but my legs gave way. I fainted. When I came to, I saw the bloody head. Someone told me they were going to wash it, curl its hair, stick it on the end of a pike, and carry it past the windows of the Temple [where the royal family were imprisoned]. What pointless cruelty!...

The number of active killers who took part in the September massacres was only about one hundred and fifty. The rest of Paris looked on in fear or approval, or stayed behind closed shutters.

### Political consequences

The political reaction to the September Massacres was divided. Some politicians turned a blind eye, most notably Danton who, as minister of justice, is surely partly to blame, as he failed to take any action to stop the violence. The massacres caused The Plain to swing towards the Girondins, who had warned against such dangers of mob rule and condemned the violence outright. Some of the Jacobins, such as Marat, had actively encouraged the bloodshed and others, like Robespierre, refused to condemn the violence, seeing it as part of the revolutionary process. Many deputies felt the Jacobins had gone too far in legitimising violence and terror, causing them to lose support in the Convention.

### Further Girondin gains

As Brissot and the Girondins had promoted the case for war so strongly (see page 209), the reputation of their faction was closely linked to the fortunes of that war. In the early months of the war, when things were going very badly for France, Brissot had come under heavy criticism. However, on 20 September 1792, there was a significant turning-point in the war. A French victory over the Prussians at the Battle of Valmy halted the Prussian advance and meant that Brunswick's threats to Paris did not become a reality. Further victories followed, notably the Battle of Jemappes, where on 6 October the Girondin general, Charles François Dumouriez, won a victory against the Austrians and conquered the Austrian Netherlands. In the south, Savoy (November 1792) and Nice (January 1793) were both annexed by France. These victories gained the Girondins even greater support.

## The trial and execution of Louis

Both the Jacobins and the Girondins had been united in their calls for a republic. Once the republic had been declared, the debate began regarding Louis' fate. Both factions agreed that Louis should be put on trial for his 'crimes' against the revolution. The Mountain, led by Robespierre, pushed not only for trial but also for execution.

SOURCE

**The following speech was made by Louis Antoine de Saint-Just in the National Convention in November 1792, during a debate on the fate of the king. It was his maiden speech at the Convention and ensured his reputation as a radical republican. Saint-Just would later become a leading Jacobin and prominent member of the Committee of Public Safety during the Terror (1793–94).**

A man of great spirit might say, in another age, that a king should be accused, not for his crimes of administration, but for the crime of having been a king, as that is an usurpation [stealing power] which nothing on earth can justify. With whatever illusions, whatever conventions, monarchy cloaks itself, it remains an eternal crime against which every man has the right to rise and to arm himself. Monarchy is an outrage which even blindness of an entire people cannot justify; that people, by the nature it gave, is guilty before nature, and all men hold from nature the secret mission to destroy such dominion wherever it may be found... Those are considerations which a great and republican people ought not to forget when judging a king.

Louis' trial began on 10 December. At great personal risk, Guillaume-Chrétien de Lamoignon de Malesherbes, a former French minister and renowned lawyer, offered to lead Louis' defence. His team argued strongly in his defence, painting a picture of a citizen-king and arguing, not unreasonably, that the king had attempted to bring liberal reforms to France even prior to the revolution. The defence, however, could do little to defend Louis when letters written by the king to the Austrian royal family were presented as evidence. Louis' chances looked even more hopeless when, in an effort to expose 'traitors', Marat insisted that all deputies declare their verdict publicly. With such pressure it is hardly surprising that, of the 721 deputies present, 693 declared Louis guilty. Yet the deputies were more divided regarding Louis' punishment. The Girondins wanted imprisonment, whereas the Jacobins argued that Louis had to die, because as long as he was alive royalists might try to restore him to the throne. The vote was close but in the end 361 voted for the death penalty against 319 voting for imprisonment.

And so it was done. On 21 January 1793, Louis was publicly executed by guillotine in the Place de la Revolution.

SOURCE 15

**On 25 January 1793, the British newspaper *The Times* published the following account of Louis' execution.**

About half past nine... Louis mounted the scaffold with composure, and that modest intrepidity peculiar to oppressed innocence, the trumpets sounding and the drums beating all the time... When the drums ceased, and Louis spoke these words. 'I die innocent; I pardon my enemies; I only sanctioned upon compulsion [being forced to agree to] the Civil Constitution of the Clergy.' He was proceeding [to speak] but the beating of the drums drowned his voice. His executioners then laid hold of him, and an instant after his head was separated from his body... Unquestionably the blood of this unfortunate monarch will invoke vengeance on his murderers. This is not the cause of monarchs only, it is the cause of every nation of the face of this earth... to crush these savage regicides [people who kill monarchs] in their dens, who aim at the ruin of all nations, and the destruction of all government... Armed with fire and sword, we must penetrate into the recesses of this land of blood and carnage.

## Conclusion

Major changes followed the storming of the Tuileries in August 1792. The Legislative Assembly was dissolved, the National Convention created, a republic declared, and Louis was tried and executed. No longer was the political battle one of constitutional monarchist versus republican. The republicans had triumphed. Instead, a new political battle emerged. This was one between the Jacobins, the most radical of the deputies who condoned the actions of the *sans-culottes* as a revolutionary force, and the Girondins, who were more moderate and condemned the actions of, as they saw them, the Parisian mob. By the end of January 1793, the Girondins had gained popularity, due to their condemnation of the September Massacres and the improving fortunes of war. Yet the Jacobin victory in ensuring Louis' execution demonstrates how much strength the more radical of the factions still possessed.

ACTIVITY
KNOWLEDGE CHECK

**How far had radicalism triumphed by January 1793?**

1 Why did the National Convention contain more left-wing leaning individuals than the Legislative Assembly had done?

2 How similar were the Girondin and the Jacobin factions?

3 Why did the Girondins gain support in September 1792? Give more than one reason.

4 Read Source 14.

a) Saint-Just mentions the 'crimes of his [Louis'] administration'. What 'crimes' do you think Saint-Just is referring to?

b) What do you think Saint-Just means when he says that Louis should be accused 'not for the crimes of his administration, but for the crime of having been a king'? What implications does this comment have regarding the fairness of Louis' trial?

c) How valuable do you consider this source to be for an enquiry into why the decision was made to execute King Louis? As well as considering what the source suggests, also consider other reasons for Louis' execution which are not alluded to.

5 Read Source 15.

a) Carefully consider the choice of language within the source and identify three words or phrases which show that the author was against the execution of King Louis.

b) Britain and France went to war in February 1793. What does this source reveal about the causes of this hostility?

c) Retaining as many words and phrases from the source as you can, edit and rewrite it in a manner that would make the source read as if it was in favour of Louis' execution. For example, you might replace the phrase 'oppressed innocence' with the words 'oppressive guilt'.

ACTIVITY
SUMMARY

**Revolution and the failure of constitutional monarchy, 1789–93**

Make a series of notes covering the periods highlighted below. Within your notes record:

- What had changed between that date and the preceding one. Which events had caused these changes?
- How had the political situation changed? Consider the extent of republican attitudes and the emergence and domination of different factions, as well as changing political institutions.
- Who had benefited or lost out from these changes? Why would some people support and others oppose the changes?

Periods to cover:

- September 1789 (reflecting on the Great Fear, the August Decrees and the Declaration of the Rights of Man)
- November 1789 (reflecting on the October Days and the sale of Church land)
- January 1791 (reflecting on the rise of political clubs, the Constitution of the Clergy and other reforms of the Constituent Assembly)
- August 1791 (reflecting on the flight to Varennes, the Champs de Mars massacre and the repression of radicalism that followed)
- June 1792 (reflecting on France's fortunes in war, Louis' vetoes and the *journée*)
- September 1792 (reflecting on the Brunswick Manifesto, the storming of the Tuileries, the creation of the Convention and the September Massacres)
- January 1793 (reflecting on Louis' trial and execution)

**WIDER READING**

Aston, N. 'Turbulent priests? The Church and the revolution', *History Today*, May 1989, pages 20–25, published online as 'Turbulent Priests? The French Church and the Restoration': www.historytoday.com/nigel-aston/turbulent-priests-french-church-and-restoration An essay exploring the role and attitudes of the clergy during the revolution; website subscription required

Cobban, A. *The Social Interpretation of the French Revolution*, Cambridge University Press (1964) A challenging academic text, this important work contests the Marxist view of the revolution as being one of class struggle

Rees, D. and Townson, D. *France in Revolution* (Access to History series, second edition), Hodder (2001) An A Level textbook that covers the whole period of 'France in Revolution'; chapter 3 addresses the constitutional monarchy phase of the revolution

Schama, S. *Citizens: A Chronicle of the French Revolution*, Viking (1989) An accessible academic text that gives an in-depth narrative of the revolution; chapters 11–14 deal with the era of constitutional monarchy

Vovelle, M. *The Fall of the French Monarchy 1787–1792*, Cambridge University Press (1984) An academic text; chapters 4 and 5 deal with the reforms of the National and Legislative Assemblies, and their impact, at great length

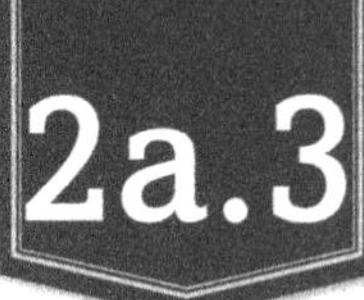

# 2a.3 The National Convention, the Jacobins and the Terror, 1793–94

**KEY QUESTIONS**

- Preconditions to Terror; why did the Jacobins rise to dominance?
- Was the Terror 'prompt, severe, inflexible' justice or simply not justice at all?
- To what extent was Robespierre the driving force of the Great Terror?
- What triggered the end of the Terror?

SOURCE

This, the last letter composed by Marie Antoinette, was written to her sister-in-law, Madame Elisabeth, on 16 October 1793.

It is to you, my sister, that I write for the last time, I have been condemned - not to a shameful death - it is such only for criminals - but to go and join your brother. Innocent like him, I hope to show the same steadfastness as he did in these last moments. I am calm, as one is when one's conscience is clear. I deeply regret leaving my poor children; you know that I lived only for them, and you, my good, loving sister, who have by your friendship sacrificed everything to be with us. What a position I leave you in!

The day she wrote this letter, nine months after the execution of King Louis, Marie Antoinette followed her husband to the scaffold. She left behind two children, a son and a daughter. While her daughter, Marie Thérèse, would survive the revolution by seeking exile in Austria and Britain, her son, Louis Charles, died in prison in 1795 at the age of just ten years old. Like his mother, he was buried in an unmarked grave. Marie Antoinette's concerns about the former king's sister's position were also not unfounded. On 10 May 1794, Madame Elisabeth was also sent to the guillotine.

The execution of the remaining royals was just one part of a period of the French Revolution known as the Terror, or the Reign of Terror. Between September 1793 and July 1794, over 2,500 people were executed in Paris alone. Including the provinces, the figure is likely to be in the region of 15,000. These were not unlicensed murders in gaols and on the streets, like the September Massacres had been. Rather, they were part of a conscious, intentional and highly organised state policy of Terror. The government, driven by a new body called the Committee of Public Safety, decreed that Terror should be the order of the day to preserve the gains of the revolution and to destroy, as they saw them, any enemies of the republic.

### Who were the victims of the Terror?

In many ways, Marie Antoinette's execution is not representative of the Reign of Terror. Many ardent royalists, or even constitutional monarchists, had fled France in 1792. So who, then, were the victims of the Terror? One historian, Donald Malcolm Greer, calculated that of those formally indicted only around 8 percent were nobles or former nobles and around 25 percent belonged to the middle class, whereas the overwhelming majority, some 60 percent, were peasants or working-class people.

It should be emphasised that these deaths are only those that were recorded, immortalised in the records of the courts of the Terror: the Revolutionary Tribunals. These figures do not take account of the thousands who died while incarcerated, awaiting trial after the infamous Law of Suspects: a law that potentially placed anyone under suspicion. They also do not take account of the tens if not hundreds of thousands who perished in the civil war that broke out in the spring of 1793. In opposition to the National Convention and the Committee of Public Safety, a number of departments rose up in open rebellion against the government.

**1793** - 1 February: France declares war on Britain
24 February: The government orders a levy of 300,000 conscripts

**1793** - 18 March: France suffers a major defeat at the Battle of Neerwinden
General Dumouriez defects to the Austrians

**1793** - 2 June: A *journée* forces the expulsion of the Girondins

**1793** - 23 August: *Levée en masse* declares total war

1793

**1793** - March: The Rising in the Vendée begins; Federalist revolts in many areas
March: The first wave of representatives on mission are deployed; watch committees are established across the country
10 March: The Revolutionary Tribunal is created in Paris

**1793** - 6 April: The Committee of Public Safety is established

**1793** - 13 July: Jean-Paul Marat is assassinated
27 July: Maximilien Robespierre and Louis-Antoine de Saint-Just are elected to the Committee of Public Safety

**1793** - 5 September: The establishment of *armées révolutionnaires*
17 September: The Law of Suspects is passed
29 September: The Law of General Maximum fixes prices on essential goods

After they were crushed, severe vengeance was reaped upon the insurgent regions. The **suppression** of the Vendée, the area that offered the greatest resistance, was so extreme that the atrocities committed there have been described as an act of **genocide**. What, then, drove this Terror?

## Causes of the Terror

**EXTRACT**

In his 2005 work, *Twelve Who Ruled*, the historian R.R. Palmer gave the following summary of the causes of the Terror.

> Anarchy within, invasion from without. A country cracking from outside pressure, disintegrating from internal strain. Revolution is at its height. War. Inflation. Hunger. Fear. Hate. Sabotage. Fanaticism. Hopes. Boundless idealism... and the dread that all the gains of the Revolution would be lost. And the faith that if they won, they would bring Liberty, Equality, Fraternity to the world.

Key within the passage in Extract 1 is the reference to 'invasion from without'. The Revolutionary War had begun in 1792, but it was in early 1793 that the conflict gained a new momentum. By spring 1793, France found itself at war with almost every other major power of Europe and, by summer, there were no less than three foreign armies on French soil. The politicians of the National Convention were not exaggerating when they spoke of the revolution having to fight for its survival. Yet there was also 'anarchy within' as towns, cities and departments rose up against the government. Some did so in opposition to the constant demands for more **conscripts** for the national army, others opposed the increasing attacks on religion. The Federalist revolt, though, was caused more by dissatisfaction with the radical Jacobin-led direction of the revolution, especially after the fall of the more moderate Girondin faction in June 1793.

By bearing these threats, both internal and external, in mind, it can be better understood why the government chose to pursue a policy of Terror, bent on ridding France of any potential enemies. However, it was not just the government that promoted such a policy. Desperately poor, and encouraged by the extremist press, it was often the *sans-culottes* who pressured the government to take more severe action against perceived enemies and counter-revolutionaries. It was *sans-culottes* action that would force the expulsion of the Girondins from the National Convention and later lead to the creation of the radical revolutionary armies that swept the provinces, hunting out any non-patriots and enforcing radical **de-Christianisation**.

### KEY TERMS

**Suppression**
To suppress something is forcibly to put an end to it. In the case of the Terror, the regions that rebelled were very harshly suppressed to stand as a lesson to others.

**Genocide**
When a large group of people from a particular nation, race, culture or religion are intentionally killed.

**Conscript**
Someone who is made to join the armed forces without volunteering to do so. The process of recruiting in this way is known as conscription.

**De-Christianisation**
A campaign to attack and destroy the institutions and beliefs of the Catholic Church.

Yet the Terror also had another side from that of violence and fear, that of 'Fanaticism. Hopes. Boundless idealism' (Extract 1). Terror needed to be justified to the people of France and no-one did more to provide that philosophical justification than Robespierre. Robespierre talked of the Terror in idealistic revolutionary terms, highlighting it as an absolute necessity in order to preserve the gains of the revolution, and arguing that only through Terror could utopia eventually be reached. Robespierre's strength of conviction was such that others found it hard to oppose him, and those who did, including Danton, were met by the guillotine. By spring 1794, Robespierre's power was so great that he has been described, both at the time and by historians since, as a dictator. His dictatorship came to a sudden end in July 1794, when his enemies, fearing for their own safety, finally rose up and overthrew Robespierre and his followers, thus ending the Reign of Terror.

**1793** - 5 October: The new revolutionary calendar comes into effect
9 October: Lyon is recaptured
16 October: Marie Antoinette is executed

**1793** - 31 October: Jacques-Pierre Brissot and other Girondin leaders are executed

**1793** - December: The Vendéan army is defeated
4 December: The Law of Frimaire

**1793** - 19 December: Toulon is recaptured by the republic

**1794**

**1794** - 5 February: Robespierre delivers his most famous speech defending the continuation of Terror

**1794** - 24 March: Jacques Hébert and his followers are executed

**1794** - 5-6 April: Georges Danton, Camille Desmoulins and other Indulgents are executed

**1794** - 8 June: The Festival of the Supreme Being
10 June: The Law of Prairial
10 June-27 July: The Great Terror

**1794** - 27-28 July: The Coup of Thermidor
28 July: Robespierre and Saint-Just are executed

**1794** - 1 August: The Law of Prairial is repealed
5 August: The mass release of political prisoners is ordered by the Convention

**1795**

# PRECONDITION TO TERROR: WHY DID THE JACOBINS RISE TO DOMINANCE?

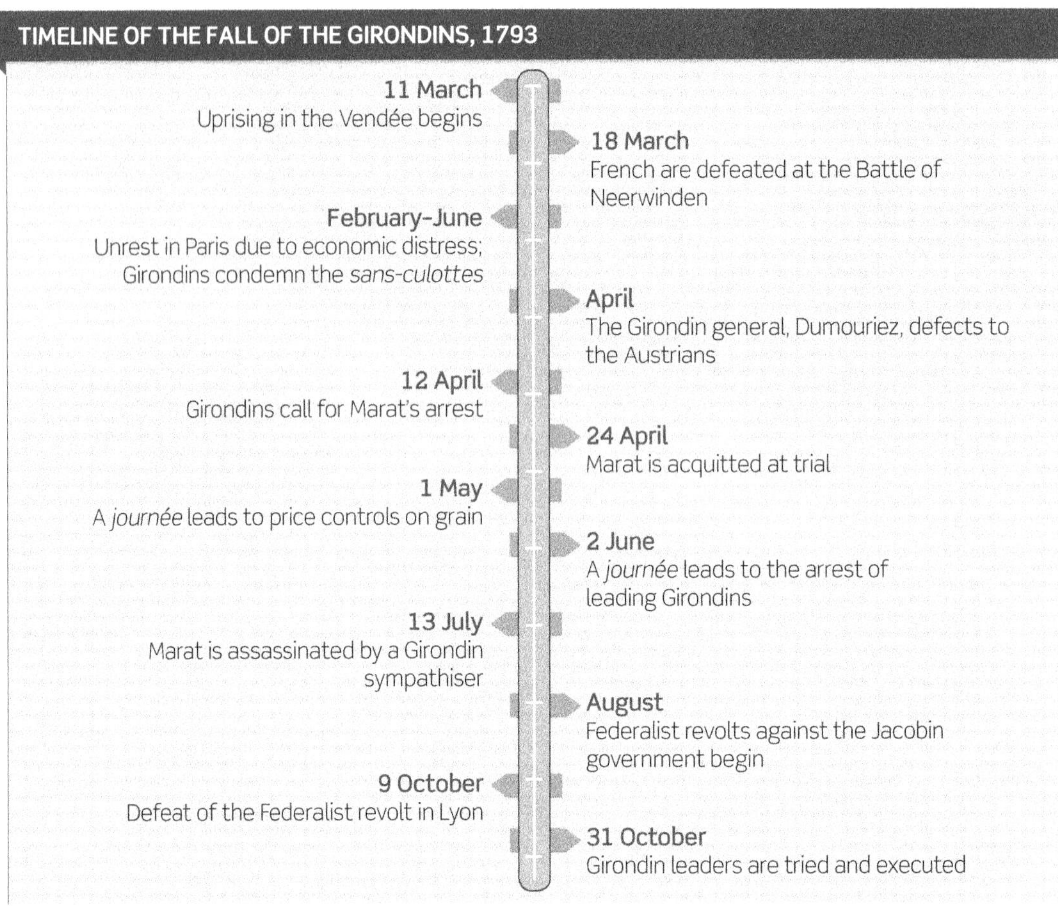


In January 1793, the month Louis was executed, the political scene in Paris remained divided. Within the Convention, the Girondins and the Jacobins competed for support from The Plain. The Girondins favoured a more moderate form of republicanism, whereas the Jacobins, especially those of The Mountain, tended towards more radical policies. Over the following months, support for the Girondins waned, ultimately leading to their fall and to Jacobin dominance. The rise of the Jacobins and the fall of the Girondins, who opposed extremist policies, were necessary **preconditions** for the Terror to develop in later 1793 and 1794.

> **KEY TERM**
>
> **Precondition**
> A change or event that has to happen before another event can. For example, the Jacobins needed to dominate the French political sphere before they could impose their policies of Terror.

## The external threat: the War of the First Coalition

War was a major factor that contributed to the changing political environment within Paris. French success in the war against Austria and Prussia was short-lived. While the French made a number of gains between September 1792 and January 1793 (see page 214), in February and March 1793 the tide of war turned against them.

In February 1793, the French National Convention declared war on Britain, the United Provinces (Holland) and Spain. The declarations can be seen as pre-emptive actions. As the French advanced north into the Austrian Netherlands, Britain feared that the United Provinces would fall into French hands. The Dutch controlled significant ports, such as Amsterdam and Antwerp, and if they fell to the French this could have threatened British dominance of the English Channel. Britain therefore demanded that France relinquish the conquered territories. Similarly, Spain was also preparing to join the coalition against France. Spain was ruled by relatives of the Bourbon family, who were deeply shocked and appalled by King Louis' execution. The Convention's declarations of war simply formalised these animosities.

By the end of February 1793, France was at war with Austria, Prussia, Britain, Holland, Spain and Piedmont-Sardinia (Italian states allied to Austria). France's enemies at this time are referred to collectively as the 'First Coalition', which was more of a collection of states with a common enemy than an organised alliance group. In the spring and summer of 1793, the War of the First Coalition went badly for France. In March, the French suffered a major defeat by the Austrians at the Battle of Neerwinden (in the Austrian Netherlands). Following the defeat, the French general, Dumouriez, **defected** to the Austrians, causing the Convention to question the loyalty of even its most renowned commanders. By August 1793, there were British, Spanish and Austrian troops on French soil. Once again, the possibility of an enemy march on Paris seemed like a reality.

KEY TERMS

**Defected**
To defect is to change allegiance from one state to another, to switch sides.

**Levy**
To enlist people for military service.

## The impact of the Vendée revolt

In addition to the external military threat, the Convention also faced the internal threat of civil war. In the Vendée, a region of western France, a major uprising occurred. In February, the Convention had ordered a **levy** of 300,000 conscripts to fight against the First Coalition. News of the levy reached the Vendée around 11 March 1793. Unwilling to fight and die for a government whose policies they objected to, many took to arms in revolt. However, the levy was only the spark for the uprising. Dissatisfaction at the direction the revolution had taken was more deeply rooted. The Civil Constitution of the Clergy had been fiercely opposed, with three-quarters of priests in the region refusing to swear the oath of allegiance. Additionally, the cost of feudal dues, supposedly abolished in August 1789, had simply been added to the leases of the land by the purchasers of the *biens nationaux* (see page 198), meaning many peasants found themselves no better off financially. However, it was not just the peasantry who rose in anger. Some monarchists, including former nobility, saw the uprising as an opportunity to attempt to restore the monarchy and the white flag of the Bourbon dynasty could be seen flying over some rebel bands.

SOURCE

An account written by a person from the Vendée region on 21 March 1793, giving his view of the causes of the revolt.

Gentleman and brothers. The inhabitants of Thouaré-sur-Loire may have taken up arms, but only because they were forced into it. On Monday 11th of this month the rebel bands began to assemble. The inhabitants had no intention of revolting because they are too peaceful for such an enterprise. The young men simply wanted to hold an assembly to agree not to send men to the national army. They were all gathered together on the Nantes road when they heard the news that a troop of National Guard was on its way from Nantes. Imagining that they were coming to seize them by force and since practically none was armed, they all rushed about, seized weapons wherever they could find them and gathered at Mauves, where unfortunately there was bloodshed. But since then the parish has been pretty quiet. In addition, the decrees on religious freedom is one of the principle causes of the revolt, because the people consider that to give them priests whom they do not want is a denial of freedom. Everyone is demanding the return of non-juring [refractory] priests, and the people are offering to pay them. This demand comes from the ordinary people and aristocrats alike - they all wish for agreement and public harmony. If this had been done more swiftly there would have been no revolt, and plenty of volunteers.

**AS Level Exam-Style Question Section A**

***Study Source 2 before you answer this question.***

Why is Source 2 valuable to the historian for an enquiry into the causes of civil war in France in spring 1793?

Explain your answer using the source, the information given about it and your own knowledge of the historical context. (8 marks)

**Tip**

*When using your contextual knowledge to explain the points raised in the source, try to use exact details to show depth of knowledge. For example, when the author writes that people did not want to send troops to the national army, what, specifically, is he referring to?*

With a mere 1,300 members of the National Guard in the Vendée to defend against unrest, the rebel armies made early gains. Over 10,000 rebels attacked and overran the town of Cholet, thus beginning the War in the Vendée. The rebels were often ill-disciplined and poorly organised but, despite increasing deployment of republican soldiers, the revolutionary forces were overwhelmed by sheer weight of numbers, suffering defeats at the Battle of Pont-Charrault (19 March 1793) and being forced to withdraw from Chalonnes (22 March).

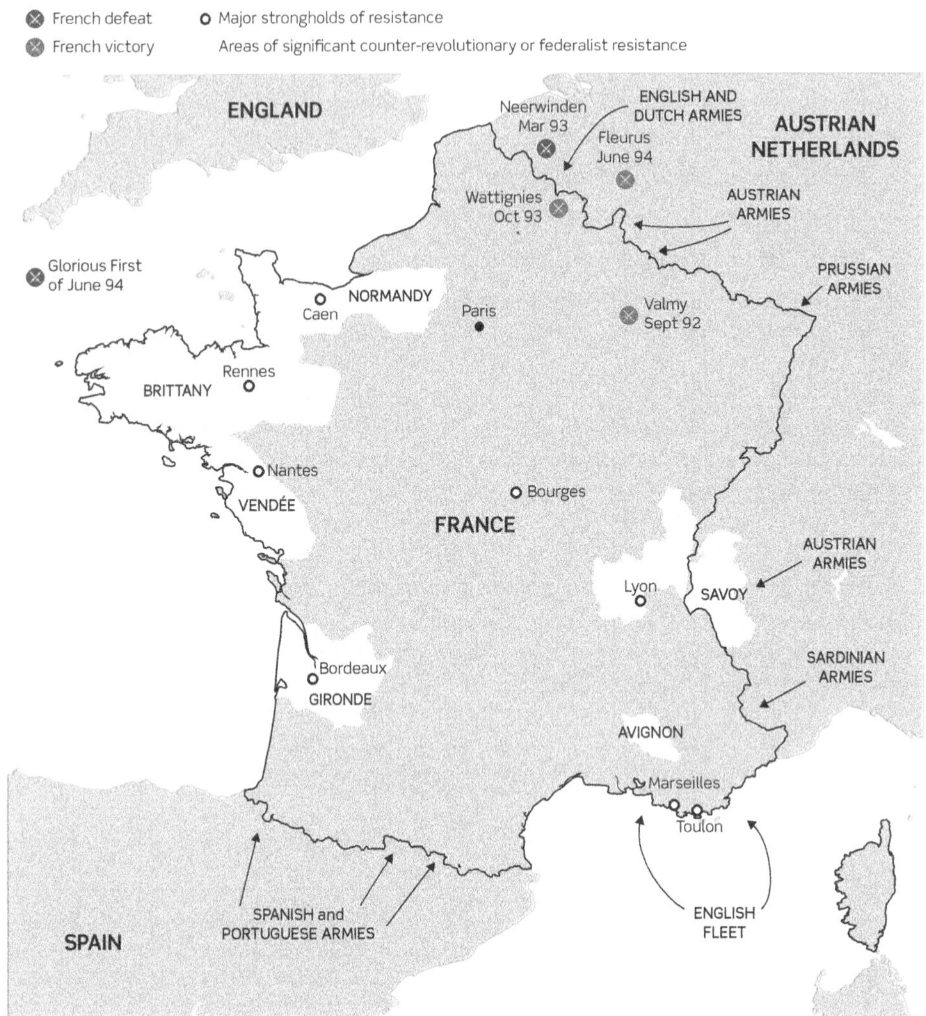


**Figure 3.1** Map of France showing both the internal and the external threats that France faced in 1793.

### The impact of the war in the Vendée

It is sometimes said that desperate times call for desperate measures and, in the spring of 1793, the situation in France did look somewhat desperate. Foreign armies advanced upon France, the leading French general defected and western France erupted into civil war. Due to the crises faced, the Convention took the decision to create a body responsible for the war effort and to defend the revolution from enemies, both internal and external. This body, created on 6 April 1793, was to be called the Committee of Public Safety.

The Committee was awarded significant power, including responsibility for determining foreign policy, with the right to appoint and dismiss commanders and for internal defence against counter-revolution, with the right to issue arrest warrants and sanction decrees.

The Committee would later become largely associated with the radical extremism of Jacobinism, dictatorship and the Terror but, when it was created, this was not the intention. Of the nine members, seven came from The Plain, with only two more radical deputies, one of whom was Danton. The Committee's existence also relied on the approval of the Convention, which renewed its powers on a monthly basis. Each week the Committee had to report directly to the Convention.

## Economic pressures and *sans-culottes* discontent

The Convention and the Committee also had to counter the threat of *sans-culottes* unrest. The war had worsened the already poor economic situation in Paris. To help fund the war effort, the government had printed more assignats, causing their value to drop by half. Supplies of bread became increasingly scarce due to the demands of feeding the army. A naval blockade of French ports by English ships further damaged France's economy as overseas trade was hampered.

As prices rose, the radical press fanned the flames of discontent. Marat blamed the price rises on hoarders and counter-revolutionaries, encouraging the *sans-culottes* to insurrection. In February 1793, the National Guard had to be deployed to bring riots in Paris, largely caused by bread prices, under control. Once again, the Convention was divided in its reaction to the *sans-culottes*. The Jacobins, and Robespierre in particular, added legitimacy to the *sans-culottes*' cause by failing to condemn them. In contrast, the Girondins attacked their actions.

The Paris Commune, reflecting the concerns of the *sans-culottes*, pushed the Convention to introduce a maximum price on bread and grain. The Girondin deputies, opposed to such demands, continued to advocate free trade. On 1 May 1793, 8,000 *sans-culottes* surrounded the Convention to force action. Brissot's newspaper, *Le Patriote français*, condemned the actions of the *sans-culottes* as 'brigandage and anarchy'. The Jacobins chose instead to embrace the demands of the Commune and the *sans-culottes*, pressing the maximum price argument. The Jacobin–*sans-culottes* alliance proved effective and, on 4 May, a law setting a maximum price for grain and bread was passed.

## Political pressures: the fall of the Girondins

The power struggle within the Convention between the Girondins and the Jacobins became more intense in April 1793. Declining French fortunes in the war had already damaged the standing of the pro-war Girondin faction. This damage was compounded by Dumouriez' defection to the Austrians. The Girondins had strongly supported Dumouriez, so his betrayal gave their political opponents a weapon to wield in the power struggle. Marat's *L'Ami du peuple* attacked the Girondins, claiming they were complicit in Dumouriez' betrayal, even going as far as to call for the lynching of the Girondin leaders. Serving as president of the Jacobin Club, Marat also published a circular sent to all provincial Jacobin Clubs, demanding the dismissal of all Girondins who had voted against the execution of Louis for harbouring monarchist sympathies. Speaking at the Convention on 10 April, Robespierre added his voice to the accusations, accusing Brissot and other leading Girondins of being members of a corrupt criminal conspiracy. He called for their trial for counter-revolutionary crimes, alongside other 'traitors' such as Marie Antoinette.

### The trial of Marat

The atmosphere in the Convention was such that, in April 1793, physical fighting even broke out between Girondin and Jacobin deputies. The Girondins counter-attacked on 12 April when Marguerite-Élie Guadet, a leading Girondin, called for Marat's indictment and trial before the Revolutionary Tribunal (see page 216) for his scandalous accusations and calls for violence. With many deputies abstaining from voting due to fear of reprisals, the Girondins managed to push through the Convention an order for Marat's arrest and trial. Yet their victory was short-lived. When Marat was brought to trial on 24 April, the applause he received from the public galleries was such that he had to ask the public to be quiet so that his defence could be heard. Judging the mood of Paris better than the Girondins had, the jury and judges took just one day to acquit Marat of all crimes.

### The *journée* of 2 June 1793 and the purge of the Girondins

On 26 May 1793, Robespierre called for the *sans-culottes* to rise up in insurrection against the Girondin deputies. He got more than he bargained for when the Commune and the sections of Paris mobilised an army of 80,000 National Guardsmen and *sans-culottes* who, on 2 June, surrounded the Convention. Their demands went further than the Jacobins had hoped, calling not only for the arrest of Girondin deputies but also for a maximum price cap on all essential goods, the establishment of a *sans-culottes* revolutionary army to deal with bread hoarders and counter-revolutionaries, and the creation of state-run arms factories. A three-day stand-off ensued and the tense situation was only resolved when Georges Couthon, a wheelchair-bound Jacobin deputy, proposed a vote within the Convention on the arrest of 29 Girondin deputies. A majority of the Convention voted in favour and the deputies were placed under arrest. While the insurrection had achieved only one of its aims, it had broken the power of the Girondins, leaving the path clear for Jacobin political dominance.

### A Level Exam-Style Question Section A

***Study Sources 3 and 4 before you answer this question.***

How far could the historian make use of Sources 3 and 4 together to investigate why the Girondins were purged in the summer of 1793?

Explain your answer, using both sources, the information given about them and your knowledge of the historical context.
(20 marks)

**Tip**

*Consider the nature of the sources, as well as their content. For example, within the content of Source 4, a number of key factors and events that contributed to the fall of the Girondins are mentioned. Yet consider the provenance of the source. It is from an extremist newspaper. How might that be relevant to the question?*

**SOURCE 3**

In his memoirs, Marc Antoine Baudot, a Jacobin deputy of The Mountain, made the following reflections on why the Girondins lost support in spring 1793. Baudot's memoirs were published in an 1893 collection, having been passed to a historian after Baudot's death in 1837.

The Girondins wanted to halt the revolution with the bourgeoisie in power, but at that time it was both impossible and impolitic [unwise]. There was open war on the frontiers, and civil war threatened; the foreign forces could only be repulsed by the masses who had therefore to be roused to support the revolution. The Mountain alone understood its mission, which was primarily to prevent foreign invasion, and it made use of the only means which could achieve success in such an enterprise. It felt constantly constrained by the circumstances, and dared to proclaim this. The Girondins either did not recognise the fact or did not wish to undergo the consequences. 'They are lawyers, fine speakers and skilled in procedure,' said Danton, 'but they have never picked up anything greater than a pen or an usher's rod.' The Girondins were tribunes [officials] without popular support. They were foolish enough, at a time when the masses were aroused, to declare war unto death on the Mountain, who understood and spoke for the same of these masses.

**SOURCE**

In his extremist newspaper, *Le Pére Duchesne* ('Father Duchesne'), the radical journalist Jacques Hébert attacked the Girondins and called on the *sans-culottes* to take action against them. Here, in edition 239, he accuses the Girondins of being royalists.

*Le Pére Duchesne*'s great denunciation address to all *sans-culottes* in all departments, concerning plotting by the Brissotins, Girondins, Rolandins, Buzotins, Pétionists, seeking to achieve the murder of the brave Montagnards [deputies of the Mountain], Jacobins, and the Paris Commune, so as to kill off freedom and restore the monarchy. Our armies are giving the republic's enemies the boot all over the place. It's in the Convention now, yes indeed, damn it, it's among the people's representatives that you will find the focus of counter-revolution. The accomplices of Capet [King Louis' family] and Dumouriez are moving heaven and earth to stir up civil war and arm the citizens from the departments against Paris... My fine *sans-culottes*, your enemies are only so bold because you stand there with your arms folded; wake up, damn it; stir yourselves and you will find them at your feet. Disarm those bastards who piss ice-water in a heatwave and who want no part in the revolution. The position of moderation is more dangerous than Austrian weapons. Strike while the iron's hot. If you slumber even a short while more you can expect to wake up to bloody slavery, damn it.

**KEY TERM**

**Purge**
An abrupt removal of a group of people, often by force.

## Marat's assassination

Marat was to pay for his part in the **purge** of the Girondins. On 13 July 1793, Charlotte Corday, a woman from Caen, a town known for its Girondin support, visited Marat in his residence in Paris. Marat was bathing at the time, seeking to sooth the pain of a chronic skin affliction. Corday asked to be allowed to deliver a note regarding counter-revolutionary activity. Upon being admitted to the room, she drew a large knife and killed Marat with one stab. Corday found the Girondins' more moderate republicanism far preferable to that offered by Marat and the Jacobins, and she hoped that killing Marat would be a blow to the radicals' cause. Corday was misguided in this as, by killing Marat, she made a martyr of him. His body was laid out for several days so the public could mourn his loss. In an act of reverence, his heart was removed, embalmed and hung in an urn from the ceiling of the Jacobin Club. Corday was tried by the Revolutionary Tribunal on 17 July, found guilty and executed by guillotine the same day.

Following the purge of the Girondins, the Committee of Public Safety became far more radical. The Committee, increased to 12 people appointed on 10 July, was composed largely of Jacobins and included some very radical individuals. They were led by Robespierre, who was closely supported by Saint-Just and Georges Couthon, a former lawyer. In charge of the war effort was Lazare Carnot, a brilliant strategist who oversaw the logistics of feeding, arming and equipping the national army. The Committee also included Jean-Marie Collot d'Herbois, a former actor, who was popular and closely associated with the *sans-culottes*.

## Federalist revolt

In spring and summer 1793, a series of protests and riots broke out across The French provinces in opposition to the purge of the Girondins and to Jacobin dominance. This 'federalist revolt', as it is known, was not counter-revolutionary, in that the rebels were not against the revolution. Instead, it was anti-Jacobin, a reaction against the radical and violent type of revolution that the Jacobins appeared to be advancing. Of the 85 departments of France, 60 witnessed disturbances.

SOURCE 5 The most famous artist of the revolutionary period, Jacques-Louis David, produced this oil painting of the death of Marat in the year he died, 1793. The portrait presents Marat as both a hero and a martyr of the revolution. In his hand he holds a letter saying 'you will give this assignat to that mother of five children whose husband died in the defense of his country'.

The most serious uprisings occurred in Bordeaux, Marseilles, Lyon and Toulon. The revolts tended to be led by the better-educated bourgeoisie, though they found support from the working classes as well. In Marseilles and Toulon, dockworkers joined the federal armies in their resistance of the Jacobins' national forces. Forces loyal to the Convention and the Committee surrounded Toulon. In response, the rebels opened their port to the British on 28 August, essentially giving over the town, as well as its fleet of 70 ships, to the enemy. French national forces besieged the town. The siege lasted from 28 August until 19 December 1793, when a young officer by the name of Napoleon Bonaparte devised a strategy for an artillery assault that forced the town into submission.

It was Lyon that perhaps posed the greatest threat. The revolt began on the same day as the purge of the Girondins. The aim of the rebels, under General de Wimpffen, was to raise a federalist army and march on Paris in opposition to the Convention and the Committee. De Wimpffen threatened to raise an army of 60,000 men to march on the capital. In reality, he raised just 2,500 from Lyon and other surrounding Federalist regions before the city was besieged by national forces. It was two months before the starving city capitulated, on 9 October 1793.

## EXTEND YOUR KNOWLEDGE

### Has the role of Jean-Paul Marat been overlooked?

Jean-Paul Marat (1743-93) was a Swiss-born journalist active in Paris during the French Revolution. From September 1789, he edited and wrote *L'Ami du peuple*, a radical newspaper. This paper demanded social equality as well as political equality for the common people of France and called for universal suffrage. It also called for radical action against aristocrats who, Marat believed, aimed to crush the revolution. Marat called for the beheading of these aristocrats and counter-revolutionaries. Marat also launched media attacks on moderates, whom he saw as traitors to the revolution. Mirabeau and Lafayette were frequent targets of such attacks, and Marat helped to turn the public mood against them.

During the period of constitutional monarchy (1789-92), Marat was frequently forced into hiding due to his inflammatory remarks. In September 1792, he was elected to the National Convention, where he continued to argue for the rights of the poor. He claimed that the Girondins, in their condemnation of popular action, were not true revolutionaries, and his newspaper played a role in the downfall and purge of the Girondin deputies (see page 221). In revenge for this role, Marat was assassinated on 13 July 1793. His death scene was immortalised in a sympathetic portrait by Jacques-Louis David, the most prominent artist of the revolutionary period.

Marat remains one of the most shadowy and controversial figures of the French Revolution, and was, according to some accounts, insane. The historian Simon Schama tells us that Marat 'glorified in rudeness' and that 'displeasing as many people as possible... was projected as a sign of his integrity.' He has often been represented as a hate-filled rebel without a cause, rather than a revolutionary leader. Some have attacked him further by portraying him as a hideously ugly individual. Yet this insane monster, as he has been portrayed, had huge popular support. When he was acquitted from the trial brought against him by the Girondins, he was paraded through the streets by thousands of followers, and his assassination triggered such a huge outpouring of grief in Paris that his torch-lit funeral pageant wound through the streets of the capital for six hours.

Why such a contradiction? In his 2012 biography of Marat, the historian Clifford D. Conner concludes that historians have detested Marat, as they feared that if such a character was treated sympathetically or even objectively it would encourage the reappearance of such individuals: individuals who condone violence as a legitimate force to forward a social or political cause. As a result it has been said that 'dispassionate evaluation of the historic Marat [has been] all but impossible'. Conner attacks claims of Marat's insanity and argues that, due to bias, the role of Marat has been overlooked in the revolution. While not excusing his calls for bloodshed, Conner presents a picture of a 'principled leader continuously seeking to advance the revolution'. He acknowledges that Marat was never as significant a figure as Robespierre, as Marat always refused to align himself too strongly with any one faction, limiting his political power. However, according to Conner, Marat was the voice of the *sans-culottes*, expressing their real views and concerns, and often leading popular feeling. Conner highlights Marat's tactical genius in pre-empting the mood of the sans-*culottes* and in channelling their discontentment into action, as he did on 10 August 1792, by 'adding an element of clarity into an otherwise confused mass movement'.

**SOURCE 6** Jean-Marie Collot d'Herbois, acting on behalf of the Committee of Public Safety, was sent to Lyon alongside Joseph Fouché to dispense revolutionary justice after the revolt had been crushed. Here, in a letter to a fellow Jacobin, he explains how and why he intended to punish the people of Lyon so harshly.

My friend and brother, our Jacobin brothers are achieving marvels; a letter from Robespierre would please them greatly and would be very effective. Here we have not restored public spirit, since there is none, but courage, the morale of a few men of energy and of a certain number of patriots who have suffered oppression for too long. We have revitalised justice in republican style, i.e. swift and terrible as the will of the nation. It will strike at traitors like a thunderbolt and leave only ashes. The destruction of one vile and rebellious city will strengthen all the others. The death of these scoundrels will assure life for generations of free men. These are our principles. We will demolish as much as we can, by cannon-fire and by exploding mines. But, as you will realise, amidst a population of a hundred and fifty thousand, there are many obstacles to such methods. The people's blade [a nickname for the guillotine] cut the heads off twenty conspirators each day and it did not frighten them. We have set up a commission which is as prompt as can be the conscience of true republicans sitting in judgement of traitors. Sixty-four of these conspirators were shot yesterday, on the same spot where they fired on patriots; two hundred and thirty will fall today. Such substantial examples will help to persuade those cities which are vacillating [uncertain where their loyalties lie].

As Collot d'Herbois' letter (Source 6) reveals, some within the government were determined to make an example of the towns and cities that had rebelled against their rule. On 12 October, Couthon called on the Convention to announce a decree to wipe Lyon off the map of France, declaring that henceforth the city would be renamed *Ville-Affranchie* ('Liberated Town'). The homes of those associated with the rising were to be torn down and in their place a column was to be erected and inscribed with the following words: 'Lyon made war on liberty. Lyon is no more.' Six hundred houses were demolished. The human cost was even higher. As well as those who had perished during the siege and bombardment of the city, nearly 2,000 people were executed: some guillotined, far more killed in mass shootings. This number included many nobles, federalist magistrates and some priests, but the greatest proportion were common workers. Far from meeting Robespierre's approval, as Collot d'Herbois had hoped, Robespierre was critical of the excesses of violence in Lyon and later called on Collot d'Herbois and Fouché to justify their severity.

## The power of the *sans-culottes* and the Paris Commune

When the *sans-culottes* and the National Guard besieged the Convention in June 1793, only one of their demands, the expulsion of the Girondins, had been met. As the value of assignats continued to fall and bread prices continued to rise, calls for economic reform and action against grain hoarders became louder. A group of extremists emerged, known as the *Enragés*. Led by a priest from a poor area of Paris, called Jacques Roux, the *Enragés* demanded action to alleviate poverty and starvation. They proposed radical solutions, including higher taxes for the rich and the execution of hoarders.

Joining the *Enragés* in their criticism of the Committee and the Convention were the Hébertists. Jacques René Hébert was a radical journalist, editor of the extremist newspaper *Le Père Duchesne*, who also criticised the government for inaction in countering poverty. Hébert also headed the revolutionary Paris Commune, a body that was instrumental in channelling the dissatisfaction of the *sans-culottes* into co-ordinated insurrection.

As well as stronger action against the internal threat of counter-revolutionary activity, the Commune and the *sans-culottes* demanded increased effort in fighting foreign enemies. Partly as a consequence, on 23 August 1793 the *levée en masse* was declared by the Convention. This was the announcement of total war. The whole nation was to be geared towards the war effort. All unmarried men aged 18–25 were to be conscripted into the army, nearly half a million men in total. Metal goods, like church bells, were to be confiscated and melted down to manufacture cannons. State munitions factories were established (as the *sans-culottes* had demanded in the *journée* of June 1793) and the government imposed increasing controls on overseas trade. The *levée en masse* was largely organised, with brilliant efficiency, by Lazare Carnot of the Committee of Public Safety and led to significant French gains in the Revolutionary War, as French forces pushed back the advancing enemy armies to outside France's borders.

Yet despite improving fortunes in the war, economic circumstances for the *sans-culottes* did not improve. As a result, on 4–5 September 1793, encouraged by Roux, Hébert and the Commune, thousands of *sans-culottes* marched on the Convention. To appease the crowd, the Convention agreed to a number of the demands of the *sans-culottes*. First, they permitted the formation of *armées révolutionnaires*: people's armies set with the task of requisitioning grain supplies and tracking down those suspected of hoarding food. An *armée* of 6,000 was recruited in Paris and provincial *armées révolutionnaires* totalled 30,000 in number. As well as seizing grain supplies, these *armées* played an active role in avenging the federalist revolts and in pursuing the cause of de-Christianisation (see page 229).

In a further effort to quell *sans-culottes* unrest, the Convention announced the law of general maximum. Introduced on 29 September, the general maximum set a maximum price on all basic commodities, as had been demanded during the *journée* of 2 June. The most significant concession, however, was in response to the *sans-culottes'* demands for tougher action against the enemies of the revolution who, as they saw it and as the extremist press told them, were responsible for their poverty and suffering. The response of the Convention was the introduction of the Law of Suspects (see page 227), the law that, to many, is seen as the beginning of the Reign of Terror.

## Conclusion

On 3 October 1793, the trial of Brissot and the other Girondin deputies began. The result was a foregone conclusion and on 31 October Brissot and 21 other Girondins were sent to the guillotine. It must be questioned why, when the Girondin faction enjoyed so much support at the beginning of 1793, they fell victim to Jacobin dominance just several months later.

A key reason was the war. It had been the Girondins who had promoted the war case most strongly so, when the war started to go unfavourably and France was placed in grave danger, it was inevitable that some blame would be laid at their feet. The defection of Dumouriez, their general, did little to help this situation. On top of this was the fear of counter-revolution. The revolt in the Vendée made the threat of counter-revolution only too real. Fuelled by the likes of Desmoulins and Marat, a culture of paranoia developed. Who were the real revolutionaries? Who could truly be trusted? To the *sans-culottes* and the Paris Commune, it did not appear that the Girondins could be trusted, as they continued to condemn the protests of 'the people' and resisted reforms (such as price regulations) aimed at alleviating their economic distress. It was this failure to engage with popular feeling in Paris that finally caused the fall of the Girondins in the *journée* of June 1793.

The Jacobins, by contrast, sided with the *sans-culottes*, a move that helped to ensure their rise in the second half of 1793. The extent of radical Jacobin dominance can be seen both in the composition of the new Committee of Public Safety of July 1793 and in the brutal revenge enacted on the towns and cities that rose in the federal revolt. The days of moderate republicanism were truly over.

ACTIVITY
KNOWLEDGE CHECK

**Preconditions to Terror; why did the Jacobins rise to dominance?**

1 Create a set of five notecards. Using one card for each of the following five factors, write an explanation of how they contributed to the rising power of the Jacobins and/or the declining popularity and power of the Girondins, culminating in the purge of June 1793:

   a) The War of the First Coalition

   b) Dumouriez' defection

   c) Marat and the radical press

   d) The Girondin stance on economic reform

   e) The *sans-culottes*

2 Turn your notecards upside down. Choose two at random. If possible, try to explain how the two are connected. Repeat the process until you feel confident that you understand the interconnections between the factors.

3 Write a one paragraph conclusion to answer the question 'Why did the Jacobins rise to dominance over the Girondins in 1793?' The conclusion should provide a brief summary of your key points before giving an overall assessment of what you believe to be the most important cause.

# WAS THE TERROR 'PROMPT, SEVERE, INFLEXIBLE' JUSTICE OR SIMPLY NOT JUSTICE AT ALL?

'Prompt, severe, inflexible' justice is how, in February 1794, Robespierre described the Terror. In 1793, a number of measures were taken in order to bring to justice those who were perceived to be a threat to the revolutionary government. The machinery of the Terror established during this time would ultimately claim thousands of lives and lead to hundreds of thousands of imprisonments. In this section, we consider why these measures were introduced and how they operated, and assess the extent to which they delivered justice or persecution.

TIMELINE OF THE INSTRUMENTS OF TERROR

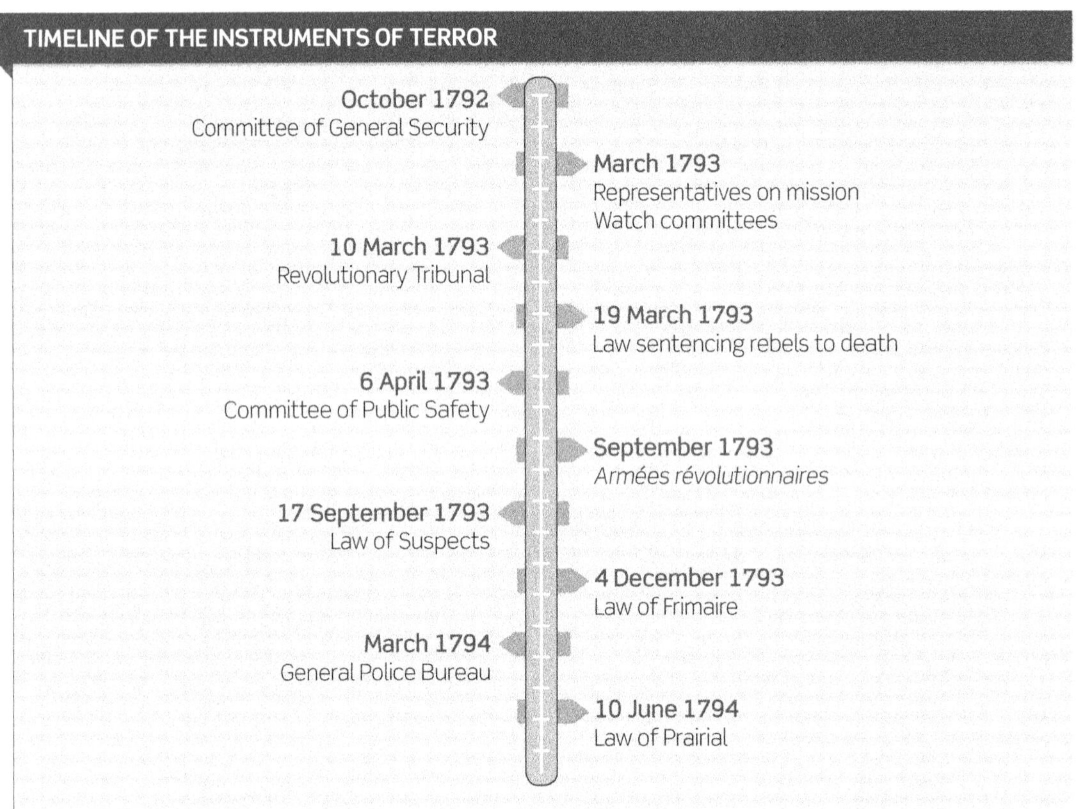


## The Committee of General Security and the Revolutionary Tribunal

The creation of the Committee of General Security was one of the first counter-revolutionary measures taken by the Convention. Established in October 1792, the Committee was essentially a police committee, consisting of 12 people responsible for overseeing the administration of revolutionary justice within Paris. The Committee's remit overlapped with that of the Committee of Public Safety (established April 1793), although the latter had greater and wider powers.

On 10 March 1793, the Revolutionary Tribunal was established in Paris under the authority of the Committee of General Security. The Tribunal was charged with the task of trying suspects accused of counter-revolutionary activity. When it was established, Danton defended its necessity by arguing that the power of revolutionary justice needed to be taken out of the hands of the *sans-culottes* and, instead, controlled by the state. With the memory of the September Massacres still fresh, this argument was a convincing one.

In some respects, the Tribunal took the form of a normal court, with a jury present and the opportunity for the accused to offer their defence. However, for anyone found guilty of crimes against the revolution, there was just one punishment: death. Jurors and judges alike were hand-picked by the

Committee, so by modern standards trials can hardly be deemed to have been fair. Furthermore, the chief prosecutor, Antoine Fouquier-Tinville, had a fearsome reputation. Over time, the very name of the Tribunal became enough to evoke fear among the people of Paris.

From March 1793 to 10 June 1794, 1,251 people were executed in Paris following hearings at the Tribunal. Of these, the majority, some 85 percent, were neither nobility nor clergy, but people who belonged to the Third Estate.

## Representatives on mission

The first wave of 'representatives on mission' were sent out in March 1793. They were representatives of the Convention, deployed to the provinces, initially with the mission of ensuring that conscription requirements for the army were being met. Two representatives were sent to each department to oversee the levy. The representatives tended to be Jacobins and, after the purge of the Girondins, were almost exclusively so. As time went on, the role of the representatives became wider and they were considered an important link between the provinces and the Committee of Public Safety (under whose authority they were placed in July 1793).

As their role was fairly poorly defined, representatives acted in varied ways. Some simply focused on the administrative duties of overseeing conscription. Others involved themselves in rooting out and denouncing local officials who they deemed to be anti-Jacobin. In this way, the representatives played an important role in the suppression of federalism. It was representatives on mission who were responsible for some of the greatest atrocities of the Terror. The representative Jean-Baptiste Carrier sanctioned the brutal executions in the Loire following the defeat of the Vendéan rebellion (see page 230) and Collot d'Herbois, a leading member of the Committee of Public Safety acting as representative for Lyon, ordered the execution of 1,900 people following the Federalist revolt there (see pages 222–224).

## Watch committees

The watch committees, or *comités de surveillance*, were established in March 1793. Each commune or department had to appoint a committee of 12 people, who were given responsibility for monitoring all foreign and suspicious individuals within their area. The war, fear of *emigrés* and counter-revolutionary plots had made the government very suspicious of foreigners. The watch committees were expected to issue and monitor citizenship cards. Individuals attracting too much suspicion could find themselves being sent to the Revolutionary Tribunal. At a time when xenophobia was the norm, and in a culture of fear, being an outsider in France in 1793 would have been a dangerous experience. After the Law of Suspects (see Source 7), the powers of the watch committees were extended and they were expected to seek out and draw up lists of counter-revolutionary suspects, who were then to be sent to trial before the Revolutionary Tribunal.

## Counter-revolutionary laws

### Law of 19 March, 1793

Prior to the Law of Suspects, those brought for trial were most frequently accused by invoking the Law of 19 March 1793. Provoked by the rising in the Vendée, this law had outlawed rebels. Any rebels captured bearing arms or possessing royalist insignia were condemned to death within 24 hours. If captured unarmed, the suspect was to be tried by the criminal courts and, if convicted, was also to be punished by death. The Law of 19 March armed the representatives on mission with a licence to enact severe vengeance upon insurgent departments. It has been calculated that as many as 10,000–12,000 people were put to death under the Law of 19 March, although with so many executions taking place without trial an accurate figure is hard to ascertain.

### Law of Suspects

The Law of Suspects was introduced by the National Convention in September 1793 in response to mounting pressure from the *sans-culottes* and the Paris Commune.

SOURCE

The Law of Suspects as decreed by the National Convention on 17 September 1793.

1. Immediately after the publication of the present decree, all suspects within the territory of the Republic and still at large, shall be placed in custody.
2. The following are deemed suspects:
   i. those who, by their conduct, associations, comments, or writings have shown themselves partisans of tyranny or federalism and enemies of liberty;
   ii. those who are unable to justify, in the manner prescribed by the decree of March 21st, their means of existence and the performance of their civic duties;
   iii. those to whom certificates of patriotism [awarded by the watch committees] have been refused;
   iv. civil servants suspended or dismissed from their positions by the National Convention or by its commissioners, and not reinstated, especially those who have been or are to be dismissed by virtue of the decree of August 14th;
   v. those former nobles, together with husbands, wives, fathers, mothers, sons or daughters, brothers or sisters, and agents of the émigrés, who have not constantly demonstrated their devotion to the Revolution;
   vi. those who have emigrated between July 1st 1789, and the publication of the decree of March 30th, even though they may have returned to France within the period established by said decree...

The Surveillance [Watch] Committees established in accordance with the law of March 21st last are responsible for drawing up lists of suspects, with issuing warrants of arrest against them, and with placing their papers under seal.

ACTIVITY
KNOWLEDGE CHECK

**The Law of Suspects**

1 Read Source 7. Under which article of the Law of Suspects could the following people have been imprisoned? Explain why. One example has been done for you.

a) Example: A young girl whose father was an aristocrat. *Article 2.v., as the families of all nobles had to be arrested.*

b) A journalist who wrote an article criticising the actions of the Committee of Public Safety.

c) A French merchant who had travelled to live and work in Britain for a few months during 1790.

d) Someone who helped to hide a refractory priest.

e) An illegal trader who made their money dealing goods on the black market.

f) A person who had been denied a citizenship card by their local watch committee for having been overheard making a negative comment about the revolution.

2 Which article of the Law of Suspects is most poorly defined? Why do you think the Convention included very loosely defined articles within the law?

With such vague definition of what constituted opposition to the revolution, the law was open to huge abuse. It could be used to revenge petty personal grievances, and any outsiders or misfits within communities could do little to defend themselves. Not publicly wearing the revolutionary cockade could be enough to lead to arrest. In Paris, the Commune drew up a list of grounds for suspicion. The list of opponents to the revolution included people who: 'in assemblies of people, arrest their energy by crafty discourses, turbulent cries and threats'; people who 'are always ready to spread bad news with affected grief' or people who 'received the constitution of the republic with indifference'. In short, not only was it a crime to say anything negative about the revolution, it was a crime not to be enthusiastic about it. You were either for the revolution or against it; there was no middle ground. It is inevitable that in such an oppressive climate people would have conformed out of fear for their own safety and opposition to the government would have been severely stifled.

The watch committees and the representatives on mission were responsible for ensuring that arrests were made. Over the next few months, thousands of arrests occurred. In Paris alone, 50 new prisons had to be created and some 7,000 suspects were detained. By the following summer, the number of detainees across France rose to 300,000. Although the majority of these were never bought to trial and many lived long enough to survive the Terror, it is estimated that as many as 10,000 may have perished while imprisoned.

In addition to the countless trials and imprisonments of unknown common people, a series of **show trials** of leading figures followed the Law of Suspects. Most famous of these was the trial of Marie Antoinette, on 14 October. Brought before the Tribunal, Marie faced unfounded accusations of incest and less improbable accusations of betraying French war secrets to the enemy. She reportedly showed great calm and dignity throughout her trial, although this had little effect on her accusers. Two days later, the trial was concluded and Marie Antoinette was sent to the guillotine.

It was the turn of the Girondins next. Imprisoned since their fall in June, on 31 October 1793 Brissot and 21 leading Girondins were sent to the guillotine, after a short trial in which there was only ever going to be one result. Other trials and executions followed. Even former leading figures of the revolution were not spared. Philippe Égalité (see page 175) perished on 6 November simply for the crime of being related to King Louis and two former revolutionary mayors of Paris, Jean-Sylvain Bailly and Jérôme Pétion, were also executed. Antoine Barnave, a leading Feuillant who had fought hard for the preservation of constitutional monarchy in the years 1789–92, was killed on 29 November. Roux, who had been imprisoned for his role in inciting the *journée* of 5 September, was also supposed to be brought before the Tribunal but, upon hearing the news of his impending trial, he committed suicide on 20 January 1794.

### Law of Frimaire

Passed on 5 December (in the new revolutionary calendar month of Frimaire), the Law of Frimaire aimed to increase greatly the central control of the revolutionary government. The law was largely a response to the federalist revolts and the rising in the Vendée. Most significantly, the law gave the Committee of Public Safety the power to purge local government officials. As local officials were elected by their communities (communes and departments), the revolutionary government might have had cause to question their loyalty to the central government in Paris. As a result, the law prescribed that all local officials had to be placed under the supervision of a national agent, who would direct those officials on central policy as well as reporting any perceived misconduct or lack of loyalty back to the Committee (in which case that official would be purged and/or brought before the Tribunal). The law placed representatives on mission under the control of the Committee and also forbade the existence of any revolutionary armies outside Paris. The Committee feared the unrestrained radicalism of the *armées révolutionnaires*, seeing them as a threat to its own authority, and therefore sought to abolish these *sans-culotte* armies. The Law of Frimaire can be seen as a step towards dictatorship, as more powers were moved from the Convention to the Committee and as the law aimed to prevent any local opposition to central government control.

## Conclusion

Due partly to internal unrest and partly to *sans-culottes'* pressure, as 1793 progressed the measures taken by the Convention and the Committee to bring to justice 'enemies' of the revolution became increasingly severe. The Committee sought to hunt out any

KEY TERM

**Show trial**
A trial where someone is publicly judged with the intention of pleasing or influencing the public as opposed to administering justice.

opposition via its network of representatives on mission and watch committees. The Law of Suspects armed this network of officials with a licence to arrest almost anyone they deemed to be the enemy. Due to the limited availability of documentary evidence, it is very challenging for the historian to assess the extent to which those arrested were actually guilty of any crime, but it is doubtful whether many of those imprisoned or executed posed a genuine threat to the revolution. A young child of a nobleman, a misfit rejected by their community, a merchant disliked for charging high prices, a common man who did not cheer at the appropriate time during a revolutionary speech – these are some of the people who were undoubtedly imprisoned. Were such people really enemies of the revolution? But was the purpose of the machinery of the Terror really to hunt out enemies? Were the Committee and the Convention actually looking to enact revolutionary justice? Or, more probably, were they actually just seeking to foster a culture of fear, where the prospect of offering any opposition to the government was just too perilous?

ACTIVITY
KNOWLEDGE CHECK

**Was the Terror 'prompt, severe, inflexible' justice?**

Draw a table as a simple summary of the instruments of the Terror. Use the following four headings: 'Law or institution', 'Date', 'Reason for introduction' and 'Function and/or responsibility'. Include an entry for each of the following: Committee of Public Safety, Revolutionary Tribunal, Representatives on mission, Watch committees, *Armées révolutionnaires*, Law of 19 March, Law of Suspects and Law of Frimaire.

# TO WHAT EXTENT WAS ROBESPIERRE THE DRIVING FORCE OF THE GREAT TERROR?

By the end of 1793, the machinery of the Terror was in place. Furthermore, in the purges of October 1793 to January 1794, the Jacobin-dominated government, the Committee in particular, had rid itself of many potential political opponents. As leader of the Committee of Public Safety, Robespierre must shoulder some of the blame for these actions. But Robespierre was not alone in the Committee and, as records of their meetings were not kept, it is difficult to judge the extent of his influence. Even if we are to accept that Robespierre's grip on the Committee was a tight one, it was often acting due to other pressures. It was the actions of the *sans-culottes* in the *journée* of September 1793 that caused the government to take more radical action, most notably the Law of Suspects. However, moving into 1794, and as the Committee further consolidated its position, its rule became more close to that of dictatorship, with Robespierre at its head.

## Religious radicalism

### De-Christianisation

In late 1793 and into 1794, a wave of religious terror swept France. De-Christianisation was not led by government policy, but was driven by the actions of the *sans-culottes*, their *armées révolutionnaires* and overzealous representatives on mission. The *sans-culottes* were encouraged in their actions by the Hébertists, who were fiercely **atheist** and anti-clerical. On 10 November 1793, Hébert organised the Festival of Reason, in which French people were encouraged to transform their local churches into Temples of Reason by removing Christian symbols and replacing them with symbols of the revolution. Secular ceremonies were held to mark this transformation, the largest of which was at Notre Dame in Paris. The Paris Commune also played its part by ordering, in November 1793, that all churches in Paris should be closed. Other areas followed Paris's example and, by spring 1794, the majority of churches in France had shut. The process of de-Christianisation was not an orderly and regulated affair. Widespread vandalism occurred: altarpieces were smashed, stained-glass windows broken and bonfires built out of prayer books and crucifixes. Priests were attacked and forced to renounce their priesthoods, and some were even forced into marriage. As a consequence, thousands of priests gave up their calling.

KEY TERM

**Atheist**
A person who does not believe in the existence of a god.

The Jacobins were divided in their reaction to de-Christianisation. Some applauded it but others, most notably Robespierre, were strong critics. Robespierre saw the religious radical fervour as immorality and mob rule pretending to pass itself off as revolutionary philosophy. Robespierre's reaction was certainly influenced by his own religious beliefs. While he was not a supporter of Catholicism (he had supported the sale of Church land earlier in the revolution), he was certainly not an atheist. Famously, he once quoted Voltaire, saying: 'If God did not exist, it would be necessary to invent him.'

EXTEND YOUR KNOWLEDGE

**The revolutionary calendar**
Another, less violent but no less radical, religious change was the introduction of the revolutionary calendar. On 20 September 1793, a committed Jacobin called Gilbert Romme proposed to the Convention that there needed to be a new organisation of time; free from the traditions and superstitions of the past, a new calendar would mark a new age.

As the Gregorian calendar dated years from the birth of Christ, this was not deemed to be appropriate in a nation denouncing religion. It was decided that this new age in history began with the creation of the French Republic and so the calendar was backdated: Year I began in September 1792.

However, it was not just years that were redefined. A ten-day week was created, Sundays and religious festival days disappeared from the calendar, and months were renamed, taking on the names of natural phenomena associated with that time of year. For example, the month during the height of summer was to be called 'Thermidor', meaning 'Heat'. Germinal ('Budding') was the first month of spring, Nivôse ('Snow') was in the depths of winter, and so on.

## Terror in the Vendée

As well as the process of radical de-Christianisation, early 1794 saw arguably the greatest humanitarian crime of the radical phase of the revolution, the suppression of the Vendée (see page 219).

While the federalist revolts had mostly been crushed by October 1793 (with the exception of Toulon), the rising in the Vendée had continued. By the autumn, the main Vendéan rebel army consisted of about 65,000 men, far larger than any force seen during the Federalist revolt. Despite a victory for government forces on 17 October near the town of Cholet, guerrilla warfare continued for the next two months. The decisive government victory came at Le Mans on 12 December, with 15,000 Vendéan rebels killed on the field. On 22 December, the last Vendéan army was defeated.

Following the defeat of the rebels, the French general, Louis-Marie Turreau, and the representative on mission, Jean-Baptiste Carrier, launched a devastating campaign to hunt out any surviving rebels and to punish the region for its disloyalty. Turreau created 'hell columns', regiments of soldiers sent across the area to burn villages, destroy crops and kill anyone who tried to prevent them. Meanwhile, Carrier authorised mass murder. 'Suspects', including 90 priests, were tied up and placed on boats on the River Loire, which were then sunk. In total, through famine, disease, murder and execution, almost a quarter of a million people died in the suppression of the Vendée.

It should be noted, however, that the devastation inflicted on the Vendée was not upon the orders of the Convention or the Committee. However, there is no doubt that they were aware of the massacres, as direct reports were made back to the Convention. Robespierre did call Carrier back to Paris on 8 February to answer for the atrocities, but no further action was taken.

## The purge of the Hébertists and the Indulgents

### The Hébertists

In February 1794, tensions once more began to rise on the streets and in the political clubs of Paris. Economic conditions had still not improved since the law of general maximum. There was talk of the poor being so desperate that they would soon be killing cats and dogs for food. There were rumours that another day of insurrection was pending, with the *sans-culottes* forcing another purge of the Convention through armed uprising. Both in the Convention and in his extreme newspaper, *Le Père Duchesne*, Hébert encouraged insurrection. A political battle emerged. The Committee, most notably Robespierre and Saint-Just, fearing for their own positions, denounced the Hébertists, their encouragement of popular unrest and their support for de-Christianisation. In response, the Hébertists accused Robespierre of defying the will of the people.

The Committee of Public Safety could not accept such a challenge to its authority. On 10 March 1794, it ordered Antoine-Quentin Fouquier-Tinville, chief prosecutor of the Tribunal, to prepare a case against Hébert and 18 of his closest allies. Fouquier-Tinville protested that there was no evidence on which to act, but for the Committee that was not important and the trial proceeded. Predictably, the jury gave a 'guilty' verdict and, on 24 March, the Hébertists were sent to the guillotine.

With the Hébertists deposed, the Committee proceeded to extend its control by closing all non-Jacobin political clubs, disbanding the Parisian *armée révolutionnaire* and purging the Paris Commune (as permitted under the Law of Frimaire), replacing the officials with Robespierre's supporters.

### The Indulgents

Between December 1793 and March 1794, the Committee had greatly broadened its power and control, both within Paris and in the provinces. This led to accusations of dictatorship. Leading these criticisms were Georges Danton and Camille Desmoulins, Robespierre's former schoolmate and closest friend. Once allies of Robespierre, in late 1793 and early 1794 they came out in moderate opposition to the Committee. Their followers were known as the 'Indulgents', a word meaning 'those who are more lenient or merciful'. They were awarded such a label because they called for an end to the Terror and for divisions in the revolutionary movement to be healed.

It may seem somewhat obscure why Danton and Desmoulins would protest against the Terror when they played such a pivotal role in bringing the Jacobins to power and in sanctioning the Terror in the first place. Yet calls for a de-escalation in Terror make good sense considering the situation of the time. By 1794, the federalist revolts had been suppressed, the Vendéan army had been defeated and French fortunes against foreign forces had improved. With France in a considerably less vulnerable position than it had been in summer 1793, arguments for the necessity of Terror appeared somewhat weaker.

Desmoulins' newspaper, *Le Vieux Cordelier* ('The Old Cordelier'), published articles calling for the release of 200,000 suspects imprisoned as a consequence of the Law of Suspects. When the newspaper first began, *Le Vieux Cordelier* had been dedicated in honour of both Danton and Robespierre, but in December 1793 it turned on the latter.

**SOURCE**

**In issue four of *Le Vieux Cordelier*, from 20 December 1793, Desmoulins made this direct appeal to his friend and former ally, Robespierre, to end the Terror.**

People apparently think that Liberty, like childhood, has to pass through crying and tears to reach maturity... A people is free the moment it wants to be such (you may recall this was Lafayette saying): 'it entered into the fullness of its rights, from the 14th July [the day the Bastille was stormed].' Liberty has neither age nor youth. It has only one age, that of strength and vigour...I think quite differently from those who tell you that terror must remain the order of the day. I am sure, on the contrary, that liberty would be strengthened, and Europe conquered, if you had a committee of clemency [mercy]... Oh! My dear Robespierre! It is you that I address these words...Oh, my old college comrade, whose eloquent speeches will be read by posterity, remember well these lessons of history and philosophy: that love is stronger and more lasting than fear; that admiration and religion are born of good deeds.

Using evidence activity (5a)

### Context is everything

Work in groups.

Take an A3 piece of paper. In the middle draw a circle about 18 cm in diameter. Within the circle is the evidence (Source 8) itself, outside the circle is the context.

Using Source 8:

1 Think of a question that the source could be helpful in answering.

2 Inside the circle, write a set of statements giving information that can be gleaned only from the source itself without any contextual knowledge.

3 Outside the circle, write down statements of contextual knowledge that relate to the source.

4 Draw annotated lines to show links between the contextual statements and the information from the source. Does context change the nature or meaning of the information?

Now answer the question:

5 Explain why knowledge of context is important when gathering and using historical evidence. Give specific examples to illustrate your point.

In publicly criticising and calling for change to the Committee's policies, Desmoulins was treading on dangerous ground. Being Robespierre's old schoolfriend could not protect him and, in the Jacobin Club on 7 January 1794, Robespierre called for his expulsion. This was followed by a greatly applauded speech in the Convention on 5 February, in which Robespierre made very clear that he had no intention of relaxing the Terror (see Sources 9 and 10) and that no man could stand in its way. As the political struggle between the Indulgents and the Committee continued into March, Robespierre was forced to confront the implications of his own speech. By placing themselves against the Terror and against the Committee, Danton and Desmoulins had placed themselves against the revolution. On 30 March, Danton, Desmoulins and other leading Indulgents were arrested in a sudden night raid. The next day, at the Convention, Saint-Just read a long report that he had written, detailing the crimes of the Indulgents. He held them responsible, with little or no evidence, for the devaluation of the assignats, for outbreaks of federalism and even, rather bizarrely, for unrest in the French overseas colonies. The Convention voted unanimously to send them to trial.

The Indulgents were brought before the Tribunal on 3 April. The show trial did not go as the Committee had hoped. Danton was a superb orator, and so used the trial as a platform to denounce Robespierre, the Committee and the Terror. He was applauded and cheered from the public galleries. To counter this, Saint-Just convinced the Convention that the prisoners were in revolt against the court and so they were to be denied the right to speak in their defence. The next day, while the accused remained in their cells, the Tribunal delivered the verdict of guilty. Danton, Desmoulins and 13 others were sent to the guillotine on 5 April 1794.

### EXTEND YOUR KNOWLEDGE

**Louis-Antoine de Saint-Just (1767–94)**

In the very early years of the revolution, Saint-Just was largely an unknown figure. He was too young to stand as a candidate for the National Assembly but, through self-promotion and political manoeuvring, he steadily built up his political reputation in Blérancourt, a town in northern France. In 1791, he published his *Esprit de la revolution* ('Spirit of the Revolution'), a text that argued that, while the revolution had made gains, the people were not yet free. He asserted that often 'the people' were not just or rational enough to know for themselves what was needed in order for them to achieve their liberty. This was an important idea, later used to justify the Terror, which implied that it was the role of the government to tell the people what was in their best interest, even if they disagreed. It was also a condemnation of popular action, namely *sans-culottes* insurrection. Although the text received only modest interest at the time, Saint-Just had built enough of a reputation to secure his election to a provincial seat in the National Convention (September 1792). He was a mere 25 years old at the time, the youngest age permitted for deputies.

It was during the debate on the fate of King Louis that Saint-Just really made his mark. He delivered a devastating speech (see page 214), arguing that Louis should receive no trial as simply by having been a king he was automatically guilty. His brilliant oratory and clear logic quickly established his position as one of the leading deputies of The Mountain and, following the purge of the Girondins, he was elected to the Committee of Public Safety. Over the next 14 months, alongside Robespierre, Saint-Just was one of the leading advocates of Terror and played a key role in the fall of the Indulgents. As his power rose, he became increasingly cold, isolated and bloodthirsty, surpassing even Robespierre in his calls for more 'revolutionary justice'. On 27 July, during the Coup of Thermidor (see page 237), Saint-Just was arrested on the orders of his enemies within the Convention. He was sent to the guillotine the next day.

### Significance of the purge

The Indulgents had initiated calls for an end to the Terror and to the dictatorship of the Committee. The execution of 15 men was not enough to end such demands. Furthermore, while Robespierre had proved the conviction of his beliefs by executing his own friend, he had also demonstrated that he was willing to stop at nothing in his pursuit of political control. This in itself caused fear, and fear causes opposition. Most significantly, though, the Committee had killed two of the most popular figures of the revolution. Many found it hard to believe that Danton could really have been an enemy of the revolution when he had been its figurehead for so long. All these issues contributed to growing opposition to the Committee and, ultimately, contributed to Robespierre's fall in July 1794.

**THINKING HISTORICALLY** Cause and consequence 6b

### Attitudes and actions

Individuals can only make choices based on their context. Prevalent attitudes combine with individual experience and natural temperament to frame the individual's perception of what is going on around them. Nobody can know the future or see into the minds of others. For example, Robespierre's decision, in early 1794, to escalate, rather than relax, the Terror caused great suffering and would, ultimately, contribute to his own downfall. Why, then, did he make this choice?

| Context | Action |
|---|---|
| There were some members of the Committee of Public Safety, such as Saint-Just and Couthon, who did not want the Terror to end.<br>The *sans-culottes* and Paris Commune continued to demand tough action against counter-revolutionaries, as they blamed them for economic hardship.<br>The *sans-culottes* had been instrumental in bringing the Jacobins to power in 1793.<br>The Law of Suspects had been introduced to appease the demands of the *sans-culottes*.<br>Robespierre had been the person who had publicly spoken most strongly in favour of Terror.<br>Although French forces had repelled enemies from French soil, the French Revolutionary Wars were far from won.<br>Many French *departments* opposed the *levée en masse*, decreed in August 1793, to raise more conscripts for the war effort. | In February–March 1794, Robespierre made the choice to continue to pursue a policy of Terror, despite calls by those close to him to end the Terror. He chose to persecute those people, such as Danton and Desmoulins, who advocated less radical action against 'enemies' of the revolution. |

Answer the following questions individually and discuss your answers in a group:

1 Why might Robespierre have believed that the *sans-culottes* would approve of his action?

2 Why might Robespierre have believed that a continuation of Terror was necessary for the war effort?

3 What do you think Robespierre might have feared would happen if he had chosen a different course of action?

4 How understandable was Robespierre's course of action, given what he understood about the situation at the time?

5 How far should the historian try to understand the context of people in the past when explaining why individuals make choices in history?

**KEY TERMS**

**Ideological**
An ideology is a system, or set, of beliefs or ideas. If something is justified on ideological grounds, it is justified based upon a set of beliefs. Someone who sticks strictly to one ideology, unwilling to change, such as Robespierre, is referred to as an ideologue.

**Utopian**
An imagined state, where everything is perfect.

## Robespierre and Saint-Just defend the Terror

Although all the members of the Committee of Public Safety share some blame for their role in implementing the Terror, none more than Robespierre provided the Terror with its **ideological** justification. To Robespierre, the Terror was not cruel or excessive, but an entirely necessary part of the process of creating a **utopian** society. He believed in Jean-Jacques Rousseau's idea of the 'general will', a concept that implied that the long-term good of society was more important than the short-term position of the individual.

**SOURCE 9** In his most famous speech to the Convention, on 5 February 1794, Robespierre outlined his view of what a utopian society would look like.

In our country, we want to substitute morality for egoism [selfishness], honesty for the love of honour, principles for convention, duties for decorum, the empire of reason for the tyranny of fashion, the fear of vice for the dread of unimportance: we want to substitute pride for insolence [rudeness], magnanimity [generosity] for vanity, the love of glory for the love of gold: we want to replace good company by good character, intrigue by merit, wit by genius, brilliance by truth, dull debauchery by the charm of happiness... we would create one [people] that is happy, powerful and stout-hearted, and replace the vices and follies of the monarchy by the virtues and astounding achievements of the republic.

Robespierre believed that it was his, and the Committee's, duty to lead France towards the vision expressed in Source 9. As it was he who held this higher truth, to oppose him meant that you were opposing **virtue** and were therefore an enemy of the revolution. This is what, in Robespierre's mind, made Terror a necessity. For utopia to be reached, all enemies and opponents had to perish. In 1794, Robespierre still believed that the time had not arrived for Terror to be relaxed, as the virtuous society was not yet complete.

### KEY TERM

**Virtue**
Behaviour showing high moral standards. When Robespierre spoke of virtue, he used it to refer to a collective state of high moral standards, a Republic of Virtue, where his utopian vision would be a reality.

### SOURCE 10

**In the same speech, Robespierre attempted to justify the continuation of the Terror, arguing that virtue could not be achieved without the application of Terror.**

If the basis of popular government in peacetime is virtue, its basis in a time of revolution is both virtue and terror - virtue, without which terror is disastrous, and terror, without which virtue has no power... Terror is merely justice, prompt, severe and inflexible. It is therefore an emanation [the origin] of virtue, and results from the application of democracy to the most pressing needs of the country.

Yet Robespierre was not alone in his impassioned and articulate defence of Terror. Saint-Just was Robespierre's closest friend and political ally during the Terror. They would often meet and talk at great length. It is hard to determine the extent to which Saint-Just influenced Robespierre's beliefs, or whether Saint-Just simply followed where Robespierre led. Saint-Just did, no doubt, have radical views of his own. He had led the call in the Convention for the execution of the king in September 1792 and, in an act pre-empting the Law of Prairial (see below), he had tried to remove the Girondins' right to defence during their trial of October 1793.

Saint-Just's speeches and writings of 1794, in which he strongly advocated the continuation of Terror, very much compare with the ideology of Robespierre. In March 1794, in a public speech, Saint-Just said: 'the revolution will devour every single friend of tyranny; not a single patriot will perish through justice... Leniency is ferocious because it threatens the Fatherland.' In saying this, Saint-Just was echoing Robespierre's sentiments that all true patriots, true republicans, had nothing to fear from the Terror, and that Terror was necessary to save France. Like Robespierre, he also believed that they were working towards creating a utopian society in which all would be happy. The Terror was simply a means to an end, a necessary part of the revolutionary process. In 1794, Saint-Just clearly did not believe this necessity was over, as he wrote in his private notes: 'No doubt it is not yet time to do good.'

### EXTEND YOUR KNOWLEDGE

**Control through fear or fascination?**
There can be no doubt that, during the Reign of Terror, many French people were controlled through fear. In a culture where any dissent could result in death, many people would certainly conform in order to protect themselves and their families. However, the radicalism of the period also had many ardent supporters, of all classes. It should not be forgotten that many of the extreme measures introduced came about due to pressure from the working classes of the *sans-culottes*. It was not just Robespierre and Saint-Just who dreamed of, and advocated, a virtuous revolutionary society. There was a revolutionary culture that ran deeper into people's everyday lives than some of the political goings-on in Paris.

Around the country, people began to call one another 'citizen', rather than using traditional titles. Whereas some people would conform to this convention for fear of suspicion if they did not, undoubtedly others did so because of the feeling of togetherness and equality that the title implied. Letters were ended with the words 'Greetings and brotherhood' rather than the more formal and submissive 'Your most humble and obedient servant'. Streets were renamed (over 1,400 in Paris alone) to remove any mention of the names of kings, queens or saints. Fashions also changed: jewellery and powdered wigs went out, long trousers and the red 'liberty' bonnet came in. Even playing cards were changed to reflect revolutionary values. While such cultural changes were centred most strongly on Paris, they probably spread as time progressed and fashions caught on.

### SOURCE 11

**The radicalism of 1793–94 penetrated into people's everyday lives. On these playing cards from the period, images of kings and queens have been removed to be replaced by the virtues of the revolution, with words referring to 'freedom', 'industry', 'liberty' and 'equality'. The card at the bottom right of the image reads 'Égalité de Couleurs' ('Freedom of Colour') and features a liberated slave. The French government abolished slavery in 1794, earlier than many European countries.**

## The Great Terror

### Increasing centralisation

With the Hébertist and Indulgent factions quashed, the Committee was free to pursue a policy of increasing Terror and centralisation. In March 1794, a General Police Bureau was created in Paris tasked with the responsibility of gathering intelligence to unearth more enemies of the revolution. Although, in theory, the bureau was answerable to the Committee of Public Safety, more commonly its members simply reported directly to Robespierre. The Police Bureau therefore gave Robespierre a powerful weapon with which to denounce and arrest his opponents. Furthermore, the Paris Commune, which had been dominated by Hébert and his supporters, was filled with those loyal to Robespierre and the Committee. The Cordeliers Club was closed down, the Parisian *armée révolutionnaire* was disbanded and representatives on mission were recalled to Paris. The Law of Frimaire had already greatly increased central control over the French provinces and, on 8 May 1794, a further law was passed that gave the Parisian Tribunal exclusive jurisdiction over counter-revolutionary trials. Provincial revolutionary tribunals were shut down.

SOURCE 12

*Executing the Executioner*, a contemporary French engraving by an unknown artist. The engraving shows that, with no-one else left to guillotine, Robespierre personally executes the executioner. The inscription on the monument behind Robespierre translates as 'Here lies all of France'. Producing anti-Robespierre propaganda such as this would have been a highly dangerous thing to do.

### Legislation of the Great Terror

There were assassination attempts on Robespierre's life on two consecutive days, on 23 and 24 May 1794. Robespierre had long been aware of reports that some people wished him dead, but these attempts unnerved him. According to some contemporaries, Robespierre became increasingly paranoid, seeing conspiracies everywhere. Sempronius Gracchus, a young militant and friend of Robespierre who would later lead his own radical faction (see page 252), said that Robespierre 'could talk only of assassination, once again of assassination, always of assassination. He was frightened that even his own shadow would assassinate him.' This fear may go some way to explain why Robespierre, along with Couthon, drafted the Law of Prairial.

The Law of 22 Prairial (10 June 1794), also known as the 'Law of the Great Terror', altered the legal process in a manner that greatly undermined the rights of anyone who stood accused at the Tribunal. It was deemed that a defence hearing was no longer necessary during a trial. Only the case of the prosecution could be heard and any witnesses presented by the prosecution could not be cross-examined or questioned by the defence. Furthermore, juries were given the power to pass verdict not simply on the basis of the material evidence presented, but also upon their own moral judgements of the defendants' actions and characters.

The Law of Prairial heralded a new era of Terror. Centred on Paris, the Great Terror is the name given to the period when the process of revolutionary justice was at its most severe. In June and July 1794, the Revolutionary Tribunal sent 1,594 people to the guillotine, a figure over 50 percent higher than the previous 14 months put together.

## Conclusion

It would be hard to blame Robespierre for all the crimes and atrocities committed during the early months of 1794. He was, after all, an open critic of de-Christianisation and the violence that surrounded it. Instead, this was very much led by the *sans-culottes*, the *armées révolutionnaires* and the representatives on mission. The devastating revenge enacted on the Vendée can also be attributed more to the actions of representatives in the provinces than to the government in Paris. However, it was the Committee of Public Safety that had created this machinery of Terror. As highlighted in the introduction to this section, establishing the extent of responsibility of individuals within the Committee of Public Safety can be problematic. Robespierre did not act alone within the Committee, Saint-Just and Couthon pushed for Terror, just as Robespierre did.

What is clear, though, is that Robespierre was the spokesperson for the Terror. It was he who made the speeches and provided the philosophical arguments for its continuation, and he did so in a passionate and convincing manner. Even at a time when others, including his closest friends, called for an end to the killing and persecution, Robespierre refused to recant, choosing instead to escalate the Terror. Whether he did this through a profound, if misguided, sense of moral duty or for fear of his own political position (or even his life), is another debate in itself.

**SOURCE 13** In July 1793, Robespierre recorded the following in his private notes. In the extract he poses questions to himself and then answers them.

What is our aim? It is to use the Constitution for the benefit of the people. Who are likely to oppose us? The rich and corrupt. What methods will they employ? Slander and hypocrisy. What factors will encourage the use of such means? The ignorance of the *sans-culottes*. The people must therefore be instructed. What obstacles are there to its [the *sans-culottes*'] enlightenment? The paid journalists, who mislead it every day by shameless impostures [deception]. What conclusion follows? That we ought to proscribe those writers as the most dangerous enemies of the country and to circulate an abundance of good literature. What other obstacle is there to the instruction [education] of the people? Its poverty. When, then, will the people be educated? When it has enough bread to eat, and when the rich and the government cease bringing treacherous pens and tongues to deceive it; when their interests are identified with those of the people. When will this be? Never. What other obstacles are there to the achievement of freedom? The war at home and abroad. By what means can this war be ended? By placing republican generals at the head of our armies, and by punishing those who have betrayed us. How can we end the civil war? By punishing traitors and conspirators, especially those deputies and administrators who are to blame; by sending patriot troops under patriot leaders to reduce the aristocrats of Lyon, Marseilles, Toulon, the Vendée, the Jura, and all other districts where the banner of royalism and rebellion has been raised; and by making a terrible example of all the criminals who have outraged liberty, and spilt the blood of patriots.

**AS Level Exam-Style Question Section B**

How far was the Terror a consequence of the actions of the *sans-culottes*? (20 marks)

**Tip**

*When addressing essay questions on the Terror, it is useful to think of the period in three phases. The first is the purge of the Girondins, the rise of the Jacobins and the creation of the early instruments of Terror (the Committee of Public Safety, the representatives on mission, the watch committees). The second is when the Reign of Terror escalated greatly following the Law of Suspects. The final phase is that of the Great Terror in June/July 1794. For each of these phases, assess the extent to which it was the* sans-culottes *or other factors, groups or individuals driving the Terror.*

**ACTIVITY**
**KNOWLEDGE CHECK**

**To what extent was Robespierre the driving force of the Terror?**

1 The following arguments could be made to support the proposition that Robespierre was to blame for the Terror. For each one, add some supporting information. This could be references to specific events or details, and/or a quotation.

**a)** Robespierre was a leading member of the Committee of Public Safety, the body that created the instruments of the Terror.

**b)** Robespierre allowed no political opposition to his rule. He purged those who dared to question his authority.

**c)** Robespierre continued to push for more Terror, even when others argued that the time had come to end it.

**d)** Robespierre provided the ideological justification for the Terror.

**e)** Robespierre played a key role in creating the law and institutions that directly led to the Great Terror.

2 For each of the arguments above, try to think of a counter-argument that could be made to challenge it directly. For example, for (a), you could counter-argue by writing that 'Robespierre was not appointed to the Committee until July 1793 and a number of key instruments of Terror, such as the representatives on mission and the Revolutionary Tribunal, were created before this time. Also, Robespierre did not act alone on the Committee. Couthon and Saint-Just also played important roles in advocating Terror.' Note how, in this example, specific details are used to support the counter-argument.

3 Now consider other aspects of the Terror that were not driven by Robespierre at all and use these to write arguments suggesting that the Terror was not his fault. Consider: de-Christianisation, the suppression of the Vendée and the federalist revolts, and the role of the *sans-culottes*.

4 Use your answers to arrive at an overall judgement about the extent to which Robespierre was to blame for the Terror.

## WHAT TRIGGERED THE END OF TERROR?

At his trial before the Revolutionary Tribunal, Danton had warned: 'You will follow us, Robespierre.' His prediction was right. On 9 Thermidor Year II (27 July 1794), Robespierre, Saint-Just, Couthon and 19 other Jacobins fell victim to the guillotine. In the following three days, another 104 supporters of Robespierre were executed. The Terror devoured its own.

Robespierre's fall, in what is known as the Coup of Thermidor, marked the end of the Jacobin Terror. We have already seen some of the causes of Robespierre's fall emerging. Opposition to Terror had grown from late 1793, accusations of dictatorship became louder, and divisions had emerged surrounding de-Christianisation and the direction of the revolution more generally. Through the purges of the Hébertists and the Indulgents, the Committee had quelled some of the open opposition to its rule, but in doing so it only fuelled further accusations of tyranny. The deaths of Danton and Desmoulins, in particular, caused many to question the judgement of the Committee. It was the events of June and July 1794, though, that would trigger the Coup of Thermidor and bring about the end of the Terror.

## Growing economic and political fear

### Economic discontent

*Sans-culotte* discontent at the removal and execution of the leaders with whom they had most closely associated themselves, notably Danton and Hébert, was exacerbated by growing economic pressures. The value of the assignats continued to drop and the Commune, now loyal to Robespierre, began to impose a maximum on wages. The limitation of wages was not a new decree, but the Commune when staffed by the Hébertists had not enforced any such controls. The new Commune did so. The application of the maximum caused wages to drop significantly, by as much as half their value. Furthermore, the Committee raised the maximum on the price of goods, causing inflation. With prices rising and wages falling, the popularity of Robespierre and the Committee with the working classes rapidly fell.

### The Cult of the Supreme Being

By June 1794, Robespierre and the Committee of Public Safety were at the height of their power and, with the likes of radical de-Christianisers such as Hébert and Roux out of the way, Robespierre was free to pursue the religious policy he desired. As already highlighted, Robespierre believed in neither the extreme atheism of the de-Christianising *sans-culottes* nor the traditions and conventions of Catholicism. He did believe, though, in the existence of God and in the importance of religion in encouraging moral behaviour and controlling society. As a result, he attempted to create a new religion, known as the Cult of the Supreme Being. All other religions were banned. To inaugurate this new religion, Robespierre planned a major festival.

Neither the Cult nor the Festival of the Supreme Being had the effect that Robespierre hoped in unifying the citizens of France through collective religion. To the atheists of the *sans-culottes*, the Cult was an abomination. To Catholics, this was a further attack on their religion. Catholicism had, essentially, been made illegal (a far cry from the freedom of belief promised by the Declaration of the Rights of Man in 1789). To others, the Cult of the Supreme Being was simply confusing. It lacked a clear system of belief and, because it was an artificial and state-imposed religion, many French people opposed it.

Furthermore, the Cult of the Supreme Being only added to accusations that Robespierre had become a power-crazed dictator. At the Festival, Robespierre personally led the ceremony, putting himself centre stage. To some, it looked like the Supreme Being was not God but Robespierre himself.

### Division within the Committee of Public Safety

In June 1794, divisions began to appear within the Committee of Public Safety. Following the Law of Prairial, there was quarrelling within the Committee. Lazare Carnot accused Robespierre and Saint-Just of being absurd dictators. Collot d'Herbois, another leading member of the Committee of Public Safety, was, as a radical de-Christianiser, appalled by the Cult of the Supreme Being. The Committee of General Security were also angered by the Law of Prairial. It had not been consulted over the law and, as the body responsible for revolutionary justice, this lay clearly within its remit. The Committee of General Security was also being increasingly sidelined, as Robespierre's Police Bureau began to take over its responsibilities.

SOURCE

14 A painting of the Festival of the Supreme Being from 1794, by the French artist Pierre-Antoine Demachy. Held on 8 June 1794, on the Champs de Mars, the Festival of the Supreme Being signified the birth of a new French religion. The event was designed on a massive scale. Under the artistic direction of Jacques-Louis David, a staged set, including the mountain seen in this image, was constructed. A woman, representing Liberty, was paraded through the crowds on a grand carriage.

It was also around this time that Saint-Just was sent on mission to oversee the war effort in Belgium, leaving Robespierre lacking one of his closest and most effective allies. As his support in the Committee waned, Robespierre began increasingly to distance himself from it. He attended less frequently, choosing instead to spend his time at his Police Bureau, and he reserved his public speech-making for the Jacobin Club. Robespierre was physically ill during this time, but the extent to which his illness or his avoidance of his opponents within the Committee determined his absence is uncertain.

Meanwhile, the Great Terror continued and Robespierre's Police Bureau drew up lists of 'suspects' at an ever-increasing rate. To be named on such a list was effectively a death sentence. Those who stood in opposition to Robespierre, Collot d'Herbois in particular, began to fear for their own lives.

### Robespierre under pressure

Collot d'Herbois, alongside Fouché, a member of the Convention, had been largely responsible for the atrocities committed in Lyon following the federalist revolt, atrocities that even Robespierre had condemned. Fouché, Collot d'Herbois and Jean-Nicolas Billaud-Varenne, another member of the Committee of Public Safety, decided to strike Robespierre's faction before they were themselves struck. They fabricated a story that Robespierre was under the influence of a woman called Catherine Théot.

Théot was an elderly woman of Paris who was convinced that she was destined to give birth to the next messiah. Despite, according to some accounts, being insane, she had built a sect of religious fanatics around her. Fouché and his allies alleged that Robespierre was under her influence and this was why he was trying to restore religion to France. They attempted to bring Théot to trial, hoping that such a trial would also name and indict Robespierre.

Robespierre discovered news of the plot. In the middle of the night, he called for Fouquier-Tinville, the chief prosecutor of the Revolutionary Tribunal, and informed him that the trial was not to go ahead. Fouquier-Tinville, fearing for his own position and safety, agreed. Despite quashing the possibility of a potentially damaging trial, Robespierre knew then for sure that his enemies were conspiring against him.

## The arrest and execution of Robespierre

Events came to a head when, on 26 July 1794, Robespierre appeared at the Convention. He told the assembly that he knew the names of more traitors of the revolution. When he was asked to name them, he refused. This proved to be a fatal error as by refusing to name who these enemies were Robespierre made everyone in the Convention feel vulnerable: they knew that any denunciation would likely spell death. The next day, 9 Thermidor Year II, desperate men, including Collot and Fouché, knowing that it was Robespierre's life or theirs, took the offensive. When Robespierre and Saint-Just (who had returned from Belgium) tried to speak to the assembly, their voices were drowned out by cries of 'Down with the tyrant'. Collot d'Herbois, as President of the Convention, gave them no chance to speak in defence of themselves. The Convention swiftly proceeded to vote for the arrest of Robespierre and his colleagues, including Saint-Just, Couthon, Augustin Robespierre (Maximilien's brother) and 18 others.

Robespierre and his supporters were taken to a prison controlled by the Commune but, proving that they still had significant support, the gaolers refused to imprison them and they were allowed to escape to the Hôtel de Ville. Once there, Robespierre untypically failed to take the initiative. He could have tried to call the sections of Paris to insurrection in protest at his arrest, but he did not. As a result, the Hôtel de Ville was stormed by the National Guard and the men were arrested for a second time. There is some confusion about what happened at the Hôtel de Ville that evening. Robespierre's jaw was shot off. Some accounts claim this was due to a failed suicide attempt, others suggest he was shot by one of the guards. Either way, the next day (28 July), witnessed by a huge crowd, Robespierre and his brother Augustin were beheaded by guillotine, followed by Saint-Just, then Couthon, and then their other close associates.

**SOURCE 15**

Following Robespierre's execution, Jean-Nicolas Billaud-Varenne reflected on how Robespierre had managed to rise to such a position of ultimate power. Billaud-Varenne had been a significant member of the Committee of Public Safety, who worked alongside Robespierre and is often considered to be one of the architects of the Terror.

Let us ask, as already has been done, why we allowed Robespierre to go so far. Not one single fact has been established, nor one single proof given, to justify that that man's power was our work. Have we forgotten that, from the time of the Constituent Assembly, he had already enjoyed an immense popularity, and that he obtained the title of the Incorruptible? Have we forgotten that, during the Legislative Assembly, his popularity only increased with the help of a very widely-known journal of which he was editor and through his frequent speeches to the Jacobins [Club]? Have we forgotten that, in the National Convention, Robespierre before long was the man who, fixing all regard upon his own person, gained so much confidence that it rendered [made] him preponderant [influential], to such an extent that when he came to the Committee of Public Safety, he was already the most important man in France? If someone asked me how he had succeeded in gaining so much ascendency [rise to power] over public opinion, I would answer that it was by displaying the most austere [strict] virtues, the most absolute devotion and the purest principles.

**AS Level Exam-Style Question Section A**

***Study Source 15 before you answer this question.***

How much weight would you give the evidence of Source 15 for an enquiry into the extent of Robespierre's role in the Terror?

Explain your answer using the source, the information given about it and your own knowledge of the historical context. (12 marks)

**Tip**

*As well as using your contextual knowledge to expand on the points Billaud-Varenne raises regarding Robespierre's role, also consider Billaud-Varenne's motives for composing such an account after Robespierre's fall. Why do you think he emphasises that Robespierre had huge power and influence even before he joined the Committee of Public Safety (a body of which Billaud-Varenne was a member)?*

## Thermidorean government established

Those who had helped overthrow Robespierre and his associates are known as the Thermidoreans. Some were members of the Committee, but far more were from The Plain of the Convention. Many opposed the Terror so, with Robespierre gone, the Convention aimed to bring about its end. The practitioners of the Terror who had not fallen with Robespierre were called upon by the Convention to defend their actions. Sixty-three were sentenced to death. Some, like Fouché, partly responsible for the Terror in Lyon, managed to defend themselves. Others, including Collot d'Herbois, were exiled to Guyana, a French colony in South America. Many former associates of The Mountain rejected their prior beliefs in an attempt at self-preservation. The result was that the political mood of the Convention swiftly became more moderate following the Coup of Thermidor.

The Convention set about abolishing the instruments of the Terror. The Thermidoreans repealed the Law of Prairial. In August 1794, the Revolutionary Tribunals were purged of Jacobin influence and all imprisoned suspects, many thousands, were released. In November, the Jacobin Club was closed down. The following month, maximum price restrictions on all goods were removed. Girondin deputies who had not been killed during the purges were restored to the Convention. Many within the Convention also opposed the radicalism of the *sans-culottes*, including de-Christianisation. On 21 February 1795, they restored freedom of worship and officially sanctioned the end of the Cult of the Supreme Being. In an attempt to avoid another emerging dictatorship, the Convention decreed that a quarter of the Committee of Public Safety had to change each month. They also abolished the Paris Commune, recognising quite rightly that it was the Commune that had often played a key role in the insurrections of the *sans-culottes*.

## Conclusion

Robespierre's fall, and the ensuing end of the Terror, was a culmination of many causes. Weariness of the Terror, anger over de-Christianisation and the purging of revolutionary figureheads all played a part. Perhaps the most significant cause, though, was Robespierre's increasing personal domination of politics. After the purge of the Indulgents, Robespierre began behaving increasingly like a dictator. The Cult of the Supreme Being, the Law of Prairial, the Police Bureau, the Great Terror: all of these could be strongly attributed to Robespierre personally. As he began to act with seemingly less concern for the mood of the Convention and the Committee, opposition grew. Yet the final trigger of his fall was fear: fear from the deputies of the Convention that no-one was safe from Robespierre's denunciations. When this fear erupted into action on 26 July 1794, Robespierre's fall was a swift one.

**ACTIVITY**
**KNOWLEDGE CHECK**

**What triggered the end of the Terror?**

1. Why did the Cult and Festival of the Supreme Being increase opposition to Robespierre's government?
2. Why else did opposition to Robespierre grow in 1794?
3. As the fall of Robespierre and Saint-Just happened so rapidly, they were given neither a trial before the Tribunal nor a chance to speak in their own defence at the Convention. Imagine this had not been the case.
   a) In a small group, prepare and stage a mock trial at the Tribunal. The case for the prosecution could be led by Collot d'Herbois and Fouché, though they may wish to call in other witnesses. How would they argue that Robespierre and Saint-Just were enemies of the revolution? What specific events and actions might they refer to in order to prove the accused's crimes?
   b) Robespierre and Saint-Just would lead their own defence (but would not be allowed to call any witnesses as the Law of Prairial had removed such a right for suspects). How would they justify their actions (use the information on pages 232–33 for ideas)? Who, or what, might they choose to blame instead to reduce their own culpability?
   c) Finally, a jury would need to arrive at a verdict. Do you think Robespierre and Saint-Just would have had any chance of being found innocent?

ACTIVITY
SUMMARY

**The National Convention and the Terror, 1793–94**

For each of the events below, create a revision flash card. On one side of the card, write the name of the event; on the reverse, write down its **date**, its **causes**, **details** about what happened (or its function) and what the **consequences** of that event were.

Cover: the War of the First Coalition; the revolt in the Vendée; Federalist revolts; the creation of representatives on mission, the Revolutionary Tribunal and watch committees; the creation of the Committee of Public Safety; the purge of the Girondins; the *levée en masse*; the creation of *armeés révolutionnaires*; the Law of Suspects; the Law of Frimaire; de-Christianisation; the purge of the Hébertists; the purge of the Indulgents; the Law of Prairial; the Coup of Thermidor; the establishment of the Thermidorean government.

These cards can then be used in a number of different ways. First, use them to consolidate your knowledge, using the 'look, cover, write and check' method, whereby you read the card, then cover it up, write what you can remember and then check your accuracy. Repeat this method until you can accurately recall all the necessary detail. Once you are confident with your knowledge, place all the cards in chronological order without looking at the dates. Then explain how each event leads to or is in some way related to the next, working your way through all the cards to tell the 'story' of the period to a classmate.

**WIDER READING**

Andress, D. *The Terror: Civil War in the French Revolution*, Abacus (2005) A highly detailed and authoritative academic study of the Terror

Doyle, W. and Haydon, C. (eds) *Robespierre*, Cambridge University Press (1999) A series of academic essays; chapter 10 by Norman Hampson on 'Robespierre and the Terror' is particularly relevant

Gough, G. *The Terror in the French Revolution* (Studies in European History series), Palgrave (1998) A readable and brief (79 pages) analysis of a key episode, with a detailed chronology of 1789-96

Martin, D. *The French Revolution*, Hodder Education (2013) An A Level textbook covering the whole period to 1799; chapter 8 addresses the Terror

Scurr, R. *Fatal Purity: Robespierre and the French Revolution*, Random House (2006) An engaging and highly readable biography of Robespierre

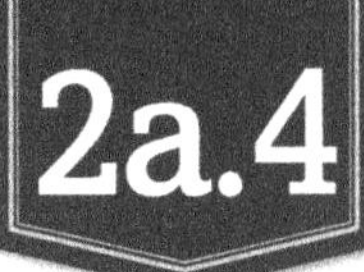


# From the Directory to Brumaire, 1795–99

## KEY QUESTIONS

- Did the Directory face insurmountable problems in 1795?
- How far did the Directory manage to achieve moderation?
- Was the Directory's dependence on the military unavoidable?
- Why was the Directory overthrown in November 1799?

After the Coup of Thermidor, the revolutionary artist Jacques-Louis David was arrested and imprisoned due to his close association with Robespierre's faction. As a personal friend of both Marat and Robespierre, David was lucky to escape execution (and perhaps only did due to his profession as an artist rather than a politician). While incarcerated in 1795, David began planning one of his most famous images: *The Intervention of the Sabine Women* (Source 1).

The painting depicts a legendary story from the beginnings of Ancient Rome. In front of the Capitol fortress of Rome, the Roman army fights against the Sabines, a local race. Central to the composition is a Sabine woman, Hersilia. She is leaping between her father, King Tatius of the Sabines, and her husband, Romulus, the founder and king of Rome. She, and other Sabine women, plead for an end to the conflict and for reconciliation between the two peoples. In the legend, Hersilia and the Sabine women's calls were heeded, and Romulus and Tatius agreed to put their grievances aside and join as one people. Towards the right of the image, a Roman soldier on horseback can be seen returning his sword to its sheath, whereas another warrior turns his horse around, leading it away from battle. In the background, helmets and hands are raised in a gesture of peace.

This historical allegory was much more than simply a romanticised classical painting. David was presenting a political statement about France and the failures of the revolution. Like Hersilia, David was making a plea for peace and reconciliation. Factionalism and divisions, economic, religious and political, had driven France apart in 1793 and 1794. Terror, persecution and civil war had characterised the period. By 1795, many people shared David's vision that the time had come to end conflict and to unite. So, when a new French constitution was fashioned in 1795, it was intended to prevent dictatorship, preserve the republic and steer a moderate course between the extremes of radical Jacobinism and royalism. The message was not lost on the people of Paris as, when the painting was first publicly displayed in the Louvre in 1799, it attracted large numbers of paying visitors and remained on display for the next six years.

The post-Thermidorean government created in 1795 was led by a five-man **executive** called the Directory. Despite general revulsion at the extremes of the Terror, and a common desire for a return

**1794** - December: Thermidorean Convention removes price controls causing inflation

**1795** - 1 April The Rising of Germinal; Parisians protest over bread shortages

**1795** - 22 August: The new constitution comes into effect

**1795** - Winter: Dire weather leads to famine

**1795** - September: The Comte d'Artois, Louis XVI's brother, launches an unsuccessful *émigré* invasion of the Vendée

**1796** - May: The Babeuf plot fails to incite a major rebellion; the Babouvist leaders are arrested

1794 | 1795 | 1796 | 1797

**1795** - Jacobins are persecuted in the White Terror

**1795** - 20 May: The Rising of Prairial; a demonstration in Paris is suppressed by government forces

**1795** - June: The Comte de Provence, King Louis XVI's brother, declares himself King Louis XVIII while in exile
June: The Convention allows military courts to be used for civil trials
28 June: An *émigré* invasion at Quiberon Bay is defeated by government forces

**1795** - 5 October: The Vendémiaire Rising is crushed by Vicomte de Barras and Napoleon Bonaparte

**1796** - Summer: The Chouannerie rebellion in Brittany is finally supressed

**1797** - February: The government scraps all paper currency in an effort to end inflation

**SOURCE 1** *The Intervention of the Sabine Women* by Jacques-Louis David was first publicly displayed in 1799, but reflects Jacques-Louis David's desires for France while he was imprisoned in 1795.

to moderation, the Directory's task was not an easy one. The economic decline was unrelenting, the War of the First Coalition continued, civil war in the provinces persisted and, as well as having to tackle Jacobinism, the Directory also had to contend with a resurgence of royalist feeling. In this chapter, we explore how the government attempted to overcome these challenges and aim to explain why the Directory failed when it was overthrown by a coup in 1799.

**KEY TERM**

**Executive**
The part of the government that held the most senior responsibilities, the executive was responsible for the daily administration of the state and the enforcement of the law. Often the executive's responsibilities included foreign affairs and defence. In France from 1795 to 1799, the executive part of the government was called the Directory.

**1797** - September: The government declares itself bankrupt, wiping out some debts but causing opposition
September: The royalists are purged from the Councils in the Coup of Fructidor

**1797** - 17 October: The Treaty of Campo-Formio concludes Napoleon's successful Italian campaign against the Austrians

**1798** - May: Napoleon launches his Egyptian campaign
11 May: The Directors overturn election results to purge Jacobins from the Councils in the Coup of Floréal

**1798** - 5 September: A new conscription laws leads to unrest, especially in the conquered territories

**1799** - June Jourdan's Law declares a *levée en masse*, increasing discontent about conscription

**1799** - July: The Law of Hostages allows for arbitrary arrest but leads to accusations of tyranny against the government

**1799** - October: Napoleon returns to Paris after his unsuccessful Syrian campaign

**1799** - 9 November :The Coup of Brumaire leads to the collapse of the Directory; Napoleon, Abbé Sieyès and Roger Ducos seize power

**1799** - 24 December: The constitution of the Consulate is presented to France by Napoleon

1798 1799 1800

# DID THE DIRECTORY FACE INSURMOUNTABLE PROBLEMS IN 1795?

With the Jacobin Terror at an end, the Thermidorean Convention began the process of writing a new constitution for France. This constitution came into effect on 22 August 1795, the new government to be led by an executive body called the Directory, consisting of five Directors. Even before the Directory was established, new problems were emerging within France and old ones were resurfacing. This section explores the challenges of the period 1794–95 and questions whether or not the Directory faced insurmountable problems from the very start.

## Political violence and the White Terror

The White Terror is the name given to the anti-Jacobin backlash that followed the collapse of Jacobin power in July 1794. White was the colour that represented the Bourbon royal family and so is the name given to this backlash. However, the name is slightly misleading as the White Terror was not exclusively a royalist reaction. While some *émigrés* and refractory priests did return to France to take advantage of the fall of the Jacobins, many of the perpetrators of the White Terror were not intent on restoring the monarchy.

It is hardly surprising that the anti-Jacobin backlash occurred most strongly in areas where the Jacobin Terror had been at its most extreme. In Paris, where the Great Terror had been largely centred, vigilante gangs of youths sought out, attacked and intimidated the Jacobins and *sans-culottes* who had played a role in driving the Terror. These youths were known as *jeunesse dorée*, meaning 'gilded youth', and, unlike the *sans-culottes*, tended to be from the bourgeois classes: many were clerks, financiers or law officials. As with the *sans-culottes*, the *jeunesse dorée* were encouraged by certain journalists, namely Louis Fréron, whose journal *L'Orateur du Peuple* ('The Spokesman of the People') advocated continual harassment of Jacobin supporters. Fréron, though, was not a royalist. While supporting the persecution of the Jacobins (with a striking level of hypocrisy, see below), Fréron was still an ardent republican.

### EXTEND YOUR KNOWLEDGE

**Louis Fréron (1754–1802)**

Louis Fréron came from a wealthy Parisian family. His father had been a successful journalist and saw to it that his son received an excellent education. Fréron followed in his father's footsteps and, in 1789, established his own newspaper *L'Orateur du peuple*.

During the constitutional monarchy phase of the revolution, *L'Orateur*, much like the publications of Marat and Desmoulins, heavily attacked the shortcomings of the new constitutional reforms. The newspaper also called for the execution of King Louis and the establishment of a republic, following Louis' abortive flight from Paris in June 1791.

After Louis' fall in August 1792, Fréron was elected to the National Convention and became a prominent member of The Mountain, as well as a close associate of Robespierre. He was sent as representative on mission to both Marseille and Toulon, where he oversaw the mass execution of hundreds of suspected counter-revolutionaries. Robespierre recalled Fréron from his mission to account for the severity of his actions. Fearing for this own life, Fréron turned on Robespierre, allying himself instead with Fouché and Collot d'Herbois, and he played an active role in the Coup of Thermidor.

Following the execution of the Robespierrists, Fréron used his newspaper to call for the harassment, imprisonment and execution of the remaining Jacobins. There was no small degree of hypocrisy in this as the Jacobin cause, and the Terror associated with it, had indeed been Fréron's cause for many years. By so strongly aligning himself against the Jacobins during the Thermidorean Reaction, Fréron managed to avoid being brought to justice for his own terrorist activities. He died of natural causes in 1802.

The *jeunesse dorée* also developed their own sub-culture, with a particular style of dress and their own songs and ballads, all of which were intentionally in stark contrast to the styles and insignia of the Jacobins and *sans-culottes*. By failing to act against them, the Directory almost granted a licence for *jeunesse dorée* violence. Due to the general revulsion created by the Terror, few were willing to speak up in defence of the Jacobins or *sans-culottes* 'terrorists'. Furthermore, the actions of the *jeunesse dorée* had a symbolic political importance: representing the shift of the political balance away from the radical politics of Jacobinism. This shift was one that the Thermidorean Convention, and later the Directory, were keen to embrace.

SOURCE

In his memoirs, written between 1830 and his death in 1838, the former Jacobin deputy of The Mountain, Pierre-René Choudieu, presented a critical view of the *jeunesse dorée*.

Fréron [a deputy often-cited as the leader of the *jeunesse dorée*] gave the watchword to the 'gilded youth', as they called the group he had organised. As a rallying sign these young people wore their hair in what they called 'victim style', that is to say well-powdered and braided at the back of the head, in contrast to the style of the patriots who wore their hair short and without powder. In imitation of the leaders of the Vendée they wore coats with black collars; nothing but a white cockade was needed for an open declaration of counter-revolution. Fréron's army consisted of enthusiastic young men who had never had anything to lose, but claimed to be pathetic victims of the Terror, with a duty to avenge their relatives who had died on the scaffold. The functions of this group were to police the Palais-Royal and the Tuileries gardens daily and to sing the 'People's Awakening', every verse of which called for the death of the republicans, whom they called 'terrorists'. The chorus ended with the words: 'They shall not escape us!' In their leisure moments they amused themselves with a dance which they called a 'farandole'. Anyone who refused to join in was picked up and thrown in the water troughs. Worthy exploits for such an army! Fréron altered his allegiance but not his character. He demanded in the Convention that the Hôtel de Ville of Paris should be torn down because it had sheltered Robespierre. He also wanted the Jacobins' club demolished.

It was not only Paris that experienced the White Terror. In Lyon, Marseilles and Toulon, cities where the memories of Jacobin atrocities were still fresh, gangs brawled with government troops and destroyed the properties of eminent Jacobins. In Lyon and the Rhône valley, the White Terror was of a particularly bloody and violent nature. In 1795, prison murders in Lyon killed hundreds and, in the Rhône valley, murder gangs would ambush victims before depositing their corpses into the river. The government and local officials turned a blind eye. In Marseilles, alleged supporters of Jacobinism were rounded up and imprisoned. The prisons were then attacked and over 100 prisoners were killed.

SOURCE

Although Louis Fréron encouraged the backlash against Jacobinism in Paris, he was shocked by what he witnessed in Marseilles, while working there as a government representative in 1794–95. In his memoirs, published in 1796, Fréron presents the view of the White Terror in Marseilles as a royalist rising.

Marseilles, worthy rival of Lyons, disgraced itself by atrocities at which nature sickens. Its prisons... were soon crammed with prisoners, most of them detained with no charge specified on the arrest warrants... The *représentant en mission* here issued a decree ordering the arrest of all persons suspected of 'terrorism'. God knows what that scope gave to the relentless aristocracy and to private vengeance. There was not one commune where, following Marseilles' example, daggers were not plunged in joy into republican hearts... Neither age nor sex were spared. Women, children and old men were ruthlessly hacked to pieces in the name of humanity by cannibals who fought over the fragments... Some of the people joined the gangs of hired murderers who went by the name of *Compagnie de Jésus* [Company of Jesus] or *Compagnie du Soleil* [Company of the Sun - French kings tended to be associated with the sun, after King Louis XIV, who was known as the Sun King]. These vile and savage perpetrators of every kind of murder committed until then penetrated into the deepest cells, they rushed upon their defenceless and starving victims. Daggers and pistols, bayonets and stilettos [a type of knife] were not enough - they loaded cannon with grapeshot and fired it point-blank into the prison yards. They threw blazing sulphur in through the ventilators; they set fire to damp straw at the entrances to the vaults where scores of prisoners were huddled and suffocated them with thick smoke. They killed, they slaughtered, they sated themselves on murder.

**A Level Exam-Style Question Section A**

***Study Sources 2 and 3 before you answer this question.***

How far could the historian make use of Sources 2 and 3 together to investigate the causes and nature of the White Terror (1794–96)?

Explain your answer, using both sources, the information given about them and your knowledge of the historical context. (20 marks)

**Tip**

*These sources suggest quite different things about the role of Fréron. How can you reconcile and explain these differences? Apply your contextual knowledge of Fréron.*

Aside from the specific documented cases from places like Lyon and Marseille, the exact scale and extent of the White Terror is largely unknown. As the deaths were unlicensed killings, unlike those executed at the behest of the Revolutionary Tribunal during 1793–94, few records were kept. An estimate of around 2,000 is often cited as the number of deaths in 1795 due to the White Terror, though this figure must be treated with caution.

## Political divisions in 1795

The political climate in Paris shifted significantly after the Coup of Thermidor. The power of the *sans-culottes* was broken. The Commune, which had been so important in mobilising and organising the *sans-culottes*, was closed down. The *sans-culottes* were closely associated with the atrocities and persecution of the Terror, from which politicians were very keen to distance themselves.

No longer did the government wish to use *sans-culotte* support as a means of legitimising their authority, as the Jacobins had done.

In 1794, the Jacobin leadership had been purged. Those not killed during the Coup of Thermidor were prosecuted over the following months. This included two of the men who had played a key role in leading the coup against Robespierre: Billaud-Varenne and Collot d'Herbois. Both were exiled to French Guyana, in South America. Jean-Baptiste Carrier, responsible for the atrocities in the Loire, was executed.

This is not to say, though, that the power of the extreme left was completely broken. There were still those who supported the radical politics of Jacobinism and who still believed in Robespierre's utopian vision. Fouché was one such person. He lost political power during the Thermidorean Reaction, due to his association with the crimes of the Terror, but he rose again in influence to lead a new wave of Jacobinism, or neo-Jacobinism as it is sometimes known. Paris also witnessed an influx of Jacobins from the provinces. They fled there to avoid the White Terror in the provinces, hoping to be protected by the anonymity of a large city.

As well as the continuation of Jacobinism, there was a resurgence of royalism. Royalists were allowed to re-enter politics, adding a new dynamic to the political landscape, one that would later threaten the stability of the government (see page 252).

Yet extreme left- and right-wing individuals were greatly outnumbered by moderates, the deputies who had formed The Plain of the National Convention and who had often been subdued into silence due to fear of repercussions. With the machinery of the Terror destroyed, their voices could once again be heard. Abbé Sieyès re-emerged as an individual of significance and influence after relative obscurity during the Terror. A number of former Girondins, those fortunate enough to survive the purge of 1793, also returned to political prominence. New men also came forward: François-Antoine Boissy d'Anglas advocated a return to government by the propertied classes (see Source 5, page 247).

While there existed idealists amongst the deputies, far more common were pragmatic men who sought to protect the positions and profits they had gained from the revolution. This meant distancing themselves from the radicalism of the *sans-culottes* and the Jacobins. However, many of the deputies were also regicides, who had previously voted for King Louis' execution. As a result, they were fearful of a restoration of the monarchy, even of constitutional monarchy.

## Economic and financial pressures

In December 1794, the Thermidoreans had abolished price controls, such as the general maximum, pursuing instead a policy of free trade. Unfortunately, the winter of 1794–95 was a particularly bad one, causing crop failures and famine. With price controls removed, the cost of essential goods, including fuel and food, rocketed. Yet, it was the winter of 1795 that was the most devastating. Temperatures were so low that rivers froze. There simply was not enough fuel available for people to heat their homes and workplaces, or to cook their food. A sack of firewood that cost 20 livres in 1790 cost 500 livres in 1795. To compound these problems, the institutions on which the poor had relied during times of hardship under the *ancien régime*, the *parlements* and Church poor relief (paid out of the tithes collected), no longer existed. The result was malnutrition, disease, famine and death.

The removal of price controls also meant that the government was now forced to pay market prices for arms and resources for the revolutionary army. To fund this, they printed more assignats and, by doing so, caused their value to plummet even further. By May 1795, the assignat had lost 96 percent of its original value. Its value became so low that farmers would not accept the paper currency in exchange for corn. This caused hunger in towns and cities, particularly Paris, as urban officials could not use their currency to buy and import food from the surrounding rural areas. When 20 percent of Parisians were so poor that they had to rely on food relief (in the form of bread rations) from such officials, their failure to secure provisions caused both anger and starvation.

No complete demographical data exists for the entire country from which to measure the extent of the famine, but if we take the town of Rouen as an example, for which data does exist, we can get some indication of the scale of hardship. In 1794, the death rate in the town was double what it would be in a normal year. In 1795, it had increased further and was then three times higher than could usually be expected. While useful to us, these figures hide the grim and tragic human reality of famine. It would be the vulnerable who would have been most likely to perish, the old, the young and the ill. Crime and prostitution increased. In the north of France, gangs of violent bandits, known as *chauffeurs*, stalked the countryside looking for isolated travellers to rob. They had a fearsome reputation for torturing their victims by burning their feet. Similar organised banditry was seen in numerous French departments. The National Guard was often insufficiently resourced to tackle this unrest.

## Popular protest

The hardship caused by the terrible winter and depreciation of the assignat sparked two uprisings in Paris. The first, the Rising of Germinal (1 April 1795) was a peaceful protest, as 10,000 people marched on the Convention demanding bread. The arrival of the National Guard was enough to disperse the crowd.

The Rising of Prairial on 20 May 1795 was a much more serious threat to the Convention. A large crowd of *sans-culottes* surrounded the assembly, this time supported by some disloyal National Guard units, and demanded action on food shortages. The Convention made a minor concession to appease the crowd, agreeing to set up a Food Commission to investigate the problem. Yet, the Convention was no longer willing to be forced into radical change by popular unrest, so it deployed 20,000 troops, from both the National Guard and the regular army, to crush the insurrection. It succeeded in doing so, making over 6,000 arrests and forcing the crowd to disperse.

### Significance of the risings

The Risings of Germinal and Prairial illustrate a number of important things about the period. First, they show the extent of dissatisfaction and desperation at the dire economic situation. These were, essentially, spontaneous bread riots and little else. Second, they reveal how the power of the *sans-culottes* had been broken. The leaders who had organised and incited the popular movements earlier in the revolution, leaders like Marat, Hébert and Roux, were no more. Without such leadership, the risings lacked clear direction and were ineffective. Yet, they also demonstrate a more significant point. They show us that, unlike the Convention during the radical phase of the Terror, the government of the post-Thermidorean period would not be dictated to by popular protest and insurrection.

SOURCE

**4** In correspondence with his brother, the Convention deputy Nicolas Ruault recorded the following on the causes of unrest in Paris in 1795. Ruault lived in Paris throughout the revolution and his letters to his brother, dating from 1783 to 1796, were published by a historian in 1976.

Public affairs are a thousand times worse in Paris than with you, my dear friend; we are lost here in an immense gulf; between us we have a hydra with 650,000 heads and the same number of stomachs, which have been hungry now for a long time. I dare not tell you all the expressions, all the curses heard in the long queues which form every evening, every night at the baker's door, in hope of getting, after five or six hours' wait, perhaps half a pound of biscuit, perhaps half a pound of bad bread, or four ounces of rice, per person. And yet half the four or five thousand men who spend half their working day waiting for this miniscule portion of wretched food, who complained about their poverty and the horror of their existence are regarded by those in authority as seditious [traitors]. It has long been known that hunger is seditious by nature; banish that, and these supposedly seditious persons will disappear. They will not break into the august French Senate [the government] as they did on the 12th of this month [the Coup of Germinal], to cry: 'Give us bread! Give us bread!' The flour intended for Paris is stopped on the way and stolen by citizens even hungrier no doubt than ourselves, if such there will be within the republic. Yet there is no lack of corn anywhere! There is still plenty in store in the departments of the Nord... The farmers absolutely refuse to sell it for paper money; you have to go to them to take linen or table silver, jewellery or gold crosses, to get a few bushels [a measure of corn]. The wretches! Brutal and grasping yokels! Discord now sits more firmly than ever within the Convention. Now we are back to where we were at the end of April '93, and a hundred times worse as far as financial matters go. Too many *assignats*, too much government slackness, too much favour shown to the enemies of democracy, too much harshness and cruelty to former patriots, too much personal bitterness.

**AS Level Exam-Style Question Section A**

***Study Source 4 before you answer this question.***

Why is Source 4 valuable to the historian for an enquiry into the causes of unrest in 1795?

Explain your answer using the source, the information given about it and your own knowledge of the historical context. (8 marks)

**Tip**

*Try to extract the more subtle points from the source, as well as the more obvious ones. It clearly makes a big point about the economic problems of 1795, but what about the fleeting references to things like 'too much favour shown to the enemies of democracy'? What might this be referring to?*

## Conclusion

When the Directory was established, the situation in France was far from stable. The White Terror went unchecked as people enacted vigilante justice against the Jacobins. The rising in the Vendée reared its head once more. A wave of royalism emerged to counter-weight the radical Jacobinism of the previous two years, and yet Jacobinism still survived, leaving a very wide political spectrum for the Directors to appease. On top of this, the economic situation was desperate, with famine in both rural and urban areas.

Despite all these challenges, to say that the Directory faced insurmountable problems would perhaps be overstating the situation. There were factors that lay in its favour. The shattered power of the *sans-culottes*, as exemplified in their failed insurrections of Germinal and Prairial, removed a very significant power threat. Also, it should be emphasised that, after the bloodshed and oppressive rule of the previous years, many people wanted a more moderate and balanced form of government. If the Directory could have provided such moderation, as well as tackling the economic crisis, then perhaps it could have succeeded.

ACTIVITY
KNOWLEDGE CHECK

**Did the Directory face insurmountable problems in 1795?**

1 Compare the White Terror of 1794-96 with the Jacobin Terror of 1793-94. What similarities and differences can you identify between the two? Consider similarities and differences between the perpetrators (*sans-culottes, jeunesse dorée* and the role of the government), the methods of Terror, the scale and the areas worse affected.

2 Identify and explain three reasons why the economic situation in France deteriorated even further in 1795.

3 Why, when the risings of Germinal and Prairial achieved so little, are they of significance to a historian?

# HOW FAR DID THE DIRECTORY MANAGE TO ACHIEVE MODERATION?

The new constitution of 1795 aimed to create a moderate form of government that would steer a central path between the extremes of neo-Jacobinism on one side and royalism on the other. This was no easy task as the Directory had to tackle severe economic problems, as well as political threats from both the left and the right.

## The 1795 constitution

The constitution of Year III came into effect on 22 August 1795. The Thermidorean Convention had attempted to create a constitution that would avoid political extremism, falling neither to the left with a return to Jacobinism nor to the right in favour of the royalists. The Thermidoreans also wished to create a system of government that would not give rise to dictatorship, as had been seen with the Committee of Public Safety.

KEY TERM

**Legislature**
The body or assembly responsible for creating laws.

### The Council of Ancients and Council of the Five Hundred

In order to create a balanced form of government, the new constitution prescribed that there should be two chambers of the **legislature**. The Council of Five Hundred consisted of elected men over the age of 30 and was the chamber responsible for initiating and drafting new legislation. These drafts, or bills, would then be passed to the second chamber, the Council of Ancients, which was composed of 250 men over the age of 40. The Council of Ancients would then either approve or refuse the bills. They had no right to amend them, nor to initiate laws themselves.

Although there was no property qualification to be a deputy in either of the two Councils (though the age requirements had to be met), there was a property qualification in order to vote. The system was similar to that of the 1791 constitution (see page 198), where elections were held in stages. All males over 21 years of age who paid direct taxes on property could vote for the electors. Electors would then vote for the deputies to the Councils. To be an elector, a man had to pay taxation equivalent to 150–200 days' labour, a very high amount, restricting the position to only the very wealthy. In an attempt to prevent dictatorship, or the dominance of any one faction, elections were also to be held annually and one-third of all members of the Councils had to be retired and replaced each year. The Thermidorean Convention feared a royalist resurgence in the first elections of 1795 and so decreed that two-thirds of those elected in the first Councils, of 1795, must have served in the Convention.

SOURCE

In summer 1795, François-Antoine Boissy d'Anglas, a member of the Council of the Five Hundred, wrote this defence of the Convention's decision to only allow limited democracy in the constitution of 1795. It was published in *Le Moniteur Universel* ('The Universal Monitor'), one of Paris' most popular newspapers during the revolutionary era.

We must be governed by the best citizens; the best citizens are those who are most educated and most interested in the keeping of the law. Now, with very few exceptions, you will find such men only among those who possess some property, who are attached to the country that contains it, the laws that protect it, and the peace that maintains it; men who owe to that property and to the affluence it affords the education which makes them fit to discuss wisely and equitably, the advantages and drawbacks of the laws that determine the fate of the country... A country governed by landowners is in a condition of social order, whereas one governed by persons other than property owners is in a state of nature.

SOURCE

Radicals were quick to condemn the constitution of 1795. Philippe Buonarroti, a former Jacobin deputy of The Mountain and later a supporter of Gracchus Babeuf (see page 252), wrote this criticism in his *History of Babeuf's Conspiracy of Equals*, published in 1828.

A mere glance at the Constitution of the Year III [1795] is enough to show that the foundation of every part of it is a continuation of wealth and poverty. First, to silence all claims and to close forever any opening for innovations which might favour the people, the latter's political rights are abolished or curtailed. The people have no share in the making of laws and no power to censure them; the constitution binds them and their descendants forever, because they are forbidden to change it. Certainly it declares the people sovereign, but any deliberation by the people is declared seditious; after confused ramblings about equal rights, the constitution none-the-less robs the great mass of citizens their rights of citizenship; and only the wealthy have the right to make appointments to the principal public offices.

## The Directory

The third body of government was that of the Directory itself, the executive, established on 2 November 1795. The Directory consisted of five men chosen by the Council of Ancients from a list drawn up by the Council of Five Hundred. They would hold office for five years, though each year one Director, chosen by lot, would be replaced. The Directory was in charge of law enforcement, foreign and military affairs. Yet their powers were rather limited, as they had no part in the creation of legislation, no right of veto, no control over finance, nor could they declare war or peace.

A brief description of the first five Directors is given below.

### *Paul Barras*

Paul Barras was the most significant member of the Directory and served as Director throughout its existence. Barras had been elected to the National Convention in 1792 and was then sent to southern France and Italy to command the French revolutionary armies. He played a key role, alongside Napoleon Bonaparte, in recapturing Toulon from rebel and British forces. He was a committed republican, who had voted for Louis' death, but he was not a radical Jacobin and had played a part in the downfall of Robespierre's faction. For more information on Barras, see page 248.

### *Lazare Carnot*

Lazare Carnot had been a member of the Committee of Public Safety, responsible for the war effort and the *levée en masse*. Due to his successes in the Revolutionary War, and his opposition to Robespierre within the Committee, Carnot was not held responsible for the Terror, as other members of the Committee of Public Safety were. He was Director until the Coup of Fructidor (see page 252) in 1797, when he was forced to flee France.

### *Jean-François Reubell*

Jean-François Reubell, like Barras, was a Director throughout the period from 1795. Reubell was a veteran of the revolution, having served in both the National Assembly and the National Convention. As a leading Feuillant (see page 201), he had been an enemy of Jacobinism. While he was not a radical, he was not a conservative either and he had supported the Civil Constitution of the Clergy and the execution of the king, as well as playing a leading role in demanding the emancipation of slaves in the French colonies. Within the Directory, he was largely concerned with foreign policy.

### *Étienne Letourneur*

Étienne Letourneur has been described as a 'non-entity with few political ideas.' He had served in the Legislative Assembly and National Convention, voted for the king's death, and, like Barras, had led French revolutionary forces in the war in the south east. Within the Directory, he was a military engineer who largely acted as an assistant to Carnot, though he was recognised as the Directory's naval expert.

### *Louis-Marie de La Revellière-Lépeaux*

Louis-Marie de La Revellière-Lépeaux had also been a member of the National Convention until, as a supporter of the Girondins, he was outlawed in June 1793. He survived to return to politics after Robespierre's fall. His brother was not so lucky and fell victim to the guillotine. It is little surprising, then, that La Revellière-Lépeaux was strongly anti-Jacobin. Yet, he was no royalist either and had voted in the Convention for the king's death. His main influence within the Directory was that of anti-clericalism.

#### EXTEND YOUR KNOWLEDGE

**Paul Barras (1755–1829)**

Paul-François-Jean-Nicolas, Vicomte de Barras, was one of the most important politicians during the Directorial period. He was born into nobility in Provence, yet became disillusioned with the *ancien régime* and welcomed the revolution of 1789.

He first entered national politics in September 1792, when he was elected to the Convention. He was then assigned the supervision of the French army in the south of France with its mission to crush counter-revolution there. He succeeded in liberating Nice from royalist forces, and was then placed in charge of recapturing Toulon from British and rebel forces (see page 250). It was here that he first worked with Napoleon Bonaparte, and the two men would become closely associated with each other.

During much of the Terror, Barras was politically shrewd, avoiding aligning himself too closely to any one faction. However, in spring 1794, realising the turn of the tide, Barras sided against the Robespierrists and played a role in the Coup of Thermidor.

Barras went on to be a leading member of the Thermidorean Convention, and was placed in charge of the Army of the Interior. It was in this role that he defended Paris against the Vendémiaire rising (see page 250), once again alongside Napoleon. As Director, Barras was strongly anti-royalist, yet he also favoured a more authoritarian form of governance than some.

As his revolutionary background was largely a military one, Barras had both the connections and the mindset to use the military for political means. It was these connections that propped up the Directory's power. For example, Barras was one of the main proponents of the Coup of Fructidor (see page 252). His reliance on the military earned him criticism, as did his excessive wealth. He earned a not underserved reputation for corruption and ostentation.

In the Coup of Brumaire (see page 260), Barras was overlooked by Sieyès in favour of Roger Ducos and Napoleon. As such, he missed out on a place within the Consulate. With no place in the new regime, Barras' prominence faded. He retired from politics and lived out his years in luxury from the wealth he had amassed during his time as Director.

## Weaknesses of the constitution

The greatest flaw in the constitution of Year III was that, in trying to create a system of checks and balances, with no one body dominating, what was actually created was a system that lacked leadership or clear direction. The Directors were supposed to enforce laws that they had no part in creating. They were supposed to deal with foreign affairs, but could not declare war or make peace.

They were supposed to organise the military, but had no control over the finances necessary to do so. There was a similar problem of responsibility between the Council of the Five Hundred and the Council of Ancients. If the Council of Ancients disapproved of a bill proposed by the Council of Five Hundred, then that bill was simply rejected, there was no room for negotiation or amendment.

Furthermore, with one-third of Council members being retired each year and with annual elections, there was no stability within the Councils. Members were constantly changing, making the emergence of any leaders or any coherent long-term policies highly challenging. Finally, the 'decree of two-thirds' (that two-thirds of Council deputies had to have sat on the Convention) caused opposition from both the left and the right. The neo-Jacobins despised the rule, as many Jacobins who had sat on the Convention had been purged by this point. Royalists also hated the rule, as there had been no royalists sitting in the Convention.

ACTIVITY
KNOWLEDGE CHECK

**How far did the Directory manage to achieve moderation?**

1 Identify three ways in which the constitution of 1795 was designed to prevent dictatorship and/or radicalism.

2 Read Sources 5 and 6. How and why do the views of the authors on the constitution of 1795 differ?

3 Read the information about the first five Directors. What similarities were there between them? Consider both the political views and the roles played by the men. What do these similarities suggest about the nature of the Directory?

## Economic and financial reforms

### Reform of the currency

One of the first priorities of the new government was to attempt to tackle the financial crisis facing the country. Inflation continued to soar and assignats had become worthless, so, in February 1796, the assignat was abolished. The following month, the Directory introduced a new paper currency, called the mandate. However, they made the mistake of valuing the mandate against the assignat (30 mandate to one assignat) and, as a result, the value of the mandate plummeted. In February 1797, all paper currency was scrapped entirely. The problem with returning to metal currency, though, was that there was not enough of it in circulation. Vast quantities had been hidden and hoarded away for safety during the revolution and, when *émigrés* fled, they had often taken their money with them. France therefore went from a situation where there was far too much money in circulation prior to 1797 to far too little thereafter. Because of this, there was a partial return to a natural economy. Deputies of the Councils were paid in grain, employees demanded payment in bread and farmers paid their land leases in produce.

### State debt

In September 1797, the Directory attempted to tackle the problem of state debt by declaring itself bankrupt and saying that it could only pay off debts to creditors by issuing them with state bonds, which could then be used to purchase *biens nationaux*. Two-thirds of state debt was wiped out in this way, reducing the government's annual expenditure by 160 million livres. Yet the move was not without controversy, as the bonds issued quickly depreciated in value, angering the creditors and making future borrowing less possible. The Council of Ancients also accused the Directory of attacking the right to property of the lenders. These lenders, or *rentiers*, as they were known, were essentially being robbed of the money owed to them, an action the Council of Ancients condemned as immoral.

### Taxation

As well as inflation and huge debts, the Directory had also inherited a failing taxation system. While the tax farmers of the *ancien régime* (see page 179) had been abolished long before, a stable system had never really replaced them. During the revolution, indirect taxes had been abolished and a universal land tax had been established. However, with limited records and few local administrators to measure land, calculate payments and oversee collection, application of the land tax was piecemeal at best. Furthermore, as half the land tax was paid in grain and the other half in assignats, the depreciation of the currency meant that state income was falling in line with this depreciation.

To try to make up for this shortfall, Dominique-Vincent Ramel-Nogaret, of the Directory's Ministry of Finance, reintroduced a number of indirect taxes. The taxes included a charge on luxuries, such as chimneys, domestic servants, and carriages, a poll tax, levied on all regardless of wealth, and a tax on windows and doors. The collection of these taxes remained inconsistent and did not entirely solve the problem of state revenue. They were also deeply unpopular and, when the government announced the reintroduction of tolls and the construction of customs barriers outside towns and cities, there were accusations that it was attempting to reintroduce the much-hated customs of the *ancien régime*. When the Directory pushed for, and the Council of Five Hundred approved, a bill proposing the reintroduction of a salt tax, the Council of Ancients used its veto. The return of the *gabelle* was a step too far.

Ramel-Nogaret's tax reforms did see an increase in state revenue. A stamp tax on newspapers and on the registration of official documents proved particularly successful. It could also be argued he had little choice other than to reintroduce indirect taxation. Direct taxation alone simply was not meeting the cost of state expenditure. Necessary or not, the tax reforms were very unpopular and, even with the new taxes, did not cover the cost of running a country during a time of war. As the 1790s progressed, the state became increasingly dependent on the wealth acquired by its armies.

## Martial law

With trouble in Brittany and the Vendée (see page 254), bread riots and banditry triggered by famine, and growing resentment of government reforms, the Directory deemed it necessary to increase policing and domestic repression. For this, it relied heavily upon the army. Troops were billeted in villages that failed to pay taxes or meet the demands of the army levy. A law introduced in June 1795 allowed the army to use military courts to try rebels and opponents of the government. Initially, these courts were temporary institutions, established as and when necessary. However, in 1797, the Directory deemed it necessary to make these courts permanent bodies. This was essentially the introduction of martial law, whereby ordinary law was replaced by military rule. Furthermore, rather than deploying units of National Guardsmen to deal with domestic unrest, as was the purpose of the guards, the Directory preferred to rely on regular soldiers whose officers they felt to be more loyal (as they were appointed by the Directors). By 1799, over 200 communes had seen policing and judicial powers being handed over from civil authorities to military ones.

**ACTIVITY**
**KNOWLEDGE CHECK**

**How far did the Directory manage to achieve moderation?**

1. 'The Directory's economic policies were effective but unpopular.' Use this page and page 249 to gather information both in support of, and opposed to, this statement. Once you have done so, try to arrive at an overall judgement about the extent to which you believe the statement to be true.
2. Why do you think the Directors preferred to rely on the regular military for domestic control, rather than the National Guard? As well as the information above, consider the backgrounds of the Directors and the earlier history of the National Guard.

## Attempts to control factionalism

### The Vendémiaire rising, 1795

The government was also dependent upon the army for quelling unrest within Paris. The 'decree of two-thirds' (see page 247) had been poorly received within Paris. Royalists correctly realised that this rule was intended to reduce the chance of any royalist revival. Many ordinary people were also unhappy about the rule, as they felt the Convention had failed to deliver them from their poverty and famine, so were keen to see an entirely new body elected.

On 5 October 1795, anger ran over into open unrest. A crowd of 25,000 gathered in Paris to seize power. The rebels vastly outnumbered the government forces, but had neither the leadership, organisation nor weaponry of the army. Barras was charged with crushing the rebellion. He was supported by a young Corsican general, called Napoleon Bonaparte, who was placed in charge of the artillery. Barras and the government soldiers succeeded in defeating and dispersing the rebels. One contemporary estimated that as many as 600 government troops and around 800 rebels were killed, some of whom were despatched by Napoleon's famous use of **grapeshot.**

KEY TERM

Grapeshot
A type of cannon or artillery shell, where numerous small metal balls are sprayed out in one shot. This type of shot was very effective at close range for hitting a wide number of targets, making it especially suited for attacks on crowds of rioters in urban areas.

EXTEND YOUR KNOWLEDGE

Napoleon Bonaparte (1769-1821)
In 1769, Napoleon was born on the island of Corsica to an Italian family, hence his name at birth: Napoleone Buonaparte (he later changed it to sound more French). Shortly before Napoleon's birth, Corsica had been taken over by France, making Napoleon a French citizen. This, and the fact he came from an aristocratic family (albeit not a particularly wealthy one), allowed him to enrol in a French military academy of the *ancien régime*, where he trained as an artillery officer.

When the revolution broke out in 1789, Napoleon welcomed political reform but saw no need for radical social change. In 1791, while a young military officer in Valence, Napoleon joined the local Jacobin Club. He soon became its president. Napoleon's rise to national significance came in August 1793 when he was placed in charge of the artillery during the siege of Toulon. His strategy played an important part in the defeat of the British and the royalists. This success brought him, not only a promotion, but also to the attention of Robespierre. Robespierre praised his command and Napoleon gained a reputation as a Jacobin general. When Robespierre fell during the Coup of Thermidor, Napoleon's career suffered, as the backlash against the Jacobins began. Napoleon was even imprisoned for a short time due to his associations with Robespierre.

Napoleon's next break came in October 1795, during the Vendémiaire rising. Napoleon happened to be in Paris at the time and Barras, whom Napoleon had fought alongside at Toulon, appointed him as commander of the artillery in defence of the city. Napoleon's role during the rising was exaggerated after the event, but he did play his part in defeating the rising and therefore a part in saving the government of the republic. This success earned Napoleon command of the Army of the Interior.

Over the next four years, Napoleon went on to become one of the most successful and famous generals of the Directorial period. Most prominent was his Italian campaign (see page 255) where he defeated France's longstanding enemy, Austria. When Napoleon personally negotiated the terms of Austria's surrender, he revealed his political, as well as his military, aspirations. Napoleon's reputation and power was such that, in 1799, when Sieyès plotted to overthrow the Directory, he chose Napoleon as the general to provide the military support for the coup.

The Coup of Brumaire was successful in bringing down the Directory (see page 260). It was also successful in bringing Napoleon to power. In the new government, Napoleon was appointed first consul. Through military victory and powerful propaganda, over the following years, Napoleon further consolidated his power: in 1804, he was declared emperor of France. He would hold this title until the collapse of the French empire in 1814. The Napoleonic period (1799-1815) would witness almost constant war, affecting all of Europe.

The Vendémiaire rising is often described as a royalist rising, though this may be too simplistic as it is difficult to discern the motives of the rebels. The sections of Paris had rejected the 'decree of two-thirds' and the *jeunesse dorée* and royalists certainly played their part, possibly inspired to revolt by the arrival of the Comte d'Artois, Louis XVI's younger brother and *émigrés* leader, in France in late September (see page 254). Many among the crowd, though, were probably driven as much by economic distress, and the failure of the government to resolve it, as they were by any desire to restore the monarchy. The fact that the rebellion was centred around the Section Lepelletier, an area populated by bankers and businessman who were increasingly impoverished by rapid inflation, supports such an assertion.

## The Babeuf Plot, 1796

It was not just royalists who posed a threat to the authority of the Directory, there were also opponents on the extreme left. Gracchus Babeuf was a radical journalist who advocated the complete redistribution of land in order to provide for all, including the most poor and needy. He opposed the policies of the Directory, seeing them as little more than preserving the gains of the bourgeoisie and doing nothing for the common people of France.

Babeuf has been accused of leading a Conspiracy of Equals, a plot to overthrow the Directory in a communist-style revolution. The reality of the situation, though, is that Babeuf was little more than a radical thinker with a small following. His newspaper, *Le Tribun du peuple* ('The People's Tribune'), had only 500 subscribers, and his influence outside of Paris was very limited. The greatest success of the Babouvists, as Babeuf's followers were known, was in encouraging three battalions of the Parisian police to mutiny in March 1796. This success was short-lived (the battalions were easily suppressed by loyal forces) and also proved to be the downfall of Babeuf, as one of the Babouvists, a man called Grisel, betrayed the plot to Director Carnot. On 10 May, Carnot oversaw the arrest of Babeuf and a number of his followers. Following his trial, Babeuf and another leading Babouvist were sent to the guillotine, while five others were exiled.

**EXTEND YOUR KNOWLEDGE**

**Gracchus Babeuf (1760–97)**

Born François-Noël Babeuf (he later took the name Gracchus after a Roman statesman of the second century), Babeuf worked as a feudal law expert under the *ancien régime* and it was through this work that he became highly conscious of the vast inequalities within French society. This led him to pursue a career as a political journalist, campaigning for political and social reform. His ideas were so radical that, in 1790, he was briefly imprisoned for the production of a particular pamphlet.

Following his release, he founded a journal, *Le Correspondant Picard*. In the journal, he proposed a radical system of land redistribution, whereby all French people, regardless of wealth or birth, would be awarded land. It is because of such ideas that Babeuf has been described as the first communist and was revered by 19th and 20th-century revolutionaries, such as the Russian Vladimir Lenin.

In February 1793, Babeuf moved to Paris. His move was ill-timed, as the Reign of Terror was about to begin. Babeuf's views were too radical for Robespierre and the Committee of Public Safety and he was imprisoned.

Following the Coup of Thermidor (July 1794), Babeuf was released and resumed his work as a journalist. In his new journal, *Le Tribun du Peuple*, Babeuf attacked the governments of the Thermidoreans and the Directory for failing to meet the needs of the poorest in society. He advocated a communist-style revolution and the overthrow of the government. His role in the failed Conspiracy of Equals (see above) led to his imprisonment. His trial began on 20 February 1797. He was found guilty and sent to the guillotine.

### The Coup of Fructidor, 1797

There were those in France under the Directory who supported the *émigré* vision of completely restoring absolute monarchy (see page 253); however, people with such views were in a minority. There were, though, a significant number of politicians who favoured a return to constitutional monarchy. These moderate royalists were led by a former Feuillant called Antoine d'André. D'André was himself an *émigré*, who had returned to France in 1797 to lead the electoral campaign for the royalists. His faction fought for the relaxation of laws against *émigrés* and refractory priests, and argued for the conclusion of peace in the Revolutionary War. Royalist clubs were established in Paris, with affiliated clubs in the provinces, and a royalist press emerged.

Such royalists had been omitted from the Council elections of 1795 due to the 'decree of two-thirds'. Yet this rule did not apply in subsequent elections, and, in the 1796 elections, the royalists made some advances. However, it was in the 1797 elections, as people became increasingly dissatisfied with the Directory's failure to solve economic problems, and its increasing reliance on military justice, that the royalists made significant gains. Of the 260 Council seats being contested, 180 were won by royalists. While this did not give them a majority in the Councils, the Directory feared that its support base was rapidly being undermined.

To add to this, also in 1797, Letourneur was removed by ballot from the Directory to be replaced by François-Marie, marquis de Barthélemy, a French politician and diplomat. This new Director was known for his support for the royalists, who had supported his appointment. Furthermore, some were beginning to question Carnot's loyalties, as he became increasingly conservative as time went on.

The remaining republican Directors felt they had to act to prevent royalist domination. On 4 September 1797, they sought help from the army and Barras called upon the assistance of Napoleon, who was by this time commander of the Army of the Interior. Napoleon was personally occupied fighting the Italian campaign (see page 255) and so sent General Augereau, an experienced and skilled officer, to Paris with troops to support the republican Directors. The soldiers surrounded the Councils and arrested Carnot, Barthélemy and 53 royalist deputies.

Barras and the republican Directors excused their actions by accusing the arrested of plotting a royalist coup. The remaining deputies of the Councils felt intimidated enough to approve a decree sanctioning the deportation of the prisoners to French Guyana though Carnot fled and sought exile in Geneva. The Councils also approved another decree, cancelling election results in numerous departments, resulting in the removal of 177 deputies from the Councils.

The Coup of Fructidor, as it is known, ensured the dominance of the Directory over the Councils and helped to prevent royalist resurgence. Yet, it came at a price. By forcibly overturning the election results, the Directory had made a mockery of democracy, significantly undermining its legitimacy. Also, once again, the Directory had been forced to rely on the military to maintain its position.

## Directorial terror

Following the Coup of Fructidor, the Directory pushed further to repress royalism. *Émigrés* who had returned to France since the Coup of Thermidor were given two weeks to leave or else they would face death. Many fled, including d'André, who escaped to Switzerland. Others were hunted down and executed.

The clergy, who were blamed for the spread of royalism, were expected to swear an oath of loyalty, declaring their hatred of monarchy. Those who refused were sentenced to deportation. Almost 10,000 priests were sentenced to the 'dry guillotine', as the long and unhealthy journey to the French colony of Guyana was known. Only a tiny fraction of these were actually captured and deported, though, as local authorities were often reluctant to act against the clergy. Only around 230 priests were sent to Guyana, with another 750 being imprisoned on islands off the coast of France.

The repression following the Coup of Fructidor took other forms. Churches were closed, mainly for the reason of preventing religious services being held, in an attempt to undermine the influence of so many priests who opposed the new oath and were often perceived to have royalist leanings. Some churches were sold off, and far more were simply demolished. In just one department alone, the Nord, over 400 parish churches were sold.

This period of Directorial 'terror', as it is sometimes known, was short-lived and was nowhere near the scale of the Jacobin Terror of 1793–94. While the Directory may have succeeded in the short term in quelling royalism, its actions only served to increase opposition, especially in more staunchly Catholic areas. The suppression of the Church also made the Directory's claims of religious neutrality appear rather shallow.

## Conclusion

The constitution of 1795 was carefully constructed to avoid dictatorship and extremism. However, the checks and balances put in place actually led to a situation where the Directory could not control the Councils without resorting to forceful measures, as seen during the Coup of Fructidor. In order to avoid extremism, the Directory became more and more dependent on the army. While it could be argued that this was necessary in order to preserve a moderate political line, the Directory's actions undermined public confidence in the political system. Similarly, the economic reforms of the government could be said to have been necessary and were, to some extent, successful in improving state finances. However, after it had reintroduced indirect taxes and failed to manage currency effectively, opposition to the Directory grew even further.

**ACTIVITY**
**KNOWLEDGE CHECK**

**How far did the Directory manage to achieve moderation?**

1. Using an internet search engine, attempt to find three differing accounts of the Vendémiaire rising. They may differ in their explanation of the causes, on the scale of the rising, and/or on the role of Napoleon. Why do you think that there is considerable uncertainty about what happened during the rising?
2. How did the Coup of Fructidor both strengthen and undermine the Directory's position?

# WAS THE DIRECTORY'S DEPENDENCE ON THE MILITARY UNAVOIDABLE?

As we have already seen, the Directory relied on the military to police the provinces through martial law and, when fearing a royalist revival, used the military to purge its political opponents during the Coup of Fructidor. As we will see in this section, internal unrest, combined with the impact of the War of the First Coalition, only added to this dependency. Yet did the Directory really have any other option?

## The Verona Declaration and the *émigré* threat

The *émigrés* were led by King Louis XVI's brothers, the Comte d'Artois and the Comte de Provence. The Comte d'Artois gathered an *émigré* army in Koblenz (a German city on the River Rhine), and the Comte de Provence built an army of *émigrés* around him in northern Italy. Prior to 1793, their aim was to restore Louis to the throne. After his execution, they proclaimed Louis' son King Louis XVII, despite his still being imprisoned in the Temple in Paris. They wished to restore France to the Bourbon absolutism that preceded the revolution.

For all their bold aims, the *émigré* threat had never been a significant one. Their armies were insubstantial and could pose little threat to the national forces of France without foreign support. Furthermore, earlier in the revolution, during the period of constitutional monarchy, the threats of the *émigrés* to restore absolute monarchy and the traditions of the *ancien régime* had put the royal family in a difficult situation, increasing anger against them and doing more harm than good to their position. As a result, Louis XVI and Marie Antoinette had preferred to look more to the intervention of foreign powers, namely Austria, as a way of restoring their authority, rather than encouraging the *émigrés*.

The states of the First Coalition also did not take the *émigrés* too seriously. While they made for useful informants, with insider knowledge of France and the French government, their aim to restore absolute monarchy was seen, by Britain in particular, as not only unrealistic but undesirable.

### Verona Declaration

On 8 June 1795, the situation with the *émigrés* changed. The child-king, Louis XVII, died while still in prison. In response to this, on 24 June, the Comte de Provence declared himself King Louis XVIII. In what is known as the Verona Declaration, as well as declaring himself king, the Comte de Provence also stated his aim to restore the estates system of the *ancien régime* and return all confiscated lands to *émigrés* and refractory clergy.

SOURCE

The Comte de Provence, the self-proclaimed King Louis XVIII, gave his Verona Declaration on 24 June 1795. The following is an extract from it.

Louis, by the grace of God, king of France and Navarre. To all our subjects, greetings. In depriving you of a king, whose whole reign was spent in captivity [referring to King Louis XVII], but even whose infancy afforded sufficient grounds for believing that he would prove a worthy successor to the best of kings, the impenetrable decrees of Providence, at the same time that they have transmitted his crown to us, have imposed on us the necessity of tearing it from the hands of revolt, and the duty of saving the country, reduced by a disastrous revolution to the brink of ruin. Impiety and revolt have been the causes of all the torments you experience: in order to stop their progress you must dry up their source. You must return to that holy religion which showered down upon France the blessings of Heaven. We wish to restore its altars; by prescribing justice to sovereigns and fidelity to subjects, it maintains good order, ensures the triumph of the laws, and produces the felicity of empires. You must restore the government which, for fourteen centuries, constituted the glory of France and the delight of her inhabitants; which rendered our country the most flourishing of states and yourselves the happiest of people.

ACTIVITY
WRITING

**Unpicking the Verona Declaration**

Using a dictionary to define any terms you do not understand, rewrite Source 7 in a simplified manner and language that is familiar to you.

The Declaration was not taken too seriously. The Comte de Provence had misjudged the mood of Paris. While, following the abuses of the Terror, more people were beginning to support the idea of a return to constitutional monarchy, few favoured a return to the absolutism of the *ancien régime*. If anything, the Declaration damaged the royalist movement within France, as it allowed the opponents of royalism to accuse it of advocating a return to despotism.

## Revolt in the provinces and reaction to conscription

### The Chouannerie and the invasion of Quiberon Bay

Potentially the greatest direct *émigré* threat was inspired by an uprising in Brittany. A rebellion against the forces of Louis-Marie Turreau (see page 230) had begun in Brittany in 1794. The unrest was led by Jean Cotterau, also known as Jean Chouan, from which the uprising acquired its name: the Chouannerie. The Chouannerie was a much more serious threat to the government than the *jeunesse dorée* or the White Terror gangs in Lyon and Toulon. As well as being an anti-Jacobin reaction, it was also a royalist movement. By the spring of 1796, the Chouans controlled most of Brittany.

The rebel leaders sought British and *émigré* support against the republic. In response, an army of 3,000 *émigrés* and British troops landed at Quiberon Bay on the south coast of Brittany on 28 June 1795, to support an even larger Chouan rebel army. However, the republican general Lazare Hoche had been warned of the coming of the *émigrés* and so met their arrival with a large force of soldiers, who outnumbered the *émigrés* by eight to one. Six thousand prisoners were taken, including both *émigrés* and Chouans. The government then came down even harder upon the Chouannerie and provided Hoche with an army of 140,000 men to supress the uprising. By the end of summer 1796, the Chouannerie was defeated. The disastrous invasion of Quiberon Bay demonstrates the poor preparation and lack of organisation that typified *émigré* resistance.

### Re-emergence of unrest in the Vendée

The early success of the Chouan movement triggered further unrest in the neighbouring region of the Vendée. The deep-rooted tensions of the region had never been resolved. The remote communities of the Vendée still harboured resentment at the Civil Constitution of the Clergy and, despite the Directory reintroducing freedom of religion, refractory clergy had not be restored and communities still found themselves lacking priests. Similarly, the position of the peasants had still not improved, with the burden of costly land leases being exacerbated by the bad winter of 1795. As a result, National Guardsmen, loyal to the Directory, frequently found themselves under attack by peasant gangs. When they tried to ensure the collection of taxes, attempted to install new priests or enforce acceptance of the new currency, there was often bloodshed.

The Comte d'Artois, who was by this time in Britain seeking support for the *émigré* cause, sought to capitalise on the unrest in the Vendée by launching another *émigré* invasion. In September 1795, he took a small fleet to capture the Isle of Yeu, off the coast of the Vendée. His intention was then to use the island as a base for an attack on mainland France. He hoped that both the British and the rebel armies in the Vendée would come to his aid. He was to be disappointed on both accounts. The British did not back his cause, no doubt partly due to the recent memory of the disaster at Quiberon Bay and partly due to their lukewarm support for the *émigré* cause more generally. The Vendéan rebels on the mainland also were not willing to risk their lives in support of the Comte d'Artois. They were largely motivated by religious and economic discontent, not by a desire to restore the *ancien régime*. The Comte d'Artois was forced to abandon his plan for a mainland invasion and he returned to Britain in humiliation.

The Vendéan revolt could never have formed the basis for a royalist overthrow of the Directory or the republic. There was limited aristocratic leadership within the movement and little evidence to suggest that the peasant rebels there had loyalties to the *émigrés* or to the British. The revolt was essentially a local one, reaching no further than the River Loire, and consisted of disorganised, often spontaneous, guerrilla attacks.

**ACTIVITY**
**KNOWLEDGE CHECK**

**Was the Directory's dependency on the military unavoidable?**

1 Read Source 7.

- a) What does the Comte de Provence write that reveals that he considered himself to be king of France when he wrote the Verona Declaration?
- b) What does he write that implies he wishes to see the hierarchy of the estates system reinstated?
- c) Write a reply to the Verona Declaration from the perspective of an ardent republican of the time. In particular, challenge what the Comte de Provence claims in the last six lines of Source 7 regarding life under the *ancien régime*.

2 Give detailed explanations of how each of the following lessened or undermined the threat from the *émigrés*:

- a) the Verona Declaration
- b) the reluctance of the states of the First Coalition to back the *émigré* cause
- c) the success of General Hoche
- d) poor planning by the Comte d'Artois
- e) the nature of the Vendéan revolt.

## The impact of war

### French military successes

By 1795, the War of the First Coalition had turned very much in France's favour. After the Battle of Fleurus (June 1794), the French conquered and occupied the Austrian Netherlands. This was followed by a successful campaign against the Dutch, and Spanish forces were also defeated in the south. In 1796, the French armies turned their attention to defeating Austria, via the Italian state of Piedmont. Due to his connections with Barras (from shared experiences during the Vendémiaire rising and in Toulon), Napoleon was placed in command of the Italian campaign (1796–97) and began his campaign on 11 April.

After a highly successful campaign, which established Napoleon's reputation as a great general, the Austrians were defeated. Napoleon ignored instructions from the Directory and chose instead to negotiate personally the terms of Austria's surrender. This was no insignificant act, as the terms were to redefine the borders and territories of Europe. The terms of the surrender were formalised in the Treaty of Campo-Formio (October 1797). The Directory was furious that Napoleon had acted independently in determining foreign policy. Yet, there was little they could do. Napoleon had, after all, led the defeat of Austria, France's enemy since 1792. He was a national hero.

## Reaction to conscription and revolt in the provinces

As the French Revolutionary Wars dragged on, the patriotic fervour that had swept France in 1792–93 waned. War weariness set in and calls for an end to conflict became louder. By the end of 1795, France had made considerable gains in the wars and had repelled all foreign enemies from French soil. Within the Councils, some of the more moderate deputies, especially the former Feuillants, began to argue for an end to the war. Within the army, there were alarming desertions after the invading foreign armies had been defeated. The famine of 1795 impacted on army provisions, just as it did on the peasants back home, increasing desertion rates further. For example, after the Spanish forces had been repelled, is it estimated that 3,000 French soldiers deserted in the Pyrenees. Yet, war continued, with a French campaign in the Rhineland and the Italian campaign. Again, in 1797, after the Treaty of Campo-Formio and the defeat of the First Coalition (with the exception of Britain), the war seemed at a point where hostilities could end. Instead, Napoleon launched the Egyptian campaign in order to threaten British interests there. As dissatisfaction with the war grew, the Directory's reputation, as the body responsible for military and foreign affairs, suffered.

As well as political opposition to continuing warfare, there was also a popular reaction. On 5 September 1798, a law was passed calling for the conscription of all men aged between 20 and 25 for a five year term. Unlike previous conscription laws, this law was to apply both in peacetime and in wartime, and it was also to apply to married men with children. This partly caused, in late 1798 and 1799, a wave of uprisings across many French provinces. In Brittany and Normandy, deserters and those avoiding conscription into the Republic's armies swelled the ranks of small, isolated rebel bands to turn them into new Chouan (see page 254) armies. These enlarged armies even managed to take control of a number of significant French towns, such as Le Mans, for short periods, before being defeated by republican forces. In the south west, a royalist conspiracy launched a rebellion that possessed both funding from the British and the wealth of a handful of returned *émigrés*. The leaders of the uprising aimed to capture Toulouse and the significant weapons arsenal that was held there. An army of 15,000 advanced on the town but, despite their significant numbers, they were poorly armed and badly led. The leaders of the army hesitated too long, allowing the authorities of Toulon to call in National Guard regiments from neighbouring departments who were successful in repelling the royalists.

While the Directory may have been successful in supressing the revolts, the spread of civil war did nothing to strengthen its position. With the threat of both internal and external enemies, demands for strong government increased. For some, this meant they looked for a return to Jacobinism, others started to look to their military generals.

In other areas, while there may not have been violent resistance to conscription, there was passive opposition. Many departments failed quite spectacularly to meet their levy requirements, as local officials resisted the levy. To take one example, the department of Mont-Terrible conscripted just 19 percent of its target. There were cases of men cutting off their own thumbs, so they could not handle a gun, or knocking out their teeth, so they could not tear open the gunpowder cartridges, to avoid being conscripted. Such was the feeling towards the prospect of serving in the army of the Republic.

### War breeds war: the vicious circle

It must be questioned why, when the ongoing war effort caused so much opposition, the Directory persisted in pursuing a policy of aggression. Extract 1 gives an explanation.

EXTRACT

In his 1975 work, *France under the Directory*, the historian Martyn Lyons gave the following explanation of why France under the Directory continued to pursue territorial expansion.

The victory of the Directorial Left in the Coup of Fructidor V inaugurated a new period of French expansion, during which Switzerland, Liguria, Rome and then Naples were occupied. The Directory saw no contradiction in levying forced loans and maintaining armies of occupation in liberated territories. The army was paid and supplied out of its own conquests, or, as the Directory preferred to put it, it was 'nourished with the fruits of its courage'... The Directory professed peaceful intentions, but it expected expansion because of financial need, and because it relied on the support of Republican generals, to whom it had already turned in Fructidor. Time and again, the Directory's hand was forced by acts of aggression committed by agents it could no control.

So then, as the French forces occupied or subjugated more lands, more soldiers were required to occupy and maintain order within the new territory. The upkeep of such forces would be very costly. It has been estimated that French profits from the Revolutionary War of 1792–99 amounted to about 360 million **francs**. However, little of this found its way back to Paris. Only one-quarter of the considerable **indemnities**, some 200 million livres, from Napoleon's Italian campaign were sent back to the Directory. Instead, the wealth tended to be spent on funding and maintaining the army. Often, army wages were in arrears by the time campaigns were won, so there were debts to clear. Then, occupying armies would have to be paid, garrisoned and supplied. This is after the considerable 'bonuses' that generals and officers were awarded for their victories. This constant need for money to finance the army trapped the Directory in a vicious circle of needing to conquer more territories, so needing to conscript more soldiers and therefore creating even greater political opposition to the regime.

Extract 1 also refers to another reason for perpetual warfare: the actions of the French generals. The government had become highly reliant on the army to maintain its position. This was true in the political sphere of Paris. During the Vendémiaire rising, forces commanded by Napoleon had defended the government. In 1797, the Directory had even used the army, under General Augereau, to purge its political opponents during the Coup of Fructidor. Yet it was also true in the provinces where martial law, as well as the actions of French generals such as Hoche, played a key role in suppressing opposition to the republic.

The more the Directory relied on its generals, the greater the power of those generals became. Within the army, officers ceased to be elected as they had been earlier in the revolution. Instead, officers would be chosen by other officers. This gave generals even greater power over their armies. In the Army of Italy, for example, Napoleon held almost total power over the appointment of officers, significantly strengthening his own position. As the power of the generals rose, they could act with growing independence from the Directory. Napoleon, in particular, began devising foreign policy without consulting the Directory. This was strongly evident after his successes in the Italian campaign, where he brokered the peace terms with Austria. Furthermore, generals could pursue aggressive policies to further their own reputations and wealth.

KEY TERMS

**French franc**
In 1795 the franc was established as the standard measure of currency in France, with one franc being valued at one and a quarter livres. Despite this change, the term livre remained in use France into the 19th century alongside the French franc.

**Indemnities**
An indemnity is an amount of money paid as compensation, or damages, by a defeated nation to a victorious one. Peace treaties would often include terms relating to how much an indemnity would be.

## Conclusion

In some respects, the Directory had little choice but to depend on the military to defend France against internal enemies. Had it not done so, the revolt of the Chouannerie and the *émigré* invasion could have posed a more serious threat. Also, while the unrest in the Vendée was a long-term drain on resources, the application of military power helped to ensure that the rebellion remained localised.

The foreign war, though, is perhaps more debatable. The Directory did not press for an end to the war, even when others pushed for it. However, even if it had done so, it would have depended on the approval of the Councils for hostilities to end. This was one of the major flaws of the constitution. The Directory was the body responsible for foreign policy and yet did not have the power to declare war or make peace. It did possess the power to appoint and dismiss commanders, but how could it justify dismissing generals like Napoleon who, despite being an increasing power threat, helped to ensure continuing victories and therefore the protection of France? Furthermore, by using the military to maintain power at the Coup of Fructidor, the Directory owed a debt to these generals.

Yet all this left the government increasingly needing more soldiers and as conscription increased so too did internal discontent.

There was also a financial side to all this. As the state economy struggled through the late 1790s, the Directory could not afford to fund the war from central finances. Instead, the army had to provide for itself. Wealth had to be acquired and, for that wealth to be acquired, military victories and conquered territories were needed. Under such circumstances, it is not surprising that military generals grew in significance. Ultimately, perhaps, the issue was not just that the Directory became dependent on the military but that the generals, Napoleon in particular, became independent of the government.

ACTIVITY
KNOWLEDGE CHECK

**Was the Directory's dependency on the military unavoidable?**

1 Explain why the ongoing war effort, despite military victories, increased opposition to the Directory.

2 Explain why a policy of ongoing war was adopted despite increasing resentment.

# WHY WAS THE DIRECTORY OVERTHROWN IN NOVEMBER 1799?

On 15 December 1799, Napoleon presented France with its new constitution. It was a constitution that placed him at the head of the government. Within five years, he had assumed almost total power and was proclaimed emperor of the French empire. The Directory, in its aim to prevent dictatorship and establish moderate government, had failed.

The event that caused the final collapse of the Directory was the Coup of Brumaire. A plot of November 1799, led by Abbé Sieyès and supported by Napoleon and his brother, Lucien Bonaparte, forcibly dismantled the Directory and led to the collapse of the constitution of 1795. While the trigger of the Directory's fall did lie in Sieyès' plot, the causes of the coup began earlier.

## The Directory under threat

### The Coup of Floréal, 1798

The Coup of Fructidor had been sufficient to break the power of the royalists and the 1798 elections saw a substantial decline in support for royalism. However, by breaking the power of the right, the Directory had had to rely on the support of the left, rather than pursuing a more moderate line. The Jacobins sought to capitalise on the situation by launching a political offensive. They attacked the Councils and the Directory for the reintroduction of indirect taxation and tolls. Although many Jacobins favoured the war, they were critical of the Directory for allowing generals to enrich themselves while their men often went unpaid and underfed. The Directory hit back against Jacobin propaganda by shutting down the presses. Eleven newspapers were suppressed.

The 1798 election results did see a shift towards Jacobinism, with 86 Jacobin deputies being elected. Of those elected, 71 had voted for the death of King Louis. While these figures reflect a swing away from royalism towards the left, they do not reflect a Jacobin majority, as 437 deputies were elected. Despite this, there was enough of a swing to the left to panic the Directory and the more moderate deputies of the Councils. As a result, the Directory instigated rumours that the Jacobins posed a threat to the republic and that they were aiming to destroy the constitution. On 22 Floréal (11 May 1798), they successfully pushed the Council of the Five Hundred into agreeing to partly or completely annul the elections in all but 53 departments, leading to 127 deputies losing their seats. In a move even more unconstitutional, these seats were then filled by people selected by the Directors themselves.

The Coup of Floréal, as it is known, did not depend on military intervention, as the Coup of Fructidor had. It did, however, demonstrate just how broken the political system was. The only way that the Directory could maintain majority support within the Councils (entirely necessary for it to wield any power) was to ride roughshod over the already limited democracy that existed.

The coups of both Fructidor and Floréal eroded people's beliefs that the constitution of 1795 was a workable one. The obvious solution was for the Council of the Five Hundred to instigate changes to the constitution. Yet this was highly problematic. It had been decreed in the constitution that any constitutional revision had to be approved by each Council, three times, over three-year intervals. Thus, even if the Councils could agree on a change (problematic in itself), it would take nine years for that amendment to be enacted. With the political system failing, people simply did not have that much patience.

### Impact of the War of the Second Coalition

We have already seen how conscription caused resentment and unrest in the French provinces and conquered territories. In 1798, warfare resumed on the European mainland. A short lull in hostilities, following the Treaty of Camp-Formio, ended when Russia declared war on France. Austria allowed Russian troops to move through its territory, triggering a French declaration of war against Austria. The War of the Second Coalition began. Some early French successes were followed by a series of defeats, as French forces were forced to retreat from Italy and the Russians occupied Switzerland.

Due to the poor military situation, the Councils introduced emergency measures. In June 1798, a law, known as Jourdan's Law (after the man who proposed it), called for another *levée en masse*, pushing conscription even further. Even more controversial was the forced loan placed upon the rich. In order to raise money for the war effort, the rich were forced to loan their wealth to the state. Unsurprisingly, there was widespread resistance to these wartime measures. Some local officials refused to enact them. Other authorities that attempted to carry them out found themselves being forcibly taken over. Deserters, royalists, brigands and disloyal officials defied the government's will and, as the Directory had tended to rely on the national army for policing, there were insufficient National Guards to control the country. In an attempt to suppress unrest and enforce obedience, the Law of Hostages (July 1799) was introduced, allowing arbitrary arrest and the confiscation of property, a move that echoed the tyranny of the Terror. With few willing or able to enforce the law, it achieved little other than increasing anger with the government.

## The role of Abbé Sieyès and the return of Napoleon

Abbé Sieyès was elected to the Council of the Five Hundred in 1798 and became one of the Directors in the following year. In many ways, Sieyès typified the kind of politician who tended to be a Director. He was a republican who believed in the values of the revolution, yet he was not a Jacobin. He had also been an active voice of The Plain during the radical phase. However, what did make Sieyès unique as a Director is that, unbeknown to those who appointed him, he aimed to bring down the Directory from within. Sieyès believed that the system of government under the Directory was failing, due to the weakness of the executive. He also supposed that, with growing unrest and political divisions, it was only a matter of time before the government was overthrown. Fearing that such a coup would result in either royalist or Jacobin dominance, Sieyès decided to take the initiative for himself.

Sieyès recognised that, to stage a successful coup, he would need military support. He also recognised that he would need a general on his side with an outstanding reputation. Napoleon Bonaparte was the man who fitted the bill.

Following his great success during the Italian campaign, Napoleon had launched an invasion of Egypt to strike at British interests. Egypt was crucial to British trade with India, the British empire's most important colony. In May 1798, Napoleon launched the Egyptian campaign with an army of 38,000. Within three months, following the Battle of the Pyramids (21 July 1798), he had captured Cairo. Napoleon then made the mistake of overextending his forces by invading the Ottoman (Turkish) controlled Syrian provinces. The campaign was a disaster and, realising his failure, Napoleon abandoned his armies and returned to Paris in October 1799.

Despite his failure in Syria, the campaign did little to damage Napoleon's reputation. His team of propagandists celebrated him as the liberator of the Egyptians, playing down his failures against the Ottomans. Furthermore, his victory over the Austrians in the Italian campaign did, in the minds of many French people, completely overshadow his failings elsewhere. This was so much so that when, on 16 October 1799, Napoleon returned to Paris, he was greeted by applauding crowds.

The timing of Napoleon's return was fortuitous for Sieyès and significant for his planned coup. Sieyès knew that force would probably be needed to overthrow the government and that a great general with a powerful reputation, like Napoleon, would help to ensure that the military remained on his side, rather than against him. Sieyès also recognised that many critics of the government now favoured a return to strong leadership, and strong leadership requires a figurehead. As he was so popular with the people of Paris, Napoleon was an obvious choice. Sieyès therefore invited Napoleon to take part in the plot and, ever keen to promote his own standing, Napoleon accepted.

## The Coup of Brumaire

On 18 Brumaire Year VIII (9 November 1799), Sieyès and fellow plotters convinced the Council of Ancients that there was a Jacobin plot being formed within the Council of the Five Hundred. They convinced the members of the Council of Ancients, in the interests of their own safety, to reconvene at a place called Saint-Cloud. Napoleon's troops then occupied the Tuileries garden outside the chamber of the Council of the Five Hundred. Jean Victor Marie Moreau, another general, surrounded the building where the Directory met. Sieyès and Ducos (who was in on the plot) immediately resigned. Barras followed suit. Of the other two Directors, one fled and the other remained under military arrest.

Whilst the Directory itself had been broken, the coup nearly failed at this point. Napoleon entered the Council of the Five Hundred with armed grenadier guards. This prompted an eruption of anger among the deputies, who accused Napoleon of being a dictator, and he was physically attacked. Rather than reject the existing constitution, as the plotters had hoped, the Council of Five Hundred instead renewed its oath to it, in defiance of the plotters. It was Lucien Bonaparte, Napoleon's brother and president of the Council of Five Hundred, who saved the coup. He claimed to the Council that, during the confusion and affray, some of the Jacobin deputies had tried to stab and assassinate Napoleon. This allowed Lucien to demand the expulsion of 61 deputies. Legislation was then quickly pushed through a depleted Council, calling for the abolition of the Directory and the establishment of a three-man executive in its place.

**SOURCE**

**8** On 10 November 1799, immediately after the Coup of Brumaire, Napoleon issued the following proclamation justifying his role in it and giving his account of the events of the two days.

On my return to Paris, I found a division reigning amongst all the constituted authorities. There was no agreement but on this single point – that the constitution was half destroyed, and could by no means effect the salvation of our liberties. All the parties came to me, confided to me their designs, unveiled their secrets, and demanded my support. I refused to be a man of any party. A council of elders [Council of Ancients] invited me, and I answered to their call... The council of elders resolved, in consequence, that the sittings of the legislative body should be removed to St. Cloud, and charged me with the disposition [use] of the force necessary to secure its independence. I owed it, my fellow-citizens, to the soldiers who are perishing in our armies, and the national glory, acquired at the price of their blood, to accept of this command.

...within [the Council of Five Hundred], assassins had established the reign of terror. Several members of the council of five hundred, armed with poniards [daggers] and fire-arms, circulated around them nothing but menaces of death... I then repaired to the council of five hundred without arms, and my head uncovered, such as I had been received and applauded by the elders. I wished to recall to the majority their wishes, and to assure them of their power... Twenty assassins threw themselves upon me, and sought my breast. The grenadiers of the legislative body, whom I had left at the door of the hall, came up and placed themselves between me and my assassins... They succeeded in bearing me away.

...Immediately after the grenadiers of the legislative body entered at the *pas de charge* into the hall, and caused it to be evacuated. The factious [conspirators] were intimidated, and dispersed themselves. The majority, released from their blows, entered freely and peaceably into the hall of sitting, heard the propositions which were made to them for the public safety, deliberated, and prepared the salutary resolution which is to become the new and provisional law of the republic. Frenchmen! You will recognise, without doubt, in this conduct, the zeal of a soldier of liberty, and of a citizen devoted to the republic. The ideas of preservation, protection, and freedom, immediately resumed their places on the dispersion of the faction who wished to oppress the councils, and who, in making themselves the most odious of men, never cease to be the most contemptible.

**AS Level Exam-Style Question Section A**

***Study Source 8 before you answer this question.***

How much weight would you give the evidence of Source 8 for an enquiry into Napoleon's role in the Coup of Brumaire?

Explain your answer using the source, the information given about it and your own knowledge of the historical context. (12 marks)

**Tip**

*Carefully consider Napoleon's motives for creating such an account. Take care, though, not to be too dismissive of the account. While Napoleon clearly has an agenda, he also reveals some important points about why and how the Coup occurred.*

## THINKING HISTORICALLY Evidence (5b)

### The importance of context

Documents (texts) are like small pieces torn from a larger tapestry (context). Historians have to reconstruct the larger pattern into which documents might fit in order to use them to construct accounts of the past. The problem is that texts can have multiple contexts. Historians often debate how best to contextualise the documents that they interpret.

Read Source 8, Napoleon's proclamation after, and account of, the Coup of Brumaire.

1 Summarise the key points from the source. According to Napoleon, who invited him to use his military influence during the coup and why did they do so? What happened when he entered the Council of the Five Hundred? How does Napoleon justify his use of force against the Council of the Five Hundred?

As well as noting the contents of the proclamation, it is important to consider Napoleon's audience. The proclamation was addressed 'To the French People' and was written just hours after he was declared Consul and would have been widely published.

The timeline below provides a possible context for the document in the wider story of the Directory. Look at this timeline and answer question 2.

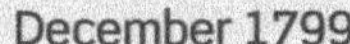

#### SEQUENCE OF EVENTS 1

**May 1799**
The Coup of Floréal: in a highly undemocratic action, the Directors overturn election results

**June 1799**
Jourdan's Law causes increased opposition to conscription

**July 1799**
The Law of Hostages leads to accusations of tyranny against the government

**November 1799**
The Coup of Brumaire marks the collapse of the Directory

**December 1799**
The constitution of the Consulship comes into effect

2 How does Napoleon's proclamation fit into the wider context of the fall of the Directory? Why might Napoleon have emphasised the weaknesses of the Directory within his proclamation?

The document might seem to have one kind of meaning when interpreted in the context of the failures of the Directory. A contrasting interpretation appears if we locate it in another context.

If we locate it in the context of Napoleon's rise to power, there is good reason to think that Napoleon was not concerned with overthrowing the Directory for the sake of the liberty and freedom of the French people. Consider the second timeline and answer the question that follows.

#### SEQUENCE OF EVENTS 2

**October 1795**
Napoleon's reputation increases due to his role in defeating the Vendémiaire rising

**1796–97**
Napoleon leads French forces to victory in the Italian campaign

**October 1797**
Napoleon defies the Directory by personally negotiating the Treaty of Campo-Formio

**November 1799**
Napoleon returns to Paris, following the Egyptian and Syrian campaigns, to rapturous applause

**November 1799**
The Coup of Brumaire marks the collapse of the Directory

**December 1799**
Napoleon ensures his place as first consul in the new constitution of the Consulship

**May 1802**
Napoleon declares himself first consul for life

**December 1804**
Napoleon makes himself emperor

3 In what way does this context suggest a different interpretation of the causes of the Coup of Brumaire to that portrayed in Source 8?

Consider what you have observed in this activity and answer the following question:

4 Why is it important for historians to spend time thinking about possible contexts for a document before they start to use it to draw conclusions about the past?

## The coup of November and the establishment of the Consulship

The new three-man executive created to replace the Directory was to be called the Consulship (also known as the Consulate). The first three consuls were the perpetrators of the Coup of Brumaire: Sieyès, Ducos and Napoleon. The coup could have ended here, with a simple down-sizing of the executive. Yet it was not to be this way, as the three consuls drew up a new constitution. Presented on 15 December 1799, this constitution recognised the position of the three-man Consulship. This executive body was awarded far greater power than the Directory had been, with full control of finance and foreign affairs. Furthermore, through skilful negotiation, Napoleon determined that one of the three consuls, the first consul, should have greater power than the other two. Naturally, Napoleon argued that, as the military leader of the coup, the position was his. The substantial country estate that Sieyès was awarded as compensation probably helps to explain why he did not offer greater resistance.

Aside from the executive, the constitution created a governing body consisting of two chambers: the Tribunate and the Legislature. These bodies were indirectly elected through universal male suffrage. They could discuss and vote on legislation, but could not initiate new bills. It was the Senate who initiated new laws. Members of the Senate were chosen by the first consul, that is, Napoleon, from among the Legislature. As such, anyone in the Legislature who sought promotion had to please Napoleon, and the Senate was filled with loyal supporters.

KEY TERM

**Plebiscite**
Where a vote of approval is held to show public support for a policy or reform.

To add legitimacy to the new constitution, Lucien Bonaparte organised a **plebiscite**. He claimed three million voters accepted the new constitution, compared with only 1,562 against. Lucien greatly falsified the figures, adding as many as 8,000 positive votes to each department, and assuming a 'yes' vote from all military personnel. Despite the massive exaggeration of figures, it would appear that the result was strongly in favour of the new constitution. A more realistic figure of 1.5 million voters in favour has been suggested. If this is accepted, then it certainly implies that the French people were calling for change. It is likely, though, that the French people's acceptance of a new constitution is as much a reflection of their dissatisfaction with the Directory than it is of any great embrace of the new leadership.

## Conclusion

The success of the Coup of Brumaire itself owes as much to the quick thinking of Lucien Bonaparte as it does to any masterly planning by Sieyès or Napoleon. The fact that the coup succeeded, and that opposition to it and to the new constitution was limited, suggest the real cause of the collapse of the Directory. That is, that by 1799 there were too few people left who were willing to support it. Even moderate republicans like Sieyès realised that the Directory was failing. The constraints of the 1795 constitution, initially intended to prevent tyranny and radicalisation, had instead left the Directory lacking power or clear leadership. The only way the Directory could exert its authority was through military means or by evading legitimate political and democratic processes. Without such challenging circumstances to contend with, including the legacy of the Terror, internal unrest, a foreign war against multiple nations and dire economic circumstances, the Directory might have stood a better chance. But the circumstances existed and it failed.

Many historians consider the Coup of Brumaire and the creation of the Consulate to be the end of the French Revolution. However, it is only with the value of hindsight that we appreciate the significance of the Coup of Brumaire. The event was treated with indifference by many at the time: just another regime change, just another purge, just more political in-fighting. Why we, as historians, tend to view the Coup of Brumaire as a turning point is that it was the event that directly brought Napoleon Bonaparte to power. Just two years after the coup, Napoleon was made consul-for-life and, within another three years, he was emperor of France. It is for this reason that the period 1789–99 is often referred to as the French Revolution and the period 1799–1815 as the Napoleonic era. As with all periods of history, the continuities from pre-1799 to post-1799 are every bit as evident and important as the changes, but it is in 1799 than our study of the French Revolution concludes.

**A Level Exam-Style Question Section B**

To what extent can the collapse of the Directory in 1799 be attributed to the pressures that war placed upon it? (20 marks)

**Tip**

*War was not a direct cause of the Coup of Brumaire, so you will need to think about the way in which war contributed to a culture in which some people, like Sieyès and Napoleon, wished to overthrow the Directory and why others, including many deputies of the Councils, were willing to stand by and let it happen.*

**ACTIVITY**
**KNOWLEDGE CHECK**

**Why was the Directory overthrown in November 1799?**

1 Identify the similarities and differences between the Coup of Floréal and the Coup of Fructidor.

2 Which one of the two do you believe undermined the authority of the Directory more? Justify your answer fully.

3 Explain how changes in the war situation increased opposition to the government in 1798–99.

4 To summarise the causes of the Coup of Brumaire, produce a Venn diagram of political, economic and military causes.

**ACTIVITY**
**SUMMARY**

**From the Directory to the Coup of Brumaire 1795–99**

As a summary of why the Directory failed, write an explanation of how each of the following nine factors contributed to the Directory's fall, substantiating your explanations with reference to specific details and events:

the weaknesses of the 1795 constitution; the strain of war; economic crisis; the royalist threat; the Jacobin threat; Directorial interference in election results; increasing Directorial dependency on the military; provincial unrest; the Coup of Brumaire.

Once you feel confident in your knowledge, draw a continuum to rate the significance of the different factors in causing the collapse of the Directory, ranging from 'Not very significant' to 'Highly significant'. Then place each of the nine factors onto that continuum according to where you think they belong, with the most significant factor at one side, ranging down to the least at the other.

Starting with what, in your view, is the most significant factor, try to explain why you think that factor is more important than the one below it. For example, 'I think that the weakness of the constitution was more significant than Directorial interference in election results because, if the constitution had given the Directory more power in the first place, then it might not have had to change election results to keep control.' Work down the continuum until you have justified your positioning of all the factors.

## THINKING HISTORICALLY Change (6a)

### Separately and together

Below are some different types of history that historians may identify.

| Political history | Economic history | Social history |
|---|---|---|
| Religious history | Military history | International history |

These are thematic histories, where a historian focuses on a particular aspect of change. For example, an economic history of the French Revolution would focus on trade and the economic reasons for the revolution, whereas a political history of the revolution would focus on governments and leaders of the revolution.

Work in groups.

1 Write a definition for each type of history.

Here are some events from across the period of the French Revolution from 1795 to 1799.

| Spring 1795 | September 1795 | September 1797 | October 1797 | July 1799 | November 1799 |
|---|---|---|---|---|---|
| The risings of Germinal and Prairial | The Comte d'Artois' unsuccessful invasion of the Vendée | The Directory wipes out much of its debt by declaring bankruptcy | The Treaty of Campo-Formio ends Napoleon's successful Italian campaign | Jourdan's Law declares a *levée en masse* | The Coup of Brumaire |

Answer the following questions:

2 The first two events, from Spring 1795, could be classified as 'social' events. What other theme(s) of history do they take into account?

3 Was the Comte d'Artois' invasion political or military, or both? Explain your answer.

4 Look at the timeline at the beginning of this chapter. Categorise the other events of 1795 according to the theme/s to which you believe they apply. How many of the events can be considered applicable to more than one theme?

5 What were the political consequences of the Directory declaring bankruptcy (an economic event)?

6 What political and economic changes came about because of the French military victories in 1797?

7 Which theme or themes of history do you believe best apply to Jourdan's Law?

8 How could the Coup of Brumaire be said to have happened for military, political, social and economic reasons?

Work in pairs.

9 Write a statement attacking 'thematic history'.

10 Write three statements defending 'thematic history'.

11 Explain why 'thematic history' occurs.

### WIDER READING

Crook, M. 'The resistible rise of Napoleon Bonaparte', 1998: http://history.org.uk/resources/student_resource_510.html An article aimed at students examining the period of the Directory and Napoleon's rise within it

Jones, P. *The French Revolution 1787–1804*, second edition, Routledge (2010) An accessible academic text aimed at undergraduate students

Lyons, M. *France under the Directory*, Cambridge University Press (1975) A challenging academic text that remains one of the most comprehensive studies of the period

Rees, D. *France in Revolution*, fourth edition, Hodder Education (2008) An A Level textbook covering the whole revolution; chapter 6 addresses the Directory with more detailed coverage of the period than many other A Level textbooks

Woronoff, D. *The Thermidorean Regime and the Directory 1794–1799*, Cambridge University Press (2009) An academic book dealing with the problems faced by the Thermidoreans and the Directory; an authoritative text based upon more recent scholarship on the period.

# Preparing for your AS Level Paper 2 exam

### Advance planning

1. Draw up a timetable for your revision and try to keep to it. Spread your timetable over a number of weeks, and aim to cover four or five topics each week.
2. Spend longer on topics which you have found difficult, and revise them several times.
3. Above all, do not try to limit your revision by attempting to 'question spot'. Try to be confident about all aspects of your Paper 2 work, because this will ensure that you have a choice of questions in Section B.

### Paper 2 overview:

| AS Paper 2 | Time: 1 hour 30 minutes | |
|---|---|---|
| Section A | Answer 1 compulsory two-part sources question | 8+12 marks = 20 marks |
| Section B | Answer 1 question from a choice of 3 | 20 marks |
| | Total marks = | 40 marks |

You should familiarise yourself with the layout of the paper by looking at the examples published by Edexcel. The questions for each section are followed by eight pages of lined paper where you should write your answer.

### Section A question

Each of the two parts of the question will focus on one of the two contemporary sources provided. The sources together will total around 300 words. The (a) question, worth 8 marks, will be in the form of 'Why is Source 1 useful for an enquiry into...?' The (b) question, worth 12 marks, will be in the form of 'How much weight do you give the evidence of Source 2 for an enquiry into...?' In both your answers you should address the value of the content of the source, and then its nature, origin and purpose. Finally, you should use your own knowledge of the context of the source to assess its value.

### Section B questions

These questions ask you to reach a judgement on an aspect of the topic studied. The questions will have the form, for example, of 'How far...', 'To what extent...' or 'How accurate is it to say...'. The questions can deal with historical concepts such as cause, consequence, change, continuity, similarity, difference and significance. You should consider the issue raised in the question, consider other relevant issues, and then conclude with an overall judgement.

The timescale of the questions could be as short as a single year or even a single event (an example from Paper 2C.2 could be, 'To what extent was Russia's involvement in the First World War responsible for the fall of the Provisional Government in 1917?'). The timescale could be longer depending on the historical event or process being examined, but questions are likely to be shorter than those set for Sections A and B in Paper 1.

### Use of time

This is an issue which you should discuss with your teachers and fellow students, but here are some suggestions for you.

1. Do not write solidly for 45 minutes on each question. For Section A it is essential that you have a clear understanding of the content of each source, the points being made, and the nature, origin and purpose of each source. You might decide to spend up to ten minutes reading the sources and drawing up your plan, and 35 minutes writing your answer.
2. For Section B answers you should spend a few minutes working out what the question is asking you to do, and drawing up a plan of your answer before you begin to write your response.

# Preparing for your AS Level exams

## Paper 2: AS Level sample answer with comments

### Section A

Part A requires you to:

- identify key points in the source and explain them
- deploy your own knowledge of the context in which events took place
- make appropriate comments about the author/origin/purpose of the source.

***Study Source 4 (page 199) before you answer this question.***

*Why is Source 4 valuable to the historian for an enquiry into the reaction to the Civil Constitution of the Clergy (1790)?*

*Explain your answer using the source, the information given about it and your own knowledge of the historical context. (8 marks)*

#### Average student answer

This source is a valuable one for enquiring into the reaction to the Civil Constitution of the Clergy as it shows how some people favoured it. The author talks about the Civil Constitution in revolutionary language, writing about 'liberty' and 'breaking our chains'. He clearly thinks that the Civil Constitution is a good thing, then, in that it is giving people their liberty from the Catholic Church. He also states that 'God is on our side' so thinks that God approves of the Civil Constitution. The source shows us how some people reacted favourably to the Civil Constitution and favoured the reduction of Catholicism's power.

Clear focus on the question. Some source details used and simple inferences made, with little contextual knowledge applied.

Yet the source has another side to it. It mentions the refusal of 'a few bishops and several priests to take the oath'. This refers to the oath that priests were required to take declaring their loyalty to the revolution. Some refused. This is valuable in that it shows that there was resistance to the Civil Constitution. The source also makes references to 'remain[ing] united' and 'letting harmony reign' suggesting there was serious opposition. The author, then, wants there to be peace.

More detailed contextual knowledge provided, with a clear mention of value and an inference on the extent of opposition. The aim of the author is considered, but the comment is undeveloped and needs to fully consider the author's motives and purpose.

Overall, I consider this to be a valuable source for an enquiry into the reaction to the Civil Constitution of the Clergy because it shows us that some people, like the author, favoured the constitution whereas others, like the priests, did not.

The conclusion is more of a summary than an overall judgement. It does not take into account the nature of the evidence.

### Verdict

This is an average response because:

- it summarises some key points from the source and makes some simple inferences from it, but misses more subtle points
- it applies a little contextual knowledge to explain some details, but not frequently enough
- it makes some comments on the value of the source
- it notes the author's intention, but does not fully consider the source's purpose or what this suggests about the topic.

Use the feedback on this response to rewrite it, making as many improvements as you can.

# Paper 2: AS Level sample answer with comments

## Section A

Part B requires you to:

- interrogate the source
- draw reasoned inferences
- deploy your own knowledge to interpret the material in its context
- make a judgement about the value (weight) of the source.

***Study Source 15 (page 237) before you answer this question.***

*How much weight do you give the evidence of Source 15 for an enquiry into the extent of Robespierre's role in the Terror (1793–94)?*

*Explain your answer using the source, the information given about it and your own knowledge of the historical context. (12 marks)*

### Average student answer

Source 15 certainly holds some weight in what it reveals to us about the extent of Robespierre's role in the Terror. The source is useful in that it can be used to suggest reasons why Robespierre came to prominence during the period. The author tells us that, even by the end of 1791, Robespierre had 'immense popularity' and had gained the nickname 'the Incorruptible'. It is certainly true that Robespierre was very popular and was known for sticking to his beliefs. Also, his speeches at the Jacobins Club, mentioned in the source, gained him a strong reputation. In this way, the source has some weight in what it says, as Robespierre was very popular and was seen by many as the leader whose ideas ultimately led to the Terror. Also, as Billaud-Varenne worked with Robespierre on the Committee of Public Safety, he gives us an interesting insight into how Robespierre was perceived at the time.

> There is no introduction. Otherwise, this is a good paragraph that considers how the source could be used. It recognises facts within the source and applies some own knowledge to show that the information is accurate.

We should be cautious, though, about taking Billaud-Varenne's account at face value. He was a member of the Committee of Public Safety. The Committee of Public Safety was the body largely responsible for the Terror. It was the Committee that controlled many aspects of the Terror, such as the Revolutionary Tribunals, and also introduced some of the laws of the Terror. So, by emphasising, and possibly exaggerating, the extent of Robespierre's role, Billaud-Varenne may be trying to downplay his own role within the Committee. As the source may have been composed to direct blame for the Terror away from the author, this may give it less weight as the reliability of his viewpoint is questionable.

> Considers the purpose of the source, but there is not enough contextual knowledge. Why, at this specific time, might Billaud-Varenne be wanting to put all the blame on Robespierre?

I would not place too much weight on Billaud-Varenne's view of Robespierre's role in the Terror as I think he is trying to blame Robespierre for the Terror so he does not get blamed himself.

> The conclusion is directly related to the enquiry. However, it is not an analytical judgement, it is one-sided.

### Verdict

This is an average response because:

- it considers how the source could be used, using some contextual knowledge (albeit not detailed)
- it considers how the purpose of the source and the position of the author affects its credibility
- it does not consider the context of the time when the source was written nor its limitations.

Use the feedback on this response to rewrite it, making as many improvements as you can.

# Paper 2: AS Level sample answer with comments

## Section A

Part A requires you to:

- identify key points in the source and explain them
- deploy your own knowledge of the context in which events took place
- make appropriate comments about the author/origin/purpose of the source.

***Study Source 4 (page 199 ) before you answer this question.***

*Why is Source 4 valuable to the historian for an enquiry into the reaction to the Civil Constitution of the Clergy (1790)?*

*Explain your answer using the source, the information given about it and your own knowledge of the historical context. (8 marks)*

### Strong student answer

This source is valuable for enquiring into the reaction to the Civil Constitution as it shows how some people favoured it and how such advocates justified themselves. The author talks about the Civil Constitution in revolutionary language, writing about 'liberty' and 'breaking our chains'. He is probably referring to liberty from the controls and power of the Catholic Church, closely associated with the ancien régime. The source shows us how some people reacted favourably to the Civil Constitution and favoured the reduction of Catholicism's power. So, this is valuable in that it reveals how revolutionaries perceived the Civil Constitution: not as an attack on religious beliefs but, rather, that the actions of the Assembly and the revolution were on the side of God.

Answer should start with an introduction that clearly focuses on the question.

Contextual knowledge is used to explain what the author means and the detail is impressive. Subtle inferences are also made.

Yet the source has another side to it. It mentions the refusal of 'a few bishops and several priests to take the oath'. This is a reference to the oath that priests were required to take declaring their loyalty to the revolution. Some refused. This is valuable in that it shows that there was resistance. However, the use of the words 'a few' and 'several' implies that they were not common, whereas this was not the case. Resistance was widespread, not just amongst the clergy, and the source makes no reference to any resistance aside from the priests. This is probably due to its purpose: to discourage resistance. Therefore, the author may be intentionally downplaying the severity and extent of opposition. The fact he has to do so, and his references to 'remain[ing] united' and 'letting harmony reign', suggest there was serious opposition, a valuable thing to learn.

A strong paragraph that takes into account the purpose of the source. It carefully analyses the specific language used. Contextual knowledge is used both to explain direct source references and limitations. The contextual knowledge applied could perhaps be more detailed.

Overall, I consider this to be a very valuable source for an enquiry into the reaction to the Civil Constitution because, taken at face value, it reveals to us how some people, like Prudhomme, strongly supported it as a part of the revolution. Furthermore, when we consider its purpose, it also reveals that resistance was considerable enough for someone to feel the need to write this defence of the Assembly's actions.

An excellent conclusion that provides a supported judgement as to the overall value of the source.

### Verdict

This is a strong response because:

- it selects valid key points and details from the source and explains valid inferences
- it applies contextual knowledge to explain these details and inferences
- it evaluates the value of the source
- it takes into account the purpose of the source.

# Paper 2: AS Level sample answer with comments

## Section A

Part B requires you to:

- interrogate the source
- draw reasoned inferences
- deploy your own knowledge to interpret the material in its context
- make a judgement about the value (weight) of the source.

***Study Source 15 (page 237) before you answer this question.***

*How much weight do you give the evidence of Source 15 for an enquiry into the extent of Robespierre's role in the Terror (1793–94)? Explain your answer using the source, the information given about it and your own knowledge of the historical context. (12 marks)*

### Strong student answer

Robespierre's role in the Terror has been the subject of much debate. Some see him as the driving force, others emphasise the role of other factors, such as the war or the actions of the sans-culottes. Source 15 suggests Robespierre's role was key, though we should be careful taking what it says at face value.

Source 15 can be used to suggest why Robespierre came to prominence during the period. The author tells us that, even by the end of 1791, Robespierre had gained 'immense popularity' and the nickname 'the Incorruptible' due to his unwavering revolutionary beliefs. He publicly stated that anyone not for the revolution was against it, and therefore should be persecuted. These beliefs, as Billaud-Varenne says, gained him great popularity as did his skilled oratory at the Jacobins Club. Billaud-Varenne worked on the Committee of Public Safety, so gives an insight into how Robespierre was perceived at the time.

This is a strong paragraph that considers how the source could be used. It also recognises facts within the source and has applied own knowledge to show that the information is accurate.

We should be cautious, though, about taking Billaud-Varenne's account at face value. Following the Coup of Thermidor, members of the Committee were held to account for their role in the Terror. By emphasising, and possibly exaggerating, the extent of Robespierre's role, Billaud-Varenne may be trying to downplay his own role so that he does not suffer the same punishment. His comment that Robespierre was 'the most important man in France' when he joined the Committee is an opinion rather than fact. As the source may have been composed to direct blame for the Terror away from the author, this may give it less weight.

A good paragraph that considers the information given about the source and how Billaud-Varenne's role as a member of the committee may have affected what the source states. It recognises the difference between fact and opinion, but this point could be further developed.

The source is also limited in that it fails to mention the responsibility of many others who were partly responsible for the Terror, and does not reveal or discuss many other causes. It gives no detail about the pressures caused by war. The fear of both the foreign enemy and the counter-revolutionary 'enemy within' were important causes of the Terror. There were far more deaths in the Vendée and in the suppression of towns like Lyon than there were in Paris and these atrocities were not the fault of Robespierre. It therefore gives a very one-sided view of the causes of the Terror, over-emphasising Robespierre's role.

Another strong paragraph that considers what the source does not tell us (i.e. its limitations) by applying detailed contextual knowledge.

### Verdict

This is a strong response because:

- it states how the source could be used, recognising facts within it and using knowledge of the period to expand on it.
- it addresses the purpose of the source, context and author
- it explains the limitations of the source by taking into account what the source does not tell us.

# Paper 2: AS Level sample answer with comments

## Section B

These questions assess your understanding of the period in some depth. They will ask you about the content you learned about in the four key themes, but may not ask about more than one theme. For these questions remember to:

- give an analytical, not a descriptive, response
- support your points with evidence
- cover the whole time period specified in the question
- come to a substantiated judgement.

*To what extent did the Directory (1795–99) fail to deal with political extremism? (20 marks)*

### Average student answer

The Directory ruled France from 1795 until 1799. It consisted of five men who ruled the country alongside two elected councils. The Directory tried to keep the politics of France balanced and to keep the country moderate. There were some people in France, though, who wanted a return to monarchy. There were others who were more left wing, such as the Jacobins. The Directory tried to stop these people from gaining power.

This introduction shows some understanding of the question. It is rather narrative, though, and gives a description rather than introducing what the debate is about.

The first political problem the Directory faced was called the White Terror. From 1794 to 1796 there was a lot of political violence in France. Armed gangs sought revenge against Jacobin supporters and sans-culottes. In Paris, a new group, known as the *jeunesse dorée*, took to the streets to attack and intimidate former Jacobins and *sans-culottes*. They were led by a journalist called Fréron. Often, the government of the Directory and local officials allowed this violence to continue. This was a bad idea as it meant that they were not dealing with political extremism.

A logical place to begin, as this was the earliest political extremism the Directory faced. The explanation at the end is one-sided, though. There needs to be analysis.

As well as the White Terror, there was a plot to overthrow the government by a communist called Babeuf. Babeuf was an extreme left-wing leader who lived in Paris. He wrote a newspaper and tried to get other people to follow him in a coup. However, the Directory found out about his plan and it captured him and his men and had them executed. So the Directory dealt with this political extremism well.

Although lacking precision, the information is largely accurate here (although Babeuf was not actually a communist). Again, though, there is no analysis. Furthermore, the structure is a little illogical here.

There were also people in France who wanted to see the power of the monarchy restored. These royalists are another example of political extremism. In the context of the time, as most deputies were republicans, this revival can be seen as political extremism. The Directory was effective in dealing with the threat of a royalist revival. When the royalists did well in the elections, the Directors felt they had to act. They called in the army and had many royalist deputies arrested. This was effective in reducing the power of royalism. The problem with the Directors' solution, though, was that they were seen to have acted undemocratically so, whilst this helped keep the councils more moderate, it also led to greater opposition.

This paragraph is more analytical as it gives both the advantages and disadvantages of the Directory's purge of the councils. The main weakness of this paragraph is that the candidate has given very little detail.

Perhaps the greatest extremist challenge to the Directory came from the rise of the Jacobins in the latter years of the Directory's rule. After the power of the royalists was forcefully reduced, there was a rise in support for the extreme Left. In the 1798 elections an increasing number of Jacobins were elected. This scared the Directors, and some moderates within the Council, as the Jacobins were highly critical of the government. In response to this, the Directory decided to spread rumours that the Jacobins were planning to stage a coup against the government. This allowed it to convince the Council of the Five Hundred to annul the election results, thereby removing the Jacobins from the Councils, a move known as the Coup of Floréal. This was a bold move that broke the power of the Jacobins.

A more detailed paragraph with reference to specific events and dates. While the focus on the question is evident, there is no real analysis: to what extent was the Coup of Floréal an effective solution to the rise of Jacobinism?

In conclusion, the Directory did quite well in dealing with political extremism. It was a mistake to let the people who created the White Terror get away with it but the Directory got tough against Babeuf, sending a lesson out to others. They also dealt with the royalists and the Jacobins in similar ways, by forcing them out of the councils when they got too many votes. This was good as it stopped them gaining power.

This conclusion provides a clear judgement and does summarise the key points from the answer. Like the body of the answer, however, it is not very analytical.

## Verdict

This is an average response because:

- it demonstrates understanding of the question, addressing the correct issues, and focusing on the question, but there is little analysis
- the knowledge deployed, though mostly accurate, lacks depth and detail
- judgements are made in relation to the question, but they are not supported or fully justified
- the work reads clearly, despite some illogical structuring.

Use the feedback on this response to rewrite it, making as many improvements as you can.

# Paper 2: AS Level sample answer with comments

## Section B

These questions assess your understanding of the period in some depth. They will ask you about the content you learned about in the four key themes, but may not ask about more than one theme. For these questions remember to:

- give an analytical, not a descriptive, response
- support your points with evidence
- cover the whole time period specified in the question
- come to a substantiated judgement.

*To what extent did the Directory (1795–99) fail to deal with political extremism? (20 marks)*

### Strong student answer

When the constitution of the Directory was created in 1795 it was done with the intention of avoiding the extremes of the preceding years. The Terror had been characterised by political extremism and violence. After the Coup of Thermidor, royalist views once again became acceptable. The Directory tried to find a balance between the extremes of radical Jacobinism and royalism. Ultimately, the Directory failed and was overthrown by a coup in 1799. Yet the extent to which this was due to the Directory's failure to tackle political extremism is arguable. It could well be said that, under the circumstances, the Directory acted decisively and effectively.

A strong introduction. It outlines issues that will be addressed within the body of the answer and hints at what line of argument will be used in the answer.

The Directory came into being in 1795 and immediately faced a new kind of political extremism – that of the White Terror. From 1794 to 1796 a wave of political violence swept France. It was felt most strongly in areas where the Jacobin Terror had been most extreme, such as Paris and Lyon. Armed gangs took to the streets to seek revenge against Jacobin supporters and *sans-culottes*. In Lyon, a prison was stormed and over 100 people, believed to be responsible for the Jacobin atrocities in the city, were murdered. In Paris, a new group, known as the *jeunesse dorée*, emerged. They took to the streets to attack and intimidate former Jacobins and *sans-culottes*. They had their own fashion and tended to wear fine clothes to separate themselves from the *sans-culottes*. They were led by a journalist called Fréron. Often, the government of the Directory and local officials turned a blind eye to this violence because, as they saw it, the people involved were on their side in opposing and punishing radical Jacobinism. It could be said that, by failing to act against the White Terror, the Directory actually legitimised political extremism.

A logical place to begin, as this was the earliest political extremism the Directory faced. The paragraph shows very impressive depth of knowledge, yet, a lot of that detail is unnecessary and the paragraph is rather descriptive.

The White Terror was so named as it is often considered to be a royalist backlash (white was the colour of the French royalty). Often, though, those involved were just seeking revenge on the 'terrorists' rather than wanting a restoration of the monarchy. Yet there were those who did want to see the power of the monarchy restored. A royalist faction emerged under d'André, royalist clubs were established in Paris and some council deputies began to argue for the withdrawal of laws against émigrés. In the context of the time, as most deputies were republicans, this revival can be seen as political extremism.

The answer makes a good link with the previous paragraph. It has also established why it is discussing royalism, in relation to the question, and sets out valid criteria for doing so.

It could well be argued that the Directory was rather effective in dealing with the threat of a royalist revival. When the constitution of 1795 was first created a rule was included that two-thirds of the deputies of the councils had to have sat in the National Convention. As few royalists were in the Convention, this helped to keep their influence down. But, in the later elections, the royalists began to gain more seats. In the 1797 elections they won many seats in the councils. The Directors felt they had to act. Barras called in the army, claiming there was a royalist conspiracy, and had many royalist deputies arrested, in what is known as the Coup of Fructidor. This was effective in ensuring that the power of royalism within the councils was reduced. The problem with the Directors' solution, though, was that they were seen to have acted undemocratically so, whilst this helped keep the councils more moderate, it also led to greater opposition.

An excellent paragraph that deploys detailed knowledge directly to answer the question. There is also some analysis towards the end. It could be improved further by evaluating these arguments – did the benefits of the Directory's actions outweigh the costs?

Threats of political extremism came not only from the royalists but also from the extreme left. The Coup of Fructidor may have effectively quelled a royalist resurgence but it also encouraged a political swing towards the left. With their opposition removed, Jacobins, or neo-Jacobins as they are sometimes known, launched a propaganda campaign attacking the failings of the Directory. Despite efforts by the Directory to shut down Jacobin printing presses, their campaign was partly successful and, in 1798, a significant number of Jacobins were elected. This scared the Directors, and some moderates within the Councils, as the Jacobins were highly critical of the government. As a result, the Directory decided to spread rumours that the Jacobins were planning to stage a coup against the government. This allowed them to convince the Council of the Five Hundred to annul the election results, thereby removing the Jacobins from the Councils; a move known as the Coup of Floréal.

The Coup of Floréal was, in some respects, a successful attempt to tackle political extremism. Over 120 deputies of the Councils lost their seats in the Coup, which were then filled by people selected by the Directors themselves. This helped to restore a much more moderate balance to the Councils. Furthermore, the Directory had achieved this without having to rely on military intervention, as they had in the Coup of Fructidor. Yet there were negative consequences of Floréal. Once again, the Directors had gone outside the democratic process, highlighting the failures of the Constitutions of 1795 as well as increasing accusations of abuse of power by the Directory. Also, it could be argued that the Coup was not necessary, as, even in the 1798 elections, the Jacobins were always a minority and were greatly outnumbered by more moderate deputies.

Strong, detailed knowledge of the Coup of Floréal. The analysis here is particularly good as both the positive consequences and the negative consequences are considered.

In conclusion, it is reasonable to argue that the Directory did act effectively in dealing with political extremism. Whilst it may have failed to act against the White Terror, to do so could have potentially caused an even greater political backlash, as it would have been seen to have been acting in favour of Jacobinism. In dealing with the royalist revival in the councils, the Directory acted decisively in removing deputies with royalist sympathies. Similarly, it tried to protect against a Jacobin resurgence in the Coup of Floréal. Whilst its actions may have undermined confidence in the legitimacy of the government, the Directory did manage to stave off a return to monarchy or Jacobin radicalism, no easy task when following the extremism of the prior years.

An excellent conclusion that provides a clear judgement, clearly explained and supported by the body of the answer. The conclusion takes into account both sides of the debate, yet still manages to provide a convincing justification.

### Verdict

This is a strong response because:

- it shows appreciation of the relationships between key features of the period, such as the White Terror and the increasing influence of royalism in the councils
- it demonstrates clear understanding of the debate, addressing the correct issues and focusing on the question, with a supported judgement reached
- the depth of knowledge and detail are impressive
- the answer is logically structured and well written.

# Preparing for your A Level Paper 2 exam

## Advance planning

1. Draw up a timetable for your revision and try to keep to it. Spread your timetable over a number of weeks, and aim to cover four or five topics each week.
2. Spend longer on topics which you have found difficult, and revise them several times.
3. Above all, do not try to limit your revision by attempting to 'question spot'. Try to be confident about all aspects of your Paper 2 work, because this will ensure that you have a choice of questions in Section B.

## Paper 2 overview

| AL Paper 2 | Time: 1 hour 30 minutes | |
|---|---|---|
| Section A | Answer 1 compulsory source question | 20 marks |
| Section B | Answer 1 question from a choice of 2 | 20 marks |
| | Total marks = | 40 marks |

You should familiarise yourself with the layout of the paper by looking at the examples published by Edexcel. The questions for each section are followed by eight pages of lined paper where you should write your answer.

## Section A question

This question asks you to assess two different types of contemporary sources totalling around 400 words, and will be in the form of 'How far could the historian make use of Sources 1 and 2 together to investigate ...?' Your answer should evaluate both sources, considering their nature, origin and purpose, and you should use your own knowledge of the context of the sources to consider their value to the specific investigation. Remember, too, that in assessing their value, you must consider the two sources, taken together, as a set.

## Section B questions

These questions ask you to reach a judgement on an aspect of the topic studied. The questions will have the form, for example, of 'How far...', 'To what extent...' or 'How accurate is it to say...'. The questions can deal with historical concepts such as cause, consequence, change, continuity, similarity, difference and significance. You should consider the issue raised in the question, then other relevant issues, and conclude with an overall judgement.

The timescale of the questions could be as short as a single year or even a single event (an example from Paper 2C.2 could be, 'To what extent was Russia's involvement in the First World War responsible for the fall of the Provisional Government in 1917?'). The timescale could be longer depending on the historical event or process being examined, but questions are likely to be shorter than those set for Sections A and B in Paper 1.

## Use of time

This is an issue which you should discuss with your teachers and fellow students, but here are some suggestions for you.

1. Do not write solidly for 45 minutes on each question. For Section A it is essential that you have a clear understanding of the content of each source, the points being made, and the nature, origin and purpose of each source. You might decide to spend up to ten minutes reading the sources and drawing up your plan, and 35 minutes writing your answer.
2. For Section B answers you should spend a few minutes working out what the question is asking you to do, and drawing up a plan of your answer before you begin to write your response.

# Preparing for your A Level exams

## Paper 2: A Level sample answer with comments

### Section A

You will need to read and analyse two sources and use them in tandem to assess how useful they are in investigating an issue. For these questions remember to:

- spend time, up to ten minutes, reading and identifying the arguments and evidence present in the sources; then make a plan to ensure that your response will be rooted in these sources
- use specific references from the sources
- deploy your own knowledge to develop points made in the sources and establish appropriate context
- come to a substantiated judgement.

***Study Sources 6 (page 178) and 13 (page 187) before you answer this question.***

*How far could the historian make use of Sources 6 and 13 together to investigate the causes of discontent in France in the 1780s?*

*Explain your answer, using both sources, the information given about them and your knowledge of the historical context. (20 marks)*

#### Average student answer

There were many causes of discontent in France in the 1780s. Sources 13 is an example of a *cahier*, which were letters of complaint that members of the French public were invited to send into the Estates General detailing their grievances. Source 6 gives a different view, that of a British visitor to France just before the revolution.

A rather short introduction. It could have briefly outlined what some of the causes of discontent were, or introduced some of the key points from the sources.

In some ways, these sources would be very useful for a historian investigating the causes of discontent in 1780s France. The sources agree on certain issues. Source 6 makes clear the problems of poverty in rural areas of France. Young refers to children looking 'terribly ragged'. He says this poverty, and the discontent it must have caused, was due to poor use of the farmland, reporting that 'one third of what [the land] I have seen in this province seems uncultivated'. Source 13 supports Young's account of poor land saying that 'we have a great deal of wasteland' and, that as they only have 'a few good fields', they get 'very small harvests'.

Both sources agree in another way. That is the feudal dues that peasants had to pay to their landlords. Feudal peasants were expected to pay a significant portion of their produce to their lord. Source 13 directly mentions these 'seigniorial' charges and states that the peasants are 'heavily burdened by these and other dues. Source 6 also partly blames the problems of France on the 'feudal nobility'.

These are sound paragraphs that address what the sources, taken together, picking up on direct similarities and summarising some of the grievances of the time. Contextual knowledge has not been fully applied, though.

Taken individually, Source 13 is also to of value to the historian as it reveals other grievances felt by the peasantry, including issues not covered in Source 6. For example, Source 13 states that 'the sale of salt it too high for poor people'. Salt was a basic necessity for preservation and the state placed a high tax upon it, called the *gabelle*. The *cahier* also asks for an end to the 'tax men' – the much hated tax farmers who were very corrupt in performing their duties. Instead the peasants are asking for 'a small tax on each young man' which would be a fairer system.

This paragraph does apply some more detailed contextual knowledge, in relation to the *gabelle*, but could have said more about the inequalities of the estates system.

There are limitations to these sources, though, that a historian would need to take into account. First, the sources only show the problems in rural areas. The urban bourgeoisie, as well as the nobility had reasons to be unhappy and these are not covered in the sources. We should also keep in mind, when considering Source 6, that it was written by an outsider who will have seen the situation in France differently to those living under it. Also, as Arthur Young was British he may be judging France harshly, as Britain and France had been enemies for many years.

In relation to Source 13, there may be vested interests at play. The *cahiers* allowed people to complain and so they would be likely to overemphasise their problems in order to get better deals for themselves. In Source 13, for example, the authors may be exaggerating their economic hardships in order to get their taxes reduced. However, it is certainly true that there were hardships in rural areas in the 1780s, so perhaps the view presented is an honest one.

Overall, these sources could be well used by a historian as they reveal some of causes of discontent in the 1780s. They show us that people were unhappy about the system of taxation (Source 13) and the problems of poor land and food shortages in rural areas (both sources).

This conclusion does give a judgement, but it is a summary rather than an analysis. It does not weigh up the strengths and limitations of the evidence.

It is good that the answer considers the limitations of the evidence provided, though an opportunity has been missed to explain what the grievances of the bourgeoisie and the nobility were (i.e. grievances not covered in the sources).

The provenance of both sources has also been considered, however, the comments on Source 6 are very generalised and contextual knowledge is not used to assess whether Young's view is accurate.

## Verdict

This is an average response because:

- it summarises the sources in relation to the enquiry specified in the question
- some contextual knowledge is used to explain the points raised in the sources
- it does consider the nature of the evidence, albeit not in a very developed fashion
- an overall judgement is reached but it is not fully justified, as it does not take into account the limitations.

Use the feedback on this response to rewrite it, making as many improvements as you can.

# Paper 2: A Level sample answer with comments

## Section A

You will need to read and analyse two sources and use them in tandem to assess how useful they are in investigating an issue. For these questions remember to:

- spend time, up to ten minutes, reading and identifying the arguments and evidence present in the sources; then make a plan to ensure that your response will be rooted in these sources
- use specific references from the sources
- deploy your own knowledge to develop points made in the sources and establish appropriate context
- come to a substantiated judgement.

***Study Sources 6 (page 178) and 13 (page 187) before you answer this question.***

*How far could the historian make use of Sources 6 and 13 together to investigate the causes of discontent in France in the 1780s?*

*Explain your answer, using both sources, the information given about them and your knowledge of the historical context. (20 marks)*

### Strong student answer

In the context of the 1789 revolution, the causes of discontent in France in the 1780s have been a subject of much study and debate. The causes of discontent were numerous and diverse, varying from harvest failures and famine to opposition to absolute monarchy. As historians we are fortunate to have access to written documents, such as Source 13 recorded in the late 1780s which reveal some of the complaints and grievances of the French people: the *cahiers de doléances*. Source 6, however, gives us a valuable different perspective, that of a British visitor, looking at the problems in France from an outsider's viewpoint.

A good introduction, as it briefly introduces what the question is about and contextualises the named sources.

In some ways, these sources would be very useful for a historian investigating the causes of discontent in 1780s France. The sources reflect the views of different nationalities but they still agree on certain issues. Source 6 makes clear the problems of poverty in rural areas of France. Young refers to children looking 'terribly ragged' and, his observation of shoe-less people leads him to speak of shoes as a luxury item. He attributes this poverty, and the discontent it must have caused, to a poor use of the farmland, reporting that 'one third of what [the land] I have seen in this province seems uncultivated'. Source 13 supports Young's account of poor land saying that 'we have a great deal of wasteland' and, that as they only have 'a few good fields', they get 'very small harvests'. Indeed the harvests in France in the later years of the 1780s were poor and no doubt contributed to discontent in rural areas. Furthermore, poor weather, such as the hail mentioned in Source 13, devastated crops causing famine.

Both sources agree on a further cause of discontent. That is the feudal dues that peasants had to pay to their landlords. Feudal peasants were expected to pay a significant portion of their produce to their lord. Source 13 directly mentions these 'seigniorial' charges and states that the peasants are 'heavily burdened by these and other dues. Source 6 is not so direct but also partly blames the problems of France on the 'feudal nobility' and their 'despotism', which could certainly include the charges they placed on the peasantry even during times of hardship.

Excellent paragraphs addressing what the sources, taken together, reveal to the historian about the enquiry. Contextual knowledge is used to expand on what the sources directly say.

Taken individually, Source 13 is also to of value to the historian as it reveals other grievances felt by the peasantry, including issues not covered in Source 6. For example, Source 13 states that 'the sale of salt it too high for poor people'. Salt was a basic necessity for preservation and the state placed a high tax upon it, called the *gabelle*. This tax was only paid by members of the Third Estate, who were often the poorest, and so became a despised symbol of the inequality of the *ancien régime*. The *cahier* also asks for an end to the 'tax men' – the much hated tax farmers

Highly detailed and precise contextual knowledge used to explain points raised in Source 13. Source 6, though, could have been similarly treated by addressing points raised in the last sentence of the source.

who were notoriously corrupt in performing their duties. Instead the peasants are asking for 'a small tax on each young man'. The idea of a universal tax on all men was a significant challenge to the privileges of the *ancien régime* but it was Enlightenment ideas of equality like this that were becoming increasingly common by the 1780s, adding to discontentment.

There are limitations to these sources, though, that a historian would need to take into account. First, neither source takes into account the views of those outside the rural peasantry. The urban bourgeoisie, as well as the nobility had reasons to be unhappy. Many nobles were concerned about Louis' proposed reforms, as the king and his ministers were trying to impose taxes upon them. This is a very different cause of discontent from those covered within the sources. As it was the nobility who defied the king during the financial crisis of 1787–89, a historian would need to take their motives into account too. Similarly, the bourgeoisie, some of whom played a key role in the 1789 revolution, were probably less motivated by rural hardship than they were by the desire to see their increasing wealth recognised though greater political participation. These sources, then, only give us a limited view of French society in the 1780s.

A strong paragraph, clearly considering the limitations of the evidence provided by addressing what the sources do not reveal about the period.

We should also keep in mind, when considering Source 6, that it was written by an outsider who will have seen the situation in France differently to those living under it. The British farming economy was superior to that of France in the 1780s so it is hardly surprising that Young finds what he witnesses in France to be so shocking. It also may be in some part due to xenophobia, as France and Britain were traditional enemies, that he is so critical of the 'detestable' habits of the French lords. That said, Source 13 does support a lot of what Young claims, adding weight to his account.

In relation to Source 13, there may be vested interests at play. When Necker sent out the request for *cahiers*, people were being invited to complain and would be likely to overemphasise their problems in order to get better deals for themselves. In Source 13, for example, the authors would have a vested interest in exaggerating their economic hardships in order to get relief from taxation. However, it is certainly true that there were hardships in rural areas in the 1780s due to population increase and harvest failures, so perhaps the view presented is an honest one.

Good interrogation of the evidence, by considering the provenance of the sources, and consideration of whether or not the sources are presenting an honest and accurate view. Contextual knowledge has been applied to make a judgement as to whether or not the sources are an accurate reflection of the period.

Overall, these sources could be used by, and are valuable to, a historian as they reveal some of the economic causes of discontent in rural areas during the 1780s, for example the complaints about the system of taxation (Source 13) and the problems of poor land and food shortages in rural areas (both sources). However, we cannot learn from them the causes of discontent amongst all classes of French society. In fact, they tell us nothing of the complaints of the nobility and the bourgeoisie. And, as it was largely these wealthier classes of society who drove the revolution in 1789, I feel that these sources are of only limited value.

A good conclusion that shows balance by summarising what the sources can be used for and their limitations. It also arrives at an overall judgement in relation to the enquiry.

### Verdict

This is a strong response because:

- it considers how the sources can be used in relation to the enquiry, i.e. what they reveal
- it uses detailed knowledge of the context to expand on the points raised in the sources
- the limitations of the sources are recognised, and contextual knowledge is used to explain these limitations
- there is interrogation of the evidence.

# Paper 2: A Level sample answer with comments

## Section B

These questions assess your understanding of the period in some depth. They will ask you about the content you learned about in the four key themes, but may not ask about more than one theme. For these questions remember to:

- give an analytical, not a descriptive, response
- support your points with evidence
- cover the whole time period specified in the question
- come to a substantiated judgement.

*How far do you agree that the collapse of constitutional monarchy in August 1792 was due to the unwise actions of Louis XVI? (20 marks)*

### Average student answer

In August 1792 the Tuileries Palace was stormed by a mob. Louis fled to the Assembly, hoping it would protect him, but the crowd burst into the Assembly, demanding the removal of the king and the end of the Assembly. Their wishes were granted and, in September 1792, France was declared a republic. The August *journée* was the final cause of the collapse of constitutional monarchy. However, the cracks and divisions that ultimately led to the *journée* had begun long before.

This is not the correct way to begin an answer. An introduction should show understanding of the question by explaining the key factor within it, as well as introducing what other key factors and arguments there are.

Louis certainly did take some unwise decisions and actions that undermined his own position. The most famous example is the flight to Varennes. King Louis and the royal family fled from Paris, hoping to get to Austrian territory. However, they were captured when they got to Varennes when a postmaster recognised Louis and they were brought back to Paris. When they were returned to the city, everyone was made to be quiet so that they did not insult or shout at the king. The flight to Varennes made people very angry as they saw Louis as a traitor to the revolution.

A logical place to begin the body of the answer: by dealing with the factor in the question. The major weakness is that it is very descriptive. It says more about what happened than it does about why the event was significant.

Louis did not only act unwisely in choosing to flee France. In 1792 he cancelled a number of laws created by the Assembly. Laws were passed demanding the exile of non-loyal priests and for the creation of an army to defend Paris. Louis tried to stop both these laws. This was highly unwise as, once again, it made him seem like he was acting against the revolution. These laws had been created by the Assembly to protect the French during the war so, by cancelling them, Louis looked like he was on the side of the enemy and a traitor to France.

This paragraph is more effective as it shows some relationship between different causes of Louis' fall – in this case Louis' mistakes and the war. What it lacks is the depth of knowledge required to support the points made.

Another cause of the fall of constitutional monarchy was the rise of political clubs and radicals. There were the Jacobins Club and the Cordeliers Club who both wanted a republic. They were led by Robespierre and Danton. These clubs produced newspapers that criticised the monarchy and told people that Louis was a traitor. This made people want to overthrow their king.

Covering the role of the political clubs is relevant to this question, however there is a missed opportunity to explain relationships between the growth of political clubs and other causes of Louis' fall.

Another cause of the failure of constitutional monarchy was the impact of war. Louis' wife, Marie Antoinette, was Austrian, so people suspected that the royal family were actively helping the opposing armies. Rumours were circulated by the press claiming not only that the king was not supporting the revolution but that he was actually an enemy and traitor of the revolution. This did considerable damage to Louis' reputation and goes some way to explain why the people of Paris overthrew him in August 1793.

There is a lack of logic in the structure of the answer here. The answer began talking about the war at an earlier point, and now returns to it again here.

The final trigger of Louis' fall, the attack on the Tuileries in August 1792, can also be considered to be a consequence of war. The war made people distrust the king but the final straw was the Brunswick Manifesto. In July, the Prussian commander, the duke of Brunswick, issued a threat to Paris, stating that if any harm came to King Louis, then he would destroy the city. With the Prussian/Austrian army advancing towards the city, this threat seemed only too real. Yet, the Manifesto did not have the effect that Brunswick desired. Instead of protecting Louis, it caused tensions in Paris to boil over. Fearing that Louis might betray the city to the enemy, the *sans-culottes* stormed the Tuileries, ultimately forcing Louis' downfall and the abolition of the Assembly.

Strong detail on the Brunswick Manifesto, but an opportunity to explore other causes of tension within Paris has been missed.

There were many reasons why constitutional monarchy failed in 1792. There were the problems caused by the war, the political clubs who ganged-up on Louis and the mistakes that Louis made. Overall, I think that Louis' unwise actions were the main cause of his fall because they made people think he was a traitor to France and a traitor cannot be a king.

This conclusion does focus on and answer the question. Yet, there is no justification given for the judgement.

## Verdict

This is an average response because:

- it addresses some of correct key issues relevant to the question
- mostly relevant and accurate knowledge is used, though it lacks depth of detail
- there is some analysis, even if it is not developed
- it reads clearly, but has some illogical structuring.

Use the feedback on this response to rewrite it, making as many improvements as you can.

# Paper 2: A Level sample answer with comments

## Section B

These questions assess your understanding of the period in some depth. They will ask you about the content you learned about in the four key themes, but may not ask about more than one theme. For these questions remember to:

- give an analytical, not a descriptive, response
- support your points with evidence
- cover the whole time period specified in the question
- come to a substantiated judgement.

*How far do you agree that the collapse of constitutional monarchy in August 1792 was due to the unwise actions of Louis XVI? (20 marks)*

### Strong student answer

France was declared a republic following the violent overthrow of the monarchy and the Assembly in August 1792. It could well be argued that Louis' unwise actions contributed to his fall. At times, his actions, not least the flight to Varennes, made it appear as if Louis was against, rather than for, constitutional monarchy, heightening anger against him. Perhaps a more convincing argument, though, could be made that it was the impact of war that brought down the monarchy. As well as being the direct cause of the August *journée,* it was the war that radicalised many people, and the war that made Louis' actions seem even more traitorous.

An excellent start. This introduces the line of argument (that war was most significant) and shows the relationship between that factor and others (e.g. economic problems and political radicalism).

Louis certainly did make actions that undermined his own position. Despite losing power in 1789, he was still the head of state and expected to uphold the values of the revolution and the constitution. Yet he made mistakes that made people feel that he did not truly support the system of constitutional monarchy. The most notable example is the flight to Varennes, when the royal family tried, and failed, to flee France. The flight confirmed people's suspicions that Louis was only pretending to be behind the revolution and it caused a backlash against him. Led by the Cordeliers, a petition was created demanding the king's dismissal. There was also a split in the Jacobin Club who, prior to then, supported constitutional monarchy but after Varennes moved towards republicanism.

A logical place to begin the body of the answer. The answer clearly explains the significance of Louis' actions and shows depth of knowledge by providing specific details to support the points.

The flight to Varennes, arguably an unwise action by the king, did move views towards republicanism. However, the impact of the flight should not be overstated. Despite Louis' admission that he felt the revolution was not working, many people remained in favour of constitutional monarchy. After the Champs de Mars massacre, there was actually a backlash against the republicans. The mood in the Assembly, although more republican than before the flight, still remained behind the constitution. If the flight to Varennes was so devastating to the king, then it has to be questioned why he remained king for over a year. Later events clearly had a part to play too.

A strong paragraph, balancing the point made in the previous paragraph with counter-arguments. Unlike the previous paragraph, though, greater depth of knowledge could have been applied.

Louis did not only act unwisely in choosing to flee France, though. In 1792 he used his right of veto to over-rule a number of laws created by the Legislative Assembly. Laws were passed demanding the deportation of all refractory priests and the creation of a *fédérés* army. Louis vetoed both these laws. This was highly unwise as, once again, it made him seem like he was acting against the revolution. Yet we have to place Louis' vetoes within context. The reason that Louis' vetoes caused such uproar, sparking a *journée* in June 1793, was because of the ongoing war. In a time of peace, Louis using his right of veto might have seemed less of a big issue, but the fact that he was vetoing laws designed to protect France against enemies during a time of war made him appear like a traitor.

This paragraph is very effective at showing the relationship between different causes of Louis' fall. The answer also skilfully turns the issue of Louis' errors around to support their argument that war was the most significant cause.

Moving on to the wider issue of war – there was some distrust of the monarchy before France went to war in spring 1792, but this distrust was heightened hugely once the war had begun. As Louis' wife, Marie Antoinette, was Austrian, people suspected that the royal family was actively helping the opposing armies. Rumours of an 'Austrian Committee' were circulated by the radical press, by the likes of Desmoulins, claiming not only that the king was not supporting the revolution but that he was actually an enemy and traitor of the revolution. This did considerable damage to Louis' reputation and goes some way to explain why the people of Paris overthrew him in August 1792.

Again, the depth of knowledge shown here is very strong, with detailed examples used to support the arguments made. There is also a clear link back to the question at the end of the paragraph.

The final trigger of Louis' fall, the *journée* of 10 August 1792, can also be considered to be a consequence of war. The war effort increased the economic burden on the already pressured Parisian working class, as food and supplies were reserved for military use, rather than for general consumption, causing inflation. On numerous occasions, the *sans-culottes* of Paris rioted over bread prices. Added to this, was an influx of *fédérés* into the city. These revolutionary soldiers were called upon to enlist to fight for the revolution and against France's enemies. As a result, many thousands of patriotic recruits would head through Paris on their way to the front, further heightening tensions within the city. The final straw was, though, the Brunswick Manifesto. In July, the Prussian commander, the duke of Brunswick, issued a threat to Paris, stating that if any harm came to King Louis, then he would destroy the city. With the Prussian/Austrian army advancing towards the city, this threat seemed only too real. Yet, the Manifesto did not have the effect that Brunswick desired. Instead of protecting Louis, it caused the already tense situation in Paris to boil over. Fearing that Louis might betray the city to the enemy, and encouraged by the radical press and the Paris Commune, the *sans-culottes* stormed the Tuileries – ultimately forcing Louis' downfall and the abolition of the Assembly. In this case, Louis' decision-making cannot be blamed. In the summer months of 1792, it was the consequences of war that mostly caused the *sans-culottes* to depose their monarch.

Strong detailed examples used to support the war argument. There is also clear linking of events, showing how pressure mounted across time due to a series of events.

To conclude, Louis certainly did make some unwise decisions that turned people more in favour of republicanism. Despite these actions the Assembly tended to remain behind him. It was only after the war began in 1792 that the pressure in Paris really began to increase. Suspicions of the king are one thing in peace time but when combined with the threat of extermination from a foreign enemy, fear of the enemy within, economic hardships worsened by war and a radical minority fanning the flames of all this, the position of the King became impossible. It is for these reasons that the *sans-culottes*, and their political influencers, overthrew Louis in August 1792.

A good conclusion that sustains the argument made throughout the answer. It also effectively re-emphasises the links between the different factors, providing balance yet still arriving at a clear judgement.

### Verdict:

This answer is a strong response because:

- it shows impressive appreciation of the relationships between key causes of the failure of constitutional monarchy
- a clear line of argument is maintained throughout the answer and a supported judgement is reached
- the depth of knowledge and detail are, for the most part, excellent
- the answer is logically structured and well written.

# Russia in revolution, 1894–1924

## The significance of the Russian Revolution

In early 1917, more than 300 years of **Tsarist** rule in Russia came to an abrupt end when Tsar Nicholas II was forced to abdicate. Nine months later, after a turbulent intervening period, the Bolsheviks – soon to rename themselves the Communists – seized power. The events of 1917 were to have momentous consequences in both Russia and the wider world. Within Russia, the revolution led first to civil war and then to economic transformation and brutal dictatorship under Josef Stalin. In the wider world, the events of 1917 inspired communists in other countries, notably China, and left anti-Communists deeply alarmed. The revolution gave rise to tensions and conflicts between Russia and the major capitalist powers, which persisted until the collapse of the Soviet Union in 1990. The Russian Revolution is unquestionably one of the most important events of modern world history.

## Preconditions of revolution in Russia

In the late 19th century, Tsarism was being undermined by a number of long-term developments. The **preconditions** of revolution in Russia were in place before Nicholas II became tsar in 1894.

### The legacy of Alexander II's 'Great Reforms'

Intended to strengthen Tsarism, the 'Great Reforms' (the most important of which was the abolition of serfdom in 1861) had the opposite effect. In key respects, they failed to live up to the hopes and expectations of the Russian people: the result was disillusionment with the Tsarist regime.

Disillusionment with the regime was nowhere stronger than in the Russian countryside. It arose out of the land settlement that accompanied the abolition of serfdom. Before 1861, serf-owners typically made some of the land on their estates available to their serfs to cultivate for subsistence purposes. Over time, serfs came to regard this land as theirs by right. In 1861, they expected to acquire it free of charge. Instead they were made to pay for it. The terms were harsh and the repayment period long (49 years): bitterness in rural Russia over the 1861 land settlement therefore persisted into the reign of Nicholas II.

#### KEY TERMS

**Tsarist**
Tsarist, or imperial, rule in Russia originated in the mid-16th century when Ivan ('the Terrible'), Grand Duke of Moscow, dispensed with his existing title and proclaimed himself tsar, or emperor, of all Russia. In 1613, the title of tsar passed to Michael Romanov, the first of the Romanov dynasty that was destined to rule Russia for the next 300 years.

In the early 17th century, Russia was already immense in size, but it grew further under Romanov rule, especially as a result of the expansionist policies of Peter the Great (1682–1725), Catherine the Great (1762–96) and Alexander II (1855–81). Late 19th-century Russia was geographically by far the largest country in the world.

**Precondition**
A long-term economic, social and attitudinal development that undermines and destabilises the established political order to the point that a revolution is a distinct possibility.

|  |  |
|---|---|
| 1861 | 1861 - Emancipation of the serfs |
| 1894 | 1894 - Nicholas II becomes tsar |
| 1906 | 1906 - First Duma |
| 1907-12 | 1907-12 - Third Duma |
| 1914 | 1914<br>August - Germany declares war on Russia |
| 1918 | 1918 - Treaty of Brest-Litovsk |
| 1921 | 1921 - Introduction of the New Economic Policy |

(Note that before February 1918 Russia used the Julian calendar, which ran 13 days behind the Gregorian calendar in use in western Europe. Dates up to 1918 in this table and throughout the unit are Julian dates.)

1864

1864 - Establishment of elected local government bodies, the *zemstva*

1905

1905 - Revolutionary turmoil throughout Russia

1907

1907 - Second Duma

1912

1912 - Fourth Duma elected

1917

1917
March - Abdication of Nicholas II

1918–20

1918–20 - Russian Civil War

1924

1924 - Lenin's death

**EXTEND YOUR KNOWLEDGE**

**The 1861 Land Settlement**

In 1861, over 80% of the inhabitants of the Russian Empire were members of peasant households. Of these, approximately half were serfs owned by private landlords, mostly Russian noblemen. The other half were state peasants who farmed land belonging to the state, paying a variety of taxes for the privilege. The 1861 land settlement applied only to privately owned serfs: state peasants were not given the right to buy the land they cultivated until 1866.

The 1861 land settlement involved the state compensating serf-owners for the land they had lost - paying them with government bonds, which could be traded for cash on the money markets - and getting its money back from the liberated serfs through 49 annual 'redemption payments'.

Peasant households did not make redemption payments on an individual basis: village communities paid them collectively.

### Industrialisation

Starting from a low base, the industrial sector of the Russian economy developed rapidly in the later 19th century. The Tsarist regime actively promoted industrial development, fearing that without it Russia would lose its Great Power status. By doing so, however, it stored up trouble for itself. In Russia, as elsewhere, industrialisation led to the emergence of an urban working class. Tsarist Russia's working class, wrestling with harsh living and working conditions, was sullen, resentful and volatile. It was small in number – around three million, or just over two percent of the total population, by the 1890s – but its influence in Tsarism's crisis years was out of all proportion to its size because it was concentrated in the major cities alongside the nerve centres of government and administration.

### Population explosion

At the time of the abolition of serfdom, the population of the Russian Empire was 74 million. By 1914, it was 164 million. One consequence of this population explosion was to add to tensions in the countryside. With more mouths to feed, peasants, who made up more than 80 percent of the population, desperately wanted to acquire extra land, but they lacked the financial means to do so. Some government help was made available through the Peasant Land Bank, founded in the 1880s, but it was not enough to satisfy peasant 'land hunger'. 'Land hunger' was one of the main drivers of peasant discontent during the revolutionary era.

### Nationalism

The Russian Empire was a multi-national state – that is, a country containing people of many different nationalities. Russians were the dominant nationality and the others were subject nationalities. In some parts of the Empire there was intense hostility to what was seen as alien Russian rule. This was true of Finland, Estonia, Latvia, Lithuania and, above all, Poland. The level of support in these places for national independence posed a serious threat to the Empire's stability.

## Tsarism's 'crisis of modernisation'

In the late 19th century the Tsarist regime found itself confronted with a disaffected peasantry, aggrieved urban workers and an educated middle class calling for political change. This situation arose in no small part out of its own urge to modernise Russia, to equip it with the kind of institutions and economy that would enable it to keep abreast of the advanced countries of western Europe. What Tsarism faced, says one historian (S.A. Smith), was 'a crisis of modernisation'. It was a crisis with which it proved unable to cope.

# 2b.1 The rule of Nicholas II, 1894–1905

**KEY QUESTIONS**

- How, and how oppressively, was Russia governed before 1905?
- How much organised opposition did the Tsarist regime face before 1905, and how did the aims of the main opposition groups differ?
- In what ways, and how seriously, was the Tsarist regime threatened by revolutionary activity in 1905?
- In what ways, and how successfully, did the Tsarist regime respond to the threats it faced in 1905?

**EXTEND YOUR KNOWLEDGE**

**Nicholas II (1868–1918)**
Nicholas II was the shy and sensitive son of an overbearing and bullying father who scorned him as a 'girlie'. He became tsar in 1894 aged only 26 when his middle-aged father, Alexander III, died suddenly. Little had been done to prepare Nicholas to carry out his responsibilities as a ruler, and he was ill at ease in the world of politics and administration. He was happiest in the company of his wife, Alexandra, and five children, to whom he was devoted.

## INTRODUCTION

The first ten years of Tsar Nicholas II's rule were less turbulent than those which followed. There were, however, clear signs during these relatively quiet years that Russia's 'crisis of modernisation' was intensifying.

- The 1890s saw a quickening in the pace of industrial growth in Russia. One historian (Hans Rogger) has spoken of 'the great industrial spurt of the 1890s'. The main growth hubs were Baku on the Caspian Sea (oil), the eastern Ukraine (coal, iron and steel), Moscow (textiles and engineering) and St Petersburg (also textiles and engineering). Total industrial output doubled in Nicolas II's first ten years as tsar.
- The industrial boom was accompanied by fast-paced urbanisation. The populations of St Petersburg and Moscow increased by 25 percent in the 1890s. Most of the new city-dwellers were industrial workers.
- Disaffected urban workers resorted to strike action with increasing frequency in the 1890s and early 1900s, despite the fact that, under Russia's harsh Penal Code, strikes and trade unions were illegal. The highest-profile individual stoppages were the 1896 and 1897 strikes by St Petersburg's textile workers.
- Unrest was not confined to the cities. The early 1900s saw outbreaks of serious peasant rioting in the fertile 'Black Earth' region in the southern part of European Russia. Landowners' estates were attacked, looted and burned. The government bore at least some of the responsibility for these disturbances. Its policy, in effect, was to make the peasantry pay for its industrialisation programme by imposing higher taxes on basic consumer items such as alcohol, sugar, tea, heating oil and matches. Some government officials feared that this squeeze on an already hard-pressed peasantry would lead to trouble, and they were proved right.

**1892** – Witte appointed finance minister (dismissed 1903)

**1894** – Nicholas II succeeds his father, Alexander III, as tsar

**1898** – Formation of the RSDLP – the Russian Social Democratic Labour Party

**1902** – Formation of the Socialist Revolutionary Party

**1903** – Bolshevik-Menshevik split

**1904** – Start of the Russo-Japanese War

1892 | 1894 | 1896 | 1898 | 1900 | 1902 | 1904

- The assassination of Tsar Alexander II in 1881 by the 'People's Will' terrorist organisation was followed by a ferocious government crackdown on radicals and agitators. Tsarism's opponents were scattered and driven underground. In the 1890s, however, they began to regroup and re-organise. The Bund, a Jewish socialist party based in Poland, was established in 1897, the Russian Social Democratic Labour Party (RSDLP) in 1898 and the Socialist Revolutionary Party in 1902.
- In 1902, the Combat Organisation, a terrorist group linked with the Socialist Revolutionary Party, launched an assassination campaign targeting senior government officials. Its most prominent early victims were Dmitry Sipyagin, the minister of the interior, in 1902 and Sipyagin's successor, Vyacheslav von Plehve, in 1904.

### EXTEND YOUR KNOWLEDGE

**Witte and the development of industry in Russia**

The driving force behind the Tsarist regime's industrial development policy in the 1890s was the dynamic but abrasive Sergei Witte (1849–1915) who was minister of finance 1892–1903. Witte attracted much-needed foreign capital into Russia by putting its currency, the rouble, on to the gold standard in 1897. This meant that roubles could, on demand, be exchanged for gold. The idea was to boost foreigners' confidence in the rouble by convincing them it would not lose its value over time due to inflation.

One project close to Witte's heart that benefited from the inflow of foreign funds was the expansion of Russia's railway network. The centre-piece of the railway building programme was the construction of the Trans-Siberian railway (begun in 1891 and finally completed in 1916).

Witte welcomed foreign investment, but kept cheap foreign imports out of Russia by means of tariffs (import duties), thereby protecting Russia's developing industries. Witte's policies produced very high growth rates in the 1890s, but their downside was the squeeze on the peasantry. This left him vulnerable to the charge made by his ministerial enemies that the over-ambitious pursuit of industrial growth was the cause of disorder in the countryside.

Nicholas II dismissed him as minister of finance in 1903, but recalled him in 1905 when the Tsarist regime had its back to the wall.

1905

**1905** - January: Bloody Sunday

**1905** - May: Battle of Tsushima

**1905** - August: August Manifesto promised the formation of a consultative Duma

**1905** - August: Witte recalled to a position of influence as the tsar's chief adviser
September: Treaty of Portsmouth between Russia and Japan

**1905** - October: Russia paralysed by a general strike
October: October Manifesto promises the formation of a Duma with law-making power

**1905** - December: St Petersburg Soviet disbanded
December: Violent suppression of the Moscow uprising

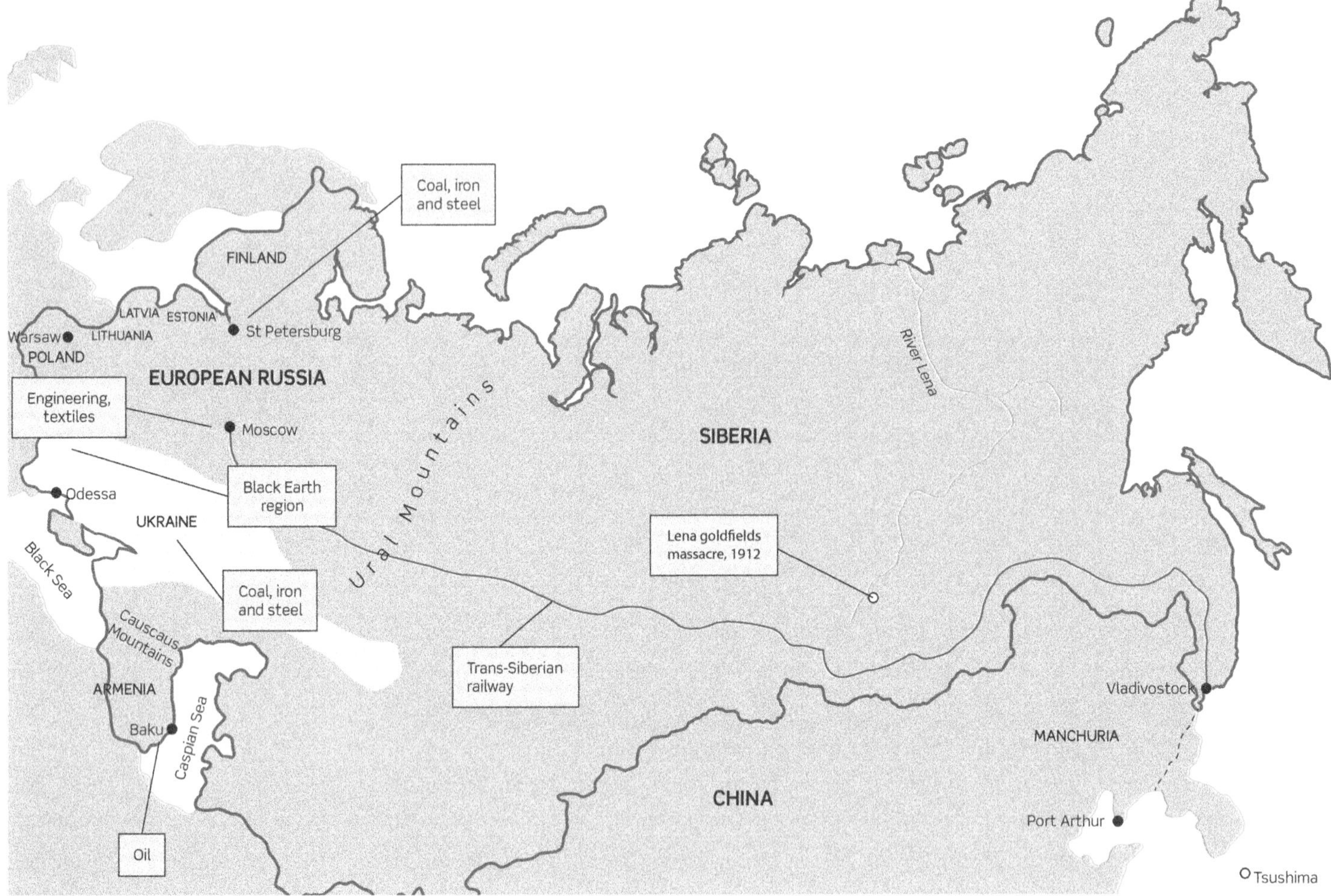


**Figure 1.1**: Nicholas II's Russian Empire.

# HOW, AND HOW OPPRESSIVELY, WAS RUSSIA GOVERNED BEFORE 1905?

## Orthodoxy, Autocracy and Nationality

The phrase 'Orthodoxy, Autocracy, and Nationality' was coined in 1833 by Sergei Uvarov, minister for education under Nicholas I, to describe the beliefs he wanted to see instilled through Russia's educational system. It subsequently became a commonly used shorthand way of summarising the basic principles on which Tsarist rule was based. Of these, autocracy was the most important.

### Autocracy

Autocracy is a form of government in which one person possesses unlimited power. Nicholas II's commitment to the principle of autocracy, like that of his predecessors, was rigid and unwavering. He believed that his right to wield unlimited power derived from the will of God and was therefore beyond challenge. He further believed that his diverse and unruly empire could not survive without the firm hand that an autocratic system could provide. Unsurprisingly, he viewed with contempt calls for reform that involved diluting the autocratic principle: early in his reign he dismissed them as 'senseless dreams'.

Late 19th-century Russia was the most autocratic state in Europe. There were no formal checks of any kind on the Tsar's power.

- Russia did not have a **constitution** setting out what the tsar could and could not do.
- There was no **parliament** – laws in Tsarist Russia were made by the tsar issuing decrees.
- There were no legal safeguards protecting the rights of individuals.
- Russia was governed on a day-to-day basis by ministers who were appointed by, and accountable to, the tsar.

**KEY TERMS**

**Constitution**
A body of rules, usually set out in a single document, which defines the functions, powers and composition of a country's main political institutions and specifies the rights that individual citizens can exercise without government interference.

**Parliament**
An assembly containing elected representatives of the people which makes laws, debates political issues and holds the government to account.

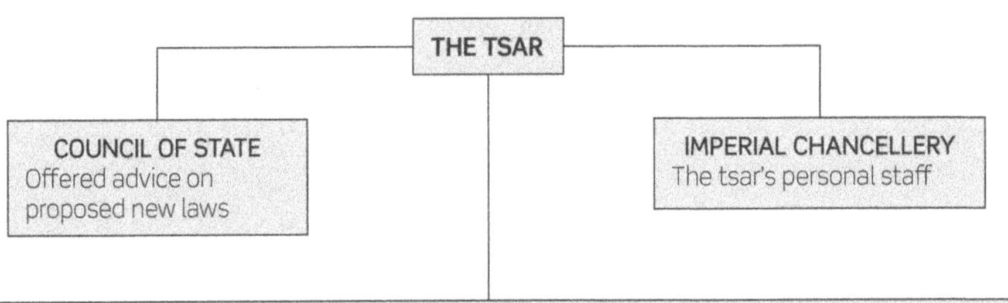


**CENTRAL GOVERNMENT DEPARTMENTS**

- There were eleven departments in all (Interior, Finance, War, Navy, Foreign Affairs, Holy Synod, Education, Agriculture, Trade, Transport, Justice).
- Ministers were responsible to the tsar on an individual basis: there was no prime minister who presented the collective view of government ministers to the tsar.
- The most important departments were the Interior Ministry (responsible for public order, policing, censorship and the supervision of local government bodies) and the Finance Ministry (responsible for taxation and economic development).

**LOCAL GOVERNMENT**

- **Provincial governors.** European Russia was divided into 78 provinces each with its own provincial governor. Governors were the tsar's representatives in their provinces and in this capacity had oversight of the whole range of government activity that went on in it. Among other things, they had the power to overrule *zemstvo* (see below) decisions. Provincial governors were answerable in the first instance to the minister of the interior.
- ***Zemstva* (singular: *zemstvo*).** The *zemstva* were elected local councils established in 1864 which operated in rural areas. They were responsible for education, health and the maintenance of roads and bridges. The *zemstva* over time became employers of large numbers of professional staff such as doctors, teachers and engineers. Although electoral arrangements for the *zemstva* were heavily weighted in favour of the upper classes, the *zemstva* became strongholds of liberal opinion. *Zemstvo* liberals were in the forefront of the campaign for reform in 1904–05. There were comparable institutions in the towns known as municipal councils.
- **Land captains.** The role of land captain was introduced in 1889. Land captains were members of the nobility who supervised peasant affairs in their localities.

**Figure 1.2**: Russia's system of government before 1905.

**SOURCE 1** Nicholas II and his wife in coronation robes, 1903.

As a ruler, Nicholas II's main strength was his sense of duty. Set against this were many weaknesses. He was naïve (he believed until the end that the vast majority of his people were devoted to him) and indecisive. He fussed over trivialities and failed to address bigger issues. In addition, he distrusted many of the politicians and officials with whom he had to deal, regarding them as devious and self-seeking. Lacking drive and imagination, Nicholas II failed to offer Russia effective leadership.

**SOURCE 2** From the memoirs of Count Sergei Witte, published in 1921. Witte was the tsar's chief minister in 1905–06, having served as finance minister 1892–1903.

His [Nicholas II's] outstanding failing is his lamentable lack of willpower. Though benevolent and not unintelligent, this shortcoming disqualifies him totally as the unlimited autocratic ruler of the Russian people.

At first any official coming into personal contact with him would stand high in his favour. His Majesty would even go beyond the limits of moderation in showering favours on his servant. Before long, however, His Majesty would become indifferent to his favourite, and, in the end, become hostile towards him.

There is an optimistic strain in His Majesty's character. He experiences fear only when the storm is actually upon him, but as soon as the immediate danger is over his fear vanishes. Thus, even after the granting of the Constitution, Nicholas considered himself an autocratic sovereign in a sense which might be formulated as follows: 'I do what I wish, and what I wish is good; if people do not see it, it is because they are plain mortals, while I am God's anointed.'

**AS Level Exam-Style Question Section A (a)**

***Study Source 2 before you answer this question.***

Why is Source 2 valuable to the historian for an enquiry into Nicholas II's abilities as a ruler?

Explain your answer using the source, the information given about it and your own knowledge of the historical context. (8 marks)

**Tip**

*You should focus tightly on the value, or usefulness, of Witte's recollections as evidence of Nicholas' strengths and weaknesses as a ruler: there is no need to consider their possible limitations.*

KEY TERM

**Russian Orthodox Church**
The largest of the Orthodox Christian churches of eastern Europe. These became distinct from the Roman Catholic Church in the Middle Ages. The Orthodox churches have their own theology and rituals, though their core beliefs are the same as those of other Christian churches.

### Orthodoxy

Orthodoxy in this case refers to the **Russian Orthodox Church** and its role and status within the Russian Empire. Orthodoxy was the religion of the tsars and the Orthodox Church was the spiritual wing of the Tsarist regime. The Orthodox Church was firmly under state control: it was run by a government department headed by a minister whose title was Procurator of the Holy Synod. As a state-controlled institution, it did the state's bidding: in its various pronouncements it preached the need for obedience to the tsar's authority.

At the end of the 19th century, the Church's value to the Tsarist regime was diminishing. It was an institution in decline: the reputation of its priests, often drunken and corrupt, was low and it was struggling to get a hearing in Russia's fast-growing towns and cities.

### Nationality

Nationality was a doctrine about Russia and its place within the tsar's Empire. It made two key claims.

- The domination of the tsar's multi-national Empire by Russia and the Russians was an entirely right and proper state of affairs. Russians, it was argued, had built the Empire and were therefore entitled to control it.
- Russia and the Russians were unique, separated from the peoples of Western Europe by a distinctive language, religion and culture. As a result, claimed supporters of Tsarism, liberal and socialist ideas had no place in Russia because they were unRussian.

In the late 19th and early 20th centuries, the doctrine of Nationality provided a justification for the regime's 'Russification' policies.

## The oppression of nationalities

The oppression of nationalities in late 19th and early 20th-century Russia took the form of Russification. Russification was a policy launched by Alexander III (1881–94) and continued under Nicholas II.

Russification was an attempt to impose Russia's language, culture and religion on the Empire's non-Russian minorities. It was implemented most aggressively in those parts of the Empire where nationalist feeling was strong. This was in the north-western borderlands (Poland, Estonia, Latvia, Lithuania, Finland) and, to a lesser extent, the Caucasus region.

- In Poland and the Baltic provinces, the use of the Russian language in court proceedings and in school lessons became compulsory, despite the fact that it was not the native language of most people in these places.
- The Orthodox Church was given government money to support its efforts to convert non-Russians to Orthodoxy. Meanwhile, churches that had deep roots in non-Russian areas were bullied and harassed. In the Baltic provinces, no new Protestant church could be built without government permission. In Armenia, the government in 1903 issued a decree confiscating the property of the Armenian Church, provoking demonstrations that culminated in troops opening fire on a crowd at Gandzak, killing 10 and wounding 70.

Russification was a counter-productive policy. Its aim was to halt the growth of nationalist movements in non-Russian areas. Instead, it aroused resentment within minority nationalities and stimulated the growth of **nationalism**.

KEY TERM

**Nationalism**
A political outlook that expresses itself in one of two main ways: either in a demand for national independence (in circumstances where a nation is denied it) or (where a nation is already self-governing) in an insistence that the nation's interests are pursued aggressively. Both outlooks derive from the assumption that the division of humankind into nations is more important than any other kind of division, such as social class. A nation is a group of people who feel a strong sense of common identity as a result of such factors as a shared language, religion, history or culture.

## Anti-Semitism

The Russian Empire acquired its Jewish population when Russia seized control of large parts of the previously independent Kingdom of Poland in the late 18th century. By 1900, there were nearly five million Jews in Russia. Virtually all of them (there were a few exceptions, including Jewish university graduates) were compelled by law to live within what was known as the Pale of Settlement, a demarcated zone stretching along Russia's western border.

No minority suffered more at the hands of the Tsarist regime than Russia's Jews. Anti-Semitic prejudice was endemic in government circles and gave rise to harsh discriminatory policies, especially in the reigns of Alexander III and Nicholas II. In the 1880s, Jewish access to higher education was severely restricted and Jews were banned from living in the Pale of Settlement's rural areas, forcing them into its towns and larger villages.

A hostile government was not the only thing the Russian Empire's Jews had to fear. They also had to contend with popular, grassroots anti-Semitism and the **pogroms** that, from time to time, arose out of it.

**KEY TERM**

**Pogrom**
Organised attack on communities, in particular minority communities, which involves murder, assault and the destruction of property. Governments may or may not be involved. The word 'pogrom' derives from a Russian word meaning 'to destroy'.

**SOURCE 3** Report from a local police chief in Balta, a town in the Ukraine, to his superiors, April 1903.

> Owing to rumours about the preparations for anti-Jewish disturbances in the Balta district I personally travelled to the town of Balta. Thanks to the timely measures that were adopted, the day when disorders were expected remained absolutely peaceful. On 18 April, however, ten peasant lads who were driving cattle began to assault Jews, but did not rob them, and said 'the Tsar permits the beating of Jews'. The Jews, though, are in a state of panicky terror: they greatly exaggerate the danger and attach significance to every trivial threat by the peasants and every foolish rumour.

**AS Level Exam-Style Question Section A (b)**

***Study Source 3 before you answer this question.***

How much weight do you give the evidence of Source 3 for an enquiry into the Tsarist regime's attitudes towards Russia's Jews before 1914?

Explain your answer using the source, the information given about it and your own knowledge of the historical context. (12 marks)

**Tip**
*Use of the phrase 'how much' suggests that the source has limitations as well as usefulness for an enquiry into the Tsarist regime's attitudes towards Russia's Jews. Offer an overall judgement on which outweighs the other at the start of your answer, then go on to give your reasons for this judgement.*

## The Okhrana

Tsarism had a number of instruments of repression at its disposal. It censored newspapers and other publications in an attempt to halt the spread of subversive ideas. In the event of large-scale disorder, it could turn to the army. At the forefront of its struggle against its internal enemies, however, was the Okhrana, Tsarism's political police force.

The role of the Okhrana was to infiltrate and destroy revolutionary and terrorist networks. In this role it was generally effective, despite being a relatively small organisation: in 1900 there were only 2,500 full-time Okhrana agents in the whole of the Empire, one-third of them stationed in St Petersburg. The key to the Okhrana's success was its use of informants: in the early 1900s, the leadership of both the Socialist Revolutionary and the Social Democratic Parties were riddled with Okhrana agents. The Okhrana had a fearsome reputation, but it was nothing like as monstrous as the secret police forces of Stalin's Russia or Hitler's Germany: it was, for example, sparing in its use of torture.

**ACTIVITY**
**KNOWLEDGE CHECK**

**The Russian Empire's system of government**

1. What would you regard as the main weaknesses of the pre-1905 Russian Empire's system of government? Give reasons for your answer.
2. To what extent was Nicholas II personally responsible for these weaknesses? Make reference to Source 2 in your answer.

# HOW MUCH ORGANISED OPPOSITION DID THE TSARIST REGIME FACE BEFORE 1905, AND HOW DID THE AIMS OF THE MAIN OPPOSITION GROUPS DIFFER?

## Unrest among peasants and workers

### Peasants

Outbreaks of peasant unrest in late 19th-century Russia were frequent but localised. They were not explicitly anti-government in character, even though government policies (**redemption payments** and high indirect taxes) were partly to blame for worsening conditions in the countryside. Usually it was local landowners who were targeted.

The underlying cause of peasant unrest was poverty and desperation. Environmental factors were one reason for rural poverty: in the northern districts of European Russia, the soil was poor and the growing season short, while in the 'Black Earth' region to the south the climate was erratic, leading to periodic crop failures and famine. Another reason was methods of production. The norm in the villages of European Russia was strip farming where the land available was divided into three large open fields, with each household being allocated a number of strips in each of the fields by the village commune or *mir*. Periodically (every 10–15 years) strips were reallocated between households to ensure fairness. Strip farming was inefficient for a number of reasons.

- Time was wasted moving from strip to strip.
- Some land was wasted because it was left uncultivated to mark the borders between strips.
- Periodic reallocation of strips meant that households had no strong incentive to improve their land.
- **Crop rotation** arrangements involved one of the three fields being left fallow each year, with the result that only two-thirds of a village's land was under cultivation at any one time.

Crop yields in Russia were very low by western European standards.

**KEY TERMS**

**Redemption payment**
A payment that a peasant community had to make to the government as a result of the 1861 land settlement.

**Crop rotation**
A practice designed to ensure that the soil retains its fertility. The three-year system of crop rotation widely used in Russia was antiquated: in western Europe it had been abandoned in favour of more sophisticated arrangements (which did not involve fallow years) and the use of fertilisers.

**EXTEND YOUR KNOWLEDGE**

**The *mir***
In the absence of a highly developed and well-manned system of local government, villages in Tsarist Russia were effectively self-governing. Village affairs were the responsibility of the village commune or *mir*. The *mir* was an all-male assembly made up of the heads of a village's households. It kept order within the village, collected taxes and redemption payments and selected conscripts for military service.

In relation to agricultural matters, apart from deciding on the periodic reallocation of strips (a practice, note, that some villages had abandoned by the early 20th century), the *mir* controlled the agricultural life of the village, making decisions about what crops were to be grown and when operations like sowing and harvesting took place.

### Workers

Working class unrest at the turn of the century mostly took the form of strikes. These were often brutal affairs: the army was called out to deal with strikers almost 300 times in 1901, a figure that increased to over 500 the following year. The willingness of workers to strike was the result of their grim living and working conditions. Pay was low; hours were long, averaging around 60 a week; factory discipline was harsh, usually enforced with a system of fines; and, with scant provision being made for health and safety, workplace injuries were frequent. Nor was there much to look forward to outside the factory gates: workers were housed in overcrowded slums, which were breeding grounds for diseases like cholera and typhus.

SOURCE 4

A satirical cartoon produced in Russia in 1900 depicting the country's social and economic structure.

The five captions on the cartoon read, from the bottom:

'We work for us, while they ...'

'Shoot at us...'

'Eat on our behalf ...'

'Pray on our behalf ...'

'Dispose of our money ...'

## Middle-class opposition and the League of Liberation

Late 19th-century Russia's middle class – industrialists, businessmen and educated professionals such as doctors and lawyers – was small but fast-expanding. Middle-class Russians were, broadly speaking, hostile to Tsarism. Their hostility had its roots in their attachment to liberal ideas. The educated middle class or 'intelligentsia' was strongly liberal in outlook: industrialists and businessmen tended to be more moderate.

Liberalism in turn-of-the-century Russia had two core principles:

- A belief in ending autocracy through the adoption of a constitution that transferred power to democratically elected institutions and guaranteed basic rights such as freedom of speech.
- A belief in an economic system based on private enterprise rather than public ownership: liberals were often enthusiastic social reformers, but they were not **socialists** who wanted to see most or all economic activity controlled by the state.

In addition, liberals had a strong preference for non-violent methods of bringing about political change. Moderate liberals usually saw a continuing role for the tsar as a British-style constitutional (or figurehead) monarch, but radical liberals often wanted Russia to become a **republic**.

One stronghold of liberalism in the Russian Empire was its university system, which in the late 19th century was expanding fast in order to supply the developing Russian economy with the higher-level skilled personnel it needed. University expansion brought an increasing number of students into contact with liberal ideas. This in turn led to conflict between liberal-minded students and officialdom. The years 1899–1901 saw a series of clashes between university students and the Tsarist authorities, one of which left 13 student protestors dead. These events had a radicalising effect on a generation of students.

### KEY TERMS

**Socialism**
A political doctrine which seeks to replace private ownership of land, industry and financial institutions with a system of public or communal ownership or regulation.

**Republic**
A country whose head of state is not a hereditary monarch but an elected or appointed president.

A second major stronghold of liberalism was the *zemstva*, Russia's elected local councils. In the 1890s the confidence of those associated with them was boosted by the contribution they made to relief efforts when famine struck southern Russia in 1891–92. Elected *zemstvo* members and technical experts, such as doctors and teachers who were employed by *zemstva*, began to call openly for a *zemstvo* voice in national affairs. They were left angry and frustrated by the government's refusal to enter into any sort of dialogue with them.

In the early 1900s, left-wing elements among the *zemstvo* liberals joined forces with radicalised students and others in the Liberation Movement. A newspaper, *Liberation*, was founded in 1902: it was printed in Germany and smuggled into Russia. In 1904, at a secret meeting in St Petersburg, the League (or Union) of Liberation was formally established. Paul Milyukov quickly emerged as its leading figure. In late 1904, with Russia at war with Japan, the League of Liberation launched its 'banquet campaign', hosting a series of public banquets in order, it claimed, to celebrate the 40th anniversary of the introduction of trial by jury in Russia. In practice, the object of the 'banquet campaign' was to mobilise liberal opinion in support of political change. Even before the shooting of demonstrators by the army on 'Bloody Sunday' in January 1905, the political temperature in Russia was rising.

**EXTEND YOUR KNOWLEDGE**

**Paul Milyukov (1859–1943)**
The son of an architect, Milyukov was a distinguished academic historian. In the 1890s, his political activism cost him his job at Moscow University and forced him abroad. Milyukov was a leader of middle-class liberal opposition to the Tsarist regime until the February Revolution in 1917. Between February and April 1917, he served as foreign minister in the Provisional Government established after the downfall of Tsarism. Milyukov was intelligent, hard-working and straight-talking, but - in the eyes of his critics - ambitious, vain, inflexible and a poor judge of character.

**SOURCE**

From the programme of the League of Liberation, 1904.

The first and main aim of the League of Liberation is the political liberation of Russia. The League considers political liberty in even its most minimal form as utterly incompatible with the autocratic character of the Russian monarchy, and for that reason will seek before all else the abolition of autocracy and the establishment in Russia of a constitutional regime. In determining the concrete forms a constitutional regime will take in Russia, the League of Liberation will make all efforts to have political problems resolved in the spirit of extensive democracy. Putting political demands in the forefront, the League also recognises as essential the definition of its attitude in principle to social-economic problems. In the realm of social-economic policy, the League of Liberation will make the direct goal of its activity the defence of the interests of the toiling masses.

## The Socialist Revolutionaries (SRs)

### Foundation

The Socialist Revolutionaries (SRs) were the heirs of an ill-fated populist movement of the 1860s and 1870s. The populists were middle-class idealists who had aimed to form a political alliance with the peasantry in order to overthrow Tsarism and build a new democratic order in Russia on the basis of the village commune or *mir*. Internal divisions, peasant indifference and government repression put paid to the original populist movement. Many on the political left nevertheless remained wedded to the idea of a distinctly Russian and largely peasant-based form of socialism. This encouraged a new generation of would-be leaders to form the Socialist Revolutionary Party in 1902.

The SRs' principal founders were Victor Chernov (1873–1952), Mikhail Gots (1866–1906), Grigory Gershuni (1870–1908) and Catherine Breshko-Breshovskaya (1844–1934), a veteran of the original populist movement who later became known as 'the little grandmother of the Russian Revolution'. All of them were middle- or upper-class in background: Chernov was a qualified lawyer; Gots was the son of a prosperous Jewish merchant; Gershuni was a pharmacist, though his father had been a serf; and Breshko-Breshovskaya was the daughter of a wealthy landowner.

The SRs aimed to win peasant support, but they were never an exclusively peasant party. They also attracted a significant following among Russia's urban workers. The line between peasants and workers in early 20th-century Russia was a blurred one: many industrial workers were first-generation migrants to the towns who retained close links with their home village, often returning to it at harvest time to help out their families.

The SRs were from the outset a relatively loosely organised and undisciplined party. A range of views was to be found in the party's ranks. There were SRs who were comparative moderates, SRs who were old-fashioned populists and SRs who were prepared to use **terrorist** methods. At no stage did the party leadership try to impose a uniform ideology on its rank and file.

### Ideas

Victor Chernov was the Socialist Revolutionaries' leading theoretician. His ideas represented what might be called mainstream SR thinking.

- Chernov was a socialist, but his socialism was of a distinctive kind. Russia's uniqueness as a country, he maintained, meant that it had to take its own special path towards socialism.
- What was unique about Russia, said Chernov, was its vast peasant population and its peasant institutions, notably the *mir*. Expecting, and wanting, Russia to remain a largely peasant country, Chernov argued that Russian socialism had to be peasant-based and built around peasant institutions rather than worker-based as suggested by the philosopher Karl Marx.
- Chernov envisaged a Russia that consisted of a vast number of largely self-governing village communities. These communities would own the land they farmed collectively. This belief in communal, rather than individual, ownership of land was a key feature of the SRs' socialism.
- Chernov did not want political life in Russia to be dominated by an immensely powerful central government. Instead, he wanted to see the decentralisation of political power. There was more than a tinge of **anarchism** in the mainstream SR outlook.

#### KEY TERMS

**Terrorism**
A political strategy that seeks, through the use of acts of violence (targeted or random), to intimidate governments and to focus attention on the terrorists' cause.

**Anarchism**
A political doctrine built around a suspicion of, and hostility towards, all forms of centralised government and state authority. It prizes individual freedom and voluntary co-operation between individuals at the local level.

### Methods

The Socialist Revolutionary Party saw the use of violence as a legitimate political weapon. Its leadership and rank-and-file were in principle united in their readiness to use force to overthrow Tsarism. In practice, however, there were differences of view about the circumstances in which the use of force was appropriate. Most mainstream SRs recognised that there was little chance of a bloodless revolution in Russia and accepted, without relish, that violence would have to be used in the course of a revolutionary uprising. Others were prepared to see violence used prior to a revolution for the purpose of raising the SRs' profile and spreading fear and alarm within the governing class. This was the position of the extremist SRs who formed the SR Combat Organisation in 1902. Their preferred tactic was the assassination of government ministers and officials, carried out using either firearms or dynamite. 'An SR without a bomb is not an SR', claimed one Combat Organisation leader. The attacks his colleagues carried out in the early 1900s left the government unmoved, but did win the SRs some support: in some quarters, the Combat Organisation's assassins were admired as selfless revolutionary heroes.

- Divisions within the SRs' ranks on the Combat Organisation's assassination campaign became apparent in 1906. A number of moderates who rejected the assassination campaign split from the SRs and established the Popular Socialist Party. At the other end of the spectrum, militants who advocated attacks, not only on government ministers and officials, but also on landowners and capitalists broke away from the main body of the SRs to form the SR Maximalists.
- In 1908, the SRs were rocked by scandal when the head of the Combat Organisation, Yevno Azef, was unmasked as an Okhrana spy. Following this revelation, the assassination campaign was suspended but the SRs did not renounce the use of violence as a political weapon.

## The Social Democrats

### Foundation

Karl Marx (1818–83) was a philosopher and economist of German descent whose ideas had, by the late 19th century, attracted a significant following in many European countries, Russia among them.

Organised Russian Marxism made its first appearance with the establishment of the Liberation of Labour Group in 1883 by a group of political exiles, G.K. Plekhanov chief among them. In 1895, it merged with another exile group, the Union of Russian Social Democrats Abroad. Also in 1895, but inside Russia, Marxists in St Petersburg founded the Union of Struggle for the Liberation of the Working Class with the aim of radicalising the city's industrial workers. Its leaders were V.I. Lenin (1870–1924), the son of a high-ranking civil servant, and Yuli Martov (1873–1923), who was brought up in a middle-class Jewish family. In 1898, representatives of these separate Marxist groups came together to form the Russian Social Democratic Labour Party (RSDLP). Lenin became active in the RSDLP's affairs on his return from a period of exile in Siberia in 1900 and, along with Martov, quickly took charge. In 1900, they started an underground newspaper, *Iskra* ('The Spark'), to disseminate their views.

## Ideas

Marxism is at root a theory about history and human progress. For Marx, history was driven by economic change and the conflict between social classes that arose out of it. All societies, he maintained, passed through a series of stages, each with its own distinctive economic system and class structure. One stage gave way to another, said Marx, when new social classes were formed as a result of economic change and proceeded to challenge, and defeat, the existing ruling class. This process was not in any way dependent on chance or human agency: it was, in Marx's view, inevitable that history would unfold in this way.

In his writings, Marx focused on three of these stages – feudalism, capitalism and communism – and on the transition from one to the other. Two revolutions were involved: a bourgeois revolution, which marked the transition from feudalism to capitalism, and a proletarian revolution, which saw the destruction of capitalism and ushered in the communist era.

### KEY TERMS

**Marxist terminology**

**Bourgeoisie**
Owners of the 'means of production' (factories, mines, banks, etc.) under capitalism.

**Proletariat**
Workers who had nothing to sell except their own labour.

**Immiseration**
Describes the process through which the proletariat got progressively poorer and more desperate.

### Marx's theory of history

| Feudal Stage | Feudalism to Capitalism | Capitalist Stage | Capitalism to Communism | Communist Stage |
|---|---|---|---|---|
| Landowners were the dominant, exploiting class and the peasantry was the subordinate, exploited class. | Industrialisation created two new social classes: the **bourgeoisie** and the **proletariat**. Owing to its superior economic muscle, the bourgeoisie would eventually oust feudalism's landowning class from political power through a bourgeois revolution. | The bourgeoisie (according to Marx) would over time get richer and numerically smaller (because the most dynamic capitalists would destroy their weaker competitors and create super-profitable monopolistic firms), while the proletariat would get poorer (because it was exploited increasingly ruthlessly by monopolists) and larger (because its ranks were swelled by failed capitalists). | The proletariat would, as a result of **immiseration**, eventually rise in revolt against the bourgeoisie. Proletarian revolutions were certain to succeed because they were risings of the many against the bourgeois few. | Proletarian revolutions would be followed by the creation of communist societies based on collective, rather than private, ownership. Society would be 'classless' and therefore free of class conflict, because there would be no division between haves and have-nots. |

The infant RSDLP quickly became mired in a bitter internal dispute about political strategy. One school of thought, taking the view that proletarian revolution in Russia was a long way off because it had yet to enter the capitalist stage of its development, argued that the party should in the interim focus on trying to bring about improvements in working-class conditions. Lenin took a different view. The outcome was the split of 1903.

### Bolsheviks and Mensheviks

The RSDLP debated the issue of political strategy at its Second Congress, held in 1903 in Brussels and then, following police intervention, London. The Congress was attended by a mere 43 delegates.

The specific issue on which the RSDLP split was a narrow one about the definition of a party member. Lenin wanted to restrict RSDLP membership to those committed to 'personal participation' in its work. His opponents, headed by Martov, called for membership to be open to anyone undertaking 'regular work' for the RSDLP or its associated organisations. Behind these rival formulas, though, lay more profound differences.

- Unlike his critics, Lenin believed that Russia was no longer a feudal country but a capitalist one, making out a case for this viewpoint in his book *The Development of Capitalism in Russia* (1896). It followed, said Lenin, that there was a realistic prospect of a proletarian revolution in Russia in the near future. In these circumstances, he argued, the RSDLP had to concentrate on making itself ready to seize the revolutionary moment. For Lenin, this meant creating a close-knit party made up of hard-core professional revolutionaries operating under centralised leadership.
- Lenin's opponents, unpersuaded of the imminence of revolution, favoured a short-term RSDLP focus on promoting the development of trade unions in Russia. They were also open to the idea of co-operating with non-Marxists. In consequence, they wanted to see an RSDLP that was more inclusive and less highly centralised than anything Lenin could accept.

Lenin won the day at the 1903 Congress. His followers became known as Bolsheviks (meaning majority), while Martov's were called Mensheviks (meaning minority). After 1903, the Bolsheviks and Mensheviks developed as separate parties. The Mensheviks interpreted Marx's ideas in a rigid, orthodox fashion: the Bolsheviks, under Lenin's leadership, were more flexible, adapting Marx's ideas to suit their own purposes.

## Reasons for the limited impact of opposition groups before 1905

### Social factors

- Russia's working class, upon whom Bolsheviks, Mensheviks and, to a lesser extent, the SRs, pinned their hopes, was numerically small (just over two percent of the population in the 1890s).
- The obstacles in the way of organising the peasantry politically and welding it into a coherent political force were immense. Russia's peasantry (over 80 percent of the population) was scattered thinly across a vast land area, living in three-quarters of a million rural settlements. In addition, the country's transport network was primitive and communication between settlements was poor.
- Levels of literacy in Russia were low. The 1897 census suggested that only 21 percent of the population could read. In these circumstances, one standard technique of political agitation – the distribution of pamphlets, newspapers and other forms of written propaganda – was of limited value.
- The leaders of the socialist groups were middle- or upper-class intellectuals. It was not easy for them to reach across the class divide and win the confidence of workers and peasants whose way of life was utterly different from their own. The socialist groups were certainly not mass membership organisations in the early 1900s: estimates suggest that at this time the SRs, Bolsheviks and Mensheviks had at most no more than 40–50,000 full members apiece.

**SOURCE 6** From a memorandum to the tsar by Peter Durnovo, former minister of the interior, written in 1914.

> The opponents of the government have no popular support. The people see no difference between a government official and an intellectual. The Russian masses, whether workmen or peasants, are not looking for political rights, which they neither want nor understand. The peasant dreams of getting a share of somebody else's land for nothing; the workman of getting hold of the entire capital and profits of the manufacturer. Beyond this they have no aspirations... Our opposition refuses to reckon with the fact that it represents no real force. The Russian opposition is intellectual throughout, and this is its weakness, because between the intelligentsia and the people there is a profound gulf of mutual misunderstanding and distrust.

**ACTIVITY**
**KNOWLEDGE CHECK**

What can be used to (i) support, and (ii) challenge Durnovo's opinions on the opposition to Tsarism?

### Repression

- Before 1905, opposition parties were illegal organisations that had to operate underground. They were further handicapped by laws restricting freedom of speech and freedom of assembly. This inhospitable legal climate made it difficult for opposition groups to win support.
- The Okhrana was adept at infiltrating and destroying revolutionary networks. It was also cold-blooded in the pursuit of its objectives: it almost certainly allowed some SR terrorist attacks that it could have prevented to go ahead in order not to blow the cover of its agents and informants.
- Repression cut revolutionary leaders off from their followers. Virtually all of Russia's leading socialists were forced to live abroad following periods of imprisonment or internal exile to Siberia. In the early 1900s, Lenin, Martov, Chernov and Gots were living in western Europe, while Gershuni and Breshko-Breshovskaya were in the USA. In these circumstances, it was difficult for opposition leaders to influence events in Russia. Note too that Okhrana surveillance and harassment of revolutionary leaders did not stop when they left Russia: the Okhrana had a Foreign Bureau based in Paris that kept tabs on those living in western Europe.
- Repression did not begin and end with the political police. Also active in defending Tsarism against its opponents were the para-military Corps of Gendarmes (of which the Okhrana was nominally a part), the regular police and the army. In the years between 1894 and 1905, the army was frequently called in to break up strikes and demonstrations: 33 times in 1900, 271 times in 1901 and more than 500 times in 1902. There was more than one incident in which unarmed demonstrators were killed. In 1901, for example, 13 people died when mounted soldiers charged into a crowd of student demonstrators in St Petersburg.

### Divisions between and within opposition groups

- The differences between liberals and socialists were of a kind that made the formation of any kind of united front between them virtually impossible. Liberals and socialists were united in wanting to overthrow Tsarism, but the socialists wanted to overthrow capitalism as well. In addition, socialist groups were willing to use force to achieve their goals, whereas liberals disliked political violence, fearing that its use could open the way to lawlessness and anarchy in Russia.
- The very different conceptions of socialism to which SRs and Marxists were committed was a formidable barrier to co-operation between them.
- There were divisions within each of the opposition groups that also limited their effectiveness. Some *zemstvo* liberals regarded Milyukov as too outspoken and preferred to follow the lead of the ultra-moderate Dmitrii Shipov; there were differences of opinion within the SRs on a range of issues, including the legitimacy of terrorist methods; and the RSDLP split into two more or less irreconcilable factions only five years after its establishment. These disputes within parties could be vicious and personalised: the terms Lenin used to describe fellow-socialists included 'cretins', 'bloodsuckers' and 'scum'.

**ACTIVITY**
**KNOWLEDGE CHECK**

**Opposition to Tsarist rule before 1905**

1. What differences were there between the aims and methods of liberals, Socialist Revolutionaries and Marxists in Nicholas II's Russia?
2. What can be inferred from Source 4 about the political sympathies of the cartoonist who produced it?
3. Does the evidence of Source 6 offer (a) an adequate and (b) a convincing explanation of the reasons why opposition groups in Russia failed before 1905 to attract mass support?
4. How accurate is it to say that repression was the main reason for the limited impact of the opposition to Tsarism before 1905?

# IN WHAT WAYS, AND HOW SERIOUSLY, WAS THE TSARIST REGIME THREATENED BY REVOLUTIONARY ACTIVITY IN 1905?

In one respect, the term '1905 revolution' is misleading. The turmoil that began in Russia in 1905 did not end within the year, but continued on into 1906 and beyond. Also, there is a case for arguing that the revolution began, not in 1905, but in 1904 with the League of Liberation's 'banquet campaign' for constitutional reform. It was, however, during 1905 that the Tsarist regime found itself engaged in a fight for its life. By late 1905, its survival was more or less assured. What the regime had to contend with after 1905 was unco-ordinated rural protest, which, though serious, was not life-threatening.

## The impact of the Russo-Japanese War (1904–05)

Nicholas II's Russia was an expansionist power. It sought to extend its influence in south-eastern Europe at the expense of the declining Turkish Empire and, in the Far East, aimed to exploit the weakness of the ramshackle Chinese Empire. In particular, Russia had designs on the Chinese province of Manchuria. The attractions of Manchuria were its mineral wealth and the 'warm water' seaport at Port Arthur, which was open all year round (Vladivostok, Russia's main Pacific seaport, was iced over in winter).

Russia's rival for influence in Manchuria was Japan, a rising military and industrial power. In the 1890s, relations between the two countries became increasingly tense. In 1895, following its victory over China in the 1894–95 Sino-Japanese war, Japan looked set to seize Port Arthur, but was forced to back-pedal by pressure from Russia and other European powers. In 1898, Russia arm-twisted China into giving it control of Port Arthur, infuriating Japan further. Attempts by the two countries in the early 1900s to settle their differences by negotiation failed. In early 1904, without warning, Japan attacked.

Russia went to war in 1904 under-prepared and over-confident. Nicholas II and his advisers viewed the Japanese as racial inferiors who would be easily swatted aside. Interior Minister Plehve reputedly claimed that a 'short, victorious war' would help the regime overcome its problems at home. In the event, Russia suffered a series of humiliating reverses.

- Japan laid siege to Port Arthur early in the war: in January 1905, it surrendered.
- In February 1905, Russian land forces lost a hard-fought major battle at Mukden.
- The greatest humiliation of all was Russia's defeat at the naval battle of Tsushima in May 1905. With Russia's main naval force in the Pacific trapped in Port Arthur, Nicholas II ordered Russia's Baltic Fleet to sail round the world to do battle with the Japanese. After an eight-month voyage, it was annihilated, with only a handful of its 52 warships escaping sinking or capture.
- The war was ended by the Treaty of Portsmouth, USA (September 1905), under which Russia agreed to abandon Port Arthur and its ambitions in Manchuria.

Russia's military defeats, and the stories of bungling and incompetence that accompanied them, affected the domestic political situation in a number of ways.

- Liberal opinion was angered by the mishandling of the war and its hostility towards the regime intensified. Liberal leaders were aware that military setbacks aided their cause. 'The worse, the better', said more radical liberals.
- Aware that military failure left the regime wounded and vulnerable, liberals challenged it more boldly. The League of Liberation's banquet campaign, launched in late 1904, reflected this new assertiveness.
- Economic life was disrupted. Unemployment and food prices rose, deepening working-class discontent.

## Bloody Sunday

In January 1905, around 150,000 unarmed demonstrators gathered at several assembly points around St Petersburg, with the intention of converging on the tsar's Winter Palace in the city centre. Before they got to their destination, columns of demonstrators were intercepted at a number of different places and fired upon by Russian army units. Estimates vary, but total casualties were in the order of 200 killed and 800 wounded. The episode was quickly labelled Bloody Sunday.

The marchers on Bloody Sunday were industrial workers, not middle-class liberals. Their plan was to present a petition to Nicholas II. The petition focused mainly on the issue of working conditions, calling for the legalisation of trade unions, higher wages and an eight-hour day, but there were, as well, pleas for free speech and political reform. There were no overt references to the evils of autocracy and no wild demands for the abolition of capitalism.

The organiser of the Bloody Sunday demonstration was Father Gapon, maverick Orthodox priest, charismatic public speaker and leader of the Assembly of Russian Factory and Mill Workers. Gapon was a sincere advocate of workers' rights, but one with a history before 1905 of links with the Okhrana. The organisation he led had begun life in 1903 as a 'police union' – an illegal trade union which was nevertheless sanctioned and funded by the Okhrana. 'Police unions' were seen by the Okhrana as a way of keeping the workers out of the clutches of the socialist parties. By 1905, though, Gapon was acting on his own. Even so, the authorities knew that neither he nor his followers nor his march (which arose out of a strike in St Petersburg's giant Putilov engineering works) represented a serious threat to the regime.

In the weeks after Bloody Sunday, a massive wave of protest swept across Russia. Nearly half a million workers went out on strike. Strikes by students led to the closure of universities for the remainder of the academic year. Meanwhile, outraged liberals bombarded the government with petitions demanding political reform. 'We can no longer live like this', declared one liberal newspaper. Russia was in disarray.

Bloody Sunday was a more important trigger of revolution than the Russo-Japanese war. The war was fought a long way off, but Bloody Sunday happened in the heart of Russia's capital city. The spectacle of peaceful demonstrators being shot down had a shock value that news of defeats in faraway places did not.

**SOURCE 7** Cordon of troops protecting the tsar's Winter Palace on Bloody Sunday, 1905.

SOURCE 8 Four texts on Bloody Sunday.

(i) 'It is impossible yet to state the exact number of casualties, but popular rumour gives the number of killed at 20,000 and the wounded at 4,000. These figures no doubt greatly exaggerate the actual state of affairs, but according to all accounts several hundreds, probably 1,300, have fallen'. **(From a report published in the *Manchester Guardian*, a British newspaper, on the day after Bloody Sunday.)**

(ii) 'At first the government had announced only 56 dead, but a later official statement gave the totals as 76 dead and 233 wounded.' **(Government figures on the number of casualties on Bloody Sunday, as described by an American historian writing in the 1970s.)**

(iii) 'Owing to the idiocy of the military authorities, the crowd was met with rifle fire. The actual victims, as certified by a public commission of lawyers of the Opposition, was approximately 150 killed and 200 wounded.' **(Opposition figures for the number of casualties on Bloody Sunday, as described by a British historian writing in the 1930s.)**

(iv) 'Over 140,000 workers gathered in the streets. They met with a hostile reception from Nicholas II. He gave orders to fire on the unarmed workers. That day over a 1,000 workers were killed and more than 2,000 wounded by the Tsar's troops.' **(Casualty figures for Bloody Sunday which appeared in a school textbook written for use in Russian schools in the 1930s.)**

THINKING HISTORICALLY — EVIDENCE (6a)

### Arguments and facts

Study Source 8. Work in groups.

1 Read texts (i) and (ii).
   a) How do these texts disagree?
   b) Which do you think is more likely to be correct? Give reasons for your answer.

2 Read texts (iii) and (iv).
   a) How do these texts disagree?
   b) What do you think is the significance of the issue of exactly who gave the order to troops to open fire on Bloody Sunday? Do you think that the author of text (iv) would have viewed the significance of this issue differently from you? Explain your answer.

3 'Finding out the exact number of casualties on Bloody Sunday is more important for the historian than establishing who gave the order to troops to open fire.' Do you agree with this statement? Give reasons for your answer.

4 If we accept that text (iv) is wrong about the number of casualties on Bloody Sunday, do we discount it as being useful? Explain your answer.

5 Why are facts important in history?

SOURCE 9 From the autobiography of Maria Shkolnik (1882–1955), a member of the SRs Combat Organisation, describing how she passed on news of Bloody Sunday to the inhabitants of the Siberian village to which she had been exiled.

At this time news of Bloody Sunday reached our village. With trembling hands, I held the letter and read to the peasants about how the workers in Petersburg, led by Father Gapon, went to request their Tsar to improve living conditions, how all of a sudden they came under fire without warning, how the Cossacks trampled them and beat them with sabres and whips, how the streets of Petersburg were transformed into a battlefield where hundreds of beaten and dead lay about. Here the peasants stopped me. 'Is it possible', they said, 'the Tsar could do this? Are his ministers not to blame?' As they thought about this, they asked me to read it all again from the beginning. On that day, their faith in Tsarism was crushed. For me, the fact that the Petersburg workers went to request the Tsar to improve their lives held a completely different meaning. I saw here an awakening of the labouring masses and looked upon this demonstration as the foreshadowing of the great revolution that would topple the Tsarist throne.

## The spread of revolutionary activity

In Russia, 1905 was a year packed with incident. Revolutionary episodes of one kind or another took place on a near-daily basis. These occurred in many different places. There is no one single thread of events that can be followed. Some generalisations are nevertheless possible.

- All of the main disaffected groups in Russian society (middle-class liberals, industrial workers, peasants and national minorities) took part in protests or other forms of revolutionary activity. In addition, there were localised mutinies in the armed forces, notably on the battleship *Potemkin* in June 1905.
- For the most part, these disaffected groups acted not in concert but in isolation from one another. 'It seemed as though Russia was undergoing not one revolution but a series of parallel revolutions', one historian (Abraham Ascher) has stated.
- Until the autumn of 1905, it was the middle-class liberals who were the dominant revolutionary force. They kept a shaken and uncertain government under continuous pressure until concessions were made, holding conferences, drafting petitions and forming new organisations, notably the Union of Unions, an association of groups representing different professions (including lawyers, doctors, teachers, engineers). Once concessions were offered, middle-class liberalism lost some momentum – partly because some liberals thought they had won, but also because liberals began to fear that Russia was starting to slide into disorder and anarchy.
- In the latter part of 1905, the labour movement came to the fore. In October, a general strike broke out. It began with a walk-out by Moscow printers, spread to the railways and mushroomed from there. The general strike was initiated and dominated by industrial workers, although students and middle-class liberals involved themselves in it as well. The strike threw the government into crisis. It also saw the rise to prominence of the St Petersburg **Soviet**, which for a short time had a higher profile than any other workers' organisation in Russia.
- The socialist parties and their leaders played a relatively small part in the events of 1905. Only Leon Trotsky, who became a leading figure in the St Petersburg Soviet, enhanced his reputation.

**KEY TERM**

**Soviet**
A Russian word meaning 'council'.

### 1905: Protest and disorder in Russia after Bloody Sunday

| | Middle Class | Working Class | Peasantry | National Minorities | Armed Forces |
|---|---|---|---|---|---|
| January–June | • Petitioning campaign.<br>• A national congress of *zemstvo* representatives held to demand reform (February). Further national *zemstvo* congresses (April, May).<br>• Union of Unions formed (April). | Wave of strikes followed by a drift back to work (January). | Outbreak of disorder in the 'Black Earth' region (March). | • Latvia: general strike – 70 killed when strikers clashed with troops in Riga (January).<br>• Poland: 93 killed when protestors clashed with troops in Warsaw (January).<br>• 30 killed in further clashes in Warsaw (May).<br>• Over 100 killed in street fighting in Lodz, Poland (June). | Mutineers from the battleship *Potemkin* joined forces with striking workers in Odessa: over 2,000 killed when troops intervened to restore order (June). |
| July–December | Supporters of the League of Liberation and the Union of Unions came together to form the Constitutional Democratic Party, generally known as the Kadets (October). | • General strike calling for an eight-hour day, basic rights and a constitution (October).<br>• Formation of the St Petersburg Soviet and soviets in other cities (October).<br>• St Petersburg Soviet disbanded (December).<br>• Armed uprising by Moscow workers crushed (December). | • SRs formed the All-Russian Peasants Union as a rural counterpart to the Union of Unions (July).<br>• Large-scale peasant disorder broke out in the 'Black Earth' region and elsewhere. | General strike in Finland (October–November). | Localised army mutinies in St Petersburg and Moscow; mutiny at the Kronstadt naval base near St Petersburg (October). |

- The countryside remained relatively quiet until the autumn of 1905. Large-scale disorder began only when peasants sensed that the Tsarist regime had lost its nerve. Disturbances in rural areas peaked in November and December, but were still going on in 1906 and even later. Peasant disorder mostly took the form of attacks on landowners' property. Land hunger lay behind these attacks: peasants aimed to drive landowners out of the countryside in the hope of gaining possession of their land.
- Trouble in the Empire's north-western border areas, where nationalistic, anti-Russian feeling was intense, began early and continued throughout 1905. Poland, in particular, was a hotbed of revolutionary activity. Demonstrators clashed repeatedly with the Russian army and, on several occasions, lives were lost. The situation in Poland was so tense that over 250,000 Russian troops had to be deployed there to maintain order.

## The St Petersburg Soviet

The St Petersburg Soviet was a council of elected representatives of the city's industrial workers. Members of the Soviet each represented around 500 workers. In October 1905, soon after its formation, the St Petersburg Soviet consisted of 562 representatives from 147 factories, 34 shops and 16 trade unions. Because the full Soviet was an unwieldy body, the decision was soon taken to form a 30-member Executive Committee. Nine of these people were nominees of the Mensheviks, Bolsheviks and SRs: the Soviet allocated each party three seats on the Executive Committee.

The St Petersburg Soviet began life as a strike committee. Its role was to organise and direct the October general strike in the capital. It quickly spawned imitators: within weeks of its formation, 50 other towns and cities in Russia had their own soviets.

When the general strike ended, the St Petersburg Soviet not only stayed in business but diversified. It published a newspaper, *Izvestia*; it established an armed **militia** to protect the city against counter-revolutionaries; and it acted as a kind of unofficial local government body, distributing food and money to those in need. Above all, it engaged in political campaigning.

The St Petersburg Soviet was an authentic working-class organisation, founded not by middle-class leaders of opposition groups but by grassroots activists. It ensured too that it retained its class identity: an attempt by the middle-class Union of Unions to affiliate with it was rebuffed. It was, however, increasingly dominated by the Menshevik faction on its Executive Committee and, in particular, by Trotsky.

Under Trotsky's influence, the St Petersburg Soviet campaigned for an eight-hour day and proclaimed its support for Polish rebels and mutineers in the Russian navy. In December 1905, the government, its confidence restored, hit back. The St Petersburg Soviet was disbanded following the arrest and imprisonment of its entire membership.

KEY TERM

**Militia**
An armed force made up of ordinary citizens rather than trained professional soldiers.

EXTEND YOUR KNOWLEDGE

**Leon Trotsky (1879–1940)**
Trotsky was born into a Jewish landowning family in the Ukraine. His real name was Bronstein: Trotsky was a pseudonym taken from one of his gaolers when exiled in Siberia. Trotsky was politically active from his late teens onwards. In 1905, he was associated with the Mensheviks but, in exile until 1917, he aligned himself with neither Mensheviks nor Bolsheviks. He eventually joined the Bolsheviks in 1917. Writer, orator and man of action, Trotsky was an extravagantly gifted revolutionary leader, but – as a result of his arrogance – he made enemies easily.

ACTIVITY
KNOWLEDGE CHECK

**Threats to the Tsarist regime in 1905**

1 To what extent does Source 7 suggest that the government believed that the workers' march on Bloody Sunday posed a major threat to the regime?

2 Which of the following do you think was most alarming from the point of view of the government in 1905: peasant unrest; strikes by industrial workers; mutinies in the armed forces or the emergence of the St Petersburg Soviet? Give reasons for your answer.

# IN WHAT WAYS, AND HOW SUCCESSFULLY, DID THE TSARIST REGIME RESPOND TO THE THREATS IT FACED IN 1905?

## The August Manifesto

In the immediate aftermath of Bloody Sunday, Nicholas II was unperturbed, failing entirely to appreciate the seriousness of the situation that was developing around him. It required some straight talking by certain of his ministers to persuade him that Russia was on the brink of full-blown revolution. In these circumstances, Nicholas' first instinct was to rely on force to suppress agitation – an instinct reinforced by the murder in February of his uncle, Grand Duke Sergei, Governor of Moscow, by the SRs Combat Organisation. Reliance on force alone, however, was not a realistic option: agitation was too widespread to be easily contained and a large part of the army was engaged in fighting the Japanese. Grudgingly, Nicholas agreed to make concessions, if only to buy time.

In January, the government promised that an inquiry would be held into the grievances of St Petersburg's factory workers – a promise that it failed to keep. More importantly, it was announced in February that an elected assembly was to be established, which would be consulted before new laws were introduced. The interior minister, Alexander Bulygin, was given the task of drawing up detailed arrangements. Liberals were unimpressed: the tsar's concessions fell a long way short of the parliament and constitution they were demanding.

Bulygin's detailed plan was set out in the 'August Manifesto', or 'Bulygin Constitution', published in August 1905. It had three key elements.

- The new elected assembly was to be called the Duma (a name deriving from the Russian verb meaning to think or consider).
- The assembly was to be purely advisory or consultative: it would be given the opportunity to discuss proposed new laws, but would have no power.
- There was to be a complex electoral system favouring peasants (reflecting the regime's belief in their fundamental loyalty) and landowners. Urban workers, the national minorities, Jews and much of the intelligentsia were to be left without the vote.

Some ultra-moderate liberals thought that the August Manifesto offered a basis for further negotiation, but almost everyone else on the opposition side dismissed it as totally inadequate. It was seen for what it was: a cosmetic proposal that left the essentials of Tsarism intact.

## The October Manifesto and the response of the opposition

The August Manifesto was quickly overtaken by events. In October, Russia was paralysed by a general strike. In desperation, Nicholas II turned to Witte, recently back from the USA, where he had negotiated the Treaty of Portsmouth with Japan. With the title of Chairman of the Council of Ministers, Witte was now effectively Russia's prime minister. He advised Nicholas II that he had two choices: military rule or significant concessions. Reluctantly, Nicholas opted for concessions. 'There was no other way out than to cross oneself and give what everyone was asking for', he wrote to his mother.

The concessions took the form of the October Manifesto. It promised:

- guaranteed basic freedoms, notably freedom of speech, assembly and association. Freedom of association meant that trade unions and political parties were legalised
- a Duma with real power in that new laws could only come into force with the Duma's approval
- the extension of the right to vote in Duma elections to all classes of the population.

On the streets, the October Manifesto was greeted with enthusiasm. Crowds gathered to celebrate what appeared to be a great victory. The general strike was called off. Opposition leaders were left to ponder their next move.

Moderate liberals and business leaders welcomed the October Manifesto. It offered the kind of balance between monarchy and democracy they favoured: they disliked autocracy, but they also feared mob rule. Their willingness to work with the government to turn its promises into detailed arrangements found expression in the formation of a new political party, the Union of 17 October. At this point, the Octobrists (as they became known) and radical liberals parted company.

Radical liberals rejected the October Manifesto, claiming that it did not go far enough. What was required, they said, was the establishment of an elected assembly to draw up a constitution for a democratic Russia. Another reason for radical hostility to the October Manifesto was distrust of the government. As soon as calm returned, radicals predicted, the government would go back on its promises. In October 1905, radical liberals formed the Constitutional Democratic or Kadet Party. It effectively replaced the League of Liberation and the Union of Unions. Its leader was Paul Milyukov.

To the left of the radicals, the socialist parties denounced the October Manifesto even more strongly than the liberals. Trotsky was the Manifesto's most eloquent socialist critic.

**SOURCE 10**

From a speech by Trotsky to a crowd in St Petersburg, October 1905.

Citizens, now we have got the ruling clique with its back to the wall, they promise us freedom. They promise us electoral rights and legislative power. Who promises these things? Nicholas the Second. Does he promise them of his own good will? Or with a pure heart?

Do not be too quick to celebrate the victory; victory is not yet complete. Is a promise of payment the same thing as real gold? Is the promise of freedom the same thing as freedom itself? What has changed since yesterday?

Citizens, our strength is in ourselves. We must defend freedom with the sword. As for the Tsar's manifesto, look, it's only a scrap of paper. Here it is before you - here it is crumpled in my fist. Today they gave it to you, tomorrow they will take it away and tear it into pieces, just as I am now tearing up this paper freedom before your eyes.

**ACTIVITY**
**KNOWLEDGE CHECK**

**Trotsky in 1905**

Write three short paragraphs explaining which of the points made in Trotsky's speech (Source 10) would have:

**a)** been endorsed by both Octobrists and Kadets

**b)** been endorsed by the Kadets, but not the Octobrists

**c)** alarmed both Octobrists and Kadets.

Shared distrust of the tsar was not by itself enough to bridge the gap between radical liberals and socialists, as Milyukov explained at the Kadets' founding conference.

**SOURCE**

From Milyukov's speech to the Kadet Party's first conference, October 1905.

Our party will never defend the interests of the landowners and industrialists at the cost of the interests of the toiling masses. Between us and our - we would like to say not opponents, but associates on the Left - there exists a certain boundary. We do not join in with their demands for a democratic republic and the socialisation of the means of production. Some of us do not support these watchwords because we regard them as generally unacceptable, others because they regard them as standing beyond the bounds of practical politics. As long as it is possible to move toward a common goal together despite this difference of motives, both groups will act as a single whole: any attempt to emphasise the demands just mentioned will result in immediate schism.

**A Level Exam-Style Question Section A**

***Study Sources 5 and 11 before you answer this question.***

How far could the historian make use of Sources 5 and 11 together to investigate the aims and priorities of Russian liberals in 1904–05?

Explain your answer using both sources, the information given about them and your own knowledge of the historical context. (20 marks)

**Tip**

*Don't base your answer solely on an evaluation of the two sources separately – consider as well whether they reinforce each other or whether one contains evidence which undermines the other.*

In the autumn of 1905, by means of the October Manifesto, the Tsarist regime split middle-class liberalism and blunted the opposition – and bought itself some breathing space. A further development that cheered it was the emergence of an aggressive right-wing movement keen to take on the radicals and socialists. The Union of Russian People was a political party founded in October 1905 to defend the principles of 'Orthodoxy, Autocracy and Nationality'. Closely linked with the Union were **para-military** gangs known as the Black Hundreds. The Black Hundreds' main target was Russia's Jews, seen as plotting the Empire's downfall. In 1905–06, the Black Hundreds were heavily involved in organising anti-Jewish pogroms. The worst single pogrom took place in late 1905 at Odessa, where 800 Jews were murdered. There were close links between the Black Hundreds and the Tsarist regime. They were subsidised and supplied with weaponry by the Interior Ministry. At the local level, some police chiefs were involved in planning Black Hundred violence. Nicholas II made no secret of his support for the Union of Russian People.

**KEY TERM**

**Para-military force**
Armed, often uniformed, military-style formation that resembles a regular armed force, but is privately organised and has no official status.

**SOURCE 12** From the autobiography of V.I. Gurko, in 1905 a senior official in the Interior Ministry.

There remained few spectators in 1905; practically all the educated elements in society were forced to declare themselves and to attach themselves to one of the four main categories into which public opinion gradually became divided. Beginning with the Right, these were (1) outright monarchists, who stubbornly insisted that an assembly of the people's representatives assisting in legislation must not diminish the authority of the monarch (2) moderate liberals, who favoured a constitutional monarchy but were ready to support the existing government and structure of the state in all other respects (3) radicals, who desired to retain a mere semblance of monarchy while striving toward democracy (4) revolutionary socialists, who regarded the changes in forms of government merely as a means of altering the existing social and economic structure.

**ACTIVITY**
**KNOWLEDGE CHECK**

**Politics and public opinion in Russia in 1905**

1. How significant were the differences between the August Manifesto and the October Manifesto?
2. In what ways, and to what extent, did the August Manifestor split the opposition to Tsarism?
3. What evidence can be offered in support of the claim of the author of Source 12 that there were, by late 1905, four distinct blocks of political opinion in Russia?

## The crushing of the Moscow Uprising

By late 1905, the government felt strong enough to silence the increasingly belligerent St Petersburg Soviet. The capital's Soviet went down without a fight. Its counterpart in Moscow did not. In early December, urged on by its militant Bolshevik members, the Moscow Soviet called for a general strike to overthrow what it called 'the criminal Tsarist government'. It went on to distribute weapons to the city's workers. An armed uprising was clearly in the making.

The government's response was savage. Army units cleared the barricades that had been erected on Moscow's streets and used artillery fire to regain control of its working-class districts. When the street battles were over, the army engaged in reprisals: mass arrests, beatings and executions without trial. More than 1,000 people died in the Moscow Uprising.

SOURCE 13 A street destroyed by government forces in the suppression of the Moscow Uprising, December 1905.

**A Level Exam-Style Question Section B**

'The Tsarist regime survived in 1905 mainly because it made massive concessions to its opponents.' How far do you agree with this statement? (20 marks)

**Tip**

*With this kind of question, which focuses on causes and their relative importance, it is generally best to begin with a consideration of the stated cause (concessions were key to Tsarism's survival) before examining and evaluating the unstated ones.*

## The extent of the recovery of Tsarist power

By the end of 1905, the Tsarist regime was in a much stronger position than it had been during the 12-day general strike in October.

- Through the October Manifesto, it had won the qualified support of a section of the educated middle class (the Octobrists) and, by doing so, had divided Russia's liberals.
- Working-class militancy and the soviets which arose out of it, arguably the biggest threat to Tsarism in the autumn of 1905, had been crushed.
- The armed forces, the nobility and the Orthodox Church had, for the most part, remained loyal to the regime.
- Elements of the propertied classes had rallied to Tsarism's defence, forming the Union of Russian People and the Black Hundreds.

- The regime had regained its confidence. One sign of its renewed confidence was the ruthlessness with which the Moscow Uprising was put down. Another was the electoral law, published in December 1905, which set out voting arrangements for the forthcoming Duma elections. The regime kept the promise made in the October Manifesto to extend the right to vote to classes of people denied it under the August Manifesto; but it also ensured that the electoral system would not be fully democratic. Under the new law, women, those under 25, soldiers and casual labourers had no voting rights. In addition, the complex system of indirect election that was adopted gave a hugely disproportionate amount of influence to landowners.

## EXTEND YOUR KNOWLEDGE

### Duma election procedures

The 1905 Duma election law divided voters into four classes: landowners, town voters, peasants and factory workers. Members of each class voted in an election to choose its delegates to Provincial Electoral Assemblies. It was these Assemblies that chose Duma members. At the Provincial Assemblies, voting power was unequally distributed between classes: landowners had a 32.7% share of the vote, the peasantry 32.3%, town voters 22.5% and factory workers a mere 2.5%. The aim of these arrangements was to maximise the power of those believed to be loyal to the regime and limit the influence of those hostile to it.

Tsarism's recovery of power by the end of 1905 was, however, partial rather than complete.

- The October Manifesto made no difference to the situation in the countryside. Levels of peasant disorder in late 1905 remained high. The authorities were not in full control of large parts of rural Russia. There were also continuing problems with national minorities, especially the Poles.
- Before the October general strike, Nicholas II's power was in theory unlimited. This was no longer the case after the publication of the October Manifesto. The promise to establish a Duma with a role in the law-making process diluted the autocratic principle. It was a promise Nicholas II bitterly regretted making but, in 1905, he did not feel himself to be in a strong enough position to go back on it.
- The legalisation of trade unions and political parties promised by the October Manifesto meant that the regime now had to contend with open criticism and opposition, something to which it was not accustomed and certainly did not welcome.

## ACTIVITY
KNOWLEDGE CHECK

### Nicholas II and Witte in 1905

1. What were the causes of the increasing self-confidence of the Tsarist regime towards the end of 1905?
2. What picture emerges from the events of 1905 of Nicholas II's capacities as a ruler?
3. How important was Witte's contribution to the survival of the Tsarist regime in 1905?

ACTIVITY
SUMMARY

**The 1905 Revolution**

1 Construct a diagram summarising key information about the political parties that had emerged in Russia by the end of 1905 and about the differences between them.

- Start by dividing the parties into liberal and socialist parties.
- Develop your diagram by making appropriate sub-divisions within each category – distinguishing, for instance, between moderate and radical liberal parties and Marxist and non-Marxist socialist parties.
- Make further sub-divisions within these categories as appropriate – distinguishing, for instance, between different Marxist parties and between moderate and extreme non-Marxist socialist parties.
- Finally, add further pieces of information, such as names of party leaders or key ideas.
- Include the Popular Socialist Party and the SR Maximalists in your diagram as well as the better-known parties.

2 Construct a graph showing the threat level to the Tsarist regime in the course of 1905. Divide the horizontal axis into 12 months, January–December. On the vertical axis, use five categories: at the top 'very severe' (meaning that the regime was under very severe threat of being toppled), then, coming down, 'severe', 'moderate', 'low' and 'no threat'.

3 Write a brief account of the role and importance of each of the following in 1905: Father Gapon; Paul Milyukov; Sergei Witte; Leon Trotsky.

4 In what ways, and to what extent, was Russia at the time of the 1905 Revolution, an unequal society? In your answer, make reference, where appropriate, to the visual as well as the written evidence in this chapter.

WIDER READING

For an accessible account of the years up to 1905 see Ascher, A. *The Russian Revolution: A Beginner's Guide*, Oneworld Publications (2014), chapters 1–2

Also valuable, and relatively brief, are:

Hutchinson, J.F. *Late Imperial Russia 1890–1917*, Longman Seminar Studies in History (1999), chapters 1–4

Wood, A. *The Origins of the Russian Revolution, 1861–1917*, Lancaster Pamphlet, Methuen (1987)

For a fuller treatment see:

Rogger, H. *Russia in the Age of Modernisation and Revolution, 1881–1917*, Longman (1983)

# 2b.2 The end of Romanov rule, 1906–17

**KEY QUESTIONS**

- What political changes took place in Russia in the years 1906–14, and to what extent did they modify the Tsarist system of government?
- To what extent did Stolypin's policies of repression and reform succeed in putting the Tsarist regime on a more stable footing?
- What impact did Russia's involvement in the First World War have on the reputation of the Tsarist regime?
- What triggered the revolution of February 1917?

**KEY TERM**

**Trudovik**
The Trudovik group can be described as the Labour group because their name derived from the Russian word for labour: a Trudovik was literally a worker or a labourer. Despite the name, their principal concern was to defend the interests of the peasantry rather than those of industrial workers. The Trudoviks' main demand was for the transfer of landowners' estates to the peasantry - but not without compensation. They also called for the democratisation of Russian political life at all levels, local as well as national. The leaders of the Trudoviks, foremost of whom was Alexis Aladin (1873-1927), were mostly middle-class intellectuals.

## INTRODUCTION

Elections to the first Duma, the elected law-making body promised in the October Manifesto, took place over several weeks in the early spring of 1906. In government circles it was assumed that the 1905 electoral law would produce a tame and pliable assembly. This assumption proved to be seriously mistaken. Milyukov's Kadets, the more radical of the two middle-class liberal parties formed in 1905, emerged from the election as the largest single party with 182 of the 448 seats that had been filled by the time the Duma met (some remained unfilled because voting was still going on). Not far behind was the **Trudovik** or Labour group, a loose association of moderate socialists concerned mainly with rural issues, with 107 seats. Of the other successful candidates, most either had no party affiliation or represented the Empire's national minorities. Only a handful of Duma members were active supporters of the Tsarist regime.

**EXTEND YOUR KNOWLEDGE**

**Witte's downfall, 1906**
The negotiator of the peace treaty with Japan and originator of the October Manifesto in 1905, Sergei Witte was a casualty of the 1906 Duma election results. Witte had promised a 'peasant Duma' that would be loyal to the tsar. His failure to deliver on this promise led to his dismissal. 'As long as I live I will never trust that man again with the smallest thing', said Nicholas II on Witte's departure from government office.

**1906** - 23 April: Fundamental Laws published
27 April: First Duma meets

**1906** - 8 July: First Duma dissolved

**1906** - 8 July: Interior Minister Stolypin appointed chairman of the Council of Ministers
10 July: Vyborg Manifesto issued

**1907** - February: Second Duma meets

**1907** - June: Second Duma dissolved; revised Duma electoral law published

**1907** - November: Third Duma meets, and goes on to serve a full five-year term

A number of factors account for the Kadets' success in the 1906 elections.

- The Socialist Revolutionaries (SRs), Bolsheviks and Mensheviks all boycotted the elections: left-wing voters switched to the Kadets or Trudoviks as the best available alternatives.
- The Kadets' election campaign was better organised and far more energetic than those of their rivals.
- The regime was counting on the support of landowners, but large numbers of them failed to turn out to vote.

Just before the Duma met, a new factor was injected into the political equation with the publication of the Fundamental Laws. These were measures that gave legal form to the promises made six months earlier in the October Manifesto. The Fundamental Laws aroused bitter controversy, with the regime's opponents claiming that it had failed to honour its promises. A furious Milyukov declared that the government was guilty of 'a fraud against the people' because the Fundamental Laws imposed limits on the Duma's power that were neither expected nor acceptable.

The 1906 Duma elections and the Fundamental Laws set the scene for two years of confrontation between the Tsarist regime and its opponents. Attempts by the first Duma to assert itself were ended when it was dissolved only two months into its five-year term. The second Duma, also dominated by opponents of Tsarism, did not last much longer. In 1907, the government broke the deadlock by changing the 1905 electoral law in ways that ensured the Duma would, in future, have a built-in conservative majority. Unsurprisingly, the third and fourth Dumas were less quarrelsome than their predecessors.

In 1914, the Tsarist regime appeared to be in a much stronger position than it had been in 1906. The Duma had been tamed; the peasantry was quiet; the economy was booming; and the revolutionary parties of the left did not appear to be gaining ground. This is not to say, however, that the regime had drawn closer to the people or that it had secured its long-term future. None of the preconditions of revolution in Russia had gone away. Tsarism was still faced with an impoverished and land-hungry peasantry, a disaffected urban working class and a hostile intelligentsia. The regime also retained its reputation for brutality: in 1912, an atrocity on the scale of Bloody Sunday took place when troops opened fire on striking gold miners in Siberia. An outburst of labour unrest followed that was comparable in size to that which had engulfed Russia in 1905.

A case can be made out both for and against the idea that revolution was imminent in Russia on the eve of the First World War. There can be no certainty one way or the other. What is not in doubt is that the First World War had a devastating impact on the credibility of the Tsarist regime. Military defeat, high casualty rates and severe economic hardship led to mounting popular discontent. Corruption and mismanagement of the war effort cost the regime the support of Russia's elites – in particular, that of the high command of the army. By early 1917, Nicholas II was isolated and friendless. In February 1917, strikers and demonstrators took to the streets of Petrograd (the new name of Russia's capital city – the government ordered the change at the start of the war because it was felt that St Petersburg sounded too German). The Petrograd army garrison refused to move against them. This was the decisive moment in what became known as the February Revolution. Within days the Tsarist regime had collapsed.

**1911** - September: Stolypin shot and dies four days later

**1912** - April: Lena goldfields massacre
November: Fourth Duma meets

**1914** - August: Germany declares war on Russia

**1915** - Russia's 'Great Retreat'
June: Formation of the 'Progressive Bloc'

**1916** - December: Murder of Rasputin

**1917** - 23 February: February Revolution begins

1911 | 1912 | 1913 | 1914 | 1915 | 1916 | 1917

# WHAT POLITICAL CHANGES TOOK PLACE IN RUSSIA IN THE YEARS 1906–14, AND TO WHAT EXTENT DID THEY MODIFY THE TSARIST SYSTEM OF GOVERNMENT?

## The Fundamental Laws, April 1906

Nicholas II associated the word 'constitution' with the demands of his political enemies. He therefore refused to allow it to be used to describe the 1906 Fundamental Laws. The Fundamental Laws nevertheless amounted to a constitution in all but name, detailing as they did the role and powers of the principal institutions of government.

In the 1905 October Manifesto, Nicholas II had promised that steps would be taken to ensure that no law could be passed without the Duma's approval and further undertook to give the Duma powers to hold government ministers to account for their actions. At the point these promises were made, in the autumn of 1905, the regime's future was uncertain. By the time government ministers came to draft the Fundamental Laws in early 1906, however, it was out of danger. As a result, the drafting of the Fundamental Laws became an exercise in clawing back as much political ground as possible. Government ministers, with the Tsar's full encouragement, set out to restrict the powers of the Duma to the barest minimum required by the wording of the October Manifesto.

- Article 4 of the Fundamental Laws insisted on the Tsar's continuing primacy within Russia's system of government: 'The All-Russian Emperor possesses the supreme autocratic power. Not only fear and conscience, but God himself, command obedience to his authority.'
- The Fundamental Laws declared a number of important areas of government activity, among them defence and foreign affairs, to be the preserve of the tsar alone and therefore outside the Duma's jurisdiction.
- Article 87 of the Fundamental Laws allowed the tsar to proclaim new laws without Duma approval at times when it was not in session. Laws made in this fashion had to be ratified by the Duma subsequently – but ratification could be delayed for months or even years. Article 87 effectively gave Nicholas II the ability to by-pass the Duma.
- The Fundamental Laws gave the tsar the right to dissolve the Duma at any time of his choosing.
- In the October Manifesto, no mention was made of a two-house (or 'bicameral') legislature. The Fundamental Laws, however, established a counterweight to the elected Duma in the shape of the unelected Imperial State Council, a revamped version of the old Council of State, the body set up in 1810 to offer the tsar advice about proposed new laws. The Imperial State Council was designed to be a solidly conservative body: half of its members were appointed by the tsar and the other half were nominated by corporate bodies such as the nobility, the Orthodox Church and the *zemstva* (elected local councils). The State Council's law-making powers were the same as those of the Duma which meant that it could block, or veto, anything the Duma did.
- Under the Fundamental Laws, the tsar alone had the right to appoint and dismiss government ministers. There was no requirement to seek Duma approval. Ministers could be summoned for questioning by the Duma and be censured by it, but it had no power to force their resignation.
- The Fundamental Laws contained provisions guaranteeing freedom of association (which legalised political parties and trades unions), freedom of assembly (which meant that peaceful demonstrations were lawful) and freedom of speech (which, among other things, allowed for a free press). In practice these guarantees were not worth all that much. There was nothing to prevent laws being introduced that restricted the exercise of individual rights and in emergencies all rights could be suspended.

## The radicalism of the first two Dumas

The first meeting of the Duma took place, not in the accommodation that had been prepared for it, but in the splendour of St George's Hall in the Tsar's Winter Palace in St Petersburg. Duma members occupied the area to the left of the Tsar's throne. Opposite them, dressed in all their finery, sat the royal family, courtiers and government officials. Nicholas II gave a brief speech, expressing the view that Russia not only needed freedom but also order based on obedience to the law.

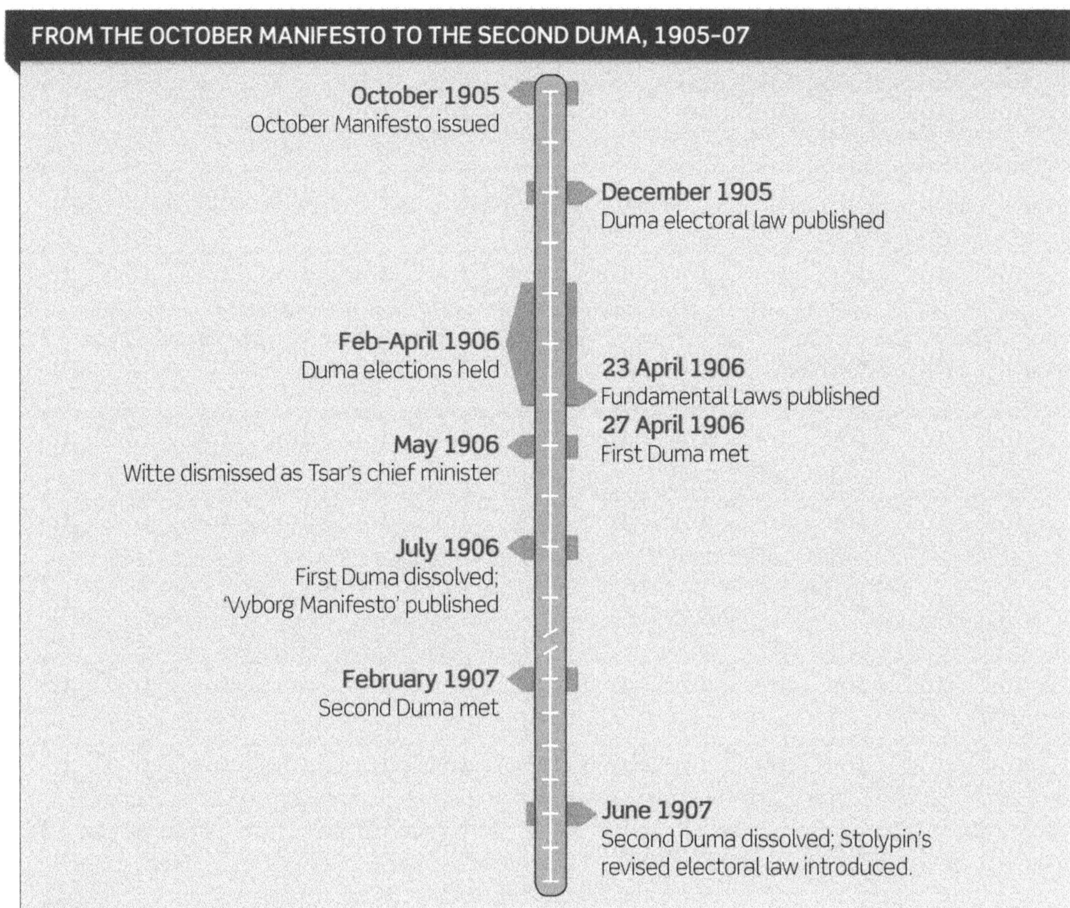


**SOURCE 1**

**From a despatch sent by the United States' ambassador to Russia to his superiors in Washington, May 1906.**

On the left of the throne were members of the Duma, in every conceivable costume, the peasants in rough clothes and long boots, merchants and tradespeople in frock coats, lawyers in dress suits, priests in long garb and almost equally long hair. On the opposite side of the hall were officers in braided uniforms, courtiers covered with decorations, generals and members of the Council of State.

At a quarter of 2, the Emperor approached. In watching the Duma members I was surprised to note that many of them did not even return the bows of His Majesty, some giving an awkward nod, others staring him coldly in the face, showing no enthusiasm, and even almost sullen indifference. He then proceeded to read his address. When he finished there was a tremendous outbreak of applause, but limited almost entirely to the right side of the hall, with the Duma members remaining quiet.

The contrast between those on the left and those on the right was the greatest one could possibly imagine, one being a real representation of the different classes of this great Empire and the other of what the autocracy and bureaucracy has been.

**SOURCE**

**From the diary of Grand Duchess Xenia, 27 and 30 April 1906. Grand Duchess Xenia was Nicholas II's sister. Note that, in Orthodox Christianity, crossing oneself is a gesture of piety or reverence: Grand Duchess Xenia thought that Duma members had failed to show the tsar proper respect.**

Sat with us were members of the State Council and high officials, to the left the members of the Duma, who included several men with repulsive faces and insolent disdainful expressions. They neither crossed themselves nor bowed, but stood with their hands behind their backs or in their pockets, looking sombrely at everyone and everything. But among the peasants there were such wonderful faces.

Nicky read the speech standing, in a loud, steady voice. Every word penetrated the soul - tears welled up in the throat. He spoke so well, saying just what was needed, asking everyone to come to his aid. When he finished a cheer broke out which was taken up by everyone.

The Duma is such filth, such a nest of revolutionaries, that it's disgusting and shaming for the rest of Russia in front of the whole world.

### A Level Exam-Style Question Section A

***Study Sources 1 and 2 before you answer this question.***

How far could the historian make use of Sources 1 and 2 together to investigate the political tensions that existed in Russia in 1906?

Explain your answer using both sources, the information given about them and your own knowledge of the historical context. (20 marks)

**Tip**

*Use your knowledge of the historical context to note the limitations of what can be gained from the source – in other words, ask yourself whether there are aspects of the political tensions that existed in Russia in 1906 about which the source has little or nothing to say.*

**KEY TERM**

**Amnesty**
An amnesty involves the government giving a pardon to, and therefore releasing, political or other prisoners. Article 23 of the Fundamental Law stated that only the tsar could pardon offenders: he refused to pardon those who had been involved in terrorism.

After the pomp of the opening ceremony, relations between the government and the Duma swiftly deteriorated. The Duma was first on to the attack, passing a resolution calling for the full democratisation of Russia, radical land reform involving the transfer of the nobility's estates to the peasantry and an **amnesty** for all political detainees. These demands were instantly dismissed by the government. The Duma responded by passing a vote of censure on the government and calling upon it to resign. Provocatively, it then began to debate a land reform measure that it knew was unacceptable to the tsar and his ministers. At this point, the government lost patience and dissolved the Duma.

Dissolution was not unexpected by the Kadets and Trudoviks in the Duma. They had made contingency plans for it. In July 1906, in accordance with their plans, around 200 Duma members left St Petersburg for nearby Finland (where they thought they would be safe from arrest) and issued an appeal to the nation. In this appeal – the so-called Vyborg Manifesto – they called upon their fellow-citizens to refuse to pay taxes until the Duma was restored. What they were hoping for was a tidal wave of protest against the regime that would sweep them into power. But the Vyborg Manifesto fell flat. Drained by the struggles of 1905, the masses did not take to the streets. The signatories of the Vyborg Manifesto were arrested for inciting disorder: they were given short prison terms and banned from taking part in further political activity. The Kadets' aggressive and unyielding tactics had backfired.

**SOURCE 3**

From the 'Vyborg Manifesto', July 1906.

Citizens of all Russia. By the decree of 8 July, the State Duma is dissolved. When you elected us as your representatives, you charged us to win land and liberty. Fulfilling your commission, we drew up laws to secure the people's freedom. We wished to issue a law distributing land to the labouring peasantry. The government refused to accept such a law, and when the Duma once again affirmed its decision, the dissolution of the people's representatives was declared.

Citizens! Stand firm behind the violated rights of the people's representatives, stand firm behind the State Duma! Russia should not remain without the people's representation for a single day. You have the means to achieve this; the government does not have the right either to collect taxes from the people or to call people to military service without the consent of the people's representation. And so, before the people's representation is convened, don't give a penny to the treasury or a soldier to the army. Be firm in your refusal, stand up for your rights, all as one man. No force can withstand the united and unwavering will of the people.

THINKING HISTORICALLY EVIDENCE (5a)

**Context is everything**

Work in groups.

Take an A3 piece of paper. In the middle of it draw a circle about 20 cm in diameter. Within the circle is the evidence itself, Source 3, outside the circle is the context.

1 Think of a question that Source 3 could be helpful in answering.

2 Inside the circle, write a set of statements giving information that can be gleaned only from Source 3 itself without any contextual knowledge.

3 Outside the circle, write down statements of contextual knowledge that relate to Source 3.

4 Draw annotated lines to show the links between the contextual statements and the information from the source. Does context change the nature or meaning of the information?

5 Explain why knowledge of context is important when gathering and using historical evidence. Give specific examples to illustrate your point.

Elections to the second Duma took place in late 1906 and early 1907. They differed from the 1906 Duma elections in two important respects.

- In 1907, the revolutionary socialist parties (SRs, Mensheviks and Bolsheviks) participated in the elections rather than boycotting them as they had done in 1906.
- In the 1906 election campaign, the government had been passive, making little effort to influence the outcome. In 1907, it was interventionist: it disrupted electioneering by the opposition parties and secretly financed the campaigns of favoured extreme right-wing candidates.

In the elections, the Kadets lost half their seats. They were now flanked on the left by some 200 socialists (104 Trudoviks, 37 SRs, 36 Mensheviks and 18 Bolsheviks) and on the right by 54 moderate liberal Octobrists, plus a number of right-wing extremists. The second Duma was more polarised between left and right than the first but, from the government's point of view, it was no more amenable. Its left-wing members were highly critical of the methods used by the government to quell peasant disorder and refused to support the land reform proposals of P.A. Stolypin, the Tsar's new chief minister.

In mid-1907, Stolypin, frustrated by the second Duma's obstructiveness, dissolved it on the pretext that some of its Bolshevik members were involved in treasonable activity. But he did not stop there. He proceeded to scrap the 1905 electoral law and replace it with a new one designed to reduce the representation in the Duma of peasants, workers and national minorities. Under the revised arrangements, the nobility (under one percent of the population) elected more than half of the Duma while the peasantry (over 80 percent of the population) elected only one-fifth of it. In this way a solid conservative majority in future Dumas was guaranteed. All this was done in violation of the 1906 Fundamental Laws and without Duma approval: Stolypin had carried out a sort of **coup d'état.**

KEY TERM

**Coup d'état**
A sudden, illegal seizure of power.

ACTIVITY
KNOWLEDGE CHECK

**The government and the Kadets, 1906-07**

1 State three ways in which government treatment of the Duma in 1906-07 outraged members of the Kadet Party.

2 What conclusions can be drawn from the events of 1906-07 about the political skill and judgement of the Kadets?

3 Why were the government and the Duma unable to establish a working relationship with each other in 1906-07?

## Nicholas II's relations with the Dumas, 1906–14

Nicholas II loathed the Duma and made little attempt to conceal his feelings towards it. In 1906, he wrote to one of his ministers to complain about 'the damned Duma'. On more than one occasion, he openly praised the Union of Russian People, the extreme right-wing party that campaigned (among other things) for the Duma's abolition.

Nicholas II could not reconcile himself to the Duma because he believed that its existence was an affront to the principle of autocracy he felt he had a duty to uphold. 'I have no right', he noted privately in 1906, 'to renounce that which was bequeathed to me by my forefathers and which I must hand down unimpaired to my son.' He claimed that he had only given the go-ahead for the Duma's establishment in 1905 because Witte had forced him into it.

Soon after the first Duma began its deliberations, its members requested an audience with the tsar. The request was turned down: Nicholas II and his advisers took the view that he should remain above the political fray. This exchange set the pattern for the remainder of the Tsar's reign: he left the day-to-day management of the Duma to his ministers and never again addressed the Duma, as he had done at the 1906 opening ceremony. In private, however, he was forthright. In 1906, although worried about the possibility of protest and disorder, he welcomed the dissolution of the first Duma and in 1907 he chided his ministers for not acting more quickly against the second.

In the elections to the third and fourth Dumas in 1907 and 1912, Tsarism's most committed opponents (Kadets, Trudoviks, socialists) won fewer than 100 seats between them. The third Duma was dominated by the Octobrists, the largest single party with 154 seats, and around 150 pro-regime right-wingers. In the fourth Duma, the right-wing parties were a little stronger, the Octobrists a little weaker. These changes in the composition of the Duma did little, however, to soften Nicholas II's hostility to it. He acknowledged that the third and fourth Dumas were much less troublesome than their predecessors, but was repeatedly infuriated by the conduct of the Octobrist leader, Alexander Guchkov.

- In a debate in 1907, goaded by Duma right-wingers describing Nicholas II as an autocrat, Guchkov insisted that post-1905 Russia was not an autocracy.
- In 1908, Guchkov made a speech in the Duma criticising the number of senior positions in the armed forces held by members of the royal family. In effect, he accused Nicholas II of **nepotism**.
- In 1912, using colourful language, Guchkov publicly attacked the growing influence in royal circles of the Siberian holy man, Grigory Rasputin. Nicholas II was outraged. So too was his wife, the Tsarina Alexandra, who hero-worshipped Rasputin because she believed he had the power to control her son's **haemophilia**. 'Hanging is too good for him', she said of Guchkov.

### KEY TERMS

**Nepotism**
The practice among those with power or influence of favouring their relatives, especially by giving them jobs.

**Haemophilia**
A genetic disorder that affects the blood's ability to clot. Nicholas II's son was therefore at risk of death from any injury that caused bleeding – not only open wounds, but also bumps and bruises that might have led to internal bleeding.

### EXTEND YOUR KNOWLEDGE

**Alexander Guchkov (1862–1936)**
Guchkov was the great-grandson of a serf who showed a talent for making money, bought his freedom and went on to make a fortune in the textile business. This kind of upward mobility was unusual, but not unique, in 19th-century Russia. Guchkov was himself a successful businessman: he was head of a major insurance company. In his political career, he was a champion of Moscow's business and financial community. A restless character with a liking for danger, Guchkov had been a soldier and an adventurer before embarking on his political career, visiting trouble spots and conflict zones around the world.

In the years immediately before the First World War, the Duma was under threat. A number of influential ministers called for it to be stripped of its powers and turned into a purely consultative body. Nicholas II clearly found their proposals tempting. In the end though, he came down on the side of other ministers who urged caution – but only after prolonged debate in government circles.

## The nature of Tsarist government and royal power in 1914

A case can be made for the view that, by 1914, autocracy in Russia had been more or less fully re-established.

- The Fundamental Laws effectively limited the Duma to the sphere of law-making which is only one aspect of the work of government. Outside of this sphere there were no serious limits on the Tsar's power. In areas such as defence, foreign affairs and public order policy, Nicholas II and his ministers were able to make decisions without reference to the Duma.
- Even within the law-making sphere, the Duma proved unable to impose itself. Nicholas II and his ministers silenced the Duma in 1906 and 1907 by using their power to dissolve it and also made extensive use of their power under Article 87 of the Fundamental Laws to make laws by decree when the Duma was not in session. Stolypin, for example, used Article 87 to enact his land reforms. By 1914, the Duma was – from the government's point of view – sometimes an irritant, but it was not a threat.
- The **rule of law** is characteristically absent in autocratic states. In countries where the rule of law is in operation, everyone in the country, including the government, is subject to the law. The rule of law was certainly not in operation in Russia before 1905. This state of affairs did not change as a result of the 1905 revolution. In 1907, the government broke the Fundamental Laws when it amended the 1905 electoral law, but nothing happened to it as a result.

Russia in 1914 is, however, perhaps best described as a *largely* rather than a *fully* autocratic state. Richard Charques, a British historian writing in the 1950s, made the same point using different language when he characterised post-1906 Russia as 'a demi-semi-constitutional monarchy'. Whatever its flaws, Russia in 1914 did have a constitution of sorts in the shape of the 1906 Fundamental Laws.

- The Duma may, by 1914, have been reduced to a talking shop but it was an elected national legislative body, something which Russia did not have before 1906.
- In 1914, political parties were within limits free to criticise the regime. This had not been the case before 1906. By 1914, there was also a relatively **free press** in Russia.

Supporters, as well as opponents, of Nicholas II often despaired of his style of government. One problem was his inaccessibility. He spent most of his time at his palace at Tsarkoye Selo, a town 15 miles outside St Petersburg, or at Livadia, his summer residence on the Black Sea: he did not make himself available to his ministers in St Petersburg on a day-to-day basis. A second, more serious, problem was that, leaving aside his determination to uphold the principle of autocracy, he had no real policies of his own. He failed to give his government clear direction. Ministers were left to their own devices, but were repudiated if their policies turned out badly. Nor for most of his reign did Nicholas II delegate authority to a recognised chief minister. This was a recipe for struggles between ministers for power and influence.

### SOURCE 4

Mikhail Rodzianko, the Octobrist President of the Fourth Duma, speaking to the tsar, 1913.

> During the last session of the Duma we debated a measure for the use of the Polish language in the schools of the western provinces. It was your imperial majesty's wish that that the language should be admitted in order to improve the position of the Poles. The measure was worked out in the Duma in that sense. Now it is being debated in the State Council and is defended by a representative of the government. Meanwhile, some members of the Council are absent, others vote against it, and the measure is rejected. Your majesty will agree that members of the government either do not wish to execute your will, or do not take the trouble to understand it. The nation feels bewildered. Each minister has his own opinion. The cabinet is generally split into two parties, the State Council forms a third, the Duma a fourth, and your own will is unknown to the nation. This cannot go on, Your Majesty; this is not Government, it is anarchy.

### ACTIVITY
### KNOWLEDGE CHECK

**The extent of change in Russia's system of government after 1905**

In what ways did Russia's system of government in 1914 differ from the system before 1905? How substantial were these differences?

### KEY TERMS

**The rule of law**
A principle that holds that states and societies should be governed in accordance with fixed rules rather than by the whims of individuals. Without the rule of law there is either anarchy (no rules at all) or arbitrary government (unaccountable rulers who can do whatever they wish).

**Free press**
Where newspapers are not restricted or controlled by government censorship.

### AS Level Exam-Style Question Section B

To what extent was Russia an autocratic state in 1914? (20 marks)

**Tip**

*If a question starts with the phrase 'To what extent' or 'How far', it indicates that the matter is not clear-cut and that there are arguments to be made both for and against the proposition contained in the question. In this case, ensure that your answer considers both arguments that support the claim that Russia was a fully autocratic state in 1914 and those that challenge it.*

### AS Level Exam-Style Question Section A (a)

***Study Source 4 before you answer this question.***

Why is Source 4 valuable to the historian for an enquiry into the nature of Tsarist rule in 1913?

Explain your answer using the source, the information given about it and your own knowledge of the historical context. (8 marks)

**Tip**

*Make sure that you offer comment not only on the information contained in the source but also on the reasons why Rodzianko's evidence can be seen as credible.*

# TO WHAT EXTENT DID STOLYPIN'S POLICIES OF REPRESSION AND REFORM SUCCEED IN PUTTING THE TSARIST REGIME ON A MORE STABLE FOOTING?

## Stolypin's policies of repression

In the years 1905–07, few parts of the countryside of European Russia escaped serious disorder. Motivated principally by land hunger, the peasantry went on the rampage. Disorder was not confined to rent strikes, land seizures and attacks on manor houses. There was also a good deal of physical violence: in 1906, over 1,000 people, many of them government officials, died in terrorist attacks. This rose to more than 3,000 in 1907. The regime was faced with a peasant revolt – though not a co-ordinated one. The need to pacify rural Russia was the most urgent task facing the Tsarist regime.

The regime's attempts to pacify the countryside began in late 1905, under Interior Minister P.N. Durnovo. Army units were sent into the areas of greatest unrest, with orders to show no mercy. Over the next six months, killings and beatings by the army left an estimated 15,000 people dead and 20,000 wounded. In addition, 45,000 people were exiled to Siberia. In some cases, whole villages were burned to the ground. The aim was not only to punish wrongdoers, but also to terrorise the mass of the rural population into submission. Durnovo's policies made the Trans-Siberian railway safe and restored order in the turbulent Baltic region, but elsewhere problems continued. Army expeditions could not be sent into all areas experiencing unrest because there were not enough troops to go round.

The government's bid to quell rural disorder in 1905 did not only involve the use of force. In late 1905, it announced that peasant redemption payments would be cut by half in 1906 and abolished altogether in 1907. This, however, was a very modest concession: redemption payments were due to end in 1910 anyway. It had little or no effect in reducing levels of unrest in the countryside.

In May 1906, Durnovo was replaced at the Interior Ministry by P.A. Stolypin. Soon afterwards, in July 1906, Stolypin was appointed Chairman of the Council of Ministers, holding both posts until his death in 1911. A member of an old-established noble family, Stolypin owed his rapid political ascent to his record as a forceful and effective provincial governor in the unruly 'Black Earth' region in the south of European Russia.

Repression in the countryside under Stolypin was as savage as it had been under Durnovo. In August 1906, Stolypin proclaimed a state of emergency covering virtually the whole of European Russia. This gave government officials the power to imprison people without trial for up to six months and to exile troublemakers. When these measures proved insufficient, he introduced arrangements that allowed courts composed of five army officers to impose punishments on peasants accused of disorder outside the ordinary framework of the law. These field courts-martial, as they were called, had a number of distinctive features:

- Cases were heard within 24 hours of an offence being committed.
- Trials were held in secret.
- The accused did not have the right to be represented by a lawyer.
- Trials lasted for a maximum of two days.
- Death sentences (by hanging) were carried out within 24 hours of the court reaching its decision.
- No appeals against verdicts or sentences were allowed.

In 1906–07, over 1,000 people were sentenced to death under these procedures. Thousands more were exiled to Siberia. F.I. Rodichev, a prominent Kadet member of the Duma, called the hangman's noose 'Stolypin's necktie'. The trains carrying off those exiled became known as 'Stolypin's wagons'. Stolypin defended himself by calling field courts-martial 'exceptional measures to fit exceptional times'.

The restoration of order in rural Russia took time. Peasant disturbances did not subside quickly or completely in 1906–07. Unrest in some areas continued on into 1908. Eventually, though, the violence unleashed by the state did its work, and the regime succeeded in reasserting its authority in the countryside.

## Actions against revolutionary parties

The revolutionary parties were not outlawed after 1905, but their leaders and organisations were subjected to repressive activity. Revolutionary leaders were either arrested or driven into foreign exile. After a year in prison awaiting trial, Trotsky and the other leaders of the St Petersburg Soviet were sentenced in 1906 to lifetime exile in Siberia: Trotsky escaped from the train taking him eastwards and made his way abroad. Lenin was in St Petersburg from November 1905 to summer 1906, when he took refuge in the relative safety of Finland: he then left Finland for western Europe with the Okhrana, the Tsarist political police force, breathing down his neck. The experiences of other revolutionary leaders, whether Bolshevik, Menshevik or Socialist Revolutionary, were not dissimilar. By 1914, most of them were following events in Russia from London, Paris, Zurich or Geneva.

The revolutionary parties were further targeted at the time of the dissolution of the second Duma in 1907. Dissolution was accompanied by the arrest of the Duma's Bolshevik members, who were charged with inciting mutiny in the armed forces. Action was also taken against Bolshevik, Menshevik and SR activists throughout the country, with large numbers being arrested. There were over 2,000 arrests in the 'Black Earth' province of Voronezh alone. The revolutionary parties, their organisational structures severely disrupted, were left weakened and demoralised.

The Bolsheviks and the Socialist Revolutionaries also attracted the attention of the authorities through their practice of 'expropriation', which meant boosting party funds by robbing banks. One bank robber's trial in 1907 saw the Bolsheviks suffer the embarrassment of being clearly implicated in criminal activity.

## Reform of agricultural landholdings and emigration to Siberia

### Stolypin's land reforms: aims and methods

Stolypin was not a **reactionary**, but a sophisticated conservative. He was unapologetic about the use of force to restore order, but insisted that reform as well as repression was required if Tsarism was to have a long-term future. 'First pacification, then reforms' was his own succinct definition of his strategy.

Stolypin saw land reform as the key to Tsarism's survival. He aimed to break up the village commune, do away with open-field strip farming and reconstruct Russian agriculture on the basis of peasants owning their own separate farms. He believed that reform along these lines would bring political, as well as economic, benefits.

**KEY TERM**

**Reactionary**
An extreme conservative opposed to any kind of political or social change.

| Political benefits | Economic benefits |
|---|---|
| • Peasants owning their own separate farms would, it was assumed, develop a strong attachment to the principle of private ownership and would therefore resist socialist calls for the communal or state ownership of land.<br>• It was further assumed that peasants who benefited from the Stolypin land reform would have a vested interest in the survival of the Tsarist regime because a new regime might undo what Stolypin had done. | • Peasant households who owned their own small farms would have a powerful incentive to develop and improve their land: incentives of this kind were absent in the existing system, where strips in open fields were often reallocated between households every 10–15 years or so.<br>• A more highly motivated peasantry would be more productive.<br>• Increased agricultural production would ensure the supply of food to Russia's growing industrial towns and eliminate the possibility of outbreaks of unrest caused by high food prices. Increased output would also enable Russia to export foodstuffs and help to generate capital that could be invested in industry. |

What Stolypin looked forward to as a result of his land reforms was the emergence of a class of prosperous, politically conservative peasant farmers. He told the Duma in 1908: 'The government has put its wager not on the drunken and the weak but on the sober and the strong – on the sturdy individual proprietor.'

The Stolypin land reform was a complex affair. Its foundations were laid by a decree issued in 1906 and the process was completed by two further laws passed in 1910 and 1911. The key features of the 1906–11 measures were as follows.

- Every peasant householder could demand that his share of communal land be turned into his own private property.

- In villages where there had been no redistribution of strips since emancipation in 1861 (so-called 'hereditary communes'), a peasant householder could request that his strips be converted into a separate small farm. If the commune was unwilling to grant his request, it had to pay him compensation.
- In villages where periodic redistribution of strips had been practised after 1861 (so-called 'repartitional communes'), separate small farms could only be created after a vote among villagers.
- The government set up local bodies called land organisation commissions to settle any disputes arising out of its land reform measures.
- The rules governing the operation of the Peasants' Land Bank, founded in 1882, were relaxed to allow enterprising peasants to borrow money at favourable interest rates to acquire more land.

### Stolypin's land reforms: impact

The implementation of Stolypin's land reforms was overtaken by war and revolution. Any estimate of their likely long-term impact would therefore be no more than guesswork. As a result it is not possible to say how successful they would have been had they been fully implemented. Their impact before 1914, however, was relatively limited.

- Initially, there was a rush to take advantage of the opportunities offered by Stolypin's reforms but, after a year or two, take-up tailed off sharply. Many peasants saw no reason to depart from their traditional customs and practices, and those that did were often victimised by their fellow-villagers.
- By 1914, only 20 percent or so of peasant householders had left the village commune and become legal owners of the land they farmed. Not all of these leavers, however, became proprietors of separate farms: around half of them owned their land in the form of strips in open fields and so still had links with the commune. In 1914, therefore, only half of those who had left the commune, around 10 percent of all peasant households, were owners of separate farms, or what are sometimes called consolidated holdings. Some 80 per cent of peasant households remained full members of village communes.
- There was a sharp increase in agricultural production in Russia in the years before 1914, but it was not attributable simply to land reform. Other factors were equally, if not more, important: a run of good harvests in 1909–13, steps towards the opening up of Siberia and greater use machinery and fertilisers.

**SOURCE**

From a report by the *zemstvo* in Kazan, 450 miles east of Moscow, into the implementation of Stolypin's land reforms in the locality, 1909.

Hostile manifestations towards separating members of the village commune often assumed bitter and barbaric forms. Fires, murders and conflicts involving bloodshed were by no means rare occurrences. There was even a case of almost unbelievable atrocity in the drenching with oil of a departing member of the commune by his fellow villagers, who burnt him like a live torch.

**AS Level Exam-Style Question Section A (b)**

***Study Source 5 before you answer this question.***

How much weight do you give the evidence of Source 5 for an enquiry into peasant attitudes towards the land reforms introduced by Stolypin in 1906?

Explain your answer using the source, the information given about it and your own knowledge of the historical context. (12 marks)

**Tip**

*Higher-level responses to questions of this type display the ability to make reasoned inferences from the factual information contained in the source. In this case, consider whether it can fairly be assumed the events described were the norm in Kazan and elsewhere.*

Stolypin's land reforms were largely concerned with making more productive use of land that peasants were already cultivating. They did not in themselves involve any transfer of additional land to the peasantry. As a result, they did not really address the issue of peasant land hunger, nor did they alleviate the problem of rural over-population in the 'Black Earth' region. Stolypin's solution to these problems was emigration to Siberia.

## Emigration to Siberia

At the turn of the century, Siberia was mineral-rich, sparsely populated and economically under-developed. Much of it – the **tundra** in the north and the **taiga** in the east – was barely habitable. In south-western Siberia, however, there was an abundance of cultivatable land. The opening of the Trans-Siberian railway made this potentially fertile area more readily accessible and mass migration became a possibility.

### KEY TERMS

**Tundra**
Treeless plain in the Arctic region, where the subsoil is permanently frozen and mosses and similar low-growing plants are the only form of vegetation.

**Taiga**
A vast area of dense coniferous forest covering much of Siberia.

### EXTEND YOUR KNOWLEDGE

**The Trans-Siberian railway**
The Trans-Siberian railway connected Moscow, in the heart of European Russia, with the port of Vladivostok on the Pacific Ocean. Construction of the line began in 1891. Most of it was open to traffic by 1905, but it was 1916 before the project was finally completed.

The Trans-Siberian railway was built to promote the economic development of Siberia. Strategic considerations were involved too: it was hoped that improved communications would facilitate the movement of troops from west to east and so help Russia to counteract the threat to its interests in the Far East posed by the rising power of Japan.

The building of the Trans-Siberian railway was a remarkable feat of engineering, but the completed line had its limitations. It was a single-track railway, which restricted the amount of traffic that could be carried, and poor-quality construction meant that in places trains had to travel at reduced speed.

Under Stolypin, peasants were offered a range of inducements to migrate to Siberia: free or cheap land, interest-free loans and reduced railway fares. A lavishly funded government advertising campaign publicised what was on offer. The results were impressive: between 1906 and 1913, some 3.5 million peasants emigrated to Siberia, though nearly 20 percent of them failed to settle and made the return journey to European Russia.

## Stolypin and his critics

Stolypin was not preoccupied with the land issue to the exclusion of everything else. He had ambitious plans for reform in other areas too. He wanted to streamline Russia's local government system, getting rid of the land captains (landowners who in 1889 had been given powers to direct and control peasant affairs in their localities) and giving the *zemstva* additional powers. He proposed to reform Russia's inadequate educational system so that all children received four years of schooling, starting at the age of eight; and he aimed to introduce a proper scheme of compensation for factory workers hurt in industrial accidents. All of these initiatives ran into opposition from powerful conservative vested interests: the nobility took issue with local government reform, the Orthodox Church resisted educational reform and industrialists complained that the workmen's compensation scheme was too expensive. With conservative Russia turning against him, Stolypin began to lose the Tsar's confidence. At the time of his assassination in 1911, he was an isolated figure facing dismissal.

As Russia's chief minister, Stolypin set out to perform a difficult balancing act. He aimed to strengthen Tsarism by reaching out to political moderates, in particular the Octobrists in the Duma, while keeping Russia's conservatives, and the tsar, on-side. He was unsuccessful: his repressive measures alienated moderates and his reforms antagonised conservatives. Nevertheless, in the judgement of one historian, Richard Pipes, he was 'arguably the most outstanding statesman of Imperial Russia'. In view of Stolypin's inability to implement many of his policies, this might appear to be a surprising judgment. What justifies it is Stolypin's toughness and the imaginative and far-sighted nature of his strategy for securing Tsarism's future.

SOURCE 6

From an article written by Lenin immediately after Stolypin's assassination, October 1911.

A landowner, he was appointed a provincial governor in 1902, gained 'fame' in the eyes of the Tsar and the reactionary court clique by his brutal reprisals against the peasants, organised Black Hundred gangs and pogroms in 1905, became Minister of the Interior in 1906 and Chairman of the Council of Ministers after the dissolution of the First Duma. That, in very brief outline is Stolypin's political biography. The biography of the head of the counter-revolutionary government is at the same time the biography of the class which carried out the counter-revolution - Stolypin was nothing more than an agent or clerk in its employ. This class is the Russian landed nobility. The estates of this class form a basis for feudal exaction which in various forms still reigns in Russia's central provinces. The 'land hunger' of the Russian peasant is nothing but the reverse side of the over-abundance of land in the hands of this class. The agrarian question, the central issue in our 1905 Revolution, was one of whether landed proprietorship would remain intact - in which case the poverty-stricken, wretched, browbeaten and downtrodden peasantry would for many years to come inevitably remain as the bulk of the population - or whether the bulk of the population would succeed in winning for themselves more or less human conditions.

ACTIVITY
WRITING

**Lenin and Stolypin**

Analyse Source 6, an extract from an article written by Lenin immediately after Stolypin's assassination, October 1911.

**1** Identify any words or phrases you don't understand and research their meanings.

**2** Identify any words or phrases that show the writer's feelings towards the Tsarist regime and its supporters. Write a short paragraph explaining his views, using quotations from the extract to back up your points.

## The Lena Goldfields Massacre, 1912

Gold was first discovered in eastern Siberia in the early 19th century. By 1900, a thriving mining industry had developed, dominated by the giant Lena Gold Mining Company. Its shareholders included the Tsar's mother and a number of government ministers.

Industrial disputes in the goldfields were not infrequent: the environment was harsh and the treatment of workers poor. The strike that culminated in the Lena massacre began as a protest against the serving of rancid horsemeat in a works canteen. This protest quickly escalated into an all-out strike, with the miners demanding a 30 percent wage increase, an eight-hour day and improvements in medical care. After a month in which the goldfields were at a standstill, the government sent in troops to arrest the strike's leaders. Striking miners responded by organising a march to demand their release. In April 1912, at Nadezhdinsk, a company of 90 soldiers opened fire on a column of 3,000 unarmed marchers. There are no definitive casualty figures, but a conservative estimate is 160 killed and 200 wounded. Despite the massacre, the Lena strikers failed to extract significant improvements in their pay and conditions from their employers. In late 1912, they and their families – nearly 10,000 people in all – gave up and left the area. The mine-owners replaced them with workers imported from Korea and China.

After the strikes of 1905, labour unrest in Russia had tailed off sharply. In the Stolypin era, the trade union movement was largely unassertive. The Lena goldfield massacre brought this period of relative calm to an end. It gave rise to a massive wave of protest strikes across Russia that only subsided when war broke out in 1914. Revolutionary leaders, who had been on the defensive since 1905, were encouraged by this upsurge in working-class militancy. The Lena shootings, claimed Lenin, had 'inflamed the masses with revolutionary fire'.

SOURCE 7 Widows and children of victims of the Lena Goldfield Massacre beside the mass grave in which they were buried, 1912.

ACTIVITY
KNOWLEDGE CHECK

**Assessing Stolypin**

1 What arguments and evidence can be offered for and against the claim that Stolypin was an 'outstanding statesman'?

2 How accurate is it to say that Stolypin's policies in 1906-11 did nothing at all to put the Tsarist regime on a more stable footing?

# WHAT IMPACT DID RUSSIA'S INVOLVEMENT IN THE FIRST WORLD WAR HAVE ON THE REPUTATION OF THE TSARIST REGIME?

## The state of the armed forces in 1914

In 1914, Russia's army was to outward appearance a formidable one. With a peacetime strength of 1.4 million men and around three million trained reservists, it was the largest army in Europe. It commanded respect for another reason: after its failure in the 1904–05 Russo-Japanese war, it had been re-armed and modernised.

Alongside these strengths, however, the Russian army had numerous weaknesses.

- Too many of its generals owed their places to nepotism rather than ability. Good-quality junior officers were also in short supply.
- The physical condition and educational standards of ordinary soldiers in the Russian army were low in comparison with those in other European armies. In addition, many conscripts identified far more strongly with their home district than they did with Russia as a whole: as a result, they were arguably less highly motivated than soldiers in other European armies, who had a more highly

developed sense of national identity. During the World War, Russian troops surrendered more quickly and deserted in larger numbers than their counterparts elsewhere.

- In some respects, the Russian army was still poorly equipped. It did not have enough heavy artillery, machine guns or motorised vehicles. There was even a shortage of rifles: in the early stages of the World War, the army needed a minimum of 100,000 new rifles a month, but Russian industry could supply only 27,000.

In 1914, Russia's generals hoped their armies would sweep all before them by sheer weight of numbers. Russia's allies, Britain and France, also had high expectations of what was optimistically called the Russian 'steamroller'. These hopes were quickly dashed. In the autumn of 1914, Russia's advance into German territory was halted at the battles of Tannenberg and the Masurian Lakes. Far worse was to come: in 1915, the year of the so-called 'Great Retreat', Russian forces were driven out of Poland, Lithuania and parts of Belorussia at a cost of one million men killed or wounded and a further one million taken prisoner. In 1916, Russia tried to regain the initiative by launching a counter-attack, known as the 'Brusilov offensive', directed against the armies of Germany's ally, Austria. The 'Brusilov offensive' was halted when German forces came to the aid of the Austrians.

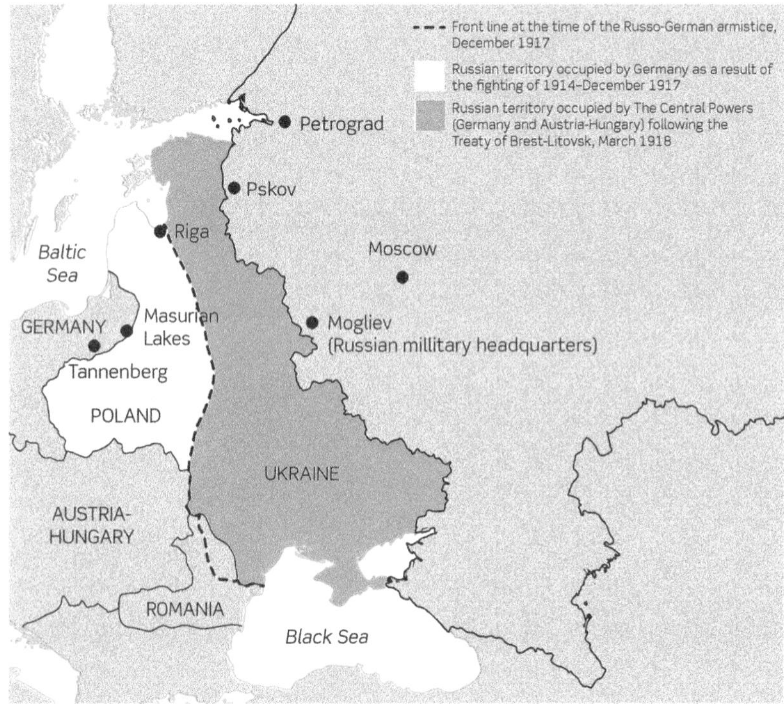


**Figure 2.1**: Russia at war, 1914–17.

## EXTEND YOUR KNOWLEDGE

### Russia and the First World War

In the late 19th and early 20th centuries Russia aimed to extend its influence in south-eastern Europe (the Balkan region) at the expense of the decaying Turkish Empire. The great prize it sought was control of the straits connecting the Black Sea to the Mediterranean. Russia's ambitions in south-eastern Europe brought it into conflict with Austria, which also had interests in the region, and its ally (from 1879 onwards) Germany. In 1894, Russia entered into an alliance with Germany's main enemy, France. The formation of this alliance gave rise to complaints by Germany that it was the victim of aggressive 'encirclement' by France and Russia.

In the years before 1914 Germany also became alarmed by Russia's growing economic and military strength. One of the main reasons why Germany went to war in 1914 was to eliminate the Russian threat before it was too late. Russia was not the aggressor in 1914, but it nevertheless had expansionist war aims: to extend its influence in south-eastern Europe and to win control of the straits.

SOURCE 8

From a report by General Polivanov, minister of war, to the Tsar's Council of Ministers, July 1915.

Only God knows where the retreat will end. The soldiers are without doubt exhausted by the continued defeats and retreats. Their confidence in final victory and in their leaders is undermined. Ever more threatening signs of demoralisation are present. Cases of desertion and voluntary surrender to the enemy are becoming more frequent.

There is growing confusion at Army Headquarters. It is also seized by the fatal psychology of defeat and is preparing to retreat deep inside Russia. Back, back, back - that is all that is heard from there. No system, no plan is evident in conduct and orders.

### ACTIVITY
### KNOWLEDGE CHECK

How far do Sources 8 and 9 offer support for the claim that Russia's armies were defeated in 1915 mainly because they were poorly equipped?

SOURCE 9

The Great Retreat: Russian prisoners being escorted away from the battlefield by their German captors, 1915.

## Economic problems in wartime

### The 1915 munitions crisis

Military planners in Russia before 1914 assumed that any war in which the country might become involved would be relatively short. With the possibility of a long war ruled out, no steps were taken to stockpile vast quantities of munitions or to build up Russia's armaments-making capacity. In 1914 and 1915, unable to supply its needs from its own resources, Russia placed huge orders with British and American arms manufacturers. In many cases, these foreign suppliers proved unable to meet the deadlines set out in their contracts. The result was the munitions crisis of spring 1915. It was a political as well as an economic crisis: the shell shortage, said the government's opponents, was symptomatic of its inability to organise Russia's war effort properly. Stung into action, the government set up a Special Committee for State Defence to control armaments production and build new factories. By 1916, the supply of munitions had improved considerably. The political damage, however, had been done: it was widely assumed that the catastrophic losses of 1915 were the result of the Tsarist regime's incompetence and mismanagement.

### Supplies for cities: transport problems

The war imposed huge strains on Russia's transport system and, in particular, on its railway network. Understandably, military traffic was given priority. The movement of ordinary freight was, as a result, seriously disrupted, not only in the areas near the battlefront but further afield too. Arms shipments from abroad mostly arrived at Vladivostock and were then transported westwards, clogging up the Trans-Siberian railway. Trains carrying food supplies to the cities were often seriously delayed, their cargo sometimes rotting away before it reached its destination. The weaknesses of the transport system were one of the main causes of wartime food shortages and rising food prices in Russia's towns and cities.

### Inflation

As the war went on, **inflation** became an increasingly serious problem. The main driver of inflation in wartime Russia was rising food prices. The supply of food to Russia's towns and cities failed to keep pace with demand, and prices rose alarmingly as a result. There were a number of reasons why foodstuffs were in short supply.

- Grain production fell in wartime, mainly because some important food-producing areas were occupied by the Germans.
- Hoarding of grain by the peasantry and speculators. In normal circumstances, peasants sold surplus grain in order to buy consumer goods. In wartime, unwilling to buy over-priced consumer goods, they held on to their grain instead.
- Hold-ups on the railway system disrupted food supplies to the towns.

**KEY TERM**

**Inflation**

Rising prices, or, to say the same thing in a different way, a fall in the purchasing power of money. If price inflation is running at an annual rate of 10%, a currency is losing 10% of its value or purchasing power each year, leaving people significantly worse off - unless, that is, they receive an equivalent pay increase to compensate for rising prices.

The urban working class was particularly badly hit by inflation. The wages of industrial workers went up during the war, but prices went up faster. In Petrograd, for example, the wages of skilled workers doubled between 1914 and 1917, but during the same period there was a fivefold increase in the cost of a bag of flour and a sevenfold increase in the cost of a bag of potatoes.

**SOURCE 10** From a report by the chief of police in Petrograd province, October 1916.

The difficult material position of the ordinary people, consigned to a half-starved existence and seeing no hope of improvement in the near future, has made them regard with sympathy any sort of plans or projects promising to improve conditions of life. As a result, a situation has been created which greatly favours revolutionary propaganda.

Despite the great increase in wages, the economic condition of the masses is worse than terrible. While wages have risen 50%, the prices on all products have increased 100-500%. The impossibility of even buying many food products and necessities, the time wasted standing in queues to receive goods, the increased incidence of disease due to malnutrition and unsanitary living conditions - cold and dampness because of lack of coal and wood - have made the workers as a whole prepared for the wildest excesses of a 'hunger riot'.

Inflation only really caught up with the peasantry in the later stages of the war, when prices of consumer goods like shoes and clothing rose sharply. As far as food was concerned, they were largely self-sufficient.

## Nicholas, Alexandra and Rasputin

The 'Great Retreat' of 1915 gave rise to panic and near-hysteria in political circles. Rumours circulated that Kiev and maybe even Petrograd were in danger. Nicholas II decided that the situation called for a dramatic gesture: in August 1915, against the advice of his ministers, who feared that he would become a target for personal criticism in the event of future defeats, he assumed overall command at the battlefront himself. His intention was to set an example and to restore calm. When the tsar arrived at the military headquarters in Mogilev, his generals were relieved to discover that he had no intention of becoming a hands-on commander: he was content to leave military decision-making to his generals and to play a largely ceremonial role.

Between late 1915 and his abdication in early 1917, Nicholas II spent very little time in Petrograd. His absence whilst at the front gave his wife, Alexandra, and her favourite, Rasputin, an opportunity to exercise greater influence in political affairs.

- Alexandra was by birth a German princess and a grand-daughter of Queen Victoria. As Tsarina (empress), she shunned St Petersburg society, which she believed to be decadent, and lived an isolated life with her family. In Russia, she was widely disliked on account of her aloofness and her German origins. Alexandra was strong-willed but unstable. In politics, she was an ultra-conservative who consistently advised her husband against making concessions to liberals and moderates.
- Rasputin (1872–1916) was a Siberian peasant who, though holding no official position in the Orthodox Church, won a reputation as a *'starets'* (holy man) and a healer. The Tsarina idolised him because she believed he could control her son's haemophilia. To the outside world, however, unaware of the boy's medical condition (which was kept a closely guarded secret) the royal family's close association with Rasputin, which began in 1906, was bewildering and unsettling. Rasputin was a thoroughly unsavoury character. His debauched private life and his links with shady financiers were the subject of unremitting gossip and rumour in wartime Petrograd. In 1916, Rasputin was murdered by a small group of conspirators, among them a nephew of Nicholas II and the husband of one of his nieces. Their aim was to cleanse and purify the monarchy.

Just how much influence Alexandra and Rasputin wielded in 1915–16 is a matter of dispute. Some historians suggest that, in Nicholas II's absence, they were in full control of domestic policy, with Rasputin the dominant partner by virtue of his ability to manipulate Alexandra. There are, however, reasons for doubting whether their joint influence was quite as great as is sometimes alleged.

- Nicholas II's presence at military headquarters was largely symbolic. Operational command of Russia's armed forces was in the hands of others. He continued to involve himself in political affairs, including ministerial appointments.
- Nicholas II naturally listened to his wife's advice, but he did not always take it.
- Nicholas II was not under Rasputin's spell to the extent that his wife was. 'Our Friend's opinions are sometimes very strange', he told his wife on one occasion.
- Some of the opposition politicians who complained most loudly about Rasputin's influence had a vested interest in exaggerating it, because they were intent on overturning the Tsarist regime.

In the end, however, what actually happened in 1915–16 was less important than what people thought was happening. What Russians saw from the outside in this period was a so-called 'ministerial leapfrog', in which jobs in the government changed hands with bewildering frequency. In the course of 1916, there were three different chief ministers (Sturmer, Trepov and Golitsyn), three Interior Ministers, three Foreign Ministers and three Ministers of Justice. People were all too ready to believe that this chaotic state of affairs was the result of Alexandra and her debauched favourite handing out jobs to their cronies. Some believed that Alexandra and Rasputin were guilty of more than mismanagement and corruption: rumours circulated that they were traitors conspiring to bring about a German victory.

The gossip and rumour that swirled around the royal family in 1915–16 did the Tsarist regime immense harm. Even conservative Russians who had stood behind the regime in 1905 now despaired of it.

**SOURCE 11** Rasputin and Tsar Nicholas II and Tsarina Alexandra: two Russian cartoons from the First World War.

ACTIVITY
KNOWLEDGE CHECK

**Rasputin, the tsar and tsarina**

What messages do the two cartoons in Source 11 seek to convey about the nature of the relationship between Rasputin and the tsar and tsarina? How accurate were these messages?

**A Level Exam-Style Question Section B**

To what extent were Tsarina Alexandra and Rasputin responsible for declining confidence in Tsarist rule in Russia in the years 1914–17? (20 marks)

**Tip**

*In your answer, identify and discuss a range of factors for declining confidence in Tsarist rule other than the stated one.*

## The Progressive Bloc and Zemgor

Only one of the political parties opposed to Tsarism was united in its opposition to the war: the Bolsheviks. The Mensheviks were divided on the issue, as were the SRs. The middle-class parties, on the other hand, were supporters of the war. Guchkov's Octobrists and Milyukov's Kadets were deeply patriotic. When war broke out, they rallied behind the government and looked forward to the destruction of Germany's armies. But they wanted to do more than to merely cheer on the war effort from the sidelines. They hoped that the government, in the spirit of wartime unity, would make it possible for them to contribute actively to the push for victory. What they had in mind was a partnership between government and Duma. The hopes of the middle-class parties were quickly dashed. The government showed little interest in enlisting the support of society at large: soon after the start of the war, the Duma was adjourned.

In these circumstances, middle-class Russians turned to voluntary action. In 1914, *zemstva* across Russia formed the Zemstvo Union to undertake war relief work – providing medical care for wounded soldiers, operating field canteens, assisting refugees escaping battle zones and digging war graves. The counterparts of the *zemstva* in the towns, the municipal corporations, formed a separate organisation, the Union of Towns, which undertook similar work. In 1915, the two Unions diversified into the manufacture of war essentials like uniforms, boots, pharmaceuticals and even munitions, joining forces for this purpose in an organisation known as Zemgor. Zemgor's contribution to total wartime production was small – no more than five percent – but the enterprise and initiative it displayed was in sharp contrast to the lacklustre performance in the economic sphere of government departments. In addition, the head of the Zemstvo Union, Prince G.E. Lvov, set an example of dedication and selflessness that few, if any, of the Tsar's wartime ministers could match. In short, the voluntary sector put the official apparatus of the state to shame.

**EXTEND YOUR KNOWLEDGE**

**The War Industries Committee**

This was an important wartime voluntary organisation, founded in July 1915 by a group of Moscow-based businessmen and industrialists in order to mobilise the support of employers and workers behind efforts to overcome the shell shortage.

Members of the War Industries Committee were not, however, motivated solely by the patriotic desire to improve the flow of weaponry to the army at the front. Self-interest was at work too. The Moscow businessmen of the War Industries Committee were angered by the fact that, in the early part of the war, most of the Russian firms that won big government contracts to supply munitions were based in Petrograd: the Muscovites wanted a bigger share of these munitions contracts and of the profits that could be made out of them.

**Prince Lvov (1861-1925)**

A landowner and member of one of Russia's oldest noble families, Prince Lvov was immensely hard-working and public-spirited. He rose to prominence through the *zemstvo* movement and through his involvement in relief work in the famine of the early 1890s and in the 1904-05 Russo-Japanese war.

In politics, he was a moderate liberal who wanted Russia to become a constitutional monarchy rather than a republic. Lvov had links with the Kadets, serving as a Kadet representative in the first and second Dumas in 1906-07, but by temperament he was a public servant rather than a party politician. Widely respected across the political spectrum, Lvov became chief minister in the Provisional Government formed after Nicholas II's abdication in early 1917.

The unity evident in Russia when it went to war in 1914 did not last for long. By mid-1915, it was gone, a casualty of the 'Great Retreat'. Opposition politicians, angered by the mismanagement of the war effort, no longer felt able to refrain from criticising the government. Under mounting pressure, Nicholas II agreed to recall the Duma. When it met, in summer 1915, around 300 of its 430 members – everyone except the extreme left and the extreme right – formed themselves into the 'Progressive Bloc' in order to press for the introduction of measures felt to be essential if the war was to be won. Members of the Progressive Bloc demanded the formation of what they called a 'unified government' – a government, that is, in which the Duma as well as the tsar had confidence. Note the limited nature of this demand: the Progressive Bloc called for partnership between government and Duma, not for the tsar to surrender to the Duma his power to appoint and dismiss ministers. Nicholas II nevertheless interpreted what was proposed as a challenge to his authority: he rejected the Progressive Bloc's demands and dismissed those of his ministers who had urged acceptance of them. After this, the Kadets in particular abandoned any thought of compromise with the Tsarist regime and turned instead to a confrontational approach. By late 1916, leading figures in the Progressive Bloc were plotting to force Nicholas II to abdicate.

EXTEND YOUR KNOWLEDGE

**The programme of the Progressive Bloc**

The Progressive Bloc did not only want 'unified government'. It also laid down a number of conditions that would have to be met before its members would enter such a government. The programme of the Progressive Bloc included demands for an amnesty for political detainees; self-government within the Russian Empire for Poland; the abolition of restrictions on Russia's Jews; greater respect for workers' and trade union rights; and changes in local government, in particular additional powers for the *zemstva* and the establishment of *zemstva* in those parts of the Empire that did not have them (Poland, Estonia, Latvia and Lithuania).

The Progressive Bloc called for a change of government in 1915 because it wanted the war effort to be managed more effectively. But this was not its only motive. Members of the Progressive Bloc feared that, in the absence of a government that enjoyed public confidence, the revolutionary parties would grow in strength. There was, warned Milyukov, the danger of a political storm breaking out and taking 'a form we do not desire'.

ACTIVITY
KNOWLEDGE CHECK

**The Tsarist regime's plummeting reputation, 1915–16**

Assess the importance of the contribution of each of the following to the Tsarist regime's plummeting reputation in 1915–16:

a) the performance of the Russian army

b) problems in the supply of munitions to the armed forces

c) the activities of Tsarina Alexandra and Rasputin

d) inflation.

# WHAT TRIGGERED THE REVOLUTION OF FEBRUARY 1917?

## Growth of unrest in town and countryside

Prices in wartime Russia did not rise steadily and evenly year by year. The rate of price inflation accelerated as the war went on. Wages failed to keep pace with prices, which meant that the purchasing power of industrial workers' incomes – in other words, how much they were able to buy with their weekly wage – fell sharply. In 1916–17, it fell by nearly a half. Rising food prices were mainly responsible for this state of affairs, but other prices were rising sharply too. In the war years, the rent workers in Petrograd had to pay for their accommodation trebled and, in the harsh winter of 1916–17, fuel for domestic heating was scarce and expensive.

Unsurprisingly, rampant inflation gave rise to labour unrest. Strikes became an increasingly serious problem in the war years. In 1916, three-quarters of a million working days were lost as a result of strike action in Petrograd alone. As well as strikes, Petrograd began to see workers' demonstrations in which calls were made for an end to the war and the removal of the tsar.

SOURCE 12

From a report by a member of staff at the American embassy in Petrograd, 7 March 1917 (dates converted to Julian calendar).

At the beginning of the week of 20 February, a shortage of black bread was noticeable. This at once caused unrest among the labouring classes. All other prime necessities within the means of the working classes had gradually disappeared as the winter advanced: meat, sugar, white flour, potatoes. Fish, poultry, eggs, cheese and butter had for a long time been so expensive that they were only within the means of the very well-to-do classes. The unrest first took visible form in the outskirts and factory districts of the city on 23 February, where the workmen struck after the dinner hours and met in groups to discuss the situation.

In the later stages of the war, unrest grew in the countryside as well as in the towns. Rural unrest had its own distinctive causes. Inflation played a part, but other reasons were arguably more important.

- Lacking a highly developed sense of Russian identity, the peasantry was never strongly pro-war. One senior government official described the mood of the peasantry in 1914 as one of 'muffled, submissive, sullen discontent'.
- The peasantry nevertheless bore most of the human cost of the war. Between 1914 and 1917, nearly 15 million men served in the Russian army. Nearly two million of them were killed and over five million were wounded or taken prisoner. The vast majority of these casualties were peasant conscripts. As the casualty lists lengthened, anti-war feeling grew.
- The loss of able-bodied men to the army meant that much of the farm work had to be done by women, children and the elderly. This extra workload was resented.
- A further source of resentment was the requisitioning by the army of horses and other livestock. The army took the best horses, leaving peasants reliant on inferior or unsuitable animals to plough their fields.
- Soldiers' wives were paid an allowance by the state when their husbands were serving in the army. This allowance was not, however, increased in line with inflation. By 1916, peasant households were finding it difficult to pay for consumer goods like sugar and clothing. This gave rise to disorder. In one case, 50 peasant women, unable to buy fabric at pre-war prices, responded by looting local shops. Incidents of this kind took place all over rural Russia in 1916. Soldiers' wives, the so-called '*soldatki*', were almost invariably prominently involved.

SOURCE 13

From a petition by a group of peasant women near Moscow to the minister of war, May 1916.

We, peasant women of the Russian soil, have given the government our sons, our brothers, our fathers. And now that is not enough for the government. It is going to exterminate us with hunger. No bread, no meat no sugar, no anything. They've begun taking our cattle. How are we supposed to support ourselves and our children? How are we supposed to live? If you do not take measures, we will rise up. Act on our demands now and do not delay. Give us bread. Down with the war. Down with the treacherous, treasonous ministers and the entire government.

## International Women's Day and the Petrograd general strike

In early 1917, Petrograd was seething with discontent. In January, nearly half of the city's workers came out on strike on the anniversary of the events of Bloody Sunday in 1905 (see page 300). A second major strike took place in early February. A week later, Petrograd's biggest factory, the giant Putilov engineering complex, was brought to a standstill by industrial action.

The day after the closure of the Putilov factory was International Women's Day, an event instituted by the international socialist movement. First celebrated in 1911, its purpose was to promote the cause of women's rights. In 1917, socialist activists encouraged Petrograd's workers to mark it by holding anti-government demonstrations.

Petrograd's working class needed little encouragement to take to the streets. This was especially true of women. Large numbers of women were employed in low-paid jobs in the city's factories. Women made up nearly 70 percent of the workforce in Petrograd's textile industry. In the engineering industry, 20 percent of all workers were women. Other women, similarly badly paid, worked in the retail sector and in domestic service. Adding to the woes of Petrograd's lower-class women was the fact that, within their households, it was they who were left to wrestle with the consequences of wartime inflation. Usually it was women, not men, who spent hours queuing for bread or foraging for firewood. On International Women's Day, women textile workers, worn down by their struggles, walked out of their factories shouting for bread and an end to the war. Their action led to five days of disorder, which saw the Tsarist regime lose control of its capital city.

### The February Revolution: events in Petrograd, 23–27 February 1917

| | |
|---|---|
| **23 February** | International Women's Day. Striking women textile workers in the Vyborg district, north of the city centre, were joined by men from nearby engineering factories in protests against food shortages. Attempts to march on the city centre were thwarted by the authorities. |
| **24 February** | The textile workers' strike spread to other industries and developed into a general strike involving more than 200,000 workers. Demonstrators reached the city centre but were beaten back by the police and the military. Observers noted that some soldiers were reluctant to act against the crowds. |
| **25 February** | Demonstrations in the city centre, involving students as well as factory workers. The demonstrations were more overtly political than previously, with marchers carrying banners with slogans like 'Down with the Tsar' and 'Down with the war'. There was further evidence of troops being reluctant to quell disorder, though most continued to obey their officers. |
| **26 February** | The authorities put into operation plans to regain control of the streets. Known agitators were arrested, strong points were set up around the city and large numbers of troops were deployed. Hundreds of demonstrators were killed in clashes with the military. |
| **27 February** | Faced with the likelihood of again being ordered to open fire on unarmed crowds, soldiers at one barracks mutinied. The mutiny quickly spread to other barracks. Army officers fled. By the afternoon, the streets were thronged with mixed crowds of workers, students and soldiers. |

## The creation of the Provisional Committee and the Petrograd Soviet

The February Revolution was a spontaneous affair, not one directed or controlled by political leaders. Its success created a political vacuum. Into this vacuum moved two bodies: the Provisional Committee of the Duma and the Petrograd Soviet.

The Provisional Committee of the Duma came into being on the day the Petrograd garrison mutinied. Dominated by the Kadet leader, Milyukov, its aim was to restore public order and to establish a new government that enjoyed public confidence. But the Provisional Committee's attempt to seize the political initiative soon ran into difficulties. One of its problems was that the Duma was not a democratically elected body: its right to take charge was therefore open to question. Another was that the Petrograd garrison was unwilling to recognise its authority. When the Provisional Committee ordered soldiers to leave the streets and return to their barracks, it was not obeyed.

The Petrograd Soviet was founded by a group of socialist intellectuals, many of them Mensheviks. Essentially it was a re-creation of the 1905 St Petersburg Soviet. There was, however, one important difference. The St Petersburg Soviet had been purely a workers' body, but members of the Petrograd Soviet were elected by soldiers as well as workers: its formal name, adopted in March 1917, was the Petrograd Soviet of Workers' and Soldiers' Deputies.

The Petrograd Soviet quickly won the allegiance of the city's workers and its garrison, but its leaders had no intention of forming a government themselves. They were content to leave the running of the country to others. There were several reasons for their self-denial.

- The Mensheviks, highly influential within the Soviet, were orthodox Marxists. They believed that early 20th-century Russia was making the transition from feudalism to capitalism: the transition from capitalism to communism via a proletarian revolution seemed to be a long way off. Their instinct was therefore to watch and wait, and not to make a futile bid for power.
- Conscious of their lack of administrative experience, Mensheviks and Socialist Revolutionaries believed themselves to be unqualified to govern.
- There were fears that the response of Russia's army commanders to the formation of a socialist-led government would be to try to seize power themselves, plunging the country into civil war.

In the immediate aftermath of the February Revolution, the Duma Committee and the Petrograd Soviet negotiated an agreement on how to proceed. The Petrograd Soviet consented to the formation of a liberal-dominated Provisional Government that would hold office while preparations were made to draw up a new democratic constitution for Russia. In return, the Duma liberals accepted that the Petrograd Soviet would act as a watchdog, monitoring events and ensuring that the Provisional Government did not betray the principles of the revolution.

## The abdication of Nicholas II

The start of the February Revolution found Nicholas II at military headquarters in Mogilev, 500 miles south of Petrograd. At this stage, he was assured by officials in the capital that there was no cause for alarm. He also received a more sobering assessment from Rodzianko, the Duma President, but took no notice of it.

SOURCE

14

A telegram from Duma President Rodzianko to Nicholas II, 26 February 1917.

> Most humbly I report to Your Majesty that the popular disturbances which have begun in Petrograd are assuming a serious character and threatening proportions. The causes are a shortage of baked bread and an insufficient supply of flour, which are giving rise to panic, but most of all a complete lack of confidence in the leadership, which is incapable of leading the nation out of this difficult situation.
>
> The war cannot be brought to a victorious end in such circumstances, as the ferment has already affected the army and threatens to spread, unless the authorities put a decisive end to the anarchy and disorder. Your Majesty, summon without delay a person whom the whole country trusts, and charge him with forming a government in which the whole population can have confidence. There is no other way out and there can be no delay.

Only after the mutiny of the Petrograd garrison did Nicholas II appreciate the seriousness of the situation. He ordered his generals to send loyal troops to Petrograd to regain control and set off for the capital himself by train. At Pskov, 150 miles outside Petrograd, he learned that the army high command had overridden his instructions and favoured his abdication. He then agreed to abdicate in favour of his brother, Grand Prince Michael. The next day, Grand Prince Michael, after conversations with Duma leaders, refused to take the throne. Monarchical rule in Russia came to an end.

Nicholas II was forced to abdicate because, by early 1917, he had lost the confidence of all sections of Russian society. Before 1914, there was no shortage of hostility towards the Tsarist regime among the educated middle class, the working classes and peasantry. In the war years, however, hostility reached new levels of intensity.

- By late 1916, military defeat and the mismanagement of the war effort had reduced the educated middle classes to despair. The Progressive Bloc's leaders were openly contemptuous of the regime, and some prominent moderates – including Guchkov, the Octobrist leader, and Prince Lvov, head of the Zemstvo Union – engaged in private discussions about the possibility of overthrowing the tsar.
- Working-class living conditions, appalling before 1914, worsened sharply during the war years. The regime might have taken steps to alleviate working-class distress, but did not. A food rationing scheme of sorts was introduced late in the war, but it was poorly organised and had little impact.
- Peasants were impoverished and land-hungry in 1905 but, in 1917, they were often bereaved as well. Peasant discontent became more overtly hostile to the regime as the war went on.

An important difference between 1905 and 1917 was the outlook of elite institutions, such as the army and the bureaucracy. In 1905, these institutions remained loyal to the Tsarist regime but, in 1917, they did not. Had he retained the backing of the army high command, Nicholas II might conceivably have survived the popular uprising in Petrograd. But, Nicholas's personal survival was not the foremost concern of Russia's military commanders in early 1917. Their priorities were winning the war and preventing the disintegration of the home front into chaos and anarchy. They decided these priorities were better served by a government of Duma politicians than by the tsar.

**SOURCE 15**

A telegram from General Alexeev, a senior member of the Russian army's high command, to Nicholas II, 1 March 1917.

> The danger that is growing by the minute of anarchy spreading all over the country, and the impossibility of continuing the war in the present circumstances, urgently demand the publication of an imperial act which could still settle the situation. This is possible only by summoning a ministry responsible to the representatives of the people.
>
> The news which reaches us gives us reason to hope that the Duma politicians can still prevent general disintegration, and that it is possible to work with them. But the loss of every hour reduces the last chances to preserve and restore order and fosters the seizure of power by extreme Left elements.

**ACTIVITY**
**KNOWLEDGE CHECK**

**Peasant and working-class discontent**

In what ways did the reasons for peasant and working-class discontent in Russia in 1916–17 differ?

**Evidence (5b)**

**Reading between the lines**

Answer the following questions on your own.

Read Sources 14 and 15.

1. Are the claims made by Rodzianko in Source 14 about the seriousness of the situation in Petrograd simple statements of fact, or did he have some ulterior motive for using words like 'panic', 'anarchy' and 'ferment'?
2. Why does General Alexeev in Source 15 make reference to the possibility of the seizure of power by 'extreme Left elements'?
3. What can be inferred from Sources 14 and 15 about the political priorities of Rodzianko and Alexeev in February 1917?
4. How does contextual knowledge help us to understand the language and arguments used by Rodzianko and Alexeev in Sources 14 and 15?

## THINKING HISTORICALLY Causation (5b)

### Causation relativity

Historical events usually have many causes. Some are crucial, while some are less important. For some historical questions, it is important to understand exactly what role certain factors played in causing historical change.

**Significant factors in the timing and nature of the February Revolution.**

| | |
|---|---|
| Food shortages and rampant inflation left workers in Russia's big cities unable to provide for their families. | Nicholas II, away at army headquarters far from the capital, did not fully understand the seriousness of the situation developing in Petrograd. |
| Russia's army chiefs reached the conclusion that a change of government was essential if Russia was to win the war. | The majority of Duma members wanted to oust Nicholas II. |
| Soldiers of the Petrograd garrison refused to obey orders to put down protests against food shortages. | The war brought misery and hardship to peasant households across Russia. |

Answer the following questions on your own.

**The timing of the February Revolution**

1 How important were food shortages in the towns in explaining the timing of the crisis that led to Nicholas II's downfall?

2 'Without the mutiny of the Petrograd garrison, there would have been no February Revolution.' How far do you agree with this claim? Give reasons for your answer.

3 Could it have made a difference to the outcome if Nicholas II had been in Petrograd in February 1917 rather than away at military headquarters?

**The nature of the February Revolution**

4 'Disillusionment with Nicholas II among army chiefs and Duma members played little part in shaping the events of February 1917.' How far do you agree with this claim? Give reasons for your answer.

5 To what extent were events in Petrograd in February 1917 shaped by peasant discontent?

## ACTIVITY SUMMARY

### Key events, personalities and groups, 1906–17

1 In table form, construct a set of notes on the four Dumas, including details, for each of the four:

a) dates between which it sat
b) its composition in terms of political parties
c) reasons why it came into conflict with the Tsarist regime
d) the circumstances in which it came to an end.

Try to add to the information in the text through your own independent reading and study.

2 Write a set of notes profiling the political career of P.A. Stolypin, in three sections:

a) biographical details (background, posts held, circumstances of his death)
b) key features of his main policies (sub-sections on pacification of the countryside, treatment of the Duma and land policy)
c) reasons why each of his major policies aroused opposition and controversy.

3 Try to summarise, in no more than two sentences apiece, the contribution made to the downfall of the Tsarist regime in 1914–17 by each of the following individuals or groups:

- Tsarina Alexandra
- Rasputin
- Zemgor
- the leaders of the Progressive Bloc
- peasant women
- Petrograd's women factory workers
- the high command of the Russian army.

## WIDER READING

All of the books listed in the Wider Reading section of Chapter 1 include coverage of the years 1906–17.

Also of value are:

Fitzpatrick, S. *The Russian Revolution*, Oxford University Press, third edition (2008), chapter 1

Pipes, R. *A Concise History of the Russian Revolution*, Vintage Books (1996), chapters 1–4

Jukes, G. *The First World War: The Eastern Front, 1914–1918*, Osprey Publishing (2002). A concise treatment of the fighting in which Russia's armies were involved.

Welch, F. *Rasputin: A Short Life*, Short Books (2014)

# 2b.3 The Provisional Government and its opponents, February–October 1917

**KEY QUESTIONS**

- Is 'dual power' an apt description of the relationship between the Provisional Government and the Petrograd Soviet in early 1917?
- Who opposed the Provisional Government in early and mid-1917, and why?
- In what circumstances did Kerensky become head of the second Provisional Government, and why did he fail to retain popular support?
- What part did Lenin and Trotsky play in the making of the October Revolution?

**KEY TERM**

**Constituent Assembly**
An elected body that has the specific function of drawing up a constitution.

## INTRODUCTION

After the February Revolution, Russia's pre-1917 political right disintegrated. The monarchists who had been prominent in the third and fourth Dumas faded from view and the far-right Union of Russian People was outlawed. As a result, the centre of gravity of Russian politics shifted to the left. The Octobrists and Kadets were now the most conservative of the major political parties. The political middle ground was occupied by the Mensheviks and Socialist Revolutionaries (SRs), with the Bolsheviks to their left.

Although the ultimate objectives of these political parties differed enormously, there was in early 1917 a wide measure of agreement between them on the immediate way forward.

- Preparations would be made to elect a **Constituent Assembly**. Constituent Assembly elections, unlike pre-war Duma elections, were to be fully democratic: there was to be universal suffrage, with all adults being entitled to vote; voting was to take place in secret; voters were to choose their representatives directly rather than indirectly; and all votes were to be of equal value, with no special weight being attached to the votes of the nobility.
- The democratically elected Constituent Assembly would devise a new constitution for Russia.
- A government would come into power under the new constitution that would have a mandate to decide on issues such as land reform.
- Until the Constituent Assembly had completed its work, Russia's affairs would be administered by a Provisional Government.

**1917**

**1917** – 2 March: Abdication of Nicholas II and formation of an all-liberal Provisional Government

**1917** – 4 April: Lenin returns to Russia and issues April Theses

**1917** – 18-21 April: Publication of the 'Milyukov Note'; mass street demonstrations

**1917** – 5 May: Reconstruction of Provisional Government as a liberal-socialist coalition

**1917** – 18 June: Start of the June Offensive

**1917** – 3-5 July: The 'July Days'; Lenin flees to Finland to avoid arrest

**1917** – 8 July: Kerensky replaces Lvov as prime minister

**1917** – 18 July: Kornilov appointed commander-in-chief by Kerensky

## EXTEND YOUR KNOWLEDGE

### Why did it take so long for elections to the Constituent Assembly to be held?

Elections to the Constituent Assembly were eventually held in November, some nine months after they were first promised. There were several reasons for this long delay.

- There were numerous issues relating to election procedures to be decided, including the minimum age of voting. The commission of lawyers the Provisional Government appointed to look into these issues got bogged down in detail.
- Local authorities (the *zemstva*) were given responsibility for administrative matters such as compiling registers of qualified voters. The *zemstva* of February 1917 were not democratically elected bodies: it was argued that they should be reformed themselves before they started work on electoral arrangements.
- Fighting at the battlefront tended to be at its most intense in the summer months: the undesirability of holding an election in the middle of a military crisis was an argument for delay until the autumn.
- The SRs argued on behalf of their peasant supporters that elections were best delayed until the harvest was safely in.

At first, it appeared that the Bolsheviks endorsed this approach. In the weeks after the February Revolution, the most influential Bolshevik in Petrograd was L.B. Kamenev. Kamenev's analysis of the political situation in Russia was virtually identical to that of the Mensheviks. He believed that the country was experiencing a bourgeois revolution, with the proletarian revolution envisaged by Marx still a long way off. Kamenev therefore adopted a policy of support for the Provisional Government. He also argued for collaboration, possibly even a merger, between Bolsheviks and Mensheviks. Then Lenin returned to Russia and everything changed.

On his arrival in Russia, Lenin announced his intention to launch an immediate bid for power. His fellow-Bolsheviks thought he had taken leave of his senses. Lenin's first political task in the spring of 1917 was to win them over. Having done so, he set about raising the Bolsheviks' profile and building a platform from which he could bring his plans to fruition. Within months, he was basking in the triumph of the October Revolution, though it only came about after a false start (the July Days) and owed much to a large slice of luck (the Kornilov affair).

The October Revolution has given rise to all sorts of controversies. One of the most important relates to its fundamental nature. Both at the time and afterwards, the Bolsheviks maintained that theirs was a popular revolution, one supported by the mass of Russian workers and peasants. This claim was derided by their enemies, who insisted that what had taken place was a seizure of power by a small and unrepresentative minority. Kerensky, for example, claimed in early 1918 that the Bolsheviks were guilty of 'pure **usurpation**'. These contrasting interpretations have been echoed in historical writings about the October Revolution. Some historians have maintained that it was a popular uprising, others that it was a *coup d'etat*. It would, however, be a mistake to assume that a choice has to be made between one or other of these viewpoints. They are interpretations that lie at opposite ends of a range of possibilities: the most persuasive view might lie somewhere between them.

### KEY TERM

**Usurpation**
The seizure of power without any lawful authority to do so.

1917

**1917** - 27–31 August: The 'Kornilov affair'

**1917** - 25 September: Trotsky becomes chairman of the Petrograd Soviet

**1917** - 12 October: Formation of the Petrograd Soviet Military Revolutionary Committee

**1917** - 24–26 October: Bolshevik seizure of power in Petrograd

**1917** - 12–15 November: Constituent Assembly elections

# IS 'DUAL POWER' AN APT DESCRIPTION OF THE RELATIONSHIP BETWEEN THE PROVISIONAL GOVERNMENT AND THE PETROGRAD SOVIET IN EARLY 1917?

The downfall of Nicholas II was welcomed in all parts of Russian society. In the weeks after his abdication, Russia was gripped by a mood of euphoria. In political circles, however, fault lines began to open up. The arrangement negotiated in the immediate aftermath of the February Revolution under which the Provisional Government ruled subject to the approval of the Petrograd Soviet – the arrangement described by Lenin as 'dual power' – soon came under strain. This was not surprising: the Provisional Government was predominantly liberal, its ministers drawn from middle or upper classes, while the leaders of the Petrograd Soviet were socialists who represented industrial workers and peasant soldiers. 'Dual power' nevertheless survived in one form or another until the October Revolution.

## The political complexion of the Provisional Government

The Provisional Government that took office in early March 1917 was essentially a Progressive Bloc government. All of its members, with the exception of Alexander Kerensky, were middle-class liberals. Its chief minister was the modest, unassuming and widely respected Prince Lvov, who also took the post of interior minister. Lvov, however, was largely a figurehead. The real driving force in the first Provisional Government was the Kadet leader, Milyukov, who became foreign minister. He was joined in the 12-man ministry by four other Kadets. The remaining places were occupied by three Octobrists, headed by Guchkov, who was appointed war minister, two non-party experts and the government's only socialist member, Justice Minister Kerensky.

Alexander Kerensky was a Petrograd lawyer who made a reputation before 1914 defending left-wing clients in political cases. In 1912, he was elected to the fourth Duma as a Trudovik. After the February Revolution, now loosely aligned to the SRs, he became vice-chairman of the newly formed Petrograd Soviet. Kerensky was charismatic, eloquent and intensely ambitious. In early 1917, he occupied a pivotal position in Russian politics because he was the only minister in the Provisional Government who was also a member of the Petrograd Soviet. Officially, the Petrograd Soviet frowned upon its members participating directly in the work of the Provisional Government, but Kerensky persuaded his colleagues that his was a special case.

## The Provisional Government's power and support

Differences in political outlook were not the only reason why the relationship between the new Provisional Government and the Petrograd Soviet was an uneasy one. A further source of difficulty was the uneven distribution of power between the two bodies.

In March 1917, the Provisional Government was in authority, but it was toothless. It had no means of compelling people to obey its orders. It had no authority over the Petrograd garrison which was firmly under the control of the Petrograd Soviet as a result of its Order Number 1 and it had no disciplined police force to call upon: Tsarist policemen made themselves scarce after the February Revolution, their place being taken by locally organised militias. The apparatus of Tsarist government in the localities also disintegrated: the post of provincial governor was abolished, while the *zemstva*, not elected on a democratic basis and dominated by the upper classes, lost credibility. In these circumstances, the Provisional Government was reliant on the power and influence of the Petrograd Soviet.

EXTEND YOUR KNOWLEDGE

**The Petrograd Soviet's Order Number 1**

The Petrograd garrison aligned itself with the Petrograd Soviet before the Provisional Government was fully set up. On 28 February, the Provisional Committee of the Duma (the forerunner of the Provisional Government), fearing that Petrograd could fall victim to mob rule, ordered the troops on the city's streets to return to their barracks.

The soldiers, distrustful of the middle-class Duma politicians and fearing that they might be disciplined for turning against their officers during the February Revolution, refused to accept the legitimacy of the order and turned to the Petrograd Soviet.

The Soviet responded on 1 March by issuing Order Number 1. This stated that the garrison was subordinate to the Soviet, and declared that the orders of the Provisional Committee were only to be obeyed if they did not conflict with those of the Soviet. As a result, the Provisional Government, when it came into being, had to have the approval of the Petrograd Soviet before it gave any orders to the garrison.

The Petrograd Soviet was in full control of the capital because it was supported by key workers and the city's army garrison.

- The loyalty of railway and postal workers to the Petrograd Soviet ensured that it controlled the city's links with the outside world.
- The backing of the army garrison gave the Petrograd Soviet the capacity to suppress opposition inside the capital, as well as protection against intervention from outside it. The garrison was a sizeable force: it consisted of around 180,000 troops in the city and a further 150,000 stationed in outlying districts. A priority of many of its members was not to be sent from the safety of Petrograd to the battlefront: when faced with this prospect, they were quick to insist that they had a duty to remain in the capital to defend the revolution against its enemies.

Note too that the Petrograd Soviet's reach extended into provincial Russia. During 1917, soviets sprang up all over the country. By October, there were something like 1,500 of them. They came in a variety of forms (workers' soviets, workers' and soldiers' soviets, peasant soviets and sailors' soviets) but all were modelled on the Petrograd Soviet and looked to it for leadership and direction. The Petrograd Soviet retained its primacy despite the formation, in June 1917, of an All-Russian Congress of Workers' and Soldiers' Deputies in which local soviets from different parts of the country were represented.

The term 'dual power' is a misleading description of the relationship between the Provisional Government and the Petrograd Soviet. It implies that power was somehow shared, or equally divided, between the two bodies. This was emphatically not the case.

SOURCE

Telegram from War Minister Guchkov to General Alexeev, commander-in-chief of the Russian army, 9 March 1917.

The Provisional Government has no power of any kind and its orders are carried out only to the extent that this is permitted by the Soviet of Workers' and Soldiers' Deputies, which controls the most essential strands of actual power, insofar as the troops, railways and post and telegraph services are in its hands. One can assert bluntly that the Provisional Government exists only as long as it is permitted to do so by the Soviet of Workers' and Soldiers' Deputies. In particular, in the military department, it is possible at present to issue only such orders as basically do not contradict the decisions of the above-mentioned Soviet.

SOURCE

N.K. Chkheidze, the Menshevik Chairman of the Petrograd Soviet, addressing a delegation of students who came to the Soviet with a banner hailing the Provisional Government, 24 March 1917.

I see on your banner the slogan 'Greetings to the Provisional Government', but for you it can be no secret that many of its members, on the eve of the Revolution, were trembling and lacked faith in the Revolution. You extend greetings to it. You seem to believe that it will carry high the new standard. If this is so, remain in your belief. As for us, we will support it for as long as it realises democratic principles. We know, however, that our government is not democratic, but bourgeois. Follow carefully its activity. We shall support all of its measures which tend towards the common good, but all else we shall unmask because at stake is the future of Russia.

**A Level Exam-Style Question Section A**

***Study Sources 1 and 2 before you answer this question.***

How far could the historian make use of Sources 1 and 2 together to investigate the nature of the relationship between the Provisional Government and the Petrograd Soviet in the period between February and April 1917?

Explain your answer using both sources, the information given about them and your own knowledge of the historical context. (20 marks)

**Tip**

*Try to work out a range of uses and limitations of the source material for the specified investigation – take care to avoid focusing exclusively or excessively on one point (the disparity in power between the Provisional Government and the Petrograd Soviet, for instance).*

## The aims and membership of the Petrograd Soviet

The Petrograd Soviet was elected by the city's factory workers and the soldiers of the Petrograd garrison. There was one representative from each battalion of soldiers (250 men) and one for every 1,000 workers. The garrison was over-represented in the Petrograd Soviet: two-thirds of its 3,000 members were soldiers' representatives, despite the fact that, in 1917, there were fewer soldiers in Petrograd than there were workers.

Elections to the Petrograd Soviet were rough-and-ready affairs. There were few set procedures: much was decided at grassroots level. Representatives did not serve for fixed terms, as is usually the case in parliamentary elections, but could be recalled by their electors and replaced at any time. As a result, the political complexion of the Soviet was constantly fluctuating.

The policies of the Petrograd Soviet were decided, not at meetings of its 3,000 members, but by its Executive Committee. This inner group was made up of seasoned political activists and professional revolutionaries: ordinary workers and soldiers were notable for their absence. In the early months of the Petrograd Soviet's existence, the Executive Committee was dominated by Mensheviks and Socialist Revolutionaries. This is unsurprising: the Mensheviks had built up a following among the capital's trade unionists before 1914 and the peasant conscripts of the army garrison had an affinity with the SRs. The most influential figure on the Executive Committee at this stage was Irakli Tsereteli (1881–1960), a Menshevik and former Duma member who returned to Petrograd from Siberian exile in mid-March 1917.

The socialist intellectuals who led the Petrograd Soviet in its early days saw its role as a temporary and relatively limited one: protecting the interests of workers and soldiers until the deliberations of the Constituent Assembly led to the establishment in Russia of a fully democratic system of government. In practice, this involved monitoring the activities of the Provisional Government and ensuring that it did not abuse its authority. Before long, however, the Petrograd Soviet began to adopt a more wide-ranging role than the one originally envisaged. It assumed command of the Petrograd army garrison; it took over responsibility for administering the capital's affairs, effectively becoming a local government body; and it began to interest itself in foreign policy issues – a development which led to conflict with the Provisional Government.

**SOURCE 3** The Petrograd Soviet in session, 1917.

## Early political reforms

The tensions between the Provisional Government and the Petrograd Soviet did not prevent the introduction of some of the reforms for which opponents of the Tsarist regime had long campaigned. In their negotiations in late February 1917, the Duma politicians and the Petrograd Soviet reached agreement, not only on an interim form of government for Russia, but also on a package of political reforms that were to take effect more or less immediately. In the spring of 1917, the Provisional Government honoured this agreement by introducing a series of measures that together turned Russia into what Lenin called 'the freest country in the world'. The measures in question were:

- an amnesty for all political prisoners, including those detained for terrorist offences
- the abolition of capital punishment
- unrestricted freedom of speech and assembly
- equal rights for all citizens regardless of class, religion or nationality (which, among other things, meant the abolition of the restrictions which prevented Jews from living outside the Pale of Settlement, a designated area on Russia's eastern borders)
- the dissolution of Tsarist police forces and their replacement by local militias with elected officers
- the election of the *zemstva* and town councils on a fully democratic basis.

SOURCE

First public statement made by the Provisional Government, 7 March 1917.

The Government will deem it to be its primary duty to open the way to the expression of the popular will with regard to the form of government and will convene the Constituent Assembly within the shortest time possible on the basis of universal, direct, equal and secret suffrage.

Realising the full gravity of the lack of rights, which oppresses the country and hinders the free creative impulse of the people at a time of grave national upheavals, the Provisional Government deems it necessary to provide the country immediately, even prior to the meeting of the Constituent Assembly, with laws safeguarding civil liberty and equality in order to enable all citizens to apply themselves to creative work for the benefit of the country.

And the Provisional Government considers it its happy duty to bring back from their exile and imprisonment, with full honours, all those who have suffered for the good of the motherland.

In fulfilling these tasks, the Provisional Government is animated by the belief that it will thus execute the will of the people.

ACTIVITY
KNOWLEDGE CHECK

**The Provisional Government and the Petrograd Soviet**

In what ways, and to what extent, did the Provisional Government and the Petrograd Soviet disagree on policy issues in early 1917? Make use of Source 4 in your answer.

## WHO OPPOSED THE PROVISIONAL GOVERNMENT IN EARLY AND MID-1917, AND WHY?

In the early months of 1917, the Mensheviks and Socialist Revolutionaries who dominated the Petrograd Soviet became increasingly critical of the middle-class liberals of the Provisional Government. The dispute between the two bodies centred on the issue of Russia's participation in the war. Matters came to a head in April 1917 when the Provisional Government's foreign minister, Milyukov, gave an assurance to Russia's allies that it would continue to fight until Germany had been defeated. This led to a political crisis which ended with Milyukov's departure from the Provisional Government. The departure of Milyukov, who was quickly followed out of the Provisional Government by War Minister Alexander Guchkov, marked the end of the phase of the Russian Revolution in which the leaders of middle-class liberalism were key players. The Provisional Government was reconstructed in April 1917 with the Mensheviks and SRs coming to the fore.

The reconstruction of the Provisional Government did not restore calm to Russian politics. Lenin returned to Russia on 3 April, just before the Milyukov crisis broke. On arrival, he signalled his opposition to the policies of the Menshevik and Socialist Revolutionary leaders of the Petrograd Soviet. In this way, the reconstructed Provisional Government found itself under immediate attack from the political left.

## Conflicting attitudes to the war

In the negotiations (28 February–2 March 1917) between the Duma liberals and the socialists of the Petrograd Soviet that led to the formation of the Provisional Government, the thorny question of Russia's participation in the war was avoided. The war was left off the agenda because it was a divisive issue: the liberals were intent on fighting until outright victory had been achieved, but the leaders of the Petrograd Soviet wanted to end the war quickly by means of a compromise peace negotiated between the Allies and the Central Powers (Germany and Austria). Disagreements over the war could not, however, be wished away: a clash was inevitable and was not long in coming. It took the form of the Milyukov crisis, otherwise known as the April crisis.

In mid-March 1917, the increasingly self-confident Petrograd Soviet published a statement on Russia's war aims. Entitled 'An Appeal to All the Peoples of the World', it set out a policy that became known as 'revolutionary defencism'. The principal architect of 'revolutionary defencism' was Irakli Tsereteli.

'Revolutionary defencism' was the product of a variety of pressures. As a socialist, Tsereteli wanted no part in an imperialist war – a war fought for financial and territorial gain between predatory capitalist countries. He was conscious too of the longing for peace among Russia's workers and peasants. On the other hand, he feared the consequences of military defeat: he suspected that a victorious Germany (a state both autocratic and capitalist) would impose a conservative and backward-looking political regime on Russia.

The policy arising out of these considerations, 'revolutionary defencism', involved three pledges.

- Russia would not make a separate peace agreement with Germany, but would try to bring about a general peace settlement involving all warring nations.
- Russia would not seek to make territorial gains at the expense of other countries.
- Until a peace settlement was reached, Russia would continue to defend its territory, and its revolution, against invading armies.

Having published its statement, the Petrograd Soviet launched a campaign to get the Provisional Government to endorse it. This campaign put it on collision course with Foreign Minister Milyukov. Milyukov's views on the war were uncomplicated: as a patriot, he wanted Russia to fight on until Germany had been defeated. He also had his eyes on a prize that could only be secured through an outright Allied victory: as a result of an agreement with its allies, Russia had been promised control of the seaway between the Black Sea and the Mediterranean after the war. This was precisely the kind of territorial gain the Petrograd Soviet repudiated.

## The Milyukov crisis

Milyukov made no secret of his opposition to 'revolutionary defencism'. But a majority of his government colleagues, including Prince Lvov, favoured a compromise with the Petrograd Soviet. The result was the Provisional Government's carefully worded Declaration of War Aims, published in late March 1917, which affirmed Russia's commitment to the war, while insisting that it would not forcibly seize territory belonging to other countries. The Petrograd Soviet accepted this formula, but did not let the matter rest there. Determined to hold the Provisional Government to its promises, it now pressed for the Declaration of War Aims to be sent to Russia's allies as a formal diplomatic note. The Provisional Government yielded to this demand, and the Declaration was duly dispatched. Milyukov, however, chose to add to it a private telegram in which he distanced himself from 'revolutionary defencism' and insisted that Russia would fight on until a 'conclusive victory' had been won. A few days later, this telegram was leaked to the press. The result was uproar. Supporters of the Petrograd Soviet took to the streets, accusing Milyukov of betrayal and demanding his resignation. There were clashes with pro-Milyukov demonstrators in which people were killed.

SOURCE 5 Paul Milyukov as Russia's foreign minister, early 1917.

ACTIVITY
KNOWLEDGE CHECK

**Milyukov**

Source 5 is an official government photograph. What impression of Milyukov does it seek to convey?

SOURCE 6 From *Izvestia*, the official newspaper of the Petrograd Soviet, 22 April 1917.

On 21 April innumerable demonstrations took place on the streets of Petrograd as a result of the conflict between the Soviet of Workers' and Soldiers' Deputies and the Provisional Government.

The inscriptions on the posters and banners testified to the fact that the demonstrators differed in their interpretations of events. There were banners expressing complete confidence in the Soviet of Workers' and Soldiers' Deputies. But there were also banners calling for complete confidence in the Provisional Government. The inscriptions expressing the attitudes of the demonstrators toward war were just as divergent. Here were all kinds of slogans ranging from 'War until final victory' to the cry 'Down with the war!'

The demonstrations varied not only in their slogans, but also in their class composition. There was a sharp contrast between the workers' demonstrations and the demonstrations of the well-to-do classes.

The Soviet took no initiative in staging the street demonstrations of its supporters. But the indignation was too great in the workers' quarters. Indignation against the phantom of a revived Tsarist policy of conquest brought the workers out on to the streets. Under conditions of highly aroused passions, the danger arose of a clash between different parties and different classes.

Some of the demonstrators were armed. As a result, the day of 21 April was darkened by regrettable and disgraceful events.

**AS Level Exam-Style Question Section A (b)**

***Study Source 11 before you answer this question.***

How much weight do you give to the evidence of Source 6 for an enquiry into the causes of the street clashes that took place during the Milyukov crisis (April 1917)?

Explain your answer using the source, the information given about it and your own knowledge of the historical context. (12 marks)

**Tip**

*If you want to argue that a source gives a one-sided or unbalanced account, you must explain what is one-sided about it by referring to one or both of:*

*(a) its content – is anything over-emphasised or omitted?*

*(b) its wording – are any of the words or phrases used 'loaded' in the sense they reveal a commitment to a particular political outlook?*

The clashes on 21 April convinced Prince Lvov that, in the interests of stability, the running battle between Provisional Government and the Petrograd Soviet had to be brought to an end. He appealed to the Soviet leadership to take office in a reconstructed Provisional Government and threatened to resign himself if they refused. Fearing anarchy, the Soviet leaders answered the call: Tsereteli came into the government as minister of posts and telegraph and Victor Chernov, the SR leader, took over as minister for agriculture. The main casualty of these manoeuvres was Milyukov, who was unacceptable to the incoming socialists: he was forced to resign. Guchkov also left the government, resigning in protest against Milyukov's treatment. His place as war minister was taken by Kerensky.

The Milyukov (or April) crisis was significant for a number of reasons.

- It demonstrated the extent of Soviet power and the weakness of the Provisional Government.
- It brought 'dual power' in its original form to an end.
- It consigned Russia's liberals to what Trotsky called 'the dustbin of history', even though 4 of the new Provisional Government's 16 ministers were Kadets.
- It ended the buoyant, optimistic mood that had been evident in Petrograd in the weeks after the February Revolution.

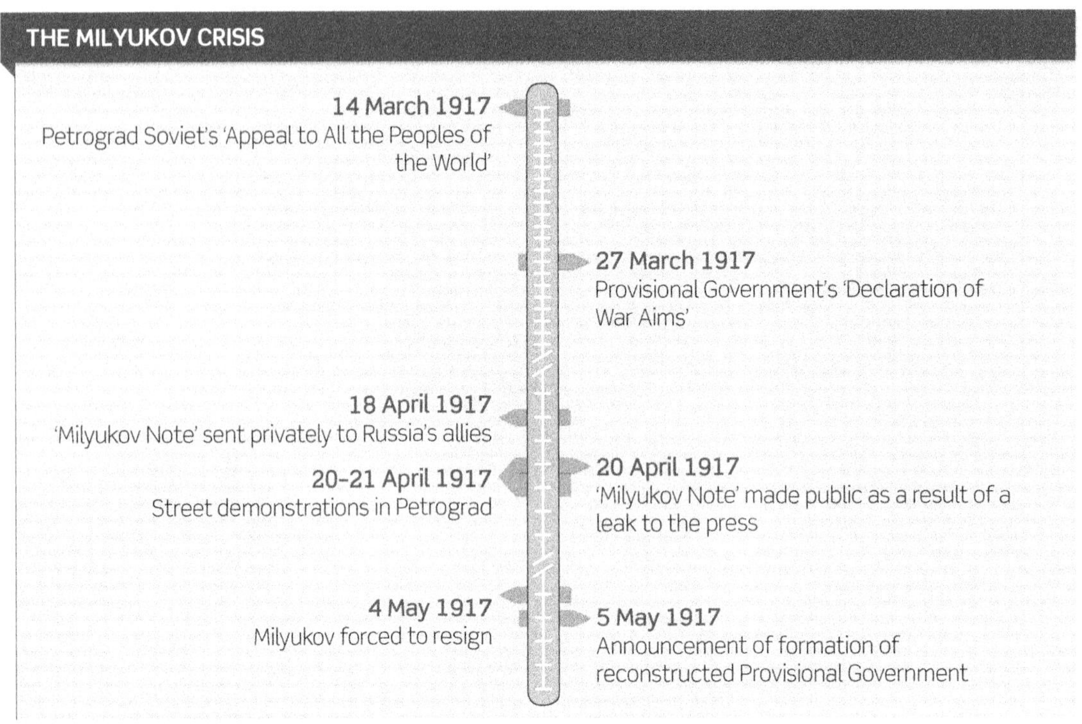


## Lenin's return to Russia and the April Theses

The February Revolution found Lenin in exile in neutral Switzerland. The only way back to Russia was through Germany. Although Lenin was a citizen of an enemy country, the German government had every reason to help him on his way: it hoped that, once back in his homeland, he would become a destabilising influence in Russian politics and thereby undermine the Russian war effort. In late March 1917, Lenin set off for Russia, travelling across Germany in a sealed train laid on by the German authorities. He then made his way through Sweden and Finland to Petrograd, arriving at Petrograd's Finland Station in early April. The circumstances surrounding Lenin's return to Russia gave rise to persistent accusations by his political enemies that he was a German spy.

**KEY TERM**

**Strategy and tactics**
A strategy is a plan of action designed to achieve a long-term objective: tactics are the methods used to implement a strategy.

Lenin spent the period between the February Revolution and his arrival at the Finland Station in April working furiously on the **strategy** and **tactics** he intended to employ on his return to Russia. The results of his thinking were published in his *Letters from Afar* (March 1917). In these observations, Lenin argued that the February Revolution, a bourgeois revolution in Marxist terms, should be swiftly followed by a second revolution in which Russia's workers, in alliance with the peasantry, would seize power. This proposal was greeted with astonishment by other leading Bolsheviks because it appeared to involve a radical departure from Marxist doctrine. Marxist theory suggested that a proletarian revolution could only take place after a long period of deteriorating working-class living standards (immiseration, in Marxist language) under capitalism – yet here was Lenin suggesting that the transition from capitalism to communism could be telescoped into a matter of months. 'Lenin takes it for granted that the bourgeois democratic Revolution is at an end and believes that an immediate transformation of our Revolution into a Socialist one is possible: we profoundly disagree with him', wrote Kamenev, one of Lenin's most senior Bolshevik colleagues, in early April 1917. Lenin was unrepentant about his flexibility in matters of doctrine. 'If you can't adjust yourself', he said, 'then you're not a revolutionary but a chatterbox.'

Lenin's first task on his return to Russia was to win his party over to his views. After a brief period of in-fighting within the Bolshevik ranks, he succeeded. His success was largely based on his force of personality, but it also owed something to the support he received from new entrants into the Bolshevik party. In February 1917, the Bolsheviks had around 25,000 members in Russia. By April, this figure had risen to 75,000. Many of the Bolsheviks' new recruits were working-class in origin and radical in outlook. Caring little for the niceties of Marxist theory, they preferred Lenin's daring to the caution of some of his lieutenants.

SOURCE

From Nikolai Sukhanov, *The Russian Revolution, 1917: A Personal Record*, published in 1955. Sukhanov sat on the Executive Committee of the Petrograd Soviet as a Menshevik and took a close interest in Lenin's activities.

Lenin's radicalism, his heedless 'Leftism' and primitive rabble-rousing, unrestrained by common sense, later secured his success among the broad proletarian-peasant masses. But the same characteristics also seduced [in April 1917] the more backward, less literate elements of the Bolshevik Party itself. Very soon after Lenin's arrival they were faced with an alternative: either keep the old principles of Marxism, but without Lenin; or stay with Lenin and conquer the masses in the easy way, having thrown overboard Marxist principles. It's understandable that the mass of party Bolsheviks decided on the latter.

Lenin's next task was to secure a wider following for his party. He recognised that, as things stood in the spring of 1917, the Bolsheviks were far too weak to mount a serious challenge for power. His tactic for drumming up new support was to announce a series of policies designed to appeal to left-wing opinion in Petrograd. These policies became known as the April Theses. Front and centre were radical Bolshevik alternatives to the Provisional Government's policies on the key issues of peace, land reform and the future government of Russia.

### Peace

The desire for peace was one of the strongest currents flowing through Russia in 1917. Anti-war feeling was especially strong in Petrograd. Immediately after the February Revolution, it seemed possible that the Petrograd Soviet's 'Appeal to the All the Peoples of the World' might spur the governments of Europe's warring powers into starting peace negotiations. By the spring of 1917, however, it had become clear that no-one outside Russia was in any hurry to negotiate. As a result, peace seemed as far away as ever, leaving the Provisional Government's 'revolutionary defencist' strategy increasingly open to criticism. In the April Theses, Lenin dismissed 'revolutionary defencism' in scathing terms and gave the impression that under Bolshevik rule there would be immediate peace.

### Land reform

The Provisional Government was fully aware of the need for land reform. It was aware, too, of the danger of peasants taking matters into their own hands and seizing the land of the nobility. It refused, however, to sanction peasant land seizures, adopting this position for three main reasons.

- It insisted that land reform was a matter for a future democratically elected parliament, not the caretaker Provisional Government.
- It argued that a disorderly peasant land grab was likely to lead to an unfair distribution of land between peasant households.
- It believed that land seizures encouraged desertions from the army, with peasant conscripts leaving their units in order to get home and claim their share of whatever was going.

In contrast to the Provisional Government, Lenin encouraged peasant land seizures. His slogan was 'All land to the peasantry'. This slogan gave the impression that the Bolsheviks were content to allow seized landowners' estates to become the peasantry's private property despite the fact that, as socialists, they were opposed to private landownership. Here was another example of Lenin's willingness to bend his principles when it suited his immediate purpose – which in this case was to sway opinion among Petrograd's workers and soldiers, both groups having a close interest in land reform because of their continuing links with their home villages.

### 'All power to the Soviets'

The Provisional Government wanted a parliament elected by all Russians to be at the heart of the country's political system. Lenin argued that the key institution in Russia's post-revolution political arrangements should be soviets elected by workers and soldiers, not a democratically elected parliament. His slogan was 'All power to the Soviets'. To some in Petrograd, and beyond, this was an attractive prospect.

- Among the workers of revolutionary Petrograd, there were those who hated the middle and upper classes and who were ready to deny them political rights.

- Lenin's plans offered a lifeline to members of soviets, who faced an uncertain future after the Constituent Assembly had done its work and left the soviets with no obvious role in Russia's political system.

Lenin's hostility towards what he called bourgeois democracy was not simply a matter of principle: he knew that the Bolsheviks stood little chance of winning a majority in nationwide free elections.

The April Theses were not an instant success. The citizens of Petrograd did not flock behind the Bolsheviks overnight. But, there were some indications of movement in the Bolsheviks' direction. 'Lenin's influence seems to have been increasing greatly in the last few days', noted the French ambassador to Russia in late April, 'he has gathered around him all the hot-heads of the revolution.'

## The June Offensive and the July Days

### The June Offensive

On 18 June 1917, following a two-day artillery bombardment, Russia's armies attacked their German and Austrian counterparts along a 120-mile front in the southern part of the battle zone.

On the face of it, the decision to launch a major offensive in mid-1917 was bizarre: Russia was war-weary and morale in the army was low. In addition, Russia's armies had been weakened by desertion: 100,000 soldiers deserted in the period between February and June 1917. The troops sent into battle in June were told by their commanders that the offensive was needed to forestall a planned German-Austrian attack on Russia. This was not, however, the whole story. The reasons behind the June Offensive (sometimes called the Kerensky Offensive) were complex and varied.

- In November 1916, Britain, France and Russia had agreed to launch a co-ordinated attack on the Central Powers in mid-1917. Members of the Provisional Government, especially the remaining Kadets, were reluctant to break this agreement.
- The Provisional Government's revolutionary defencists saw an offensive as a way of getting their plans for Europe-wide peace negotiations back on track. A major victory, they reasoned, would give the Provisional Government leverage: Britain and France would be unable to ignore the wishes of a victorious Russia, while a Germany forced on to the defensive would be ready to enter peace talks.
- Kerensky, now war minister, had visions of leading Russia to victory and covering himself with glory. Before the offensive was launched he rushed around the battlefront trying to whip up enthusiasm for it.
- Russia's army chiefs were dismayed by the way in which discipline in the army had broken down since the February Revolution. Soldiers' committees had been established with the blessing of the Provisional Government that challenged the authority of officers. The generals saw a successful offensive as a means of restoring the army's discipline and morale.

In the event, the June Offensive was a disaster. Initial Russian gains were followed by a German counter-attack. Russia's armies broke and ran, looting as they went. Within a week, German forces had advanced 150 miles deeper into Russian territory.

The failure of the June Offensive was a pivotal moment in the history of the revolution. It left the plans and hopes of the revolutionary defencists in tatters; it undermined the credibility of the entire Provisional Government; and it increased the attractions of the Bolshevik alternative – an immediate peace and a transfer of power to the soviets.

### The July Days

The First Machine Gun Regiment was one of the largest units in the Petrograd garrison, with 10,000 men and 1,000 machine guns. It was stationed in Petrograd's Vyborg factory district. On 20 June 1917, it received orders to send 500 of its guns, along with their operators, to the battlefront to support the June Offensive. The soldiers refused, claiming that they had the right to remain in the capital to defend the revolution. They appealed to other units of the Petrograd garrison and to Vyborg's radical factory workers for support.

At this point, mid-level Bolshevik activists in Petrograd – but not the party's top leaders – became involved. These activists were intent on exploiting the Machine Gun Regiment's mutiny for their own purposes. Acting on their own initiative, without the approval of Lenin or other high-ranking Bolsheviks, they set out to persuade the soldiers and their civilian supporters that the moment had come to overthrow the Provisional Government by force.

On 3 July, soldiers and workers took to the streets calling for power to be transferred to the soviets. They returned the next day, this time reinforced by the arrival of 20,000 sailors from Kronstadt, the island naval base 20 miles outside Petrograd. The Kronstadt sailors were disciplined, militant and fearsome. Treated badly by their superiors before 1917, they took their revenge during the February Revolution, murdering their base commander and establishing the Kronstadt Soviet to govern the island.

All the elements for a successful Bolshevik insurrection now appeared to be in place. But, at the crucial moment, Lenin, called upon to address the crowds, hesitated. He did not urge them on: instead he appealed for calm. He seems to have believed that, if the Bolsheviks seized power, they would be unable to hold on to it. Without leadership and direction, the crowds dispersed. As they did so, the Provisional Government hit back at the Bolsheviks. Loyal troops were rushed to the capital by Kerensky, who had been outside Petrograd on government business; documents purporting to prove that Lenin was a German spy were passed to the newspapers; and a series of repressive measures was introduced.

- Warrants were issued for the arrest of Lenin and other leading Bolsheviks: Lenin, heavily disguised, fled to Finland to avoid being taken into custody.
- 800 prominent Bolsheviks were arrested and imprisoned.
- Bolshevik offices were ransacked.
- The Red Guards – armed pro-Bolshevik factory workers – had their weapons taken away from them.
- Army units that had taken part in the July disturbances were disbanded.

The July Days were a calamity for the Bolsheviks. Their organisation was broken and their leaders were either in prison or in hiding. They appeared to have missed out on their opportunity to seize power.

ACTIVITY
KNOWLEDGE CHECK

**Milyukov, Tsereteli and Lenin in early 1917**

1. Write a paragraph explaining the ways in which, in early 1917, the attitudes of Milyukov, Tsereteli and Lenin and their respective followers to the issue of Russia's participation in the war differed. In your paragraph make use of Source 6.
2. Lenin is often depicted as a masterly political operator. To what extent does his record between April and July 1917 support this view? Make use of Source 7 in your answer.

# IN WHAT CIRCUMSTANCES DID KERENSKY BECOME HEAD OF THE SECOND PROVISIONAL GOVERNMENT, AND WHY DID HE FAIL TO RETAIN POPULAR SUPPORT?

In the summer and early autumn of 1917, the flamboyant Kerensky was the dominant figure in Russian politics. He owed his rise to power to the widespread belief that he was a political strong man who could unite the nation and ensure that the revolution was not derailed either by the Bolsheviks on the left or by counter-revolutionaries on the right. In the event, Kerensky failed to live up to the hype that surrounded him. As chief minister, he was neither decisive nor ruthless. His reputation was damaged by stories about his vanity and his extravagant lifestyle. There were failures of policy too: he failed to control inflation or develop a land policy that was acceptable to the peasantry. In the end, though he was an adept political tactician, he was comprehensively out-manoeuvred by Lenin.

## Kerensky as prime minister

In the late summer of 1917, Germany's armies were only 300 miles from Petrograd. All that stood in their way was a Russian army that appeared to have lost the will to fight.

SOURCE

A report from the Army Committee of the South-West Front, a largely socialist body representing the views of soldiers and junior officers, to the Provisional Government, 22 July 1917.

Most units are in a state of increasing disintegration. Persuasion and argument have lost their power. They provoke only threats and even shooting. Some units desert their positions without even waiting for the approach of the enemy. There have been cases when orders for immediate advance to assist hard-pressed units were discussed for hours at meetings. Positions are not infrequently being deserted at the very first shot of the enemy. Long columns of deserters, with and without rifles, are moving along without any consciousness of possible punishment. At times whole units desert in this manner.

**AS Level Exam-Style Question Section A (a)**

***Study Source 8 before you answer this question.***

Why is Source 8 valuable to the historian for an enquiry into the condition of the Russian army in mid-1917?

Explain your answer using the source, the information given about it and your own knowledge of the historical context. (8 marks)

**Tip**

*Try to identify three or four distinct reasons why the source has value, and devote a short paragraph to each one. Consider what different things are being said about the conduct of Russian soldiers and the nature of the body that is describing their conduct.*

SOURCE 9
Alexander Kerensky meeting troops at the battle front, June 1917.

In these desperate circumstances, calls were soon heard for a change at the top. The mild-mannered Prince Lvov recognised that he was unable to provide the kind of inspirational, single-minded and ruthless leadership the situation appeared to demand. He was in any case exhausted, worn down by the effort of trying to make 'dual power' work. On 7 July, he resigned as prime minister.

Kerensky was the obvious successor. In the run-up to the June Offensive, his popularity had reached extraordinary levels. He was, a British diplomat noted, 'the man who all Russia feels can save the country from ruin'. Nor, despite the fact he had championed it so vocally, did his reputation plummet when the June Offensive failed. One reason why he survived largely unscathed was his role in preventing a Bolshevik takeover in July. Another was the adroit way in which he off-loaded blame for the June Offensive's failure onto the Bolsheviks, claiming that it could have succeeded but for the activities of so-called traitors and German spies behind the front lines.

## The membership of the new government

Even though the military situation was dire, Kerensky did not find it easy to put a government together. He wanted his ministry to be a liberal-socialist coalition, just as its predecessor had been, so as to give it the appearance of a government of national unity. The problem he faced was that the combination of political forces that had come together after the February Revolution was starting to fall apart.

- In the summer of 1917, the Kadets were moving to the right. Their hopes of a complete and decisive victory for Russia had been shattered. The condition of the army, and of the country at large, left them in despair. They were increasingly exasperated by the soviets and the socialists who dominated them. What they wanted was a government willing to restore discipline in the army and order in the country: what they were uncertain about was whether Kerensky would be willing to take drastic action against his fellow socialists.
- In the SR ranks, a split was opening up between the moderates who supported 'revolutionary defencism' and 'dual power' and a left-wing that was increasingly sympathetic to Leninist ideas of immediate peace and soviet power. Leading figures among the Left SRs, as they became known, included M.A. Natanson and Maria Spiridonova. Estimates suggest that, by the summer of 1917, up to 40 percent of party members were Left SRs. Victor Chernov, the leader of the SRs and agriculture minister in the Provisional Government, did not have the confidence of the whole party.
- The Mensheviks also split. In opposition to Tsereteli there arose an anti-war faction who became known as the Menshevik Internationalists. The leader of this faction was Martov, one of the last exiled political leaders to make his way back to Russia. On his return, he was fiercely critical of the policies the party had adopted in his absence. He condemned 'revolutionary defencism', arguing instead for a separate peace with Germany if all other attempts at negotiation failed. Martov won the support of around one-third of Menshevik activists.

Inter-party talks about the composition of the new government opened in early July. They soon broke down, the Kadets refusing to serve alongside the SR leader, Chernov, and the SRs threatening to walk out unless Chernov remained a minister. Kerensky ended the squabbling by resigning himself, stating that he would only reconsider his position if he were allowed to choose his own ministers. On this basis, a government was formed, consisting of nine socialists (four SRs, three Mensheviks and two Trudoviks), three Kadets and four others. The socialists included Chernov, but not Tsereteli, who refused office because he feared Kerensky would not pay sufficient attention to the wishes of the Petrograd Soviet.

Kerensky had got the liberal-socialist coalition he wanted, but it looked fragile from the outset and certainly had a narrower base of support than its predecessors. Another problem for the government was that it was short of big hitters: Kerensky apart, all of the political heavyweights from the early days of the revolution, such as Guchkov, Milyukov and Tsereteli, were now on the political sidelines.

**ACTIVITY**
**KNOWLEDGE CHECK**

**Kerensky**

On the basis of his record between March and July of 1917, what conclusions can be reached about Kerensky's strengths and weaknesses as a political leader? Make reference in your answer to Source 9.

## Problems in industry and agriculture

The military situation was very far from being the incoming government's only headache. It was also faced with economic chaos in the cities and large-scale disorder in the countryside.

### Industry

The February Revolution transformed the political environment within which the Russian labour movement operated. Under Tsarism, it had been treated with suspicion and hostility. After the February Revolution, thanks to the power of the soviets, it had nothing to fear from the authorities. Trade union membership increased rapidly in the course of 1917. Another feature of the industrial scene in 1917 was the emergence of factory committees. These were elected bodies of senior workers who spoke on behalf of everyone employed in individual factories.

Workers were quick to take advantage of their changed circumstances. In Petrograd and elsewhere, they first used their new-found strength to get rid of unpopular foremen and managers, often carting them out of factories in wheelbarrows. Next, they turned their attention to the redress of long-standing grievances, demanding big pay rises and the eight-hour day. With no Tsarist army or police force to fall back on, employers felt powerless to resist. In Petrograd, workers' wages doubled or even trebled in early 1917 and an eight-hour day became the norm in Russian industry.

These gains soon proved illusory. The benefits of wage increases, however spectacular, were quickly wiped out by rampant inflation. Prices in Russia's cities soared in 1917 as a result of ongoing shortages in the supply of food. The Provisional Government fared little better than its Tsarist predecessor when it came to sorting out problems with the railway system or preventing hoarding of grain by the peasantry.

## EXTEND YOUR KNOWLEDGE

### The rate of inflation in Petrograd in 1917

The figures below show the movement of prices in Petrograd in the course of 1917. They are a price index with price levels in 1913 being expressed as a base of 1. Prices in January 1917 were over three times higher than they had been in 1913. Prices in October 1917 were four times higher than they had been in January.

| 1913: | 1 |
|---|---|
| January 1917: | 3.5 |
| April 1917: | 4.5 |
| June 1917: | 6.0 |
| August 1917: | 10.5 |
| Sept. 1917: | 11.4 |
| October 1917: | 14.3 |

In mid-1917, workers began to demand a further round of wage increases to compensate for rising prices. This time, they met employers in a more determined mood. Businessmen complained that higher wage costs and falling **productivity** (a consequence of the eight-hour day) had left them facing bankruptcy. Workers responded by calling strikes to force their employers' hands. At this point, a significant number of employers simply gave up and shut their businesses down, thereby adding unemployment to Russia's other economic woes. Some factory committees took over businesses abandoned by their owners and ran them on the basis of workers' control.

## KEY TERM

### Productivity

A measure of how much each employee in a factory, industry or country makes over a period of time. It is calculated by dividing total output by the number of workers in question.

SOURCE

A Menshevik worker in Petrograd's biggest factory, the Putilov armaments works, reporting to the district committee of his party, September 1917.

There is not a shadow of discipline in the working masses. Thefts have become more frequent recently. The numbers of instances of workers being drunk is also increasing. But what is most terrible is the sharp fall in the productivity of labour. Just how low this is is shown, for example, by the fact that formerly 200 gun carriages were being produced each month, but now there are 50 to 60. The Putilov works is hurtling towards the abyss. It is already in a catastrophic state.

Russia's economic problems, which included inflation, strikes, rising unemployment and falling productivity, were a major factor in the rising tensions between social classes that were evident in Russia in the summer of 1917. Some historians have called this development 'social polarisation'. Middle- and upper-class Russians accused industrial workers of unpatriotically refusing to make the sacrifices required by the war effort. Workers retorted that the propertied classes, clinging to their wealth and privileges, were failing to come to terms with the revolution.

'Social polarisation' had political consequences: it undermined the Provisional Government, which preached co-operation between classes, and benefited the Bolsheviks, who advocated class war.

## Agriculture

A basic assumption among Russia's peasants was that the land should belong to those who worked on it. On this basis they had long insisted that all land owned by private landlords, the Orthodox Church and others should be confiscated and handed over to village communities. They greeted the February Revolution with enthusiasm mainly because it cleared away obstacles that had in the past stood in the way of land reform along the lines they favoured.

Peasants did not instantly take the law into their own hands. At first, there was a readiness to wait for the Provisional Government to come forward with a land reform programme. But patience soon wore thin. In the spring of 1917, peasants started to resort to direct action. To begin with, this took forms such as illegally gathering landowners' timber and grazing cattle on landowners' estates without permission but, before too long, whole estates were being seized by force. In a parallel development, peasants who had taken advantage of Stolypin's land reforms to leave the village commune were pressured by their fellow-villagers into rejoining it.

As the peasant rebellion gathered momentum in the course of 1917, the Provisional Government looked on impotently. It had neither the will nor the means to impose order in the countryside. Landowners who appealed to it for support went away disappointed. This failure to uphold the rights of property contributed to growing upper- and middle-class disenchantment with the revolution in late 1917.

## EXTEND YOUR KNOWLEDGE

### Peasant disillusionment with the Provisional Government in 1917

The Provisional Government's reluctance to act on land reform was not the only reason for peasant disillusionment with it. Peasants were also angered by the Provisional Government's policy on food supply. In March 1917, aiming to ensure that urban Russia was fed, the Provisional Government introduced a system under which the state became the only legal buyer of grain, paying sellers (the peasantry) at a fixed price.

Peasants were unimpressed with this arrangement, because the fixed price they were paid did not keep pace with inflation. Rather than sell their grain for what were, in practice, lower and lower prices, they hoarded it.

## ACTIVITY
KNOWLEDGE CHECK

### Disillusionment and despair in Russia in late 1917

1 Write down three reasons why many middle- and upper-class Russians believed in mid-late 1917 that their country was heading towards complete breakdown.

2 How much weight can be attached to Source 10 as a source of information about morale among Petrograd's factory workers in late 1917?

## The Kornilov affair and its impact on the government and the Bolsheviks

### Kerensky and Kornilov

On 18 July 1917, in the middle of negotiations about the make-up of his new government, Kerensky appointed General Lavr Kornilov (1870–1918) commander-in-chief of Russia's armies. Kornilov owed his appointment to his reputation for toughness and to his popularity among the middle and upper classes – a section of the population Kerensky was keen to see represented in his government.

Kornilov was a fighting general from humble origins: his father was a peasant. He was decorated for gallantry in the 1904–05 Russo-Japanese war and served with distinction on the front line against Germany and Austria in 1914–16. In 1917, he had a close-up view of the revolution as commander of the Petrograd military district and was increasingly disgusted with what he saw. After the July Days, he made little attempt to conceal his wish to restore order in Petrograd, if necessary by force. Kornilov was suicidally brave, but his political grasp was limited. One of his fellow-generals said of him that he had 'the heart of a lion, the brain of a sheep'.

When appointed commander-in-chief, Kornilov left Kerensky in no doubt that he had his own political agenda. He indicated he would only take up his post if a series of conditions were met. These conditions were the subject of negotiations between Kerensky and Kornilov, largely conducted through intermediaries, which occupied the next five weeks. In the course of these negotiations, Kornilov added to his original demands. Here is the full list of what he wanted.

- Desertion and acts of treason by soldiers in the rear areas of the battle-zone to be punishable by death (deserters from the front line were already being shot).
- The army commander-in-chief was to be accountable for his actions not to the government but to his conscience and the people.
- No interference by civilian politicians in military affairs.
- Railway workers and workers in defence-related industries to be placed under army control and made subject to military punishments.
- Strikes in all industries to be banned for the duration of the war, with violations of the ban to be punishable by death.

SOURCE

Order to the citizens of Petrograd by the Petrograd Soviet, August 1917.

РАЙОННЫМЪ
Совѣтамъ Рабочихъ Депутатовъ
Фабрично-Заводскимъ Комитетамъ

**ПРИКАЗЪ.**

Корниловскія банды Керенскаго угрожаютъ подступамъ къ столицѣ. Отданы всѣ необходимыя распоряженія для того, чтобы безпощадно раздавить контръ-революціонное покушеніе противъ народа и его завоеваній.

Армія и Красная Гвардія революціи нуждаются въ немедленной поддержкѣ рабочихъ.

Приказываемъ районнымъ Совѣтамъ и фабр.-зав. комитетамъ:

1) выдвинуть наибольшее количество рабочихъ для рытья окоповъ, воздвиганія баррикадъ и укрѣпленія проволочныхъ загражденій;

2) гдѣ для этого потребуется прекращеніе работъ на фабрикахъ и заводахъ, немедленно исполнить;

3) собрать всю имѣющуюся въ запасѣ колючую и простую проволоку, а равно всѣ орудія, необходимыя для рытья окоповъ и возведенія баррикадъ;

4) все имѣющееся оружіе имѣть при себѣ;

5) соблюдать строжайшую дисциплину и быть готовыми поддержать армію революціи всѣми средствами.

Предсѣдатель Петроградскаго Совѣта Раб. и Солд. Депутатовъ
Народный Комиссаръ ЛЕВЪ ТРОЦКІЙ.

Предсѣдатель Военно-Революціоннаго Комитета
Главнокомандующій ПОДВОЙСКІЙ.

TO THE DISTRICT
SOVIETS OF WORKER'S DEPUTIES AND
SHOP-FACTORY COMMITTEES

**ORDER**

THE KORNILOV BANDS OF KERENSKY ARE THREATENING THE OUTSKIRTS OF OUR CAPITAL. ALL NECESSARY ORDERS HAVE BEEN GIVEN TO CRUSH MERCILESSLY EVERY COUNTER-REVOLUTIONARY ATTEMPT AGAINST THE PEOPLE AND ITS CONQUESTS.

THE ARMY AND THE RED GUARD OF THE REVOLUTION ARE IN NEED OF IMMEDIATE SUPPORT OF THE WORKERS.

THE DISTRICT SOVIETS AND SHOP-FACTORY COMMITTEES ARE ORDERED:

1) To bring forward the largest possible number of workers to dig trenches, erect barricades and set up wire defenses;

2) Wherever necessary for this purpose to SUSPEND WORK in shops and factories, it must be done IMMEDIATELY.

3) To collect all available plain and barbed wire, as well as all tools FOR DIGGING TRENCHES AND ERECTING BARRICADES;

4) ALL AVAILABLE ARMS TO BE CARRIED ON PERSONS;

5) Strictest discipline must be preserved and all must be ready to support the Army of the Revolution to the utmost.

President of the Petrograd Soviet of Workers & Soldiers Deputies
People's Commissar LEV TROTSKY.

President ot the Military-Revolutionary Committee
Chief Commander PODVOISKY.

*[Reproduction in English of the Russian text on opposite page.]*

Startling though these demands were, Kerensky did not break off his negotiations with Kornilov. He was reluctant to alienate the army's leaders because he knew that he might have to call on them at some point in the future to suppress disorder in Petrograd. On 26 August, however, it was reported to Kerensky (through an intermediary) that Kornilov had upped the stakes still further, and was now calling for the imposition of martial law in Petrograd and for all civil and military authority to be placed in his hands. Kornilov, it appeared, was intent on making himself a military dictator. On 27 August, Kerensky dismissed him as commander-in-chief.

An outraged Kornilov responded by ordering a detachment of troops under the command of General Krymov to march on Petrograd. Here, it seemed, was a counter-revolution in the making. Kerensky was forced to turn to the Petrograd Soviet for assistance. It duly mobilised in defence of the capital the considerable resources it had at its disposal: the soldiers of the Petrograd garrison, the Kronstadt sailors and the Red Guards, disarmed after the July Days but now issued with weapons on Kerensky's orders. In the event, Krymov's advance on Petrograd petered out without a shot being fired.

- Railwaymen loyal to the Petrograd Soviet held up troop trains heading towards the capital.
- Crucially, representatives of the Petrograd Soviet, many of them Bolsheviks, infiltrated Krymov's advancing forces and succeeded in turning the ordinary soldiers against their officers.

ACTIVITY
KNOWLEDGE CHECK

**Bolshevik propaganda**

Source 11 is on the face of it an order issued by the Petrograd Soviet. What evidence is there in its language and content which suggests that it was in fact a piece of Bolshevik propaganda?

Kornilov was subsequently placed under arrest. He escaped from custody during the October Revolution and was killed in one of the early battles of the civil war. Krymov committed suicide after his advance on Petrograd was halted.

### Impact of the Kornilov affair on the government and the Bolsheviks

The Kornilov affair left Kerensky badly damaged. He found himself under fire from both left and right.

- On the left, Kerensky was widely suspected of having been a willing participant in Kornilov's counter-revolutionary schemes. Another left-wing claim was that Kerensky had, through his apparent willingness to place Petrograd's workers under military control, shown himself to be an enemy, not a friend, of the working class. An indication of left-wing disillusionment with Kerensky after the Kornilov affair was the resignation of Victor Chernov, the SR leader, as minister of agriculture.
- Those clamouring for the restoration of order and discipline in Russia – industrialists, the nobility, senior army officers and the propertied classes generally – accused Kerensky of political cowardice. The right-wing argument was that Kerensky, having done the right thing by appointing Kornilov commander-in-chief in the first place, should have stood by him and implemented his programme.

The big winners in the Kornilov affair were the Bolsheviks. Bolshevik sympathisers led the successful defence of Petrograd. Many of those who infiltrated Krymov's army were Bolsheviks and the political orientation of the Red Guards and the Kronstadt sailors was Bolshevik. The Bolsheviks were therefore able to project themselves in their propaganda as saviours of the revolution. On the defensive after the fiasco of the July Days, they were now in a position to go back on to the attack.

After the Kornilov affair, there was a surge in popular support for the Bolsheviks. Membership of the party increased sharply. The Bolsheviks polled strongly in city council elections that took place in August and September, winning 33 percent of the vote in Petrograd and 51 percent in Moscow. Most significantly, they started to win control of soviets in major cities. At the end of September, Trotsky, who had returned from exile in May and committed himself to the Bolsheviks in July, became chairman of the Petrograd Soviet. By this time, the Bolsheviks also controlled the Moscow Soviet. In several other cities, soviets were dominated by loose coalitions of Bolsheviks, Left SRs and Menshevik Internationalists. The stranglehold of the mainstream SRs and the 'revolutionary defencist' Mensheviks on the soviets, had been broken. Note, however, that on the eve of the October Revolution, the Bolsheviks did not have majority support, or anything like it, across Russia as a whole.

The Kornilov affair was not the only reason for this shift of opinion in the Bolsheviks' direction. Other factors were at work too. The Bolsheviks were better led and organised than their rivals and had fewer internal divisions. The policies Lenin had set out in the April Theses grew in appeal as 1917 wore on. In an increasingly polarised society, the Bolshevik idea of depriving the middle and upper classes of political rights was attractive to many in the lower classes. The entry into the Bolshevik ranks of Trotsky, arguably the best-known revolutionary in Russia and an electrifying public speaker, was significant too.

ACTIVITY
KNOWLEDGE CHECK

**The Kornilov affair**

What arguments can be offered in support of the view that the Kornilov affair was a decisive turning-point in the history of the Russian Revolution?

## WHAT PART DID LENIN AND TROTSKY PLAY IN THE MAKING OF THE OCTOBER REVOLUTION?

The Kornilov affair put the Bolsheviks in a position where they could think in terms of seizing power in Russia. Without Lenin, however, they would never have got to this position and nor, in all likelihood, would they have gone on to take advantage of it.

- Left to themselves, other Bolsheviks in the spring of 1917 would almost certainly not have thought in terms of making a bid for power. The chances are that they would have adopted the Menshevik position of qualified support for the Provisional Government.

- The policies Lenin set out in the April Theses were the basis on which the Bolsheviks were able to increase their strength in the spring and early summer of 1917.
- Lenin's demand for an uprising in the autumn of 1917 was decisive. Whether other Bolsheviks would have gone ahead without his urgings is open to question.

Lenin did not, though, bring about the October Revolution single-handedly. Others were involved, notably Trotsky. It was Trotsky, not Lenin, who determined the way in which power was seized in Petrograd in October 1917. Lenin's role in the detailed planning and execution of the seizure of power was surprisingly limited.

## Lenin's influence on the Central Committee

'History will not forgive us if we do not assume power now.' This claim was made by Lenin in one of two impassioned letters he sent to the Bolshevik party's Central Committee after the Kornilov affair. The letters were sent from Finland, where Lenin had been in hiding since the July Days. The 22-strong Central Committee was the Bolsheviks' key decision-making body, elected by representatives of the grassroots membership at irregularly held party Congresses. If Lenin's plan for an immediate armed insurrection was to go ahead, the Central Committee would have to approve it.

The Central Committee more or less ignored Lenin's letters. They were discussed at a meeting in mid-September, but no action was taken. Back in Finland, Lenin grew increasingly agitated. On 10 October, he travelled secretly to Petrograd in order to put his case in person to a meeting of the Central Committee. The meeting was a stormy one. Lenin's plans were opposed by two of his most senior lieutenants, Kamenev and Zinoviev. They maintained that the success of an insurrection could not be guaranteed. In place of Lenin's high-risk strategy, they proposed a more cautious one of seeking to maximise the Bolshevik vote in the forthcoming Constituent Assembly elections, with a view to entering government in coalition with the Left SRs and the Menshevik Internationalists. The debate ended with a 10–2 vote in favour of an insurrection. However, no date was fixed.

Kamenev and Zinoviev reopened the issue at a further meeting of the Central Committee that took place a week later. Again, they were defeated. Detailed planning for a seizure of power in Petrograd and Moscow now got under way.

SOURCE

**Extracts from the minutes of the meeting of the Bolshevik party's Central Committee, 16 October 1917.**

Comrade Lenin: The masses trust the Bolsheviks and demand deeds, from them, not just words. They demand a decisive policy of struggle against the war and against ruin. All this leads to a clear conclusion that there must be an armed uprising.

Comrade Sverdlov (Central Committee member) reports on the state of affairs in the localities of Petrograd:

Vasilevsky Island: Not in a fighting mood.

Vyborg District: The same, but preparing for an insurrection.

City District: The mood is hard to gauge.

Nevsky District: The mood has swung sharply in our favour.

Okhtensky District: Things are bad for us.

Porokhovsky District: The mood is strengthening in our favour.

Shlisselburg District: The mood is in our favour.

Comrade Shmidt (Central Committee member) from the trade unions: The total number of organised unionists is over 500,000. Our party has predominant influence. The mood is such that we cannot expect active support for an uprising.

Comrade Zinoviev: He doubts it is possible for the insurrection to succeed. Above all else, the railway and postal telegraph apparatus is not in our hands. And we are not yet strong enough in Petrograd. The mood in the factories is not what it was in June.

Comrade Kamenev: We must exercise great caution.

Comrade Stalin: The result of Kamenev and Zinoviev's proposal would be that the counter-revolution becomes organised; we will retreat endlessly and lose the whole revolution.

Comrade Lenin proposed the following: This meeting calls on all organisations and all workers and soldiers to make comprehensive and intensive preparations for an armed insurrection.

Lenin's resolution is voted on: 20 for, 2 against, 3 abstaining.

There was a postscript to the Central Committee's debates. Kamenev published an article in a non-Bolshevik newspaper condemning Lenin's rashness. Lenin was beside himself with anger, not only because of the disloyalty involved, but also because the Bolsheviks' intentions had been signalled to the general public. Petrograd knew what was coming days before the October Revolution got under way. Not that it made much difference: very few of those uneasy about the prospect of Bolshevik rule were in any hurry to fight for Kerensky.

The Central Committee's deliberations in October 1917 over whether to launch an armed insurrection are instructive. They demonstrate that debate among senior Bolsheviks before the October Revolution was open and could be hard-hitting. They show that, after the Kornilov affair, there was considerable uncertainty in Bolshevik circles about how best to exploit their newly acquired popularity. Above all, they reveal the extent of Lenin's mastery over his followers: in October 1917, he bullied and cajoled a hesitant party into taking a course of action it would not otherwise have taken.

## Trotsky and the Military Revolutionary Committee

Lenin played no part in the detailed planning of the October Revolution. Having agreed to his demand for an armed insurrection, the Bolshevik Central Committee kept him on the sidelines, presumably because it thought of him as a strategist, not a tactician. At the tactical level, the Bolshevik seizure of power was organised and directed by Trotsky.

One of Trotsky's priorities was to 'camouflage' (his term) the Bolshevik seizure of power. He wanted it to appear after the event that the Provisional Government had been overthrown, not by the Bolsheviks acting in their own interest, but rather by the soviets acting in the name of the people. This is where the Military Revolutionary Committee came in.

The Military Revolutionary Committee (MRC) was formed by the Petrograd Soviet at the instigation of the Mensheviks after the Kornilov affair. Its role was to organise Petrograd's defences against the possibility of an attack by German forces or by domestic counter-revolutionaries. It was a perfect vehicle for Trotsky because, to outward appearance, it was an instrument of the Petrograd Soviet, not of the Bolsheviks. Behind the scenes, though, it was firmly under Bolshevik control. The MRC gave the Bolsheviks access to valuable military intelligence and to stockpiles of weaponry. It also enabled them to secure key strongpoints in Petrograd in advance of their insurrection. Any objections to its activities could be brushed aside with the claim that it was acting on behalf of the Petrograd Soviet.

On the eve of the October Revolution, Kerensky's military advisers assured him that most of the Petrograd garrison remained loyal to him. This was entirely untrue: most of the garrison was either pro-Bolshevik or uncommitted. Only a handful of soldiers were ready to fight in defence of the Provisional Government. Trotsky, by contrast, had a sizeable force at his disposal, consisting of the Kronstadt sailors, the Red Guards and some units of soldiers. It was not, however, without its weaknesses.

SOURCE

Trotsky's appraisal of the forces under his command in October 1917, from Trotsky's *History of the Russian Revolution*, published in 1932.

For active operations it was possible to count firmly upon the Red Guard, upon the advanced group of sailors and upon the better preserved regiments. The different elements of this collective army supplemented each other. The numerous garrisons lacked the will to fight. The sailor detachments lacked numbers. The Red Guard lacked skill. The workers together with the sailors contributed energy, daring and enthusiasm. The regiments of the garrison constituted a rather inert reserve, imposing in its numbers and overwhelming in its mass.

## The events of 24-26 October

The Bolshevik insurrection got under way on the evening of 24 October. It was almost entirely bloodless. Lenin said later that taking power in Petrograd was easier than picking up a feather.

### 24-26 October in Petrograd: key events

| | |
|---|---|
| **24 October** | • On the evening of 24 October, the Bolsheviks began to take control of railway stations, post and telegraph offices, bridges and other key installations. Some of these places had been guarded by soldiers, but these guards moved off without a fight. By the early morning of 25 October, most of Petrograd was under the Bolsheviks' control. |
| **25 October** | • Kerensky left Petrograd on the morning of 25 October in search of support from army units stationed outside the capital.<br>• The lightly defended headquarters of the Provisional Government at the Winter Palace in Petrograd was surrounded by pro-Bolshevik soldiers and Red Guards. A number of government ministers were inside.<br>• In the early afternoon, Trotsky announced the overthrow of the Provisional Government at a meeting of the Petrograd Soviet - a little prematurely, because the Winter Palace had not yet been taken.<br>• Late in the evening, a meeting of the second Congress of Soviets began (the first Congress took place in June). Arrangements for the Congress had been made a month earlier. Delegates from soviets across the whole of Russia were present. Around 300 of the 670 delegates were Bolsheviks. |
| **26 October** | • In the early hours, Mensheviks and moderate SRs walked out of the Congress of Soviets in protest against the Bolshevik seizure of power.<br>• The Winter Palace surrendered (2am) without much of a fight. There was no storming, or frontal assault, of the Winter Palace by heroic workers and soldiers, as later Bolshevik propaganda claimed. Provisional Government ministers found in the Winter Palace were arrested.<br>• The Bolsheviks announced the formation of a soviet-based government at the Congress of Soviets (5am).<br>• Lenin appeared before the Congress of Soviets in the evening and announced a Decree on Peace, a Decree on Land and the formation of a new government.<br>• The Decree on Peace demanded an immediate ceasefire in the world war and called on the governments of combatant countries to enter peace negotiations at once.<br>• The Decree on Land confiscated without compensation landed estates belonging to the nobility, the Orthodox Church and others and promised that all land would 'pass into the use of those who cultivated it'.<br>• These announcements were approved by the Congress. Support from the Congress was important to the Bolsheviks because it gave the impression that the country had somehow risen to acclaim their seizure of power. |

Bolshevik leaders were alive to the danger of being left isolated after a successful uprising in Petrograd. They recognised that their survival prospects depended on the revolution spreading quickly across Russia. An insurrection in Moscow was therefore planned in parallel with the one in Petrograd. Things did not go smoothly. Moscow's Bolsheviks were under-prepared and only won control of the city after a week's fighting against forces loyal to the Provisional Government. One thousand people died in the struggle for Moscow.

## The formation of the Bolshevik government

The Decree on Establishment of the Workers and Peasants Government announced by Lenin on 26 October stated that the new administration would govern Russia until the Constituent Assembly was convened. It further stipulated that the new government would be accountable to the Congress of Soviets and its central committee. In these early days, the Bolsheviks were careful to give the impression that they were marching in step with public opinion.

Trotsky disliked the title 'minister', which he thought sounded un-revolutionary and bourgeois. On his recommendation, the new government adopted the title 'People's Commissars' instead. The collective name for the new government was the Council of People's Commissars, or **Sovnarkom** for short.

**KEY TERM**

**Sovnarkom**
The abbreviation 'Sovnarkom' derives from the initial letters of the Russian words for council (*soviet*), people (*narodnykh*) and commissar (*komissar*).

In the first instance, all of Sovnarkom's members were Bolsheviks. Some Left SRs joined later. Lenin became Chairman of the Council of People's Commissars. Trotsky took the post of Commissar for Foreign Affairs. Towards the bottom of the governmental pecking order was the Commissar for Nationalities, Josef Stalin.

## The Constituent Assembly elections

The long-awaited elections to the Constituent Assembly were held in most of Russia between 12 and 15 November 1917. Some provinces failed to keep to the timetable that had been laid down. The results of these elections are key evidence in any discussion about whether the October Revolution was a popular uprising, a *coup d'etat* or something in between.

**SOURCE 14** Constituent Assembly elections results, November 1917.

| | Total votes (rounded) | Number of seats won | % share of the vote (rounded) |
|---|---|---|---|
| Socialist Revolutionaries | 17.1 million | 380 | 41.0% |
| Bolsheviks | 9.8 million | 168 | 23.5% |
| Kadets | 2.0 million | 17 | 4.8% |
| Mensheviks | 1.4 million | 18 | 3.3% |
| Others (including parties representing national minorities) | 11.1 million | 120 | 26.9% |

These overall results mask considerable differences between regions. The Bolsheviks polled strongly in the major cities, especially in Petrograd and Moscow. In the working-class districts of these cities, they won 60–70 percent of the vote. Soldiers serving at the front came out in favour of the Bolsheviks in large numbers. The Bolsheviks did least well in the rural areas, where the SRs held sway.

**SOURCE 15** Percentage Bolshevik share of the vote in selected regions.

| | Bolsheviks | SRs | Mensheviks | Kadets | Others |
|---|---|---|---|---|---|
| Soldiers serving on Russia's Western Front | 67% | 19% | 1% | 2% | 11% |
| Petrograd | 50% | 26% | 1% | 14% | 9% |
| Moscow | 57% | 26% | 5% | 7% | 5% |
| Kursk (a rural 'Black Earth' region province) | 11% | 82% | 1% | 5% | 1% |

The Bolsheviks may have won less than a quarter of the vote overall in the Constituent Assembly elections, but their position was rather stronger than this headline figure suggests. The ballot papers used in the elections did not differentiate between the various elements of the SR party, which in late 1917 was disintegrating. The Left SRs at this point were allies of the Bolsheviks. In late 1917, six Left SRs took up posts in Sovnarkom. A fair proportion of the SR votes in the Constituent Assembly elections were cast for candidates who favoured collaboration with the Bolsheviks.

At the same time, it should be borne in mind that that some of those who did support the Bolsheviks in the Constituency Assembly elections were only lightly attached to the party. Public opinion in Russia in 1917 was fickle and volatile. Many of those who voted Bolshevik in the Constituent Assembly elections were fair-weather supporters who subsequently became disillusioned. 'Their Bolshevism', said one Menshevik, 'was nothing but hatred for the coalition and longing for land and peace.'

## Weaknesses and failings of the Provisional Government, February-October 1917

- The different Provisional Governments were all, to some degree, coalitions involving liberals and socialists: the gulf between the two in terms of attitudes and aspirations meant that they were inherently unstable coalitions.
- The Provisional Government did not have the means to enforce its will. As a result, it was forced to bargain and to compromise with institutions and individuals who did have power – notably the Petrograd Soviet and General Kornilov.
- Conscious of its status as an interim government, the Provisional Government insisted that decisions on major issues such as land reform had to wait until after the Constituent Assembly had done its work. This gave an impression of indecision and delay. Lenin exploited this to the full, offering a mocking summary of Provisional Government policy: 'As to land, wait until the Constituent Assembly. As to the Constituent Assembly, wait until the end of the war. As to the end of the war, wait until complete victory.'
- The Provisional Government proved unable to prevent the deterioration of economic conditions in Russia, failing in particular to control inflation. Its attempt to prevent runaway increases in food prices by introducing a state monopoly on the sale of grain did not succeed because peasants were unwilling to supply the government at the low prices they were offered.
- Kerensky, the most talented of the Provisional Government leaders, was deeply flawed, he was vain, driven by personal ambition and deficient in political judgement.
- The Provisional Government after April 1917 was up against skilled, resourceful and ruthless opponents in Lenin and Trotsky.

**ACTIVITY**
**KNOWLEDGE CHECK**

**The Bolsheviks on the eve of the October Revolution**

1 What picture emerges from Source 12 about the level of support for the Bolsheviks among Petrograd's workers in October 1917? To what extent does it support Zinoviev's claim that 'we are not yet strong enough in Petrograd'?

2 What does Source 13 tell us about the strengths and weaknesses of the forces available to the Bolsheviks on the eve of the October Revolution?

**ACTIVITY**
**SUMMARY**

**Bolsheviks and anti-Bolsheviks in 1917**

1 Write a paragraph on each of the following, explaining why they were significant figures in 1917 and what political errors they made:
- Paul Milyukov
- Alexander Kerensky
- General Kornilov.

2 Write a paragraph on each of the following, explaining why they were an asset to the Bolsheviks in 1917:
- Lenin
- Trotsky
- the Red Guards
- the Kronstadt sailors.

3 Construct a two-column table summarising the arguments and evidence for and against the view that the October Revolution was 'a classic *coup d'etat*, the capture of governmental power by a small minority' (Richard Pipes).

**A Level Exam-Style Question Section B**

How far was the Provisional Government responsible for its own downfall? (20 marks)

**Tip**

*Start your answer with a succinct 'thesis statement' that sets out your judgement on the extent to which (a) the Provisional Government's own errors and failings, and (b) others factors, were responsible for the Provisional Government's downfall. Structure the remainder of your answer around the reasons that can be offered in support of this thesis.*

## Interpretations (5c)

### Good questions, bad questions

Below are approaches associated with three participants in the Russian Revolution who subsequently wrote historical accounts of it.

| **Leon Trotsky** | **Paul Milyukov** | **Alexander Kerensky** |
|---|---|---|
| As a Marxist, Trotsky believed that political change was shaped and determined by economic developments and conflict between social classes. As a result, he did not believe that the actions of individuals were a critical factor in deciding historical outcomes. | Milyukov did not accept that conflict between social classes is the only, or main, driver of change in history. He argued that individuals, and the judgements they made, had a profound effect on the course of events. | In his writings on the history of the Russian Revolution, Kerensky focused heavily on the motives of the key participants in the Revolution, including his own. He made no attempt to be impartial or objective. |

Work in groups.

1 Devise three criteria of what makes a good historical question (note: you will have to consider the difference between historical and unhistorical questions).

2 Consider what you know about the October Revolution.

a) Each write a historical question about the October Revolution.

b) Put these in rank order, with the best question based on your criteria first.

3 Using a piece of A3 paper, write the names of the three writers above so that they form a large triangle.

a) Write your questions on the piece of paper so that their positions reflect how likely each of the writers is to be interested in that question. For example, a question about Lenin's motives and thinking in the autumn of 1917 would interest Kerensky and Milyukov more than it would Trotsky, so it would be somewhere between these two but nowhere near Trotsky.

b) Add some further questions. Try to think of questions that only one of the three would be interested in.

4 Take it in turns to try to answer the questions you have created in the style of one of the writers. See if the other members of the group can work out which one it was.

Answer the following questions individually, using the examples created by the above activity.

5 Does one approach to writing history lead to better reasoning than others? Explain your answer.

6 Explain why all writers of historical accounts who deploy rigorous methodology are, to an extent, useful sources for the study of the past.

### WIDER READING

For accessible short histories of the Russian Revolution with full coverage of 1917 see:

Fitzpatrick, S. *The Russian Revolution*, Oxford University Press, third edition, (2008)

Smith, S.A. *The Russian Revolution: A Very Short Introduction*, Oxford University Press (2002)

Service, R. *The Russian Revolution, 1900-1927*, Macmillan (1986)

Williams, B. *The Russian Revolution, 1917-21*, Historical Association Studies, Blackwell (1987)

Also worth exploring is the website *Seventeen Moments in Soviet History* at www.sovietthistory.macalester.edu, an archive of short essays, audio and visual materials, primary sources and maps.

# 2b.4 Defending the Bolshevik revolution, October 1917–24

**KEY QUESTIONS**

- What steps did the Bolsheviks take after the October Revolution to consolidate their hold on power?
- How did Bolshevik economic policy evolve in the years 1917–21?
- Why were the Bolsheviks able to defeat their domestic enemies in the Russian Civil War?
- For what reasons, and with what results, did foreign powers intervene in Russia in the civil war era?

## INTRODUCTION

The October Revolution marked the beginning, not the end, of the Bolsheviks' seizure of power. In late 1917, the task of securing their position and extending their influence across Russia as a whole still lay ahead. The difficulties involved in this enterprise were massive. Immediately after the October Revolution, the Bolsheviks only controlled Petrograd, Moscow and a handful of other major cities. In the countryside, they had no real presence at all. In the border regions, there were minority nationalities intent on breaking away from Russia. Small wonder that many well-informed observers believed that the Bolshevik regime would be short-lived.

The Bolsheviks were faced with three main enemies that had to be either defeated or neutralised.

- First, there was Germany, whose forces were in late 1917 camped deep inside Russian territory. The Russian army facing these forces had more or less completely disintegrated as a fighting force and offered no sort of barrier against further German advances. Ending the war with Germany was therefore crucial to the Bolsheviks' survival prospects.
- Second, there were the liberals, moderate socialists and others within Russia who opposed the October Revolution and what it stood for. Middle-class liberals were, of course, hostile to Bolshevik rule from the outset. So, too, were the Right Socialist Revolutionaries (SRs), who in late 1917 set up a Committee for the Salvation of the Revolution. Before the end of 1917, upper-class conservatives and army officers had begun to congregate in the south-eastern part of European Russia with the intention of organising counter-revolutionary activity.
- Third, there were the minority nationalities who refused to accept Bolshevik rule. In the months after the October Revolution, there were declarations of independence in Finland, Estonia and the Ukraine. Georgia, Azerbaijan and Armenia followed suit in early 1918. Poland and Lithuania, both occupied by German forces during the war, gained their independence after Russia and Germany made peace in March 1918.

**1917** - 20 November: Peace talks between Russia and Germany open at Brest-Litovsk

**1918** - 5-6 January: Constituent Assembly meets and is disbanded

**1918** - 3 March: Treaty of Brest-Litovsk signed

**1918** - 8 April: Trotsky appointed People's Commissar for War

1917

1918

**1917** - 7 December: Decree issued establishing the Cheka

**1918** - 6 March: Bolsheviks rename themselves the Russian Communist Party

**1918** - 9 March: British troops land at Murmansk: beginning of Allied intervention

**1918** - 17 July: Nicholas II and his family murdered at Ekaterinburg

A key advantage the Bolsheviks had in their struggle to consolidate their rule was the disparate nature of the forces arrayed against them. Apart from a shared anti-Bolshevism, their opponents had nothing at all in common. As a result, there was never the faintest chance of any kind of unity among them or joint action by them. This meant that the Bolsheviks were able to pick off their enemies one by one.

In their first years in power, however, the Bolsheviks found more than once that steps taken to overcome one problem had a knock-on effect and gave rise to difficulties elsewhere. The Treaty of Brest-Litovsk, for example, removed the threat from Germany but intensified hostility to Bolshevik rule inside Russia. Similarly, repressive measures introduced within Bolshevik-held territory in 1917–18 to silence critics and opponents alienated sections of opinion that had previously been pro-Bolshevik.

In the era of civil war, the Bolsheviks staggered from emergency to emergency. Immediately after the civil war, they faced a major rebellion against their rule. Governing in these circumstances of near-continuous crisis was challenging and exhausting. It required leadership of exceptional resilience, ruthlessness and flexibility. Lenin and Trotsky rose to the challenge. In Lenin's case, the experience wore him down physically and contributed to his premature death.

ACTIVITY
KNOWLEDGE CHECK

**Anti-Bolshevism**

What devices does the creator of Source 1 use to express his deep hostility towards Bolshevik rule? Is there any evidence which suggests that he was an extreme right-wing, rather than a liberal, opponent of Bolshevism?

**SOURCE**

'Peace and freedom in Sovdepia', an anti-Bolshevik poster produced in 1919. 'Sovdepia' was a term used by the Bolsheviks' opponents in the civil war to refer to the area of Russia under Bolshevik control.

**1918** – 30 August: Attempted assassination of Lenin by Fanya Kaplan: 'Red Terror' at its peak

**1919** – October–November: Red Army defeats Kolchak's army and forces Denikins to retreat

**1920** – April–October: Russo-Polish War

**1921** – 2–18 March: Kronstadt mutiny
**1921** – March: Compulsory grain requisitioning abandoned: introduction of the NEP

**1922** – December: Formation of the Union of Soviet Socialist Republics (USSR)

**1924** – 21 January: Lenin's death

1919 1920 1921 1922 1923 1924

# WHAT STEPS DID THE BOLSHEVIKS TAKE AFTER THE OCTOBER REVOLUTION TO CONSOLIDATE THEIR HOLD ON POWER?

## The closing of the Constituent Assembly

In their decree of October 1917, establishing the Council of People's Commissars (Sovnarkom), the Bolsheviks appeared to commit themselves to the view that the Constituent Assembly alone had the authority to decide Russia's political future. Appearances were deceptive. Having seized power, Lenin had no intention of surrendering it to the Constituent Assembly.

In the weeks after the October Revolution, Lenin tried in vain to persuade his colleagues to postpone the Constituent Assembly elections, knowing that the Bolsheviks were unlikely to win a majority. When the results became known, with the Bolsheviks winning less than a quarter of the popular vote, he made little attempt to conceal his intention to ignore them. He attacked the newly elected Assembly as both unrepresentative and illegitimate.

- He claimed that the make-up of the Constituent Assembly did not reflect voters' true preferences because ballot papers had not offered them a choice between pro-Bolshevik Left SRs and anti-Bolshevik Right SRs – the elections having taken place before the split in the SR ranks was formalised.
- He asserted that the soviets were a higher type of democratic institution than the Constituent Assembly, which he dismissed as an organ of bourgeois democracy. His argument on this point derived from Marx. Marx argued that, between the workers' revolution and the establishment of a full-blown communist society, there would have to be a temporary dictatorship of the proletariat in order to sweep away the remnants of bourgeois resistance to change. In this transitional period, said Lenin, it was the soviets, untainted by the presence of anti-socialist bourgeois politicians, which best reflected the will of the people.

Causation (6b)

**Attitudes and actions**

Individuals can only make choices based on their context. Prevalent attitudes combine with individual experience and natural temperament to frame the individual perception of what is going on around them. Nobody can know the future or see into the minds of others.

| Context | Action |
|---|---|
| • Immediately after seizing power in October 1917, the Bolsheviks promised that they would submit themselves to the Constituent Assembly.<br>• The Bolsheviks won under a quarter of the votes cast in the Constituent Assembly elections of November 1917.<br>• In December 1917, the Left SRs joined the government as allies of the Bolsheviks.<br>• In 1917–18, many Russian workers favoured a system of government based on soviets elected by workers and peasants.<br>• Public opinion in Russia in 1917–18 was volatile. | In January 1917, the Constituent Assembly was disbanded on Lenin's orders. |

Answer the following questions individually and discuss your answers in a group.

1. Why was the decision to disband the Constituent Assembly so controversial?
2. How much of a political risk did Lenin take when he ordered the disbandment of the Constituent Assembly?
3. Were there any courses of action open to Lenin in January 1918 that would have allowed the Bolsheviks to retain power, but did not involve the disbandment of the Constituent Assembly?
4. To what extent was Lenin's distinctive personality and temperament a factor in the decision to disband the Constituent Assembly?
5. How far should the historian try to understand the context of the beliefs and values of people in the past when explaining why individuals make choices in history?

Before the Constituent Assembly met, Sovnarkom imposed a number of conditions upon it. Voters were to have the right to recall and replace 'awkward' representatives; members of the Constituent Assembly were required to have their credentials approved by a Bolshevik-controlled election commission; and it was laid down that the Constituent Assembly could only meet if half of its members were present. It was not difficult to work out the direction in which events were heading.

On 5 January 1918, the day the Constituent Assembly was scheduled to open, 50,000 anti-Bolshevik demonstrators gathered in Petrograd. Bolshevik forces opened fire on them, killing ten. The meeting of the Constituent Assembly nevertheless went ahead but the Bolsheviks permitted it to remain in session for only one day. It was then forcibly disbanded. Its Right SR members left Petrograd and established a base in eastern Russia, where they formed an alternative government called the 'Committee of Members of the Constituent Assembly'.

## Making peace at Brest-Litovsk

Peace talks between Russia and Germany began in November 1917. Lenin was desperate for a quick settlement.

- In the absence of a peace agreement, Russia was wide open to German invasion.
- Lenin had promised Russia's war-weary workers and peasants peace and needed to deliver on his promise if he was to retain his credibility.
- Lenin wanted to be free to concentrate on overcoming the Bolsheviks' internal enemies. 'The bourgeoisie has to be throttled', he said, 'and for that we need both hands free.'

Germany, for its part, was more than willing to negotiate with Russia. The entry of the USA into the war in April 1917 left it facing the prospect of having to fight against three major powers in France: it therefore aimed to shut down its Eastern Front and transfer men and equipment to its Western Front in order to defeat the British and French before the Americans arrived.

A cease-fire between Russia and Germany was agreed soon after the peace talks opened. Negotiations on the terms of a permanent peace settlement proved more difficult. The price Germany demanded for ending the war was high: the loss of Finland, Estonia, Latvia, Lithuania, Poland, the Ukraine and parts of Armenia. These areas contained 26 percent of Russia's population, 27 percent of its arable land and 74 percent of its coal and iron ore.

The severity of Germany's demands threw the Bolshevik leadership into disarray. Left-wing Bolsheviks, headed by the 30-year old Nikolai Bukharin, called for the rejection of the terms and the launching of a 'revolutionary war' against Germany. This would have involved guerrilla activity behind enemy lines and stirring up the German working class against its government. Trotsky, by contrast, argued for a policy of 'neither war nor peace', under which Russia would declare the war was over but refuse to sign a peace treaty. Lenin, injecting a dose of realism into proceedings, urged acceptance of Germany's terms and threatened to resign from Sovnarkom if his wishes were not met.

**SOURCE 2** Lenin in early 1918.

**ACTIVITY**
**KNOWLEDGE CHECK**

**Lenin's style of leadership**

In what ways, and to what extent, would Source 2 be of use to a historian investigating the manner in which Lenin conducted himself as head of government?

**EXTEND YOUR KNOWLEDGE**

**Nikolai Bukharin (1888–1938)**

Although he was nearly 20 years younger than Lenin, Bukharin was one of the Bolsheviks' most influential leaders. An impulsive character, more gregarious and less calculating and ruthless than some of his senior colleagues, Bukharin was widely liked within the party. He was also almost the only senior Bolshevik who used his real name rather than an alias.

After the October Revolution, Bukharin, in political and economic terms, veered wildly from one extreme to another: in 1918, apart from advocating a 'revolutionary war' against Germany, he was an economic radical, calling for a rapid transition to socialism; but, after 1921, he emerged as a leading economic moderate.

**SOURCE 3** Lenin arguing for acceptance of Germany's peace terms in the Bolshevik Central Committee, 24 January 1918.

It is now a question of how we must defend the homeland. The army is utterly exhausted by war. There is no doubt that it is a shameful peace which we are forced to conclude now, but if we embark on a war, our government will be swept away and another government will make peace. Now we not only have the support of the proletariat but of the poor peasants too, and that will leave us if we continue the war. Those who advocate a revolutionary war point out that this will awaken revolution in Germany. But Germany is only just pregnant with revolution and we have given birth to a completely healthy child, a socialist republic, which we may kill if we start a war.

What comrade Trotsky suggests - halting the war, refusing to sign a peace and demobilising the army - this is international political showmanship.

The Brest-Litovsk treaty, signed in March 1918, solved a problem for the Bolsheviks, but also gave rise to some new ones.

- The Left SRs, deeply hostile to Brest-Litovsk because it involved the loss of huge amounts of territory in the parts of Russia where they were strongest, stormed out of Sovnarkom in protest against it.
- Russia's army chiefs and its middle and upper classes, all strongly nationalist in outlook, were appalled by what they saw as the shameful Bolshevik surrender at Brest-Litovsk. Their aim was now to overthrow Bolshevism and re-start the war against Germany.

It was after Brest-Litovsk that civil war in Russia began in earnest.

## The formation of the Cheka

The Bolsheviks created a political police force within weeks of seizing power in Petrograd. Its full name was the 'All-Russian Extraordinary Commission for Combating Counter-Revolution and Sabotage' (Cheka for short). The Sovnarkom decree (December 1917) that established the Cheka defined its purpose as the suppression of counter-revolution and sabotage across the whole of Russia. At first, the Cheka employed only a handful of people. By 1921, its numbers had swelled to nearly 150,000. Not all Chekists were secret policemen: almost from the start there were also heavily-armed military-style Cheka units that were instruments of mass repression.

The Cheka operated outside the framework of the ordinary law. It had the power to arrest and punish alleged counter-revolutionaries as it saw fit. 'My powers are such that I can shoot anybody', bragged one provincial Cheka leader. Suspected counter-revolutionaries and saboteurs were punished without trial and had no right of appeal against Cheka decisions. Often, they were simply executed on the spot. The Cheka was accountable only to Sovnarkom.

The Cheka quickly acquired a reputation for savagery. It became notorious, not only for its on-the-spot executions, but also for its use of torture. Here the lead came from the top. The leader of the Cheka was Felix Dzerzhinsky (1877–1926), a Polish nobleman turned Communist and a bloodthirsty fanatic. Dzerzhinsky wanted the Cheka to be feared as 'the sword and shield of the revolution'.

**EXTEND YOUR KNOWLEDGE**

**The Bolsheviks rename themselves**

Before March 1918, the Bolsheviks' formal name was the Russian Social-Democratic Labour Party of Bolsheviks. In March 1918, they renamed themselves the Russian Communist Party (Bolsheviks). There was a further name-change in 1925, this time to All-Union Communist Party (Bolsheviks). By this point, it had become customary, inside and outside Russia, to refer to Russia's ruling party as the Communists, with the term Bolsheviks falling into disuse. When referring to the party in the Lenin era, however, both 'Bolshevik' and 'Communist' are accurate, and can be used interchangeably.

SOURCE

From Alexander Berkman, *The Russian Tragedy*, a pamphlet published in 1922. Alexander Berkman (1870–1936) was a Russian-born anarchist who spent most of his adult life in the USA, but returned to Russia in 1920 full of enthusiasm for the Revolution – only to leave, disillusioned, two years later.

Arrests, night searches, executions are the order of the day. The Cheka, originally organised to fight counter-revolution and speculation, is becoming the terror of every worker and peasant. Its secret agents are everywhere, always unearthing 'plots', signifying the shooting of hundreds without hearing trial or appeal. From the intended defence of the Revolution the Cheka becomes the most dreaded organisation, whose injustice and cruelty spread terror over the whole country. All-powerful, owing no-one responsibility, the Cheka is a law unto itself, possesses its own army and makes its own laws which supersede those of the official state. The prisons and concentration camps are filled with alleged counter-revolutionaries and speculators, 95% of whom are starved workers, simple peasants and even children of 10-14 years of age.

**AS Level Exam-Style Question Section A (b)**

***Study Source 4 before you answer this question.***

How much weight do you give the evidence of Source 4 for an inquiry into the role of the Cheka in Lenin's Russia, 1917–24?

Explain your answer using the source, the information given about it and your own knowledge of the historical context. (12 marks)

**Tip**

*Try in your answer to maintain a broadly equal balance between consideration of a source's strengths and its limitations – and avoid excessive concentration on its limitations. Here, there is information about Cheka activities (potentially a strength) but, in light of the origins of the source, there are questions to be asked about whether its claims are exaggerated (potentially a weakness).*

In the era of revolution and civil war, Bolsheviks sometimes spoke of the Cheka as a regrettable necessity, a product of the desperate circumstances in which they found themselves. However, under a variety of names (it became the GPU, or State Political Administration, in 1922, and the OGPU, or Unified State Political Administration, in 1924), it went on to become a permanent feature of Communist rule in Russia.

## Attacks on Bolshevik opponents

The Bolsheviks were, from the outset, aggressively intolerant of criticism and opposition. Within days of taking power, they issued a Decree on the Press that shut down hostile newspapers. But they did not wage all-out war on all of their political enemies at once. At first, they concentrated their fire on the Kadets, proclaiming them to be 'a party of enemies of the people'. The Kadet party was outlawed in November 1917 and those of its leaders who had not left Bolshevik-held territory were arrested and imprisoned. When, in 1918, Bolshevik Russia equipped itself with a constitution – it called itself the Russian Soviet Federated Soviet Republic (RSFSR) – the middle classes, the section of the population on which the Kadets had relied for support, were denied the right to vote in elections to soviets.

**EXTEND YOUR KNOWLEDGE**

**The RSFSR and the USSR**

The RSFSR formally came into existence in July 1918 when its constitution was adopted by the Congress of Soviets. At this point, most of the eastern and southern parts of the old Russian Empire were not under secure Bolshevik control. In 1922, after the civil war, the Ukraine, Transcaucasia and Belarus, now Bolshevik-controlled 'soviet republics', signed a treaty of union with Russia. The name given to the new unified state was the Union of Soviet Socialist Republics (USSR, or Soviet Union). The USSR was only fully up and running in 1924, when its constitution came into force. Other 'soviet republics' joined the USSR later. The USSR was dissolved in 1991.

The Bolsheviks turned their attention to their socialist rivals in the course of 1918. In mid-1918, the Mensheviks and SRs (Left and Right) were expelled from the soviets at all levels, which prevented them from taking part in open political activity. At no point, however, were they formally outlawed. Until 1921–22, they were allowed to lead a shadowy, semi-legal existence. They were then harassed into extinction, most of their leaders being either forcibly deported from Russia by the Bolsheviks or choosing to exile themselves from it. Thousands of lower-level Mensheviks and SRs were arrested and sent to Bolshevik prisons and labour camps in Siberia. To all intents and purposes, Bolshevik Russia was a one-party state from 1918 onwards. 'Our party has for some years been the only legal party in the country', wrote Zinoviev in 1921.

## The Red Terror

In the course of 1918, the number and scale of Cheka atrocities rose sharply. By the latter part of the year, the Cheka had embarked on a systematic campaign to terrorise the population of Bolshevik-controlled Russia into submission. This campaign, the so-called 'Red Terror', arose out of a series of reverses the Bolsheviks suffered in the spring and summer of 1918.

- The Bolsheviks' prestige was seriously dented by the treaty of Brest-Litovsk. In the spring of 1918, they did poorly in elections to the soviets. This setback contributed to their growing sense of insecurity.
- The civil war began in earnest in the spring of 1918. The Bolsheviks' hold on power became precarious. The temptation to lash out at their enemies, real and imagined, became overwhelming.
- In the summer of 1918, extremist Left SRs, embittered by the Brest-Litovsk treaty, reverted to the tactic of assassination used in the Tsarist era. Prominent victims included Germany's ambassador to Russia and the head of the Petrograd Cheka. There was also an attempt on the life of Lenin himself: in August 1918, his would-be assassin, Fanya Kaplan, shot Lenin twice from close range, but Lenin survived. It was after the attempted murder of Lenin that the Cheka was let fully off the leash.

Bolshevik propaganda maintained that the 'Red Terror' targeted bourgeois 'wreckers' who were trying to prevent the establishment of socialism in Russia. In practice, the victims of the 'Red Terror' came from a variety of backgrounds. In the civil war era, the Bolsheviks did not use the term 'bourgeois' to refer to a social class: they used it to describe anyone who opposed them.

The highest-profile victims of the 'Red Terror' were Nicholas II and his family. After the February Revolution, they had been placed in protective custody, first near Petrograd, then in Siberia. In July 1918, the entire royal family was murdered by Chekists, almost certainly on Lenin's direct orders. According to Trotsky, Lenin feared that Nicholas II was a potential rallying-point around whom his enemies could assemble.

The 'Red Terror' involved numerous acts of stomach-churning brutality. There were reports of Cheka victims being scalped, crucified and pushed into vats of boiling water. Estimates of the number of people who died at the hands of the Cheka in the 'Red Terror' in 1918 vary, but the figure appears to have been at least 10,000. In the years between 1917 and 1923, the Cheka and its successor organisation, the GPU, may have claimed as many as 200,000 lives. The Bolsheviks' opponents in the civil war declared themselves to be shocked and horrified by the scale of Cheka violence but, in some cases, they conducted themselves in a not dissimilar fashion in the areas under their control: there was a '**White** Terror' as well as a 'Red Terror'.

**KEY TERM**

**Whites**
The Bolsheviks' conservative opponents in the civil war were called Whites because white was a colour traditionally associated with absolute monarchy: the background of the flag of the Bourbon absolute monarchs who ruled France before the French Revolution was white.

THINKING HISTORICALLY **Causation (6a)**

Different times and different places have different sets of ideas. Beliefs about how the world works, how human societies should be governed or the best way to achieve economic prosperity, can all be radically different from our own. It is important for the historian to take account of these different attitudes and be aware of the dangers of judging them against modern ideas.

Read the observations below about Russia in the civil war era, and then answer the questions that follow.

*In the civil war era, the propertied classes living in Bolshevik-held territory were brutally persecuted. The Bolsheviks' hostility to the bourgeoisie derived in part from their Marxist principles, but also owed something to the crude anti-bourgeois prejudices that were common among Russian workers and peasants at the time. Another factor was Bolshevik outrage over the anti-communist atrocities committed during the civil war by the counter-revolutionary bourgeoisie, the Whites.*

1 How did Marxist theory provide a basis for the Bolshevik hostility towards Russia's propertied classes?

2 Do you think it would have made any difference to Bolshevik attitudes towards Russia's propertied classes if the Whites had conducted themselves in a more humane manner during the Russian Civil War?

3 In early 20th-century Russia, class prejudices were stronger than they are in contemporary Britain.

a) Can you think of any other ways in which attitudes in early 20th-century Russia differed dramatically from those that are current in Britain now?

b) Why do you think that they are different?

4 How important is it for historians to deal with events in the context of the beliefs and values of people in the past as well as seeing them as part of a greater pattern?

ACTIVITY
KNOWLEDGE CHECK

**The Bolshevik consolidation of power**

1 Explain three ways in which, in their first six months in power, the Bolsheviks alienated some of the people who had supported them at the time of the October Revolution.

2 How accurate is it to say that in their first year in power the Bolsheviks showed themselves to be far more brutal and repressive than ever Nicholas II's regime had been?

# HOW DID BOLSHEVIK ECONOMIC POLICY EVOLVE IN THE YEARS 1917–21?

## State capitalism (October 1917–July 1918)

In the economic sphere, the incoming Bolshevik regime had only limited freedom of manoeuvre. It was boxed in by a number of conflicting pressures.

- The Bolsheviks inherited an economy in a dire condition: inflation was running out of control, unemployment was rising and productivity was falling. There was a need to arrest economic decline.
- There were expectations among industrial workers and the peasantry that their grievances would be addressed by the Bolsheviks as a matter of urgency. They could not be ignored: their support was essential if the fledgling Bolshevik regime was to survive.
- Left-wing Bolsheviks, headed by Bukharin, were calling for a more or less instant transition to a fully socialist economy – a policy that, in Lenin's estimation, was certain to have a seriously destabilising impact on economic life.

Lenin's strategy in these difficult circumstances was to do what he could to restore economic stability, while not dismissing the demands of the workers, peasants and left-wing Bolsheviks. Unsurprisingly, given the way he had to juggle priorities, his early economic policy lacked coherence.

- An important and sometimes overlooked fact about the early months of Bolshevik rule is that much of Russian industry remained under private ownership. The activities of private companies were, however, monitored and directed by the state. This combination of private ownership and state control can be described as a system of state capitalism. In December 1917, a new body, the Supreme Council of National Economy (VSNKh, or Vesenkha), was created to supervise industry and manage the economy. It reported directly to Sovnarkom.
- The peasantry was appeased by the Decree on Land (November 1917), which legitimised the peasant land seizures of 1917. The Decree drew heavily on the land policy of the Socialist Revolutionaries (SRs) and was instrumental in persuading the Left SRs to join Lenin's government.
- The Decree on Workers' Control (November 1917) pandered to the wishes of industrial workers by giving them a say in how their factories were run and ensuring that managers treated them properly. It did not, however, authorise workers to seize control of their factories and run them themselves.
- A limited and unsystematic programme of **nationalisation** was implemented. The banking industry was taken over by the state. A number of individual factories, including the giant Putilov works in Petrograd, were also nationalised. There were also cases of 'nationalisation from below', where workers took control of enterprises and declared them to be state property.

KEY TERM

**Nationalisation**
A term used to describe the process of a government taking control of a privately owned company or industry.

## War Communism (July 1918–March 1921)

In the spring of 1918, the context in which Bolshevik economic policy was made changed radically. The treaty of Brest-Litovsk and the onset of full-scale civil war meant that the Bolsheviks no longer had access to the resources of the Ukraine and other areas. The loss of the Ukraine's coal, iron ore and grain left Lenin's government facing dire economic problems in the areas where it remained in control.

- Industrial output slumped.
- In the cities, there were acute shortages of food and fuel.
- Prices soared: the value of the rouble, Russia's currency, collapsed more or less completely.
- The peasantry were unwilling to sell their produce for worthless paper money so cutting the supply of food to the cities further and driving prices even higher.
- Desperate for food, urban workers deserted the cities in massive numbers and returned to their native villages. Between 1918 and 1920, Petrograd lost three-quarters of its population. The population of Moscow halved in the same period. On top of all the other difficulties, factories found themselves short of labour.

Fighting for their lives, the Bolsheviks implemented a series of measures that together are known as War Communism. The core aims of War Communism were to ensure that the cities were fed and that industrial production was maximised. Its key features were compulsory requisitioning, a ban on private trade, rationing, wholesale nationalisation of industry and a return to 'one-man management'.

- Compulsory requisitioning was the Bolshevik solution to peasant grain hoarding. 'Food brigades' were sent out from the cities to extract grain from the peasantry by force. Where necessary, the 'food brigades' were assisted by the army and the Cheka. In theory, peasants were supposed to be paid a fixed price for their grain but, in practice, requisitioning often meant straightforward theft.
- The ban on private trade was designed to prevent peasants from supplying grain to middlemen and speculators who then sold it on at inflated prices. The ban did not succeed: a thriving '**black market**' in illegally traded foodstuffs soon developed.

KEY TERM

**Black market**
A sector of the economy in which goods or services are traded illegally. Black-market sellers may have legal ownership of the goods they are selling: what is illegal is the act of trade itself. In a black market transaction both the seller and the buyer act illegally.

- In the cities, food was distributed on the basis of a strict rationing system. The way in which food rationing worked reflected the Bolsheviks' priorities and values. The biggest rations went to the army and workers in heavy industry. Then came the civil servants and workers in light industry, who received barely enough to live on. At the bottom of the scale were 'capitalists, landlords and parasites', in other words, the middle classes, who, said Zinoviev, were given 'just enough bread so as not to forget the smell of it'.
- Large-scale industrial enterprises were put under direct state control in mid-1918. Smaller firms were nationalised later. Nationalised industries operated under the overall supervision of the Vesenkha. Individual industries were controlled by departments, or *glavki*, of the Vesenkha.
- The experiment with workers' control in industry was ended. In its place came a return to traditional, top-down methods of management – 'one-man management', as the Bolsheviks called it. The idea was to make the industrial workforce more disciplined and productive. In addition, the Bolsheviks introduced a system of internal passports in an attempt to halt the flight of industrial workers to the countryside. Trotsky wanted to go further and impose military-style discipline in the factories. Lenin, however, overruled him.

SOURCE

From an article in the independent socialist newspaper *New Life*, 19 April 1918. *New Life*'s publisher was the famous Russian novelist and playwright, Maxim Gorky. *New Life* was shut down by the Bolsheviks in July 1918.

News is arriving of the bread war which is now taking place in Voronezh, Smolensk, Tambov, Riazan, Simbirsk, Kharkov, Ufa, Orenburg, Kursk and a number of other provinces. Armed detachments of Red Guards and hired soldiers are roaming over villages and hamlets in quest of bread, making searches, laying traps with more or less success. Sometimes they return with bread; at other times they come back carrying the dead bodies of their comrades who fell in the fight with the peasants. Many of the villages are now well-armed, and seldom does a bread expedition end without victims. At the first report of a requisitioning expedition, the whole district is mobilised and comes to the defence of the neighbouring village.

ACTIVITY
KNOWLEDGE CHECK

**Feeding the towns, 1918**

What can be inferred from Source 5 about the importance that the Bolsheviks attached to increasing the supply of food to the towns?

SOURCE

Victor Serge, *Memoirs of a Revolutionary*, published in 1951. Serge (1890–1947), the son of a Russian political exile, was a one-time anarchist who returned to Russia in 1919 and joined the Bolsheviks. In the winter of 1920–21, he was based in Petrograd.

The rations issued were minute: black bread, or sometimes a few cupfuls of oats instead; a few herrings each month, a very small quantity of sugar for people in the 'first category' (workers and soldiers) and none at all for the third category (non-workers). The words of St. Paul that were posted up everywhere, 'He that doth not work, neither shall he eat' became ironical, because if you wanted any food you really had to resort to the black market instead of working. In the dead factories, the workers spent their time making pen-knives out of bits of machinery, or shoe-soles out of the conveyor belts, to barter them on the underground market. If you wished to procure a little flour, butter or meat from the peasants who brought these things illicitly into town, you had to have cloth or articles of some kind to exchange.

Winter was torture for the townspeople: no heating, no lighting and the ravages of famine. Children and feeble old folk died in their thousands. Typhus was carried everywhere by lice, and took a frightful toll.

**AS Level Exam-Style Question Section A (a)**

***Study Source 6 before you answer this question.***

Why is Source 6 valuable to the historian for an enquiry into the impact of War Communism in Russia in 1918–21?

Explain your answer using the source, the information given about it and your own knowledge of the historical context. (8 marks)

**Tip**

*Unsupported assertions about why a source has value won't impress: each of the reasons you give should be accompanied by some explanation.*

**ACTIVITY**
**WRITING**

Use the words in the box below to complete these sentences so that they best describe the nature and characteristics of War Communism.

| autonomy | improvisation | ideology | productivity | retrospect |
|---|---|---|---|---|
| acquisition | viable | antipathy | discriminate | |

War Communism was a label applied in ________ to the economic policies introduced in 1918.

Some historians claim that War Communism was primarily the result of the application of Marxist ________, with its deep-rooted ________ to the market economy, but others suggest that it was an ________ in the face of military emergency.

The core of War Communism was the compulsory ________ of grain from the peasantry.

Under War Communism, average labour __________ was one-third of 1913 levels.

Under War Communism, the __________ of trade unions was restricted.

The rationing system under War Communism was designed to ___________ in favour of workers.

In conditions of peace, War Communism was no longer ________.

## The Tambov rising and the Kronstadt mutiny

### The Tambov rising

The Bolshevik policy of *prodrazverstka* (grain requisitioning) caused enormous resentment in the countryside. During the Civil War, though, peasant hostility towards the Bolsheviks was to some extent kept in check by fears of a White victory and its possible consequences – above all, the return of the land seized in 1917 to landowners. But, in 1920, as the fighting wound down and a poor harvest reduced villages to near-starvation, it boiled over. By 1921, much of the countryside was in open revolt against Bolshevik rule.

The fiercest fighting took place in Tambov province, to the south of Moscow, where a 40,000-strong peasant force led by Alexander Antonov (1889–1922) waged a guerrilla campaign against the Red Army. Antonov was a former SR with a long history of militancy. Between 1909 and 1917, he was in prison for terrorist offences and he died in a shoot-out with a Cheka unit in 1922.

**SOURCE 7** From an article about events in Tambov province in 1920–21 in *Volia Rossii*, a newspaper published by Socialist Revolutionary exiles in Czechoslovakia, March 1921.

In the autumn of 1920 the Tambov peasantry revolted, and the movement developed at first so successfully that the peasants resolved to march on the city of Tambov. The army of peasants presented a striking appearance. Along the highway there were moving forward, amid clouds of dust, silently and ominously, a multitude of thousands of peasants. They had their own cavalry as well as infantry. Most of them were only armed with weapons made by themselves such as axes, pitchforks and clubs. The villages along the road welcomed the marching peasants with the ringing of church bells, and furnished them with provisions and arms.

The Bolshevik authorities at Tambov were in a panic. To their luck, however, aid arrived from neighbouring provinces, and the insurgents were forced to retreat. New punitive expeditions were organised and sent to the insurgent regions. Wholesale shootings and fires concluded the first period of the Tambov peasant uprising. That period was one of spontaneous, unorganised mass risings, without definite leadership. The second period commences from the moment when Antonov takes over leadership of the defeated insurgents. The peasants are aiding him gladly, regarding him as the avenger of their downtrodden rights, while the Bolsheviks call him a bandit but have failed to catch him.

In late 1920 Antonov discharged poorly armed insurgents, retaining only those who had either guns or rifles. His very first engagement with Bolshevik troops ended in the defeat of the latter. The first engagement was followed by others, and many of these, too, were victorious for the men of Antonov.

With the beginning of 1921 the insurgents began to form large regiments, organised according to sound military strategy under the direction and command of regular staffs. Although a Red Army of 100,000 men had been massed against Antonov by the beginning of February, the soldiers were reluctant to take the offensive against him.

The insurgents are acting with energy and precision, delivering short but telling blows.

ACTIVITY
KNOWLEDGE CHECK

**Alexander Antonov**

What can be inferred from Source 7 about the leadership qualities of Alexander Antonov?

The government response to the Tambov rising, spearheaded by the Red Army, was brutal in the extreme. Poison gas was used against the rebels and thousands of their wives and children were taken hostage. The uprisings in Tambov and elsewhere brought Russia close to paralysis. Large parts of the country were effectively out of the authorities' control. Railway transport was seriously disrupted. There was a food crisis in the towns. The Red Army was stretched to the limit. In these circumstances, Lenin was forced to start thinking about major concessions to the peasantry.

Rural discontent had its parallel in the cities. Urban protest was largely fuelled by food shortages, but there were also calls for the restoration of trade union rights, lost under War Communism, and allegations of widespread corruption within the Bolshevik ranks. Anger in the towns expressed itself mainly in the form of strikes. In February 1921, Moscow was virtually paralysed by strike action, and huge crowds of demonstrators took to the streets. In one incident, Cheka units opened fire on a crowd of strikers, killing several of them. Days later, a similar clash took place in Petrograd: a crowd of striking workers from the city's engineering factories, docks and shipyards was fired upon by soldiers. At least 30 people were killed or wounded.

### The Kronstadt mutiny

The Bolsheviks suffered a further blow in March 1921 when 10,000 sailors of the Baltic fleet based at Kronstadt mutinied in support of strikers in nearby Petrograd. The mutineers published a 15-point manifesto (sometimes called the Petropavlosk Resolution, named after the battleship on which it was drafted) that condemned Bolshevik abuses of power. The manifesto called for the legalisation of all socialist and anarchist parties, new soviet elections, rights for trade unions and an end to special privileges for senior Bolsheviks.

The Kronstadt mutiny lasted only a fortnight – it was suppressed by 50,000 Red Army troops who staged a frontal assault on the island fortress across the icebound Gulf of Finland, losing 10,000 killed in the process – but it was (from the Bolshevik point of view) a profoundly embarrassing episode. In 1917, the Kronstadt sailors had been among the Bolsheviks' strongest supporters. Trotsky had called them 'the pride and glory of the Russian Revolution'. Their mutiny in 1921 showed just how extensive disillusionment with the Bolsheviks had become.

## The economic and political results of the New Economic Policy

### The New Economic Policy

In March 1921, Lenin announced that compulsory grain requisitioning was to be abandoned. This was the first step in the introduction of the New Economic Policy (NEP). Other changes followed in piecemeal fashion over the next 18 months. The transition to the NEP was complete by the end of 1922. The overall effect of the introduction of the NEP was to create a **mixed economy** in Soviet Russia.

KEY TERM

**Mixed economy**
One in which some industries are owned and run by the government while others are privately owned and operated on the basis of the market forces of supply and demand.

The NEP had four main features:

- Compulsory grain requisitioning was replaced by a 'tax in kind'. This meant that peasants had to hand over to the state a fixed proportion of the grain they produced. Any surplus left over after this 'tax in kind' had been paid could be sold for profit on the open market. The amount of grain demanded by the state in 1921 totalled about half the amount requisitioned in 1920. In 1924, the 'tax in kind' was replaced by money payments. The abandonment of compulsory grain requisitioning took the steam out of peasant discontent.
- Under the NEP, private trading and the private ownership of small-scale businesses were legalised. Many of the privately-owned businesses that emerged were in the service sector, such as, shops, market stalls, cafés and the like, but there was also a significant amount of private manufacturing. Privately owned manufacturing companies typically produced consumer goods such as clothes and footwear.
- The 'commanding heights' of the economy, as Lenin called them, remained under state control. The 'commanding heights' included not only heavy industries like coal and steel, but also the railway network and the banking system. Foreign trade continued to be a state monopoly.
- The industries that remained under state control after 1921–22 were expected to trade at a profit. If they got into difficulties, they were not bailed out by the government. One of the consequences of this new regime was an increase in unemployment as state-run industries shed surplus workers in order to increase efficiency.

When Lenin introduced the NEP, he called it a 'retreat' and 'a peasant Brest-Litovsk' – a surrender for the sake of survival. What was surrendered in 1921–22 was socialist principle, because the NEP involved the partial restoration of capitalism in Russia. Lenin insisted, however, that the retreat would only be a temporary one, implying that, at some point in the future, the NEP would be abandoned in favour of an authentically socialist policy. But, on the issues of exactly how long the NEP would last and exactly what would replace it, he remained largely silent. These issues remained unresolved at the time of his death.

### Economic results of the NEP

- The NEP was introduced too late to prevent a major famine. In the summer of 1921, a drought in the 'Black Earth' region (southern European Russia) led to major crop failures. As a result of the requisitioning policy under War Communism, peasant households were left with no reserves of grain to fall back on. The consequence was a famine affecting 25 million people. The death toll may have reached as high as five million. 'The 1921 famine in Russia was the greatest human disaster in European history, other than those caused by war, since the Black Death', one historian (Richard Pipes) has claimed. In desperation, some people resorted to cannibalism.
- After 1921, the Soviet economy recovered strongly. By the time of Lenin's death in 1924, industrial output was rising sharply and grain production had bounced back from the catastrophically low levels of 1920–21. In both sectors of the economy, though, output in 1924 remained below pre-1914 levels.

SOURCE

Economic recovery under the NEP. (Note that these figures do not show actual quantities produced, but production in different sectors of the economy expressed as a proportion of the 1913 level of production, with 1913 production being expressed in the form of a base of 100.)

| | 1913 | 1920 | 1921 | 1922 | 1923 | 1924 | 1925 | 1926 |
|---|---|---|---|---|---|---|---|---|
| Industrial production (by value) | 100 | 14 | 20 | 26 | 39 | 46 | 76 | 108 |
| Coal production (tonnage) | 100 | 30 | 31 | 33 | 47 | 56 | 62 | 95 |
| Electricity production (kilowatt hours) | 100 | na* | 27 | 40 | 59 | 80 | 150 | 180 |
| Iron production (tonnage) | 100 | na* | 3 | 4 | 7 | 18 | 36 | 58 |
| Steel production (tonnage) | 100 | na* | 4 | 9 | 17 | 27 | 51 | 74 |
| Grain production (tonnage) | 100 | 58 | 47 | 63 | 71 | 64 | 91 | 96 |

*= not available

- Russia's economic recovery was erratic and uncertain rather than smooth and unbroken. Difficulties arose in 1923 because agriculture recovered from War Communism more quickly than industry. The price of food, relatively plentiful, fell: the price of consumer and manufactured goods, relatively scarce, rose. The result was the 'scissors crisis', so named (by Trotsky) because the lines on a graph showing trends in agricultural and industrial prices resembled a pair of scissors being opened. The government acted to correct the imbalance, pushing industrial prices down.
- The success of the NEP did not mean that the issue of how long it should last was put completely to one side. At the time of Lenin's death, a vigorous debate was taking place within the Bolshevik leadership on the question of long-term economic strategy. Bukharin, one of the leading Bolshevik economic theorists, called for the NEP and the mixed economy that arose out of it to be made permanent. An opposing view was put forward by E.A. Preobrazhensky, another prominent Bolshevik economic guru. Preobrazhensky wanted to phase out the NEP and move in the direction of socialism by expanding the state-owned industrial sector of the economy. This was to be financed by taxing the peasantry more heavily. Preobrazhensky was backed by Trotsky, whereas Stalin appeared to side with Bukharin.

SOURCE 9 Armand Hammer, an American with business interests in Russia, describing Moscow in 1921.

I had been away little more than a month, but short as the time was, I rubbed my eyes with astonishment. Was this Moscow, the city of squalor and sadness that I had left? Now the streets that had been so deserted were thronged with people. Everyone seemed in a hurry, full of purpose, with eager faces. Everywhere one saw workmen tearing down the boarding from the fronts of stores, repairing broken windows, painting, plastering. From high-piled wagons goods were being loaded into stores. Everywhere one heard the sound of hammering. My fellow-travellers, no less surprised than I, made inquiries. 'NEP, NEP' was the answer.

SOURCE 10 The Smolensk Market in Moscow, 1921.

## Political results of the NEP

One danger attached to the introduction of the NEP (from the Bolshevik point of view) was that relaxation of state control in the economic sphere would give rise to expectations of a similar relaxation in the political sphere. Lenin's response was to make it clear there would be no let-up in what he called 'iron rule'. The introduction of the NEP was accompanied by a tightening of the Bolsheviks' political grip in Russia.

- The SRs and Mensheviks, just about tolerated in the civil war era, were now suppressed. In 1921, 5,000 allegedly counter-revolutionary Mensheviks were arrested. In 1922, 34 prominent SRs were put on trial in Moscow, accused of terrorist activities: 11 of them were condemned to death.
- The Cheka, rebranded in 1922 as the GPU (the State Political Administration), enlarged its network of concentration camps for political detainees.

Another way in which the Bolsheviks made it clear there was to be no softening in 'iron rule' was a renewed onslaught on the Orthodox Church. The Orthodox Church had initially come under attack from the Bolsheviks in their first year in power. In 1917–18, the Church was separated from the state and stripped of its privileges. The pretext for the Bolsheviks' new offensive against the Church in 1921–22 was the claim that it had refused to sell its treasures to aid famine victims. Soviets were ordered to remove all precious items from churches in their localities. In many places, priests and congregations resisted. This led to clashes between congregations and the Bolshevik authorities in which up to 8,000 people were killed.

**ACTIVITY**
**KNOWLEDGE CHECK**

**The impact of the New Economic Policy**

'The introduction of the NEP brought about a swift and spectacular economic recovery in Russia - an economic miracle.' How far do you agree with this claim? Making use of Sources 8, 9 and 10, give reasons for your answer.

## The ban on factions, 1921

During the civil war, the Bolshevik leaders sometimes encouraged their followers to think of War Communism, not as a purely temporary expedient, but as part of Russia's transition to socialism. Many rank-and-file Bolsheviks were therefore dismayed and bewildered by the partial restoration of capitalism under the NEP. 'We felt as though the Revolution had been betrayed', one Bolshevik activist later recalled. Concerns of this kind were reinforced after 1921 by the emergence of a class of get-rich-quick private businessmen – the so-called 'nepmen' – who were quick to flaunt their new wealth. This they did in the bars, nightclubs and casinos which re-opened in Russia's major cities. It was a spectacle that angered dedicated Bolsheviks. Some disillusioned party members put it about that the initials NEP really stood for 'New Exploitation of the Proletariat'.

**KEY TERM**

**Faction**
An organised group within a political party or movement with its own distinctive viewpoint and agenda.

Lenin's response to criticism from within the Bolshevik ranks was to stifle it. In 1921, at the Tenth Party Congress, the establishment of **factions** within the party was banned. Violations of the ban on factions were to be punishable by expulsion from the party. Existing organised groups within the party were to be dissolved. The ban on factions brought to an end the Bolshevik culture of open and vigorous internal debate until a decision had been reached. The kind of exchanges that had seen Kamenev and Zinoviev question the wisdom of attempting to seize power in October 1917, and Bukharin opposing the acceptance of the Brest-Litovsk peace terms in 1918, became a thing of the past.

The immediate targets of the ban on factions were two organised groups that had emerged within the Bolshevik party in 1920–21: the Democratic Centralists, who deplored the increasingly bureaucratic nature of Bolshevism; and the Workers' Opposition, who disliked the way in which the return to 'one-man management' under War Communism had weakened the influence of trades unions.

**EXTEND YOUR KNOWLEDGE**

**Alexandra Kollontai (1872–1952)**
A leading figure in the Workers' Opposition movement, Kollontai was the most prominent woman in the male-dominated world of Bolshevik politics. The daughter of a Tsarist general, Kollontai was in 1917–18 People's Commissar for Social Welfare in Lenin's government. Out of favour politically after the defeat of the Workers' Opposition, she became one of the world's first female ambassadors, serving as Soviet ambassador to Norway, Mexico and Sweden. A prolific writer on women's rights and gender issues, Kollontai is best remembered as a pioneer feminist.

The ban on factions was followed by a major purge of the party's membership. On the eve of the introduction of the NEP, there were 730,000 party members but, by early 1923, this figure had shrunk to 500,000. The message to survivors of the purge was clear: the decisions of the party leadership had to be accepted without question.

**KEY TERM**

**Oligarchy**
A political system in which power rests in the hands of a very small group of people.

By 1924, the Soviet Union was an **oligarchy**. Its rulers were accountable to no-one. In the early days of Bolshevik rule, Sovnarkom was answerable to the Congress of Soviets, composed of delegates elected by city and provincial soviets, and its Central Executive Committee. Before long, however, soviet elections became a charade as Russia became a one-party state and Sovnarkom and other state institutions, such as government departments, were increasingly marginalised. Bolshevik party bodies grew in power at the expense of the institutions of the Soviet state. The Bolshevik party's Political Bureau, or Politburo, established in 1919, emerged as the key decision-making body. With the erosion of internal party democracy after the 1921 ban on factions, its decisions could not be challenged by ordinary party members.

**ACTIVITY**
**KNOWLEDGE CHECK**

**The introduction of the NEP**

Why was the New Economic Policy introduced in 1921? (Note: try to reach conclusions about the relative importance of political and economic considerations.)

# WHY WERE THE BOLSHEVIKS ABLE TO DEFEAT THEIR DOMESTIC ENEMIES IN THE RUSSIAN CIVIL WAR?

The first shots in the Russian Civil War were fired in October 1917, when army units loyal to Kerensky, the Provisional Government's chief minister, marched on Petrograd and were sent packing. Bolshevik forces also saw action in late 1917, in the Volga region of southern Russia, where an anti-Bolshevik Volunteer Army had been assembled by Generals Alexeev and Kornilov. These early clashes were, however, small-scale affairs. Descent into all-out civil war came later and owed much to two developments.

- The dissolution of the Constituent Assembly by the Bolsheviks in January 1918 outraged liberals and Socialist Revolutionaries (SRs) whose sights were set on a democratic political settlement in Russia.
- The treaty of Brest-Litovsk in March 1918 was the final straw for many of the Bolsheviks' enemies because it stripped Russia of so much territory and amounted to a national humiliation.

The Russian Civil War was one of the 20th century's most bitterly contested wars. It cost over three million people their lives. A million or more died in the fighting and more than two million as a result of disease. In addition, two million Russians left the country as political exiles.

The Russian Civil War was also an episode of bewildering complexity. The main conflict was the one between the Bolsheviks (or Reds) and the Whites, but the Red-White struggle was only part of the story: the Bolsheviks also fought against peasant (or 'Green') armies, in which SRs were often prominent, and against separatist movements.

## The Socialist Revolutionaries, national minorities and the Whites

### Socialist Revolutionaries

After the dissolution of the Constituent Assembly, the Right SR leadership fled to Samara, 500 miles to the east of Moscow. There they established an alternative government called the 'Committee of Members of the Constituent Assembly' ('**Komuch**'). Its aim was to champion the cause of what they called the 'democratic counter-revolution'.

**KEY TERM**

**Komuch**
A word made up out of the initial letters of the Russian words for 'committee' and 'constituent assembly'.

Also based in eastern Russia was the Provisional Siberian Government, a body backed by conservatives, ex-Tsarist army officers and Kadets. In September 1918, Komuch and the Provisional Siberian Government came together to form the Provisional All-Russian Government. This unlikely alliance did not last for long. In a bout of political in-fighting in late 1918, the conservatives saw off the Right SRs and expelled their leaders from Russia. This episode marked the end of the Right SRs as a significant force in Russian politics.

At no point in 1918 did the SRs in eastern Russia have a sizeable armed force of their own to deploy. They did, however, benefit from the presence in the region of the 50,000-strong Czech Legion. The Czech Legion consisted of Czech soldiers from the Austrian army who, having been taken prisoner by the Russians in the First World War, agreed to fight for them – believing that the defeat of Austria would help bring about an independent Czechoslovakia. After the Brest-Litovsk treaty, the Bolsheviks agreed to send the Czechs back to western Europe via Siberia so that they could fight with the British and French on the Western Front. On the journey down the Trans-Siberian railway, the Czechs became suspicious of the intentions of their Bolshevik escorts and overpowered them. Encouraged by Britain and France to fight against the Bolsheviks, the Czechs swiftly won control of most of western Siberia. After their initial success, however, they were weakened by mutinies and a lack of supplies, and lost effectiveness.

Left SRs were active in some of the peasant, or 'Green', armies that fought in southern and central Russia during the civil war. Some of these peasant armies, though, were freelance units concerned mainly with the defence of their locality. An example is the 15,000-strong 'Revolutionary Insurgent Army of the Ukraine' led by the anarchist Nestor Makhno (1889–1935).

### National minorities

In his 'Declaration of the Rights of the Peoples of Russia' (November 1917), Lenin promised non-Russian minorities the right to separate themselves from Russia if they wished. In practice, he was not prepared to see the resources of the national minority areas lost to the Bolshevik state. Where breakaway or separatist regimes were set up, the Bolsheviks tried to overthrow them. The Red Army fought, for example, against the Ukrainian separatist regime of Simon Petluria in 1918–20, Baltic separatists (Estonians, Latvians and Lithuanians) in 1918–19 and Transcaucasian separatists (Armenians, Georgians and Azerbaijanis) in 1920–21.

### The Whites

The White armies were commanded by former chiefs of the Tsarist armed forces. Ex-Tsarist army officers provided the backbone of the White armies.

The Whites were political conservatives:

- They were strong believers in property rights. Peasants were left in no doubt that a White victory would mean the restoration of land they had seized in 1917 to its former owners.
- They were nationalists who believed in a Russia 'Great, United and Indivisible' – in other words, they wanted to re-establish Russia with its pre-1917 borders. They were unwilling to make any concessions to national minorities. This was a problem, because in some of the areas in which the Whites were based such as the Ukraine and Transcaucasia, separatist feeling was strong.

- Some of the White generals were monarchists, but others favoured some sort of military dictatorship.
- Their hatred of Bolshevism was intense. They despised the Bolsheviks as traitors, atheists and hijackers of private property.

The three main White armies were: the forces led by Admiral Kolchak in Siberia and the Urals; the Armed Forces of Southern Russia (AFSR), commanded by General Anton Denikin and, later, by Baron Wrangel; and, smallest of the three, the North-Western Army headed by General Nikolai Yudenich.

## Trotsky and the Red Army

At the time of the October Revolution, the Bolsheviks had a miscellaneous collection of armed men at their disposal, but no properly organised army. As full-scale civil war loomed, their first thought was to create an all-volunteer 'Socialist Guard' with elected officers. The hope was that such a force would sweep all before it by virtue of its revolutionary enthusiasm. Lenin soon became impatient with this kind of idealistic thinking. In March 1918, Trotsky was appointed People's Commissar for War and, with Lenin's backing, proceeded to build a 'Red Army' on traditional lines.

- The election of officers was scrapped and replaced by an old-fashioned system of appointment from above. This enabled Trotsky to appoint ex-Tsarist officers ('military specialists', the Bolsheviks called them) to senior positions in the Red Army. Some ex-Tsarist officers joined the Red Army willingly. Others volunteered because they had no other way of making a living. Many were **conscripted** and prevented from deserting by the threat of reprisals against their families if they did so.
- The Bolsheviks needed the 'military specialists', but did not fully trust them. Trotsky kept them under control by establishing a system of 'dual command', under which every ex-Tsarist commander was supervised by a political commissar, or minder, who was a Bolshevik of proven loyalty. Every order issued by a military commander had to be counter-signed by the political commissar before it could come into force.
- Compulsory military service for the mass of the population was reintroduced in May 1918. Discipline in the Red Army was ferocious. Deserters and those guilty of unjustified retreat were liable to execution.

By the end of 1918, there were one million men in the Red Army. By 1921, this figure had risen to over five million. It was not, however, quite as formidable a force as these figures might suggest. Some of its units were poorly trained and equipped. Desertion was an ongoing problem, despite the death penalty for offenders: in mid-1919, for example, at harvest time, men were deserting at the rate of 250,000 a month. The Red Army was also ravaged by disease: in 1920, nearly one-third of its men contracted typhus.

**KEY TERM**

**Conscription**
A practice under which governments compel citizens to undertake military service, with penalties for refusal. In the Russian Civil War, both Bolsheviks and Whites regarded themselves as legitimate governments, and both therefore felt entitled to impose compulsory military service on people in the areas they controlled.

**SOURCE 11** From a report from a political commissar fighting with a Red Army division in southern Russia, May 1919.

I may say that as far as politics goes the mood of the Red Army men is generally very good. There are no politically unreliable units in the division. The Red Army men show a tremendous interest in newspapers, but unfortunately papers only reach us very irregularly.

I must tell you our strength has come down to 80–100 infantry per regiment instead of the former strength of 2,000. Spanish influenza and typhus have accounted for many of the losses and we have suffered many casualties in battles.

The men are without footwear or clothing, since it is impossible to offer them any articles of uniform. Because of that they have refused to advance, making their demands as follows: 'first of all put some clothes on me, and after that if I refuse, you can shoot me if you wish'. In the 203rd Regiment alone there are 600 men who are barefoot.

They are simply in rags - there is no other word to describe them. Faced with the lack of uniform they requisition things from the local people, sometimes robbing them, and that poisons people's minds against us. I have shouted and made a great fuss to get someone to attend to this, for there is neither tobacco, nor sugar, nor fat bacon, to say nothing of uniform and forage for horses.

Trotsky's personal contribution to the Bolshevik victory in the civil war was immense. He was not a great battlefield commander, but he built the Red Army out of nothing and moulded it into an effective fighting force. In addition, he was an inspirational figure, moving from front to front in his famous armoured train, rallying Red Army units with rousing speeches. He was supported by some gifted generals, notably Mikhail Tukhachevsky, a former Tsarist officer turned Bolshevik; Semyon Budenny, a farm labourer before being conscripted into the Tsarist army in 1903 and rising through the ranks; and Mikhail Frunze, a hardened Bolshevik activist who, as a 20-year-old, had been sentenced to ten years hard labour for his part in the 1905 Moscow uprising.

ACTIVITY
KNOWLEDGE CHECK

**The Red Army's weaknesses**

'The Red Army's main weakness in the civil war was low morale among its soldiers.' To what extent does the evidence of Source 11 support this claim?

## The geography of the civil war

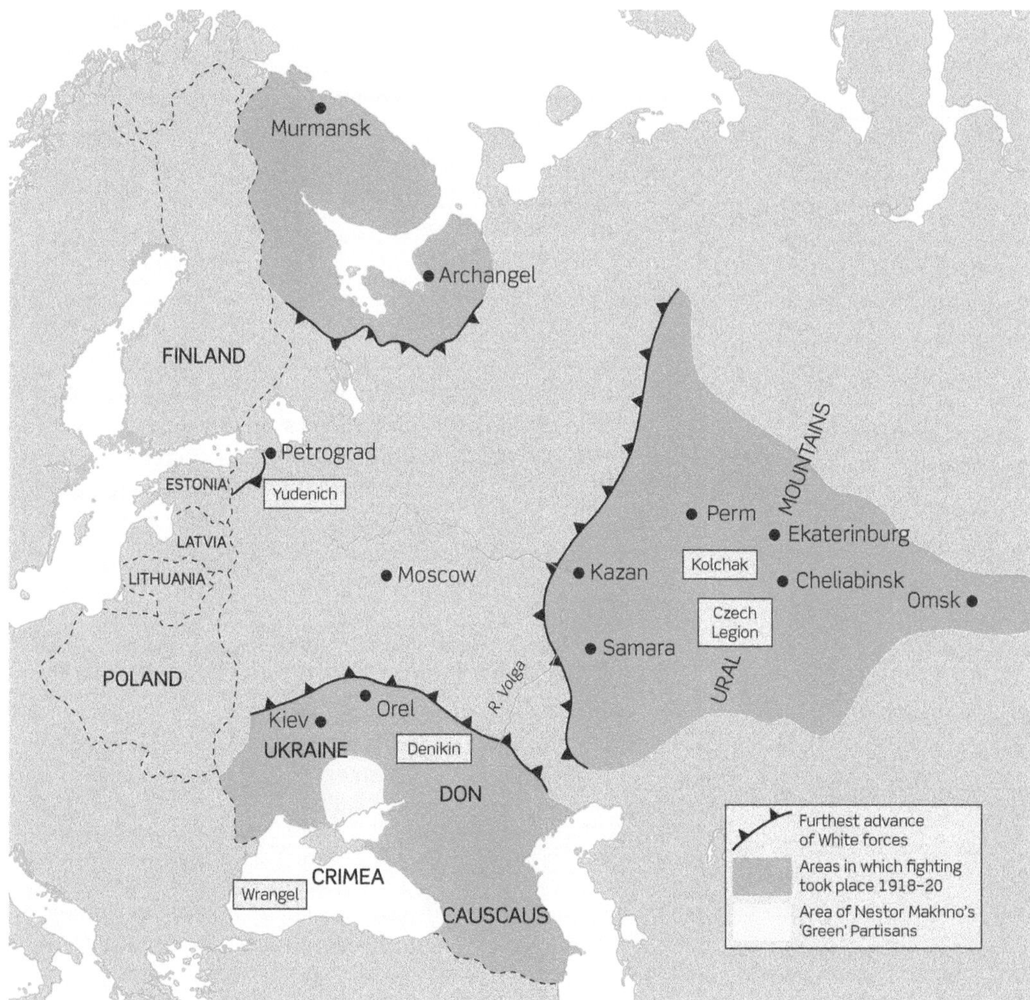


**Figure 4.1**: The Russian Civil War.

The Bolsheviks were in more or less secure control of northern and central European Russia throughout the Civil War. Their geographical position gave them a number of advantages over their enemies.

- The Bolsheviks controlled the most densely populated parts of Russia. In 1918–19, Bolshevik-held territory contained some 70 million people compared with approximately 20 million in the White-controlled areas. This mattered, because the Bolsheviks and the Whites both relied on compulsory military service to raise their armies. The Bolsheviks had a larger pool of manpower available to them than the Whites. One consequence of this was that, in major battles, the Red Army had a significant numerical advantage over the Whites.
- Russia's main engineering factories were located within territory controlled by the Bolsheviks, notably the giant Putilov works in Petrograd, giving them the capacity to manufacture armaments. The Whites, by contrast, relied heavily on handouts from foreign powers. In addition, almost the whole of the munitions stockpile of the old Tsarist army fell into Bolshevik hands in 1917–18. One estimate suggests that it amounted to 2.5 million rifles, 12,000 artillery pieces and 28 million shells.
- The Bolsheviks controlled the hub of the Russian railway network, which radiated outwards from Moscow. This enabled the Bolsheviks to rush reinforcements to any battlefront on which they were seriously threatened. The Whites, in contrast, had to operate around the circumference of Bolshevik-held territory. Communications between the different White armies were limited, so it was virtually impossible for their commanders to co-ordinate their activities.

## The defeat of Kolchak, Denikin and Yudenich

### Kolchak

Admiral Alexander Kolchak (1873–1920) was a noted polar explorer and a former commander of Russia's Black Sea Fleet. In late 1918, he took over the leadership of White forces in the Urals-Siberia region, with the title of 'Supreme Ruler of Russia'. As a politician and a general he had serious flaws: he was a poor administrator, he was thin-skinned and temperamental; and he had no experience of land warfare. He nevertheless built up, with British assistance, a fighting force of some 150,000 men, which in the spring of 1919 went on to the offensive and pushed the Red Army back more than 250 miles. But Kolchak's armies were unable to keep up the momentum: in the summer of 1919, they were broken and driven back by a determined Red Army counter-attack. In early 1920, retreating eastwards along the Trans-Siberian Railway, Kolchak fell into the hands of the Bolsheviks and was executed.

### Denikin

General Anton Denikin (1872–1947) came to the fore after the deaths of the first two White commanders (Kornilov and Alexeev) in southern Russia. Denikin's social origins were humble and his political outlook was, by the standards of other White generals, relatively liberal. In late 1918, he had an army of 150,000 men at his disposal. There were, however, tensions within his forces. The Armed Forces of Southern Russia (AFSR), the name by which Denikin's armies were known after January 1919, contained 40,000 Don Cossacks (descendants of runaway serfs who settled in the Don region from the 15th century onwards and developed a distinct identity) who were principally concerned with the defence of their homeland and cared little for the fate of Russia as a whole.

Despite these tensions, the AFSR were (to begin with) highly successful. In the summer and autumn of 1919 they advanced on a broad front, reaching Orel, only 250 miles from Moscow, in October. They were then rolled backwards by a massive Red Army counter-attack. In March 1920, after retreat had degenerated into panic and collapse, Denikin resigned his command and went into exile. He was replaced by Baron Peter Wrangel (1878–1928).

In 1920, the remnants of the AFSR were bottled up in the Crimean peninsula. Though heavily outnumbered by the Bolsheviks, they held out under Wrangel's leadership for nine months before admitting defeat. In November 1920, 150,000 civilian and military refugees, Wrangel among them, were evacuated from the Crimea in a fleet of Allied warships.

### Yudenich

General Nikolai Yudenich's 15,000-strong North-Western Army was the smallest of the White forces. In 1919, it advanced out of its bases in Estonia and, in October (at about the same time as Denikin reached Orel), came within sight of Petrograd. It was then defeated by a much larger Bolshevik force commanded by Trotsky. By the time it was threatened by Yudenich, Petrograd did not have the strategic importance it had once had, as Lenin had made Moscow the Bolshevik capital in March 1918.

SOURCE

Reminiscences of Ekaterina Olitskaia, who in 1919 was a young SR sympathiser living in the southern Russian city of Kursk.

The rumours concerning Kolchak and Yudenich were followed by rumours of an offensive by General Denikin. Denikin's army was moving towards us, and moving incredibly fast. The Communist press talked about the outrages perpetrated by the Whites, about their ties to foreign invaders, about the estate and factory owners who followed the Denikin army, about the return of the land and factories to the capitalists, and about atrocities, floggings, hangings and anti-Jewish pogroms. All this I could believe, but they also said that the SRs were supporting General Denikin and his army. This I absolutely refused to believe.

SOURCE

Paul Milyukov, the Kadet leader, commenting on Denikin's rule in southern Russia in *Russia Today and Tomorrow*, published in 1922. Milyukov was in southern Russia in 1918 acting as a political adviser to Generals Kornilov and Alexeev, but went into foreign exile in early 1919.

The newcomers who joined Denikin's army at the time of its growing success had no scruples against making up for their mockingly low pay by speculating with army supplies or even by looting the population. Plunder, not only by individuals, but by whole units, became almost a profession. Bribery, drunken orgies and every kind of violence became customary, especially in the large cities and among the chief commanders.

But this is not all. Former landowners were also coming back with the army. Each one endeavoured to return to his own former estate, which had been taken by the peasants. Occasionally the landlord was intent on revenge for the mistreatment or murder of some members of his family by the peasants. His return was then coupled with relentless reprisals. This was enough for the peasant to come to the conclusion that the estates of the nobles were to be taken from him by the new power.

In a civil war everything depends on the state of mind of the population living under competing systems of government. We have seen how favourable that state of mind was for the liberators and how much it changed owing to the utterly bad tactics of the White armies.

**A Level Exam-Style Question Section A**

***Study Sources 12 and 13 before you answer this question.***

How far could the historian make use of Sources 12 and 13 together to investigate the reasons for the failure of the Whites in the Russian Civil War?

Explain your answer using both sources, the information given about them and your own knowledge of the historical context. (20 marks)

**Tip**

*Since you are expected to write for 45 minutes in response to questions of this type, your answer needs to be clearly structured around three components: an introduction offering an overall judgement on the extent of the usefulness of the sources; the main body of the answer giving reasons for the usefulness and limitations of the sources as evidence of the Whites' failure; and a conclusion.*

## THINKING HISTORICALLY Change (6a)

**Separately and together**

Below are some of the different types of historical writing that historians may identify.

| Political history | Economic history | Social history |
|---|---|---|
| Religious history | Military history | International history |

These are thematic histories, where a historian focuses on a particular aspect of change. For example, an economic history of Nicholas II's Russia would focus on the growth of industry, railway building and developments in agriculture, whereas a political history would focus, among other things, on support for, and opposition to, the Tsarist regime.

Work in groups.

**1** Write a definition for each type of history.

Here are some events in the history of Lenin's Russia, 1917–14.

| 1918 Treaty of Brest-Litovsk | 1918 Decision taken to employ ex-Tsarist officers in the Red Army | 1918 War Communism introduced | 1921 War Communism abandoned in favour of the NEP | 1921 Intensification of Bolshevik persecution of the Orthodox Church |
|---|---|---|---|---|

Answer the following.

**2** From what different thematic perspectives could the Treaty of Brest-Litovsk be studied?

**3 a)** How would an analysis by a military historian of the decision to employ ex-Tsarist officers in the Red Army differ from that of a political historian?

**b)** How would an analysis by a religious historian of Bolshevik persecution of the Orthodox Church differ from that of a political historian?

**4** What were the social and economic consequences of the introduction of the policy of War Communism?

**5** Was the NEP introduced primarily for political reasons?

Work in pairs.

**6** Write a statement attacking 'thematic history'.

**7** Write three statements defending 'thematic history'.

**8** Explain why 'thematic history' is written.

**ACTIVITY KNOWLEDGE CHECK**

**Reasons why the Bolsheviks were successful in the Civil War**

Why were the Bolsheviks able to defeat their domestic enemies in the Russian Civil War?

(Suggestion: organise your ideas under three main headings:

**a)** the Bolsheviks' advantages in terms of geography and resources

**b)** other Bolsheviks strengths, including the contribution of Trotsky

**c)** the military and political weaknesses of the White Russians.)

Make use of Sources 12 and 13 in your answer.

# FOR WHAT REASONS, AND WITH WHAT RESULTS, DID FOREIGN POWERS INTERVENE IN RUSSIA IN THE CIVIL WAR ERA?

## Reasons, nature and extent of intervention

### Reasons

The Bolsheviks opened peace talks with Germany in November 1917. A cease-fire to enable negotiations to take place on a full peace treaty was agreed in December. These developments dismayed Russia's principal wartime allies, Britain and France. It seemed certain not only that a separate peace between Russia and Germany was imminent, but also that Germany was about to make huge gains of both territory and influence at Russia's expense. This prospect alarmed the Allies for a number of reasons.

- With Russia out of the war, Germany would no longer have to fight a war on two fronts, but could concentrate its forces on the Western Front. In 1917, the effectiveness of France's armies on the Western Front had been undermined by large-scale mutinies and American forces were still to arrive in significant numbers: as a result, it was far from certain that the Allies would be able to withstand an all-out German offensive.
- There appeared to be every chance that Germany's gains at Russia's expense would include access to the economic resources of the Ukraine and Transcaucasia (coal, oil and iron ore). This would greatly enhance Germany's economic power and its ability to continue fighting.
- Between 1914 and 1917, Russia received sizeable amounts of military aid from its allies. There were huge armaments and supply dumps in the Arctic ports of Archangel and Murmansk, and at Vladivostok on the Pacific. If these were seized by the Germans, it would tip the military balance further in their direction.

Discussions among the Allies about intervention in Russia began in late 1917. The first Allied troops arrived in Russia in the spring of 1918. The objectives of Allied intervention at this stage were, in descending order of importance: to establish in Russia a government willing to reopen an Eastern Front against Germany; to deny Germany access to Russia's economic resources; and to prevent Allied supply dumps falling into German hands.

The original case for Allied intervention in Russia disappeared when the war with Germany ended in November 1918. Allied forces were not, however, immediately withdrawn. Allied politicians had different reasons for wanting a continued military presence in Russia.

- A small minority, headed by Winston Churchill, War Secretary in the British Cabinet, wanted to fight an ideological crusade against communism. Churchill regarded Bolshevism as a contagious disease that had to be eradicated before it spread throughout Europe. 'It is not a creed', he declared. 'It is a pestilence.'
- There were economic reasons for intervention. France had economic interests in the Ukraine it wanted to protect. Britain was intent on retaining control of its supply dumps at Archangel and Murmansk. Japan aimed to profit from Russia's difficulties by carving out an economic sphere of influence in eastern Siberia.
- The USA felt that it had a humanitarian obligation to ensure that the Czech Legion was safely evacuated from Russia.

### Nature

Allied intervention after November 1918 was a half-hearted affair, reflecting the uncertainty and differences of opinion about its purposes. The troops of the most reluctant interventionist power, the USA, were more or less under orders to avoid involvement in combat. French forces were withdrawn from southern Russia in early 1919, only a few months after they had landed. The Japanese, primarily concerned with furthering their own economic interests, confined themselves to Russia's Pacific coast and shunned contact with the Bolsheviks.

Britain was by far the most active of the interventionist powers. Four hundred British soldiers were killed in action in Russia in 1918–20. Three Victoria Crosses were awarded. In addition, Britain made supplies worth £100 million available to the Whites. Through incompetence and corruption some of these supplies found their way into Bolshevik hands. General Knox, the British military representative in Siberia, received a letter purportedly written by Trotsky thanking him for his assistance in equipping the Red Army.

### Extent

In late 1918, there were over 200,000 foreign troops on Russian soil. Their impact on the outcome of the civil war was, however, limited. There were few direct clashes between the interventionist forces and the Red Army. The interventionist forces were mostly occupied in guarding supply dumps, patrolling railway lines and occupying towns in areas outside of the battle zones.

Allied forces were concentrated in three main areas: Murmansk and Archangel in the Arctic, where Britain took the lead; the Ukraine and Crimea, where the French were in charge; and eastern Siberia, where there was an uneasy partnership between the Americans and the Japanese.

**SOURCE**

**14** Allied forces in Russia, 1918–22.

| Region | Nationality | Numbers | Date of arrival | Date of departure |
|---|---|---|---|---|
| White Sea (Archangel-Murmansk) | British | 10,000 | March 1918 | October 1919 |
| | American | 5,000 | August 1918 | July 1919 |
| | French, Canadian, Italian, Serbian | small detachments | mid-1918 | September 1919 |
| Baltic | British | naval squadron | December 1918 | March 1920 |
| Siberia | Czech Legion | 55,000 | May 1918 | April 1920 |
| | American | 12,000 | August 1918 | January 1920 |
| | British | 1,000 | August 1918 | November 1919 |
| | Japanese | 65,000 | April 1918 | October 1922 |
| South (Crimea, Ukraine, Transcaucasia) | French | 10,000 | December 1918 | April 1919 |
| | Greek | 30,000 | December 1918 | April 1919 |
| | Romanian | 30,000 | December 1918 | April 1919 |
| | Polish | 3,000 | December 1918 | April 1919 |
| | British | 1,000 | August 1918 | December 1919 |

## The impact of war weariness and the lack of support in the west for intervention

In none of the major interventionist powers was there any real appetite for a no-holds-barred fight with Bolshevik Russia. Churchill, agitating for Lenin's regime to be strangled at birth, was an isolated figure.

Woodrow Wilson, the American President, was no friend of communism as an ideology and was angered by what he saw as Russia's treachery at Brest-Litovsk. He nevertheless took the view that Russia should be left to settle its affairs in its own way: he approved intervention only for the limited purpose of protecting supply dumps and rescuing the Czech Legion. Similarly, Georges Clemenceau, the French premier, was strongly anti-communist in outlook but, as a hard-nosed realist, never gave serious consideration to the idea of an ideologically motivated assault on Bolshevism. Clemenceau maintained that any threat Lenin's Russia posed to western Europe was best contained by the creation of a strong Poland on its western border. In Britain, meanwhile, Churchill's ideas were dismissed by Prime Minister David Lloyd George, who argued that Britain could not afford to intervene in Russia on the scale needed to exert a decisive influence on the course of events. He was backed by his Chancellor of the Exchequer, who at the end of the war in 1918 was looking for big cuts in public spending.

The state of public opinion contributed to the reluctance of western political leaders to be dragged too deeply into Russia's internal affairs. In the USA, the end of the war against Germany was followed by calls in the press and in Congress for the withdrawal of all American troops from Russia. A Senate motion in February 1919 demanding an immediate pull-out was defeated by only the narrowest of margins. Wilson acknowledged that the continued presence of American troops in Russia after the November 1918 armistice was 'very unpopular'. In Britain and France, Clemenceau and Lloyd George were conscious of the war-weariness of their fellow-citizens. Both men also led countries with powerful and well-organised labour movements within which there was a good deal of sympathy for the Bolshevik cause. In 1919, left-wingers in Britain started a 'Hands Off Russia' campaign, which enjoyed a notable success in 1920 when London dockers refused to load a ship, the *Jolly George*, with weapons destined for use by White Russian forces.

The end of Allied intervention in Russia was hastened by the unwillingness of the troops sent there to engage in combat. In early 1919, one of the commanders of French land forces in southern Russia noted that 'our men and even our officers are very reluctant to advance into Russia'. An American officer reported, in June 1919, that members of the small American expeditionary force sent to Archangel and Murmansk were in a state of near-mutinous resentment at being forced to meddle in Russia's internal affairs. Morale was no better among British forces in the Arctic region. In September 1919, two detachments of Royal Marines refused to go into battle when ordered to do so. There were also small-scale mutinies on British warships.

## The end of intervention

It is not hard to understand why the Allies were interested in regime change in Russia in early 1918: they were facing a critical military situation in western Europe and thought that the re-opening of an anti-German front in eastern Europe by a friendly Russian government would relieve the pressure on them. The continued presence of Allied troops on Russian soil after the November 1918 armistice is a different matter. Allied intervention in Russia in the post-war period was confused, unco-ordinated and unpopular. It was also counter-productive, in that it allowed Bolshevik propaganda in Russia to depict Lenin and his associates as patriotic defenders of the homeland against foreign invaders and to portray the Whites as tools of foreign capitalism. By early 1920, Allied intervention in Russia was effectively over, though financial assistance to the Whites continued for a little longer.

ACTIVITY
KNOWLEDGE CHECK

**The Allies and the Whites**

In what ways does Source 15 give a misleading impression of the relationship between the interventionist powers and the White Russian forces?

SOURCE 15

A poster produced in 1919 by the Bolshevik poster artist Viktor Deni. It depicts the White generals – Denikin (left), Kolchak (centre) and Yudenich (right) – and the interventionist powers.

The withdrawal of the Allies did not bring Lenin's troubles entirely to an end. In 1920, Russia faced a further foreign incursion when it was attacked by Poland.

The Russo-Polish war arose out of arrangements made at the 1919 **Paris Peace Conference**. The peacemakers were committed to re-establishing Poland as an independent state, but were not in a position to fix its borders with Russia because Russia was not invited to the peace conference. They did recommend a border, known as the Curzon Line, but it failed to satisfy the ambitions of Pilsudski, the Polish leader. Pilsudski laid claim to large tracts of territory to the east of the Curzon line on historical grounds. In April 1920, Poland, intent on eastwards expansion, attacked Russia.

The 1920 Russo-Polish war was a see-saw affair. Initially, Polish forces advanced deep into the Ukraine, capturing Kiev. They were then driven back to the outskirts of Warsaw by a spectacular Red Army counter-attack. This was followed by a crushing Polish victory outside Warsaw – the so-called 'miracle of the Vistula' – that forced the Red Army into headlong retreat. In October 1920, Russia agreed to a cease-fire and, under the subsequent Treaty of Riga (1921), ceded more than 30,000 square miles of territory on its eastern border to Poland.

The borders of Lenin's Russia after the civil war differed significantly from those of Nicholas II's Russia. Finland, Estonia, Latvia, Lithuania and Poland were now fully independent states. The Bolsheviks had, however, succeeded in regaining control of the Ukraine, Transcaucasia and Siberia.

## SOVIET RUSSIA IN 1924

At the time of Lenin's death in 1924, the Soviet Union was a highly centralised and repressive one-party state. The rights and freedoms guaranteed to the citizens of Russia by the Provisional Government in early 1917 had either disappeared or been seriously eroded. On the other hand, the economy, thanks to the NEP, was growing. Standards of living were rising, though from a very low base.

In the years 1917–21, Lenin's workload as head of government was enormous. It took its toll on his health. From mid-1921 onwards, he was no longer capable of a full day's work. In May 1922, he suffered a major stroke which left the right side of his body paralysed and he also had difficulty speaking. He made a recovery of sorts, but it was slow and incomplete. In December 1922 and March 1923 he had further strokes. In the last year of his life he was an invalid, living at a country house outside Moscow. He died in January 1924 following another stroke.

Lenin left behind a number of major unsolved problems. One was the future of the NEP. Another was the amount of power wielded by the fast-growing army of Communist Party officials and bureaucrats headed by Stalin, appointed General Secretary of the Party in 1922. Above all, though, there was the problem of who would succeed Lenin as leader. In his so-called 'political testament', drafted in December 1922, Lenin made it clear that he wanted to be succeeded by a collective leadership and not by any one individual. But he no longer possessed the drive and energy needed to impose his wishes on his Communist Party colleagues. His death was followed by a prolonged leadership struggle involving Trotsky, Stalin, Zinoviev, Kamenev and Bukharin. Stalin emerged triumphant, going on to become one of the most bloodstained rulers in modern history.

### KEY TERM

**The Paris Peace Conference**
A meeting of representatives of the Allied powers, headed by Britain, France and the USA, held in January 1919. Its purpose was to decide what peace terms were to be imposed on the Allies' defeated enemies (Germany, Austria, Hungary, Turkey and Bulgaria). Bolshevik Russia was not invited to the peace conference because the Allies did not recognise the Bolsheviks as the legitimate rulers of Russia.

The Paris peace-makers decided in 1919 to create an independent Poland out of (i) territory formerly belonging to Germany and Austria, and (ii) former Russian territory that had been taken by Germany under the 1918 Treaty of Brest-Litovsk. The absence of Russia from the peace conference meant that the borders of newly independent Poland and Russia could not be decided by international agreement.

### AS Level Exam-Style Question Section B

To what extent were the weaknesses of their opponents responsible for the survival of the Bolshevik government in the years 1917–24? (20 marks)

**Tip**

*With this type of question about causes, devote around a third of your answer to the cause given in the question and around two-thirds to other, unstated, causes.*

## EXTEND YOUR KNOWLEDGE

### Lenin and world revolution

Allied intervention was an ineffective attempt by the outside world to influence the course of events in Russia. Under Lenin, there was a parallel attempt by Russia, also ineffective, to influence the course of events in the outside world. As Russia's head of government, one of Lenin's main priorities was to bring about communist revolutions elsewhere in Europe. It was a priority in part because the Bolsheviks were committed in principle to the overthrow of capitalism on a world-wide basis, but mostly because Lenin believed that Bolshevism in Russia could only survive if communist revolutions took place in the industrialised countries of western Europe. 'It is the absolute truth that without a German revolution we are doomed', he told a Communist Party Congress in 1918.

As a Marxist, Lenin assumed that industrial workers were natural or instinctive communists, whereas peasants, strongly attached to the idea of private property, were not. This assumption gave rise to another: that the position of communist regimes in industrialised countries with large proletariats would be secure, but that of similar regimes in peasant countries was bound to be insecure. Lenin's aim, therefore, was to establish solidly based communist regimes in industrialised countries like Britain and Germany which would then prop up his own embattled regime in peasant Russia.

In 1919, the Communist International, usually referred to as Comintern, was founded in Moscow. To outward appearance, it was a free and equal association of communist parties from different parts of the world. In practice, it was the instrument through which the Bolsheviks tried to incite revolution in western Europe. Lavishly financed, Comintern initially had some success, with Soviet republics being formed in 1919 in Hungary and Bavaria but neither survived for long. Capitalism proved more resilient than Lenin expected. In the 1920s, as it became clear that communism in Russia could survive in the absence of revolutions in western Europe, Comintern lost its importance.

## ACTIVITY
SUMMARY

**Civil War and Bolshevik rule in Russia, 1917–24**

1 During the civil war era, the Bolsheviks faced enemies of differing importance at different times. Construct a table containing a set of notes:
- Germany
- the Czech Legion
- Kolchak
- Denikin
- Yudenich
- Poland,

showing the date at which each of these enemies posed its most serious threat to the Bolsheviks and the way in which the Bolsheviks removed or overcame each of these threats.

2 Write two or three sentences on each of the following terms, explaining its meaning in the context of economic life in Lenin's Russia:
- Vesenkha
- workers' control
- one-man management
- *prodrazverstka*
- tax in kind
- 'commanding heights'
- nepmen.

3 Some historians have claimed that Bolshevik ruthlessness and brutality in the civil war era was an unavoidable response to the counter-revolutionary activities of the regime's opponents. Construct a two-column table detailing arguments that could be used to support this claim and arguments that could be used to challenge it.

## WIDER READING

There are concise accounts of the years 1917–24 in:

Fitzpatrick, S. *The Russian Revolution*, Oxford University Press, third edition (2008), chapters 3 and 4.

Smith, S.A. *The Russian Revolution: A Very Short Introduction*, Oxford University Press (2002), chapters 2–5

For the military aspects of the civil war, there is:

Bullock, D. *The Russian Civil War, 1918–22*, Osprey Publishing (2008)

and a fuller treatment in:

Mawdsley, E. *The Russian Civil War*, Birlinn Publishing, new edition (2008)

A sense of what living through the Russian Civil War entailed for ordinary people can be gained from two novels:

Bulgakov, M. *The White Guard*, Collins (1967)

Pasternak, B. *Doctor Zhivago*, Collins (1958)

For specialist, but accessible and concise, treatments of the Russian economy in 1917–24 see:

Davies, R.W. *Soviet Economic Development from Lenin to Khrushchev*, Cambridge University Press, (1998), chapters 3 and 4

Nove, A. *An Economic History of the USSR*, Penguin Books (1969), chapters 2–5

The *Seventeen Moments in Soviet History* website at www.soviethistory.macalester.edu has a range of material relating to the introduction of the NEP.

# Preparing for your AS Level Paper 2 exam

## Advance planning

1. Draw up a timetable for your revision and try to keep to it. Spread your timetable over a number of weeks, and aim to cover four or five topics each week.
2. Spend longer on topics which you have found difficult, and revise them several times.
3. Above all, do not try to limit your revision by attempting to 'question spot'. Try to be confident about all aspects of your Paper 2 work, because this will ensure that you have a choice of questions in Section B.

## Paper 2 overview:

| AS Paper 2 | Time: 1 hour 30 minutes | |
|---|---|---|
| Section A | Answer 1 compulsory two-part sources question | 8+12 marks = 20 marks |
| Section B | Answer 1 question from a choice of 3 | 20 marks |
| | **Total marks =** | **40 marks** |

You should familiarise yourself with the layout of the paper by looking at the examples published by Edexcel. The questions for each section are followed by eight pages of lined paper where you should write your answer.

## Section A question

Each of the two parts of the question will focus on one of the two contemporary sources provided. The sources together will total around 300 words. The (a) question, worth 8 marks, will be in the form of 'Why is Source 1 useful for an enquiry into …?' The (b) question, worth 12 marks, will be in the form of 'How much weight do you give the evidence of Source 2 for an enquiry into …?' In both your answers you should address the value of the content of the source, and then its nature, origin and purpose. Finally, you should use your own knowledge of the context of the source to assess its value.

## Section B questions

These questions ask you to reach a judgement on an aspect of the topic studied. The questions will have the form, for example, of 'How far…', 'To what extent…' or 'How accurate is it to say…'. The questions can deal with historical concepts such as cause, consequence, change, continuity, similarity, difference and significance. You should consider the issue raised in the question, consider other relevant issues, and then conclude with an overall judgement.

The timescale of the questions could be as short as a single year or even a single event (an example from Paper 2C.2 could be, 'To what extent was Russia's involvement in the First World War responsible for the fall of the Provisional Government in 1917?'). The timescale could be longer depending on the historical event or process being examined, but questions are likely to be shorter than the those set for Sections A and B in Paper 1.

## Use of time

This is an issue which you should discuss with your teachers and fellow students, but here are some suggestions for you.

1. Do not write solidly for 45 minutes on each question. For Section A it is essential that you have a clear understanding of the content of each source, the points being made, and the nature, origin and purpose of each source. You might decide to spend up to ten minutes reading the sources and drawing up your plan, and 35 minutes writing your answer.
2. For Section B answers you should spend a few minutes working out what the question is asking you to do, and drawing up a plan of your answer before you begin to write your response.

# Preparing for your AS Level exams

## Paper 2: AS Level sample answers with comments

### Section A

Part A requires you to:

- identify key points in the source and explain them
- deploy your own knowledge of the context in which events took place
- make appropriate comments about the author/origin/purpose of the source.

***Study Source 5 (page 294) before you answer this question.***

*Why is Source 5 valuable to the historian for an enquiry into opposition to Tsarism before 1905?*

*Explain your answer using the source, the information given about it and your own knowledge of the historical context. (8 marks)*

#### Average student answer

This source is valuable because it tells us about the outlook of one element in the opposition to Tsarism before 1905, namely the middle-class liberals. The League of Liberation was formed in 1904 to represent the views of liberals associated with the zemstva. The leading figure in the League of Liberation was Paul Milyukov.

'Own knowledge' is used here to expand on the information contained in the source, but some of it is inaccurate and it doesn't relate clearly to the source's value for the specified enquiry.

One valuable thing the source tells us is that middle-class liberals before 1905 were not calling for the introduction of reforms by the Tsarist regime but rather for its abolition. The Union's programme suggests the regime would never grant basic freedoms because to do so would be 'utterly incompatible with the autocratic character of the Russian monarchy'. This indicates that liberals had no belief in the capacity of the regime to reform itself – not surprisingly, because Nicholas II in 1894 had described the hopes of zemstvo liberals as 'senseless dreams'.

This paragraph offers an inference from the content of the source about liberal attitudes to Tsarism and its capacity to reform itself, which is valid though not highly penetrating.

The source also indicates what kind of Russia liberals wanted to see after the abolition of Tsarism. They wanted a 'constitutional regime' – a Russia equipped with a constitution that would impose limits on the power of the government. Furthermore, liberals wanted 'extensive democracy' – a political system in which everyone had the right to vote in elections to parliament and the ballot was secret. Lastly, liberals wanted to see improvements in the lives of 'the toiling masses'. What is said on this point is vague, but it can be inferred that liberals did not see socialist measures involving the nationalisation of industries as part of the solution to Russia's 'social-economic problems'.

A positive here is the selection and explanation, using own knowledge, of key points from the source. However, the commentary in this paragraph, as in the preceding ones, focuses entirely on the content of the source. There is no reasoning based on the source's origins and nature.

#### Verdict

This is an average response because:

- it does not focus tightly on the reasons why the source is valuable for the specified inquiry
- it lacks reasoning based on the nature and purpose of the source.
- it doesn't offer an overall judgment on the source's value for this enquiry.

Use the feedback on this response to rewrite it, making as many improvements as you can.

# Paper 2: AS Level sample answers with comments

## Section A

Part B requires you to:

- interrogate the source
- draw reasoned inferences
- deploy your own knowledge to interpret the material in its context
- make a judgement about the value (weight) of the source.

***Study Source 9 (page 301) before you answer this question.***

*How much weight do you give to the evidence of Source 9 for an enquiry into responses to Bloody Sunday (January 1905) in Russia? Explain your answer using the source, the information given about it and your own knowledge of the historical context. (12 marks)*

### Average student answer

The main value of the source lies in what it tells us about peasant reactions to Bloody Sunday. It implies that before 1905 the peasantry respected the tsar but turned against him as a result of Bloody Sunday. There may be some element of truth in this – the tsar, for example, believed that peasants looked up to him as their 'little father'. However, if peasant attitudes to the tsar had changed drastically in January 1905, an immediate upsurge in peasant protest might have been expected – but large-scale disorder in the countryside only broke out towards the end of the year. And it seems likely that these disorders were caused by land hunger. This is a reason for doubting the source's account.

This paragraph contains an inference from the source about changing peasant attitudes towards the tsar and there is use of own knowledge. The reasoning, however, is not always persuasive – for example, the tsar's assumptions about peasant feelings towards him can't really be used as evidence of what these feelings actually were.

There is a further reason for questioning the value of the source for an enquiry into responses to Bloody Sunday. It relates only to responses in one Russian village – one of the thousands that there were in Tsarist Russia.

This paragraph makes a valid point, but one that might have been developed further.

It also needs to be borne in mind that this source is an extract from an autobiography. The difficulty with autobiographies is that their writers tend to exaggerate their own importance. Here the writer gives the impression that she was single-handedly responsible for changing a whole village's attitudes to the tsar. This seems unlikely. In addition, the writer, as a member of the SR Combat Organisation, was deeply hostile to the tsar. Her bias means that the account she gives of how the peasants reacted to what she told them about Bloody Sunday can't really be believed.

This paragraph relies heavily on generalised assertions about the nature of autobiographical writing and the consequences of interpreting events from a particular viewpoint. There needs to be a tighter focus on the value and limitations of the source in relation to the specified enquiry.

This source has some value for an enquiry into responses to Bloody Sunday, but its value is relatively limited. It tells us something about how peasants reacted, but only in one village. Also, the writer is biased and therefore had a motive for exaggerating the amount of anger peasants felt towards him in 1905.

The first sentence offers an overall judgement on how much weight can be given to the source in relation to the specified enquiry – but the second merely repeats points already made.

### Verdict

This is an average response because:

- its attempts at evaluation are not always based on sound reasoning
- it doesn't use all of the material in the source: the author's own response to Bloody Sunday is neglected
- it does not focus tightly on the value and limitations of the source in relation to the specified inquiry.

Use the feedback on this response to rewrite it, making as many improvements as you can.

# Paper 2: AS Level sample answers with comments

## Section A

Part A requires you to:

- identify key points in the source and explain them
- deploy your own knowledge of the context in which events took place
- make appropriate comments about the author/origin/purpose of the source.

***Study Source 5 (page 294) before you answer this question.***

*Why is Source 5 valuable to the historian for an enquiry into opposition to Tsarism before 1905?*

*Explain your answer using the source, the information given about it and your own knowledge of the historical context. (8 marks)*

### Strong student answer

The programme of the League of Liberation is valuable for an enquiry into opposition to Tsarism before 1905 because it reveals the reasons for, and the depth of, anti-Tsarist feeling within Russia's middle classes. The League of Liberation, founded in 1904, was an attempt to establish a broadly based liberal party that united zemstvo leaders and student radicals. Its programme incorporated demands on which all liberals were agreed.

> A strong paragraph in which detailed own knowledge is used to highlight the main reason for the source's value.

The source shows that liberals opposed Tsarism mainly for political reasons. What they wanted was 'liberty', a 'constitutional regime' and 'extensive democracy' – that is, a parliament with real power elected on the basis of universal suffrage and a secret ballot. It is clear too that liberals had no belief in the Tsarist regime's capacity to reform itself, which helps to explain the depth of their hostility to it.

> This paragraph contains valid and well-supported inferences from the source about the reasons for, and strength of, liberal opposition to Tsarism.

The source also reveals something of the priorities of middle-class liberalism. The League put 'political demands in the forefront'. The 'defence of the interests of the toiling masses' seems to have been less of a priority. This is reflected in the vagueness of the League's proposals for tackling Russia's 'social-economic problems'.

> A valid inference is made about the political priorities of Russian liberals, and it is supported by well-selected material from the source.

Finally, the source is valuable because it shows the growing confidence of the liberal movement in 1904. Political parties were illegal in Russia before 1905, yet liberals were prepared to organise and to challenge the Tsarist regime openly. By doing so, they risked imprisonment and exile – but they nevertheless went ahead.

> A strong paragraph that uses 'own knowledge' and awareness of the nature of the source as the basis for a well-reasoned inference.

Overall, this source is valuable to the historian because it gives us an insight into the attitudes and values of Tsarism's liberal opponents. As an organisation's agreed programme, it reflected the views of a large number of people, not just one or two individuals, and this makes it particularly valuable.

> A paragraph that offers a well-founded overall judgment on the source's value.

### Verdict

This is a strong response because:

- it focuses tightly throughout on the source's value for the specified enquiry
- it offers reasoning based on the source's origins and nature, and it uses own knowledge to good effect
- it evaluates the source's value for the specified enquiry in a well-organised and perceptive way.

# Paper 2: AS Level sample answers with comments

## Section A

Part B requires you to:

- interrogate the source
- draw reasoned inferences
- deploy your own knowledge to interpret the material in its context
- make a judgement about the value (weight) of the source.

***Study Source 9 (page 301) before you answer this question.***

*How much weight do you give to the evidence of Source 9 for an enquiry into responses to Bloody Sunday (January 1905) in Russia?*

*Explain your answer using the source, the information given about it and your own knowledge of the historical context. (12 marks)*

### Strong student answer

Quite a lot of weight can be given to the evidence of the source for an enquiry into responses to Bloody Sunday, mainly because it has rarity value. However, for a number of reasons it needs to be treated with caution.

A paragraph that suggests one reason why weight can be attached to the source, but that also indicates that it has its limitations.

The principal value of the source lies in the account it gives of peasant anger at the news of Bloody Sunday. Direct evidence of the peasant political attitudes in the early 1900s is scarce. Widespread illiteracy meant that peasants left little written evidence behind. Historians studying their attitudes have to rely on official documents such as police reports. This source, however, was produced by someone unconnected with the regime who witnessed peasant responses to Bloody Sunday first hand. But the reliability of the source is open to question. Its author belonged to an extremist organisation that killed Interior Minister Plehve in 1904, and so it cannot be relied upon to give an impartial account of peasant attitudes. In addition, the account of Bloody Sunday given to the villagers was phrased in highly emotive language, almost certainly designed to elicit the kind of reaction it allegedly produced. Lastly, the source's value is limited by the fact that it relates to only one village – a remote Siberian village at that.

A strong paragraph that evaluates convincingly the weight that can be given to the source as evidence of peasant responses to Bloody Sunday. The evaluation is based on a consideration of the nature of the source as well as its content of the source. In addition, 'own knowledge' is used effectively to support the explanation.

The source is also valuable because it gives an indication of the ways in which extreme opponents of Tsarism responded to Bloody Sunday. There was horror at the regime's conduct, revealed in the phrase 'with trembling hands', but there was also elation that an event had taken place that seemed likely to hasten Tsarism's downfall.

A paragraph that makes a valid inference from the source's content about the responses of supporters of revolutionary parties to Bloody Sunday.

It is interesting too that a Socialist Revolutionary Party, often seen as the peasant party, should attach so importance to a movement of the 'labouring masses' – in other words, urban workers. It indicates that the SRs aimed to win support in the cities as well as in the countryside.

Own knowledge is deployed effectively in this paragraph to make a point that is valid but far from obvious.

The source gives some indication of the reactions to Bloody Sunday of peasants and revolutionaries, but it has nothing to say about the reactions of urban workers, the middle classes or the Tsarist regime itself.

A paragraph that sums up the value and limitations of the source in relation to the specified enquiry.

### Verdict

This is a strong response because:

- it focuses throughout on evaluating the source in relation to the specified enquiry
- it is based on a consideration of the nature as well as the content of the source, and deploys 'own knowledge' effectively
- it is well-organised and incisive.

# Paper 2: AS Level sample answers with comments

## Section B

These questions assess your understanding of the period in some depth. They will ask you about the content you learned about in the four key topics, but may not ask about more than one theme. For these questions remember to:

- give an analytical, not a descriptive, response
- support your points with evidence
- cover the whole time period specified in the question
- come to a substantiated judgement.

*How accurate is it to say that Lenin's leadership was the most important reason for the Bolsheviks' success in the revolution of October 1917? (20 marks)*

### Average student answer

At the time of the February Revolution, the Bolsheviks were not a major political force. In the course of 1917 things changed dramatically. Lenin's leadership was certainly a significant factor in their eventual success in October 1917. However, there were other factors too. The Provisional Government did not deal with the problems that the people of Russia faced. Furthermore, the Kornilov affair in August was important to the Bolsheviks' success.

This is not a strong introduction. It does show an understanding of the need to discuss both the factor stated in the question – Lenin's leadership – and unstated factors, but it doesn't give an indication of the line of argument which is going to be developed in the main body of the essay.

Lenin returned to Russia from exile in April 1917. On his return, he persuaded members of his party to give up any thought of supporting the Provisional Government and to concentrate instead on preparing a bid for power. He then set out a series of policies known as the April Theses. He committed the Bolsheviks to opposition to the war and to the transfer of the nobility's estates to the peasantry and called for political power to be given to the soviets. These policies proved to be popular; the mass of the Russian population was war-weary, and peasants had for a long time been intent on seizing the nobility's estates. The Bolsheviks' increasing popularity gave them a platform on which they based their eventual bid for power. In July 1917, things went badly wrong for Lenin and the Bolsheviks. They had an opportunity to seize power during the 'July Days', but failed to take it because Lenin did not act decisively enough. A number of Bolshevik leaders were arrested in the subsequent Provisional Government crackdown, and Lenin was forced to flee to Finland. Fortunately for the Bolsheviks, they were able to recover their position thanks to the Kornilov affair. Kornilov, commander-in-chief of the Russian army, tried to stage a counter-revolution but was thwarted, mainly because Bolsheviks infiltrated his forces and turned them against their officers. After the Kornilov affair, the way was open to the Bolsheviks to launch a bid for power. There were some Bolsheviks (Kamenev and Zinoviev) who thought that the time was not ripe for an insurrection, but Lenin was able to persuade his party otherwise. This was one of the most significant ways in which Lenin contributed to the Bolsheviks' success in 1917. Lenin, however, played only a limited part in the planning of the take-over of power in October. It was Trotsky who planned the insurrection, cleverly making it look like a seizure of power by the soviets rather than the Bolsheviks.

The weakness of this paragraph is that it is a narrative of what Lenin did between April and October 1917, rather than an attempt to explain the significance of his contribution to the Bolsheviks' seizure of power. There are, though, some analytical comments embedded within the narrative, for example, in the paragraph's two closing sentences. These would be credited.

An important failing of the Bolsheviks' opponents was their attitude towards the war. The Russian people were desperate for peace, but the Bolsheviks' opponents failed to give the people what they wanted. The Provisional Government talked about starting negotiations for a peace settlement involving all the combatant countries, but they did not pursue the matter with real urgency and were not prepared to think in terms of a separate peace between Russia and Germany. In the meantime, the Provisional Government continued to fight the war. People began to despair of it, and turned to the Bolsheviks, who were the most committed opponents of the war in Russia in 1917.

> This paragraph offers some relevant comment, but it is flimsy and uncertain. It makes no attempt, for example, to identify the Bolsheviks' opponents and assumes, incorrectly, that these opponents held similar views on the issue of war and peace.

Another failing of the Bolsheviks' opponents was their policy on the land issue. There was widespread agreement in 1917 that the estates of the nobility should be transferred to the peasantry, but disagreement over how this should be done. The Bolsheviks said that the transfer should take place immediately, but the Provisional Government insisted that the matter could only be dealt with by the democratically elected Constituent Assembly. This was the position not only of middle-class liberals but also of the main peasant party, the Socialist Revolutionaries. The Socialist Revolutionaries' popularity among the peasantry was demonstrated by their success in the Constituent Assembly elections in November 1917, where they won 40 percent of the votes cast compared with the Bolsheviks' 23 percent. In the summer of 1917, though, they could not persuade the peasantry to wait for the Constituent Assembly to settle the land issue. The Bolsheviks became stronger as a result.

> This paragraph also contains some relevant comments, pointing out the differences between the Provisional Government and the Bolsheviks on the land issue but it does not go on to explain why this issue had a bearing on the outcome in October 1917. In addition, when the paragraph summarises the results of the Constituent Assembly elections (which took place in November 1917), it drifts outside the time-scale of the question.

The Kornilov affair was a slice of luck for the Bolsheviks. Before the Kornilov affair, the Bolsheviks were in trouble. They had tried and failed to seize power in July 1917, and as a result the Provisional Government came after them, forcing Lenin to flee to Finland. But when the right-wing military commander Kornilov tried to take control of Russia, the Bolsheviks played an important part in stopping him. This enabled them to regain popularity, and their regained popularity put them in a position to attempt an insurrection of their own. The insurrection took place in late October. Bolshevik forces occupied key points in Petrograd, encountering little resistance because Kerensky, prime minister, had fled the capital in search of support.

> At the end of this paragraph, where the events of the October Revolution are briefly described, there is a further lapse into narrative writing – that is, into story-telling.

In conclusion, it can be seen that other factors apart from Lenin's leadership were involved in the Bolsheviks' success in October 1917. These factors were probably more important than Lenin's leadership.

> This brief conclusion begins by restating a point made in the introduction. It then addresses directly, for the first time, the issue of the importance of Lenin's leadership to the Bolsheviks' success in October 1917 in relation to other factors. The claim made is defensible, but it is not one that has been supported by argument and evidence in the course of the answer (or indeed in the conclusion). As such, it is an assertion rather than a piece of reasoned argument.

## Verdict

This is an average response because:

- it doesn't address the question directly enough – it doesn't offer, or support, a clear judgment on the issue of the relative importance of Lenin's leadership to the Bolsheviks' success in October 1917
- it contains some lapses into narrative writing
- at some points it lacks depth, and it also lacks range – there is no mention, for example, of the significance of the Provisional Government's failure to control inflation and only very limited reference to the impact of the Bolsheviks' 'All power to the soviets' policy.

Use the feedback on this answer to rewrite it, making as many improvements as you can.

# Paper 2: AS Level sample answers with comments

## Section B

These questions assess your understanding of the period in some depth. They will ask you about the content you learned about in the four key topics, but may not ask about more than one theme. For these questions remember to:

- give an analytical, not a descriptive, response
- support your points with evidence
- cover the whole time period specified in the question
- come to a substantiated judgement.

*How accurate is it to say that Lenin's leadership was the most important reason for the Bolsheviks' success in the revolution of October 1917? (20 marks)*

### Strong student answer

Lenin's leadership was a significant factor in the Bolshevik's success in October 1917, but it was not the only or even most important one. A more important factor than Lenin's leadership in the Bolsheviks' success was the failings of their political opponents. The Bolsheviks also benefited from a slice of luck.

This introduction addresses the question directly, offering a clear judgement on the importance of the stated factor – Lenin's leadership – in relation to the unstated ones. Also, by identifying the unstated factors it proposes to discuss, it gives an indication of the shape and structure of the discussion to follow.

Lenin contributed to the Bolsheviks' success in October 1917 in three main ways. First, on his return from exile in April 1917 he persuaded the Bolsheviks to adopt a strategy aimed at seizing power in a 'second revolution'. This was not easy to do. A number of senior members of the party, including Kamenev and Zinoviev, shared the Menshevik view that Russia was living through a bourgeois revolution and that the overthrow of capitalism by a proletarian revolution predicted by Marx was a long way off. Lenin had to win the party over to his flexible interpretation of Marxism which held that the gap between a bourgeois and a proletarian revolution could be very short. Next, Lenin raised the Bolsheviks' political profile by setting out in the April Theses a number of policies: opposition to the war, immediate transfer of the nobility's estates to the peasantry and insistence that the soviets should be the basis of the future government of Russia. These policies were at odds with those of the Provisional Government and did not bring overnight success. But by the summer of 1917 they became increasingly attractive to workers and soldiers in Petrograd who were losing patience with the Provisional Government on account of its failure to make radical changes. Popular support in the capital for the Bolsheviks increased, giving them a launch-pad for a second revolution. Lastly, Lenin successfully urged his party to launch a bid for power in the aftermath of the Kornilov affair. In the Kornilov affair, Bolshevik Red Guards, who were armed factory workers, played a key role in preventing a counter-revolution. As a result the Bolsheviks' popularity and prestige rose, creating circumstances in which the Bolsheviks could bid for power with a realistic chance of success. As in April, though, there were Bolsheviks who favoured caution and delay. Lenin got his way by the weight of his arguments and the strength of his personality. Had he failed, there would have been no October Revolution.

This paragraph analyses, that is, breaks down into its component parts, the nature of Lenin's contribution to the Bolsheviks' success in October 1917. It also gives some idea of the difficulties that he faced. It does not simply tell the story of what Lenin did between April and October 1917.

Lenin's actions in 1917 show beyond doubt that he was a forceful and decisive leader. But his undoubted skills would have counted for little had the failings of the Bolsheviks' opponents not opened the way for them to take power.

This is a useful, short, linking paragraph that signals that the discussion is now going to turn to causes of the Bolsheviks' success other than the one stated in the question.

The Bolsheviks were helped most of all by their opponents' attitudes to the war. By 1917, the war had become deeply unpopular with much of Russian public opinion. But the Bolsheviks' opponents failed to satisfy the demand for peace. The liberals of the first Provisional Government, headed by Milyukov, wanted to fight on until victory had been won – a policy which saw Milyukov forced out of the government in May 1917. The Mensheviks, who dominated the Petrograd Soviet in early 1917 and who joined the Provisional Government after the April Crisis, promised an end to the war through their policy of 'revolutionary defencism' but it failed to deliver and became discredited. Kerensky also lost touch with popular opinion after launching the June Offensive, he looked more like a warmonger than a peacemaker. The Bolsheviks were the most committed opponents of the war in Russia in 1917 and this helped put them in a position to launch a bid for power.

Another important failing of the Bolsheviks' opponents was their policy on the land issue. The various Provisional Governments maintained that the issue of land reform could only be settled by a democratically elected Constituent Assembly. To an impatient peasantry, this looked like a policy of delay, and gave rise to doubts about whether the Provisional Government was really serious about land reform. The Bolsheviks exploited the hesitancy of the Provisional Government by calling for the immediate transfer of the nobility's estates to the peasantry. This policy of 'All land to the peasantry' may not have won the Bolsheviks all that much support in the countryside, where they were an unknown quantity, but it undoubtedly helped them in Petrograd, where industrial workers often retained close ties with their home villages.

The Bolsheviks' slice of luck in 1917 came in the shape of the Kornilov affair. Before the Kornilov affair, the Bolsheviks were in disarray. They had been given an opportunity to seize power in the July Days, but had failed to take it. As a result, they found themselves on the receiving end of a Provisional Government crackdown. Lenin was forced to flee to Finland. Kornilov's intervention in politics saved the day for the Bolsheviks. The Bolsheviks played a major part in defeating Kornilov's attempted counter-revolution, infiltrating Kornilov's forces and turning them against their officers, and were therefore able to present themselves as saviours of the revolution. They exploited their new-found strength skilfully, Lenin urging an immediate insurrection and Trotsky, who planned the insurrection, cleverly making the October Revolution look like a seizure of power by the soviets rather than the Bolsheviks.

The almost universal expectation in Russia in early 1917 was that following Constituent Assembly elections a democratic government would come into being. Lenin's leadership, bold and decisive though it was, was not the main reason why things did not work out in this way. The key factor was that in the course of 1917 the Provisional Government lost control of the country, thereby opening the way for a Bolshevik seizure of power. In October 1917, the Bolsheviks took advantage of a situation they did not create.

These two paragraphs do not merely describe what the Provisional Government and the Bolsheviks did in relation to the issues of war and peace and the land, but try to analyse the political consequences of their actions.

Note the way in which each of these paragraphs begins with a 'topic sentence' that states what the paragraph is going to be about. 'Topic sentences' not only introduce the detailed explanation that follows, but also give an indication of the role of the paragraph within the overall argument of the answer.

To achieve the highest level, responses are expected to be written in a well-organised way and to communicate their arguments with clarity: topic sentences help to achieve these objectives.

This conclusion is brief, but it summarises effectively the case for not regarding Lenin's leadership as the main reason for the Bolsheviks' success in October 1917. The claim that the Bolsheviks fed off the failings of others, as opposed to sweeping into power on the basis of the positive appeal of their brand of socialism, is a plausible one and has been argued for throughout the answer.

## Verdict

This is a strong response because:

- it offers and supports a clear judgement on the relative importance of Lenin's leadership as a factor in the Bolsheviks' success in October 1917
- it focuses tightly on the question throughout
- it is well organised, and the argument is communicated with a high degree of clarity
- it deploys a range of accurate material in support of the points it makes (although it is not without its limitations, for example, no reference is made to the deteriorating economic situation in Russia in 1917, and there is only scant discussion of the role of Trotsky).

# Preparing for your A Level Paper 2 exam

## Advance planning

1. Draw up a timetable for your revision and try to keep to it. Spread your timetable over a number of weeks, and aim to cover four or five topics each week.
2. Spend longer on topics which you have found difficult, and revise them several times.
3. Above all, do not try to limit your revision by attempting to 'question spot'. Try to be confident about all aspects of your Paper 2 work, because this will ensure that you have a choice of questions in Section B.

## Paper 2 overview

| AL Paper 2 | Time: 1 hour 30 minutes | |
|---|---|---|
| Section A | Answer 1 compulsory source question | 20 marks |
| Section B | Answer 1 question from a choice of 2 | 20 marks |
| | **Total marks =** | **40 marks** |

You should familiarise yourself with the layout of the paper by looking at the examples published by Edexcel. The questions for each section are followed by eight pages of lined paper where you should write your answer.

## Section A question

This question asks you to assess two different types of contemporary sources totalling around 400 words, and will be in the form of 'How far could the historian make use of Sources 1 and 2 together to investigate ...?' Your answer should evaluate both sources, considering their nature, origin and purpose, and you should use your own knowledge of the context of the sources to consider their value to the specific investigation. Remember, too, that in assessing their value, you must consider the two sources, taken together, as a set.

## Section B questions

These questions ask you to reach a judgement on an aspect of the topic studied. The questions will have the form, for example, of 'How far...', 'To what extent...' or 'How accurate is it to say...'. The questions can deal with historical concepts such as cause, consequence, change, continuity, similarity, difference and significance. You should consider the issue raised in the question, then other relevant issues, and conclude with an overall judgement.

The timescale of the questions could be as short as a single year or even a single event (an example from Paper 2C.2 could be, 'To what extent was Russia's involvement in the First World War responsible for the fall of the Romanovs in 1917?'). The timescale could be longer depending on the historical event or process being examined, but questions are likely to be shorter than the those set for Sections A and B in Paper 1.

## Use of time

This is an issue which you should discuss with your teachers and fellow students, but here are some suggestions for you.

1. Do not write solidly for 45 minutes on each question. For Section A it is essential that you have a clear understanding of the content of each source, the points being made, and the nature, origin and purpose of each source. You might decide to spend up to ten minutes reading the sources and drawing up your plan, and 35 minutes writing your answer.
2. For Section B answers you should spend a few minutes working out what the question is asking you to do, and drawing up a plan of your answer before you begin to write your response.

# Preparing for your A Level exams

## Paper 2: A Level sample answers with comments

### Section A

You will need to read and analyse the two sources and use them in tandem to assess how useful they are in investigating an issue. For these questions, remember to:

- spend time, up to 10 minutes, reading and identifying the arguments and evidence presented in the sources, then make a plan to ensure that your response will be rooted in these sources
- use specific references from the sources
- deploy own knowledge to develop points made in the sources and establish appropriate context
- come to a substantiated judgement.

***Study Sources 5 and 6 (page 367) before you answer this question.***

*How far could the historian make use of Sources 5 and 6 together to investigate the impact of the policy of War Communism in Russia in 1918–21?*

*Explain your answer, using both sources, the information given about them and your knowledge of the historical context. (20 marks)*

#### Average student answer

The 'New Life' article would be extremely useful to the historian because it contains a number of points of information about the impact of War Communism in the countryside. It tells us that the peasantry was bitterly opposed to the policy of grain requisitioning which was a key element in the policy of War Communism. It also tells us that violent clashes took place between peasants opposed to requisitioning and the Red Guard and Red Army requisitioning squads which were sent out from the cities in search of grain. These clashes, it seems, occurred across the whole of European Russia. We have no means of knowing where 'New Life' got its information from, but we know from other sources that its account is accurate. We know, for example, that in Tambov province, one of the provinces 'New Life' mentions, Alexander Antonov raised a large peasant army to fight against the grain requisitioning squads.

An abrupt start, with no attempt made to offer an overview of the lines of argument that are to be developed in the answer. There is within the paragraph some use of 'own knowledge' to confirm and expand on the information contained in the source, but it is not very extensive.

The fact that other sources corroborate what it says is not the only reason for believing the 'New Life' account of the impact of War Communism in the countryside. It appeared in a newspaper that was socialist in its political sympathies but was not a pro-Bolshevik newspaper. Bolshevik newspapers like 'Pravda' pumped out propaganda, and would not have published an account of the 'bread war' like the one which appeared in 'New Life' – an account that highlighted the extent of the opposition to government policy. It was presumably this sort of honesty that led to 'New Life' being banned.

This paragraph addresses the issue of the source's reliability to good effect, though the point made is a relatively straightforward one.

Victor Serge's memoirs are a source of information about living conditions in Petrograd under War Communism. It's true that Serge only tells us about living conditions in one Russian city, but we know from other sources that life was just as bad in places like Moscow. Serge says a number of things that make his account useful to the historian. First, he tells us about how the rationing system worked, how much food people got ('minute' quantities) and what sort of food it was. It is noticeable that rations did not include nourishing foods like meat and vegetables. Serge does not, though, say anything about how hard life was under War Communism for 'non-workers' – that is, middle-class people – who got the smallest amount of rations, except to point out they got no sugar. Next, Serge tells us that under War Communism trading on the 'black market' became very widespread among all classes of the population. Because the peasantry refused to hand over grain to the requisitioning squads, food in the shops in the cities was scarce, and so the only way to get food was to trade with the peasant 'bagmen' who brought food into the cities unofficially and illegally. If you were caught by the Cheka, the penalties involved in this kind of trading, which the Bolshevik government regarded as economic sabotage, were harsh. The source does not explore this aspect of War Communism. Lastly, Serge explains how vulnerable cold and half-starved city populations were to the ravages of disease.

In this paragraph, understanding of the source is demonstrated and key points of its content are selected and discussed. However, there is only limited evidence, in the suggestion that 'black market' trading became widespread, of a capacity to make reasoned inferences from the source material. In addition, although there is some use of 'own knowledge' to consider the limitations of the source, it is relatively limited.

Evidence from other sources supports Serge's description of life in Petrograd. Because food was so scarce in the cities, large numbers of their inhabitants left, returning to their home villages in the expectation that there would at least be something to eat there. The population of Petrograd and Moscow went down by something like half in the War Communist era. Another reason for believing Serge's account was that he had Bolshevik sympathies. You would expect a Bolshevik to cover up the extent of the problems which arose under Bolshevik rule out of loyalty to the party, but Serge does not. Instead, he describes bluntly just how bad things were, talking about 'dead factories', 'torture', the 'frightful' death toll and the 'ravages of famine'. Admittedly, Serge was an unusual Bolshevik, having lived abroad for most of his life and having been an anarchist, so perhaps he was more prepared to be honest and open than some party members might have been. It's also possible that his political views had changed by the time he wrote his memoirs, which seems to have been a long time after the era of War Communism.

This paragraph contains reasonable, if straightforward, points that go some way towards establishing that Victor Serge's memoirs are a credible source.

Taken together, the two sources paint a bleak picture of the impact of War Communism: violent conflict in the villages, hunger in the towns. It is, though, a credible and accurate picture, one which other sources confirm. For these reasons, historians could make a lot of use of the two sources. There are, however, aspects of the impact of War Communism they do not tell us anything about, for example, the changes that took place in the way that industry was run.

The usefulness to the historian of the two sources in combination needs fuller consideration than the sentence or two offered here. Also, discussion of the limitations of the two sources, both in this paragraph and elsewhere in the answer, is limited.

## Verdict

This is an average response because:

- it is uneven – there are sound discussions of the reliability of the sources in the light of their nature and origins, but the analysis of their content is less successful
- it is somewhat unbalanced, Victor Serge's memoirs receive quite a lot more attention than *New Life*
- use of own knowledge to consider the limitations of the sources, or to confirm and expand on the information they contain, is relatively limited
- consideration of the usefulness to the historian of the two sources in combination is under-developed.

Use the feedback on this answer to rewrite it, making as many improvements as you can.

# Paper 2: A Level sample answers with comments

## Section A

You will need to read and analyse the two sources and use them in tandem to assess how useful they are in investigating an issue. For these questions, remember to:

- spend time, up to 10 minutes, reading and identifying the arguments and evidence presented in the sources, then make a plan to ensure that your response will be rooted in these sources
- use specific references from the sources
- deploy own knowledge to develop points made in the sources and establish appropriate context
- come to a substantiated judgement.

***Study Sources 5 and 6 (page 367) before you answer this question.***

*How far could the historian make use of Sources 5 and 6 together to investigate the impact of the policy of War Communism in Russia in 1918–21?*

*Explain your answer, using both sources, the information given about them and your knowledge of the historical context. (20 marks)*

### Strong answer

The historian could make considerable use of these sources to investigate the impact of War Communism. Both sources are written from a distinctive and valuable perspective, and both contain important points of information. They do, however, have their limitations.

This paragraph gives a helpful brief overview of the lines of argument that are to be developed in the main body of the answer.

The authors of the two sources were not White Russian opponents of the regime, determined to present the grimmest possible picture of the impact of Bolshevik policies, but nor were they totally committed supporters of the regime who were blind to its faults. It can be inferred that both authors were what might be called critical friends of the Bolsheviks. In the case of 'New Life', the fact that it was eventually shut down by the Bolsheviks suggests that before July 1918 it had spoken out against the regime but the fact that it continued to be published after the November 1917 Bolshevik Decree on the Press, which suppressed Kadet newspapers, suggests that the Bolsheviks' view of it was not entirely unsympathetic. As for Victor Serge, he was an outsider, in 1919 new to both Russia and Bolshevism. His confession that he traded on the 'black market' – behaviour which Lenin's government condemned as economic sabotage, and which the Cheka used brutal methods to prevent – suggests that he was not among the most committed and inflexible of Bolsheviks. He makes no attempt to hide the fact that conditions in Bolshevik-run Petrograd in 1920–21 were appalling. Although his account seems to have been written long after the era of War Communism, there is no reason to doubt the truth of it. It would have been impossible for him to publish an honest account of conditions under War Communism at the time. Perhaps it became easier later on. The authors of the two sources, then, were to some degree independent-minded. Because of this, their evidence, which focuses on the harmful consequences of War Communism, has a high degree of credibility.

This is a closely argued paragraph that focuses on the issue of the reliability of the two sources in the light of their origins and content. Valid inferences are made from information given about the origins of the sources, and these inferences are supported by detailed own knowledge.

Both sources contain valuable information about the impact of War Communism. 'New Life' reports how brutally government forces implemented the policy of grain requisitioning, which was an integral part of War Communism. It also indicates, by listing the provinces in the grip of 'the bread war', just how widespread peasant resistance to forcible requisitioning was. And it reveals something of the intensity of peasant resistance, noting the frequency of violent clashes between peasants and the authorities. Admittedly, we have no means of knowing where the journalist who wrote the 'New Life' article got his or her information from. But there is plenty

The strength of this paragraph is that it does not simply summarise, paraphrase or recycle the content of the source, but instead makes reasoned inferences from it – about, for example, the extent and intensity of peasant resistance to government forces trying to requisition grain.

of other evidence which corroborates the 'New Life' account. In Tambov province in 1920–21, for example, Alexander Antonov's 40,000-strong peasant army fought a guerrilla war against the Red Army. The Red Army used vicious methods to overcome Antonov's guerrillas, using poison gas against them and taking their wives and children hostage.

Victor Serge's memoirs are informative about the working of the rationing system and the kinds of food people received. They also indicate that under War Communism trading on the 'black market' became universal. Less obvious, but important, is what Serge implies about the impact of War Communism on industrial production. Workers, it seems, did not produce what they were supposed to be producing. In addition, though this is not mentioned in the source, we know that many workers left the cities in 1918–21 and returned to their home villages in search of food. The result was 'dead factories', in other words, a slump in industrial output. It is true that Serge only had first-hand knowledge of conditions in Petrograd, but things were no different in Moscow (which lost half of its population in the War Communist era) or other major cities.

Once again, there is reasoned inference from the content of the source – this time about the impact of War Communism on factory output. Own knowledge is then deployed to offer a further reason for the decline in industrial production. More might have been said, however, about the rationing system and 'black market' trading.

Taken together, the two sources could be used by the historian to support the claim that War Communism had an extremely damaging impact on the lives of ordinary Russians. The two sources, moreover, complement each other: 'New Life' describes the impact of War Communism on peasant lives in rural areas, while Victor Serge gives an account of its impact on industrial workers in the big cities. In addition, the descriptions given in the two sources are reliable. However, there are, unsurprisingly, aspects of the impact of War Communism that they do not cover. They focus on its social impact and have little to say about its economic consequences (for example, the drop in industrial and agricultural output and the return to 'one-man management' in industry) or its political consequences (the growing importance of the Cheka, for instance). On the matters they do describe, though, the two sources are exceptionally useful to the historian.

This paragraph contains well-founded comments on both the usefulness to the historian of the two sources in combination and on the limitations of the sources. The comments on the limitations of the sources might, however, have been developed more fully through the deployment of own knowledge.

## Verdict

This is a strong response because:

- it focuses tightly throughout on the issue of the sources' usefulness to the historian for the specified purpose
- it is well-balanced, not concentrating excessively on one source at the expense of the other
- it displays a highly developed capacity for making reasoned inferences from the content of the sources and from the information given about their origins and nature
- it deploys detailed own knowledge in support of the arguments and explanations it offers
- it makes well-founded comments on the usefulness to the historian of the two sources in combination
- it makes clear the limitations of the two sources in relation to the purpose specified.

# Paper 2: A level sample answers with comments

## Section B

These questions assess your understanding of the period in some depth. They will ask you about the content you learned about in the four key topics, but may not ask about more than one theme. For these questions remember to:

- give an analytical, not a descriptive, response
- support your points with evidence
- cover the whole time period specified in the question
- come to a substantiated judgment.

*To what extent did Russia undergo profound political and economic reform in the years 1906–14? (20 marks)*

### Average student answer

After the 1905 revolution, a shaken Tsarist regime introduced a number of reforms in both the political and economic spheres. These reforms did not have a really profound impact on either the functioning of the Russian Empire's government or its economy. It is therefore wrong to say that in the years 1906–14 Russia underwent a period of profound political and economic reform.

A sound introduction that indicates the line of argument that is going to be developed in the main body of the answer.

In the political sphere, the Tsarist regime promised a lot more in 1905 than it went on to deliver in 1906. In his 1905 October Manifesto, Nicholas II promised to create an elected Duma with real power. The 1906 Fundamental Law, however, issued when the Tsarist regime was no longer in serious danger of going under, gave the Duma only a limited amount of power. In the Fundamental Law, the tsar declared that he retained supreme autocratic power. Under the provisions of the Fundamental Law, he could appoint and dismiss his ministers without reference to the Duma, and he could dissolve the Duma at any time of his choosing. Nor did the Duma have any power in relation to the army and navy and foreign policy – these were matters for the tsar alone. Most important of all, the tsar could use Article 87 of the Fundamental Law to make laws by decree when the Duma was not in session.

This is a poorly focused paragraph. It contains potentially relevant information, but it is offered in the form of a description of the main provisions of the 1906 Fundamental Law rather than being deployed as evidence in support of a clearly stated argument. In addition, what is said about the October Manifesto is misleading: it did not contain a promise to establish a Duma with real power, but instead stated that in future no law would come into effect without Duma confirmation.

Weak in 1906, the Duma became even weaker in 1907. Relations between the government and the first two Dumas in 1906–07 broke down because anti-Tsarist parties were in the majority and were unco-operative. As a result, Stolypin lost patience with the Duma, and in 1907 changed the way in which it was elected. The new rules favoured the nobility and the upper classes, and ensured that future Dumas would have a built-in conservative majority. The third and fourth Dumas which sat after 1907 were docile bodies which were not a threat to the regime. The 1906 Fundamental Law and Stolypin's 'coup' in 1907 had deprived the Duma of real power and ensured that the Russian Empire remained to all intents and purposes an autocracy. Since this was so, the political reforms introduced after 1906 can hardly be described as profound. Many of the conservative advisers who surrounded Nicholas II did not want profound reform in any case. They were suspicious of Prime Minister Stolypin's intentions, and set out to undermine him. By 1911 they had won Nicholas II over to their point of view, and had Stolypin not been assassinated he would probably have been dismissed.

An uneven paragraph: there is relevant comment on the reasons why reforms introduced by the Tsarist regime in 1906–07 cannot reasonably be described as 'profound', but the early part of the paragraph is a narrative of relations between the regime and the Duma in 1906–07 rather than a piece of analytical writing. Nor is the relevance of the comments on Stolypin's downfall at the end of the paragraph clear.

Reform in the economic sphere took the shape of the land reform driven forward by Stolypin. Stolypin wanted to abolish the system of open-field farming which was widely used across Russia. Open-field farming, in which each household was given strips within open fields to cultivate, was inefficient because time was wasted moving from strip to strip. Also, because strips were periodically reallocated, peasants had no incentive to improve the land they cultivated. Stolypin's plan was to replace the strip-farming system with one in which each peasant household owned its own separate farm. This involved breaking the power of the village commune, or mir, which organised the cultivation of arable land under the strip-farming system. In practice, many peasants were cautious and unenterprising and so were unwilling to leave the commune. By the time the First World War broke out, only 10 percent of households owned separate farms. The vast majority of peasantry still belonged to the commune and were still growing crops on strips within open fields. Their lives had not been transformed. Stolypin's land reform had only had a limited amount of impact, and cannot therefore be described as a profound reform. Perhaps it would have been different had the reform been fully implemented.

A paragraph that in itself is sound enough, offering support for the judgement set out in the introduction. However, the treatment of post-1906 economic reform is brief in comparison with the amount of space devoted to political reform above and this leaves the answer as a whole lop-sided and unbalanced.

Little changed in Russia as a result of the reforms introduced after 1906. It was still an autocratic country. The power of the secret police was undiminished. The regime remained brutal, as the 1912 Lena goldfield massacre showed. In the economic sphere, all of the problems which had existed before 1906 were still there in 1914. The working and living conditions of the industrial workers in the towns were still terrible. The peasantry remained poor and were still land-hungry. If profound economic and political reforms had been introduced in Russia after 1906, this would not have been the case. People would have had more freedom and political power, and would have been more prosperous. These things, however, did not happen.

This conclusion contains relevant and well-founded comments but the quality of the argument and evidence offered in support of them in the main body of the answer is patchy.

### Verdict

This is an average response because:

- it is unbalanced, focusing more heavily on political reform than on economic reform
- it does not focus tightly throughout on the question set
- it contains descriptive passages that do not offer support for the judgement given in the introduction and conclusion
- it includes some material that is not relevant to the question set
- it lacks range – there is, for instance, no reference to Stolypin's efforts to promote emigration to Siberia.

Use the feedback on this answer to rewrite it, making as many improvements as you can.

# Paper 2: A level sample answers with comments

## Section B

These questions assess your understanding of the period in some depth. They will ask you about the content you learned about in the four key topics, but may not ask about more than one theme. For these questions remember to:

- give an analytical, not a descriptive, response
- support your points with evidence
- cover the whole time period specified in the question
- come to a substantiated judgment.

*To what extent did Russia undergo profound political and economic reform in the years 1906–14? (20 marks)*

### Strong student answer

In the years 1906–14, the Tsarist regime, shaken by revolution, introduced reforms in both the political and economic spheres. The economic reforms, notably Stolypin's land reforms, were more profound – that is, thoroughgoing and far-reaching – than the political ones, but they had not by 1914 had a transformative effect on the Russian economy. The political reforms left Russia's system of government largely unaltered.

A short but incisive introduction that makes clear the approach that is going to be taken. There is, as well, a welcome attempt to define what 'profound' means in this context.

The political changes introduced after 1906 restricted the tsar's power to only a limited extent. The key promise made in the 1905 October Manifesto was to establish a Duma, or parliament, which would be given a real say in law-making. The regime failed to honour its promise. The powers given to the Duma in the 1906 Fundamental Law were restricted to the point that opponents of the regime, such as Milyukov's Kadets, claimed that they had been cheated. There was to be an unelected upper house, the Imperial Council of State, which could block measures passed by the Duma, and Article 87 of the Fundamental Law enabled the tsar to by-pass the Duma by giving him the power to issue decrees when it was not in session. Further inroads into the power of the Duma came in 1907, when Stolypin high-handedly changed the basis on which the Duma was elected, introducing arrangements which were massively weighted in favour of the nobility. After 1907, the Duma was an unrepresentative talking-shop.

A well-focused, tightly argued paragraph based on in-depth knowledge and one which resists the temptation simply to list the provisions of the 1906 Fundamental Law.

This is not to say that in the political sphere everything after 1906 went back to where it had been before 1905. However limited its powers, the Duma was an elected national body, and some of its members, even in the conservative Third and Fourth Dumas, were prepared to speak out against the regime. In addition, after 1906 political parties were legal and the press enjoyed a certain amount of freedom. These were in their way significant changes, but to describe them as 'profound' is over-generous. They certainly fell a long way short of the expectations of opponents of the regime, whether Guchkov's Octobrists, the Kadets, the SRs, the Mensheviks or the Bolsheviks.

A paragraph that demonstrates an informed awareness of the extent of political change in Russia after 1906.

In the economic sphere, Stolypin ambitiously set out to reconstruct the communal system of agriculture operating across much of European Russia, in which the mir, or village commune, allocated (and periodically reallocated) strips of land in three open fields to each of the village's households. The prize for breaking up the communal system and replacing it with one in which peasant households had their own separate farms was, from the Tsarist regime's point of view, great – giving a more efficient and productive agricultural sector, because peasants would have more incentive to work hard. And a property-owning peasantry would be immune to the appeal of socialism. Had Stolypin's reforms been fully implemented they might well have merited the description 'profound'. But Stolypin's assassination in 1911 and the outbreak of war in 1914 together put paid to his plans. By 1914, only 20 percent of peasant households had left the village commune and only half of these were owners of separate farms. During the First World War those who had left the commune were reabsorbed into it. In 1917, Russia's agricultural system was pretty much back where it had been before Stolypin.

This paragraph maintains a sharp focus on the extent to which Stolypin's land reforms can be regarded as 'profound'. The verdict offered – that the intention was to make profound changes, but the impact of the measures introduced was relatively limited – is well-founded.

Stolypin had more success in his efforts to unlock the economic potential of Siberia. In the years before 1914, over three million peasants left the over-populated parts of European Russia and emigrated to Siberia. They were lured by the promise of free or cheap land and assisted by interest-free loans and subsidised railway fares. This was a major reforming project, but those who migrated to Siberia in the Stolypin era constituted under 2 percent of the Russian Empire's 164 million population. But government encouragement of emigration to Siberia does not qualify as a 'profound' reform: it did little to relieve the problems of peasant poverty and discontent in European Russia.

A well-informed paragraph that recognises that land reform was not the only kind of economic reform attempted after 1906 and so brings breadth to the answer.

From the point of view of the Tsarist regime, the reforms introduced after 1906 must have seemed profound in that they involved a radical break with the past: the Fundamental Law, which was a constitution of sorts, and the establishment of the Duma, diluted the autocratic principle on which Romanov rule had been based since the early 17th century, and the attempt to abolish open-field farming threatened to overturn customs and practices which had been in existence for generations. On the other hand, from the point of view of revolutionaries, the reforms were of no great consequence. In their view, despite the post-1906 reforms, the Russian Empire remained an autocratic, poverty-stricken state with a backward economy. A more impartial judgement of the reforms would be that they were significant but not profound.

A thoughtful and well-judged conclusion: the point that what counts as 'profound' is to some degree a matter of perspective is a persuasive one. The reaction of the revolutionary parties to Stolypin's reforming project might have been explored further.

## Verdict

This is a strong response because:

- it weighs carefully the case for and against the idea that the post-1906 economic and political reforms were 'profound' and reaches a secure conclusion
- it focuses tightly throughout on the question set
- factual material is at all times deployed as evidence in support of the arguments that are put forward and there are no lapses into description or narration
- it is well-organised and the argument is communicated with clarity and precision
- consideration might, however, have been given to the question of whether Stolypin's priorities in promoting land reform were political rather than economic.

# Index

# Acknowledgements

*The authors and publisher would like to thank the following individuals and organisations for permission to reproduce photographs and text in this book.*

### Photographs

(Key: b-bottom; c-centre; l-left; r-right; t-top)

**akg-images Ltd:** 236, 241, Jean-Claude Varga 171; **Alamy Images:** Art Reserve 59, Classic Image 25, 87, 98, David Humphreys 45, FineArt 17, INTERFOTO 130, Mary Evans Picture Library 49, National Geographic Collection 6, Pictorial Press Ltd 81, The Art Archive 34, 68, 96, World History Archive 106, 118; **Bibliothèque nationale de France:** 173; **Bridgeman Art Library Ltd:** De Agostini Picture Library/M. Seemuller 166; **Château de Versailles:** 181; **DK Images:** 311br, 327bl; **Getty Images:** Fine Art Images/Heritage Images 287, 307, Hulton Archive 9, 43, 334, 346, Sovfoto/UIG 323, The Print Collector 28, Topical Press Agency 371; **Mary Evans Picture Library:** 69, 85, 135, 233, Albert Harlingue/Roger-Viollet 202, BeBa/Iberfoto 211, Epic/Tallandier 194, Iberfoto 216, 223, Illustrated London News Ltd 300, J. Bedmar/Iberfoto 234, John Massey Stewart Collection 293, Musee Carnavalet/Roger-Viollet 169t, 193, Robert Hunt Collection/Imperial War Museum 325, SZ Photo/Scherl 358, 361, The Everett Collection 349; **© National Portrait Gallery, London:** 127; **TopFoto:** Fine Art Images/Heritage Images 359bl, 380, IMAGNO/Austrian Archives 286, 289, ITAR-TASS 335, 338, RIA Novosti 327br, 341, SCRSS 359tr

**Cover images:** *Front:* **Bridgeman Art Library Ltd:** Private Collection/Archives Charmet

All other images © Pearson Education

### Figures

Figures 2.1 and 4.1 adapted from *Lenin's Russia* by Alan White, Collins Educational, 1998, p.11. Reproduced by permission of HarperCollins Publishers Ltd.

### Tables

Table 5.1 adapted from *The Financial Revolution in England* by Peter George Muir Dickson, Macmillan, 1967, pp.48–49. Reproduced with permission of Palgrave Macmillan; Table p.354 adapted from 'Lenin and the First Communist Revolution' by Bryan Caplan, from the Museum of Communism, George Mason University, Washington DC, http://www.gmu.edu/departments/economics/bcaplan. Reproduced by kind permission of Bryan Caplan; Table p.354 adapted from *The Election to the Russian Constituent Assembly of 1917* by Oliver Henry Radkey, Harvard University Press, 1950, pp.78–80. Reproduced by permission of Harvard University History Department; Table p.370 from *An Economic History of the USSR 1917–1991* by Alec Nove, Penguin Books 1969, Pelican Books 1972, p.94, copyright © Alex Nove, 1969, 1976, 1982. Reproduced by permission of Penguin Books Ltd.

### Text

Extract p.17 from *Three British Revolutions: 1641, 1688, 1776* Ed John Greville Agard Pocock, Princeton University Press, 2014, pp.185, 192, copyright © 1980; p.217 from *Twelve Who Ruled: The Year of the Terror in the French Revolution* by Robert Roswell Palmer, Princeton University Press, 2005, copyright © 1941 © renewed 1969; p.301 from *The Road to Bloody Sunday: The Role of Father Gapon and the St. Petersburg Massacre of 1905* by Walter Sablinsky, Princeton University Press, 1976, p.266; and p.376 from *In the Shadow of Revolution: Life Stories of Russian Women from 1917 to the Second World War* by Sheila Fitzpatrick and Yuri Slezkine, Princeton University Press, 2000, p.43. Reproduced by permission of Princeton University Press; Extract p.20 from "What was the English Revolution?" by John Morrill, *History Today Ltd,* Vol. 34, (3), pp.11–12, March 1984, http://www.historytoday.com/john-morrill/what-was-english-revolution. Reproduced with permission; Extract p.20 from *The Outbreak of the English Civil War* by Anthony Fletcher, Hodder Education, 1985, pp.407, 413, 415, copyright © Anthony Fletcher, Bloomsbury Academic, an imprint of Bloomsbury Publishing Plc; Extract p.25 from 'Venice: May 1653', *Calendar of State Papers Relating To English Affairs in the Archives of Venice*, ed. Allen B Hinds, Vol. 29, 1653–1654, pp.63–80, London, 1929, http://www.british-history.ac.uk/cal-state-papers/venice/vol29/, pp.63–80, accessed January 2015; Extract p.41 from *The Emergence of a Nation State, 1529–1660*, 2/e by Alan G.R. Smith, Longman, 1997, p.263, Taylor & Francis; Extracts pp.46, 63, 67 from *The Stuart Age: England, 1603–1714* by Barry Coward, Routledge, 2011, pp.20, 153, 251, copyright © 2011; Extract p.121 from *The Nature of the English Revolution* by John Morrill, Routledge, 1993, p.452, copyright © 1993; Extract p.123 from *Century of Revolution*, 2/e by Christopher Hill, Routledge, 2001, pp.242, 244, copyright © 2001. Extract p.133 from *The Glorious Revolution*, 2/e by John Miller Routledge, 1997, p.40, copyright © 1997; Extract p.134 from *William III* by A.M. Claydon, Routledge, 2002, p.76, copyright © 2002; and Extract p.286 from *Russia in the Age of Modernisation and Revolution 1881–1917* by Hans Rogger, Longman, 1983, p.102, copyright © 1983. Reproduced by permission of Taylor & Francis Books UK; Extract p.54 from *Puritans and Puritanism in Europe and America*, eds Francis J. Bremer and Tom Webster, ABC-CLIO Ltd, 2006, p.346; Extract p.61 from "Oliver Cromwell's Policy towards the English Catholics: The Appraisal by Diplomats" by Albert J. Loomie, *The Catholic Historical Review* Vol. 90, No. 1, pp.29–44, Catholic University of America Press, Jan., 2004; Extract p.228 from

*University of Chicago Readings in Western Civilization, Vol 7: The Old Regime and the French Revolution* by Keith Michael Baker, University of Chicago, 1987, pp.338–9. Permission conveyed through Copyright Clearance Center; Extract p.72 from *The Problem of the Poor in Tudor and Early Stuart England* by A. L. Beier, Routledge, 1983, p.11. Reproduced with kind permission from Professor Lee Beier; Extract p.74 from 'The Rise of the Gentry, 1558–1640' by R.H Tawney, *The Economic History Review*, Vol. A11, (1), pp.1–38, 2008, copyright © 2008, John Wiley and Sons; Extract p.75 from *The Gentry 1540–1640* by Hugh R Trevor-Roper, Economic History Review, Cambridge University Press, 1953; Extract p.123 from *Toleration in Enlightenment Europe* by Ole Peter Grell and Roy Porter, Cambridge University Press, 2000, pp.134, copyright © 2000; Extract p.134 from 'Constitutions and Commitment: The Evolution of "Institutional Governing Public Choice in Seventeenth-Century England" by Douglass C. North and Barry R. Weingast, *The Journal of Economic History*, Vol. 49, (4), pp.803–832, December 1989, copyright © The Economic History Association 1989; Extracts pp.178, 276, 278 from *Travels in France during the years 1787, 1788 & 1789* by Arthur Young, ed Constantia Maxwell, Cambridge University Press, 1929, p.109; Extract p.214 from *Regicide and Revolution, Speeches at the Trial of Louis XVI* by Michael Walzer, translated by Marian Rothstein, Cambridge University Press, 1974, pp.124–5, copyright © 1974 Columbia University Press; Extracts pp.248, 257 from *France Under the Directory* by Martyn Lyons, Cambridge University Press, 1965, pp.22, 204; and Extracts pp.294, 384 from *The Liberation Movement in Russia 1900–1905* by Shmuel Galai, Cambridge University Press, 2002, p.90. Reproduced by permission of Cambridge University Press and the authors; Extract p.93 from *The Penguin Economic History of Britain: Reformation to the Industrial Revolution 1530–1780* by Christopher Hill, Penguin Books, 1999, copyright © Christopher Hill, 1999; Extracts pp.117, 136 from *Revolution: The Great Crisis of the British Monarchy* by Tim Harris, Penguin Books, 2006, p.243, copyright © Tim Harris, 2006; and Extracts pp.194, 237 from *A History of Modern France: 1715–1799, v.1*, 3/e, by Alfred Cobban, Penguin Books, 1990, pp.164, 240, copyright © Alfred Cobban 1990 Reproduced by permission of Penguin Books Ltd; Extract p.105 from 'October 1651: An Act for increase of Shipping, and Encouragement of the Navigation of this Nation.', in *Acts and Ordinances of the Interregnum, 1642–1660*, ed. C.H. Firth and R.S. Rait, London, 1911, pp.559–562 http://www.british-history.ac.uk/no-series/acts-ordinances-interregnum/ accessed 18 December 2014, Crown © Copyright. Reproduced with permission under the terms of the Click-Use Licence; Extract p.107 from *Great Power Rivalries* by Jack S Levy, ed: William Thompson, University of South Carolina Press, 1999, pp.189, 190. Reproduced by permission; Extract p.108 from *Stuart Economy and Society* by Nigel Heard, Hodder Education, 1995; and Extract p.205 from *Access to History: France in Revolution* 4/e by Duncan Townson and Dylan Rees, Hodder Education, 2008, p.63. Reproduced by permission of Hodder Education; Extract p.118 from *1688: The First Modern Revolution* by Dr Stephen Pincus, Yale University Press, 2011, p.294; and Extract p.234 from *Robespierre: A Revolutionary Life* by Peter McPhee, Yale University Press, 2012, p.201. Reproduced with permission from Yale University Press; Extract p.125 from *The Glorious Revolution: 1688 – Britain's Fight for Liberty* by Edward Vallance, Abacus, 2007; and Extract p.233 from *The Terror: Civil War in the French Revolution* by David Andress, Abacus, 2005, p.373, Reproduced by permission of Little, Brown, Books Ltd; Extracts pp.175, 180, 184, 196, 199, 201 from *Documents and Debates: The French Revolution* by Leonard W. Cowie, Palgrave Macmillan, 1988, pp.7, 11, 29, 61, 71, 77. Reproduced with permission of Palgrave Macmillan; Extract p.184 from *French Revolution Documents 1787–92*, Vol. I, edited by John Morris Roberts, Basil Blackwell, 1966, p.8; and Extract p.188 from *Revolution From 1789 to 1906* by Raymond William Postgate, Harper & Row, 1962, p.26. Reproduced by permission of Peters Fraser & Dunlop, www.petersfraserdunlop.com on behalf of the Estates of John Morris Roberts and Raymond William Postgate; Extracts from p.185 from *The French Revolution: Voices from a momentous epoch 1789–1795* by Richard Cobb and Colin Jones, Simon & Schuster, 1988, pp.24, 26, 32, 38, 132, 176, 182, 184, 198, 200–1, 234, 236, 238, 240, 242. Reproduced by kind permission of Professor Colin Jones; Extract p.188 from *Paris in the Revolution: A collection of eye-witness accounts* by Reay Tannahill, The Folio Society, p.25, 1966, 1967, text copyright © The Folio Society Limited. Reproduced with permission; Extract p.189 from *English Witnesses of the French Revolution* by James Matthew Thompson, Basil Blackwell, 1938, p.56. Reproduced by permission of the RNLI; Extract p.190 from *Revolutionary Europe 1783–1815* by George Rudé, Collins, 1964, p.74, Reproduced by permission of Harvey J. Kaye, Professor of Democracy & Justice Studies University of Wisconsin on behalf of the Estate of George Rudé; Extract p.195 from 'Declaration of Rights of Man' by Alexis Francois Pison de Galland, 26/08/1789, http://www1.curriculum.edu.au/ddunits/downloads/pdf/dec_of_rights.pdf, Prepared by Gerald Murphy (The Cleveland Free-Net - aa300) Distributed by the Cybercasting Services Division of the National Public Telecomputing Network (NPTN); Extracts pp.199, 230, 266, 270 from *Press in the French Revolution* by John Gilchrist and William James Murray, Ginn & Co, imprint of Harcourt, 1971, pp.71, 87; Extract p.205 from *France in Revolution 1776–1830* by Sally Waller, Heinemann Advanced History, 2002, p.41, copyright © Sally Walker 2002. Reproduced by permission of Pearson Education Ltd; Extract p.205 from *French Revolutionaries and English Republicans: The Cordeliers Club, 1790–1794* by Rachel Hammersley, Royal Historical Society, 2005, p.30. Reproduced by permission of Boydell & Brewer Ltd; Extracts p.208 'Cordeliers petition', 1792, http://alphahistory.com/contact.html, page 227 from 'The Law of Suspects', 1793, http://alphahistory.com/frenchrevolution/law-of-suspects-1793/ and page 210 'Brunswick Manifesto', 1792, http://alphahistory.com/frenchrevolution/brunswick-manifesto-1793/, All text © Alpha History; Extract p.213, 223 from *Citizens: A chronicle of the French Revolution* by Simon Schama, Alfred A. Knopf Inc. 1989, Viking 1989, Penguin Books 1989, 2004, pp.361, 734, copyright © Simon Schama 1989. Reproduced by permission of Penguin Books Ltd and Peters Fraser & Dunlop, www.petersfraserdunlop.com on behalf of Simon Schama; Extract p.221 as discussed in *The Making of Insurrection: Parisian Sections and the Gironde* by Morris Slavin, Harvard University Press, 1986, p.16; Extract p.223 from *Jean Paul Marat: Tribune of the French Revolution (Revolutionary Lives)* by Clifford D. Conner, Pluto Press, 2012, pp.1, 8, 153. Reproduced by permission; Extracts pp.229, 232, 233 from *Fatal Purity: Robespierre and the French Revolution* by Ruth Scurr, Chatto & Windus, 2007, pp.266, 275, copyright © Ruth Scurr. Reproduced by permission of The Random House Group Limited and Henry Holt and Company, LLC. All rights reserved; Extract p.233 from *Morning Glory* by Marie-Hélène Huet, University of Pennsylvania Press, 1997, p.93. Reproduced by permission; Extract p.235 from *The French Revolution* by C. Hibbert, Penguin, 1982, p.248. Reproduced by permission of David Higham Associates; Extracts pp.237, 268, 272 from *The Ninth of Thermidor: The Fall of Robespierre* by Richard Bienvenue, Oxford University Press, 1968, p.317; and Extract p.317 from *The Twilight of Imperial Russia* by Richard Charques, Oxford University Press, 1974, p.130. Reproduced by permission of Oxford University Press, USA, www.oup.com; Extract p.247 from *The Thermidorians* by Georges Lefebvre, translated by Robert Baldock, Routledge & Kegan Paul Plc, 1965, p.189, copyright © 1965, Taylor & Francis; Extract p.260 from "Napoleon's Proclamation to the French People on Brumaire", http://www.napoleon-series.org/research/government/legislation/c_proclamation.html, copyright © 1995–2002, The Napoleon Series, All Rights Reserved; Extracts pp.285, 348 from *The Russian Revolution: A Very Short Introduction* by S. A. Smith, Oxford University Press, 2002, pp.6, 29. Reproduced by permission of Oxford University Press, www.oup.com; Extracts pp.291, 301, 387 from *Everyday Life in Imperial Russia: Select Documents 1772–1914* edited by ChaeRan Y. Freeze and Jay M. Harris, Brandeis University Press, 2013, pp.554, 579. Reproduced with permission of University Press of New England; Extract p.294 from *Russia in Revolution* by Lionel Kochan, Paladin Grafton Books, 1970, p.114, copyright © 1970 Lionel Kochan; and Extracts pp.321, 355 from *The Russian Revolution, 1899–1919* by Richard Pipes, Fontana Press, 1992, p.166, copyright © 1992 Richard Pipes. Reproduced by permission of HarperCollins Publishers Ltd; Extract p.301 from "Soldiers massacre demonstrators in St. Petersburg", *The Guardian Archive*, 23/03/1905, copyright © Guardian News & Media Ltd; Extract p.301 from *The Fall of the Russian Monarchy: A Study of the Evidence* by Bernard Pares, Jonathan Cape, 1939, p.79. Reproduced by permission of The Random House Group Ltd; Extract p.302 from *The Russian Revolution: A Beginner's Guide* by Abraham Ascher, Oneworld Publications 2014, p.29. Reproduced with permission; Extract p.311 from *The Revolution of 1905: Authority Restored* by Abraham Ascher, Stanford University Press 1994, p.79. Reproduced with permission; Extract p.313 from *A Lifelong Passion: Nicholas and Alexandra, Their Own Story* by Andrei Malyunas and Sergei Mironenko, Weidenfeld & Nicolson, 1996, p.292. Reproduced by permission of The Orion Publishing Group, London; Extracts pp.357, 382 from 'Seventeen Moments in Soviet History' www.soviethistory.macalester.edu, copyright © 2014; Extract p.367 from *Memoirs of a Revolutionary* by Victor Serge, translated by Peter Sedgwick, University of Iowa Press, 2002, pp.115–116. Reproduced by kind permission of Richard Greeman; Extract p.370 from *Russia under the Bolshevik Regime* by Richard Pipes, Vintage, 1995, p.419, copyright © 1994 Richard Pipes. Reproduced by permission of The Wylie Agency (UK) Ltd; Quote p.378 from Winston Churchill gathered by Clive Ponting, Churchill, 1994, pp.229–230, Sinclair-Stevenson, Hamish Hamilton, copyright © Winston S. Churchill. Reproduced with permission of Curtis Brown, London on behalf of the Estate of Sir Winston Churchill; and Extract p.380 from "The French Army and Intervention in Southern Russia, 1918–1919" by J.K. Munholland, *Cahiers du Monde russe et soviéique*, Vol. XXII (1), pp.43–66, janv-mars 1981, Paris, EHESS. Reproduced by permission of CERCEC Cahiers du Monde russe.

Every effort has been made to contact copyright holders of material reproduced in this book. Any omissions will be rectified in subsequent printings if notice is given to the publishers.